Microsoft®

Visual Basic 2010

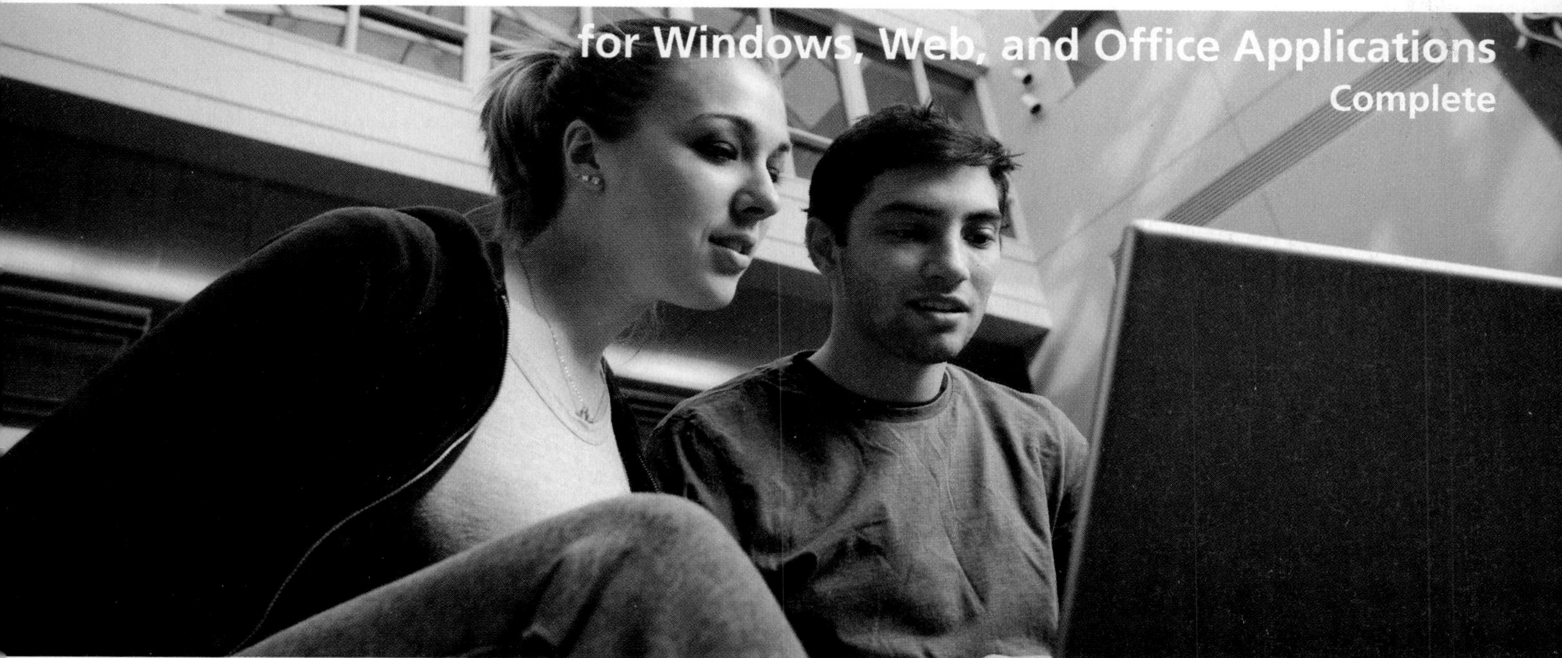

for Windows, Web, and Office Applications
Complete

Gary B. Shelly
Corinne Hoisington
Central Virginia Community College

COURSE TECHNOLOGY
CENGAGE Learning™

Australia • Brazil • Japan • Korea • Mexico • Singapore • Spain • United Kingdom • United States

Microsoft® Visual Basic 2010 for Windows, Web, and Office Applications: Complete
Gary B. Shelly
Corinne Hoisington

Vice President, Publisher: Nicole Pinard
Executive Editor: Kathleen McMahon
Product Managers: Crystal Parenteau and Nada Jovanovic
Associate Product Manager: Aimee Poirier
Editorial Assistant: Lauren Brody
Director of Marketing: Cheryl Costantini
Marketing Manager: Tristen Kendall
Marketing Coordinator: Stacey Leasca
Print Buyer: Julio Esperas
Production Director: Patty Stephan
Content Project Manager: Heather Hopkins
Development Editor: Lisa Ruffolo
Copyeditor: Michael Beckett
Proofreader: Andrew Therriault
Indexer: Sharon Hilgenberg
QA Manuscript Reviewers: Serge Palladino and Danielle Shaw
Art Director: Marissa Falco
Cover Designer: Lisa Kuhn, Curio Press, LLC
Cover Photo: Tom Kates Photography
Text Designer: Joel Sadagursky
Compositor: PreMediaGlobal

Library of Congress Control Number: 2010929660

ISBN-13: 978-0-538-46848-0

ISBN-10: 0-538-46848-3

Course Technology
20 Channel Center Street
Boston, MA 02210
USA

Cengage Learning is a leading provider of customized learning solutions with office locations around the globe, including Singapore, the United Kingdom, Australia, Mexico, Brazil, and Japan. Locate your local office at: **international.cengage.com/region**

Cengage Learning products are represented in Canada by Nelson Education, Ltd.

To learn more about Course Technology, visit **www.cengage.com/coursetechnology**

To learn more about Cengage Learning, visit **www.cengage.com**

Purchase any of our products at your local college store or at our preferred online store **www.cengagebrain.com**

Printed in the United States of America
1 2 3 4 5 6 7 16 15 14 13 12 11 10

CONTENTS

CHAPTER 4
Variables and Arithmetic Operations

CHAPTER 5
Decision Structures

PREFACE

The Shelly Cashman Series® offers the finest textbooks in computer education. This *Microsoft Visual Basic 2010* book utilizes an innovative step-by-step pedagogy, which integrates demonstrations of professional-quality programs with in-depth discussions of programming concepts and techniques and opportunities for hands-on practice and reinforcement. The popular Guided Program Development section supports students as they work independently to create useful, realistic, and appealing applications, building their confidence and skills while guiding them to select appropriate Visual Basic 2010 programming methods. Online Reinforcement boxes direct students to online videos that show how to perform a series of steps. Other marginal elements, such as In the Real World boxes, provide expert tips to add interest and depth to topics. A robust and varied collection of exercises, including a series of practical case-based programming projects, ensures students gain the knowledge and expertise they need to succeed when developing professional programs.

Visual Basic 2010 builds on the features of Visual Basic 2008, which introduced coding once and deploying on multiple devices. Some of the major enhancements to Visual Basic 2010 include rapid application development tools, a redesigned interface that supports Windows Presentation Foundation, dual-monitor support, improved IntelliSense features to increase productivity, and a more helpful debugging experience. Using Visual Basic 2010, you can design, create, and deploy Windows, Web, and Office applications. Visual Studio 2010 includes several productivity enhancements including IntelliSense tools, new and updated project types, Silverlight expanded sample applications, and more.

Objectives of this Textbook

Microsoft Visual Basic 2010 for Windows, Web, and Office Applications: Complete is intended for a semester-long course that introduces students to the correct ways to design and write programs using Visual Basic 2010. The goal of this text is to provide a complete course in computer programming for students with little or no previous programming experience. The objectives of this book are:

- To teach the fundamentals of the Microsoft Visual Basic 2010 programming language
- To understand and apply graphical user interface design principles
- To emphasize the development cycle when creating applications, which mirrors the same approach that professional developers use
- To illustrate well-written and readable programs using a disciplined coding style, including documentation and indentation standards
- To create Visual Basic applications that deploy on multiple platforms such as Web pages, Windows, and Office environments
- To demonstrate how to implement logic involving sequence, selection, and repetition using Visual Basic 2010
- To write useful, well-designed programs that solve practical business problems

- To create appealing, interactive Web applications that can be delivered and executed on the Internet
- To organize complex programs by using procedures and to anticipate and prevent errors by managing exceptions
- To encourage independent study and help those who are working on their own in a distance education environment

The Shelly Cashman Approach

Features of this *Microsoft Visual Basic 2010* book include:

- **Realistic, Up-to-Date Applications** Each programming chapter focuses on building a sample project, a complete, useful application that showcases Visual Basic 2010 features and the latest technology.
- **Guided Steps to Encourage Independence** After observing how a professional developer would build the chapter project and exploring related programming concepts and Visual Basic 2010 techniques, students create the sample application on their own in the Guided Program Development section. This step-by-step section provides enough guidance for students to work independently, with Hint Screens that verify students are performing the tasks correctly.
- **More Than Step-By-Step** Each chapter offers clear, thorough discussions of the programming concepts students need to understand to build the sample application. Important Visual Basic 2010 design and programming features are also highlighted, including time-saving techniques such as using IntelliSense, code snippets, and the Toolbox. As appropriate, students design and prepare for applications the way professional developers do — by creating or analyzing requirements documents, use case definitions, and event planning documents.
- **Online Reinforcement Boxes** The Online Reinforcement boxes send students to the Online Companion at scsite.com/vb2010 to watch videos illustrating each step in the chapter project. Students can refer to the Online Reinforcement boxes when they work through or review the chapter, watching videos as they prepare to create the chapter application on their own.
- **Heads Up Boxes** Heads Up boxes appear in the margin to give advice for following best programming practices and tips about alternative ways of completing the same task.
- **In the Real World Boxes** This marginal feature provides insight into how developers use Visual Basic tools or programming techniques to save time or enhance professional development projects.
- **Watch Out For Boxes** These boxes explain how to avoid common pitfalls when using a particular command, programming structure, or technique.

Organization of this Textbook

Microsoft Visual Basic 2010 for Windows, Web, and Office Applications: Complete provides detailed instructions on how to use Visual Basic 2010 to build authentic, effective, and appealing applications for Microsoft Windows personal computers and the Web. The material is divided into eight chapters, an enrichment chapter, and five appendices.

End-of-Chapter Activities

A notable strength of this *Microsoft Visual Basic 2010* book is the extensive student activities at the end of each chapter. Well-structured student activities can make the difference between students merely participating in a class and retaining the information they learn. These end-of-chapter activities include the following:

- **Learn It Online** The Learn It Online section directs students to Web-based exercises, which are fun, interactive activities that include chapter reinforcement (true/false, multiple choice, and short answer questions), practice tests, and a crossword puzzle challenge to augment concepts, key terms, techniques, and other material in the chapter.
- **Knowledge Check** The Knowledge Check section includes short exercises and review questions that reinforce concepts and provide opportunities to practice skills.
- **Debugging Exercises** In these exercises, students examine short code samples to identify errors and solve programming problems.
- **Program Analysis** The Program Analysis exercises let students apply their knowledge of Visual Basic 2010 and programming techniques. In some exercises, students write programming statements that meet a practical goal or solve a problem. In other exercises, students analyze code samples and identify the output.
- **Case Programming Assignments** Nine programming assignments for each chapter challenge students to create applications using the skills learned in the chapter. Each assignment presents a realistic business scenario and requires students to create programs of varying difficulty.
  - ● Easiest: The first three assignments provide most of the program design information, such as a requirements document and use case definition, for a business application. Students design an application, create an event planning document, and write the code for the application.
  - ●● Intermediate: The next three assignments provide some of the program design information, such as a requirements document. Students create other design documents, such as a use case definition and event planning document, and then build the user interface and code the application.
  - ●●● Challenging: The final three assignments provide only a description of a business problem, and students create all the design documents, design the user interface, and code the application.

To the Instructor

Each chapter in this book focuses on a realistic, appealing Visual Basic 2010 application. A chapter begins with a completed application, which you can run to demonstrate how it works, the tasks it performs, and the problems it solves. The chapter introduction also identifies the application's users and their requirements, such as running the program on the Web or validating input data.

The steps in the next section of a chapter show how to create the user interface for the application. You can perform these steps in class — each step clearly explains an action, describes the results, and includes a figure showing the results, with callouts directing your attention to key elements on the screen. Some marginal features, such as the Heads Up boxes, provide additional tips for completing the steps. The Online Reinforcement boxes direct students to videos that replay the steps, which is especially helpful for review and for distance learning students.

This section also explains the Visual Basic 2010 tools and properties needed to understand and create the user interface. For example, while placing a text box in an application, the chapter describes the purpose of a text box and why you should set its maximum and minimum size. You can discuss these ideas and strategies, and then continue your demonstration to show students how to apply them to the chapter application.

After completing the user interface, the chapter explores the programming concepts students should understand to create the application, such as proper syntax, variables, data types, conditional statements, and loops. This section uses the same types of steps, figures, and marginal features to demonstrate how to enter code to complete and test the application.

To prepare students for building the application on their own, the chapter next considers the program design and logic by examining planning documents:

- *Requirements document* — The requirements document identifies the purpose, procedures, and calculations of the program, and specifies details such as the application title, restrictions, and comments that help to explain the program.
- *Use case definition* — The use case definition describes what the user does and how the program responds to each action.
- *Event planning document* — The event planning document lists each object in the user interface that causes an event, the action the user takes to trigger the event, and the event processing that must occur.

You can discuss these documents in class and encourage students to review them as they create a program, reinforcing how professional developers create applications in the modern workplace.

In the innovative Guided Program Development section, students work on their own to create the chapter application. They complete the tasks within each numbered step, referring to Hint Screens when they need a reminder about how to perform a step or which method to use. Many tasks reference figures shown earlier in the chapter. Students can refer to these figures for further help — they show exactly how to use a particular technique for completing a task. Steps end with a results figure, which illustrates how the application should look if students performed the tasks correctly. To reinforce how students learned the chapter material, the Guided Program Development section also focuses first on designing the user interface and then on coding the application. A complete program listing appears at the end of this section, which students can use to check their work.

At the end of each chapter, you'll find plenty of activities that provide review, practice, and challenge for your students, including a summary table that lists skills and corresponding figures and videos, descriptions of online learning opportunities, and exercises ranging from short, focused review questions to assignments requiring complete programs and related planning documents. You can assign the Learn It Online, Knowledge Check, Debugging Exercises, and Program Analysis activities as necessary to reinforce and assess learning. Depending on the expertise of your class, you can assign the Case Programming Assignments as independent projects, selecting one from each level of difficulty (easiest, intermediate, and challenging) or concentrating on the level that is most appropriate for your class.

Important to Note: In previous editions of Visual Basic we covered mobile applications. However, Microsoft has not yet included this in Visual Basic 2010. They are currently developing a new mobile application platform for Visual Studio 2010 called Microsoft® Phone 7. When this feature becomes available for Visual Basic 2010, online updates to Chapter 5 will be available at scsite.com/vb2010/mobile.

INSTRUCTOR RESOURCES

The Instructor Resources include both teaching and testing aids.

- **Instructor's Manual** Includes lecture notes summarizing the chapter sections, figures and boxed elements found in every chapter, teacher tips, classroom activities, lab activities, and quick quizzes in Microsoft Word files.
- **Syllabus** Easily customizable sample syllabi that cover policies, assignments, exams, and other course information.
- **Figure Files** Illustrations for every figure in the textbook in electronic form.
- **PowerPoint Presentations** A multimedia lecture presentation system that provides slides for each chapter. Presentations are based on chapter objectives.
- **Solutions to Exercises** Includes solutions for all end-of-chapter and chapter reinforcement exercises.
- **Test Bank & Test Engine** Test Bank includes 112 questions for every chapter, featuring objective-based and critical thinking question types, including page number references and figure references, when appropriate. Also included is the test engine, ExamView, the ultimate tool for your objective-based testing needs.
- **Data Files for Students** Includes all the files that are required by students to complete the exercises.
- **Additional Activities for Students** Consists of Chapter Reinforcement Exercises, which are true/false, multiple-choice, and short answer questions that help students gain confidence in the material learned.

Book Resources

- Instructor's Manual
- PowerPoint Presentations
- Solutions to Exercises (Windows)
- Syllabus
- Test Bank and Test Engine
- Additional Student Files
- Data Files for Students (Windows)

About Our Covers

The Shelly Cashman Series® is continually updating our approach and content to reflect the way today's students learn and experience new technology. This focus on student success is reflected on our covers, which feature real students from University of Rhode Island using the Shelly Cashman Series in their courses, and reflect the varied ages and backgrounds of the students learning with our books. When you use the Shelly Cashman Series®, you can be assured that you are learning computer skills using the most effective courseware available.

To the Student

Getting the Most Out of Your Book

Welcome to *Microsoft Visual Basic 2010 for Windows, Web, and Office Applications: Complete*. To save yourself time and gain a better understanding of the elements in this text, spend a few minutes reviewing the descriptions and figures in this section.

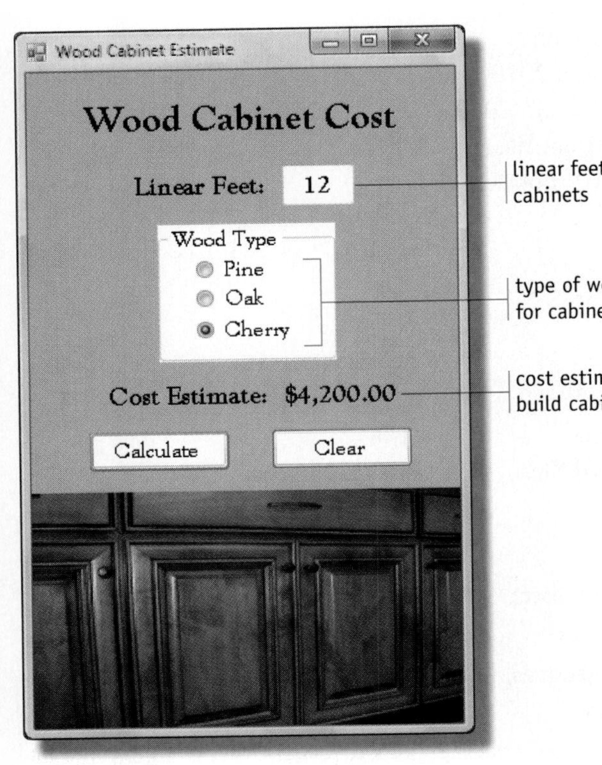

Introduction and Initial Chapter Figures Each chapter presents a programming project and shows the solution in the first figure of the chapter. The introduction and initial chapter figure let you see first-hand how your finished product will look and illustrate your programming goals.

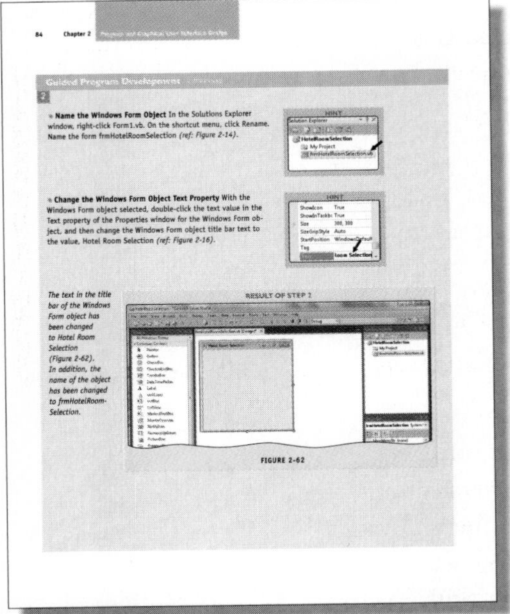

84 Chapter 2

Guided Program Development

2

» **Name the Windows Form Object** In the Solutions Explorer window, right-click Form1.vb. On the shortcut menu, click Rename. Name the form frmHotelRoomSelection *(ref: Figure 2-14)*.

HINT

» **Change the Windows Form Object Text Property** With the Windows Form object selected, double-click the text value in the Text property of the Properties window for the Windows Form object, and then change the Windows Form object title bar text to the value, Hotel Room Selection *(ref: Figure 2-16)*.

HINT

The text in the title bar of the Windows Form object has been changed to Hotel Room Selection (Figure 2-62). In addition, the name of the object has been changed to frmHotelRoom-Selection.

RESULT OF STEP 2

FIGURE 2-62

Guided Program Development After reading through the chapter and observing how to create the chapter application, the Guided Program Development section takes you through building the chapter project step by step. As you perform each task, you can refer to Hint Screens that remind you how to complete a step or use a particular technique. If you need further help, some steps include references to figures shown earlier in the chapter — you can revisit these figures to review exactly how to perform a task. Each step ends with a results figure, so you can make sure your application is on the right track. A complete program listing also appears at the end of the Guided Program Development section, which you can use to check your work.

Visual Basic 2010 Online Reinforcement Videos The first of their kind, the Shelly Cashman Online Companion provides video reenactments of every new Visual Basic process that is introduced in each chapter. These animated tutorials provide a Web-based visual instruction on how to complete a Visual Basic task. You can watch these videos to learn how to perform the steps shown in the book or to review the steps and techniques.

To access the Online Reinforcement videos, you need only a computer with an Internet connection. Use your Web browser to visit scsite.com/vb2010, click the link to the appropriate chapter, and then click the link to a figure to play a video.

Marginal Boxes Marginal elements include Heads Up boxes, which offer tips and programming advice, In the Real World boxes, which indicate how professional developers use Visual Basic 2010 tools, and Watch Out For boxes, which identify common errors and explain how to avoid them.

HEADS UP

During the development of the program, periodically you should save the program so you do not lose your work.

IN THE REAL WORLD

Program names can contain spaces and some special characters, but by convention most developers use a name with capital letters at the beginning of each word in the name. This naming convention is called camel case.

WATCH OUT FOR

If you make an error while typing a property, such as the Name, you can press the BACKSPACE key to erase your mistake, and then type the correct data. You also can double-click the property you want to change and start all over again.

Learn It Online Reinforcing what you're learning is a snap with the Chapter Reinforcement exercises, Practice Test, and other learning games on the Learn It Online page of the Online Companion. Visit scsite.com/vb2010 to access these fun, interactive exercises.

96 Chapter 2 Program and Graphical User Interface Design

Learn It Online

Start your browser and visit scsite.com/vb2010/ch2. Follow the instructions in the exercises below.

1. **Chapter Reinforcement TF, MC, SA** Click one of the Chapter Reinforcement links for Multiple Choice, True/False, or Short Answer below the Learn It Online heading. Answer each question and submit to your instructor.
2. **Practice Test** Click the Practice Test link below the Learn It Online heading. Answer each question, enter your first and last name at the bottom of the page, and then click the Grade Test button. When the graded practice test is displayed on your screen, submit the graded practice test to your instructor. Continue to take the practice test until you are satisfied with your score.
3. **Crossword Puzzle Challenge** Click the Crossword Puzzle Challenge link below the Learn It Online heading. Read the instructions, and then click the Continue button. Work the crossword puzzle. When you are finished, click the Submit button. When the crossword puzzle is redisplayed, submit it to your instructor.

Knowledge Check To verify you've learned the essential information in the chapter, you can work through the Knowledge Check exercises. Use these short exercises to test your knowledge of concepts and tools and to prepare for longer programming assignments.

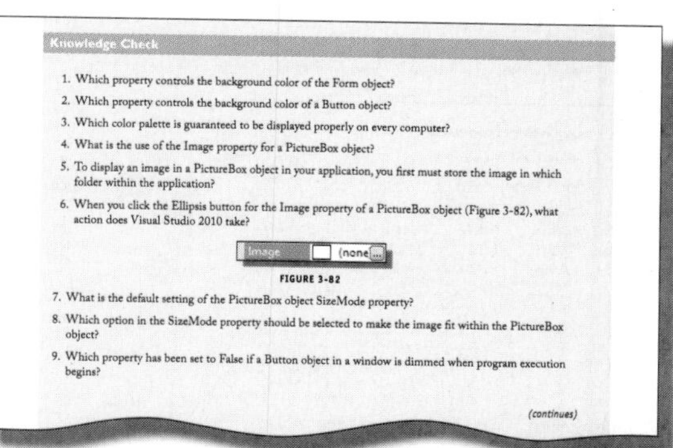

Knowledge Check

1. Which property controls the background color of the Form object?
2. Which property controls the background color of a Button object?
3. Which color palette is guaranteed to be displayed properly on every computer?
4. What is the use of the Image property for a PictureBox object?
5. To display an image in a PictureBox object in your application, you first must store the image in which folder within the application?
6. When you click the Ellipsis button for the Image property of a PictureBox object (Figure 3-82), what action does Visual Studio 2010 take?

Image (none)

FIGURE 3-82

7. What is the default setting of the PictureBox object SizeMode property?
8. Which option in the SizeMode property should be selected to make the image fit within the PictureBox object?
9. Which property has been set to False if a Button object in a window is dimmed when program execution begins?

(continues)

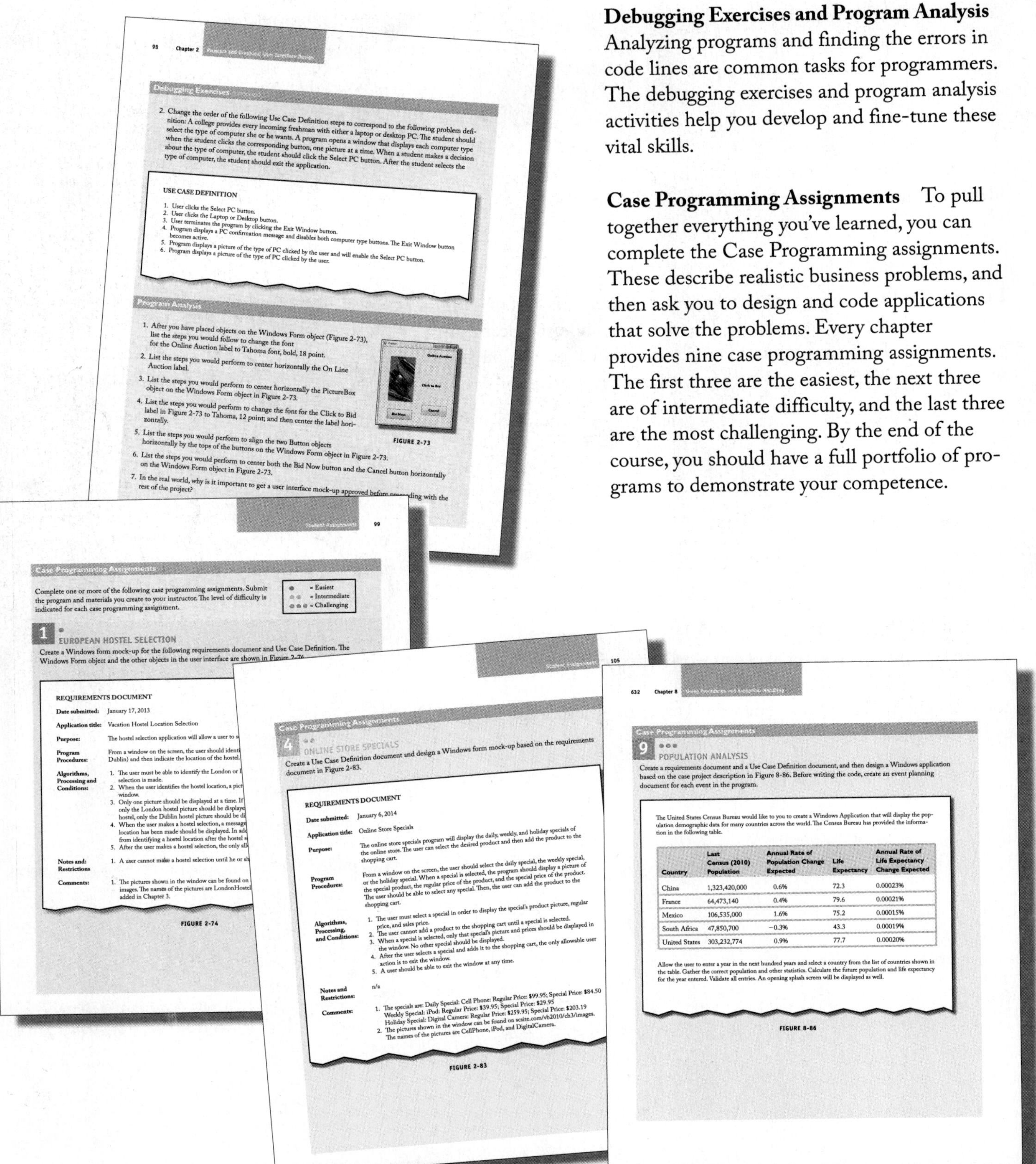

Debugging Exercises and Program Analysis Analyzing programs and finding the errors in code lines are common tasks for programmers. The debugging exercises and program analysis activities help you develop and fine-tune these vital skills.

Case Programming Assignments To pull together everything you've learned, you can complete the Case Programming assignments. These describe realistic business problems, and then ask you to design and code applications that solve the problems. Every chapter provides nine case programming assignments. The first three are the easiest, the next three are of intermediate difficulty, and the last three are the most challenging. By the end of the course, you should have a full portfolio of programs to demonstrate your competence.

CHAPTER 1

Introduction to Visual Basic 2010 Programming

OBJECTIVES

You will have mastered the material in this chapter when you can:

- Understand software and computer programs
- State the role of a developer in creating computer programs
- Specify the use of a graphical user interface and describe an event-driven program
- Specify the roles of input, processing, output, and data when running a program on a computer
- Describe the arithmetic operations a computer program can perform
- Explain the logical operations a computer program can perform
- Define and describe the use of a database
- Identify the use of a computer programming language in general, and Visual Basic 2010 in particular
- Explain the use of Visual Studio 2010 when developing Visual Basic 2010 programs
- Specify the programming languages available for use with Visual Studio 2010
- Explain the .NET 4.0 Framework
- Explain RAD
- Describe classes, objects, and the .NET Framework 4.0 class libraries
- Explain ADO.NET 4.0, ASP.NET 4.0, MSIL, and CLR
- Specify the types of Visual Basic 2010 applications

Introduction

A computer is an electronic device that completes tasks, under the direction of a sequence of instructions, to produce useful results for people. The set of instructions that directs a computer to perform tasks is called **computer software**, or a **computer program**.

When controlled by programs, computers can accomplish a wide variety of activities. For example, computers can interpret and display a page from the World Wide Web, compute and write payroll checks for millions of employees, display video and play audio from the Web or from digital video discs (DVDs), create messages on mobile phones, and be used to write a book (Figure 1-1).

FIGURE 1-1

FIGURE 1-2

Two vital components of a computer must interact with one another for any activity to be performed. These components are computer hardware and computer software. **Computer hardware** is the physical equipment associated with a computer. This includes the keyboard, mouse, monitor, central processing unit (CPU), random access memory (RAM), hard disk, DVD drive, printer, and other devices (Figure 1-2).

Computer software, or a computer program, is a set of electronic instructions that directs the computer hardware to perform tasks such as displaying a character on the monitor when a key on the keyboard is pressed, adding an employee's regular time pay and overtime pay to calculate the total pay for that employee, or displaying a picture from an attached digital camera on the monitor. Computer hardware cannot perform any activity unless an instruction directs that hardware to act. In most cases, the instruction is part of a computer program a developer has created to carry out the desired activity.

A third component required is data. **Data** includes words, numbers, videos, graphics, and sound that programs manipulate, display, and otherwise process. The basic function of many programs is to accept some form of data (sometimes called **input data**), manipulate the data in some manner (sometimes called **processing**), and

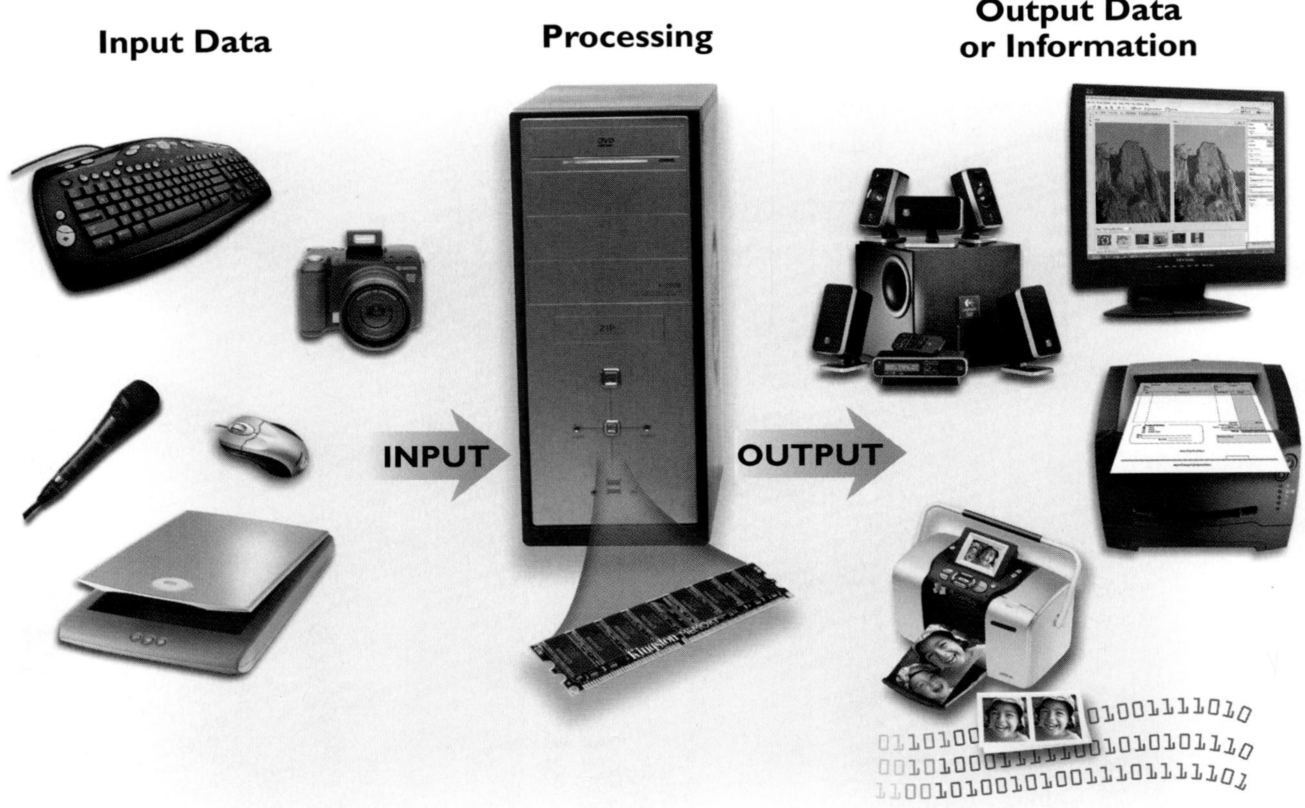

FIGURE 1-3

create some form of data usable by people or other computers (sometimes called **output data**, or **information**) (Figure 1-3). In short, many computer programs perform the following general steps: accept input data, process the data, and create output data. The data that acts as input to a program, the processing that occurs, and the output that is created varies with the requirements of the program.

In order for the computer to execute a program, both the program and the data must be placed in the computer's **random access memory (RAM)** (Figure 1-4). Once the program is stored in RAM, the **central processing unit (CPU)** of the computer can access the instructions in the program and the data in RAM to perform activities as directed by the program.

One other activity that hardware and software typically carry out is saving both the data and other software. **Saving**, or **storing**, data refers to placing the data or software electronically on a storage medium such as hard disk or Universal Serial Bus (USB) drive. The software and data are stored so they can be accessed and retrieved at a later time. Stored data is said to be **persistent** because it remains available even after the computer power is turned off.

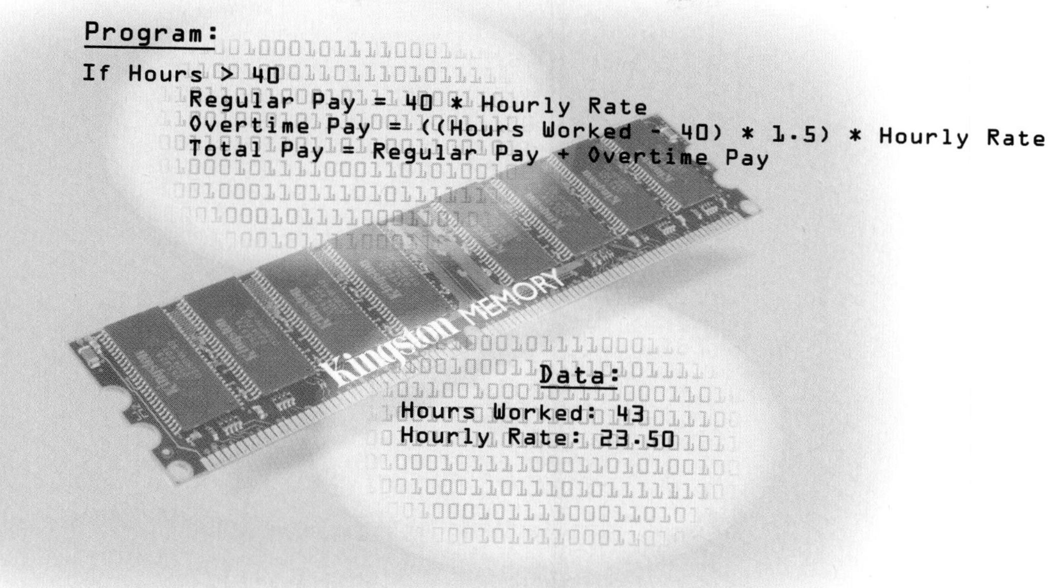
Program:
If Hours > 40
Regular Pay = 40 * Hourly Rate
Overtime Pay = ((Hours Worked - 40) * 1.5) * Hourly Rate
Total Pay = Regular Pay + Overtime Pay
Kingston MEMORY
Data:
Hours Worked: 43
Hourly Rate: 23.50

FIGURE 1-4

Computer Programmers and Developers

A computer program is designed and developed by people known as **computer programmers**, or developers. **Developers** are people skilled in designing computer programs and creating them using programming languages. Some computer programs are small and relatively simple, but often a problem to be solved on a computer requires more than one program. Thus, you will find that developers speak of developing an **application**, which can mean several computer programs working together to solve a problem.

When designing a program, developers analyze the problem and determine how to solve it. Once a computer program or an application is designed, the developer must create it so it can be executed on a computer. In most cases, the developer creates the program by writing the code for the program(s) using a **programming language**, which is a set of words and symbols that can be interpreted by special computer software and eventually executed as instructions by a computer. In this book, you will learn the skills required to both design and create computer programs using the Visual Basic 2010 programming language (Figure 1-5).

Event-Driven Computer Programs with a Graphical User Interface

Most Visual Basic 2010 programs are **event-driven programs** that communicate with the user through a **graphical user interface (GUI)**. The GUI usually consists of a window, containing a variety of objects, that can be displayed on various devices

```
Private Sub btnSelectRoom_Click(ByVal sender As System.Object, ByVal e As System.Ev
    ' This code is executed when the user
    ' clicks the Select Room button. It
    ' disables the Standard Room button,
    ' the Select Room button, and the
    ' Deluxe Room button. It hides the
    ' Instructions label, displays the
    ' Confirmation Message label, and
    ' enables the Exit Window button.

    btnStandardRoom.Enabled = False
    btnSelectRoom.Enabled = False
    btnDeluxeRoom.Enabled = False
    lblInstructions.Visible = False
    lblConfirmationMessage.Visible = True
    btnExitWindow.Enabled = True

End Sub

Private Sub btnDeluxeRoom_Click(ByVal sender As System.Object, ByVal e As System.Eve
    ' This code is executed when the user
    ' clicks the Deluxe Room button. It
    ' displays the Deluxe Room picture,
    ' hides the Standard Room picture, and
    ' enables the Select Room button.

    picDeluxeRoom.Visible = True
    picStandardRoom.Visible = False
    btnSelectRoom.Enabled = True

End Sub
```

FIGURE 1-5

such as a computer monitor or a mobile phone screen. Users employ the GUI objects to select options, enter data, and cause events to occur. An **event** means the user has initiated an action that causes the program to perform the type of processing called for by the user's action. For example, a user might enter data into the program, and then click a button. Clicking the button triggers an event, resulting in the program performing the processing called for by clicking the button.

To illustrate the process of entering data when using a graphical user interface and then triggering an event, consider the window shown in Figure 1-6.

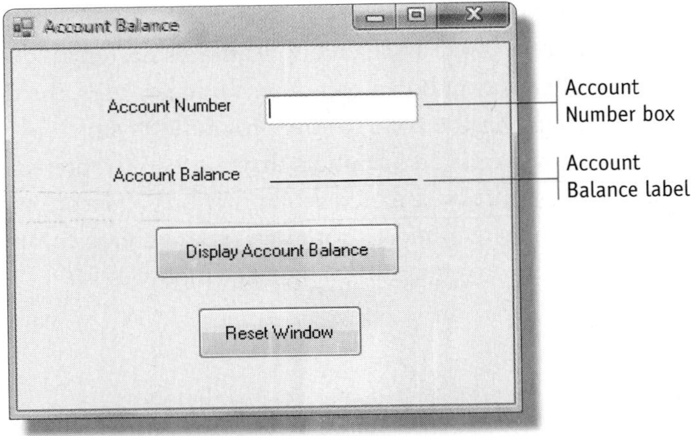

FIGURE 1-6

This window is part of a banking application. When it is displayed, the teller at the bank or a user on the Web can enter an account number. Then the user can click the Display Account Balance button (that is, trigger an event) and the program displays the account balance. The following steps illustrate the dynamics of the interaction with the program:

STEP 1 The user enters the account number in the Account Number box.

The account number the user entered is displayed in the Account Number text box (Figure 1-7). The Account Balance label displays no information.

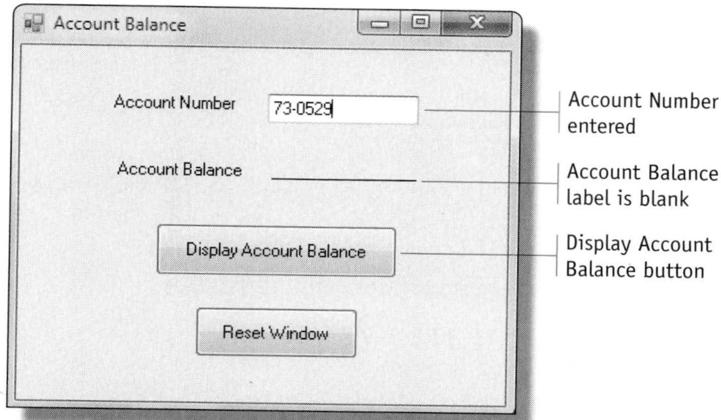

FIGURE 1-7

STEP 2 The user clicks the Display Account Balance button.

The account balance is displayed in the Account Balance label (Figure 1-8). Clicking the Display Account Balance button triggered the event that caused the program to determine and display the account balance based on data that the program accessed.

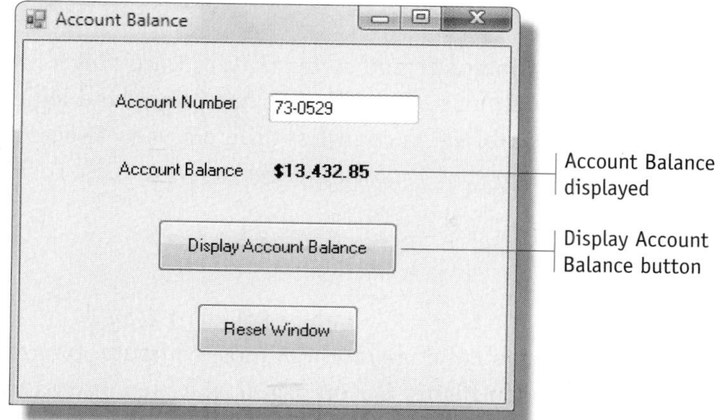

FIGURE 1-8

STEP 3 The user clicks the Reset Window button to clear the text box and the label and prepare the user interface for the next account number.

Clicking the Reset Window button triggers another event. The text box and the label are cleared and the insertion point is placed in the Account Number text box (Figure 1-9). The user now can enter a new account number to determine the account balance.

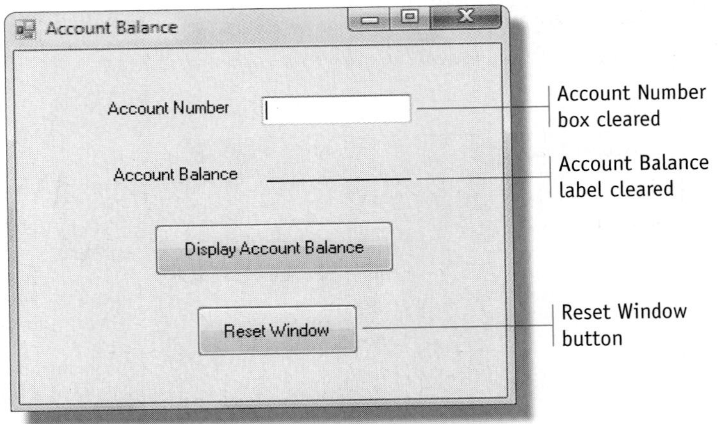

FIGURE 1-9

The events in the previous example consist of clicking the Display Account Balance button and clicking the Reset Window button. The program reacts to the events by performing specific actions (showing the account balance and resetting the text box and label). This is an example of an event-driven program. The Visual Basic developer designs the user interface and writes the program code that performs these event-triggered actions.

Basic Program Operations

All programs, regardless of their size and complexity, execute only a few fundamental operations: input, output, basic arithmetic operations, and logical operations. These operations can be combined in countless different ways to accomplish the tasks required of the program. The following pages describe these basic program operations.

Input Operation

As noted previously, a fundamental operation in most computer programs is the user entering data. For instance, in Figure 1-7 on page 7, the user entered the account number. The steps that occurred when the user typed the account number are shown in Figure 1-10.

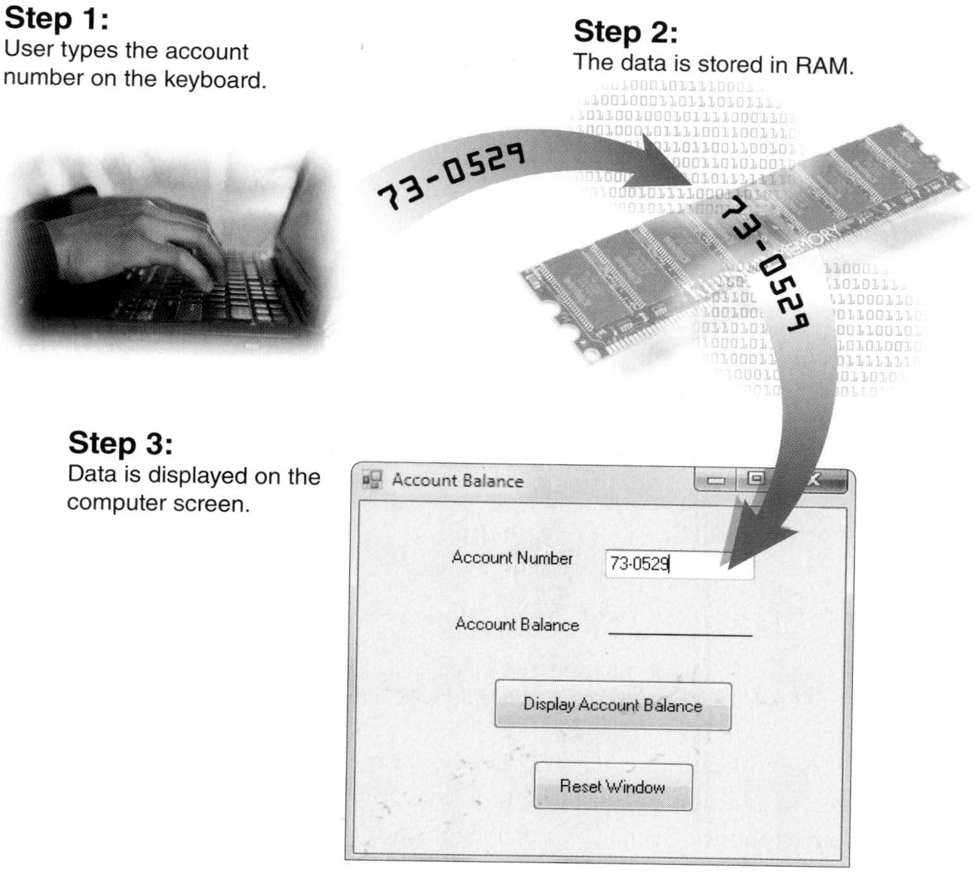

Step 1:
User types the account number on the keyboard.

Step 2:
The data is stored in RAM.

Step 3:
Data is displayed on the computer screen.

Account Balance

Account Number 73-0529

Account Balance

Display Account Balance

Reset Window

FIGURE 1-10

In Figure 1-10, the banking computer program that processes the user's request is stored in RAM. The data entered by the user also is stored in RAM. Depending on the input device, data entered might also be displayed on the computer screen. The input device used to enter data depends on the application. In Figure 1-10, the user typed the account number on a keyboard. Other applications might allow data to be entered with a scanner, digital camera, video camera, mouse, or other device. In each instance, the data is stored in the computer's RAM. When the data is in RAM, instructions in the program can operate on the data.

Output Operation

The second basic program operation is creating output, or information. As you learned previously, a major goal of most computer programs is to create output data, or information, that is useful to people. In Figure 1-8 on page 7, the information requested of the program is the account balance. The process of creating output is shown in Figure 1-11.

As always, the program must be stored in RAM to control the operations of the computer. In the example, the program sets the text of the Account Balance label equal to the account balance, and then displays it on the screen.

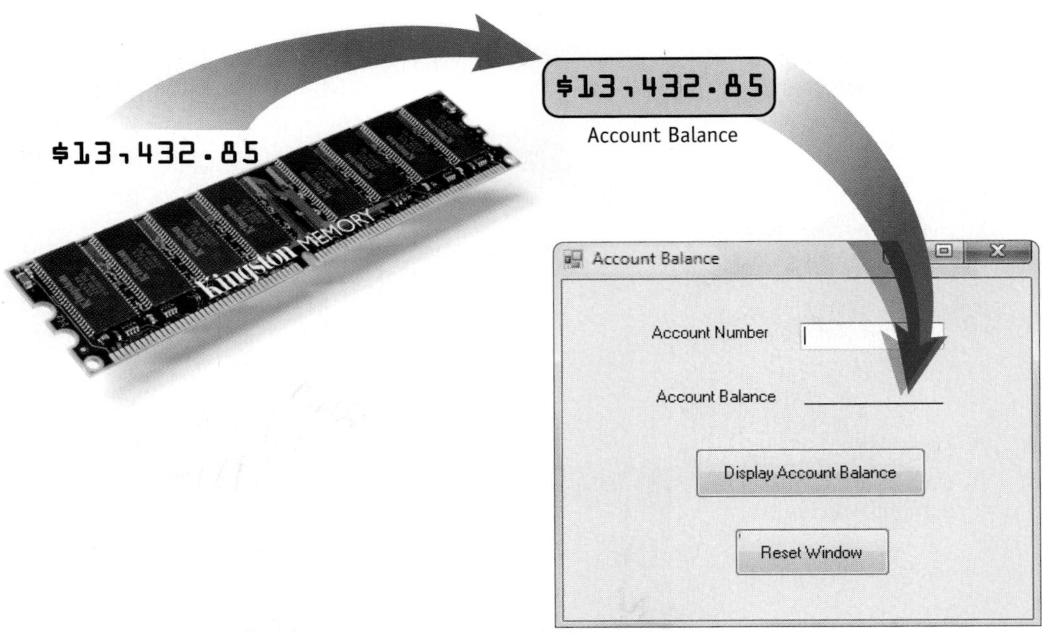

FIGURE 1-11

As with input operations, a variety of devices can present output. Common output devices, in addition to computer monitors, include printers, gaming console screens and smartphone screens (Figure 1-12).

Input and output operations are basic to all computers and most computer programs. It is the ability to enter data, process it in some manner, and create output in the form of useful information that makes a computer valuable. Understanding input/output operations is essential because they provide the foundation for many of the programs you will write in this text.

Basic Arithmetic Operations

Once data is stored in main computer memory as a result of an input operation, the program can process it in some manner. In many programs, arithmetic operations (addition, subtraction, multiplication, and division) are performed on numeric data to produce useful output.

Prior to performing arithmetic operations, the numeric data used in calculations must be stored in RAM. Then, program instructions that also are stored in RAM can direct the computer to add, subtract, multiply, or divide the numbers. The answers from arithmetic operations can be used in additional calculations and processing, stored for future use, and used as output from the program.

The example in Figure 1-13 illustrates the steps an application performs to calculate an average test score. The average test score is calculated from the three test scores a user enters.

In the example in Figure 1-13, the program adds the three test scores the user enters, and then divides the total by 3 to obtain the average score. As always, both

FIGURE 1-12

the program and the data required to calculate the average test score must be stored in the computer's RAM. As you can see, when the user enters data in a text box, the data is stored in RAM and is available for arithmetic and other operations.

This example demonstrates the three fundamental operations of input (entering the three test scores), processing (calculating the average test score), and output (displaying the average test score). Although most applications are more complex than the one illustrated, the input, process, and output operations are used; and arithmetic operations commonly part of the processing step.

Logical Operations

It is the ability of a computer to perform logical operations that separates it from other types of calculating devices. Computers, through the use of computer programs, can compare numbers, letters of the alphabet, and special characters. Based on the result of these comparisons, the program can perform one processing task if the

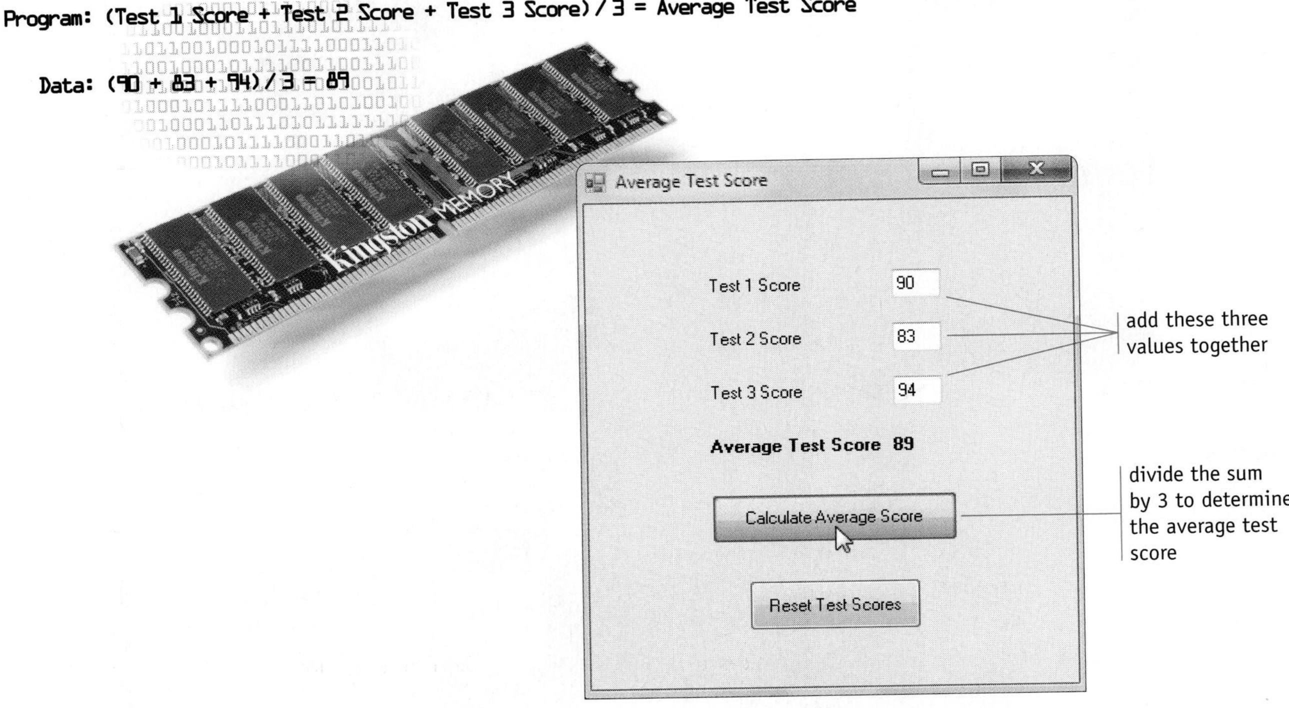

FIGURE 1-13

condition tested for is true and another processing task if the condition is not true. Using a program to compare data and perform alternative operations allows the computer to complete sophisticated tasks such as predicting weather, formatting and altering digital photographs, editing digital video, and running high-speed games.

A program can perform the following types of logical operations:

- Comparing to determine if two values are equal.
- Comparing to determine if one value is greater than another value.
- Comparing to determine if one value is less than another value.

Based on the results of these comparisons, the program can direct the computer to take alternative actions.

Comparing — Equal Condition

A program can compare two values stored in RAM to determine whether they are equal. If the values are equal, one set of instructions will be executed; if they are not equal, another set of instructions will be executed.

Comparing to determine if two values are equal requires comparing one value to another. In an application for calculating student tuition, different rates might apply based on the student's residence. If the school is located in Texas, and the student resides in Texas, the tuition per unit is one value; if the student does not reside in Texas, the tuition per unit is another value (Figure 1-14).

BEFORE:

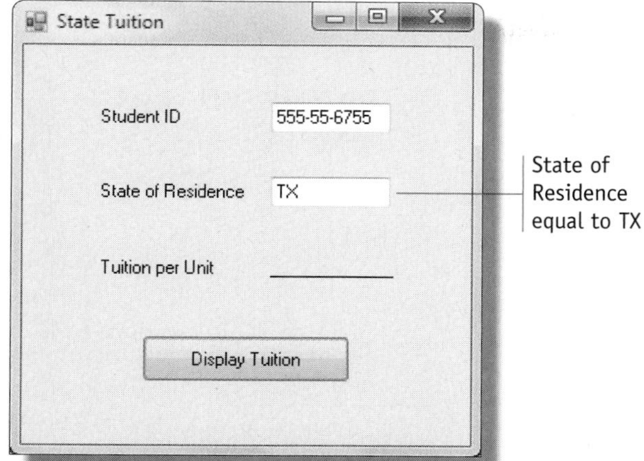

AFTER:

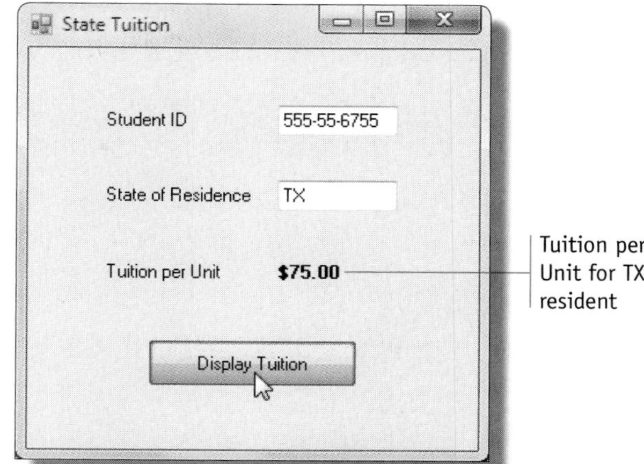

BEFORE:

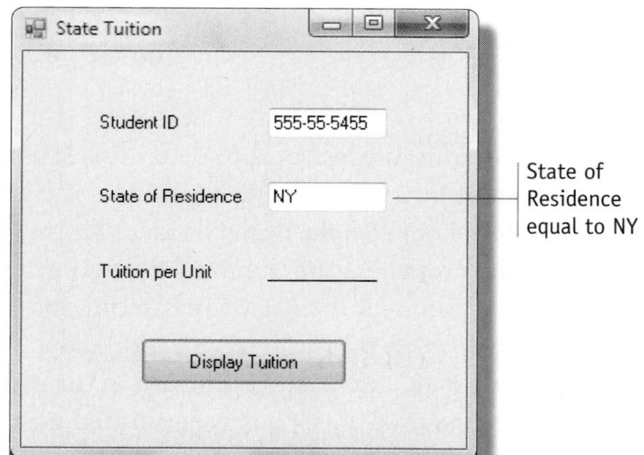

AFTER:

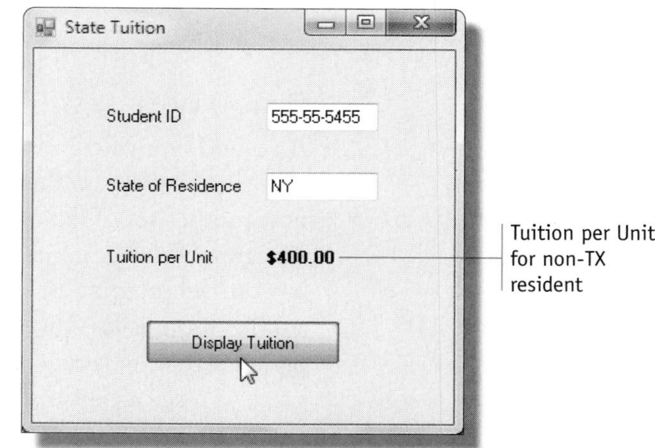

FIGURE 1-14

When the Display Tuition button is clicked and the state is equal to TX, the program displays the in-state tuition per unit. If the state is not equal to TX, the program displays the out-of-state tuition per unit.

Comparing can be used to determine if a condition is selected. For example, in Figure 1-15, the Campus Parking Fees window contains a Student Name text box that provides space for the student name On-Campus Housing and Off-Campus Housing option buttons, or radio buttons, that allow the user to select either on-campus housing or off-campus housing. When the user clicks the Calculate Parking Fees button, the program displays the appropriate parking fee.

In Example 1, the user name is Phyllis Gomez and the On-Campus Housing option button is selected. When the user clicks the Calculate Parking Fees button, by comparing, the program determines that the On-Campus Housing button is selected. Because it is selected, the result of the comparison is true and the program displays the parking fee for on-campus housing. In Example 2, the Off-Campus Housing button is selected, so the program displays the parking fee for off-campus housing.

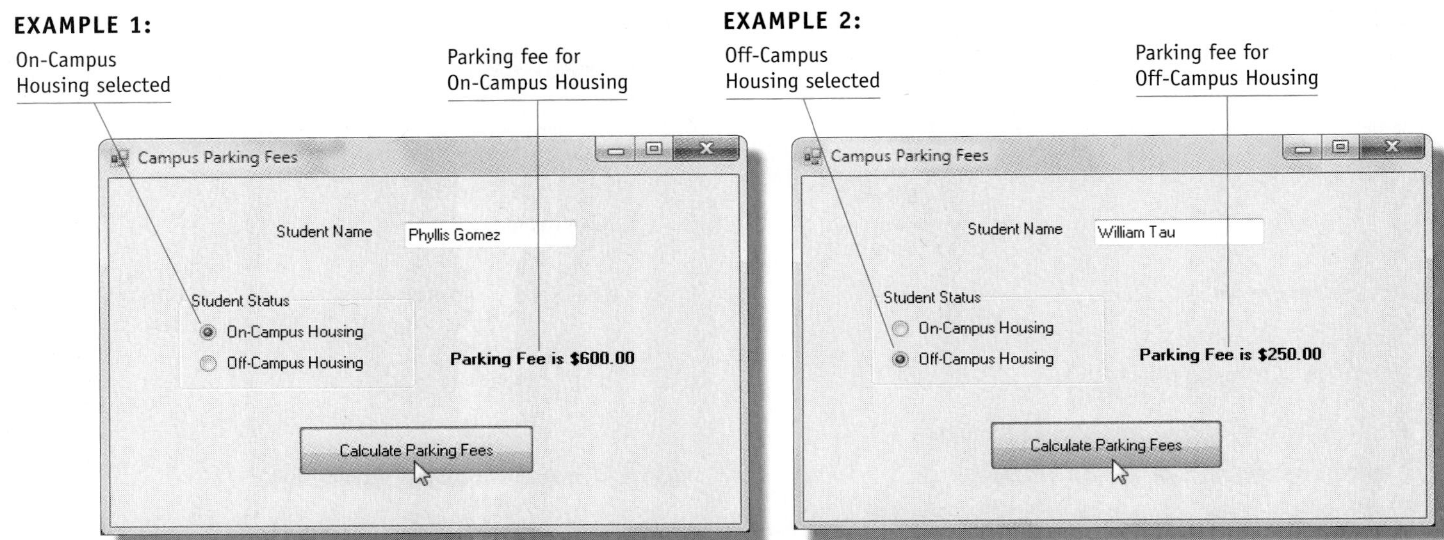

FIGURE 1-15

Comparing — Less Than Condition

A second type of comparison a computer program can perform is to determine if one value is less than another value. If it is, one set of instructions will be executed; if it is not, another set of instructions will be executed. For example, in the Student Dorm Assignment program in Figure 1-16, when the user clicks the Submit Application button, the program makes a comparison to determine if the person registering for a dorm room is less than 18 years old. If so, the person is considered a minor and a parent signature is required. If not, no signature is required. An instruction in the program to place a check in the Parent Signature Required check box is performed if the age is less than 18, and the instruction is not executed if the age is 18 or more.

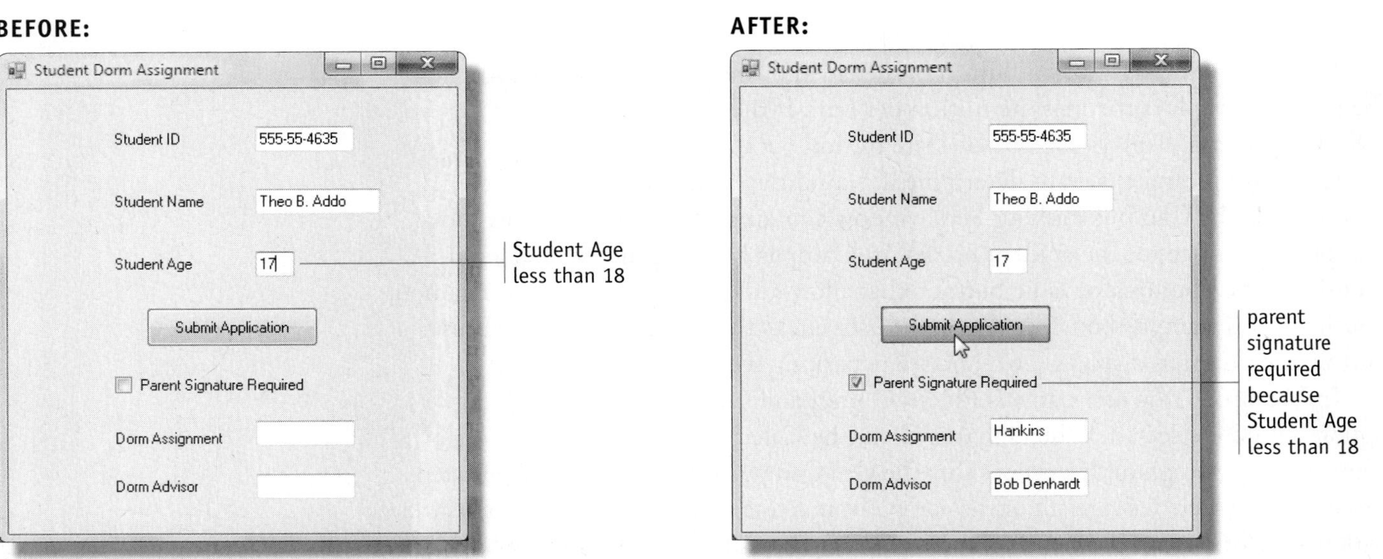

FIGURE 1-16 (*continues*)

BEFORE:

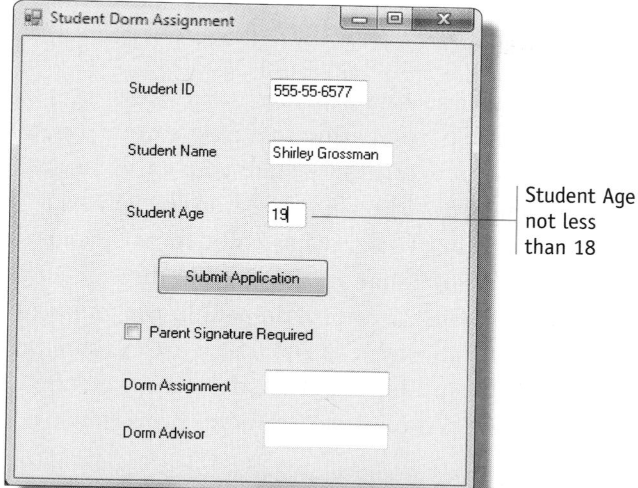

AFTER:

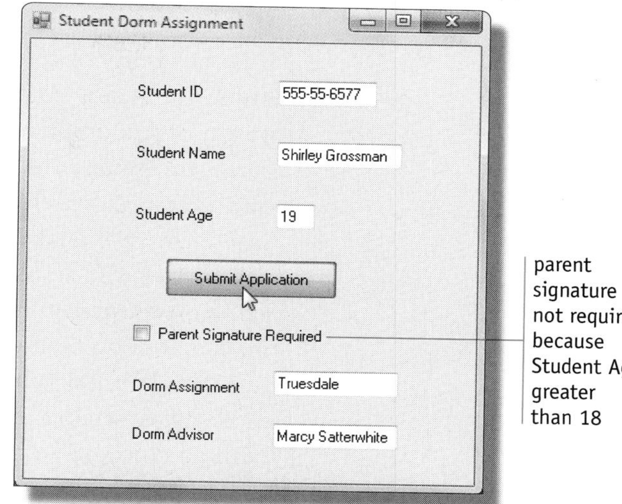

FIGURE 1-16 (*continued*)

Comparing — Greater Than Condition

The other condition a computer program can determine is whether one value is greater than another value. For example, in a payroll application, the hours worked by an employee can be compared to the value 40. If the hours worked are greater than 40, then overtime pay (1.5 times the hourly rate) is calculated for the hours over 40 worked by the employee. If the employee worked 40 hours or less, no overtime pay is calculated. This comparing operation is shown in Figure 1-17.

In Figure 1-17a, the Hours Worked box contains 42, so the program calculates overtime pay for employee Anna Junga. In Figure 1-17b, George Ortega worked 30 hours, so no overtime pay is calculated. When the Hours Worked value is greater than 40, the program executes one set of instructions; if the Hours Worked value is not greater than 40, the program executes another set of instructions.

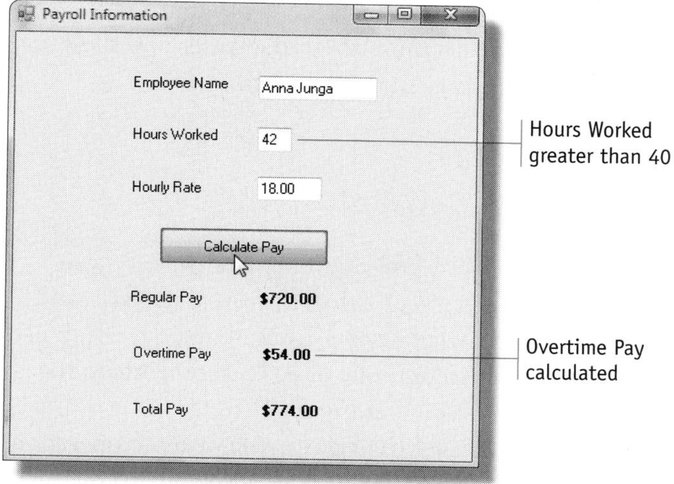

FIGURE 1-17a

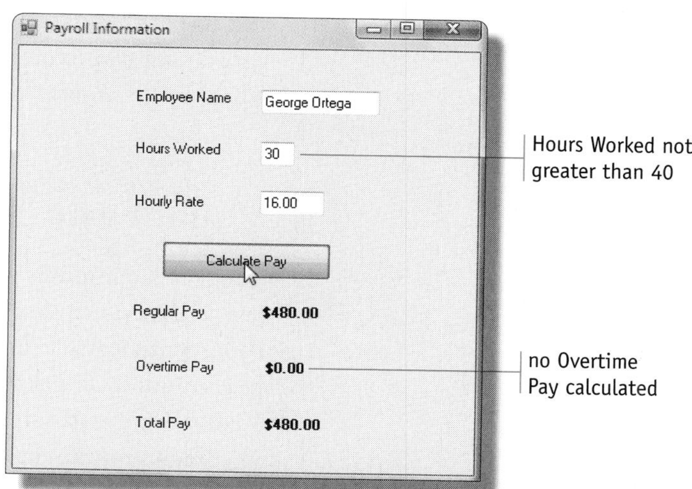

FIGURE 1-17b

Logical Operations Summary

While the logical operations shown in the previous examples might seem simple, it is the ability of a computer running under the control of a program to perform millions of these comparisons in a single second that provides the processing power of a computer. For example, if you are participating in a road race computer game, the game program uses comparisons to determine where your car is located on the screen, which graphic road elements should be displayed on the screen, where the car you are racing is located, whether your car has collided with your competitor, and so on. All of the many decisions that are required to display your game on the screen and respond to your actions as you participate in the game are made based on comparisons to determine if one value is equal to, greater than, or less than another value. As you can imagine, millions of these decisions must be made every second in order for your high-speed road race game to provide you with an enjoyable experience.

Saving Software and Data

When you develop and write a program, the code you write and the other features of the program you create, such as the graphical user interface, must be saved on disk. Then, when you want the program to run, you can cause the program to load into RAM and execute. By saving the program on disk, you can execute the same program many times without rewriting it each time you want to run it.

The program you write, however, also can save data. This data, which can be generated from the processing in the program, can be saved on disk for future use. For example, in a banking application, a customer might open an account. The computer program that is used to open the account saves the customer's information, such as name, address, account number, and account balance, on disk. Later, when the customer makes a deposit or withdrawal, the customer information will be retrieved and modified to reflect the deposit or withdrawal.

In most cases, data such as a customer's name and address is saved in a database. A **database** is a collection of data organized in a manner that allows access, retrieval, and use of that data. Once the data is saved in the database, any programs with permission can reference the data. You will learn more about databases and their use when programming using Visual Basic 2010 later in this textbook.

Visual Basic 2010 and Visual Studio 2010

To write a computer program, a developer uses a programming language. As you learned previously, a programming language is a set of written words, symbols, and codes, with a strict set of usage rules called the language **syntax,** that a developer uses to communicate instructions to a computer. An example of code statements in the Visual Basic 2010 programming language is shown in Figure 1-18.

Each program statement causes the computer to perform one or more operations. When written, these instructions must conform to the rules of the Visual Basic

```
        Do Until intNumberOfEntries > intMaximumNumberOfEntries _
            Or strVehicleSpeed = strCancelButtonClicked

            If IsNumeric(strVehicleSpeed) Then
                decVehicleSpeed = Convert.ToDecimal(strVehicleSpeed)
                If decVehicleSpeed > 0 Then
                    lstRadarSpeed.Items.Add(decVehicleSpeed)
                    decTotalOfAllSpeeds += decVehicleSpeed
                    intNumberOfEntries += 1
                    strInputBoxMessage = strNormalBoxMessage
                Else
                    strInputBoxMessage = strNegativeNumberErrorMessage
                End If
            Else
                strInputBoxMessage = strNonNumericErrorMessage
            End If

            If intNumberOfEntries <= intMaximumNumberOfEntries Then
                strVehicleSpeed = InputBox(strInputBoxMessage & intNumberOfEntries, _
                                           strInputBoxHeading, " ")
            End If

        Loop

        ' Makes label visible
        Me.lblAverageSpeed.Visible = True
```

FIGURE 1-18

2010 language. Coding a program is a precise skill. The developer must follow the syntax, or **programming rules**, of the programming language precisely. Even a single coding error can cause a program to execute improperly. Therefore, the developer must pay strict attention to coding an error-free program.

When writing Visual Basic 2010 programs, most developers use a tool called Visual Studio 2010. **Visual Studio 2010** is a software application that allows you, as the developer, to create Visual Basic 2010 programs using code you write, code prewritten by others that can be incorporated into your program, and sophisticated tools that speed up the programming process significantly while resulting in better executing and more reliable programs. In this book, you will be using Visual Studio 2010 to write Visual Basic 2010 programs.

Visual Studio 2010 is a type of **integrated development environment (IDE)**, which provides services and tools that enable a developer to code, test, and implement a single program, or sometimes the series of programs that comprise an application. Visual Studio 2010, which was developed by Microsoft Corporation, works specifically with Visual Basic 2010 as well as other programming languages to develop program code.

After you start the Visual Studio 2010 application, the Visual Studio 2010 window is displayed. In this window, you can develop and write your Visual Basic 2010 program, as shown in Figure 1-19.

The following are general guidelines for using this window. In subsequent chapters, you will learn to use each of the elements found in the Visual Studio 2010 window.

Title Bar: The title bar identifies the window and the application open in the window. In Figure 1-19, the open application is Payroll.

HEADS UP

Various versions of Visual Studio 2010 are available, including Visual Studio Standard Edition, Visual Studio Professional Edition, Visual Studio Express Edition, and Visual Studio Team System. The MSDN Academic Alliance allows students to get a free copy of Microsoft Visual Studio Professional 2010 if the school is part of the Academic Alliance. For more information, see the MSDN link at http://msdn2.microsoft.com/en-us/academic/bb676724.aspx.

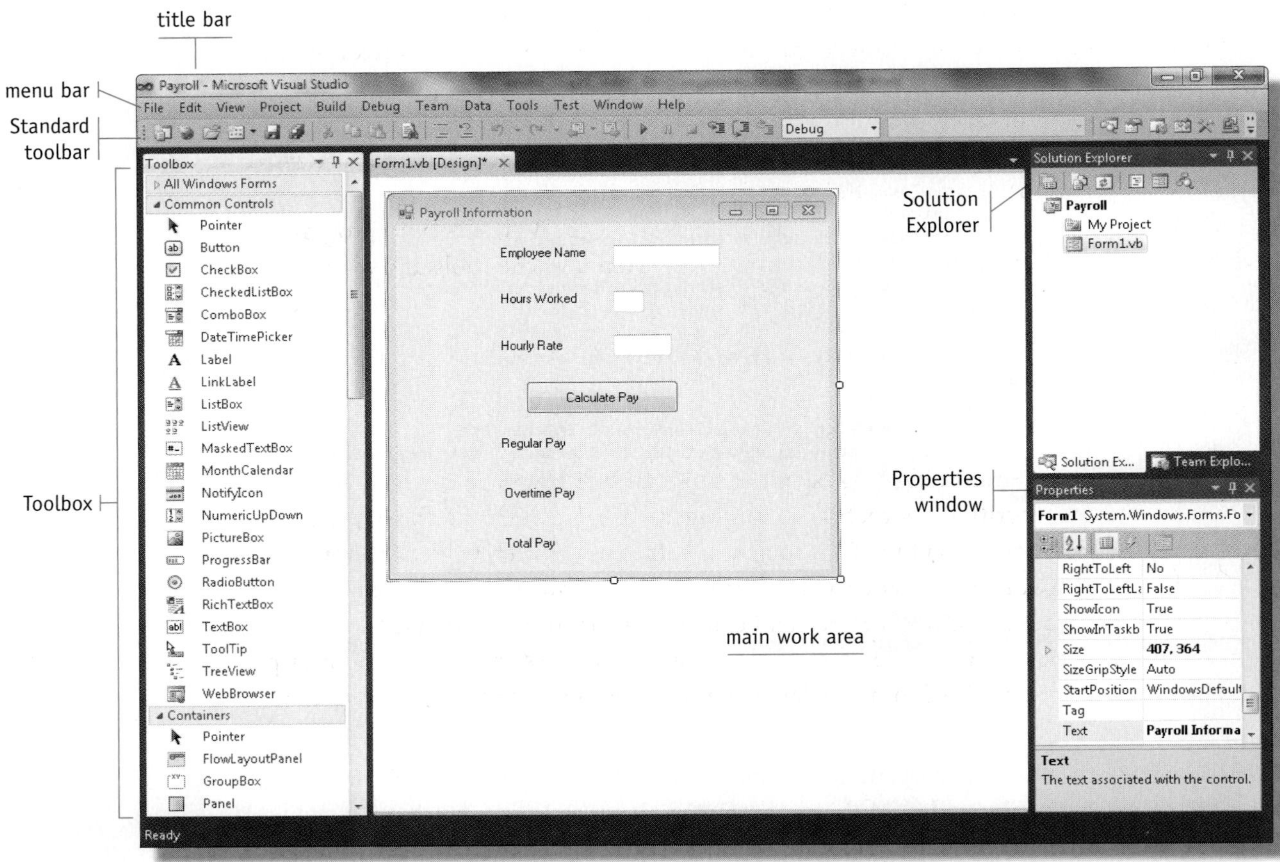

FIGURE 1-19

Menu Bar: The menu bar displays the Visual Studio 2010 menu names, each representing a list of commands that allow you to create, edit, save, print, test, and run a Visual Basic program, as well as perform other functions that are critical to the development of Visual Basic programs.

Standard Toolbar: The Standard toolbar contains buttons that execute frequently used commands such as Open Project, New Project, Save, Cut, Copy, Paste, and Undo.

Toolbox: The Toolbox contains **.NET components** that you can use to develop the graphical user interface for the program. For example, through the use of the Toolbox, you can place buttons, picture boxes, labels, radio buttons, and other Windows GUI objects in the window you develop for your program.

Main Work Area: The main work area is used to contain the item on which you are working. In Figure 1-19, it contains the Payroll Information window, which has been developed in the Payroll program.

Solution Explorer: The Solution Explorer window displays the elements of the **Visual Basic solution**, which is the name given to the Visual Basic program and other items that are generated by Visual Studio so the program will execute properly. You will learn about these items and how to use the Solution Explorer window throughout this book.

CHAPTER 2

Program and Graphical User Interface Design

OBJECTIVES

You will have mastered the material in this chapter when you can:

- Open and close Visual Studio 2010
- Create a Visual Basic 2010 Windows Application project
- Name and set the title bar text in a Windows Form object; resize a Windows Form object
- Add a Label object to a Windows Form object; name the Label object; set the text in the Label object; change the Font properties of the text in the Label object
- Add a PictureBox object to the Windows Form object; name the PictureBox object; resize the PictureBox object
- Add a Button object to the Windows Form object; name the Button object; set the text in the Button object; change the Button object size
- Align objects on the Windows Form object
- Save and open Visual Basic projects
- Understand and implement graphical user interface design principles
- Understand and implement the first two phases of the program development life cycle

Introduction

Before a program actually can be coded using Visual Basic 2010, it must be designed. Designing a program can be compared to constructing a building. Before cement slabs are poured, steel beams are put in place, and walls are built, architects and engineers must design a building to ensure it will perform as required and be safe and reliable. The same holds true for a computer program. Once the program is designed, it can be implemented through the use of the Visual Basic 2010 programming language to perform the functions for which it was designed.

To illustrate the process of designing and implementing a computer program in the Visual Basic 2010 programming language using **Visual Studio 2010** as the integrated development environment, the application shown in Figure 2-1 will be designed and implemented in this chapter and in Chapter 3.

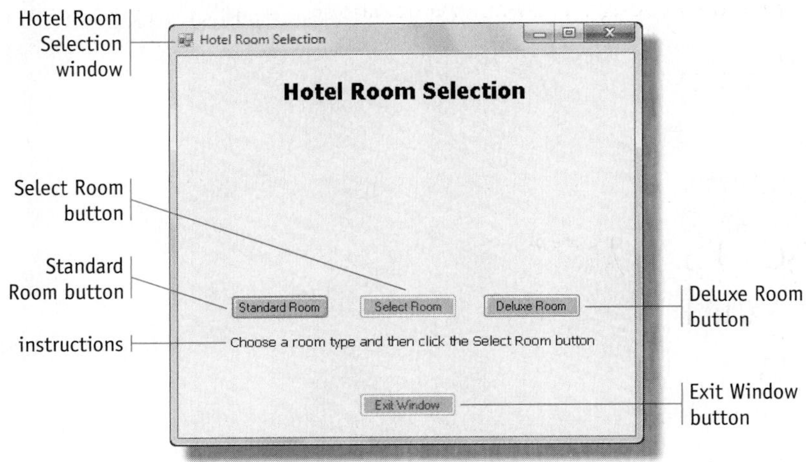

FIGURE 2-1a

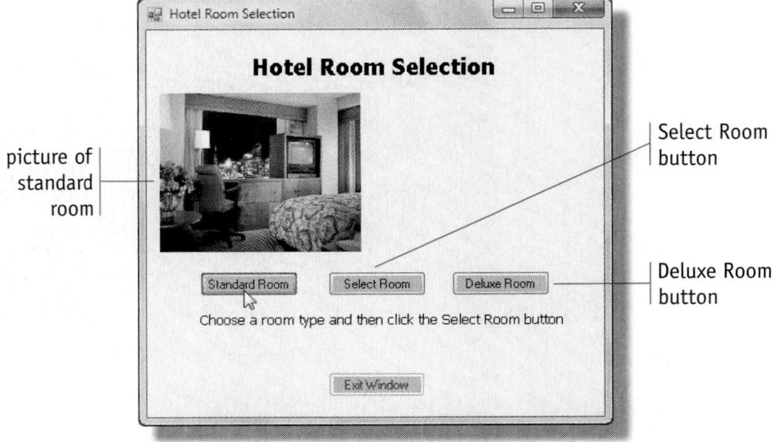

FIGURE 2-1b

The application in Figure 2-1 could be part of a larger computer application that is used to make hotel reservations. The program that creates the window in Figure 2-1 will run on a personal computer using the Windows operating system and will allow a reservation clerk or a customer to select the room type for a hotel reservation.

In Figure 2-1a, the program begins by displaying the Hotel Room Selection window on a PC monitor. The program provides instructions that tell the user to choose the room type (by clicking the Standard Room or Deluxe Room button), and then click the Select Room button to make a room selection. If the user clicks the Standard Room button, a picture of a standard room is displayed (Figure 2-1b). If the user clicks the Deluxe Room button, a picture of a deluxe room is displayed (Figure 2-1c). After choosing a room type, the user can click the Select Room button and the program informs the user the room selection has been completed (Figure 2-1d). To close the window and exit the program, the user can click the Exit Window button after making a room selection.

By the end of Chapter 3, you will have completed the design and implementation of this program.

ONLINE REINFORCEMENT

To view a video of the program execution shown in Figure 2-1, visit scsite.com/vb2010/ch2 and then click Figure 2-1. Turn on your speakers to listen to the audio walkthrough of the steps.

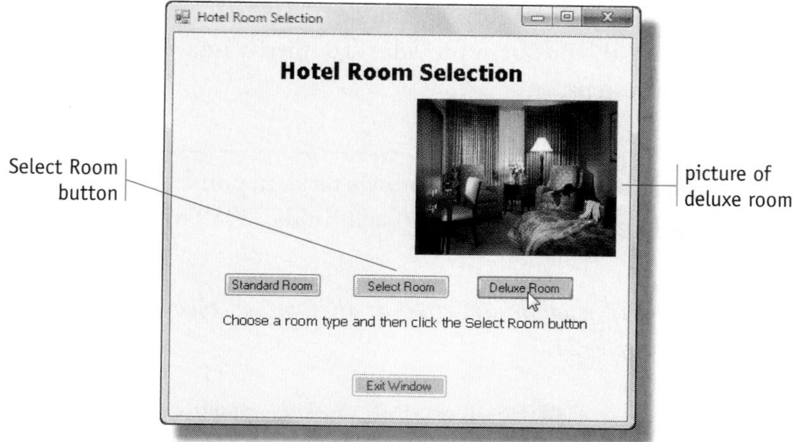

FIGURE 2-1c

FIGURE 2-1d

Using Visual Studio 2010

When designing an event-driven program that uses a graphical user interface (GUI), such as the program in this chapter, one of the first steps is to design the user interface itself. Recall that the user interface is the window that is displayed on the screen when the program is running, together with the variety of objects such as buttons that are displayed in the window. Before beginning to design the user interface, however, the developer should know how to use certain Visual Studio and Visual Basic **rapid application development** (**RAD**) tools because these tools are used in the design process. For example, you use the Visual Studio tools to place a button on the window. So, before starting the design of the user interface for the program in this chapter, you should know how to accomplish the Visual Studio tasks described in the following pages.

Open Visual Studio 2010

To design a user interface using Visual Studio, the developer must open Visual Studio 2010 and then use the tools the program provides. To open Visual Studio 2010, you can complete the following steps:

STEP 1 Click the Start button on the Windows taskbar, point to All Programs on the Start menu, and then point to Microsoft Visual Studio 2010 on the All Programs submenu.

The program name, Microsoft Visual Studio 2010, is displayed on the Microsoft Visual Studio 2010 submenu (Figure 2-2).

HEADS UP

Visual Basic 2010 can be run on Windows 7, Windows Vista, or Windows XP. In this book, the default operating system is displayed as Windows 7, but all the programs work in the three operating system environments.

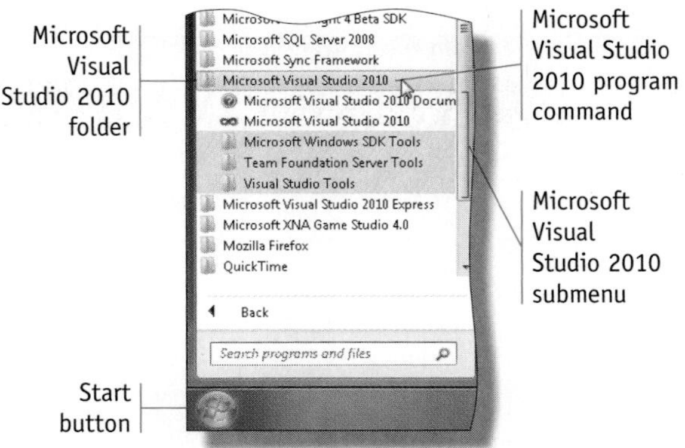

FIGURE 2-2

STEP 2 Click Microsoft Visual Studio 2010 on the submenu.

For a short time, a Visual Studio splash screen appears, and then Microsoft Visual Studio 2010 opens (Figure 2-3). The title of the window is Microsoft Visual Studio. The menu bar and the Standard toolbar are displayed at the top of the window. The Start Page contains information regarding Visual Basic. To close the Start Page, click the Close button on the Start Page title bar. You will learn the other elements of this window as you progress through this book.

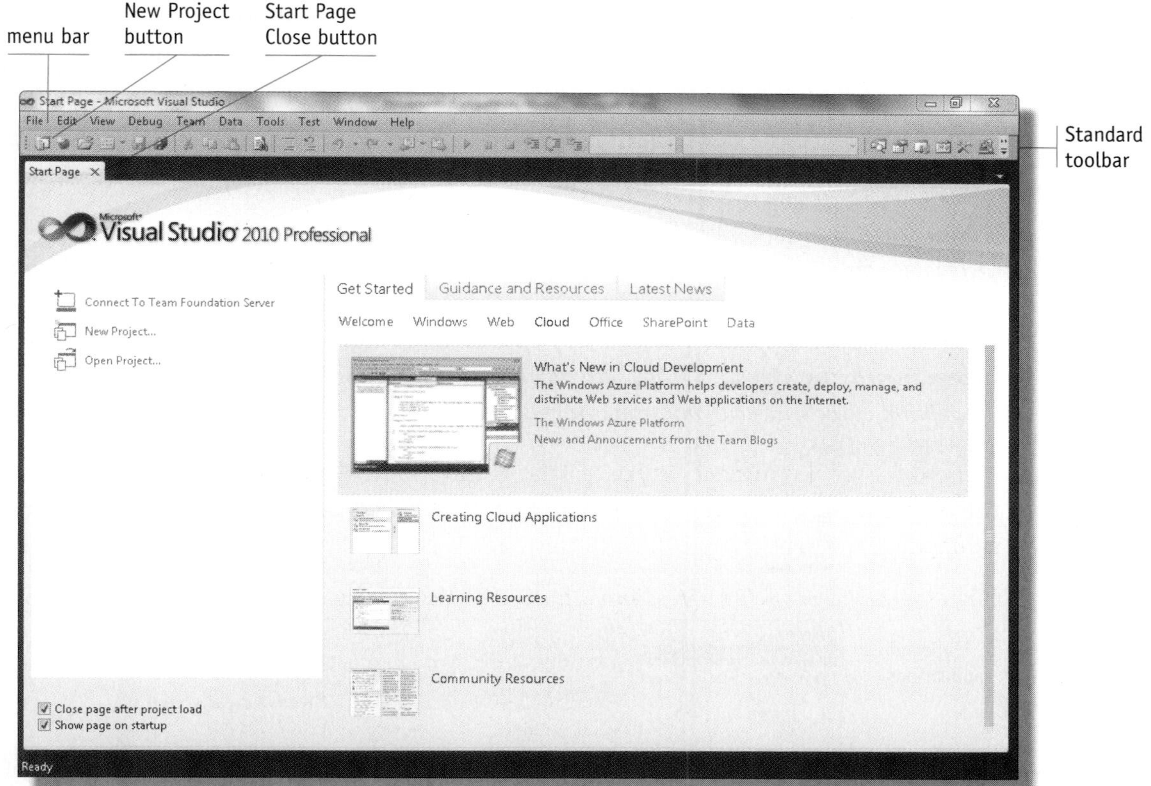

FIGURE 2-3

ONLINE REINFORCEMENT

To view a video of the process in the previous steps, visit scsite.com/vb2010/ch2 and then click Figure 2-2.

Create a New Visual Basic 2010 Windows Application Project

A **project** is equivalent to a single program created using Visual Studio. A **Windows Application project** is a program that will include, as the user interface, a window on the screen of a computer using the Windows operating system. When the program is executed, the user will interact with the program by using the window and its components (the user interface).

To create a new project using Visual Studio, you must specify the programming language you want to use and the type of program, or application, you will create. To create a new Visual Basic Windows Application project, you can take the following steps:

STEP 1 Click the New Project button on the Standard toolbar.

Visual Studio opens the New Project window (Figure 2-4). The New Project window on your computer might be displayed differently, depending on selections made at the time Visual Studio was installed on your computer. The left pane contains the programming languages and other types of templates available in Visual Studio. The middle pane contains the types of applications you can create within each programming language. The right pane displays a description of the selected application. At this time, you want to create a Windows Application using Visual Basic.

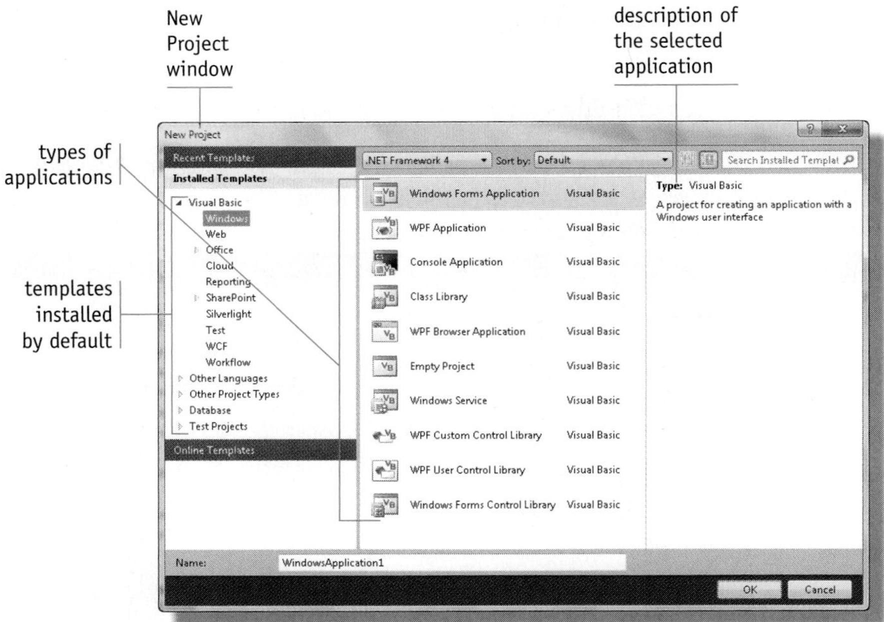

FIGURE 2-4

STEP 2 If necessary, in the left pane, click Windows so it is selected.

Windows is highlighted in the left pane and the types of Windows projects you can create using Visual Basic are listed in the middle pane (Figure 2-5).

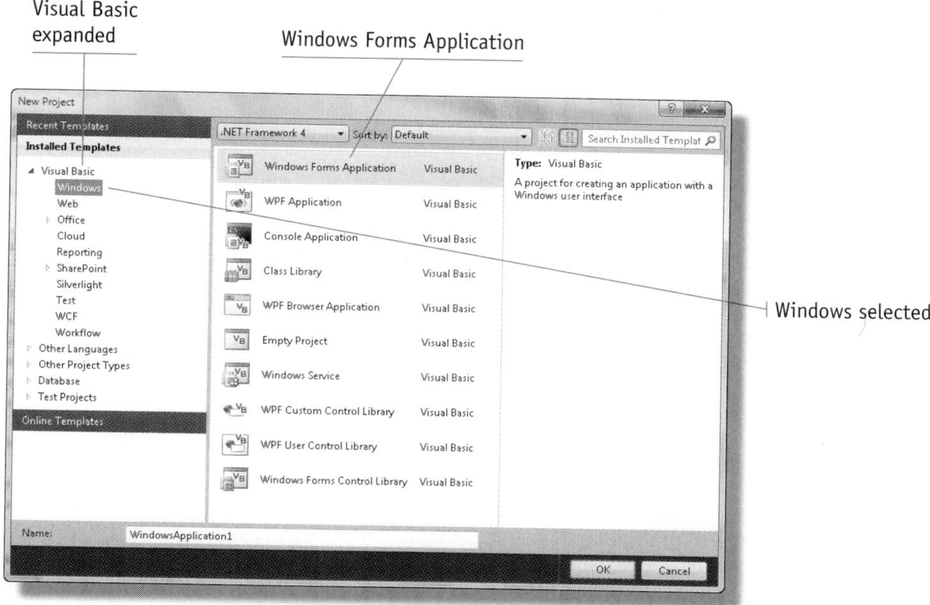

FIGURE 2-5

STEP 3 If necessary, click Windows Forms Application in the middle pane.

Windows Forms Application is selected in the middle pane (Figure 2-6). By making this selection, you have specified you want to create a program that will run under the Windows operating system using the Windows graphical user interface.

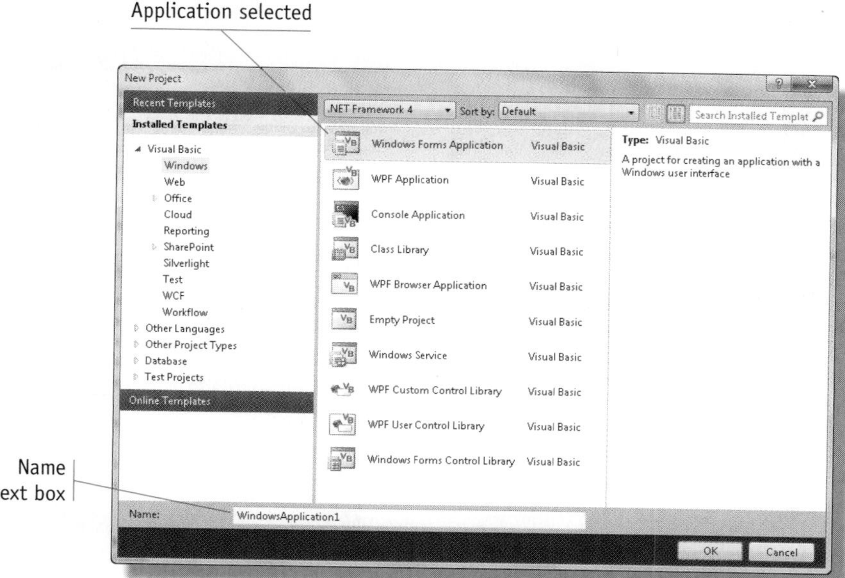

FIGURE 2-6

IN THE REAL WORLD

Program names can contain spaces and some special characters, but by convention most developers use a name with capital letters at the beginning of each word in the name. This naming convention is called camel case.

STEP 4 Double-click the text, WindowsApplication1, in the Name text box to select the text. Type the project name. For this example, you could type `HotelRoomSelection` as the name.

The project name appears in the Name text box (Figure 2-7).

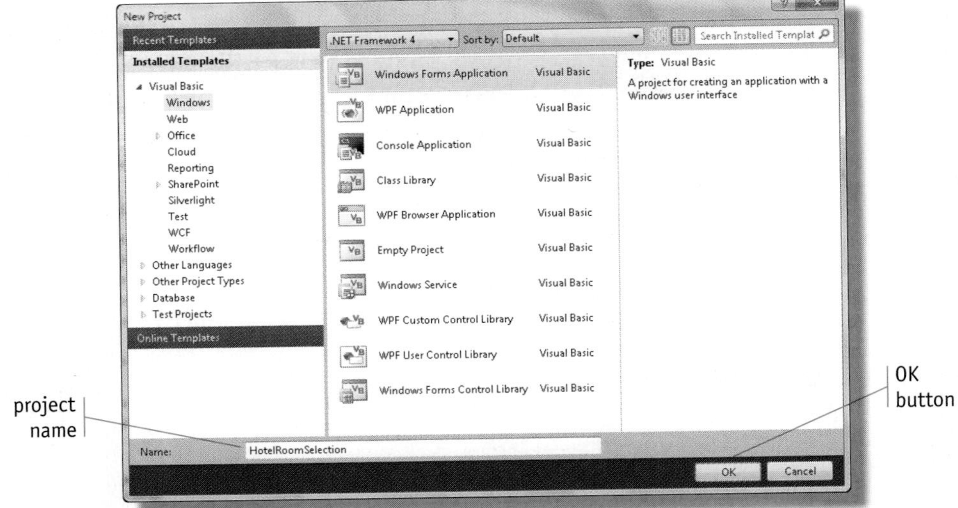

FIGURE 2-7

STEP 5 Click the OK button in the New Project window.

Visual Studio creates a new project (Figure 2-8). The project name is displayed in the title bar of the window.

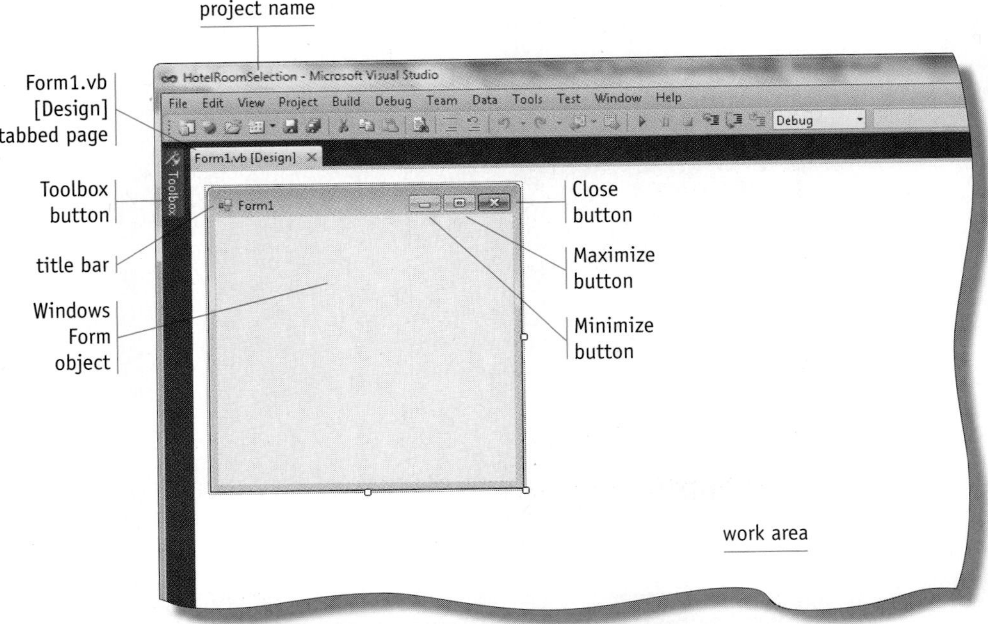

FIGURE 2-8

ONLINE REINFORCEMENT

To view a video of the process in the previous steps, visit scsite.com/vb2010/ch2 and then click Figure 2-4.

The Visual Studio window contains several important features of which you should be aware. First, in the portion of the window known as the **work area**, a tabbed page named Form1.vb [Design] contains a Windows Form object called Form1. A **Windows Form object** is the window you will use to build the program and is the window that will be displayed on your screen when you execute the program. The Windows Form object is the fundamental object in the graphical user interface you will create using Visual Studio tools. Notice in Figure 2-8 that the Windows Form object contains a blue title bar, a window title (Form1), a Minimize button, a Maximize button, and a Close button.

A second important element is displayed on the left of the window. Depending on the settings within Visual Studio, the left portion of the window will appear as shown in Figure 2-8 or as shown in Figure 2-9. In Figure 2-8, the left margin contains the Toolbox button. The Toolbox button also appears on the Standard toolbar.

Display the Toolbox

You can use the **Toolbox button** to display the Toolbox. The **Toolbox** is the primary tool you will use to place objects such as buttons on the Windows Form object. To display the Toolbox, you can take the following steps:

STEP 1 If the window does not already display the Toolbox, point to the Toolbox button in the left margin of the window.

When you point to the Toolbox button, the Toolbox is displayed on the window (Figure 2-9). Notice that the Toolbox hides part of the Form1 Windows Form object.

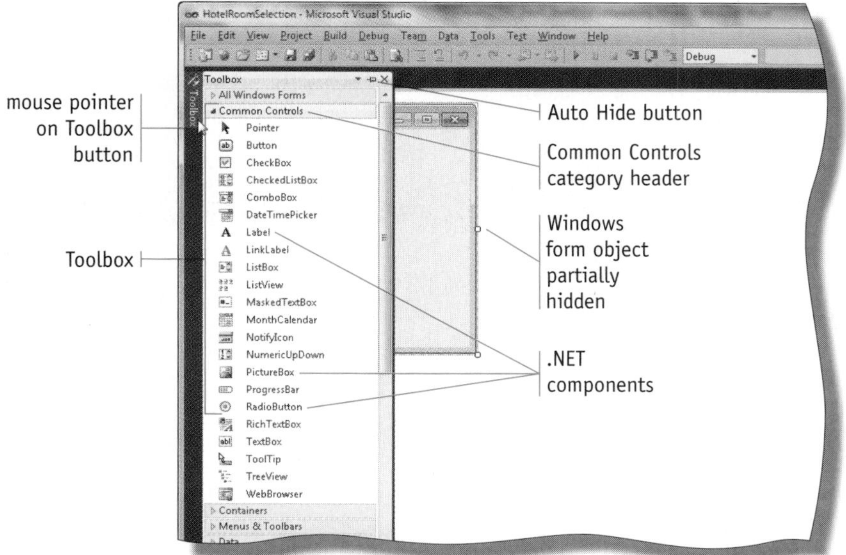

FIGURE 2-9

WATCH OUT FOR

In Figure 2-9 the Common Controls category of tools is open and all the tools in the category are visible. If the Common Controls Category is not open, a triangle is placed to the left of the category header (Common Controls). To open the category, click the expand triangle.

ONLINE REINFORCEMENT

To view a video of the process in the previous step, visit scsite.com/vb2010/ch2 and then click Figure 2-9.

The Toolbox contains, among other things, many graphical elements called **.NET components** that you can place on the Windows Form object as graphical user interface objects. For example, it contains buttons that can be placed on the Windows Form object. You will learn how to perform this activity in the next section of this chapter.

IN THE REAL WORLD

When the Toolbox is not displayed, you can display it using two different techniques. If you point to the Toolbox button, the Toolbox is displayed as long as the mouse pointer is within the Toolbox. When you move the mouse pointer out of the Toolbox, the Toolbox is hidden. If you click the Toolbox button, the Toolbox is displayed until you click somewhere else within the Visual Studio window. When the Toolbox can be displayed or not, depending on your actions, it is said to be in **Auto Hide mode.** To cause the Toolbox to be displayed at all times, follow the step shown in Figure 2-10.

Permanently Display the Toolbox

As long as the mouse pointer is within the Toolbox, the Toolbox is displayed. If, however, you move the mouse pointer off the Toolbox, it no longer is displayed.

When you are designing the graphical user interface, normally it is advantageous to display the Toolbox at all times. To keep the Toolbox on the window at all times, you can complete the following step:

STEP 1 If necessary, point to the Toolbox button in the left margin of the window to display the Toolbox. Then, click the **Auto Hide button** on the Toolbox title bar.

When you click the Auto Hide button, the Pushpin icon on the Auto Hide button on the Toolbox title bar changes from being horizontal, which indicates Auto Hide, to vertical, which indicates the Toolbox has been "pinned" to the window and will remain there (Figure 2-10). Form1 is moved to the right so you can see both the Toolbox and all of Form1.

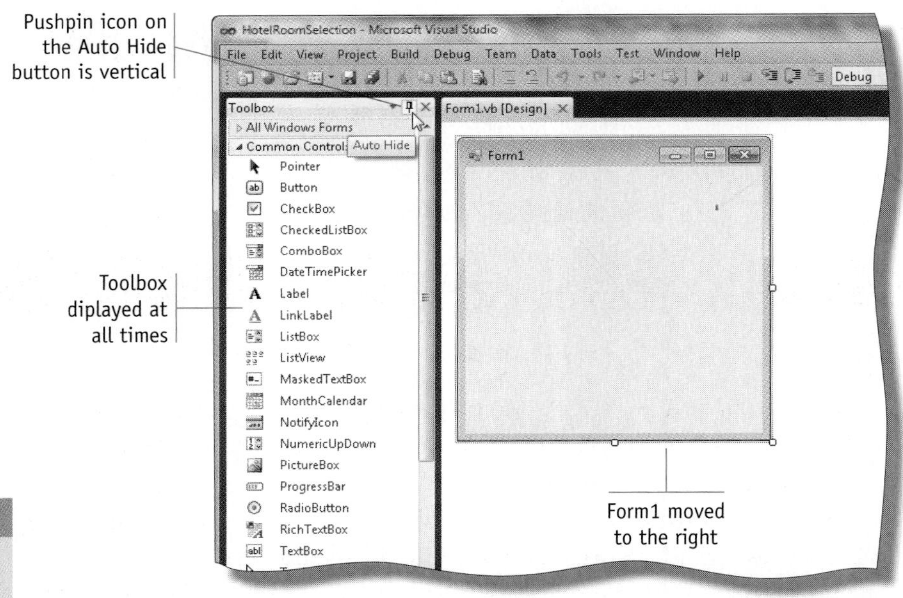

FIGURE 2-10

ONLINE REINFORCEMENT

To view a video of the process in the previous step, visit scsite.com/vb2010/ch2 and then click Figure 2-10.

When the Pushpin icon is vertical, the Toolbox is said to be in Dockable mode, which means it can be dragged around and placed anywhere within the Visual Studio window. In most applications, it should remain on the left of the window as shown in Figure 2-10. Later, you can change the Toolbox back to Auto Hide mode by clicking the Auto Hide button again.

View Object Properties

Every object you create in the user interface, including the Windows Form object, has properties. **Properties** can describe a multitude of characteristics about the object, including its color, size, name, and position on the screen. You will learn about the properties of all the objects you create using the Toolbox.

To view the properties for an object in Visual Studio, you use the Properties window. By default, the Properties window is displayed in the lower-right section of the Visual Studio window (Figure 2-11).

HEADS UP

If the Solution Explorer window is not displayed on your screen, you can display the window by taking the following steps: 1) Click View on the menu bar; 2) Click Solution Explorer on the View menu. The Solution Explorer window will be displayed in the location shown in Figure 2-11.

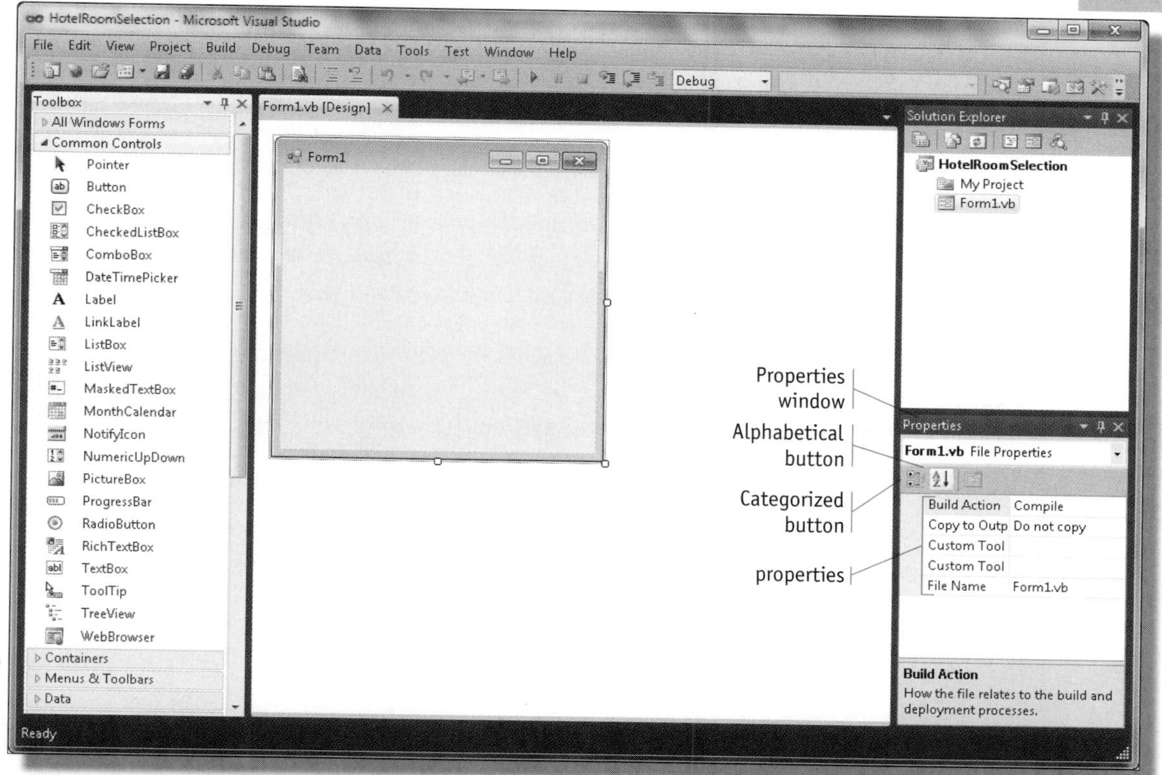

FIGURE 2-11

In the **Properties window** shown in Figure 2-11, the property names in the left list appear in Alphabetical view. Many developers find the Alphabetical view the easiest to use when searching for properties. Some developers, however, prefer the Categorized view, where properties are organized according to type. You can change the order of the properties into Categorized if you click the Categorized button on the Properties window toolbar (see Figure 2-11). In this book, the properties are shown in Alphabetical view, which is achieved by clicking the Alphabetical button on the Properties window toolbar.

HEADS UP

If the Properties window is not displayed on your screen, you can display the window by taking the following steps: 1) Click View on the menu bar; 2) Click Properties Window on the View menu. The Properties window will be displayed in the location shown in Figure 2-11.

Name the Windows Form Object

Visual Studio gives every object in a Visual Basic graphical user interface a default name. For example, the name for the first Windows Form object in a project is Form1. In virtually every instance, a developer should assign a meaningful name to

HEADS UP

If the properties in the Properties window do not appear in alphabetical order, click the Alphabetical button to place them in alphabetic order.

an object so the program can reference it if required. The name for an object should reflect the object's use. For example, a good name for the Hotel Room Selection window might be HotelRoomSelection. Notice in the name that each word is capitalized and the remaining letters are lowercase. You should always follow this naming method when naming objects.

No spaces or other special characters are allowed in the object name. Also, by convention, each object name should begin with a prefix that identifies the type of object. For Windows Form objects, the prefix is frm. Therefore, the complete name for the Windows Form object would be frmHotelRoomSelection. The form name should be changed in the Solution Explorer.

To give the name, frmHotelRoomSelection, to the form in Figure 2-11, you can complete the following steps:

STEP 1 Click anywhere in the Windows Form object to select it.

When you click within any object, including a Windows Form object, that object is selected (Figure 2-12). Sizing handles and a heavier border surround the selected object. In addition, the Properties window displays the properties of the selected object.

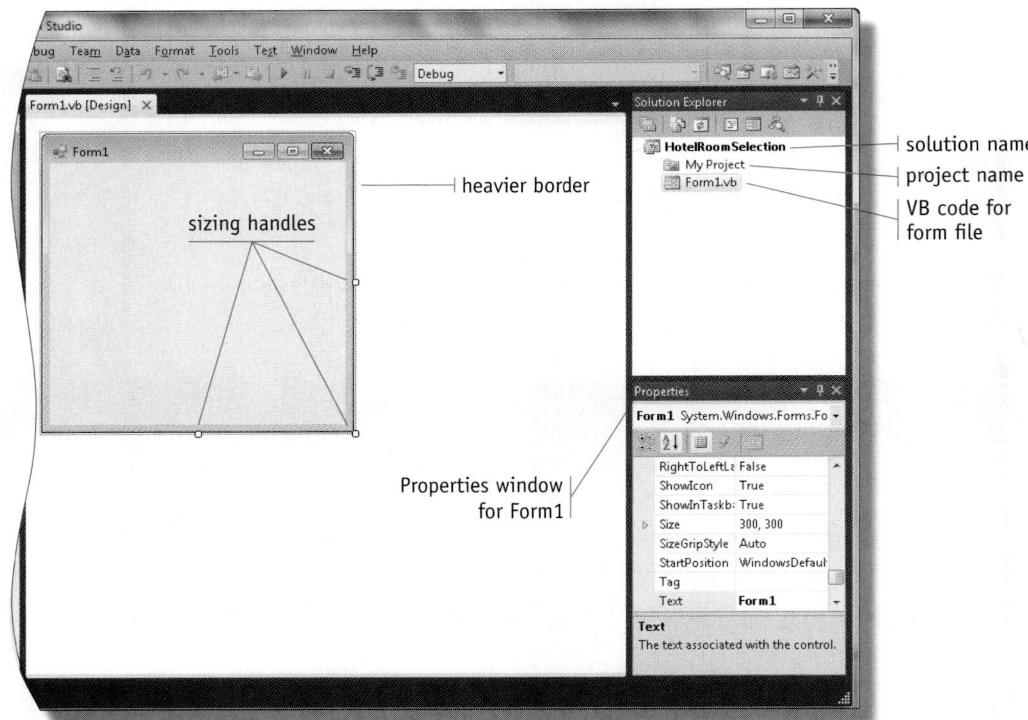

FIGURE 2-12

STEP 2 In the Solution Explorer window, right-click the Form1.vb filename. On the shortcut menu, point to Rename.

The name, Form1, is right-clicked in the Solution Explorer window. The shortcut menu for the Form1.vb file appears. Rename is highlighted (Figure 2-13).

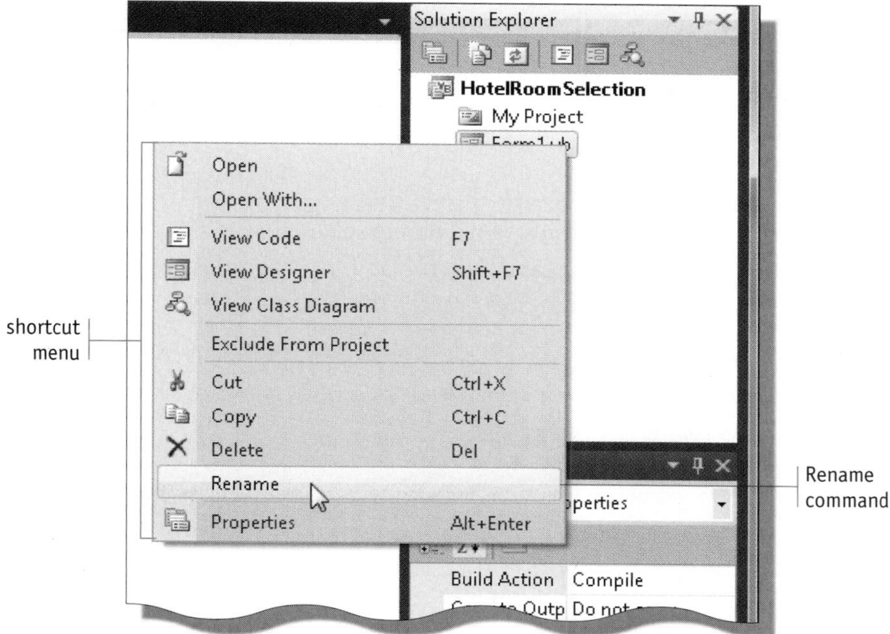

FIGURE 2-13

STEP 3 Click Rename. Type `frmHotelRoomSelection.vb` and press the ENTER key.

The Form1.vb form file is given the new name frmHotelRoomSelection.vb in the Solution Explorer window (Figure 2-14).

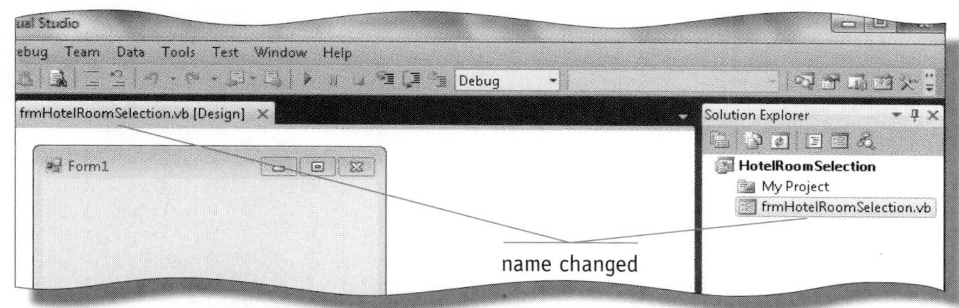

FIGURE 2-14

ONLINE REINFORCEMENT

To view a video of the process in the previous steps, visit scsite.com/vb2010/ch2 and then click Figure 2-12.

Set the Title Bar Text in a Windows Form Object

After you name the Windows Form object, often the next step in the graphical user interface design is to change the title bar text so it reflects the function of the program. In this example, the name used is Hotel Room Selection. The **Text property** in the Windows Form object Properties window contains the value that is displayed in the title bar of the window. You can set the Text property using the following steps:

STEP 1 With the Windows Form object selected, scroll in the Properties window until you find the Text property. (Remember: The properties are in alphabetic order.) Then, double-click in the right column for the Text property.

The text, Form1, is selected in the Properties window (Figure 2-15). Form1 is the default text value for the first Windows Form object created in a project. Whenever a property is selected, you can change the property.

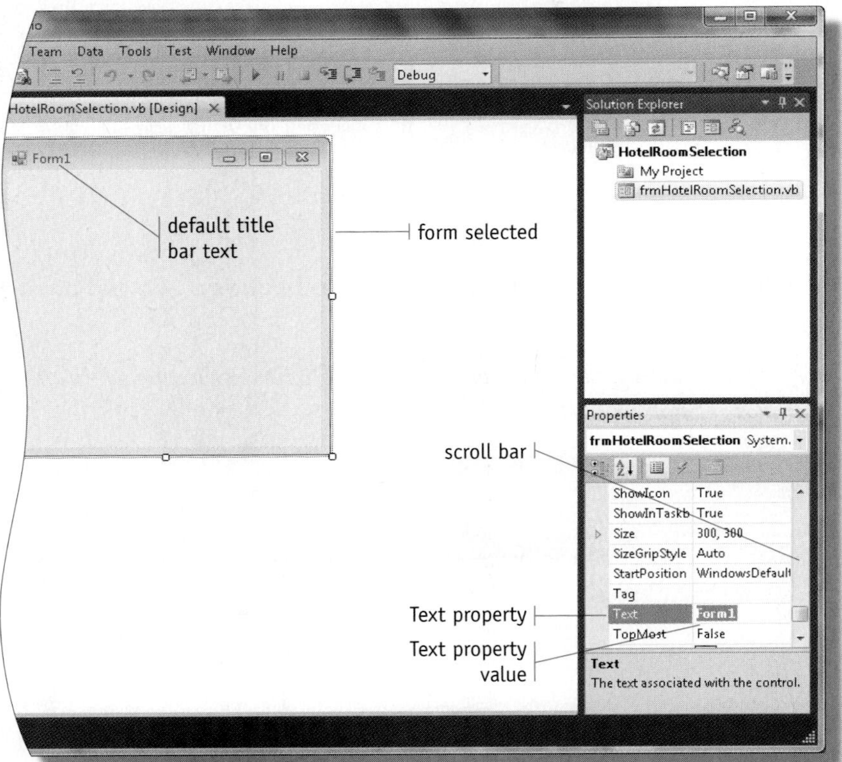

FIGURE 2-15

STEP 2 Type `Hotel Room Selection` and then press the ENTER key.

The value, Hotel Room Selection, is displayed for the Text property in the Properties window and also is displayed in the title bar of the Windows Form object (Figure 2-16). You can enter any value you like for the Text property of the Windows Form object.

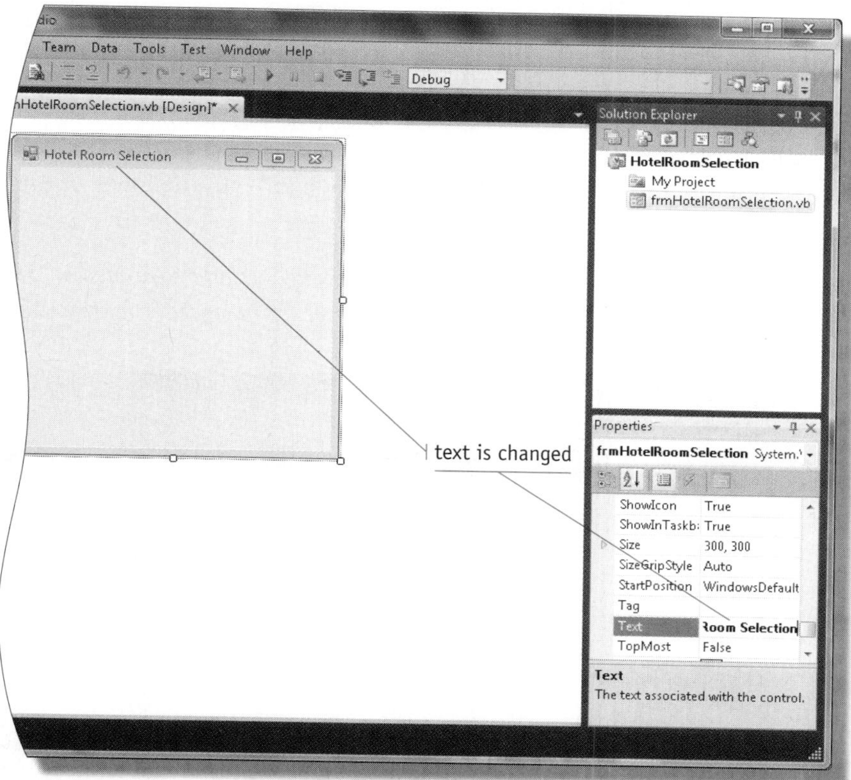

FIGURE 2-16

ONLINE REINFORCEMENT

To view a video of the process in the previous steps, visit scsite.com/vb2010/ch2 and then click Figure 2-15.

You can change many of the properties for any object in the graphical user interface using the techniques just illustrated.

Resize a Form

To resize a Windows Form object, you can change the **Size property** in the Properties window to the exact number of horizontal and vertical pixels you desire. You also can change the Windows Form object size by dragging the vertical border to change the width of the window or the horizontal border to change the height. Another way to change the size is to drag a corner sizing handle, which allows you to change both the width and the height at the same time.

The following steps illustrate using the sizing handles to change the size of the Windows Form object shown in Figure 2-17:

STEP 1 Place the mouse pointer over the sizing handle in the lower-right corner of the Windows Form object.

When the mouse pointer is over the sizing handle, it changes to a two-headed arrow that indicates you can drag to change the size of the Windows Form object (Figure 2-17).

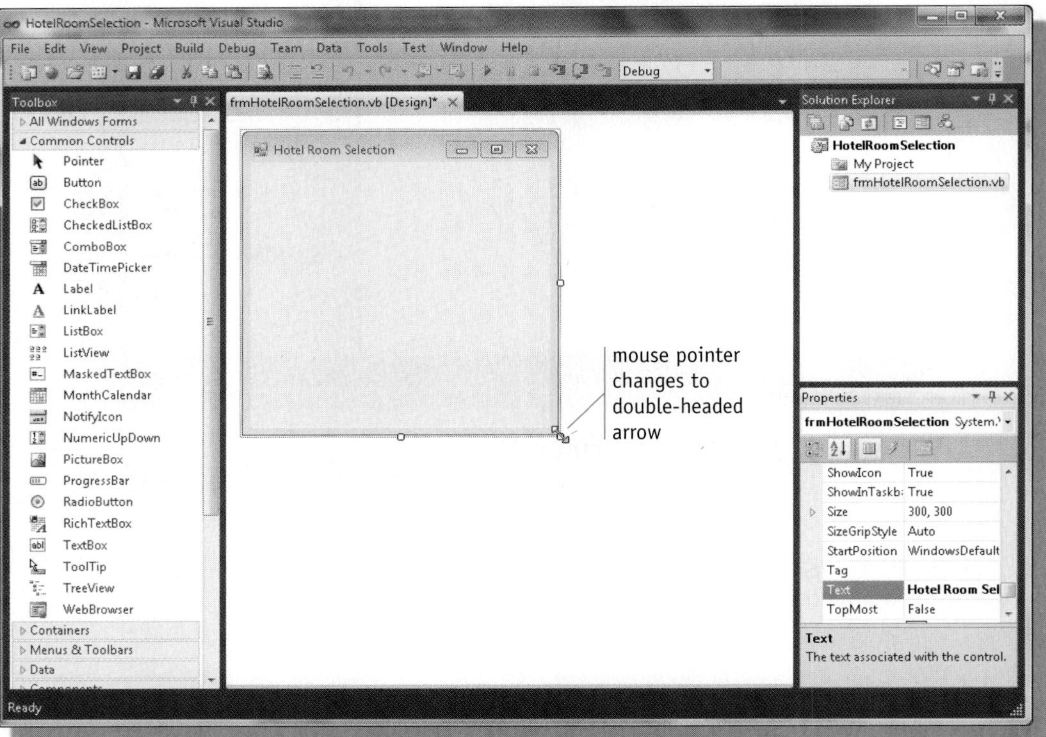
mouse pointer changes to double-headed arrow

FIGURE 2-17

STEP 2 Drag the sizing handle to the right and down until the window is the size you want. Then, release the left mouse button.

The Windows Form object has been resized (Figure 2-18). The exact size of the Windows Form object is shown on the Status bar as (number of horizontal pixels, number of vertical pixels). In Figure 2-18, the size of the Windows Form object is 430 pixels horizontally by 395 pixels vertically.

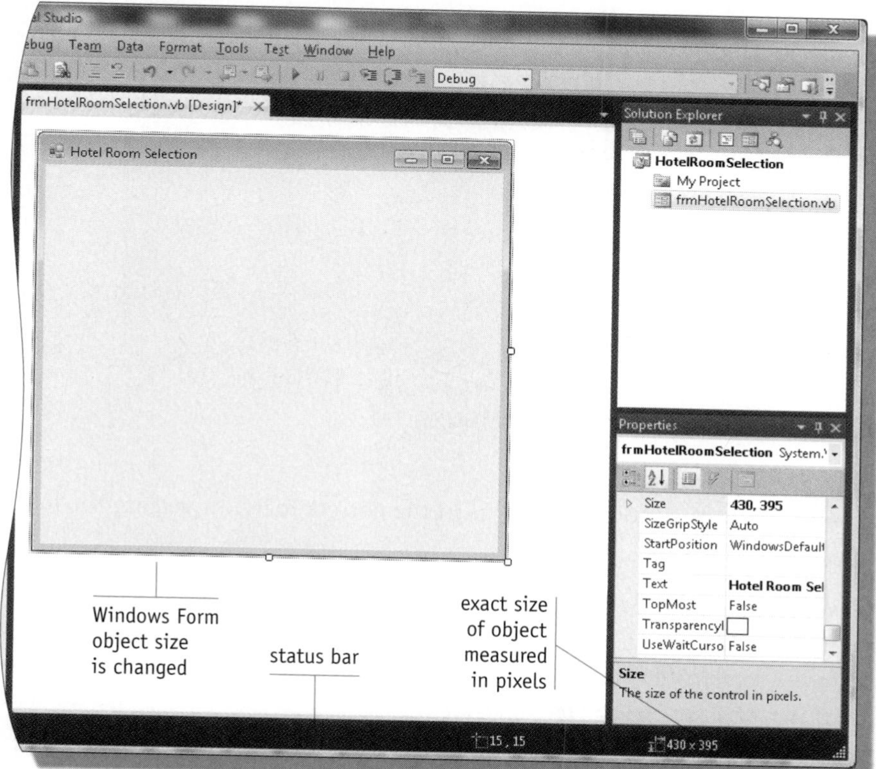

FIGURE 2-18

ONLINE REINFORCEMENT

To view a video of the process in the previous steps, visit scsite.com/vb2010/ch2 and then click Figure 2-17.

Add a Label Object

After sizing the Windows Form object, you can use the Toolbox to add other GUI objects as required. For example, a graphical user interface often displays a message or labels an item in the window. To accomplish this, you can use the **Label .NET component** in the Toolbox to place a **Label object** on the Windows Form object. To add a Label object to a Windows Form object, you can complete the steps on the next page.

STEP 1 Drag the Label .NET component button from the Common Controls category in the Toolbox over the Windows Form object to the approximate location where you want to place the Label object.

The mouse pointer changes to a crosshair and small rectangle when you place it over the Windows Form object (Figure 2-19). The Label object will be placed on the form at the location of the small rectangle in the mouse pointer.

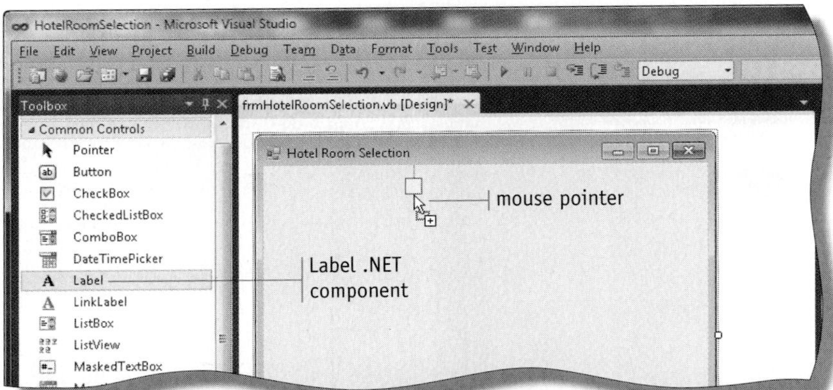

FIGURE 2-19

IN THE REAL WORLD

In addition to dragging a .NET component from the Toolbox to the Windows Form object, you can place an object on the Windows Form object by double-clicking the .NET component in the Toolbox. You can move and resize the object after it has been placed on the Windows Form object. You also can click the .NET component in the Toolbox and then click the Windows Form object at the desired location for the object. The object will be placed where you clicked. Developers use the technique they find most convenient.

STEP 2 When the mouse pointer is in the correct location, release the left mouse button.

The Label object is placed on the Windows Form object at the location you selected (Figure 2-20). The label is selected, as identified by the dotted border surrounding it. The default text within the label is Label1. In virtually all cases, you must change the label text to reflect the needs of the interface.

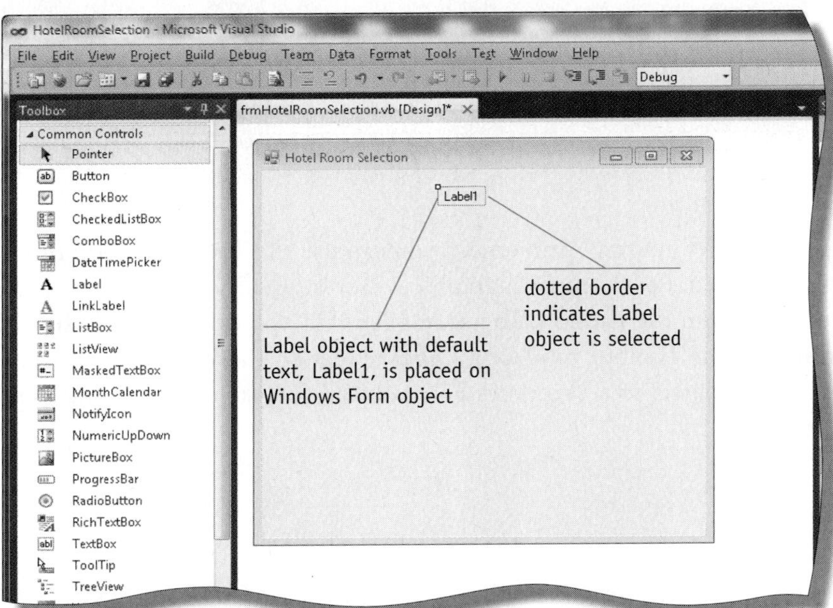

FIGURE 2-20

ONLINE REINFORCEMENT

To view a video of the process in the previous steps, visit scsite.com/vb2010/ch2 and then click Figure 2-19.

Name the Label Object

As with most objects you place on the Windows Form object, the first step after creating the object should be to name the object. To give the Label object the name, Heading, together with the Label prefix, lbl, complete the following steps:

STEP 1 With the Label object selected, scroll in the Properties window until you find the (Name) property. Then double-click in the right column for the (Name) property.

The default name, Label1, is selected (Figure 2-21). When a property is selected, you can change the property.

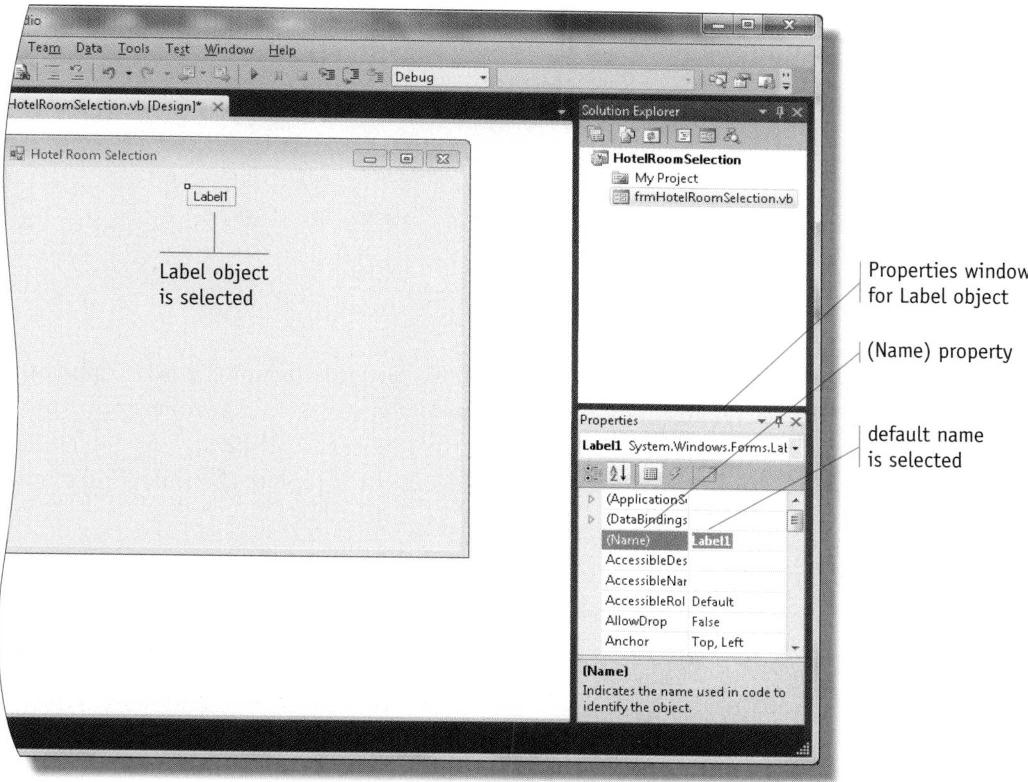

FIGURE 2-21

WATCH OUT FOR

If you make an error while typing a property, such as the Name, you can press the BACKSPACE key to erase your mistake, and then type the correct data. You also can double-click the property you want to change and start all over again.

ONLINE REINFORCEMENT

To view a video of the process in the previous steps, visit scsite.com/vb2010/ch2 and then click Figure 2-21.

STEP 2 Type the new name, `lblHeading` and then press the ENTER key.

The name you entered is displayed in the Name property in the Properties window (Figure 2-22). You now can reference the Label object by its name in other parts of the program.

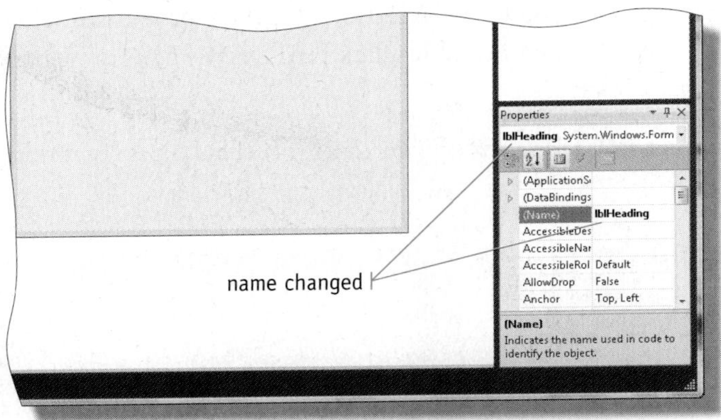

FIGURE 2-22

Change the Text in a Label Object

The default text in a Label object, Label1, normally is not the text you want to display in the label. Therefore, you should change the Text property for the Label object to the desired value. To change the text that is displayed on the label in Figure 2-21 to Hotel Room Selection, you can complete the following steps:

STEP 1 With the Label object selected, scroll in the Properties dialog box until you find the Text property. Then, double-click the Text value in the right column.

The text value in the right column of the Text property, which is the text that is displayed in the label, is selected (Figure 2-23). When the Text value is selected, you can change it.

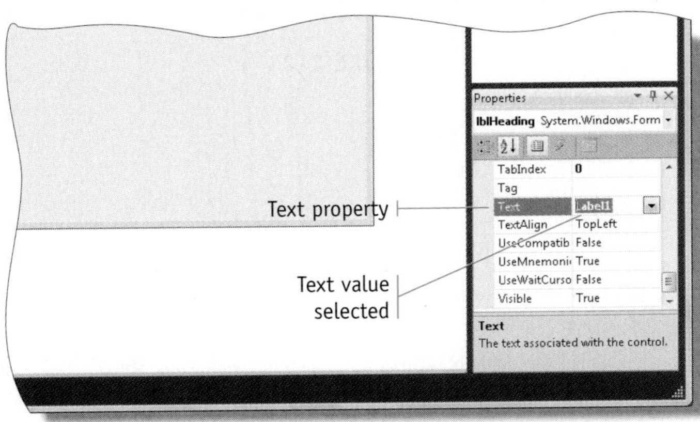

FIGURE 2-23

STEP 2 Type `Hotel Room Selection` for the Text property.

The text you typed, Hotel Room Selection, is displayed in the Text property for the Label object (Figure 2-24).

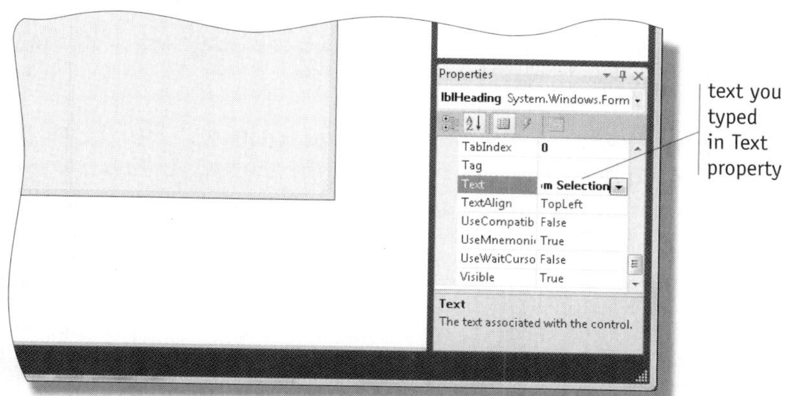

FIGURE 2-24

STEP 3 To enter the Text property, press the ENTER key.

The text you entered, Hotel Room Selection, is displayed in the Text property and also in the label itself (Figure 2-25). The text is, by default, 8 points in size. The Label object automatically expanded horizontally to accommodate the text you typed. By default, Label objects change size so they are just the right size for the text in the Text property.

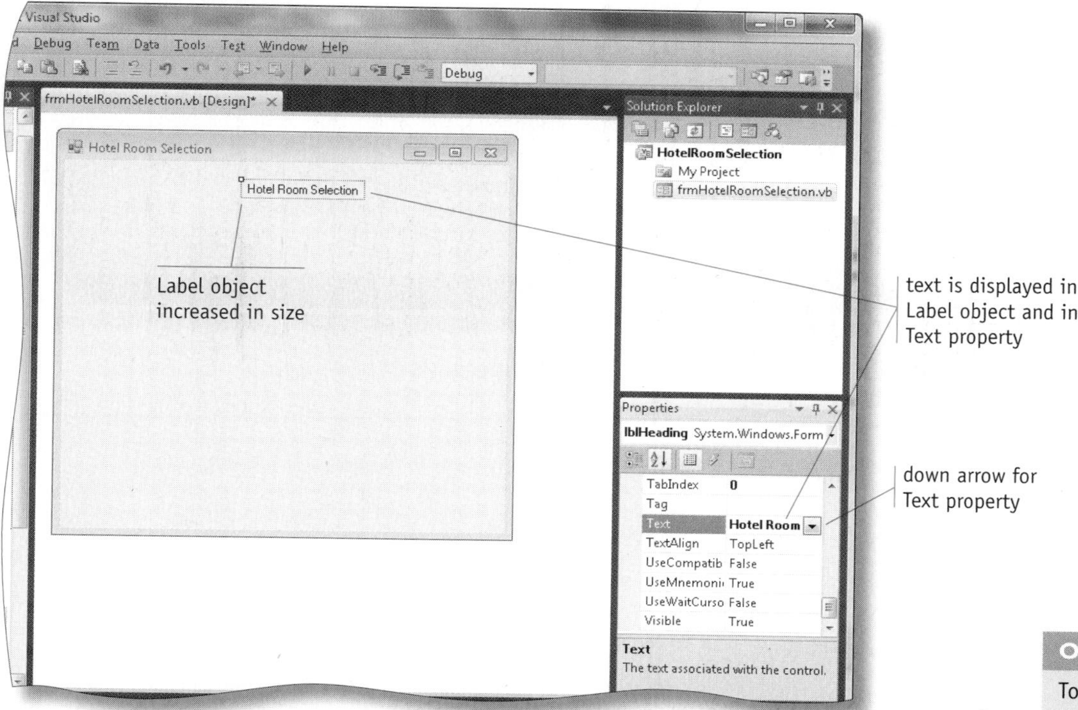

FIGURE 2-25

ONLINE REINFORCEMENT

To view a video of the process in the previous steps, visit scsite.com/vb2010/ch2 and then click Figure 2-23.

The text in a Label object can be multiple lines. To enter multiple lines for a Label object, you can complete the following steps:

STEP 1 With the Label object selected, click the Text property name in the left column of the Properties window. Then, click the down arrow in the right column of the Text property.

A box opens in which you can enter multiple lines (Figure 2-26). As you type, you can move the insertion point to the next line by pressing the ENTER key. To accept the text for the label, press CTRL + ENTER (this nomenclature means you hold down the CTRL key, press the ENTER key, and then release both keys).

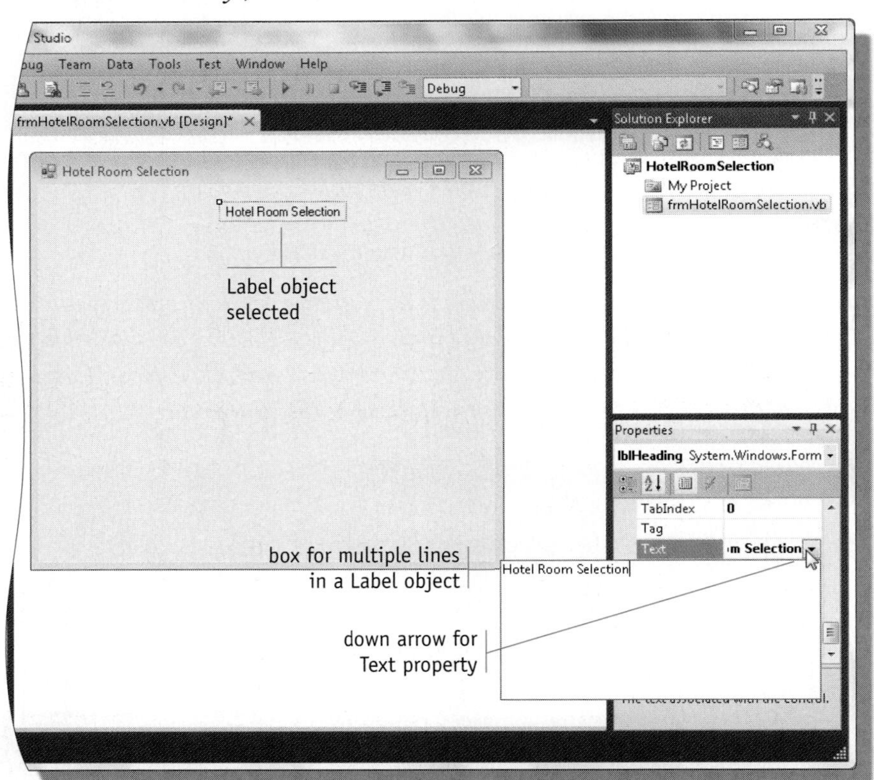

FIGURE 2-26

ONLINE REINFORCEMENT

To view a video of the process in the previous step, visit scsite.com/vb2010/ch2 and then click Figure 2-26.

Change Label Font, Font Style, and Font Size

Many times, the default font, font style, and font size of the text in a Label object must be changed to reflect the purpose of the label. For example, in a label that is used as a heading for a window, the text should be larger than the default 8-point font used for Label objects, and should be bold so it stands out as a heading. To change the font, font style, and font size of a label, you can select the label and then use the **Font property** to make the change. To change the text that appears in the lblHeading label to Tahoma font, make the font bold, and increase the font size to 16 point, you can complete the following steps:

STEP 1 Click the Label object to select it. Scroll until you find the Font property in the Properties window. Click the Font property in the left column of the Label property window.

The Label object is selected as shown by the dotted border surrounding it (Figure 2-27). When you click the Font property in the Properties window, an ellipsis button (a button with three dots) is displayed in the right column. In the Properties window, an ellipsis button indicates multiple choices for the property will be made available when you click the button.

WATCH OUT FOR

When you click an object to select it, you might double-click it accidentally. If you do, a tabbed page with programming code opens. To return to the form and continue developing the user interface, click the [Design] tab for your form, such as the frmHotelRoomSelection.vb [Design] tab.

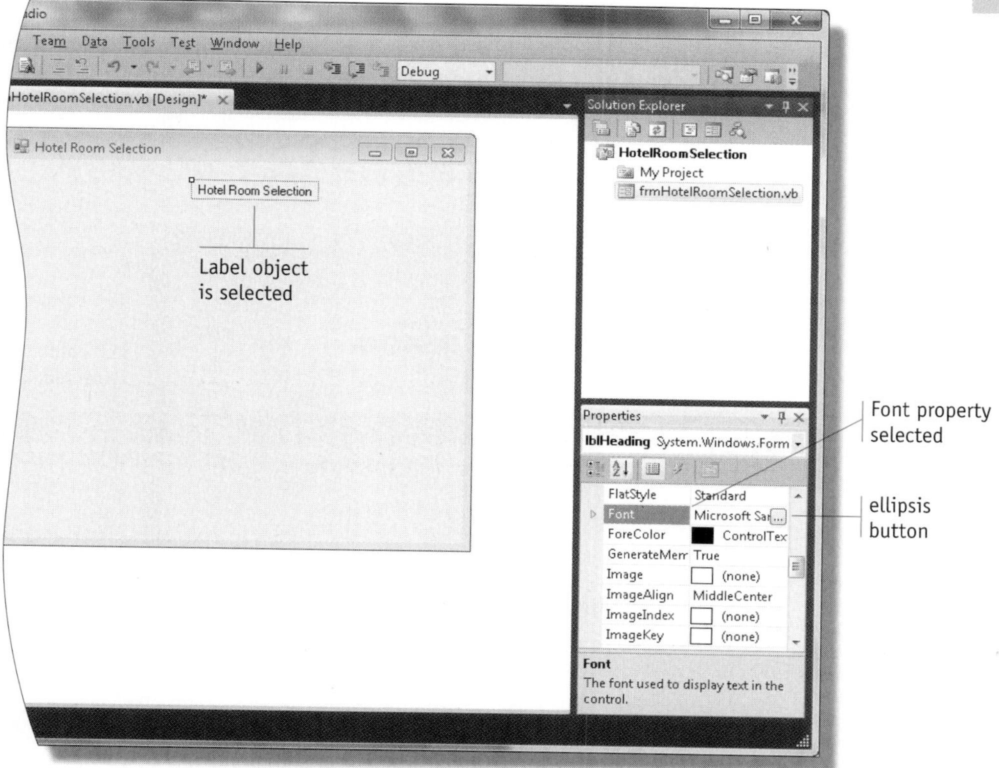

FIGURE 2-27

STEP 2 Click the ellipsis button for the Font property.

The Font dialog box is displayed (Figure 2-28). Using the Font dialog box, you can change the Font, Font style, and Size of the text in the Label object.

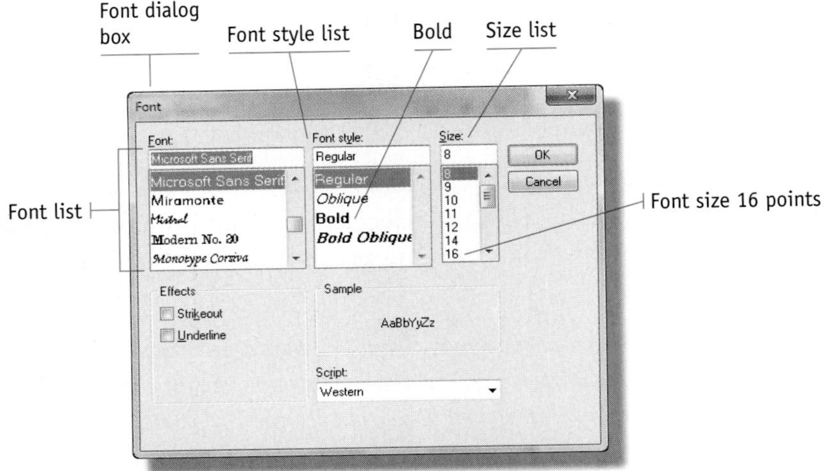

FIGURE 2-28

STEP 3 In the Font dialog box, scroll to find Tahoma in the Font list and then click Tahoma in the Font list. Click Bold in the Font style list. Click 16 in the Size list.

The selections are highlighted in the Font dialog box (Figure 2-29).

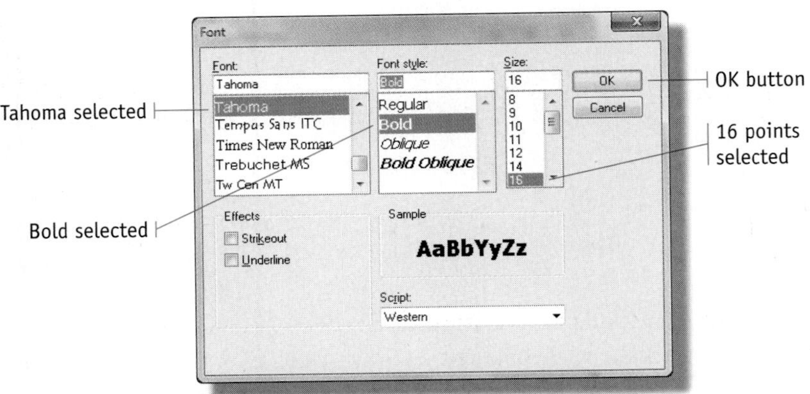

FIGURE 2-29

STEP 4 Click the OK button.

The font, font style, and font size in the Label object are changed as specified in the Font dialog box (Figure 2-30). The Label object automatically expands to accommodate the changed font. The changes also are made for the Font property in the Properties window.

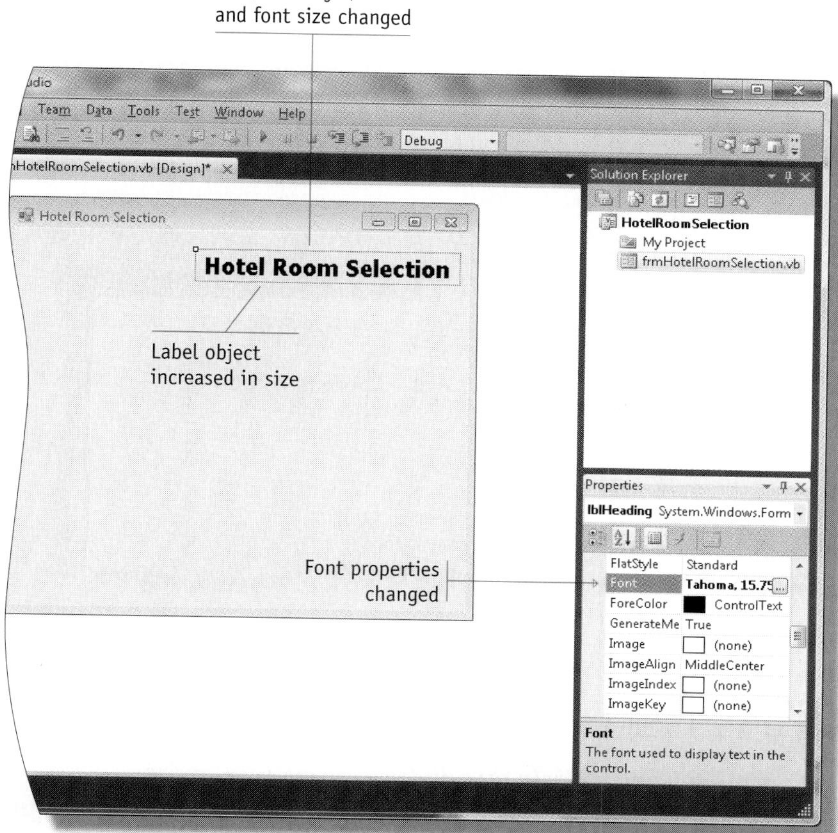

FIGURE 2-30

ONLINE REINFORCEMENT

To view a video of the process in the previous steps, visit scsite.com/vb2010/ch2 and then click Figure 2-27.

Center a Label Object in the Windows Form Object

When you place an object on the Windows Form object, the object you place may not be located in precisely the correct position. So, you must align the object in the window. A single label often is centered horizontally in the window; that is, the distance from the left frame of the window to the beginning of the text should be the same as the distance from the end of the text to the right frame of the window. To horizontally center the label containing the heading, you can complete the following steps:

STEP 1 With the Label object selected, click Format on the menu bar and then point to Center in Form on the Format menu.

The Format menu is displayed and the mouse pointer is located on the Center in Form command (Figure 2-31). The Center in Form submenu also is displayed. The two choices on the Center in Form submenu are Horizontally and Vertically. Horizontally means the label will be centered between the left and right edges of the window. Vertically means the label will be centered between the top edge and the bottom edge of the window.

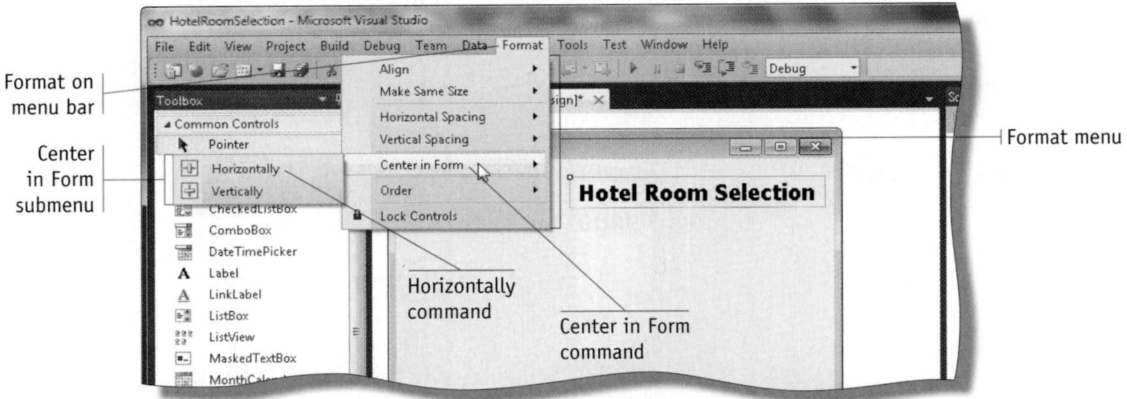

FIGURE 2-31

STEP 2 Click Horizontally on the Center in Form submenu.

The label is centered horizontally in the window (Figure 2-32).

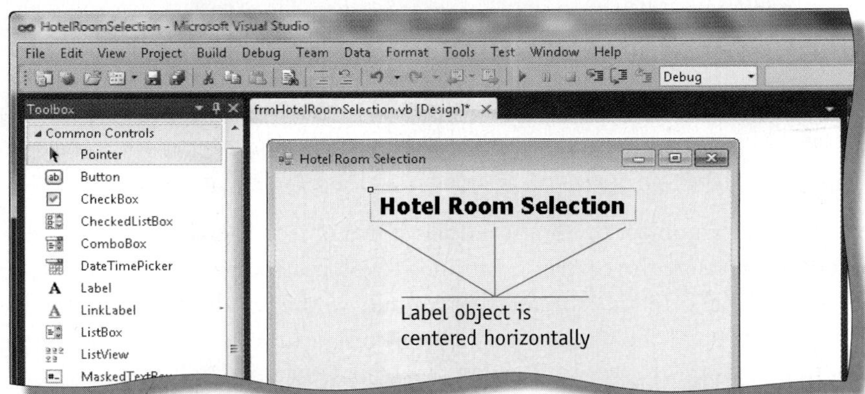

FIGURE 2-32

ONLINE REINFORCEMENT

To view a video of the process in the previous steps, visit scsite.com/vb2010/ch2 and then click Figure 2-31.

Object alignment is an important aspect of user interface design because carefully aligned objects in an interface make them and the interface easy to use. Centering within the Windows Form object is the first of several alignment requirements you will encounter in this chapter.

Delete GUI Objects

In some instances, you might find that you add an object to the Windows Form object and later discover you do not want or need the object in the user interface. When this occurs, you should delete the object from the Windows Form object. Visual Studio provides two primary ways to delete an object from the Windows Form object: the keyboard and a shortcut menu. To delete an object using the keyboard, perform the following steps:

STEP 1 Select the object to be deleted by clicking it.

When you click an object, such as the label in Figure 2-33, the object is selected. When a label is selected, it is surrounded by a dotted border. As you saw with the Windows Form object (Figure 2-12), other objects are surrounded by a heavier border and sizing handles.

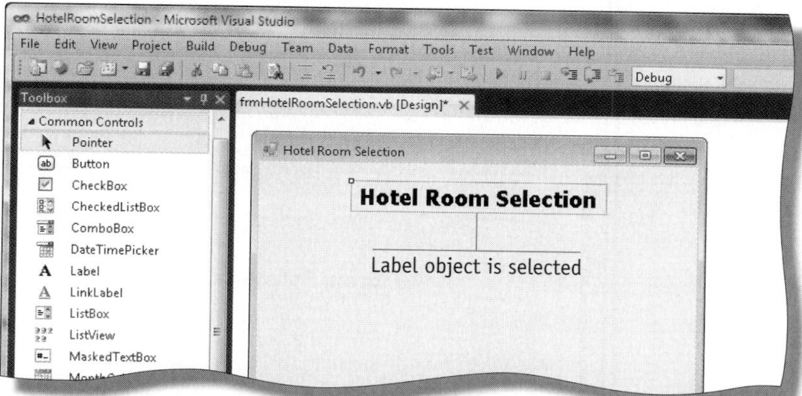

FIGURE 2-33

STEP 2 Press the DELETE key on the keyboard.

When you press the DELETE key, Visual Studio removes the object from the screen (Figure 2-34).

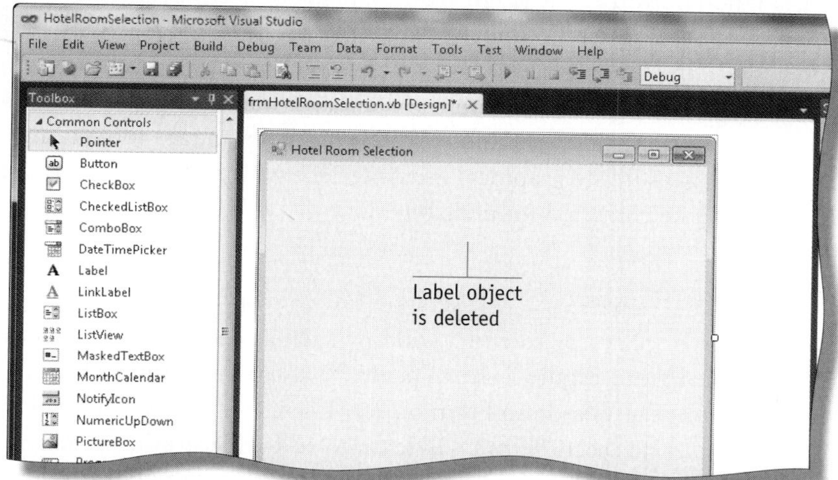

FIGURE 2-34

ONLINE REINFORCEMENT

To view a video of the process in the previous steps, visit scsite.com/vb2010/ch2 and then click Figure 2-33.

A second way to delete an object is to use a shortcut menu. To use a shortcut menu, right-click the object to be deleted and then select Delete on the shortcut menu.

Use the Undo Button on the Standard Toolbar

As you work in Visual Studio to create a graphical user interface, you might delete an object or perform another activity that you realize was an error. You can undo an action you just performed by clicking the Undo button on the Standard toolbar. To undo the action of deleting the heading label, you can perform the following step:

STEP 1 Click the Undo button on the Standard toolbar.

When you click the Undo button, the last action performed in Visual Studio is "undone." In Figure 2-35, the action that deleted the label (Figure 2-34) is undone and the Label object now appears on the Windows Form object again.

FIGURE 2-35

ONLINE REINFORCEMENT

To view a video of the process in the previous step, visit scsite.com/vb2010/ch2 and then click Figure 2-35.

You can use the Undo button to undo more than just the last action performed. If you click the Undo button arrow (Figure 2-35), many of the previous activities are shown in a list. You can undo a number of activities by clicking an activity in the list.

When you use the Undo button, you might undo something you do not want to undo. You can click the Redo button on the Standard toolbar to redo an action.

Learning to use the Undo and Redo buttons on the Standard toolbar means you can add or delete items in the graphical user interface with the assurance that any error you make can be corrected immediately.

Add a PictureBox Object

When you want to display a picture in a window, such as the hotel room pictures shown in Figure 2-1b and Figure 2-1c on pages 30 and 31, you must place a PictureBox object on the Windows Form object. Then, the picture is placed in the PictureBox object. In this section, you will learn to add a PictureBox object to the Windows Form object. In Chapter 3, you will learn how to place a picture in the PictureBox object.

A **PictureBox** is an object much like a label. To add a PictureBox object to the window, you can use the Toolbox, as shown in the following steps:

STEP 1 With the Toolbox visible, drag the PictureBox .NET component on the Toolbox over the Windows Form object to the approximate location where you want the PictureBox object to be displayed.

The mouse pointer changes when you place it over the Windows Form object (Figure 2-36). The upper-left corner of the PictureBox object will be placed on the form at the location of the small square in the mouse pointer.

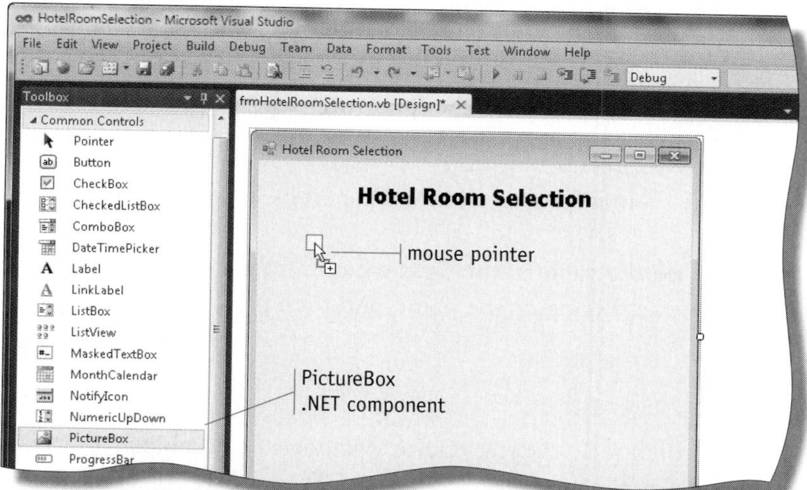

FIGURE 2-36

STEP 2 When the mouse pointer is in the correct location, release the left mouse button.

A PictureBox object is placed on the Windows Form object in the default size (Figure 2-37). The PictureBox object is selected as indicated by the sizing handles and the heavier border. Notice that when the mouse pointer is inside the PictureBox object, it changes to a crosshair with four arrowheads. This indicates you can drag the PictureBox object anywhere on the Windows Form object.

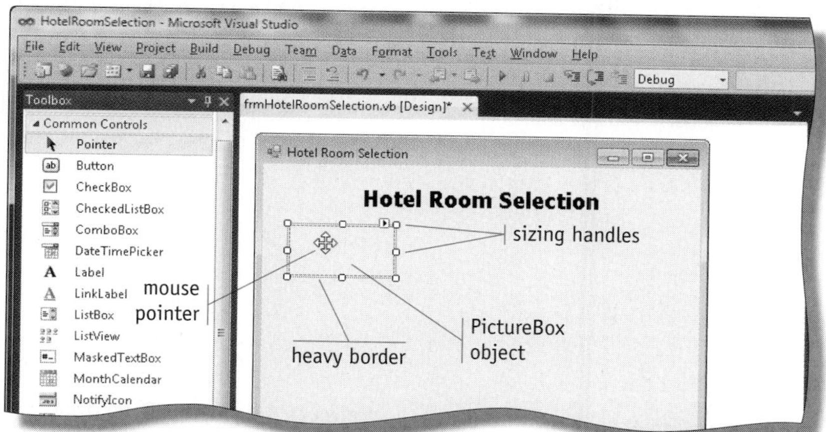

FIGURE 2-37

ONLINE REINFORCEMENT

To view a video of the process in the previous steps, visit scsite.com/vb2010/ch2 and then click Figure 2-36.

As you can see, placing a PictureBox object on the Windows Form object is similar to placing a Label object on the Windows Form object. You will find you can use the same technique for most objects within the Toolbox.

Name a PictureBox Object

When you add an object to the Windows Form object, the first action you should take is to name the object. The technique for naming a PictureBox object is identical to that used for naming a Label object except that the prefix for a PictureBox object is pic. For example, to give the name, picStandardRoom, to the PictureBox object just added to the form, you can complete the following steps:

1. Select the PictureBox object.
2. Locate the (Name) property in the Properties window for the PictureBox object.
3. Double-click the value in the right column for the (Name) property, type `picStandardRoom` as the name, and then press the ENTER key.

Resize a PictureBox Object

When you place a PictureBox object on the Windows Form object, it often is not the size required for the application. You can resize a PictureBox object using the same technique you used to resize the Windows Form object. The step on the next page will resize the Picture Box object:

STEP 1 With the left and right PictureBox objects selected as shown in Figure 2-42, click Format on the menu bar and then point to Align on the Format menu.

The Format menu and the Align submenu are displayed (Figure 2-43). The left PictureBox object is the "controlling" object as indicated by the white sizing handles, so the right PictureBox object will be aligned horizontally with the left PictureBox object.

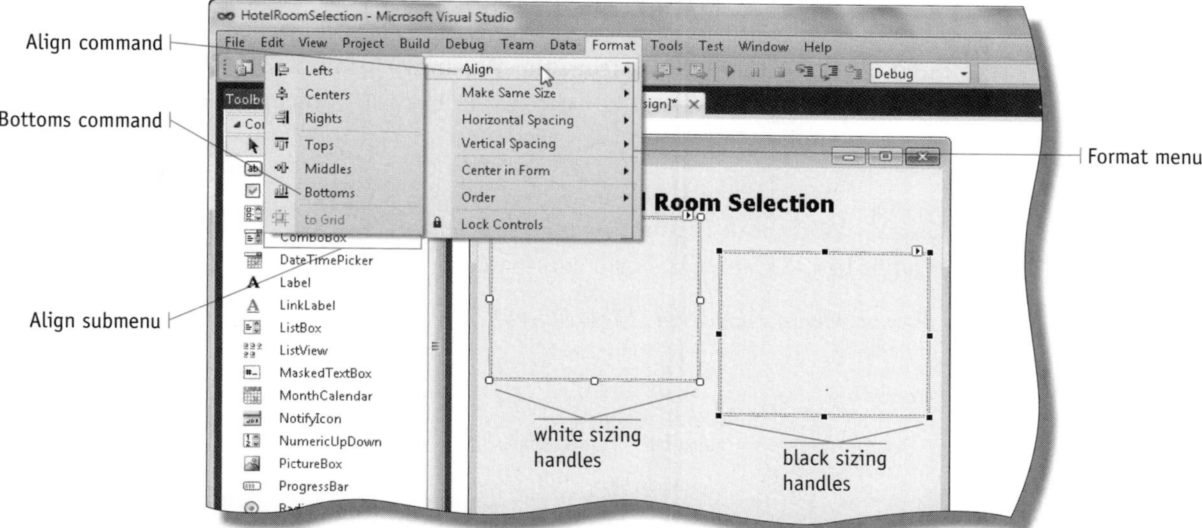

FIGURE 2-43

STEP 2 Click Bottoms on the Align submenu.

The bottom of the right PictureBox object is aligned horizontally with the bottom of the left PictureBox object (Figure 2-44). In addition, because the PictureBox objects are the same size, the tops also are aligned.

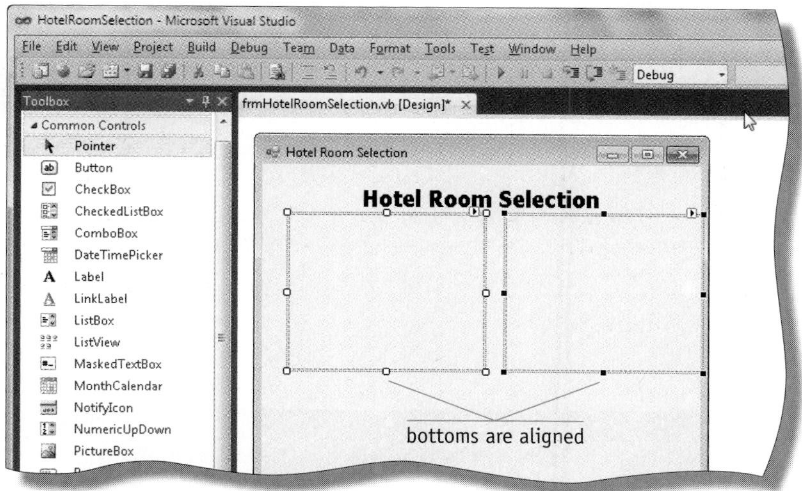

FIGURE 2-44

ONLINE REINFORCEMENT

To view a video of the process in the previous steps, visit scsite.com/vb2010/ch2 and then click Figure 2-43.

Notice on the Align submenu in Figure 2-43 that Visual Studio offers seven choices for alignment. When you are aligning objects horizontally, you should choose from the Tops, Middles, and Bottoms group. When you are aligning objects vertically, you should choose from the Lefts, Centers, and Rights group. Aligning to a grid will be covered later in this book.

Center Multiple Objects Horizontally in the Window

From Figure 2-44 on page 63 you can see that the PictureBox objects are not centered horizontally in the Windows Form object. As you learned, you can center one or more objects horizontally within the Windows Form object by using a command from the Format menu. To center the two PictureBox objects as a unit, you can complete the following steps:

STEP 1 With both PictureBox objects selected, click Format on the menu bar and then point to the Center in Form command.

The Format menu is displayed (Figure 2-45). The Center in Form submenu also is displayed.

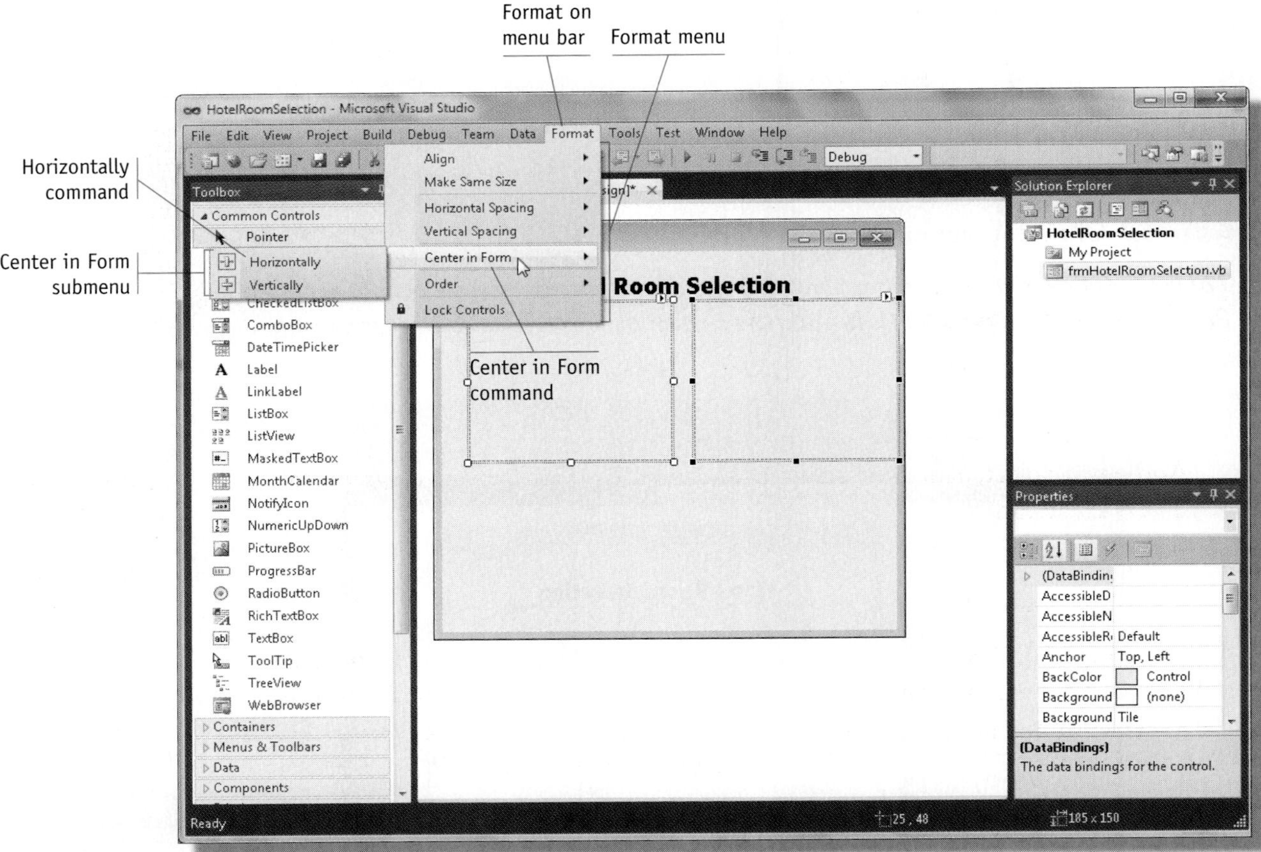

FIGURE 2-45

STEP 2 Click Horizontally on the Center in Form submenu.

The two PictureBox objects, as a unit, are centered horizontally in the Windows Form object (Figure 2-46). The left border for the left PictureBox object is the same distance from the window frame as the right border for the right PictureBox object.

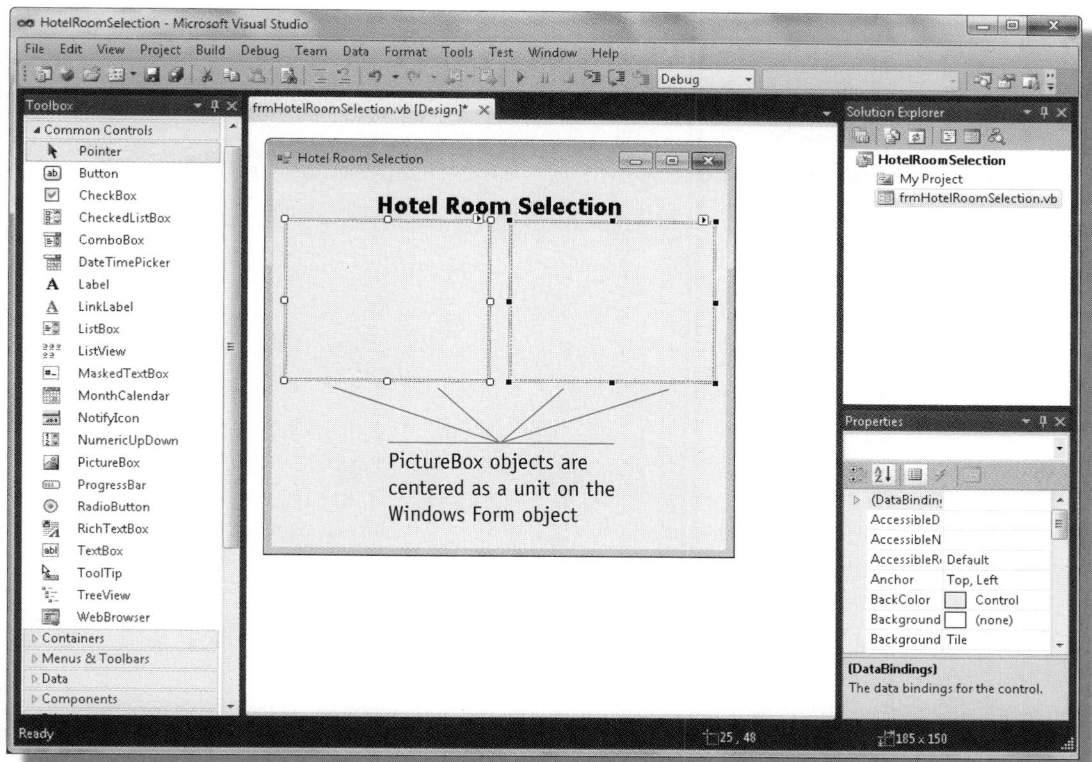

FIGURE 2-46

Adding an object, naming it, sizing it, and aligning it are basic to all graphical user interface design.

ONLINE REINFORCEMENT

To view a video of the process in the previous steps, visit scsite.com/vb2010/ch2 and then click Figure 2-45.

Add a Button Object

A **Button object** is a commonly used object in a graphical user interface. For example, you probably are familiar with the OK button that is used in many applications. Generally, when the program is executing, buttons are used to cause an event to occur. To place a Button object on the Windows Form object, you use the Toolbox. To create a Button object, you can complete the steps on the next page:

STEP 1 With the Toolbox displayed in the Visual Studio window, drag the Button .NET component in the Toolbox over the Windows Form object to the position where you want to place the button.

When you drag the button over the Windows Form object, the mouse pointer changes (Figure 2-47). The upper-left corner of the Button object will be placed where the upper-left corner of the rectangle is located.

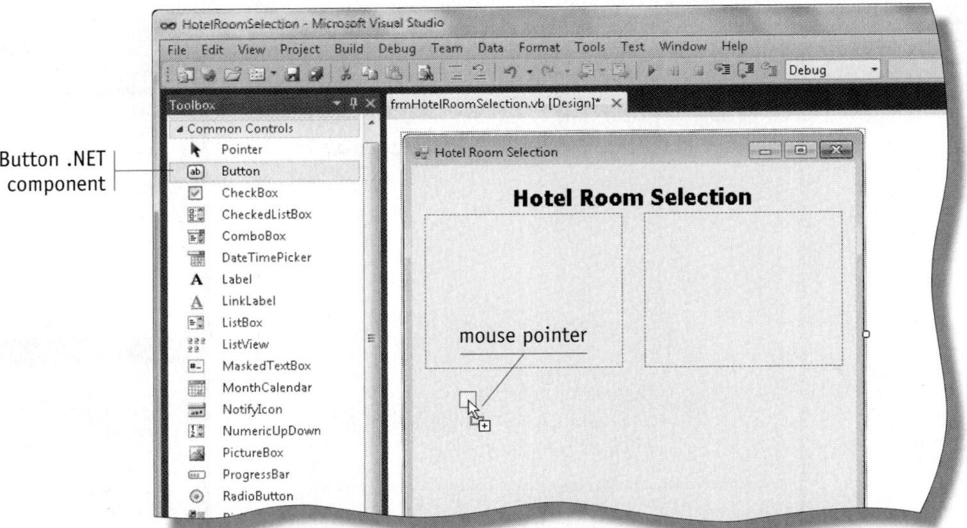

FIGURE 2-47

STEP 2 When the mouse pointer is positioned properly, release the left mouse button.

A standard-sized Button object is added to the Windows Form object (Figure 2-48). The text on the button is the default, Button1. In addition, the button is selected as indicated by the heavier border and sizing handles.

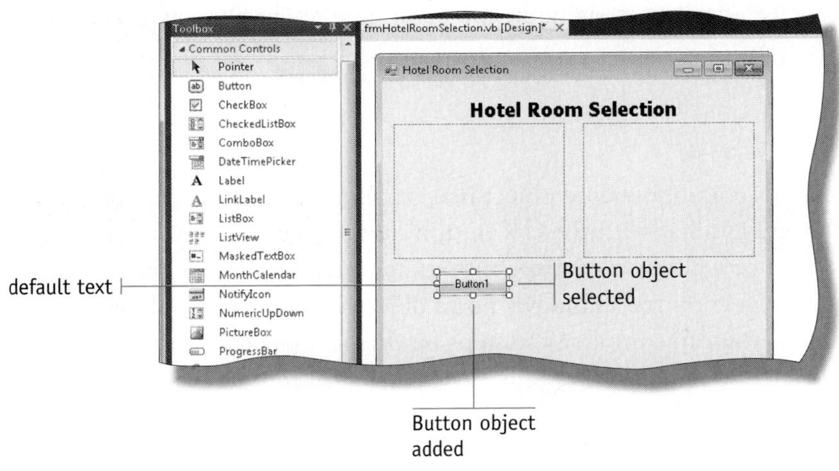

FIGURE 2-48

ONLINE REINFORCEMENT

To view a video of the process in the previous steps, visit scsite.com/vb2010/ch2 and then click Figure 2-47.

Name and Set Text for a Button Object

As with other objects added to the Windows Form object, the first step after adding the Button object is to name it. A Button object name should contain the prefix, btn. For example, the name for the button you just added could be, btnStandardRoom.

In most cases, you also will change the text that appears on the Button object. To change the text on the btnStandardRoom button, you can do the following:

HEADS UP

In this chapter, you have named four different objects: a Windows Form object, a Label object, a PictureBox object, and a Button object. As you learned, each object name should have a prefix that identifies the type of object. In this chapter, the prefixes are:

Type of Object	Name Prefix
Windows Form object	frm
Label object	lbl
PictureBox object	pic
Button object	btn

STEP 1 With the Button object selected, scroll in the Properties dialog box until you find the Text property. Double-click the Text value in the right column, type `Standard Room` and then press the ENTER key.

The text for the Standard Room button is changed both on the button and in the Properties window (Figure 2-49). The button is not large enough to contain the words, Standard Room, so only the word, Standard, is displayed. In the next set of steps, you will learn how to enlarge the size of the Button object.

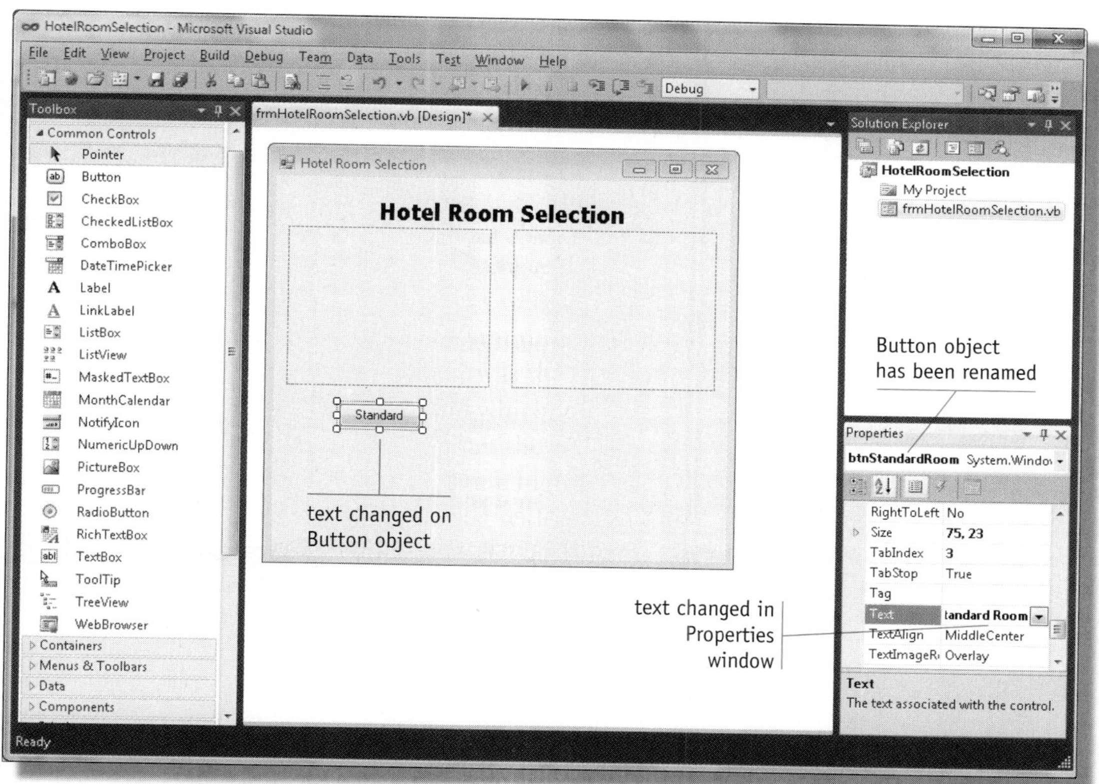

FIGURE 2-49

ONLINE REINFORCEMENT

To view a video of the process in the previous step, visit scsite.com/vb2010/ch2 and then click Figure 2-49.

Change Button Object Size

Sometimes, the button size may not be big enough to display the button text (see Figure 2-49 on the previous page). To change a Button object size to accommodate the text, you can perform the following steps:

STEP 1 Place the mouse pointer over the right edge of the Button object until the pointer changes to a double-headed arrow.

The mouse pointer changes to a double-headed arrow, which indicates you can drag the border of the button to increase or decrease its size (Figure 2-50).

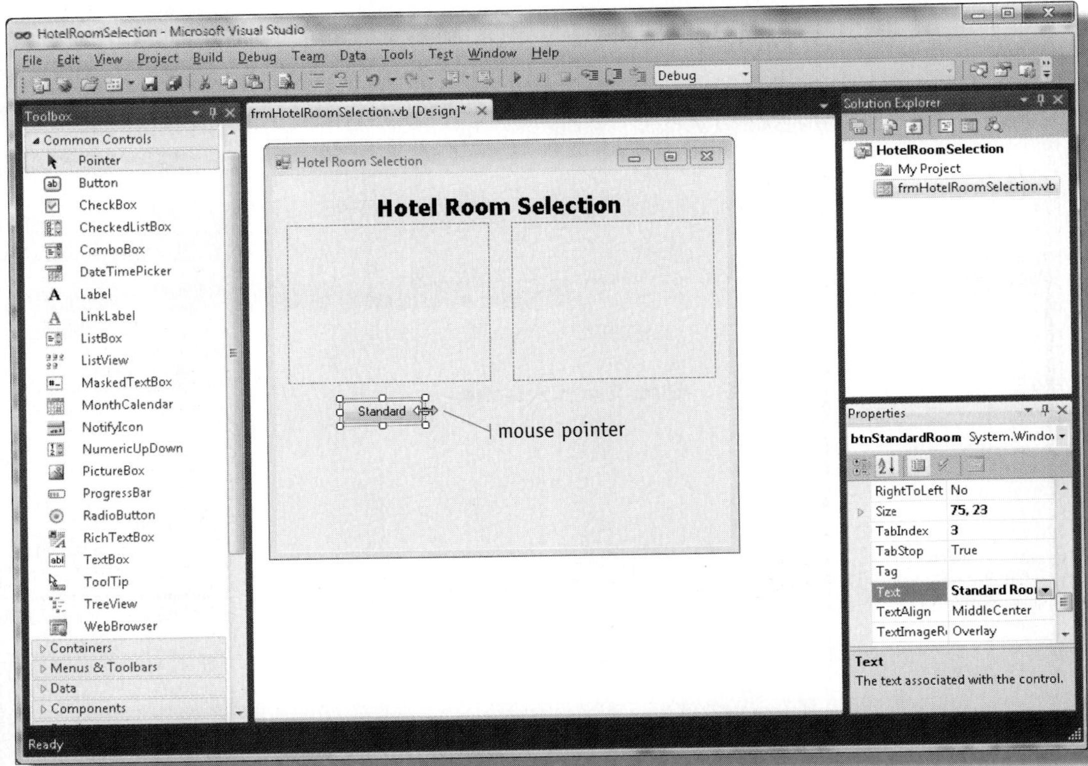

FIGURE 2-50

STEP 2 Drag the mouse pointer to the right until the Button object is just big enough to display the text, Standard Room, and then release the left mouse button.

As you drag the mouse pointer to the right, the button is made bigger (Figure 2-51). When the button is big enough to display the text, it is the right size.

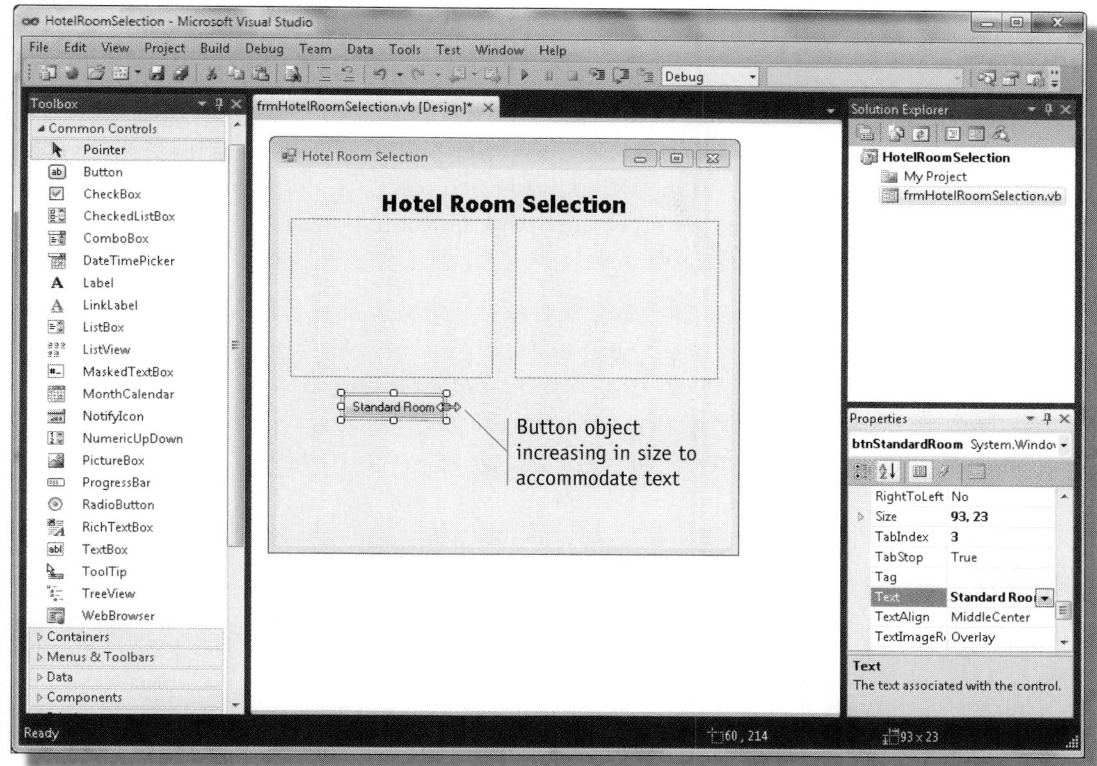

FIGURE 2-51

You can move a Button object by placing the mouse pointer on the button (the mouse pointer changes to a crosshair with four arrowheads) and then dragging the button to any location on the Windows Form object. You can move other objects on the Windows Form object using the same technique.

ONLINE REINFORCEMENT

To view a video of the process in the previous steps, visit scsite.com/vb2010/ch2 and then click Figure 2-50.

IN THE REAL WORLD

Some developers use the AutoSize property for a Button object to ensure the button always is large enough for text. By setting the AutoSize property for a Button object to True in the Properties window, the Button object will expand or contract when you change the text so the text fits precisely in the button.

Add and Align a Second Button

Often, a window requires more than one button. When a second button is added to the window, a normal requirement is that the buttons be aligned. As with PictureBox objects, you can align Button objects horizontally or vertically.

With the PictureBox objects, you saw that you can align objects after they have been placed on the Windows Form object. You also can align objects when you place them on the Windows Form object. To add a second button to the Windows Form object in Figure 2-51 and align it horizontally at the same time, you can complete the following steps:

STEP 1 Drag the Button .NET component from the Toolbox to the right of the Standard Room button on the Windows Form object. Align the top of the rectangle in the mouse pointer to the top of the Standard Room button until a blue line displays along the tops of the buttons.

*The blue line, called a **snap line**, indicates the top of the Standard Room button is aligned with the top of the Button object being added to the Windows Form object (Figure 2-52). You can drag the Button object left or right to obtain the desired spacing between the buttons. If the blue line disappears while you are dragging, move the mouse pointer up or down until the blue line reappears, signaling the objects are horizontally aligned.*

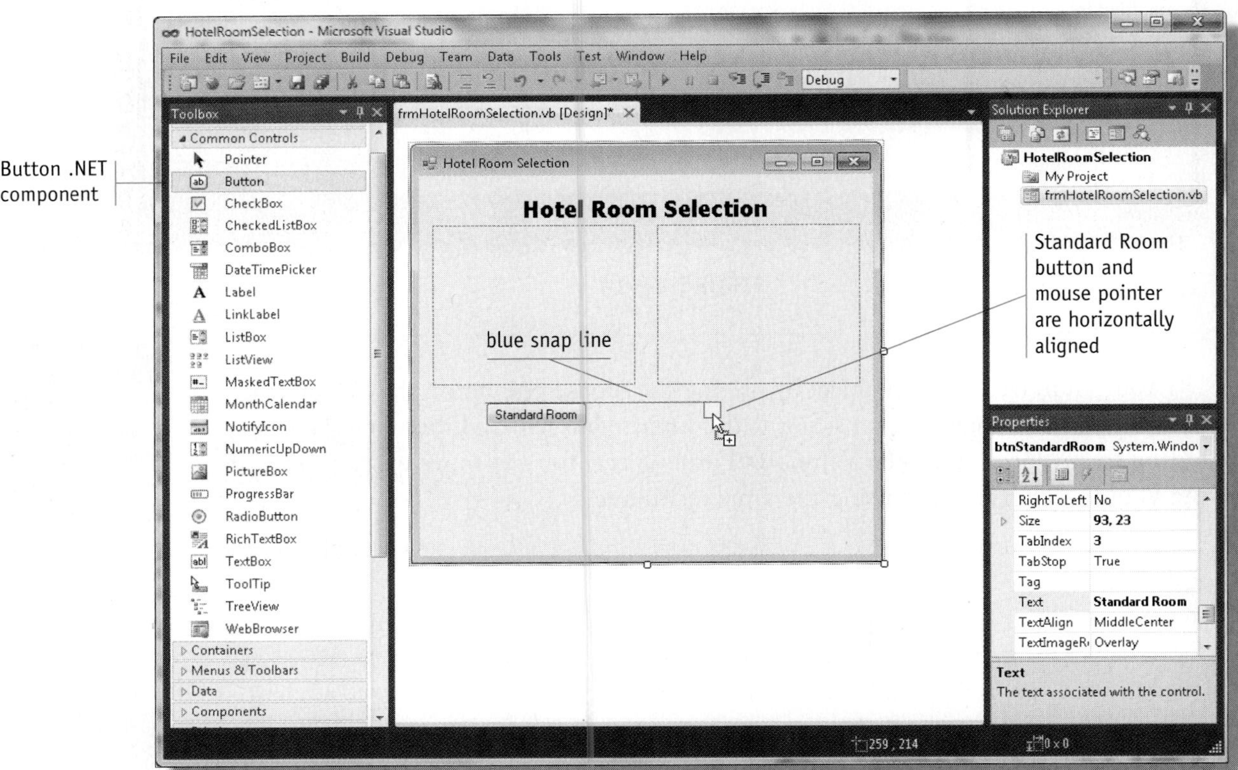

FIGURE 2-52

STEP 2 When the buttons are aligned and spaced as you like, release the left mouse button.

The Button1 object is aligned horizontally with the Standard Room button (Figure 2-53). Their tops are on the same line and, because they are the same vertical size, their bottoms are aligned as well.

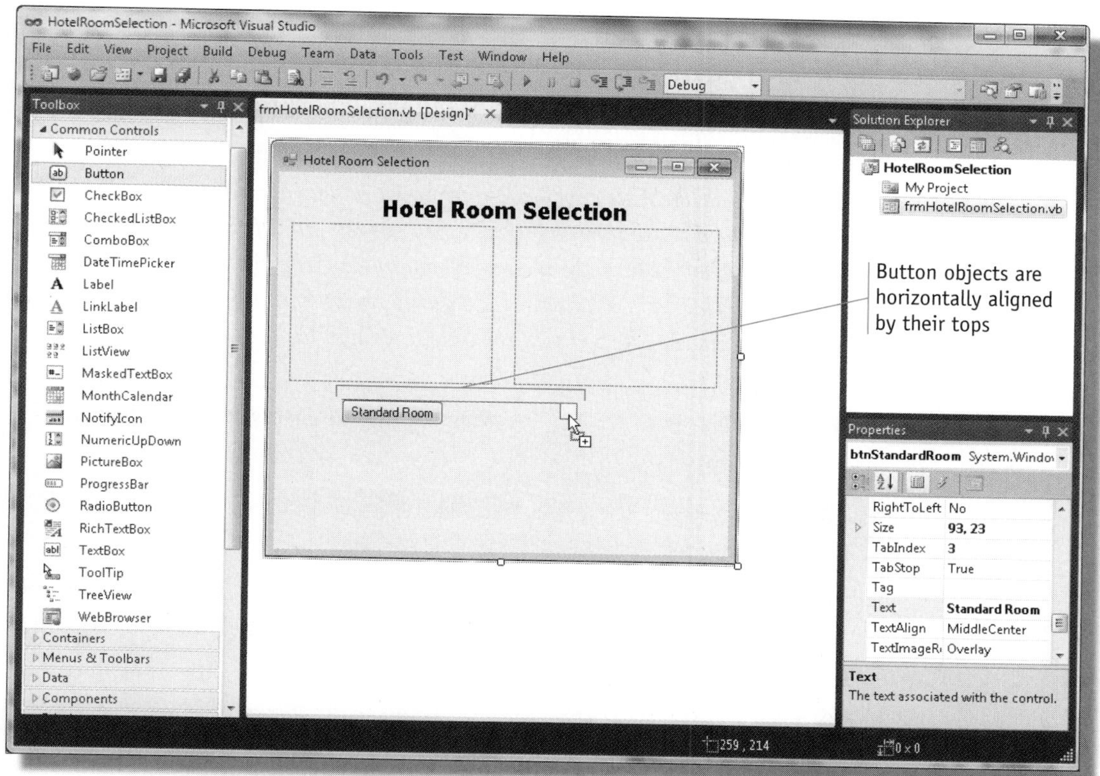

FIGURE 2-53

After adding the second Button object, you should name it, change the text as needed, and size the Button object if necessary. For the second Button object, assume you have named it btnDeluxeRoom, have changed the button text to Deluxe Room, and have made the two buttons the same size. You will recall that you can make the Deluxe Room button the same size as the Standard Room button by completing the following steps:

Step 1: Click the Standard Room button and then, while holding down the CTRL key, click the Deluxe Room button.

Step 2: Click Format on the menu bar, point to Make Same Size on the Format menu, and then click Both on the Make Same Size submenu.

Step 3: To unselect the Button objects, click anywhere on the Windows Form object except on another object.

ONLINE REINFORCEMENT

To view a video of the process in the previous steps, visit scsite.com/vb2010/ch2 and then click Figure 2-52.

Align Objects Vertically

The buttons in Figure 2-53 are aligned horizontally. They also can be aligned vertically. To illustrate this and to show how to align objects already on the Windows Form object using snap lines, assume that the Standard Room button and the Deluxe Room button should be vertically aligned on the left side of the Windows Form object with the Standard Room button above the Deluxe Room button. To vertically align the Button objects, you can complete the following steps:

STEP 1 If necessary, click anywhere in the Windows Form object to deselect any other objects. Then, slowly drag the Deluxe Room button below the Standard Room button until vertical blue snap lines are displayed.

*As you drag, **blue snap lines** indicate when the sides of the objects are aligned vertically. In Figure 2-54, since the buttons are the same size, when the left side of the Standard Room button is aligned with the left side of the Deluxe Room button, the right sides are aligned as well, so two blue vertical lines are displayed. If you drag the button a little further to the left or right, the buttons will not be aligned and the blue lines will disappear.*

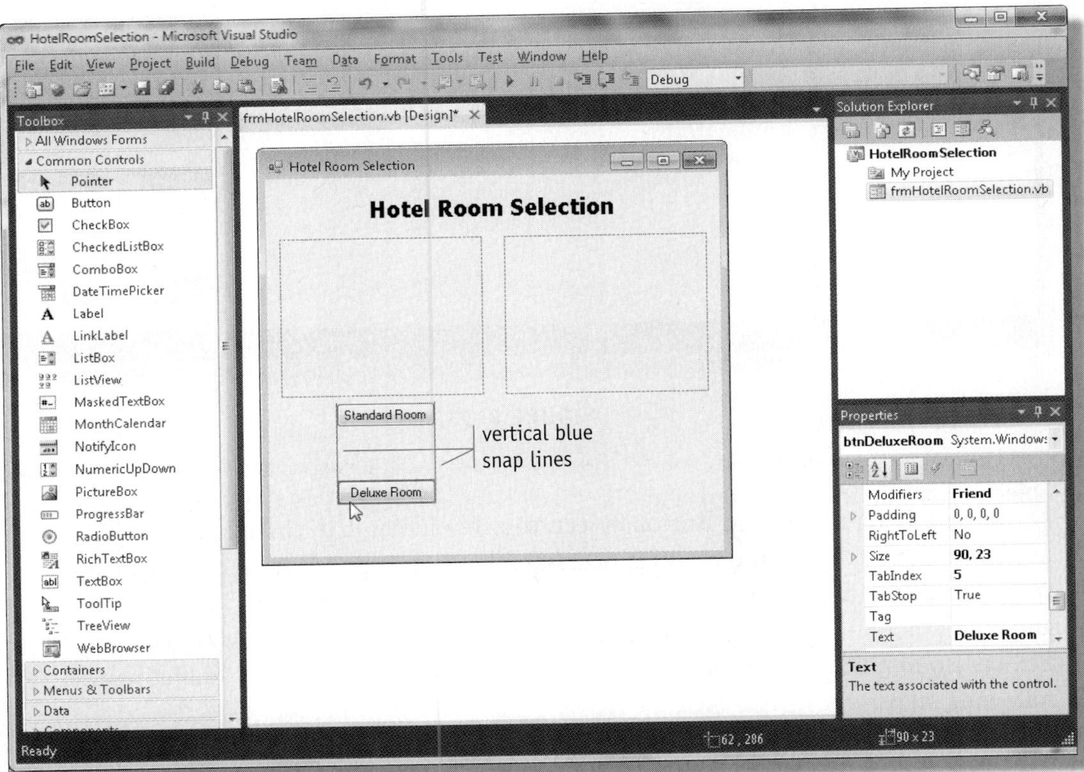

FIGURE 2-54

STEP 2 When the blue lines appear, indicating the buttons are aligned vertically, drag the Deluxe Room button up or down to create the proper spacing between the buttons, and then release the left mouse button.

The vertical distance between the buttons is a judgment call, based on the needs of the application, the size of the Windows Form object, and the number of other elements within the window (Figure 2-55). As with many aspects of GUI design, the eye of the developer will be critical in determining the actual placement of objects in the window.

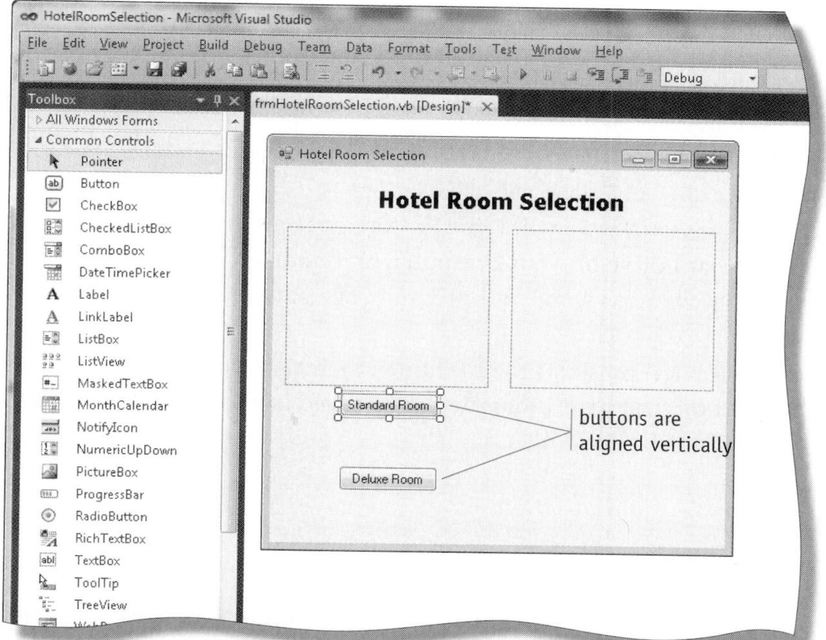

FIGURE 2-55

ONLINE REINFORCEMENT

To view a video of the process in the previous steps, visit scsite.com/vb2010/ch2 and then click Figure 2-54.

In the previous examples, you have seen the use of blue snap lines. As you drag objects, you also might see red snap lines flash on the screen. A **red snap line** indicates text within an object is aligned. For example, if you drag a button and the text in the button you are dragging aligns horizontally with the text in another button, a red snap line will be displayed. The use of red and blue snap lines allows you to align objects on the Windows Form object by dragging instead of selecting the objects and using the Format menu.

Visual Studio offers a variety of tools to create and align elements in the graphical user interface, and to make the user interface as effective and useful as possible.

Save a Visual Basic Project

As you are working on a Visual Basic project, a mandatory practice is to save your work on a regular basis. Some developers save every 10-15 minutes while others might wait for a natural break to save their work. Regardless, it is important to develop the habit of regularly saving your work.

To save the work you have completed, you can click the Save All button on the Standard toolbar. The first time you save a project, the Save Project dialog box shown in Figure 2-56 is displayed.

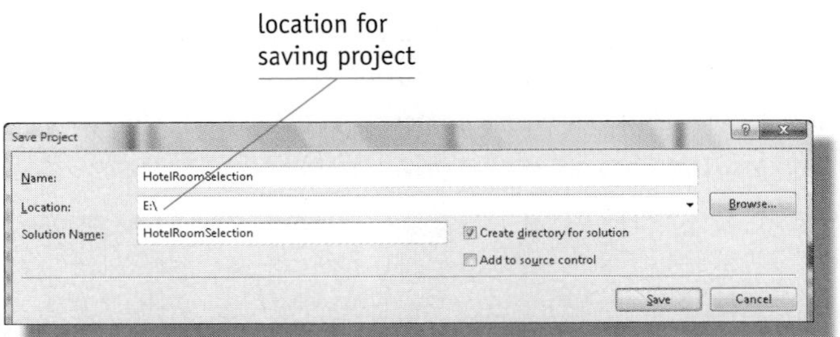

FIGURE 2-56

Select the location where you want to store your program. You might use a USB drive, the hard drive on your computer, or a network drive. If you have any questions concerning where to store your program, check with your instructor or network administrator.

After you save the program the first time, each time you click the Save All button on the Standard toolbar, your program will be saved in the same location with the same name.

Close Visual Studio 2010

To close Visual Studio, you can click the Close button on the right of the Visual Studio window title bar. If, when you close Visual Studio, you have never saved your program, Visual Studio will display the Close Project dialog box (Figure 2-57).

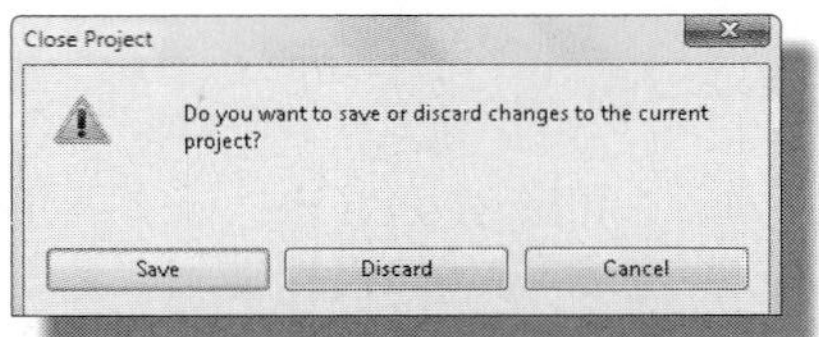

FIGURE 2-57

You can choose to save your program or to discard your program. If you click the Save button, the Save Project dialog box will be displayed (Figure 2-56) and you can save your program. If you click the Discard button, your program will be discarded and not saved.

If, when you close Visual Studio, you have accomplished work since you last saved your project, Visual Studio will ask if you want to save the elements of the project that have changed since you last saved the project. In most cases, you should choose Yes.

Open a Visual Basic Project

After you save a project and close Visual Studio, you often will want to open the project and work on it again. To open a saved project, you can follow one of several methods:

Method 1: Double-click the solution file in the folder in which it is stored. This method will open the solution and allow you to continue your work.
Method 2: With Visual Studio open, click the Open File button on the Standard toolbar, locate the solution file, and open it in the same manner you use for most programs running under the Windows operating system.
Method 3: With Visual Studio open, click File on the menu bar and then point to Recent Projects and Solutions on the File menu. A list of the projects most recently worked on is displayed. Click the name of the project you want to open. This method might not work well if you are using a computer that is not your own because other persons' projects might be listed.

After using one of these methods, you can continue the work on your project.

WATCH OUT FOR

Sometimes when you open a Visual Basic project, the Form1.vb[Design] tabbed page is not displayed. (This page is renamed as frmHotelRoomSelection.vb in your project.) To display it, double-click Form1 or the new name in this project, frmHotelRoomSelection.vb, in the Solution Explorer window at the upper-right section of the Visual Studio window.

Program Development Life Cycle

Now that you have learned the Visual Studio and Visual Basic skills necessary to design a user interface, you are ready to learn about the program development life cycle. The **program development life cycle** is a set of phases and steps that are followed by developers to design, create, and maintain a computer program. The phases of the program development life cycle are:

1. **Gather and Analyze the Program Requirements** — The developer must obtain the information that identifies the program requirements and then document these requirements.
2. **Design the User Interface** — After the developer understands the program requirements, the next step is to design the user interface. The user interface provides the framework for the processing that will occur within the program.
3. **Design the Program Processing Objects** — A computer program consists of one or more processing objects that perform the tasks required within the program. The developer must determine what processing objects are required, and then determine the requirements of each object.
4. **Code the Program** — After the processing object has been designed, the object must be implemented in program code. **Program code** consists of the instructions written using a programming language such as Visual Basic 2010 that ultimately can be executed by a computer.
5. **Test the Program** — As the program is being coded, and after the coding is completed, the developer should test the program code to ensure it is executing properly. The testing process is ongoing, and includes a variety of stages.
6. **Document the Program/System** — As a program is being designed and coded, and after that process is completed, the developer should be documenting the program. **Documenting a program** means writing down in

a prescribed manner the instructions for using the program, the way in which a program performs its tasks, and other items that users, other developers, and management might require.

7. **Maintain the Program/System** — After a program is put into use, the program likely will have to be changed, or modified, some time in the future. For example, in the hotel room selection program, if a third type of room, such as a suite, is added to the rooms available in the hotel, the program must be changed to reflect the new room type. The process of changing and updating programs is called **program and system maintenance**.

The program development life cycle rarely is accomplished in a linear fashion, with one phase complete before the next phase starts. Rather, programs are developed iteratively, which means phases and steps within phases might have to be repeated a number of times before the program is completed. For example, the requirements for a program might be changed after the developer has begun coding the program. If this occurs, the developer must return to Phase 1 and gather and document the new requirements. Then, changes might have to be made to the user interface or other parts of the program to accommodate the updated requirements. This process of moving back and forth within the program development cycle is normal when developing a computer program.

The next sections in this chapter explain in detail Phase 1 and Phase 2 of the program development life cycle. The remaining phases are explained in Chapter 3.

Phase 1: Gather and Analyze the Program Requirements

An old programming adage states, "If you don't understand the problem to be solved, you will never develop a solution." While this seems self-evident, too often a program does not perform in the desired manner is because the designer did not understand the problem to be solved. Therefore, it is mandatory that, before beginning the user interface design, the developer understand the problem to be solved.

In many programming projects in industry, the developer is responsible for gathering the program requirements by interviewing users, reviewing current procedures, and completing other fact-gathering tasks. The emphasis in this book is on learning to program using the Visual Basic 2010 language, so the process of gathering program requirements is beyond the scope of the book. You will be given the program requirements for each program in this book.

When the requirements have been determined, they must be documented so the developers can proceed to design and implement the program. The exact form of the requirements documentation can vary significantly. The format and amount of documentation might be dictated by the application itself, or by the documentation standards of the organization for which the program is being developed. For Windows applications in this book, two types of requirements documentation will be provided for you. The first is the requirements document.

A **requirements document** identifies the purpose of the program being developed, the application title, the procedures to be followed when using the program, any equations and calculations required in the program, any conditions within the program that must be tested, notes and restrictions that must be followed by the program, and any other comments that would be helpful to understanding the problem.

Recall that the program to be developed in this chapter and in Chapter 3 is the Hotel Room Selection program (see Figure 2-1 on pages 30 and 31). The requirements document for the Hotel Room Selection program is shown in Figure 2-58.

The requirements document contains all the information that should be needed by a developer to design the program. In an event-driven program such as the Hotel Room Selection program, however, one additional document often is developed in

REQUIREMENTS DOCUMENT

Date submitted:	January 23, 2013
Application title:	Hotel Room Selection
Purpose:	The hotel room selection program will allow a user to view different room types and make a room selection.
Program Procedures:	From a window on the screen, the user should choose the room type and then make a room selection.
Algorithms, Processing, and Conditions:	1. The user must be able to view a standard room and a deluxe room until he or she makes a room selection. 2. When the user chooses a room type, a picture of that room type should appear in the window. 3. Only one picture should be displayed at a time, so if a user chooses a standard room, only the standard room picture should be displayed; if a user then chooses a deluxe room, the deluxe room picture should be displayed and the standard room picture should not be displayed. 4. When the user makes a room selection, a confirming message should be displayed. In addition, the user should be prevented from identifying a room type after the room selection is made. 5. After the user makes a room selection, the only allowable action is to exit the window.
Notes and Restrictions:	1. The user should not be able to make a room selection until he or she has chosen a room type.
Comments:	1. The pictures shown in the window should be selected from the pictures available on the Web.

FIGURE 2-58

order to clarify for the developer exactly what should occur in the program. The document is the Use Case Definition.

A **use case** is a sequence of actions a user will perform when using the program. The **Use Case Definition** specifies each of these sequences of actions by describing what the user will do and how the program will respond. The Use Case Definition for the Hotel Room Selection program is shown in Figure 2-59.

USE CASE DEFINITION

1. User clicks Standard Room or Deluxe Room button.
2. Program displays a picture of the room chosen by the user and enables the room selection button.
3. User clicks room buttons to view rooms if desired. Program displays the picture of the chosen room.
4. User clicks the Select Room button.
5. Program displays a room selection confirmation message, and disables both room buttons and the Select Room button. The Exit Window button becomes active.
6. User terminates the program by clicking the Exit Window button.

FIGURE 2-59

As you can see, the Use Case Definition specifies the actions performed by the user and the actions the program is to take in response.

The Use Case Definition is an important part of the requirements documentation for two reasons: 1) It defines for the developer exactly what is to occur as the user uses the program; 2) It allows the users to review the requirements documentation to ensure the specifications are correct before the developer actually begins designing the program.

When gathering and documenting the program requirements, it is critical that the users be involved. After all, the program is being developed for their use. When the users concur that the program requirements documentation is correct, the developer can move forward into the design phases for the program with the most confidence possible that the program will fulfill the needs of the users.

For the programs you will design in this book, the program requirements, including the requirements document and the Use Case Definition, will be provided to you. You should be aware, however, that in many cases in industry, an experienced developer must gather the requirements as well as implement them in a program.

IN THE REAL WORLD

The general term, users, as used in this text can refer to widely different groups of people. In some cases, the actual users of the program, such as bank tellers in a banking application, and their management must approve the user interface design. This does not mean, of course, that every teller in a bank must approve, but a representative group should be involved in the approval process.

In other cases, users might refer to people who are not actual users but who represent the users. For example, in the hotel reservation program in this chapter, all the people who might be registering at a hotel do not have to approve the user interface design. But, the hotel might select certain actual customers to participate in a focus group to review the user interface and make their comments.

The important point is that people who will actually use the interface or their representatives should review it. Then, management can give the final approval.

Phase 2: Design the User Interface

Virtually all programs developed for a graphical user interface are driven by the user's actions when using the interface. It is these actions that dictate the processing the program should execute. Therefore, by designing the user interface, the developer will obtain a foundation for designing the rest of the program. In addition, by designing the user interface early in the design process, the developer can interact with users and ensure that the interface will fulfill the user requirements.

Guided Program Development

1

- **Open Visual Studio 2010** Open Visual Studio using the Start button on the Windows taskbar and the All Programs submenu *(ref: Figure 2-2)*. If necessary, maximize the Visual Studio window. If necessary, close the Start page.

HINT

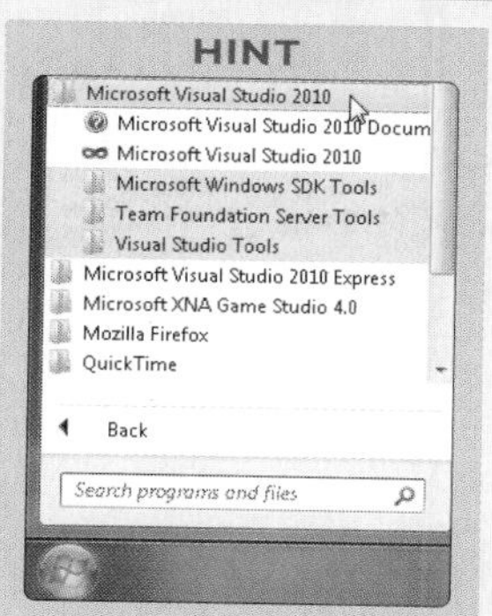

HEADS UP

During the development of the program, periodically you should save the program so you do not lose your work.

- **Create a new Visual Basic Windows Application** Create a new Visual Basic Windows Forms Application project by clicking the New Project button, selecting Visual Basic in the left pane, selecting Windows Forms Application in the right pane, naming the project, and then clicking the OK button in the New Project dialog box *(ref: Figure 2-3)*.

HINT

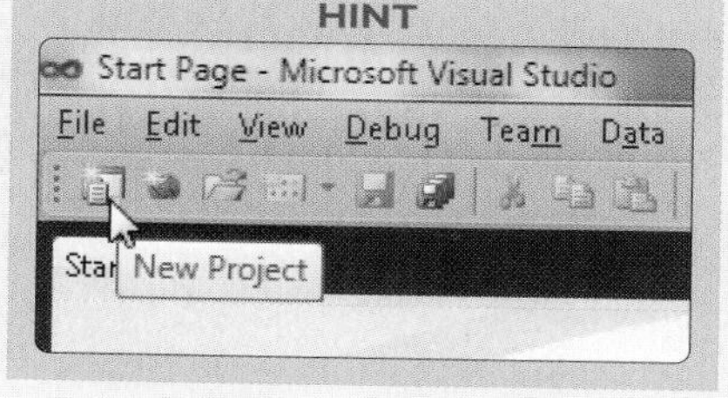

- **Keep the Toolbox Visible** If necessary, click the Auto Hide button to keep the Toolbox visible *(ref: Figure 2-10)*.

HINT

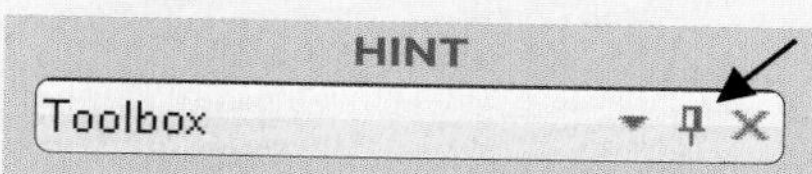

RESULT OF STEP 1

The Visual Studio application opens and a new project is displayed in the window (Figure 2-61). The Toolbox remains visible regardless of the location of the mouse pointer.

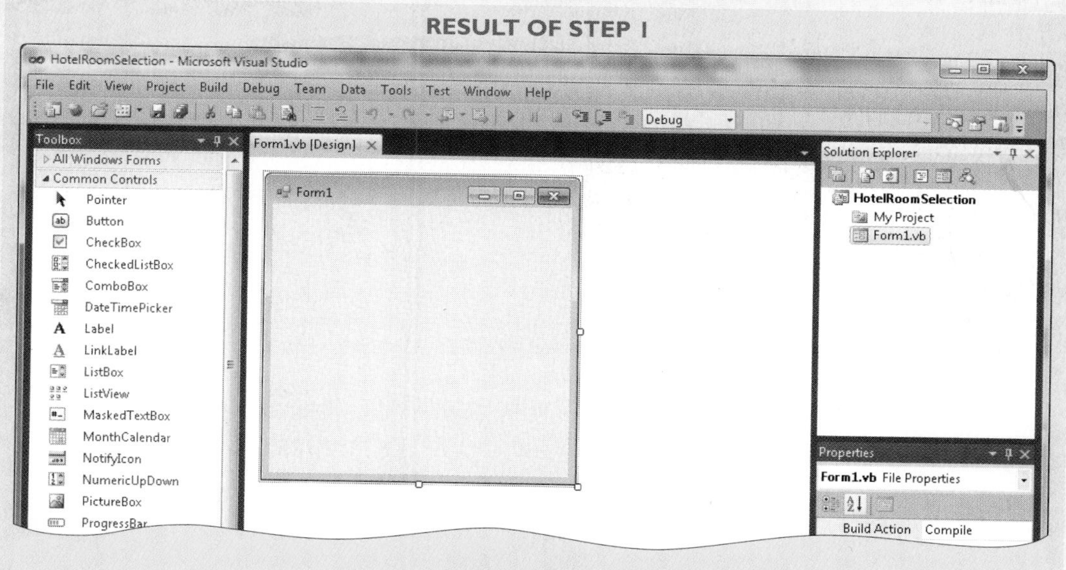

FIGURE 2-61

(continues)

Guided Program Development *continued*

2

• **Name the Windows Form Object** In the Solutions Explorer window, right-click Form1.vb. On the shortcut menu, click Rename. Name the form frmHotelRoomSelection *(ref: Figure 2-14)*.

HINT

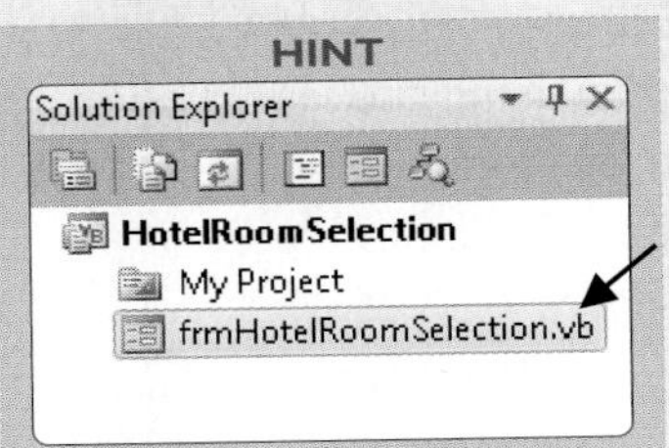

• **Change the Windows Form Object Text Property** With the Windows Form object selected, double-click the text value in the Text property of the Properties window for the Windows Form object, and then change the Windows Form object title bar text to the value, Hotel Room Selection *(ref: Figure 2-16)*.

HINT

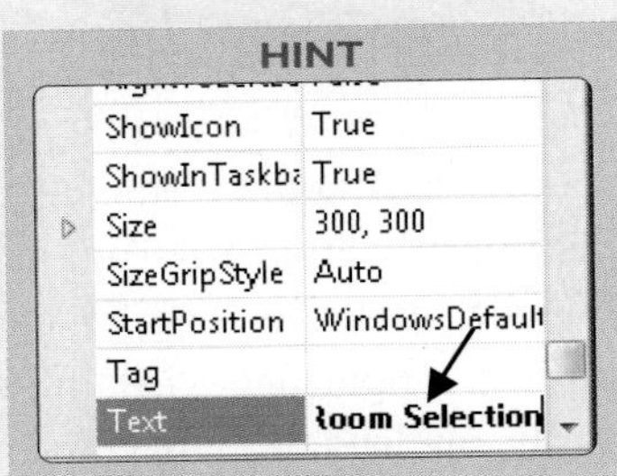

The text in the title bar of the Windows Form object has been changed to Hotel Room Selection (Figure 2-62). In addition, the name of the object has been changed to frmHotelRoom-Selection.

RESULT OF STEP 2

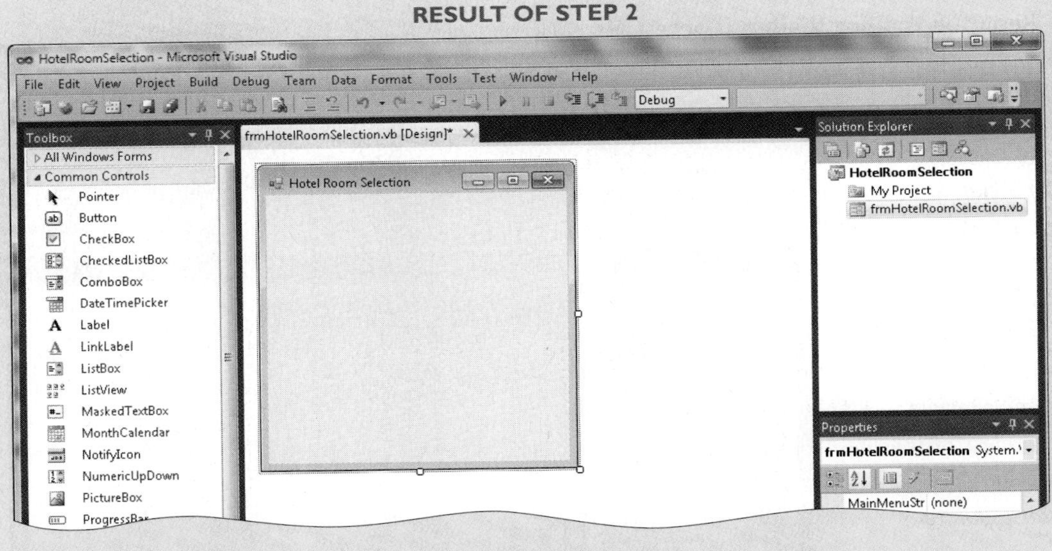

FIGURE 2-62

Guided Program Development *continued*

3

- **Resize the Windows Form Object** Resize the Windows Form object to the approximate size shown in Figure 2-60 (430 × 395) by dragging the sizing handle in the lower-right corner of the Windows Form object *(ref: Figure 2-18)*.

4

- **Add a Label Object** Add a Label object by dragging the Label .NET component from the Toolbox to the Windows Form object. Place the label near the center and top of the Windows Form object *(ref: Figure 2-19)*.

- **Name the Label Object** Change the name of the Label object to lblHeading by using the (Name) property in the Properties window for the Label object *(ref: Figure 2-21)*.

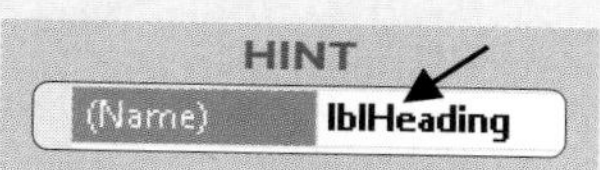

- **Change the Label Object Text Property** Double-click the text value in the Text property in the Properties window for the Label object, and then change the Text property of the lblHeading Label object to Hotel Room Selection *(ref: Figure 2-23)*.

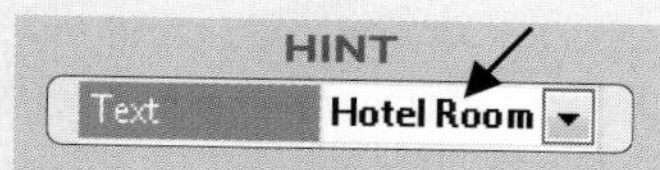

- **Open the Font Dialog Box** Click the Font property in the Properties window for the Label object and then click the ellipsis button (...) for the Font property *(ref: Figure 2-27)*.

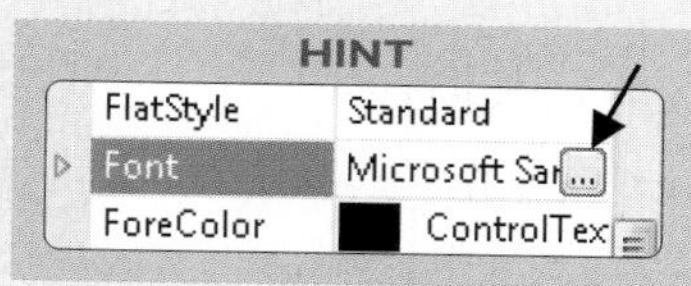

- **Change the Font for the Label Object** In the Font list of the Font dialog box, change the font in the lblHeading Label object to Tahoma *(ref: Figure 2-29)*.

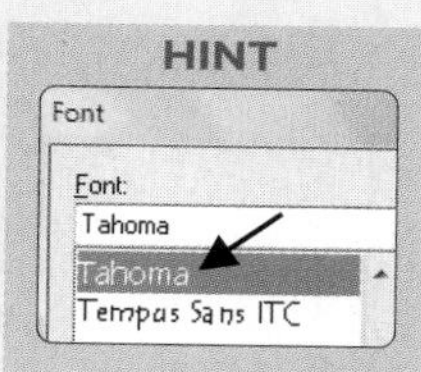

- **Change the Font Style for the Label Object** Using the Font style list in the Font dialog box, change the Font style in the lblHeading Label object to Bold *(ref: Figure 2-29)*.

(continues)

Guided Program Development *continued*

- **Change the Size for the Label Object** Using the Size list in the Font dialog box, change the font size in the lblHeading Label object to 16 point *(ref: Figure 2-29)*.

HINT

- **Center the Heading Horizontally** If necessary, select the lblHeading Label object. Then, using the Center in Form command on the Format menu, click the Horizontally command on the Center in Form submenu to center the lblHeading Label object horizontally on the Windows Form object *(ref: Figure 2-31)*.

HINT

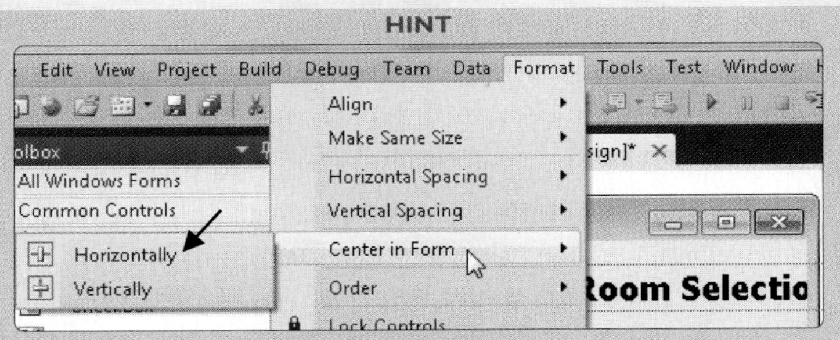

The Heading Label object text has been changed and the Label object is centered horizontally on the Windows Form object (Figure 2-63). The vertical placement of the label, that is, the distance from the top of the window frame, is dependent on the eye of the developer, the size of the Windows Form object, and the other objects that are part of the graphical user interface. While you may have placed the label in your window a little higher or a little lower, your window should closely resemble the one in Figure 2-63.

RESULT OF STEPS 3 AND 4

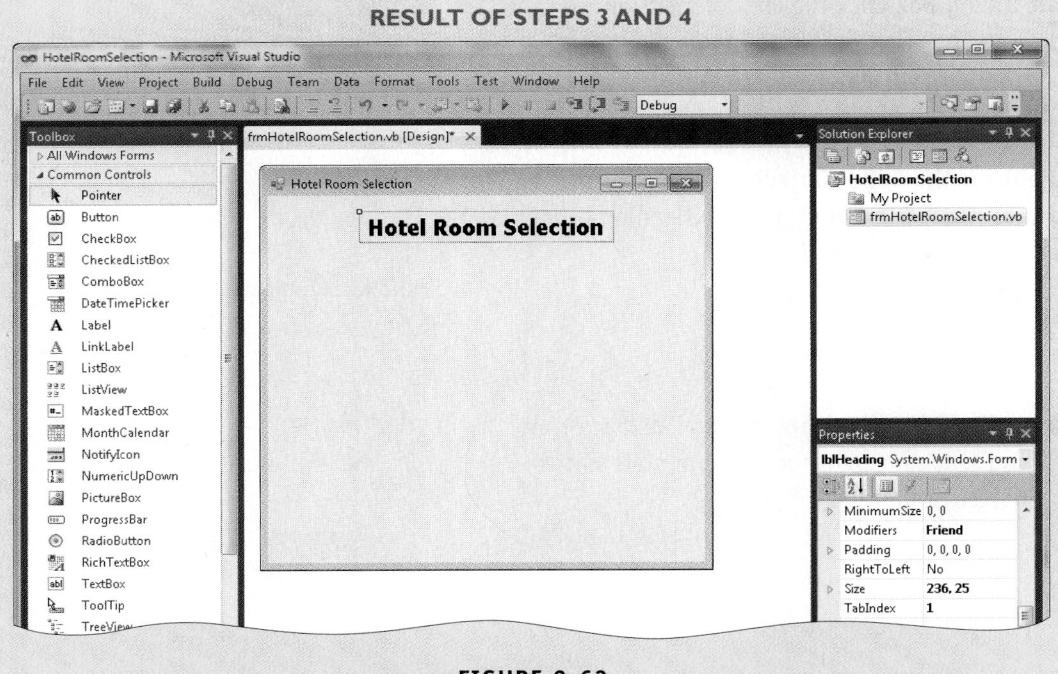

FIGURE 2-63

Guided Program Development *continued*

5

- **Add a PictureBox Object** Add a PictureBox object to the Windows Form object by dragging a PictureBox .NET component from the Toolbox to the Windows Form object. Place the PictureBox object below and to the left of the heading label in a location similar to that shown in Figure 2-64 *(ref: Figure 2-36)*.

- **Name the PictureBox Object** Using the (Name) property in the PictureBox Properties Window, name the PictureBox object, picStandardRoom.

- **Resize the PictureBox Object** Resize the PictureBox object to the approximate size of the PictureBox object in Figure 2-64 (185 × 150) by dragging the sizing handle in the lower-right corner of the PictureBox object *(ref: Figure 2-38)*.

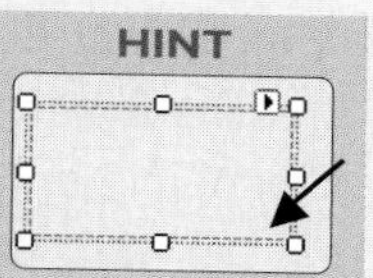

A properly sized PictureBox object is displayed in the Windows Form object (Figure 2-64). This PictureBox object will be used to display a picture of a standard room when the program is completed in Chapter 3.

RESULT OF STEP 5

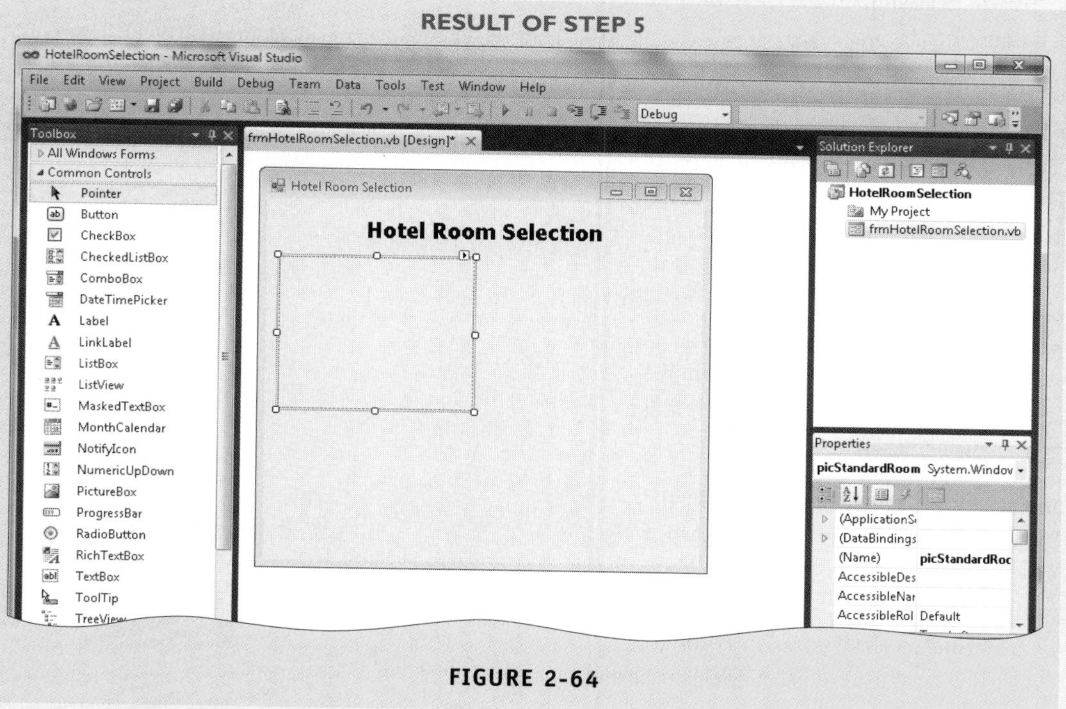

FIGURE 2-64

(continues)

Guided Program Development *continued*

6

- **Add a PictureBox Object** Add a second PictureBox object to the Windows Form object by dragging a PictureBox .NET component from the Toolbox to the Windows Form object. Place it to the right of the PictureBox object already in the Windows Form object *(ref: Figure 2-39)*.

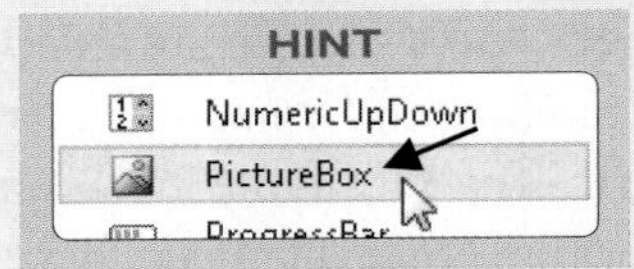

- **Name the PictureBox Object** Using the (Name) property in the PictureBox Properties window, name the PictureBox object picDeluxeRoom.
- **Size the PictureBox Object** Make the second PictureBox object on the right of the Windows Form object the same size as the PictureBox object on the left of the Windows Form object by using the Both command on the Make Same Size submenu of the Format menu *(ref: Figure 2-41)*.

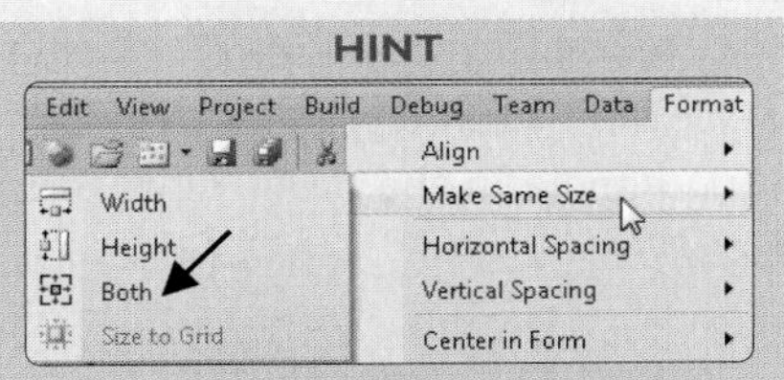

- **Align the PictureBox Objects Horizontally** Align the two PictureBox objects so their bottoms are horizontally aligned by using the Bottoms command on the Align submenu of the Format menu *(ref: Figure 2-43)*.

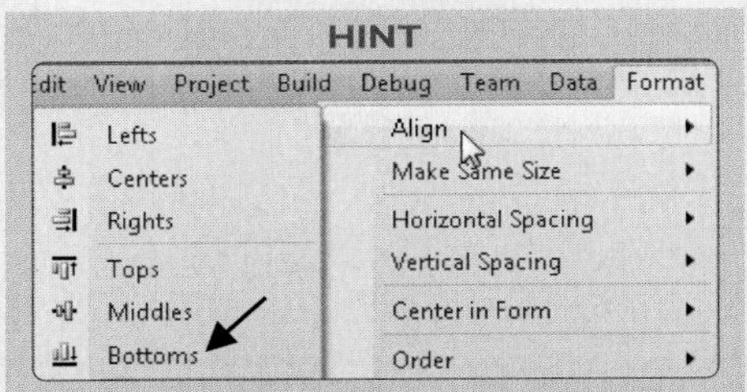

- **Set the Distance Between the PictureBox Objects** If necessary, adjust the distance between the two PictureBox objects so it is approximately the same as the distance in Figure 2-65. To do so, click the Windows Form object to unselect the two PictureBox objects. Then, place the mouse pointer in the right PictureBox object and drag the object left or right to set the correct distance. As you drag, blue snap lines should appear to indicate the PictureBox objects still are horizontally aligned. When the PictureBox objects are the correct distance apart, release the left mouse button.
- **Center the PictureBox Objects in the Windows Form Object** Center the PictureBox objects as a unit horizontally within the Windows Form object by selecting both PictureBox objects, displaying the Center in Form command on the Format menu, pointing to the Center in Form command, and then clicking Horizontally on the Center in Form submenu *(ref: Figure 2-45)*.

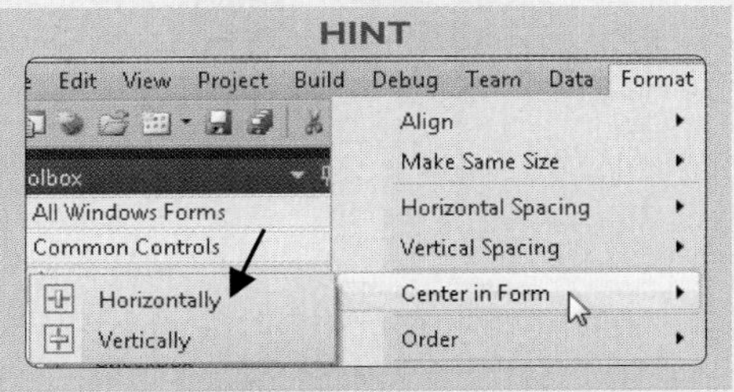

Guided Program Development *continued*

The PictureBox objects are sized and located properly within the Windows Form object (Figure 2-65).

RESULT OF STEP 6

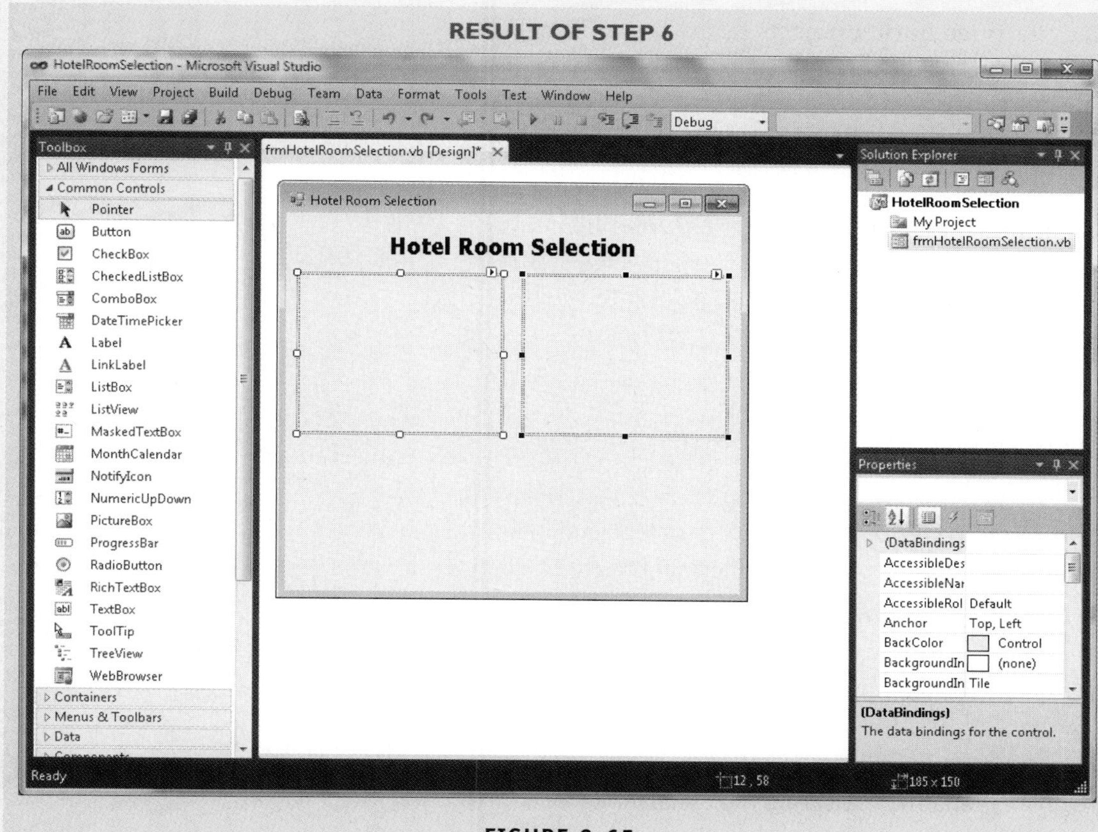

FIGURE 2-65

7

- **Add Three Button Objects to the Windows Form Object** Add three Button objects to the Windows Form object by dragging three Button .NET components onto the Windows Form object. They should be horizontally aligned below the PictureBox objects at about the same locations as shown in Figure 2-60 on page 82. Use blue snap lines to horizontally align the buttons on the Windows Form object as you drag them onto the form *(ref: Figure 2-47, Figure 2-52)*.

HINT

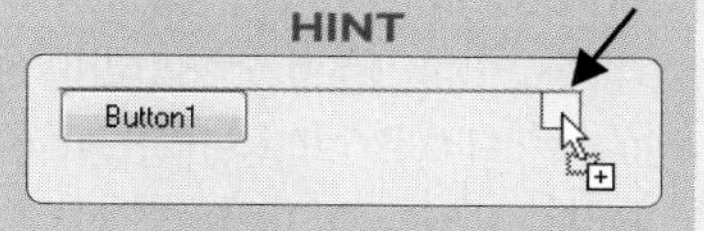

(continues)

Guided Program Development *continued*

- **Name the Three Button Objects** By using the (Name) property in the Properties window, name the leftmost Button object, btnStandardRoom; the center Button object, btnSelectRoom; and the rightmost Button object, btnDeluxeRoom.

- **Change the Text Property for Three Button Objects** By using the Text property in the Properties window, change the text for each of the Button objects to the text shown in Figure 2-66 on the next page *(ref: Figure 2-49)*.

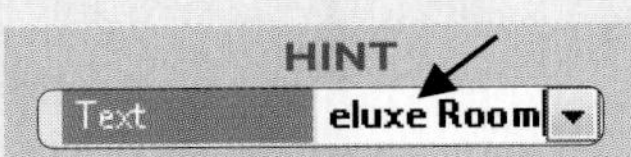

- **Change the Button Object Size** Change the size of the Standard Room button to accommodate the text, Standard Room *(ref: Figure 2-50)*.

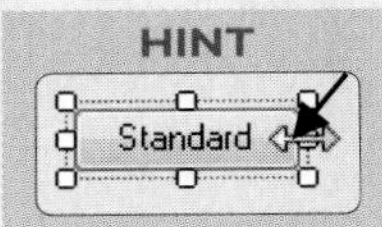

- **Resize the Button Objects** Using the same technique you used for sizing the PictureBox objects, make all three Button objects the same size as the Standard Room Button object.

- **Align the btnStandardRoom Button Object** Center the Standard Room Button object under the standard room PictureBox object by: (a) selecting the standard room PictureBox first and then selecting the Standard Room Button object through the use of the CTRL key and clicking *(ref: Figure 2-40)*; (b) With the standard room PictureBox object as the controlling object, use the Centers command on the Align submenu of the Format menu to align the PictureBox object and the Standard Room Button object *(ref: Figure 2-43)*.

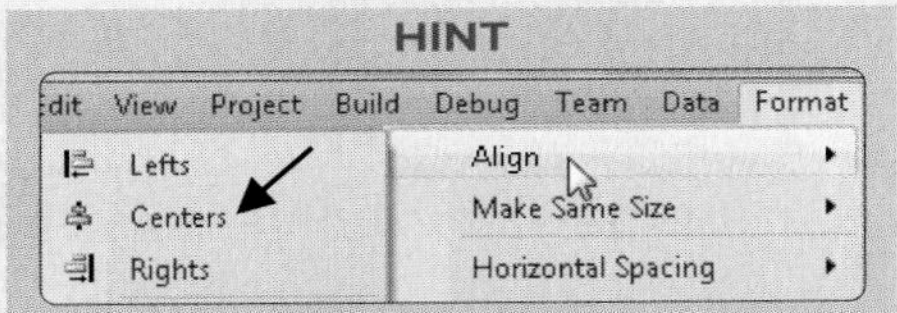

- **Align the btnDeluxeRoom Button Object** Using the same technique, center the Deluxe Room Button object beneath the deluxe room PictureBox object.

- **Center the btnSelectRoom Button Object** Center the Select Room Button object horizontally within the Windows Form object by selecting the Select Room Button object and then using the Horizontally command on the Center in Form submenu of the Format menu *(ref: Figure 2-31)*.

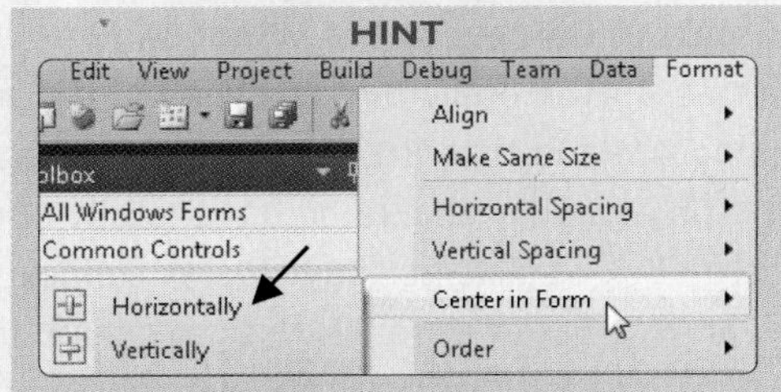

Guided Program Development *continued*

The Button objects are sized and placed properly within the Windows Form object (Figure 2-66). All three buttons are the same size. The Standard Room and Deluxe Room buttons are centered under their respective PictureBox objects, while the Select Room button is centered in the Windows Form object.

RESULT OF STEP 7

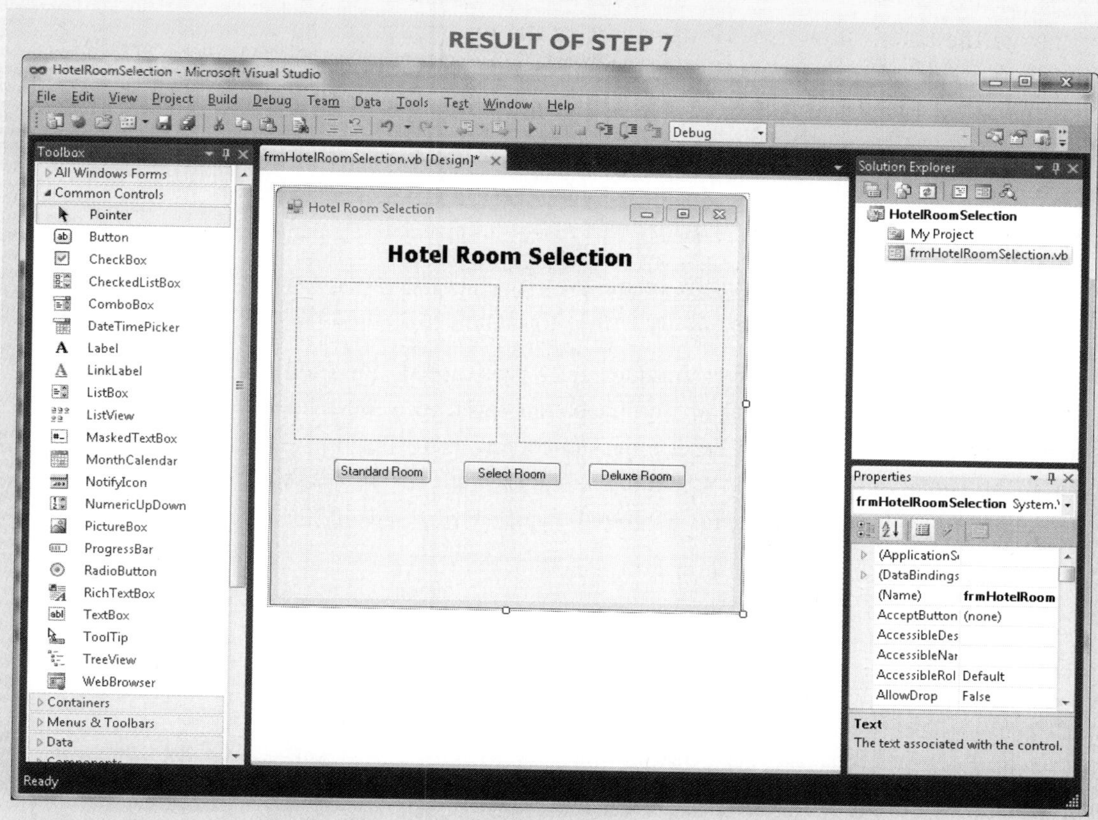

FIGURE 2-66

8

- **Add a Label Object** Add the instructions Label object to the Windows Form object by dragging a Label .NET object from the Toolbox to the Windows Form object. Place it below the Button objects at the approximate location shown in Figure 2-60 on page 82 (*ref: Figure 2-19*).

HINT

- **Name a Label Object** Using the techniques you have learned, give the Label object the name, lblInstructions.

(continues)

Guided Program Development *continued*

- **Change the Label Object Text Property** Using the techniques you have learned, change the text in the lblInstructions Label object to, Choose a room type and then click the Select Room button.

- **Change the Label Object Font** Using the techniques you have learned, change the font for the lblInstructions Label object to Tahoma, change the Font style to Regular, and change the Size to 10 point.

- **Center the Label Object** Using the techniques you have learned, center the lblInstructions Label object horizontally within the Windows Form object.

- **Add a Label Object** Using the techniques you have learned, add the final message Label object whose text should read, You have completed your room selection, to the Windows Form object. Place the Label object in the location shown in Figure 2-67. Give it the name, lblConfirmationMessage. Change the font to Tahoma, the Font style to Regular, and the Size to 10 point. Center the Label object within the Windows Form object.

The two Label objects contain the correct text and are centered horizontally in the Windows Form object (Figure 2-67).

RESULT OF STEP 8

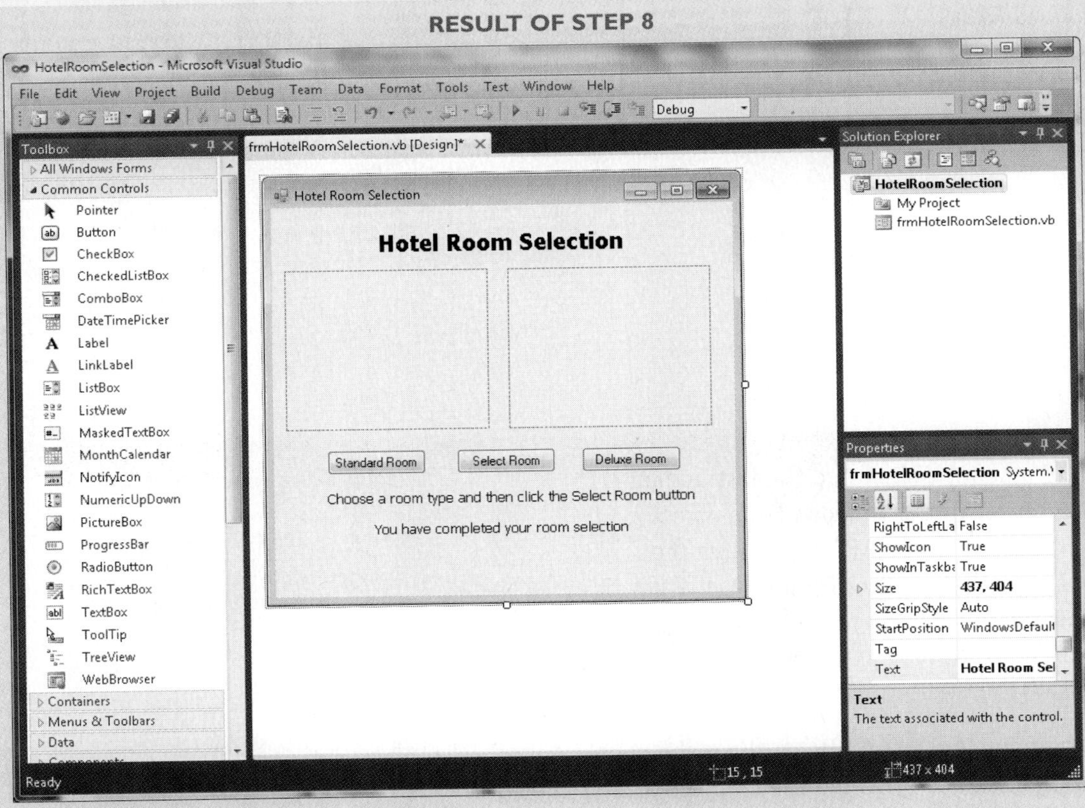

FIGURE 2-67

Knowledge Check *continued*

6. What does RAD stand for?
7. What is the purpose of the Auto Hide button on the Toolbox title bar?
8. What is the difference between red and blue snap lines?
9. Which Windows Form object property was changed to display the words "Welcome Screen" on the title bar in Figure 2-71?
10. A Button, a Label, and a PictureBox are all ______________.

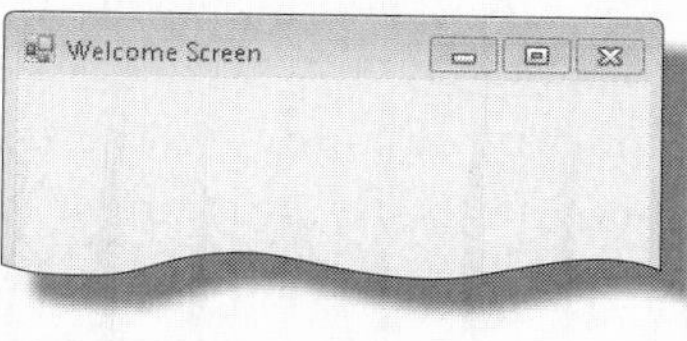

FIGURE 2-71

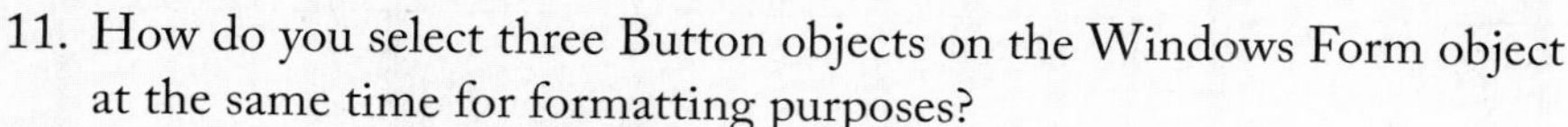

11. How do you select three Button objects on the Windows Form object at the same time for formatting purposes?

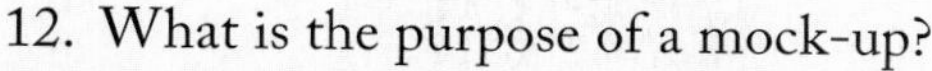

12. What is the purpose of a mock-up?
13. What are the first two phases of the program development life cycle?
14. Write the Label object name, Title, together with the correct prefix.
15. Write the Button object name, Submit, together with the correct prefix.
16. Write the PictureBox object name, Computer, together with the correct prefix.
17. Which property of the Label object do you use to change the name of the label from Label1 to a new name?
18. What is the name of the button you can click to sort the property names in the Properties window from A to Z?
19. How do you save the project you have created for the user interface mock-up?
20. Name the four objects you learned in Chapter 2 together with the purpose of each object.

Debugging Exercises

1. List the steps required to change the poorly aligned buttons on the left to the properly aligned buttons on the right.

BEFORE

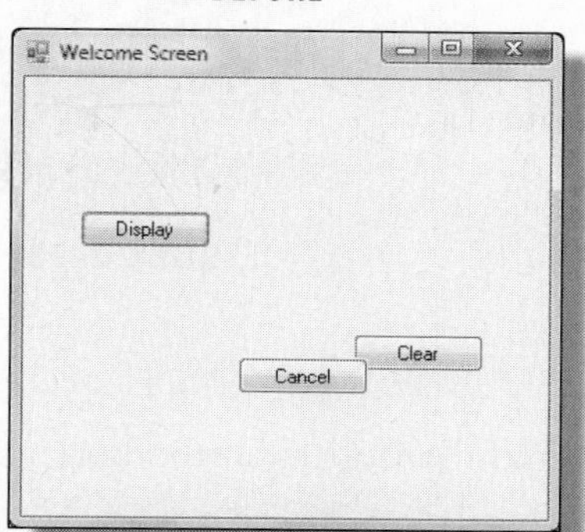

FIGURE 2-72a

AFTER

FIGURE 2-72b

(continues)

Debugging Exercises *continued*

2. Change the order of the following Use Case Definition steps to correspond to the following problem definition: A college provides every incoming freshman with either a laptop or desktop PC. The student should select the type of computer she or he wants. A program opens a window that displays each computer type when the student clicks the corresponding button, one picture at a time. When a student makes a decision about the type of computer, the student should click the Select PC button. After the student selects the type of computer, the student should exit the application.

USE CASE DEFINITION

1. User clicks the Select PC button.
2. User clicks the Laptop or Desktop button.
3. User terminates the program by clicking the Exit Window button.
4. Program displays a PC confirmation message and disables both computer type buttons. The Exit Window button becomes active.
5. Program displays a picture of the type of PC clicked by the user and will enable the Select PC button.
6. Program displays a picture of the type of PC clicked by the user.

Program Analysis

1. After you have placed objects on the Windows Form object (Figure 2-73), list the steps you would follow to change the font for the Online Auction label to Tahoma font, bold, 18 point.
2. List the steps you would perform to center horizontally the On Line Auction label.
3. List the steps you would perform to center horizontally the PictureBox object on the Windows Form object in Figure 2-73.
4. List the steps you would perform to change the font for the Click to Bid label in Figure 2-73 to Tahoma, 12 point; and then center the label horizontally.

FIGURE 2-73

5. List the steps you would perform to align the two Button objects horizontally by the tops of the buttons on the Windows Form object in Figure 2-73.
6. List the steps you would perform to center both the Bid Now button and the Cancel button horizontally on the Windows Form object in Figure 2-73.
7. In the real world, why is it important to get a user interface mock-up approved before proceeding with the rest of the project?

Case Programming Assignments

Complete one or more of the following case programming assignments. Submit the program and materials you create to your instructor. The level of difficulty is indicated for each case programming assignment.

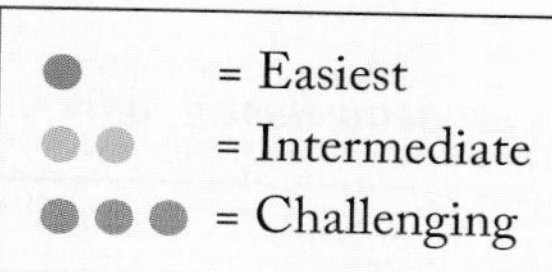

1 • EUROPEAN HOSTEL SELECTION

Create a Windows form mock-up for the following requirements document and Use Case Definition. The Windows Form object and the other objects in the user interface are shown in Figure 2-76.

REQUIREMENTS DOCUMENT

Date submitted: January 17, 2013

Application title: Vacation Hostel Location Selection

Purpose: The hostel selection application will allow a user to select the location in London or Dublin.

Program Procedures: From a window on the screen, the user should identify a hostel location (London or Dublin) and then indicate the location of the hostel.

Algorithms, Processing and Conditions:

1. The user must be able to identify the London or Dublin hostel, back and forth until the selection is made.
2. When the user identifies the hostel location, a picture of that hostel should appear in the window.
3. Only one picture should be displayed at a time. If a user identifies the London hostel, only the London hostel picture should be displayed; if a user identifies the Dublin hostel, only the Dublin hostel picture should be displayed.
4. When the user makes a hostel selection, a message stating that the selection of a hostel location has been made should be displayed. In addition, the user should be stopped from identifying a hostel location after the hostel selection has been made.
5. After the user makes a hostel selection, the only allowable action is to exit the window.

Notes and: Restrictions

1. A user cannot make a hostel selection until he or she has identified a hostel location.

Comments:

1. The pictures shown in the window can be found on scsite.com/vb2010/ch3/images. The names of the pictures are LondonHostel and DublinHostel. Images will be added in Chapter 3.

FIGURE 2-74

(continues)

Case Programming Assignments

European Hostel Selection (continued)

USE CASE DEFINITION

1. User clicks London Hostel button or Dublin Hostel button.
2. Program displays a picture of the hostel identified by the user and enables the location selection button.
3. User clicks hostel buttons to view hostel locations if desired. Program displays the picture of the identified hostel.
4. User clicks the Select Location button.
5. Program displays a hostel selection confirmation message, and disables both hostel buttons and the Select Location button. The Exit Window button becomes active.
6. User terminates the program by clicking the Exit Window button.

FIGURE 2-75

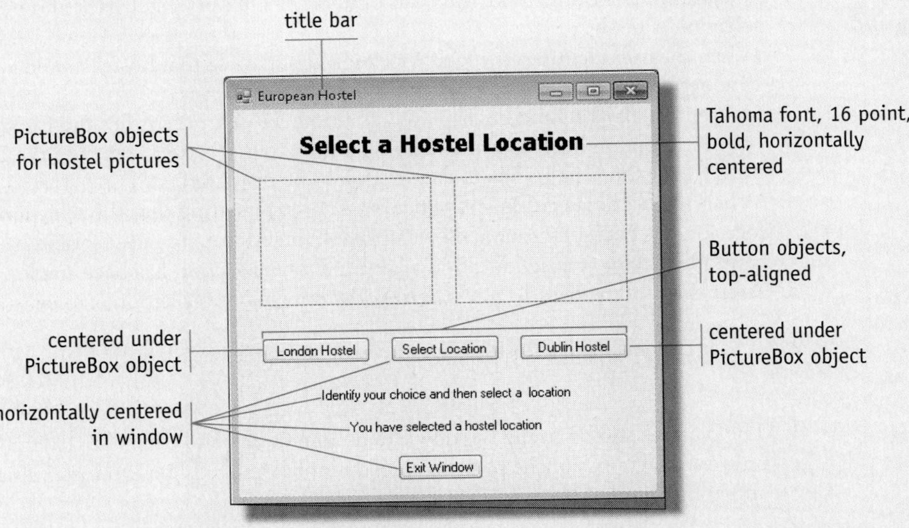

FIGURE 2-76

Case Programming Assignments

2 • BANKING

Create a Windows form mock-up for the following requirements document and Use Case Definition. The Windows Form object and the other objects in the user interface are shown in Figure 2-79.

REQUIREMENTS DOCUMENT

Date submitted: January 14, 2013

Application title: Bank Welcome Screen with Banking Hours

Purpose: This application displays a welcome screen for the First Corner National Bank. The user can choose an option to view the hours of the bank.

Program Procedures: From a window on the screen, the user makes a request to see the bank's open hours.

Algorithms, Processing and Conditions:

1. The user first views a welcome screen that displays the bank's name (First Corner National Bank), bank picture, and a phrase that states the bank is FDIC insured.
2. When the user opts to view the bank hours, the following hours are displayed:

Monday – Thursday	9:00am – 5:00pm
Friday	9:00am – 8:00pm
Saturday	9:00am – 1:00 pm

3. After the user views the hours, the only allowable action is to exit the window.

Notes and Restrictions: n/a

Comments:

1. The picture shown in the window can be found on scsite.com/vb2010/ch3/images. The name of the picture is BankBuilding. Images will be added in Chapter 3.

FIGURE 2-77

(continues)

Case Programming Assignments

Banking *(continued)*

USE CASE DEFINITION

1. The window opens, displaying the title of the bank, the bank's picture, and a message that the bank is FDIC insured. All buttons are enabled.
2. User clicks the View Banking Hours button.
3. Program displays the banking hours above the buttons. The View Banking Hours button is disabled.
4. User clicks the Exit Window button to terminate the application.

FIGURE 2-78

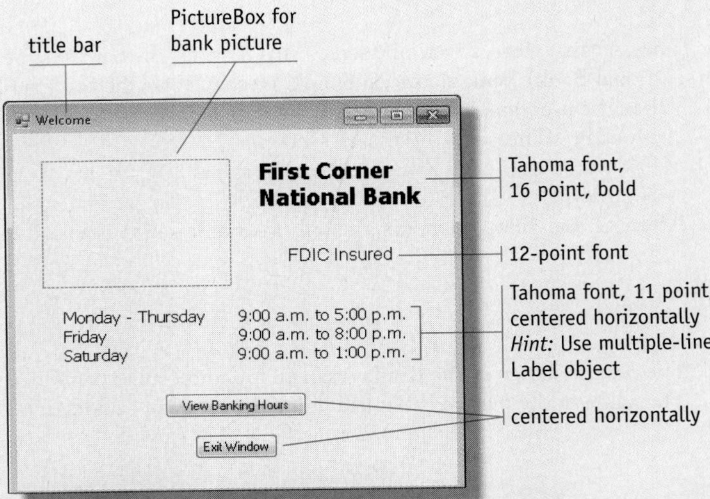

FIGURE 2-79

Case Programming Assignments

3 • VISUAL BASIC 2010 TERMS

Create a Windows form mock-up for the following requirements document and Use Case Definition. The Windows Form object and the other objects in the user interface are shown in Figure 2-82.

REQUIREMENTS DOCUMENT

Date submitted:	August 16, 2013
Application title:	Visual Basic 2010 Terms
Purpose:	This application displays the definitions of common Visual Basic terms. When the user chooses to view a definition, the term's definition is displayed.
Program Procedures:	From a window on the screen, the user makes a request to see one of three VB definitions.
Algorithms, Processing, and Conditions:	1. The user first views a screen that displays three VB terms. 2. An image of a computer is displayed at the top of the window throughout the running of the application. 3. The user can select any of the three terms displayed on the buttons, and the definition appears after each selection is made. 4. The user can click any of the term buttons and the definition will appear. Any previous definitions will disappear. 5. An exit button is available at all times, allowing the user to end the application.
Notes and Restrictions:	1. Only one definition should be displayed at a time, so if a user selects a second term, the second definition only should be displayed.
Comments:	1. The computer picture shown in the window can be found on scsite.com/vb2010/ch3/images. The name of the picture is Computer. Images will be added in Chapter 3.

FIGURE 2-80

(continues)

Case Programming Assignments

Visual Basic 2010 Terms (continued)

USE CASE DEFINITION

1. The window opens and displays a computer image, the title (Visual Basic 2010 Terms), three buttons labeled with VB terms, and an Exit Window button. All buttons are enabled.
2. User clicks each of the term buttons to review the definitions.
3. Program displays the definitions to the right of the buttons.
4. Only one definition shows at a time.
5. User clicks the Exit Window button to terminate the application.

FIGURE 2-81

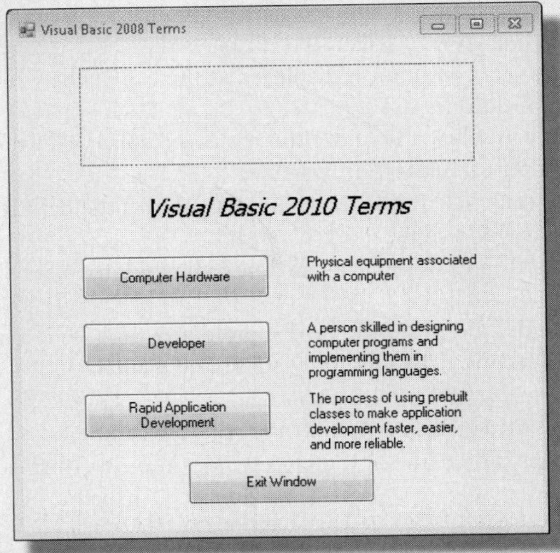

FIGURE 2-82

Case Programming Assignments

4 ●● ONLINE STORE SPECIALS

Create a Use Case Definition document and design a Windows form mock-up based on the requirements document in Figure 2-83.

REQUIREMENTS DOCUMENT

Date submitted:	January 6, 2014
Application title:	Online Store Specials
Purpose:	The online store specials program will display the daily, weekly, and holiday specials of the online store. The user can select the desired product and then add the product to the shopping cart.
Program Procedures:	From a window on the screen, the user should select the daily special, the weekly special, or the holiday special. When a special is selected, the program should display a picture of the special product, the regular price of the product, and the special price of the product. The user should be able to select any special. Then, the user can add the product to the shopping cart.
Algorithms, Processing, and Conditions:	1. The user must select a special in order to display the special's product picture, regular price, and sales price. 2. The user cannot add a product to the shopping cart until a special is selected. 3. When a special is selected, only that special's picture and prices should be displayed in the window. No other special should be displayed. 4. After the user selects a special and adds it to the shopping cart, the only allowable user action is to exit the window. 5. A user should be able to exit the window at any time.
Notes and Restrictions:	n/a
Comments:	1. The specials are: Daily Special: Cell Phone: Regular Price: $99.95; Special Price: $84.50 Weekly Special: iPod: Regular Price: $39.95; Special Price: $29.95 Holiday Special: Digital Camera: Regular Price: $259.95; Special Price: $203.19 2. The pictures shown in the window can be found on scsite.com/vb2010/ch3/images. The names of the pictures are CellPhone, iPod, and DigitalCamera.

FIGURE 2-83

Case Programming Assignments

5 ●●

RAFFLE PRIZE SELECTION

Create a Use Case Definition document and design a Windows form mock-up based on the requirements document in Figure 2-84.

REQUIREMENTS DOCUMENT

Date submitted: March 21, 2013

Application title: Raffle Prize Selection

Purpose: Your school has started selling raffle tickets for a scholarship fund that provides the winner a choice of raffle gifts. The winner can choose one of three prizes. So they can choose, the program must display each of the prizes upon request of the raffle winner. The winner then can make the choice of the prize he or she would like to receive.

Program Procedures: From a window on the screen, the user selects one of three raffle prizes. A picture of the prize is displayed in the window. The user then can choose the prize he or she wants to receive.

Algorithms, Processing, and Conditions:

1. The user selects a prize. Then, a picture of the prize is displayed in the window.
2. The user can select any of the three prizes. Only the picture for the selected prize should be displayed.
3. The user can select prizes back and forth to see the pictures for the prizes.
4. After the user finds a prize he or she wants, the user chooses that prize for delivery.
5. After the user chooses a prize, a message stating that a raffle prize has been chosen should be displayed.
6. After the user chooses a prize, the only allowable action is to exit the window.

Notes and Restrictions:

1. The user should not be able to choose a prize until they have viewed the picture of at least one raffle prize.

Comments:

1. The raffle prizes available are a gas grill, a flat-screen television, and a laptop.
2. The pictures shown in the window can be found on scsite.com/vb2010/ch3/images. The names of the pictures are Grill, TV, and Laptop.

FIGURE 2-84

CHAPTER 3

Program Design and Coding

OBJECTIVES

You will have mastered the material in this chapter when you can:

- Change the BackColor property of an object
- Add images to a PictureBox object
- Locate and save an image from the World Wide Web
- Import an image into the Program Resources folder
- Size an image
- Set the Visible property in the Properties window
- Set the Enabled property in the Properties window
- Run a Visual Basic 2010 program
- Enter Visual Basic 2010 code
- Understand Visual Basic 2010 code statement formats
- Use IntelliSense to enter Visual Basic 2010 code statements
- Using code, set the Visible property of an object
- Using code, set the Enabled property of an object
- Enter comments in Visual Basic 2010 code
- Correct errors in Visual Basic 2010 code
- Write code to use the Close() procedure
- Print code
- Prepare an Event Planning Document

Introduction

In Chapter 2 you completed the design of the graphical user interface (GUI) mock-up. While users and others can approve the mock-up as being functional, the developer normally must make a variety of changes to the GUI to prepare it for the actual production version of the program. Among these changes are:

1. Adding color to the interface to make it more visually appealing.
2. Acquiring and including images that are required for the program.
3. Setting interface object properties in accordance with the needs of the program.

Once these tasks have been completed, Phase 2 of the program development life cycle (PDLC) has been completed.

The next two phases of the PDLC are:

Phase 3: Design the program processing objects
Phase 4: Code the program

This chapter will provide the skills and knowledge necessary first to complete phase 2 of the PDLC and then complete phases 3 and 4.

Sample Program

You will recall that the sample program for Chapter 2 and this chapter is the Hotel Room Selection program. Windows for the program are shown in Figure 3-1.

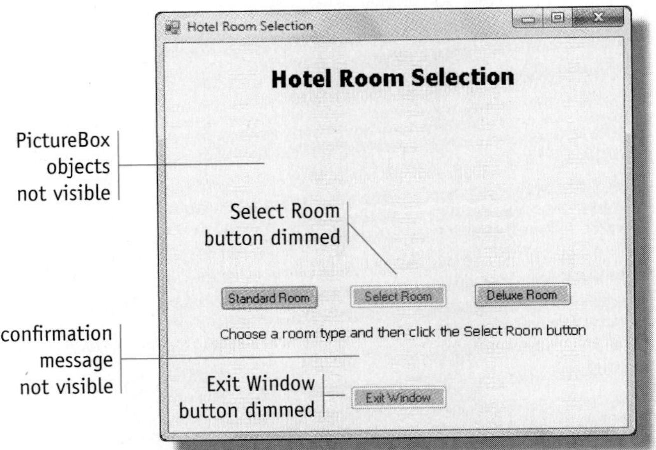

FIGURE 3-1a

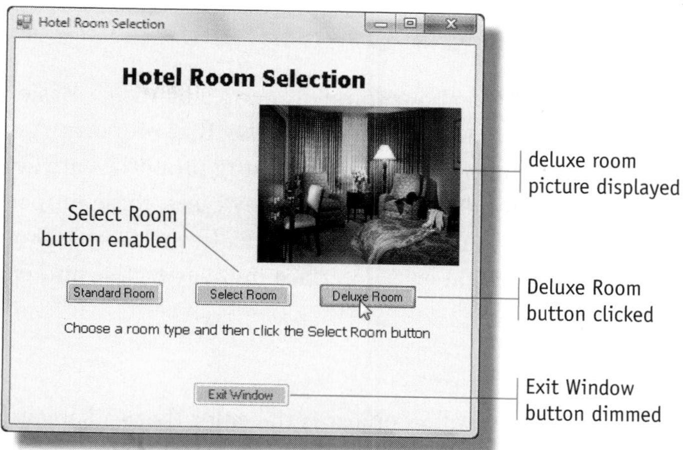

FIGURE 3-1b

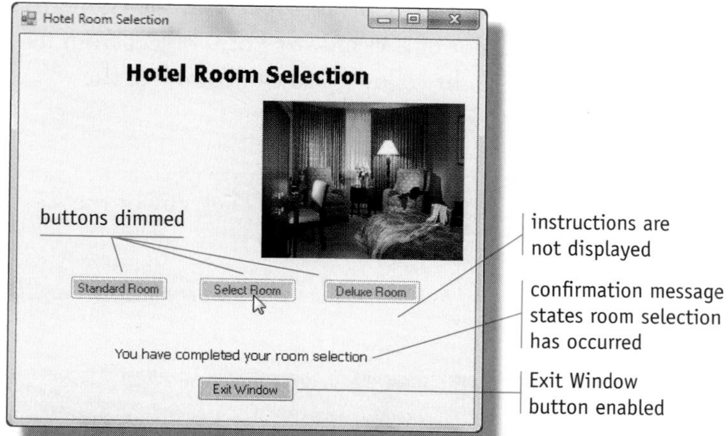

FIGURE 3-1c

ONLINE REINFORCEMENT

To view a video of program execution, visit scsite.com/vb2010/ch3 and then select Figure 3-1. Turn on your speakers to listen to the audio walk-through of the steps.

In the opening window (Figure 3-1a), you can see that no images appear in the PictureBox objects that are included in the window, and that the Select Room button and the Exit Window button are dimmed, which means they are disabled when the program begins. In Figure 3-1b, the user clicked the Deluxe Room button, so the picture is displayed. In addition, the Select Room button is enabled. The Exit Window button still is dimmed. In Figure 3-1c, the user has selected a room, so the room selection confirmation message is displayed; the Standard Room, Select Room, and Deluxe Room buttons are dimmed; and the Exit Window button is enabled. Each of these changes occurs through the use of code you enter into the program, as you will discover later in this chapter.

Fine-Tune the User Interface

You have learned about some properties of Visual Basic objects in Chapter 2, including the Name property and the Text property. As you probably noted in the Properties window in Chapter 2, more properties are available for each of the objects in a graphical user interface. In many cases, these properties are used to fine-tune the user interface to make it more usable. In the sample program, the BackColor property is used to make the user interface more attractive and effective.

BackColor Property

The **BackColor** of an object is the color that is displayed in its background. For example, in Figure 3-1 the BackColor of the Windows Form object is a light yellow, while the BackColor of the Button objects is an orange shade. You can select the BackColor of an object through the use of the **BackColor property** in the Properties window. For example, to change the BackColor of a Windows Form object from its default color of Control (gray) to Cornsilk (light yellow), you can complete the following steps:

STEP 1 Click the Windows Form object to select it. (Do not click any of the objects on the Windows Form object.)

The Windows Form object is selected, as indicated by the thick border and the sizing handles (Figure 3-2).

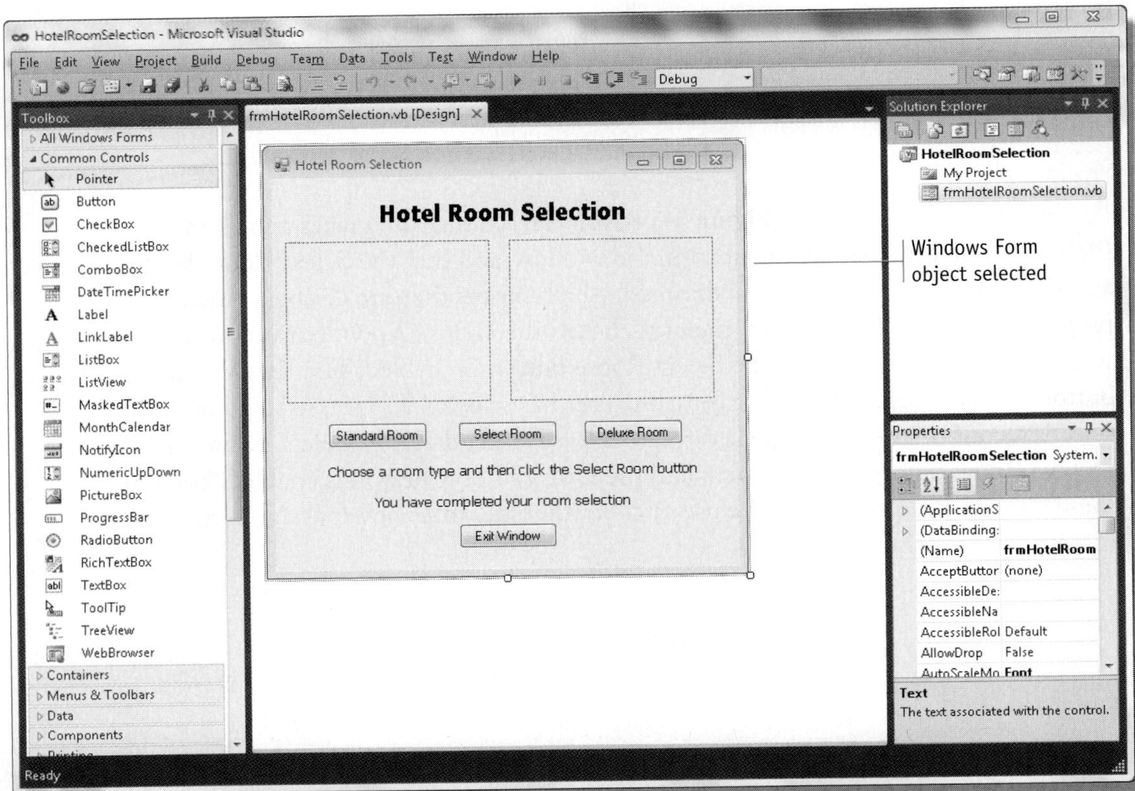

FIGURE 3-2

STEP 2 If necessary, scroll in the Properties window until the BackColor property is displayed, and then click the right column of the BackColor property.

The BackColor property is selected, and the BackColor arrow is displayed (Figure 3-3).

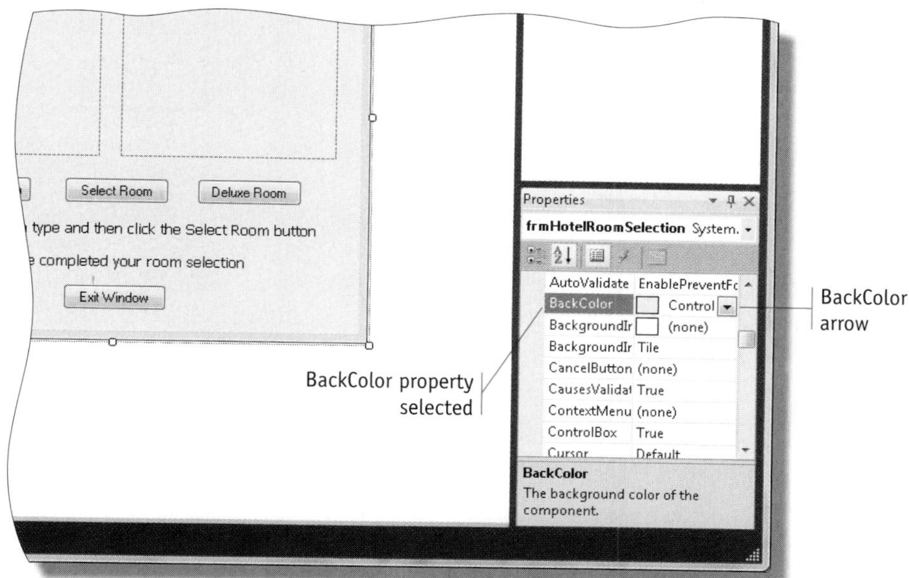

FIGURE 3-3

STEP 3 Click the BackColor arrow. Then, if necessary, click the Web tab to display the Web tabbed page.

The color window within the Properties window opens (Figure 3-4). The Web tabbed page contains more than 100 named colors you can select to display as the BackColor for the selected object, which in this case is the Windows Form object.

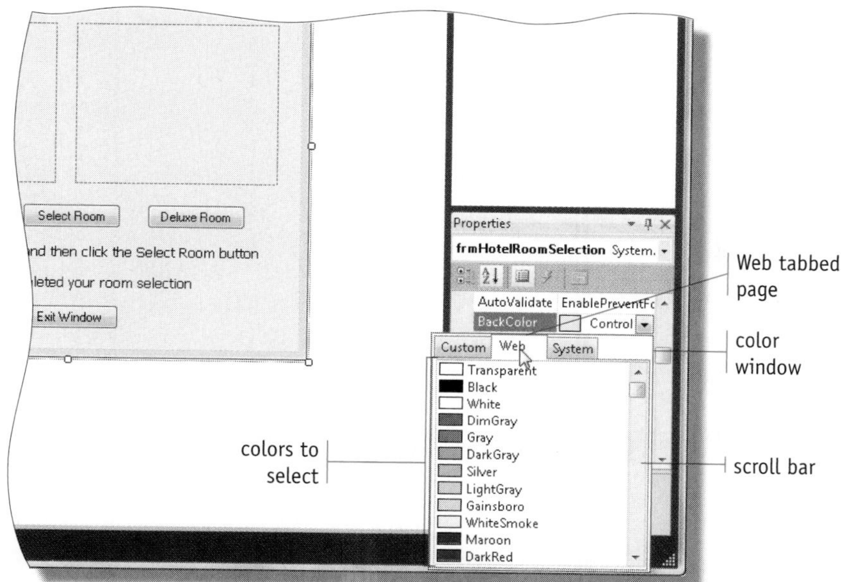

FIGURE 3-4

IN THE REAL WORLD

Visual Studio 2010 offers three palettes for BackColors and ForeColors — the **Custom palette**, the **Web palette**, and the **System palette**. In the Custom palette, 48 colors are available for selection; in addition, 16 white color chips are available in which you can select your own color by right-clicking the color chip and then identifying the exact color you want from the Define Color window. You should be aware that some of the colors you select from the Define Color window might not be displayed properly on all computers. When the Web palette is open, you can choose from 141 colors that are guaranteed to be displayed properly on every computer. The System palette contains fewer colors, listing only those that correspond to the colors selected in other areas of the computer system.

HEADS UP

Carefully consider your choice for the BackColor of a window. Generally, use light colors so the objects in the window are easily visible. In some instances, you might choose a darker color, but then you should use lighter colors for the objects within the window. If you choose a darker BackColor and the object contains text, such as a Button or Label object, then the text color, as specified by the **ForeColor property**, should be a light color. The choice of a BackColor can be critical to the usability of the window.

STEP 4 Scroll until the Cornsilk color is displayed in the list of colors.

The name and a sample of the Cornsilk color are displayed (Figure 3-5).

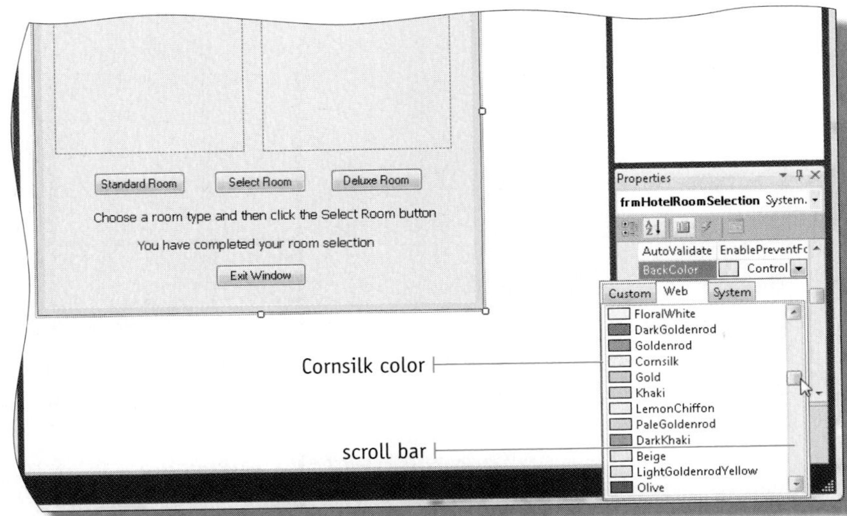

FIGURE 3-5

STEP 5 Click Cornsilk on the color list.

The background color in the Windows Form object is changed to Cornsilk (Figure 3-6).

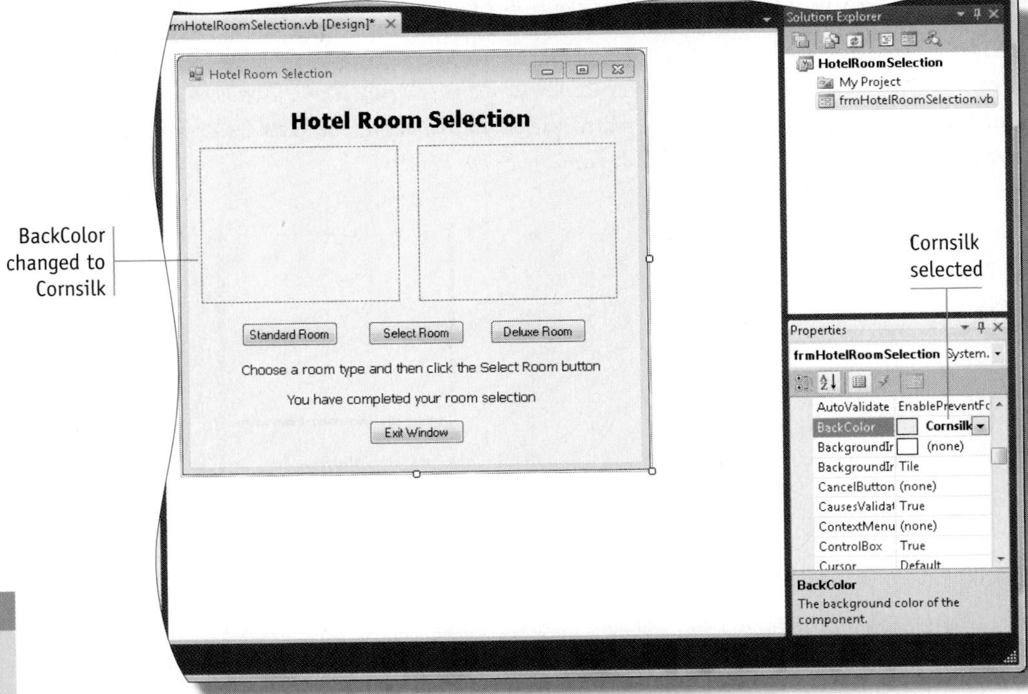

FIGURE 3-6

ONLINE REINFORCEMENT

To view a video of the process in the previous steps, visit scsite.com/vb2010/ch3 and then select Figure 3-2.

You can use the same technique to change the BackColor on any object that contains the BackColor property, including Button and Label objects.

Adding Images to a PictureBox Object

PictureBox objects are used to display a graphic image. In the sample program, a picture of both a standard room and a deluxe room are displayed. You must specify the image that will be displayed in a particular PictureBox object. Before specifying the image, however, you must locate the image and then place it in the Resources folder that is linked to the application. The steps for displaying an image in a PictureBox object are:

1. Locate the image to be displayed in the PictureBox object. You might locate this image on the Web, in which case you must then store the image in a folder on your computer; or it might already be stored on your computer or a local network.
2. Import the image into the **Resources folder**. This step makes the image available for display within the PictureBox object. Multiple images can be placed in the Resources folder.
3. Specify the image to be displayed within the PictureBox object.

Each of these steps will be shown on the following pages.

HEADS UP

While many Web sites offer images you can select, three sites are particularly useful. These sites are: bing.com/images, www.google.com/images, and www.webshots.com. When you visit sites, not all images are available for free download. In some cases, the images are copyrighted and you must acquire rights to use the image. In addition, some sites require a fee to be paid before the image can be used. Therefore, you should download only those images for which you have paid, or acquired the rights to use or those images that are free of copyright and can be used by anyone.

Locate and Save an Image from the World Wide Web

Images are available from a multitude of sources, ranging from your own digital camera to millions of publicly available images on the Web. If you work for a company, the company might have photos and graphic images that can be used in company applications.

For purposes of the images used in this book, you can use the scsite.com/vb2010 Web site to retrieve an image. For example, to retrieve the standard room image from this site, you could complete the steps beginning on page 118:

STEP 1 Open your Internet browser (in this example, Internet Explorer is used. Steps for other browsers might vary slightly). Then, enter `scsite.com/vb2010/ch3/images` in the Address box and press the ENTER key.

The browser window is open and the scsite.com/vb2010/ch3/images Web page is displayed (Figure 3-7). The names and thumbnails of the images used in this chapter are displayed on the Web page.

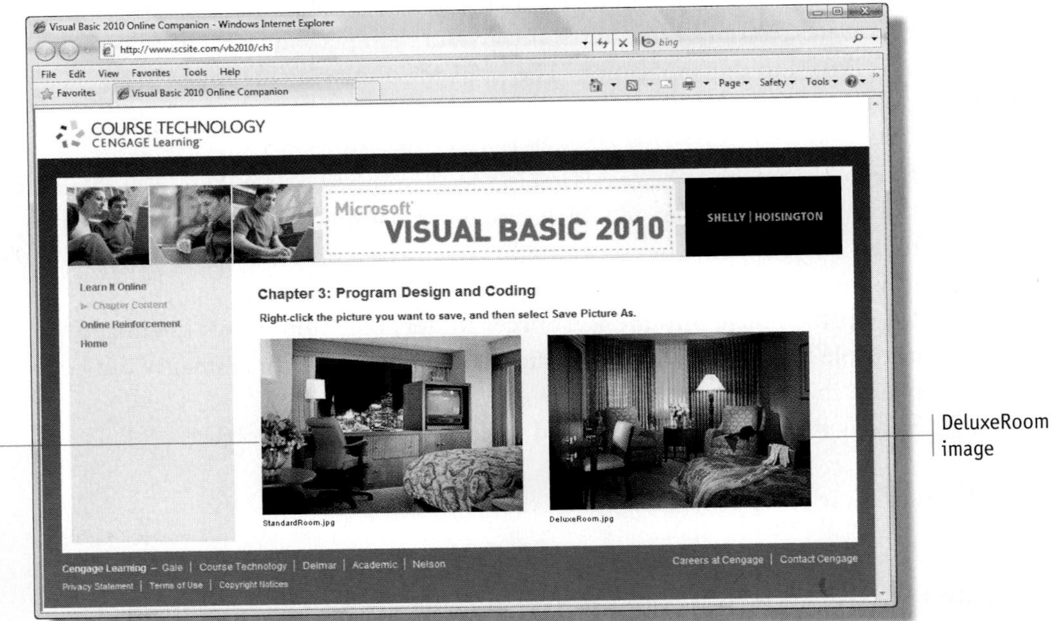

FIGURE 3-7

HEADS UP

When selecting an image, it is advisable to choose one that is the approximate size of the PictureBox object where you will place the image. You can determine the size (in pixels) of a selected PictureBox object by looking at the Size property in the Properties window. To determine the size of the image on the Web, right-click the image and then click Properties on the menu. The size, in pixels, is displayed in the Properties dialog box. By choosing an image of the same approximate size, you minimize the distortion of the image when it is fitted into the PictureBox object. If you cannot find an image that is about the same size, then less distortion will occur if you select a larger image with approximately the same relative dimensions as the Picture Box object. In general, avoid selecting an image considerably smaller than the PictureBox object.

STEP 2 Locate the StandardRoom.jpg image and then right-click the image.

The shortcut menu is displayed (Figure 3-8).

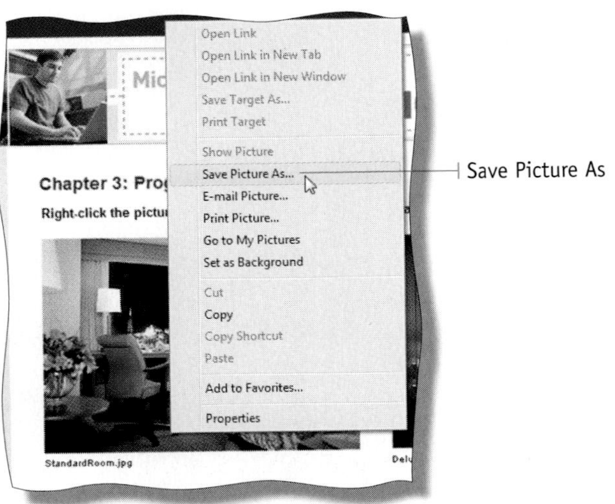

FIGURE 3-8

STEP 3 Click Save Picture As on the shortcut menu.

The Save Picture dialog box opens (Figure 3-9). You must identify the drive and folder in which you want to store the image. Each of these items will be unique for your computer and drives. In all sample programs in this book, images are stored on a USB drive that is designated as drive E. You also must enter a file name under which the image will be stored.

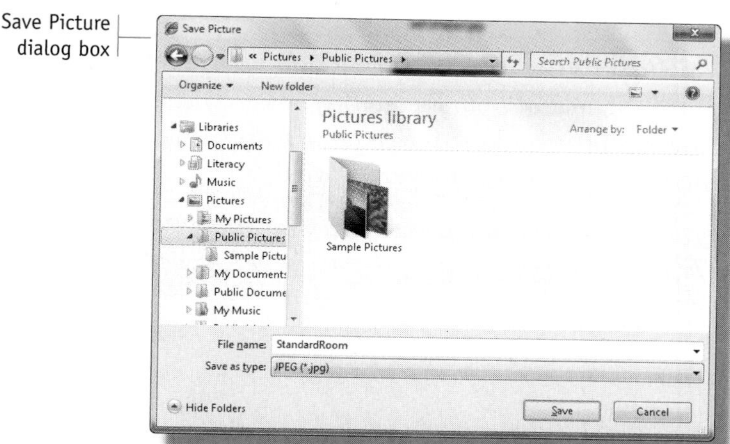

FIGURE 3-9

STEP 4 Identify the drive and folder where the image will be stored. Enter the image file name, `StandardRoom`, in the File name text box.

The information required to store the image is entered in the Save Picture dialog box (Figure 3-10). You must remember where you save the images because later you must locate them when you import them into the Resources folder for use within the program. Image file names should not contain spaces.

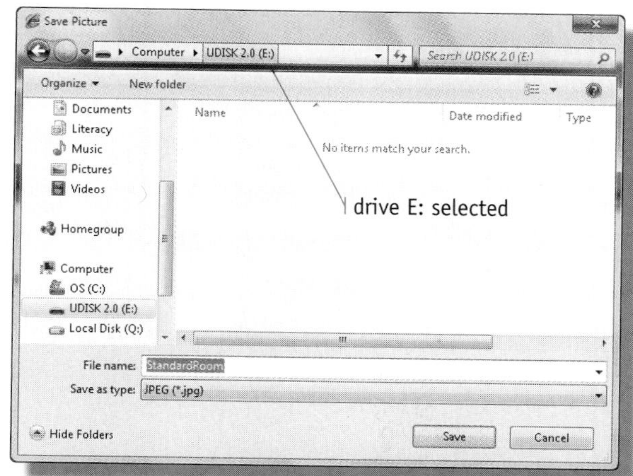

FIGURE 3-10

STEP 5 Click the Save button in the Save Picture dialog box to save the image in the selected location.

ONLINE REINFORCEMENT

To view a video of the process in the previous steps, visit scsite.com/vb2010/ch3 and then select Figure 3-7.

Import the Image into the Program Resources Folder

After you have saved an image on a storage device available to your computer, you should import the image into the Resources folder of the program so the image is available for use by the program. To import the Standard Room image into the Resources folder, you can complete the following steps:

STEP 1 With Visual Studio 2010 and the Hotel Room Selection Visual Basic program open, select the picStandardRoom PictureBox object by clicking it. Scroll in the PictureBox Properties window until the Image property is visible. Click the Image property name in the left list in the Properties window.

With the PictureBox object selected, the Properties window displays all the properties of the object (Figure 3-11). The ***Image property*** *specifies the image that should be displayed in the selected PictureBox object. The Image property is selected in the Properties window. The Image property Ellipsis button is displayed in the right column of the Image property.*

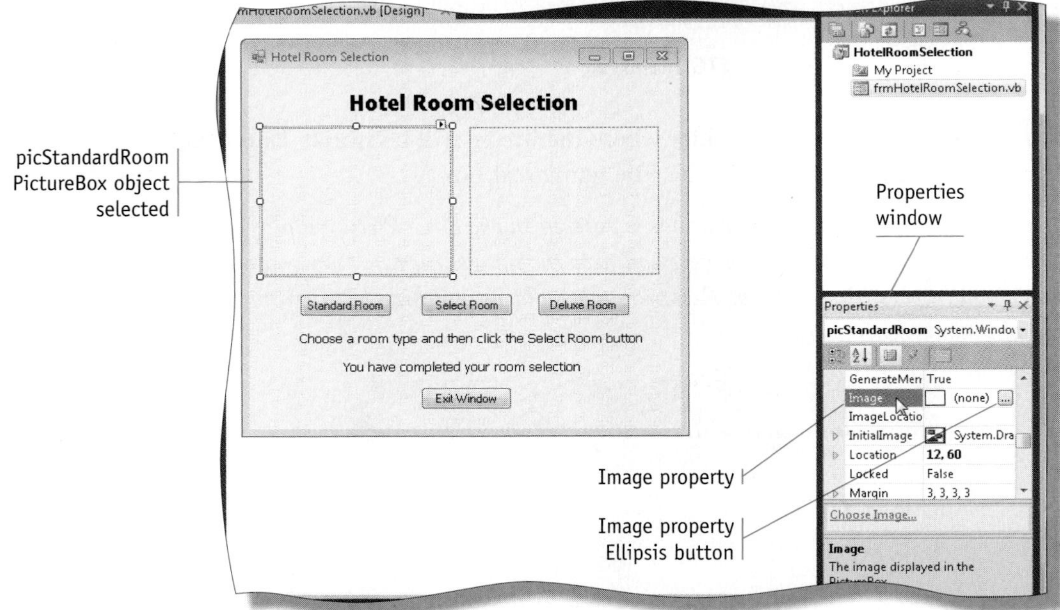

FIGURE 3-11

STEP 2 Click the Ellipsis button in the right column of the Image property.

*The **Select Resource dialog box** opens (Figure 3-12), and displays the resources that have been imported for the program. In Figure 3-12, no resources have been imported.*

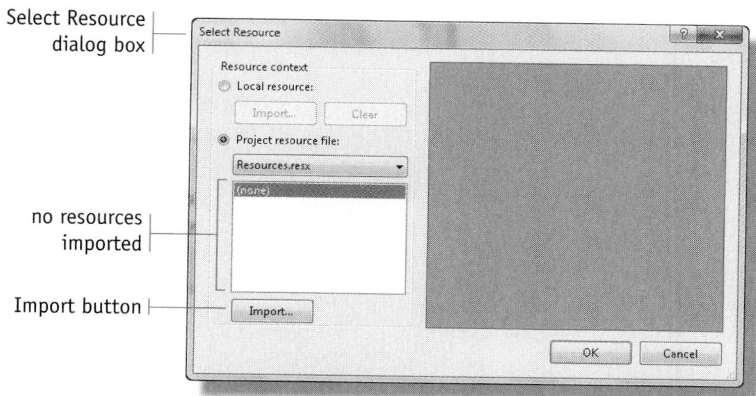

FIGURE 3-12

STEP 3 Click the Import button in the Select Resource dialog box. Then, using the features of the Open dialog box, locate the file you want to import into the program. In this case, the file is the StandardRoom.jpg file that is stored on drive E, which is a USB drive.

The Open dialog box opens when you click the Import button (Figure 3-13). The location of the StandardRoom.jpg file is on drive E.

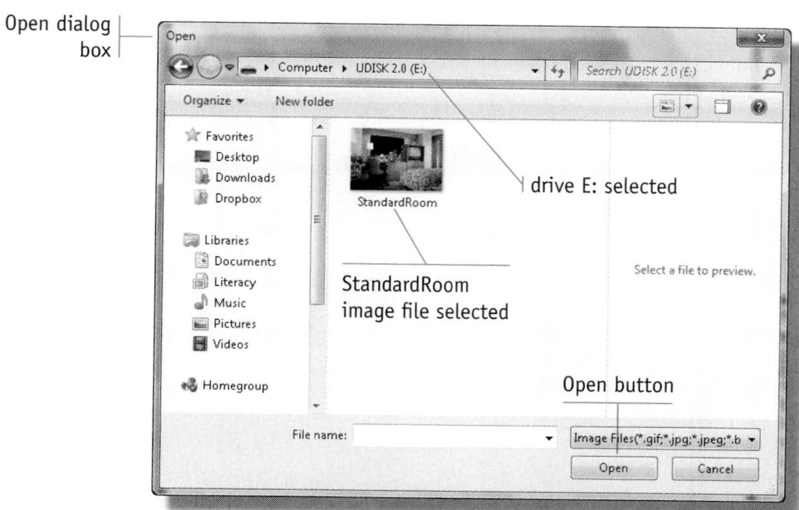

FIGURE 3-13

STEP 4 Click the Open button in the Open dialog box.

The Select Resource dialog box is displayed again, but now the StandardRoom image is identified in the Project resource file list (Figure 3-14). The image appears in the preview window. This means the image has been made a part of the resources for the program. It no longer is necessary to locate the image on the USB drive in order to include the image in a PictureBox object.

FIGURE 3-14

STEP 5 With the StandardRoom file name selected in the Project resource file list, click the OK button in the Select Resource dialog box.

The StandardRoom image becomes the image displayed in the picStandardRoom PictureBox object (Figure 3-15). In addition, the Resources folder is added to the Solution Explorer window, indicating the Resources folder now is part of the program.

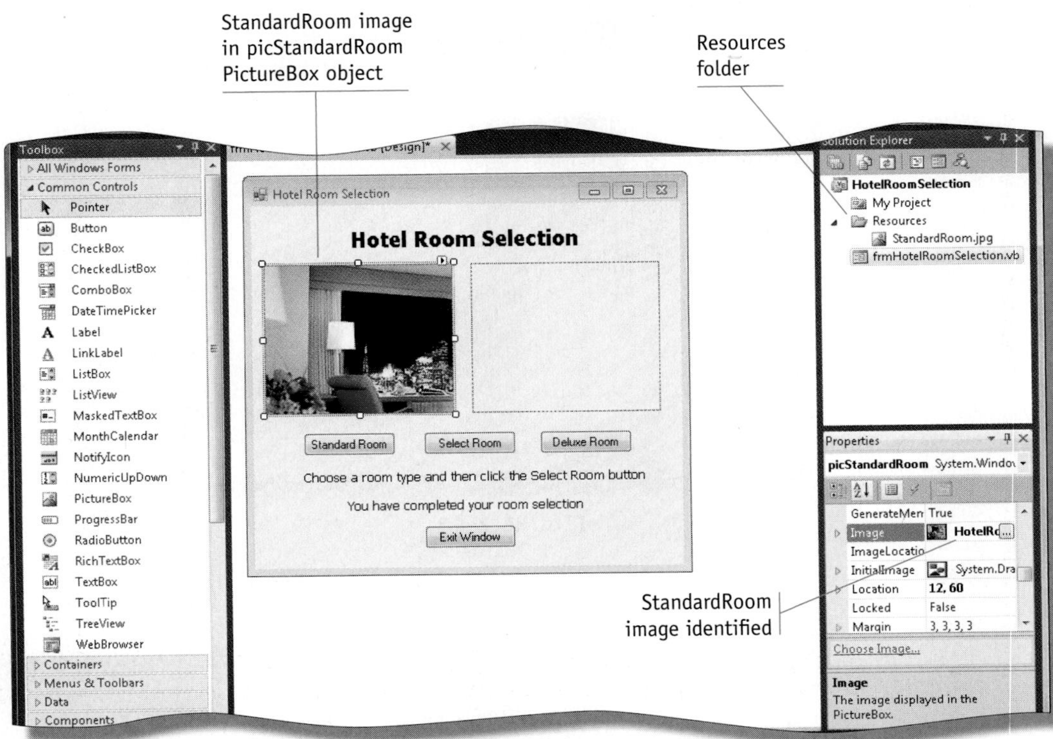

FIGURE 3-15

ONLINE REINFORCEMENT

To view a video of the process in the previous steps, visit scsite.com/vb2010/ch3 and then select Figure 3-11.

Size an Image

In most cases, when you import an image into a program, the image will not fit in the PictureBox object perfectly. This occurs for two reasons: the image is a different size from the PictureBox object, and/or the image has a dimension different than the PictureBox object. In both cases, the developer must adjust the size of the image to fit in the PictureBox object, or adjust the size of the PictureBox object to accommodate the image.

In Figure 3-15, you can see that the image is larger than the PictureBox object (compare the image in Figure 3-14 to the image in Figure 3-15). Because the PictureBox object must remain its current size, the image must be adjusted using the **SizeMode property**. To adjust an image size to fit in a PictureBox object, you can complete the following steps:

STEP 1 With the PictureBox object containing the StandardRoom image selected, scroll in the picStandardRoom Properties window until you see the SizeMode property. Click the SizeMode property name in the left column and then click the SizeMode arrow in the right column of the SizeMode property.

The SizeMode property list is displayed (Figure 3-16). The list contains five choices you can use to change either the size of the image or the size of the PictureBox object. Normal is selected because it is the default value.

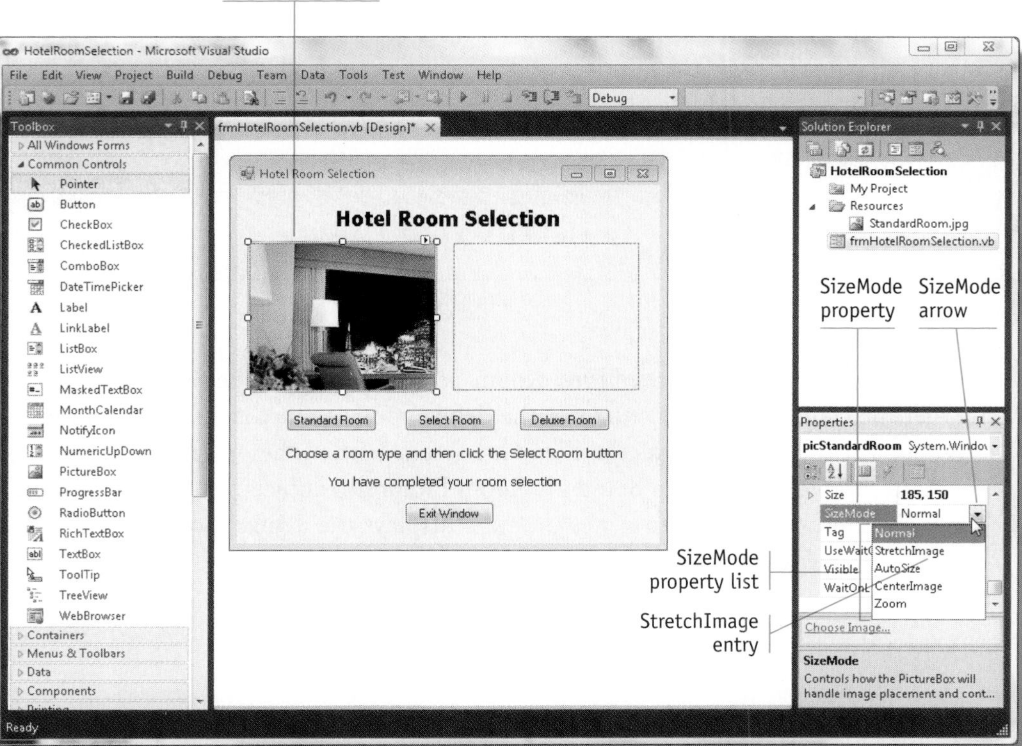

FIGURE 3-16

HEADS UP

StretchImage is not the only choice on the SizeMode list in the Properties window for PictureBox objects (see Figure 3-16). The other choices and their actions are: a) **Normal:** No changes are made to the image size or the size of the PictureBox object. Visual Studio places the image in the PictureBox object with the upper-left corner of the image and the upper-left corner of the PictureBox object aligned; b) **AutoSize:** Visual Studio increases or decreases the size of the PictureBox object to accommodate the size of the image. The entire image is visible and fits precisely in the PictureBox object; c) **CenterImage:** No changes are made to the image size or the size of the PictureBox object. Visual Studio places the image in the PictureBox object with the center of the image aligned with the center of the PictureBox object; d) **Zoom:** The image size is either reduced or enlarged so it fits in the PictureBox object. The fit can be left and right or up and down, depending on the dimensions of the image and the PictureBox object. If the image and PictureBox object are not exactly proportional to another, the image will not fill out the entire PictureBox object.

STEP 2 Click StretchImage in the SizeMode list.

The SizeMode list is closed and the image is resized to fit within the picStandardRoom PictureBox object (Figure 3-17). When you use the ***StretchImage option****, some distortion of the image might occur in order to make the image fit within the PictureBox object. This is why it is important to select an image that has the same approximate dimensions (or at least the same aspect ratio) as the PictureBox object in which the image will be placed.*

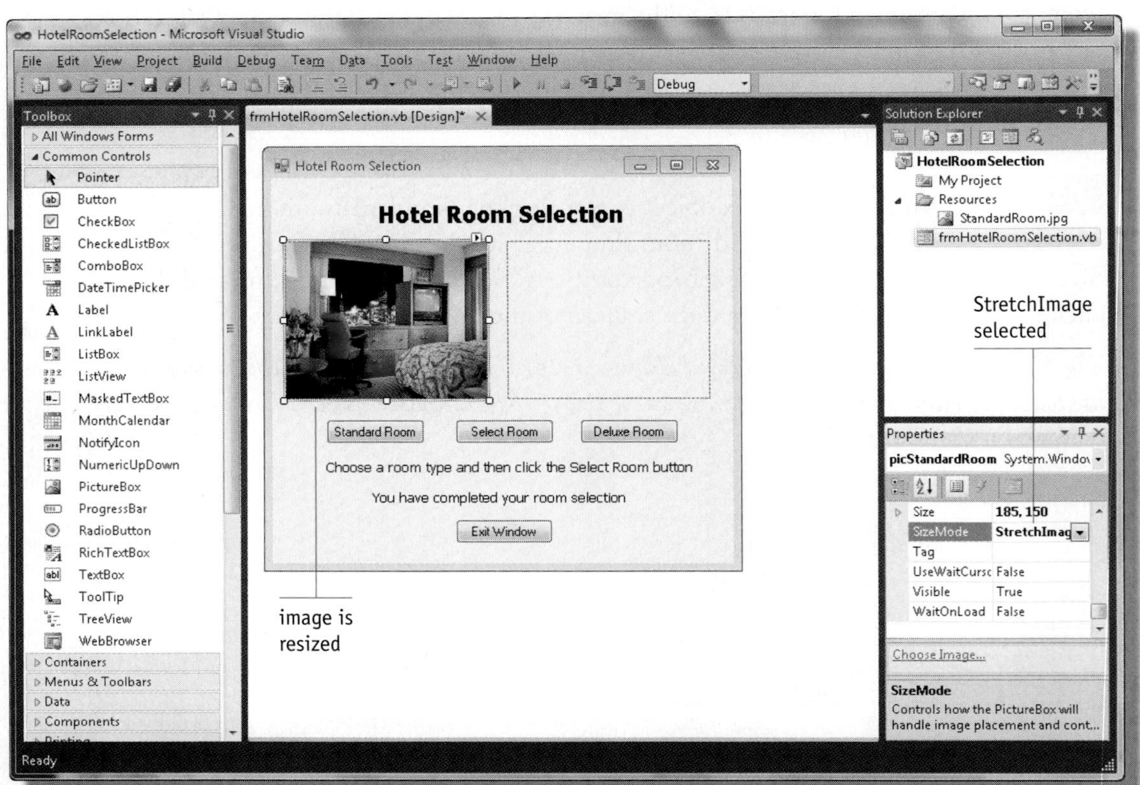

FIGURE 3-17

ONLINE REINFORCEMENT

To view a video of the process in the previous steps, visit scsite.com/vb2010/ch3 and then select Figure 3-16.

Visible Property

As you have learned, when the Hotel Room Selection program begins execution, neither the standard room picture nor the deluxe room picture is displayed in the window. When the user clicks the Standard Room button, the program displays the standard room picture in the Standard Room PictureBox object; and when the user clicks the Deluxe Room button, the program displays the deluxe room picture in the Deluxe Room PictureBox object.

The property that controls whether an object is displayed on the Windows Form object is the **Visible property**. By default, the Visible property is set to True so that any object you place on the Windows Form object will be displayed when the program runs. To cause the object not to display, you must set the Visible property to False. To set the Visible property for the picStandardRoom PictureBox object to False, you can complete the following steps:

STEP 1 If necessary, select the picStandardRoom PictureBox object. Scroll in the Properties window until the Visible property is displayed. Click the Visible property name in the left column, and then click the Visible arrow in the right column of the Visible property.

When you click the Visible arrow, the list displays the words True and False (Figure 3-18). To make the object visible when the program starts running, select True. To make the object not visible when the program starts running, select False.

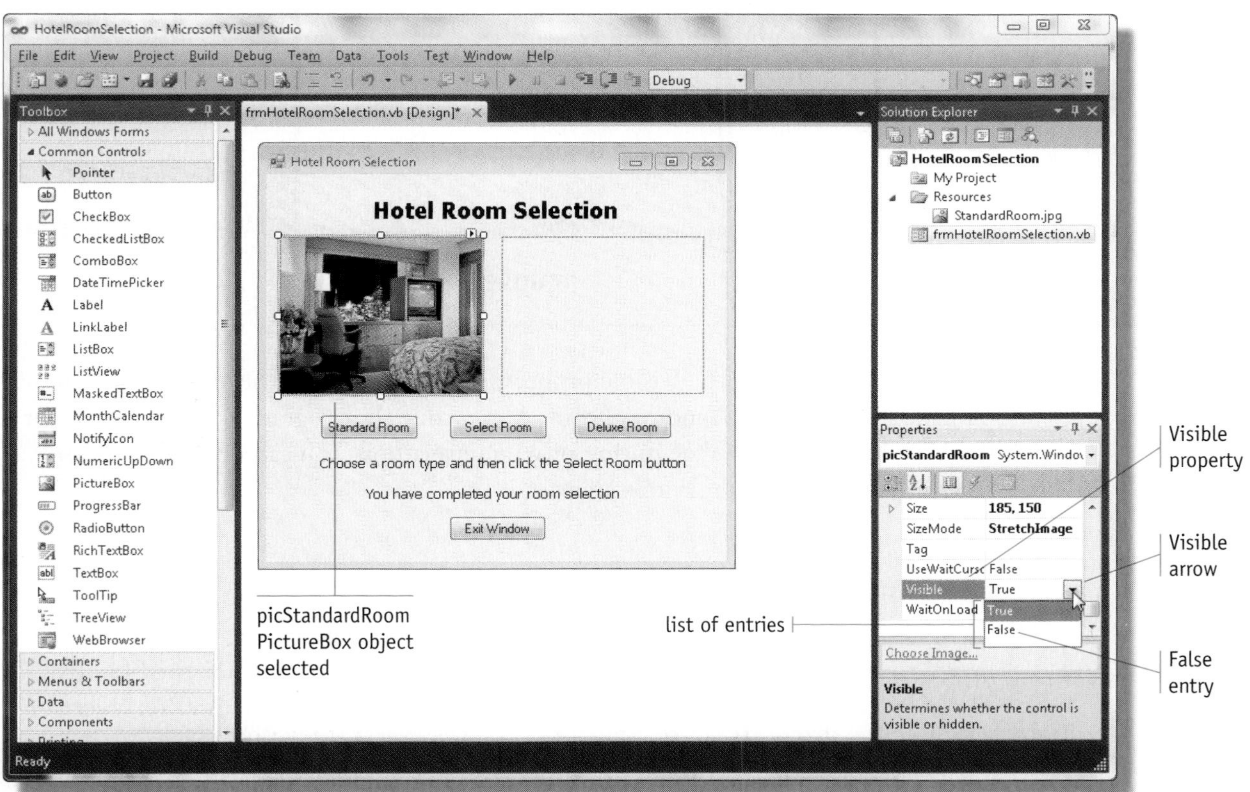

FIGURE 3-18

STEP 2 Click False on the Visible property list.

The Visible property is set to False (Figure 3-19). When the program begins running, the picStandardRoom object will not be displayed on the Windows Form object. Note that the image and object are displayed on the frmHotelRoomSelection.vb [Design] tabbed page regardless of the Visible property setting.

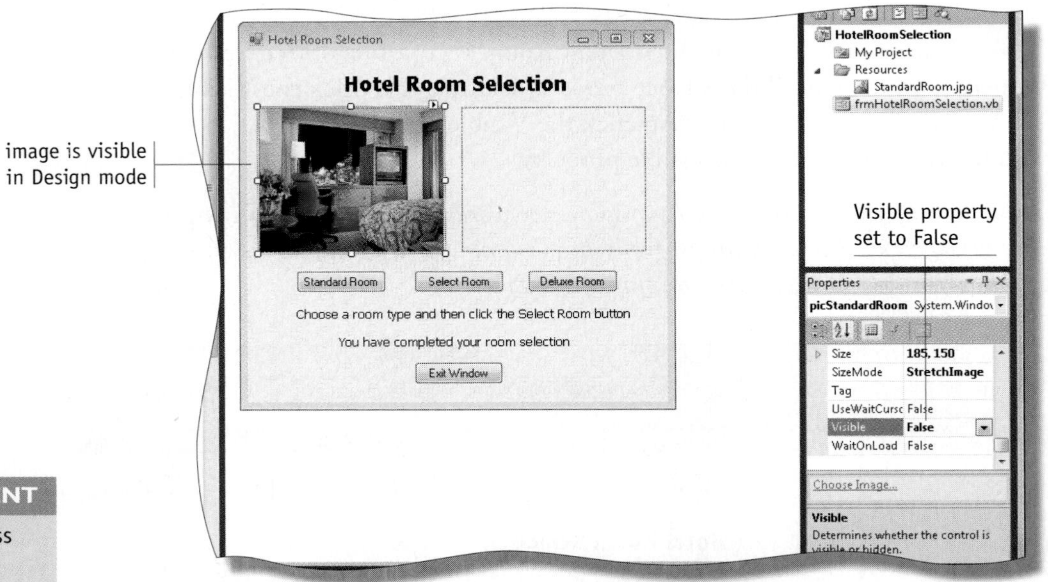

FIGURE 3-19

ONLINE REINFORCEMENT

To view a video of the process in the previous steps, visit scsite.com/vb2010/ch3 and then select Figure 3-18.

Once you have set the Visible property for an object to False, the only way to display the object on the Windows Form object while the program is running is to set the Visible property to True during program execution. You can do this by writing code, as you will see later in this chapter.

Enabled Property

In an event-driven program, objects such as Button objects can be used to cause events to occur. For example, in the sample program, when you click the Standard Room button, a picture of a standard room is displayed in the PictureBox object. In addition, the Select Room Button object becomes **enabled**, which means it can be clicked to cause an event to occur. When the program begins execution, however, the Select Room button is **disabled**, which means nothing will happen when you click the button. A disabled button is displayed as a dimmed button (see Figure 3-1a) on page 112).

The **Enabled property** controls when a Button object is enabled, which means clicking the button can cause an event to occur, and when a Button object is not enabled, which means clicking the button causes no action to occur. The default for the Enabled property is True, which means the associated Button object is enabled. To set the Enabled property to False for the Select Room button, you can complete the steps on the next page:

STEP 1 Select the btnSelectRoom object. Scroll in the Properties window until the Enabled property is displayed. Click the Enabled property name in the left column, and then click the Enabled arrow in the right column of the Enabled property.

The list displayed when you click the Enabled arrow contains the words, True and False (Figure 3-20). To make the object enabled when the program starts running, select True. To make the object not enabled when the program starts running, select False.

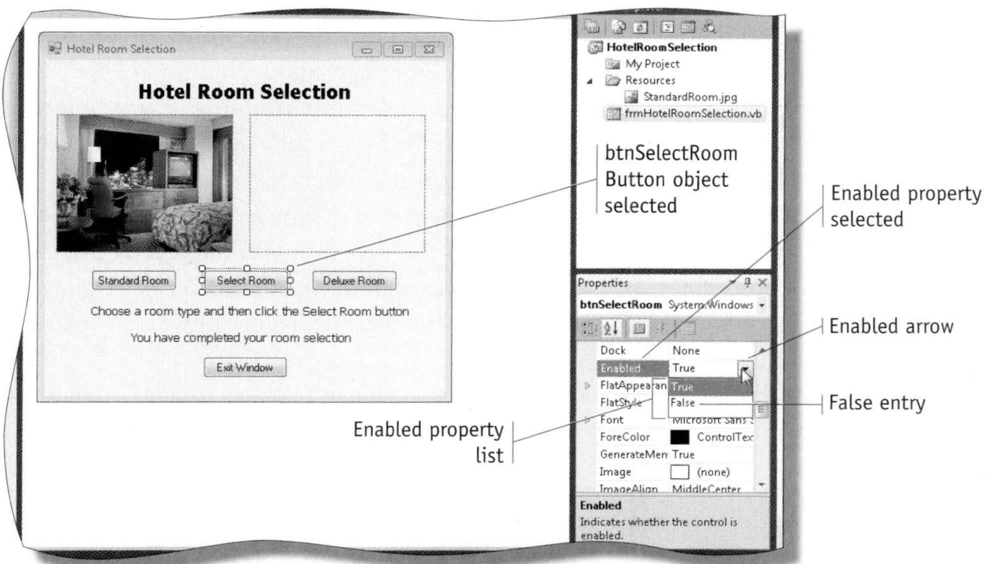

FIGURE 3-20

STEP 2 Click False on the Enabled property list.

The Enabled property is set to False (Figure 3-21). When the program begins running, the btnSelectRoom Button object will not be enabled on the Windows Form object.

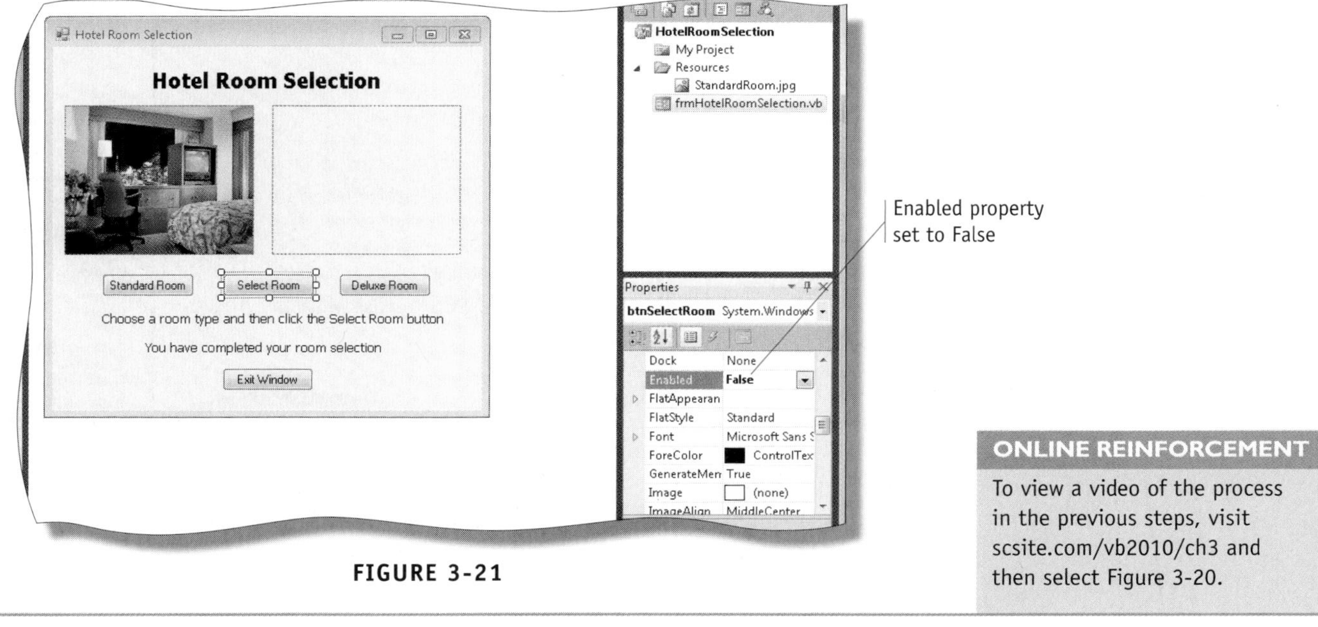

FIGURE 3-21

ONLINE REINFORCEMENT

To view a video of the process in the previous steps, visit scsite.com/vb2010/ch3 and then select Figure 3-20.

Once you have set the Enabled property to False, the only way to cause a Button object to be enabled on the Windows Form object while the program is running is to set the Enabled property to True. You can do this by writing code, as you will see later in this chapter.

Running a Program

When you set some object properties, the effect of the property change might not be evident until you run the program. For example, you have set the Visible property for the picStandardRoom PictureBox object to False, and you have set the Enabled property for the btnSelectRoom Button object to False. Neither change is evident, however, when you view the Hotel Room Selection Windows Form object on the frmHotelRoomSelection.vb [Design] tabbed page in Visual Studio. These settings will take place only when you actually run the program.

To ensure the settings are correct for the user interface, you must run the program. **Running the program** means the program is compiled, or translated, from the instructions you have written or generated in the Visual Basic language into a form of instructions that the computer can execute eventually. These instructions are saved and then executed as a program.

To run the program you have created, you can click the Start Debugging button on the Standard toolbar, as shown in the following steps:

STEP 1 Point to the Start Debugging button on the Standard toolbar.

The pointer points to the Start Debugging button (Figure 3-22).

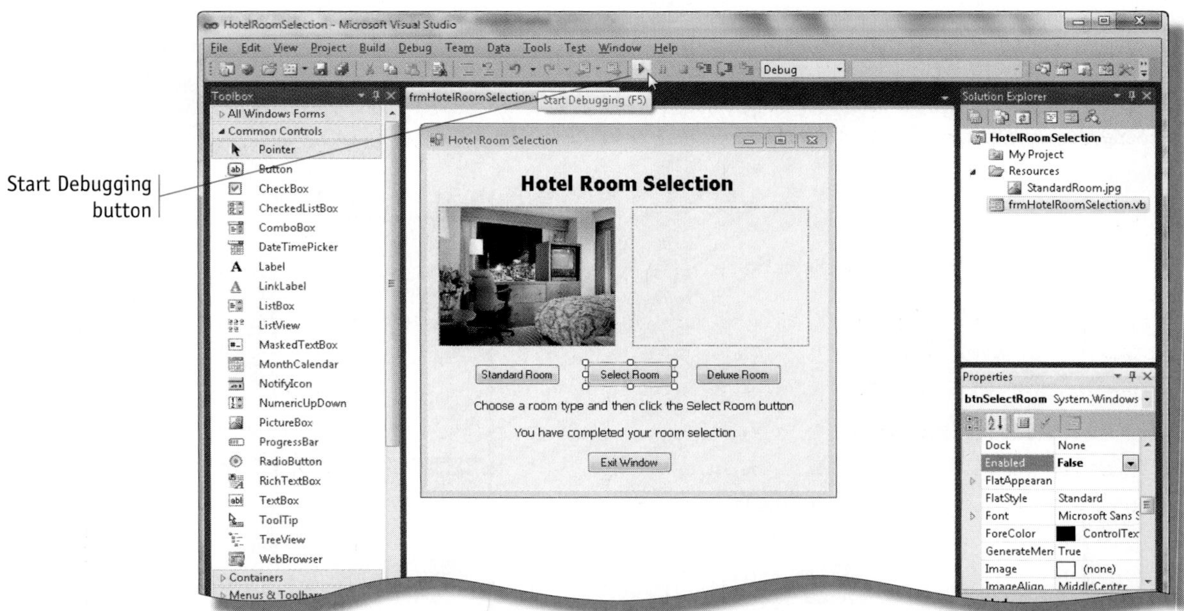

FIGURE 3-22

STEP 2 Click the Start Debugging button on the Standard toolbar.

The program is compiled and saved, and then is run on the computer. When the program runs, the Hotel Room Selection window is displayed on the screen (Figure 3-23). Notice that the Standard Room image is not displayed in the window because the Visible property for the picStandardRoom PictureBox object was set to False (see Figure 3-19 on page 126). Notice also that the Select Room button is dimmed, which indicates its Enabled property is set to False.

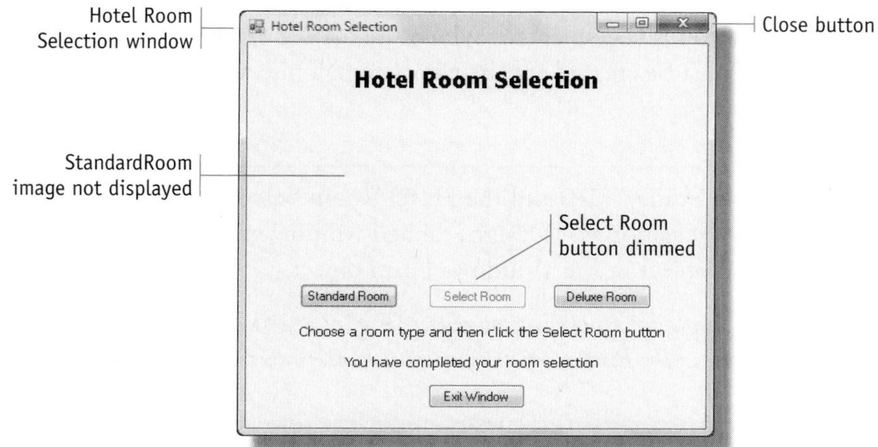

FIGURE 3-23

ONLINE REINFORCEMENT

To view a video of the process in the previous steps, visit scsite.com/vb2010/ch3 and then select Figure 3-22.

Once you have started running the program, it will continue to run until you close it. To close a program, click the Close button on the right of the window title bar (see Figure 3-23).

Once you have set all the properties for the objects in the user interface, the design of the user interface is complete. You now are ready to move to the next phase of the program development life cycle — designing the program processing objects.

Visual Basic Program Coding

Prior to beginning the design of the program processing objects, the developer must understand certain program coding principles and techniques so he or she can apply this knowledge to the program design. **Program code** is the set of instructions written by the developer that direct the program to carry out the processing required in the program. The following sections explain the Visual Basic 2010 code required for the Hotel Room Selection program.

Entering Visual Basic Code for Event Handling

As you have learned, most program processing in an event-driven program occurs when the user triggers an event. For example, when a user clicks a button on the graphical user interface, this activity can trigger an event and the program performs the required processing. The developer writes program code to carry out the processing. This code is placed in a section of the program called an **event handler** — so-called because it "handles" the event that the user action triggers by executing code that performs the required processing.

To write the code for an event handler, the developer first must identify the GUI object that will be used to trigger the event. For example, in the sample program, you have learned that when the Standard Room button is clicked, the standard room picture should appear in the picStandardRoom PictureBox object. To write the code that will display the standard room picture, the developer must inform Visual Studio that the Standard Room button is the object for which the code is to be written, and that an event handler must be created for the click event. This can be done using the following steps:

STEP 1 With Visual Studio 2010 and the Hotel Room Selection program open and the frmHotelRoomSelection.vb [Design] tabbed window visible, point to the Standard Room Button object in the Windows Form object.

The pointer points to the Standard Room Button object (Figure 3-24). The four-headed arrow pointer indicates you can drag the Button object to another location in the window if desired.

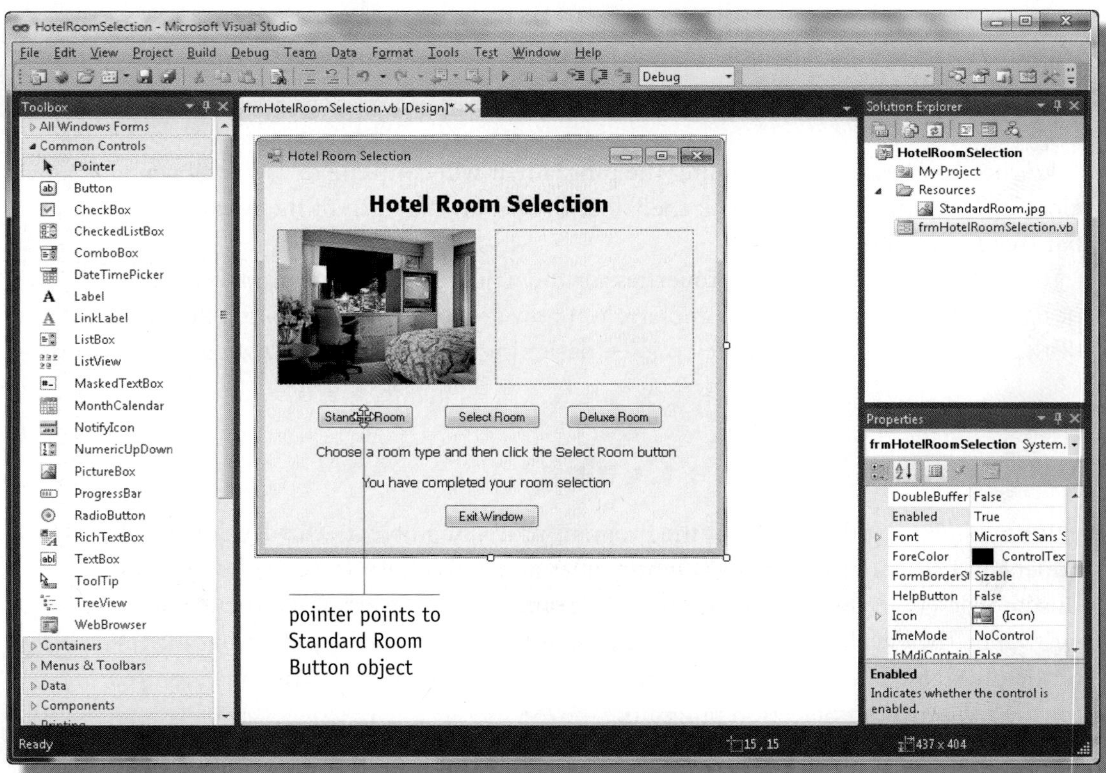

FIGURE 3-24

STEP 2 Double-click the Standard Room Button object.

The code window is displayed on the frmHotelRoomSelection.vb tabbed page (Figure 3-25). The code in the window is generated by Visual Studio. This code identifies an event handler, which is the code that executes when an event is triggered. In this case, when the Standard Room button is clicked, the code in this event handler will be executed by the program. The list box at the upper-left of the tabbed page identifies the object for which the event hander will execute — in this case, the btnStandardRoom object. The list box at the upper-right of the tabbed page identifies the event that must occur in order to execute the code in the event handler. The event identified in Figure 3-25 is Click. So, when the user clicks the Standard Room button, the program will execute the code between the Private Sub statement and the End Sub statement. In Figure 3-25, no code other than the event handler identification code generated by Visual Studio has been entered. The insertion point is located where the developer should begin entering the code that executes when the user clicks the btnStandardRoom Button object.*

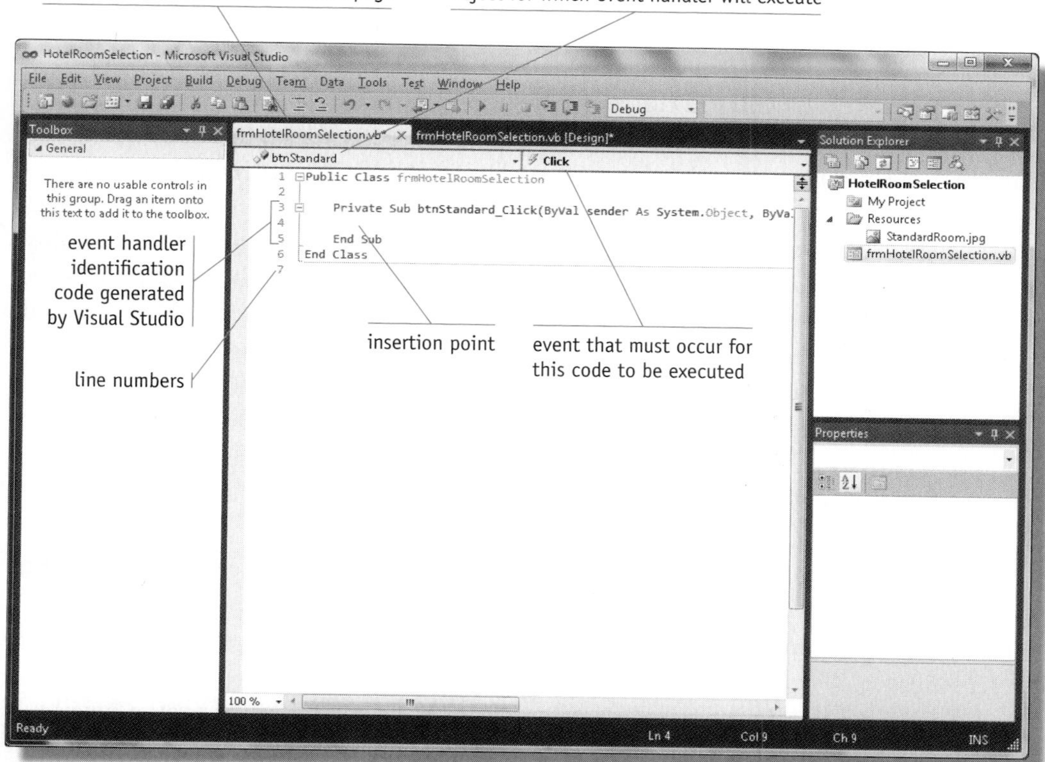

FIGURE 3-25

> **HEADS UP**
>
> In the left column of the coding window in Figure 3-25, line numbers appear. These line numbers help identify each line of code in the coding window. They do not appear by default, however, so you must instruct Visual Studio to display the line numbers. If line numbers do not appear in the coding window on a computer you are using, you can display them by completing the following steps: 1) Click Tools on the menu bar; 2) Click Options on the Tools menu; 3) If necessary, click the triangle next to Text Editor in the Options dialog box; 4) If necessary, click the triangle next to Basic in the list below Text Editor; 5) Click Editor in the list below Basic; 6) Place a check mark in the Line numbers check box; 7) Click the OK button in the Options dialog box.

> **ONLINE REINFORCEMENT**
>
> To view a video of the process in the previous steps, visit scsite.com/vb2010/ch3 and then select Figure 3-24.

Visual Basic 2010 Coding Statements

A Visual Basic 2010 coding statement contains instruction(s) that the computer eventually executes. Visual Basic has a set of rules, or **syntax**, that specifies how each statement must be written.

In the Hotel Room Selection program, you will recall that when the user clicks the Standard Room Button while the program is running, the standard room image should be displayed in the picStandardRoom PictureBox object. Figure 3-26 shows a Visual Basic coding statement that sets the Visible property for the picStandardRoom PictureBox object to True so the image is displayed in the picture box after the statement is executed.

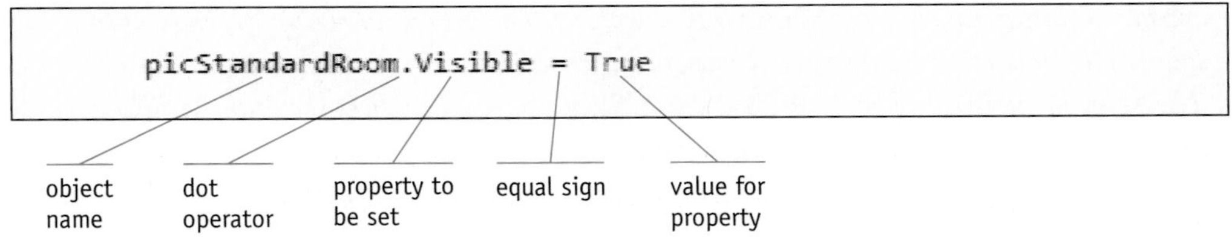

FIGURE 3-26

The first part of the statement, picStandardRoom, identifies the object containing the property to set. The name of the object is followed by the dot operator (period) with no intervening spaces. The dot operator separates the name of the object from the next entry in the statement and is required.

Following the dot operator is the name of the property to set. In Figure 3-26, the name of the property is Visible. You will recall that the Visible property determines whether an image is displayed in the PictureBox object when the program is running. In Figure 3-19 on page 126, the Visible property for the picStandardRoom PictureBox object was set to False so the image would not be displayed when the program was started. This statement sets the Visible property to True so the image will be displayed.

The property name is followed by a space and then an equal sign. The space is not required, but good coding practice dictates that elements within a statement should be separated by a space so the statement is easier to read. One or more spaces can be used, but most developers use only one space. The equal sign is required because it indicates that the value to be used for setting the property follows. A space follows the equal sign for ease of readability.

The word True follows the space. The value True in the Visible property indicates that the image in the PictureBox object should be displayed. When the program is running, as soon as the Visible property is set to True, the image appears in the picture box.

Each entry within the program statement must be correct or the program will not compile. This means the object name must be spelled properly, the dot operator must be placed in the correct location, the name of the property must be spelled properly, the equal sign must be present, and a valid entry for the property must follow the equal sign. For the Visible property, the only valid entries are True and False, so the word True or the word False must follow the equal sign.

General Format of a Visual Basic Statement

The general format of the Visual Basic statement shown in Figure 3-26 appears in Figure 3-27.

General Format: Property Value Assignment Statement

```
objectname.property = propertyvalue
```

EXAMPLE	*RESULT*
picStandardRoom.Visible = True	Picture is visible
btnSelectRoom.Enabled = False	Button is dimmed

FIGURE 3-27

In the general format, the object name always is the first item in the Visual Basic statement. The object name is the name you specified in the (Name) property in the Properties window. In Figure 3-26, the object name is picStandardRoom because that is the name given to the standard room PictureBox object.

The dot operator (period) is required. It follows the object name with no space between them. Immediately following the dot operator is the name of the property that will be set by the statement. The property name must be spelled correctly and must be a valid property for the object named in the statement. Valid properties that can be specified in the statement are identified in the Properties window associated with the object.

The equal sign must follow zero or more spaces in the statement. Visual Basic statements do not require spaces, nor is there is a limit on how many spaces can be contained between elements in the statement. The equal sign identifies the statement as an **assignment statement**, which means the value on the right side of the equal sign is assigned to the element on the left side of the equal sign. When setting properties, it means the value on the right side of the equal sign is assigned to the property identified on the left side of the equal sign.

The property value specified in the assignment statement must be a valid value for the property identified on the left side of the equal sign. You can see the valid values for a given property by looking in the Properties window for the object whose property you are setting.

After you have entered the property value, the Visual Basic statement is complete. Because correct programming protocol states that only one statement should appear on a line, the next step is to press the ENTER key to move the insertion point to the next line in the coding window.

The general statement format shown in Figure 3-27 is used for all statements in which the code sets the value of an object property.

HEADS UP

Unlike some programming languages, in Visual Basic capitalization of object names, properties, property values, and other values is not important. Therefore, the object name picStandardRoom is equivalent to the object name picstandardroom. The reason for capitalization within the object name is to make the name easier to read.

IN THE REAL WORLD

Microsoft created IntelliSense in response to the needs of developers in a rapid application development environment so they can enter statements accurately and easily. Most developers use IntelliSense and its use is the standard within the software industry.

IntelliSense

In Figure 3-25 on page 131, the insertion point is located in the coding window. To enter the statement in Figure 3-26 into the actual program in the coding window, you can type the entire statement. Visual Studio, however, provides help when entering a statement so that you will be less prone to make an error when entering the statement. This help is called IntelliSense.

IntelliSense displays all allowable entries you can make in a Visual Basic statement each time a dot (period), equal sign, or other special character required for the statement is typed. When you type the prefix pic as shown in Figure 3-28, an IntelliSense window opens with all the objects that begin with that prefix. Instead of possibly misspelling the object name, you can select it from the IntelliSense list. Therefore, when using IntelliSense, the complete Visual Basic statement would be as shown in Figure 3-28:

```
picStandardRoom.Visible = True
```

FIGURE 3-28

When you type the first few letters of the object name, IntelliSense displays a list of all the entries, including all the objects, that can be specified in the statement.

Enter a Visual Basic Statement

To enter the Visual Basic statement in Figure 3-28 using IntelliSense, you can complete the following steps:

STEP 1 With the code editing window open and the insertion point positioned as shown in Figure 3-25 on page 131, type `pic`.

The characters pic are displayed in the code window (Figure 3-29). IntelliSense displays a list of all the entries that can follow the prefix in the statement. Sometimes the entry selected in the list is the correct entry for the statement you are entering, but often it is not the correct entry. Therefore, you must identify the correct statement in the list before entering it.

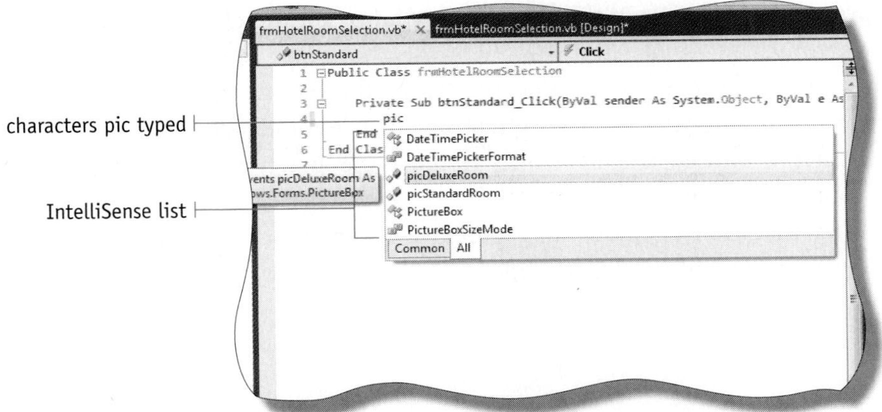

FIGURE 3-29

STEP 2 To identify the correct entry, type the next letter of the entry until the entry is selected. In this case, type s on your keyboard.

When you type characters, IntelliSense highlights in the list an entry that begins with the letters you type (Figure 3-30). When you enter pics, IntelliSense highlights the only term in the list that begins with pics, which is picStandardRoom. This is the object name you want to enter into the Visual Basic statement.

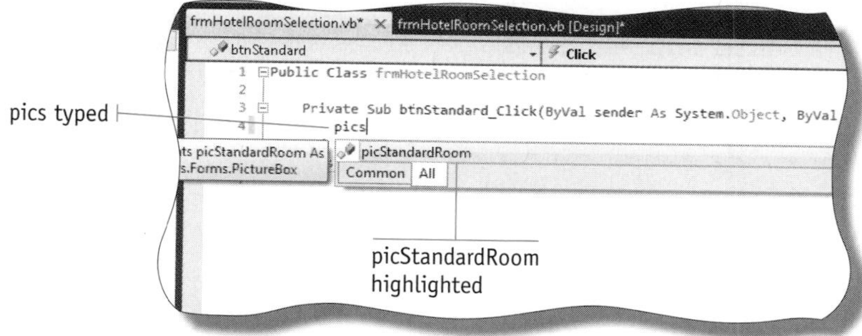

FIGURE 3-30

STEP 3 When IntelliSense highlights the correct object name, press the key on the keyboard corresponding to the entry that is to follow the object name. In this case, press the PERIOD key.

IntelliSense automatically enters the entire object name into the Visual Basic statement and the period (the character you typed) following the object name (Figure 3-31). In addition, because IntelliSense realizes that the dot you entered means more information is required in the statement, a list of the allowable entries following the dot is displayed.

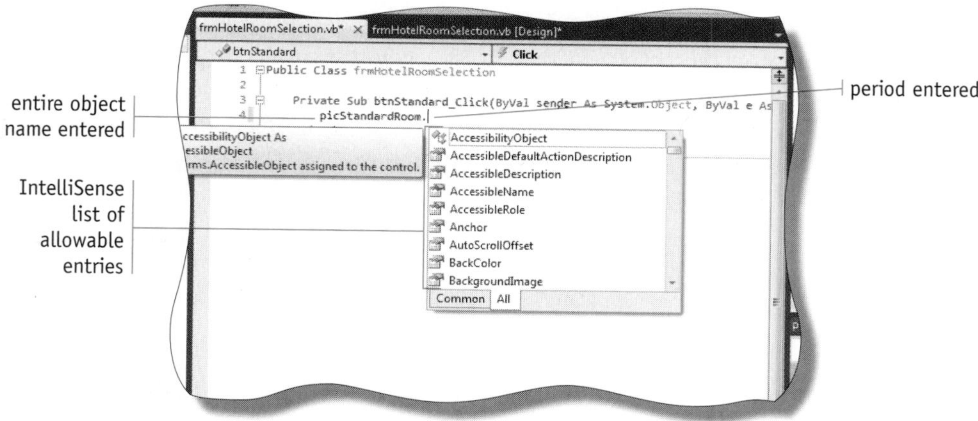

FIGURE 3-31

STEP 4 As with the object name in Step 2, the next step is to enter one or more characters until IntelliSense highlights the desired property in the list. Type the letter v on your keyboard.

IntelliSense highlights the properties in the list that begins with the letter v (Visible), or that contains the letter v such as in ProductVersion (Figure 3-32). Because the Visible property is highlighted, no further action is required to select the Visible property.

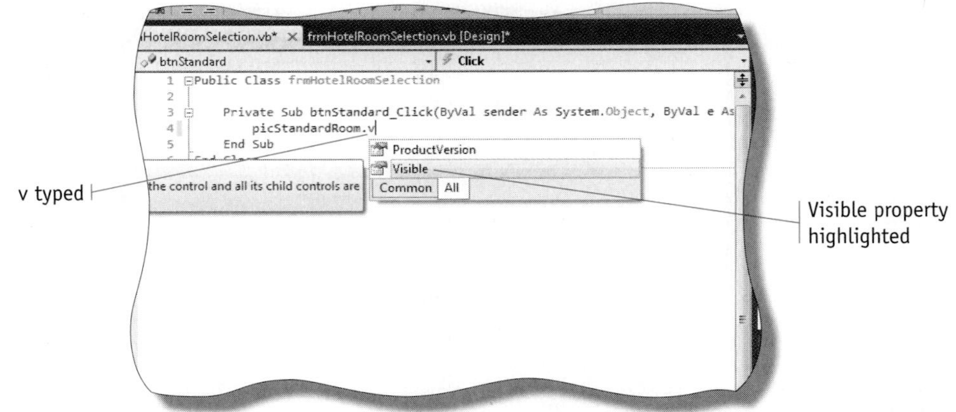

FIGURE 3-32

IN THE REAL WORLD

When you enter a statement using IntelliSense, by default IntelliSense will format the statement after you press the ENTER key. So, if you did not enter spaces in the statement before and after the equal sign, IntelliSense automatically would insert the spaces when you press the ENTER key. You can choose whether to enter spaces as you enter the statement, or let IntelliSense insert the spaces when you press the ENTER key.

STEP 5 Press the key for the character that is to follow the property name. In this case, press the SPACEBAR on the keyboard.

IntelliSense enters the highlighted property name (Visible) followed by the character you typed (space) (Figure 3-33). The space indicates to Visual Basic that the object name and property name entry is complete. Notice also that the IntelliSense tip specifies what the statement will be able to do. In Figure 3-33, it states that the statement "gets or sets a value indicating whether the control is displayed." This means the Visible property indicates whether the picStandardRoom PictureBox object is displayed.

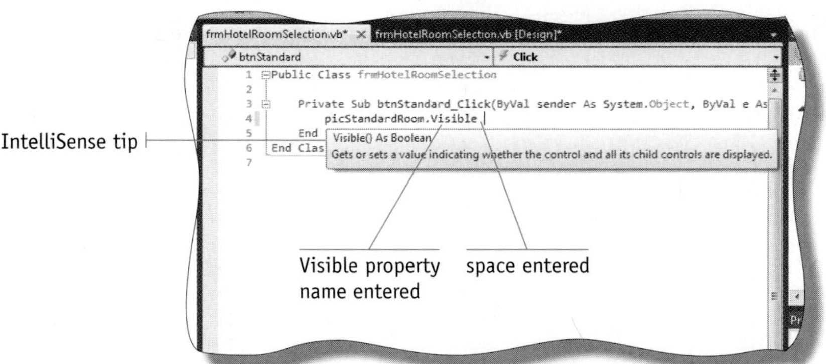

FIGURE 3-33

STEP 6 Press the EQUAL SIGN key on the keyboard and then press the SPACEBAR. On the IntelliSense list, click the Common tab to display the most common results.

The equal sign and a space are displayed and then IntelliSense displays a list containing the entries you can make (Figure 3-34). For the Visible property, the only possible entries following the equal sign are False (which indicates the PictureBox object should not be visible) and True (which indicates the PictureBox object should be visible).

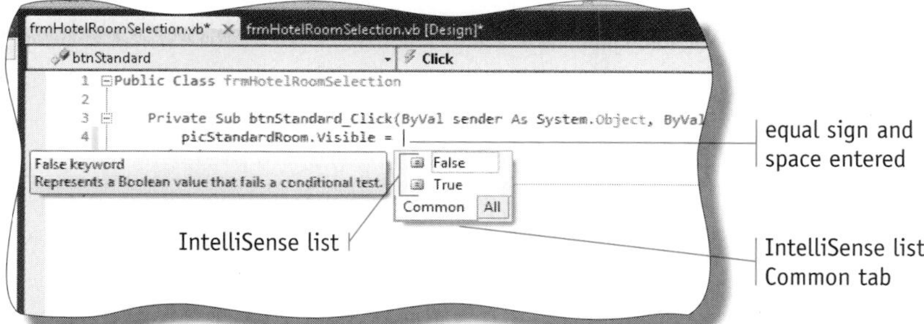

FIGURE 3-34

STEP 7 Type t on the keyboard.

IntelliSense highlights the True entry (Figure 3-35).

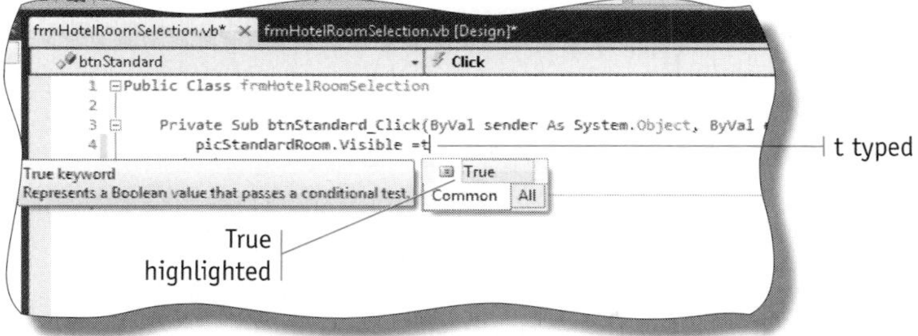

FIGURE 3-35

STEP 8 Press the key for the character that is to follow the True entry. In this case, press the ENTER key.

Because you pressed the ENTER key, IntelliSense enters True into the statement and then Visual Studio moves the indented insertion point to the next line (Figure 3-36). The Visual Basic statement now is completely entered.

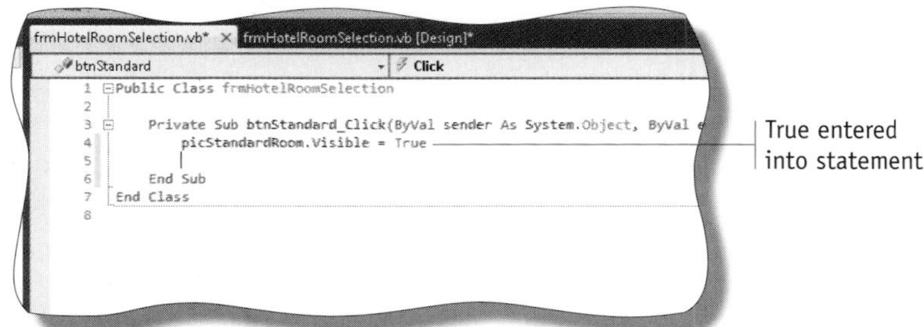

FIGURE 3-36

IN THE REAL WORLD

You can highlight the entries in the lists IntelliSense displays in a variety of ways. In the example, typing the first character of the entry was used. Other ways to highlight an entry include pressing the UP ARROW key and the DOWN ARROW key until the entry is highlighted, and using the mouse to scroll in the list until the entry is visible and then clicking the entry.

To enter an entry from the list, the example illustrated pressing the key for the character to follow the entry from the list. Other ways include pressing the Tab key, and double-clicking the entry in the list. In both these cases, you still must enter the next character in the statement, whereas in the example, that character is entered when you press the correct key to select the IntelliSense entry from the list.

ONLINE REINFORCEMENT

To view a video of the process in the previous steps, visit scsite.com/vb2010/ch3 and then select Figure 3-29.

Visual Studio and IntelliSense automatically create the indentations in the program statements in Figure 3-36 because the indentations make the statements easier to read and understand. As programs become more complex, proper indentation of program statements can be an important factor in developing error-free programs.

The following steps summarize the procedure for using IntelliSense to enter a Visual Basic statement that sets a property:

1. Type the first letter(s) of the name of the object whose property will be set until the object name is selected in the IntelliSense list.
2. Press the PERIOD key.
3. Type the first letter(s) of the name of the property to be set until the name is highlighted in the IntelliSense list.
4. Press the SPACEBAR to complete the first portion of the statement.
5. Press the EQUAL SIGN key.
6. Press the SPACEBAR.
7. Press the first letter(s) of the entry you want to select in the list until the entry is highlighted; or if IntelliSense does not display a list, type the value for the property.
8. Press the ENTER key.

Using IntelliSense to enter a Visual Basic statement provides two significant advantages: 1) It is faster to enter a statement using IntelliSense than it is to enter a statement by typing it; 2) Using IntelliSense reduces the number of errors committed when entering a statement to almost zero. By using only the entries contained on the IntelliSense lists, the developer seldom will make a mistake by entering an invalid entry. In addition, because the entry is chosen from a list, it is not possible for the entry to be misspelled or mistyped.

Entering a programming statement is a fundamental skill of a Visual Basic programmer. You should understand thoroughly how to enter a programming statement using IntelliSense.

Set Visible Property to False

In Figure 3-36 on page 137, the programming statement set the Visible property for the picStandardRoom PictureBox object to True, which will cause the image in the picture box to be displayed when the statement is executed. The statement will be executed when the user clicks the Standard Room button because the statement is within the btnStandardRoom_Click event handler.

Another setting that must take place when the user clicks the Standard Room button is to set the Visible property for the picDeluxeRoom PictureBox to False so the deluxe room picture is not displayed when the standard room picture is displayed. To set the Visible property for the picDeluxeRoom PictureBox object to False, you could complete the steps on the following pages:

STEP 1 With the insertion point on the second line of the code editing window for the Click event of the Standard Room button, type `pic` on your keyboard.

The letters you typed are displayed in the code editing window and the IntelliSense list shows the valid entries you can choose (Figure 3-37). The entry picStandardRoom is highlighted because it is the last entry that was selected from this list.

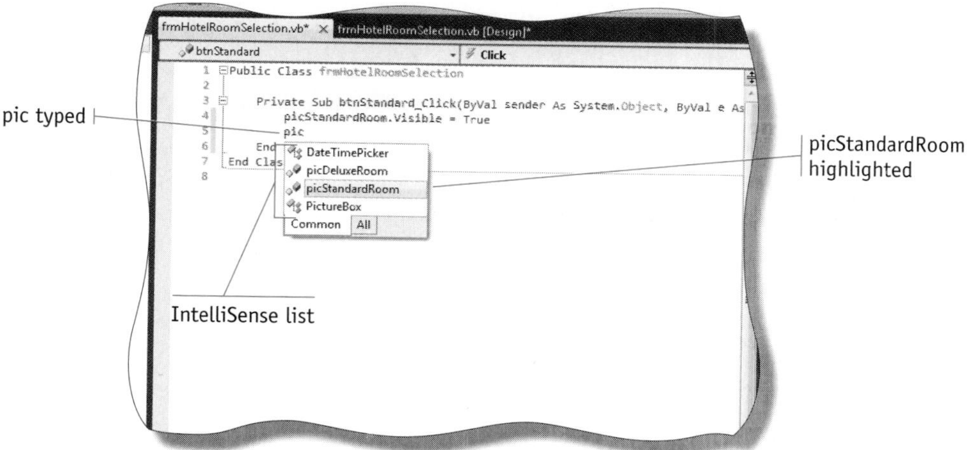

FIGURE 3-37

STEP 2 Type `d` to highlight the picDeluxeRoom entry in the IntelliSense list.

IntelliSense highlights picDeluxeRoom in the list because this is the only entry that starts with the characters, picd (Figure 3-38).

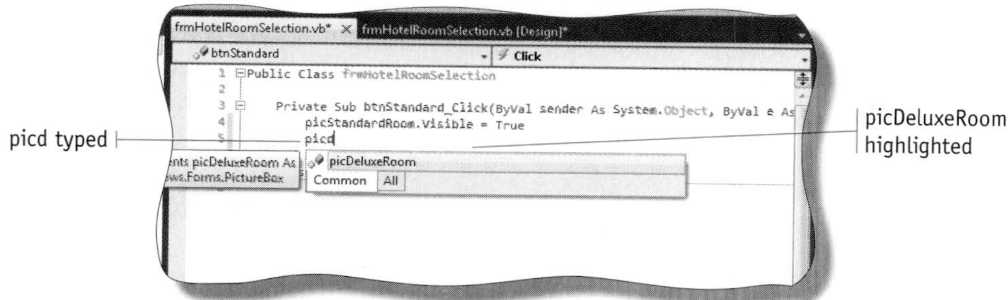

FIGURE 3-38

STEP 3 Press the key on the keyboard for the character that is to follow the object name. In this case, press the PERIOD key.

The picDeluxeRoom entry is placed in the statement followed by the dot operator (period) you typed (Figure 3-39). In addition, IntelliSense displays the list of allowable entries.

Visible is highlighted in the list because it was the entry selected the last time the list was used. If Visible was not highlighted, you could type the letter v to highlight Visible in the list.

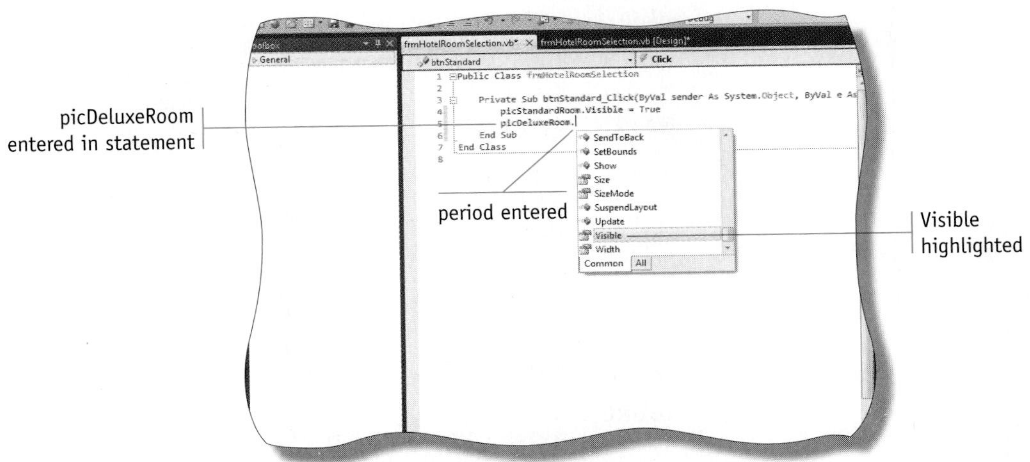

FIGURE 3-39

STEP 4 Press the SPACEBAR, press the EQUAL SIGN key, and then press the SPACEBAR.

IntelliSense places the Visible entry in the statement (Figure 3-40). Next, the space you typed appears, followed by the equal sign and the space you typed. When you typed the equal sign, IntelliSense displayed the list of allowable entries following the equal sign.

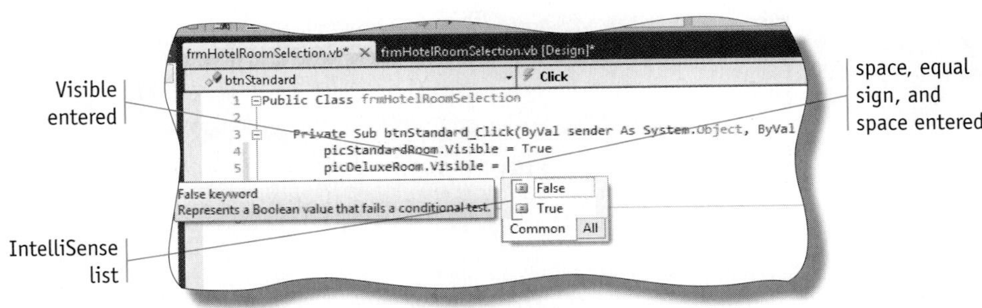

FIGURE 3-40

STEP 5 Type `f` and then press the ENTER key.

When you type the letter f, IntelliSense highlights False in the list. When you press the ENTER key, IntelliSense inserts False (Figure 3-41).

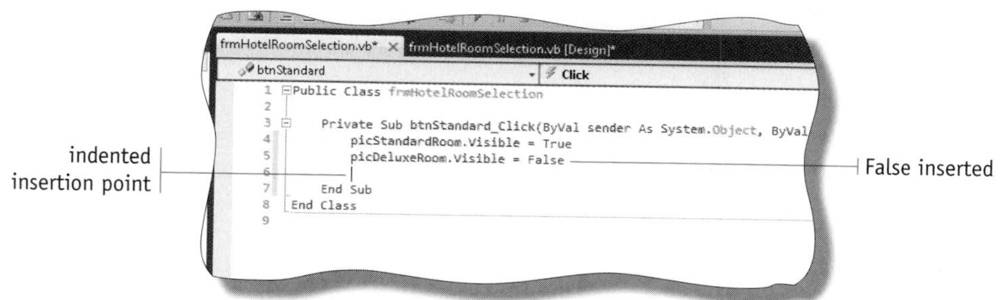

FIGURE 3-41

ONLINE REINFORCEMENT

To view a video of the process in the previous steps, visit scsite.com/vb2010/ch3 and then select Figure 3-37.

Once again, using IntelliSense to enter a Visual Basic programming statement results in a correct statement in minimum time with reduced chance of error.

Enabled Property

You learned earlier that if the Enabled property for a Button object is True, the click event code for the button will be executed when the user clicks the button. If the Enabled property for a Button object is False, the event code for the button will not be executed. In Figure 3-21 on page 127, the Enabled property for the Select Room button was set to False so that the button is not active when the program begins execution. When a picture button such as the Standard Room button is clicked, however, the Enabled property must be set to True so the Select button is active. To set the Enabled property to True, a coding statement to set the Enabled property for the btnSelectRoom Button object is required. To enter the coding statement into the btnStandardRoom_Click event handler, you can complete the following steps:

STEP 1 Type `btn` to display the IntelliSense list (Figure 3-42).

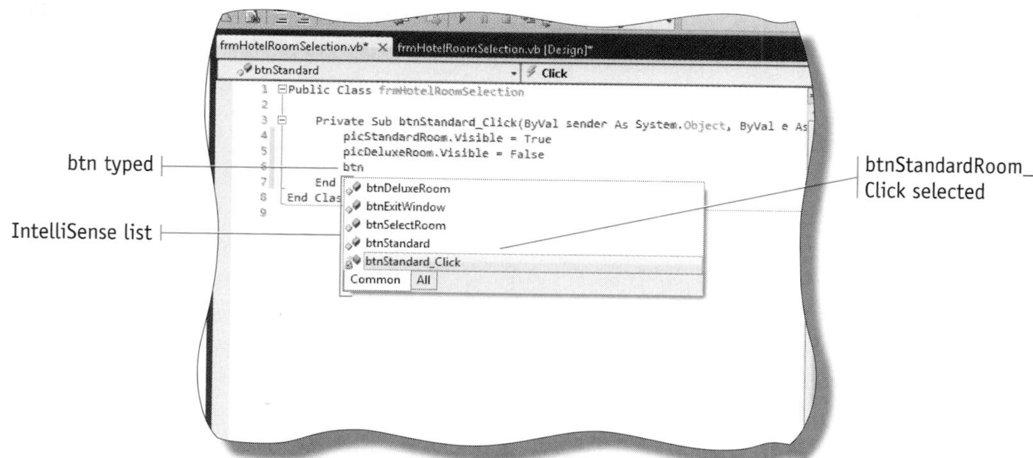

FIGURE 3-42

STEP 2 Type se (or more characters if necessary) until IntelliSense highlights the btnSelectRoom entry in the list.

IntelliSense highlights btnSelectRoom, the only entry that starts with the characters, btnse (Figure 3-43). Sometimes, the correct entry will be highlighted before you type all the distinguishing characters. If so, you need not type any more characters.

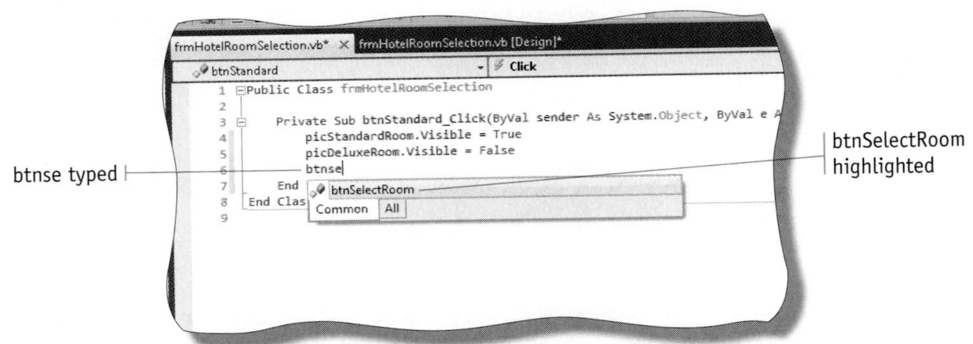

FIGURE 3-43

STEP 3 Type a period, type e, press the SPACEBAR, press the EQUAL SIGN key, press the SPACEBAR again, and then type t to select True in the IntelliSense list.

IntelliSense places the highlighted entry (btnSelectRoom) into the statement and displays a list of the next allowable entries. When you typed e, Enabled was selected in the list. Pressing the SPACEBAR caused IntelliSense to place the entry, Enabled, and then the space into the statement. When you typed the equal sign and space, IntelliSense inserted the equal sign and space, and displayed the list of entries that can follow the equal sign (Figure 3-44). When you typed the letter t, IntelliSense highlighted True in the list.

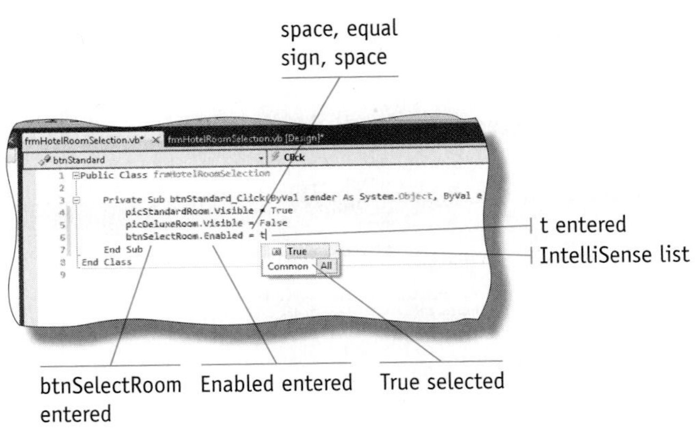

FIGURE 3-44

STEP 4 Press the ENTER key to enter the completed statement and place the insertion point on the next line.

IntelliSense enters the entry, True, into the statement (Figure 3-45). Pressing the ENTER key completes the statement and moves the indented insertion point to the next line.

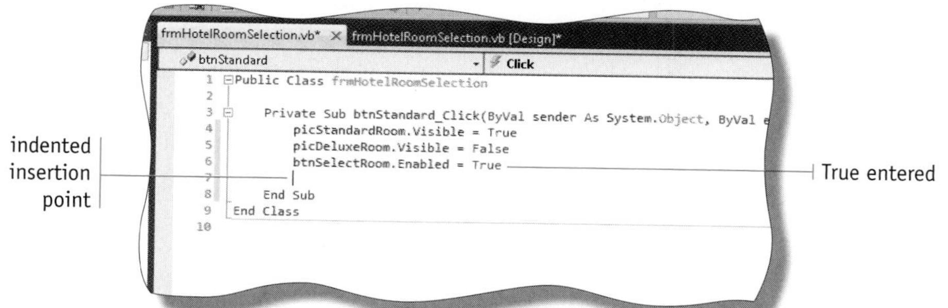

FIGURE 3-45

ONLINE REINFORCEMENT

To view a video of the process in the previous steps, visit scsite.com/vb2010/ch3 and then select Figure 3-42.

Learning the process of entering program statements through the use of IntelliSense is fundamental to writing programs using the Visual Basic 2010 language.

Comments in Program Statements

A well-written Visual Basic 2010 program normally contains **comment statements** within the code itself to document what the code is doing. An example of comment statements in code is shown in Figure 3-46.

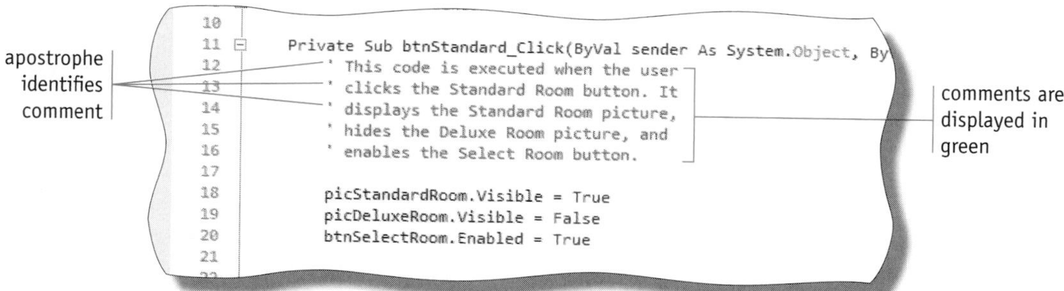

FIGURE 3-46

A comment is preceded by an apostrophe. Whenever the Visual Basic compiler encounters an apostrophe in the code, it ignores the remaining characters on the line. To the compiler, it's as if the comments do not exist.

The comments in the code, which are displayed in green text, describe the processing that will occur in the code that follows. Because comments are ignored by the Visual Basic compiler, no programming language syntax must be followed within the comments. Any letters or characters are allowed within comments. The general reason for comments is to aid the code reader in understanding the purpose of the code and how it accomplishes its tasks.

To enter comments, type an apostrophe in the code. All characters following the apostrophe on that line of code are considered a comment. To enter the comment code shown in Figure 3-46, you could complete the following steps:

STEP 1 To insert a blank line following the event code generated by Visual Studio that begins with the word Private, click anywhere in that line and then press the END key on your keyboard.

Visual Studio positions the insertion point at the end of the line that you clicked (Figure 3-47).

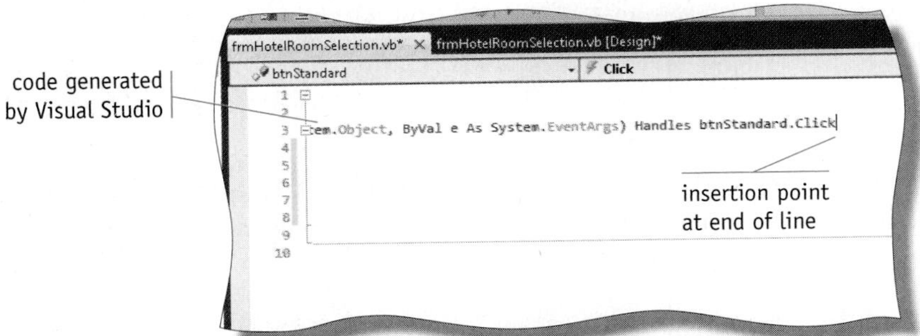

FIGURE 3-47

STEP 2 Press the ENTER key.

Visual Studio inserts a blank line in the code and then moves the insertion point to the blank line (Figure 3-48). The comments can be inserted on the blank line.

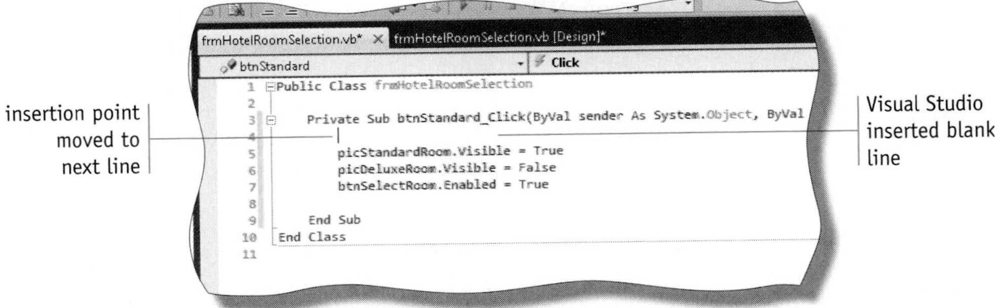

FIGURE 3-48

STEP 3 Type the first line of the comments, beginning with an apostrophe, as shown in Figure 3-46 on page 143, and then press the ENTER key.

The apostrophe as the first character typed identifies the rest of the line as a comment (Figure 3-49). The comment line is displayed in green text. When you press the ENTER key, Visual Studio creates a new blank line and places the indented insertion point on that line.

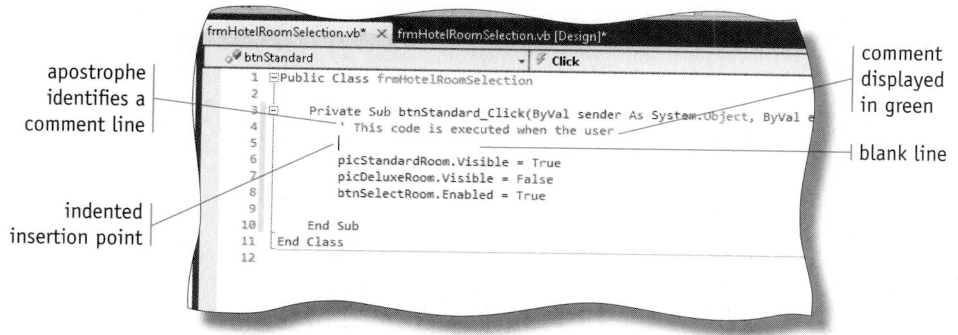

FIGURE 3-49

ONLINE REINFORCEMENT

To view a video of the process in the previous steps, visit scsite.com/vb2010/ch3 and then select Figure 3-47.

You can continue to enter lines of comments by typing an apostrophe and the comment, and then pressing the ENTER key until all comments are completed.

Same Line Comments

Because the Visual Basic compiler treats all characters following an apostrophe as comments, it is possible to place a comment on the same line as executable code. In Figure 3-50, a comment is shown on the same line as the statement that sets the btnSelectRoom Enabled property to True.

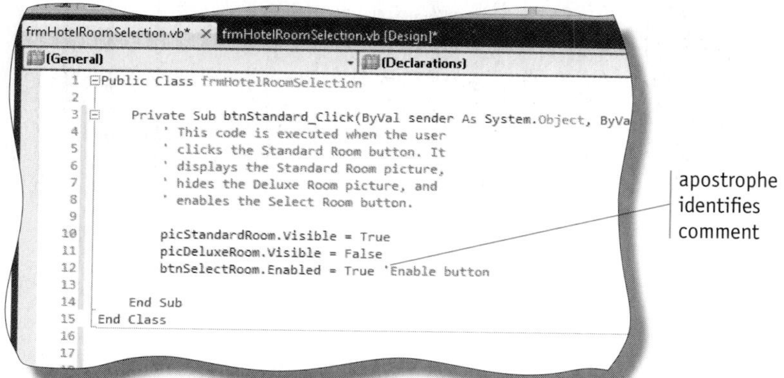

FIGURE 3-50

In Figure 3-50, the apostrophe specifies that all characters remaining on the line are to be treated as comments. Therefore, the text, Enable button, is displayed in green and is treated as a comment. To enter a comment on any line, enter an apostrophe and then type the comment. Remember that all characters following an apostrophe on a line of code are treated as comments.

Introductory Comments

Every program should begin with comments that state the name of the program, the developer's name, the date, and the purpose of the program. These comments should precede any other statements in the program (Figure 3-51).

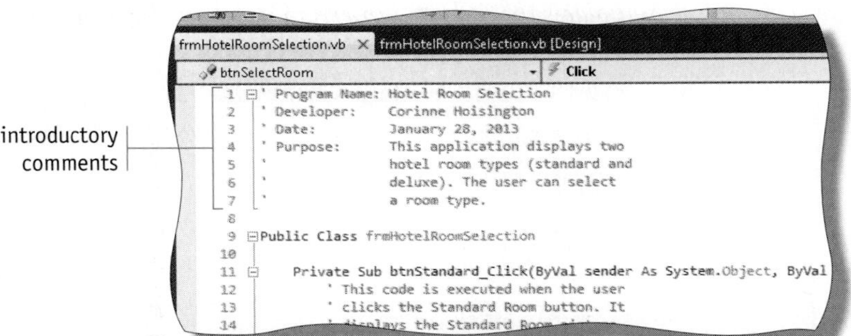

FIGURE 3-51

Notice that the introductory comments precede all code in the program — even the code generated by Visual Studio. To enter introductory comments, you can complete the following steps:

STEP 1 Click to the left of the word Public on line 1 in the program to place the insertion point on that line.

The insertion point is positioned at the beginning of line 1 in the code (Figure 3-52).

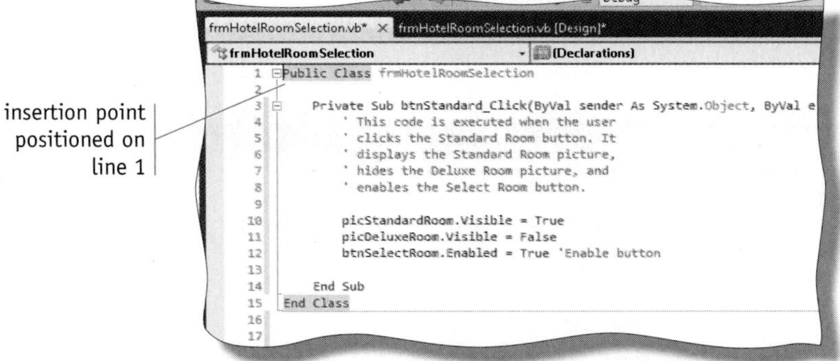

FIGURE 3-52

STEP 2 Press the ENTER key one time, and then press the UP ARROW key one time.

When you press the ENTER key, Visual Studio inserts a blank line on line 1 of the code and moves the line that begins with the words, Public Class, down to line 2 (Figure 3-53). Visual Studio also moves the insertion point to line 2 when you press the ENTER key. When you press the UP ARROW key, the insertion point moves to the first line, which is blank.

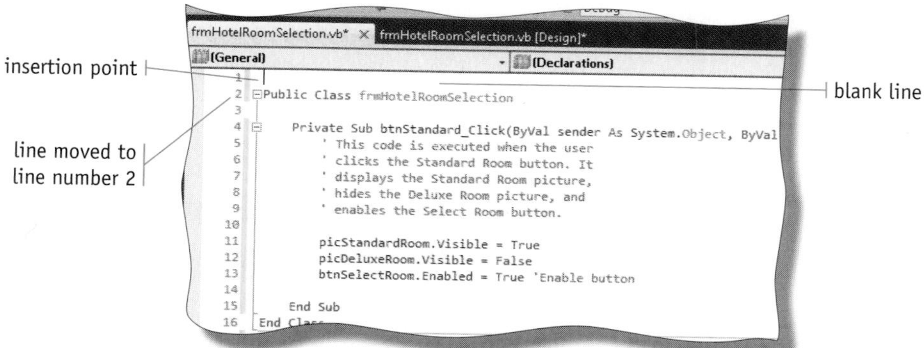

FIGURE 3-53

STEP 3 Type an apostrophe, a space, the text, `Program Name:` and then press the TAB key one time.

The apostrophe identifies all characters and words that follow as comments, so the characters are displayed in green (Figure 3-54). The first line of introductory comments normally specifies the name of the program. Pressing the TAB key moves the insertion point to the right.

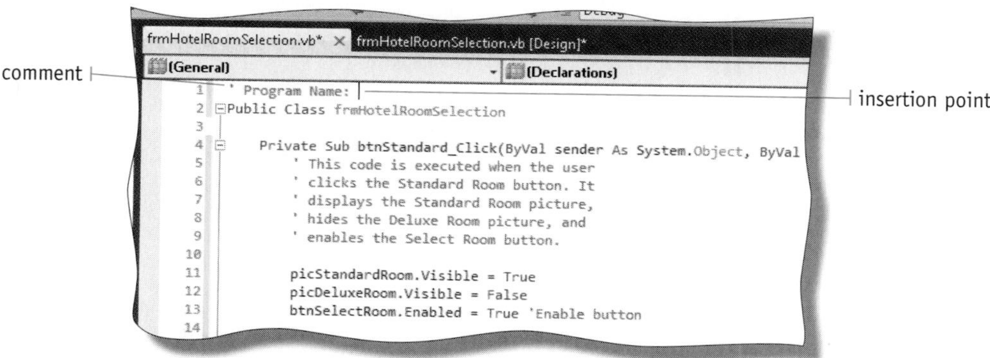

FIGURE 3-54

STEP 4 Type `Hotel Room Selection` as the name of the program. Then, press the ENTER key.

The program name appears in the first line of comments and the insertion point is moved to line 2 (Figure 3-55).

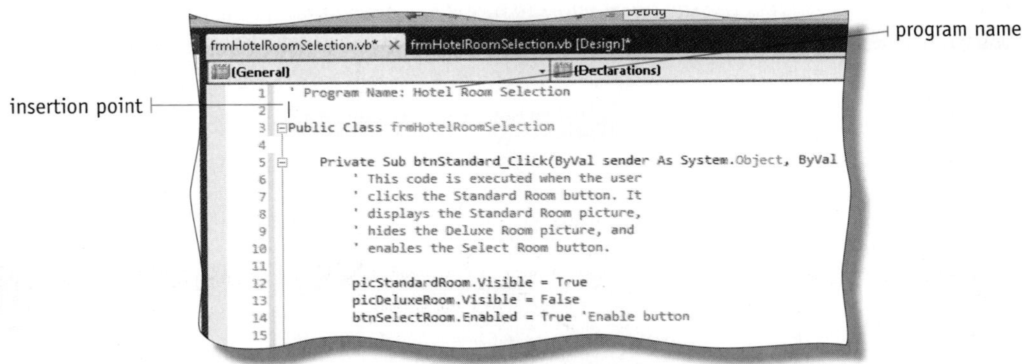

FIGURE 3-55

ONLINE REINFORCEMENT

To view a video of the process in the previous steps, visit scsite.com/vb2010/ch3 and then select Figure 3-52.

You can enter the remaining comments using the same techniques. Press the TAB key one or more times to align vertically the paragraphs on the right so they appear as shown in Figure 3-51 on page 146.

Correcting Errors in Code

Using IntelliSense to assist you when entering code reduces the likelihood of coding errors considerably. Nevertheless, because you could create one or more errors when entering code, you should understand what to do when a coding error occurs.

One possible error you could commit would be to forget an apostrophe in a comment statement. In Figure 3-56, a comment was entered without a leading apostrophe.

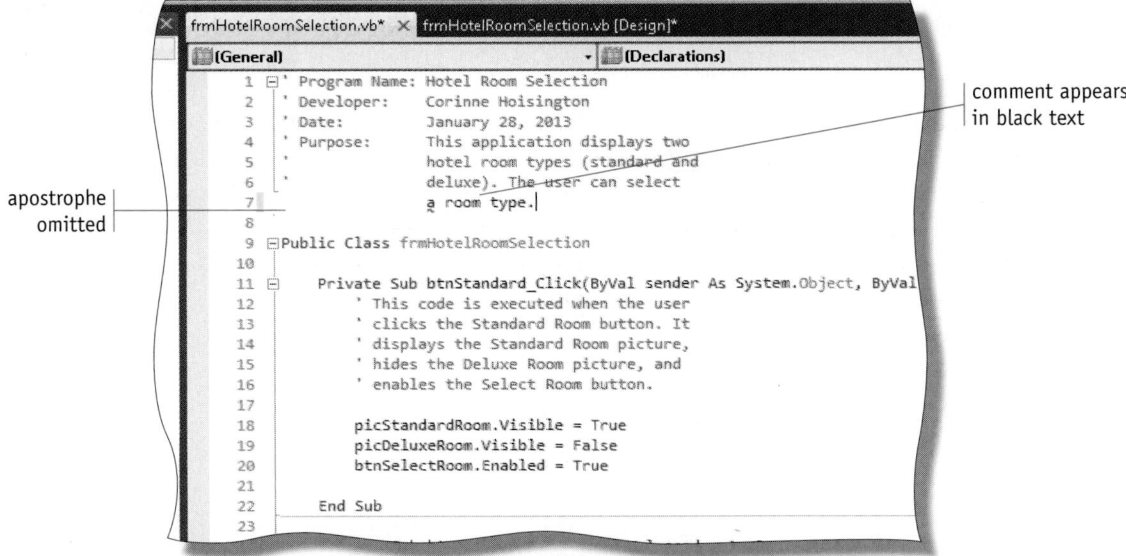

FIGURE 3-56

In Figure 3-56, the comment words are displayed in black text, which is a clue that this is an error because comment characters normally are displayed in green text. Nonetheless, Visual Studio gives no other indication that an error has occurred.

From this point where the error occurred, the developer might take any course of action. For example, she might immediately run the program. Or, she might click anywhere in the window to move the insertion point, or press the ENTER key to insert a blank line. If the program in Figure 3-56 is executed immediately by clicking the Start Debugging button on the Standard toolbar, the window shown in Figure 3-57 will be displayed.

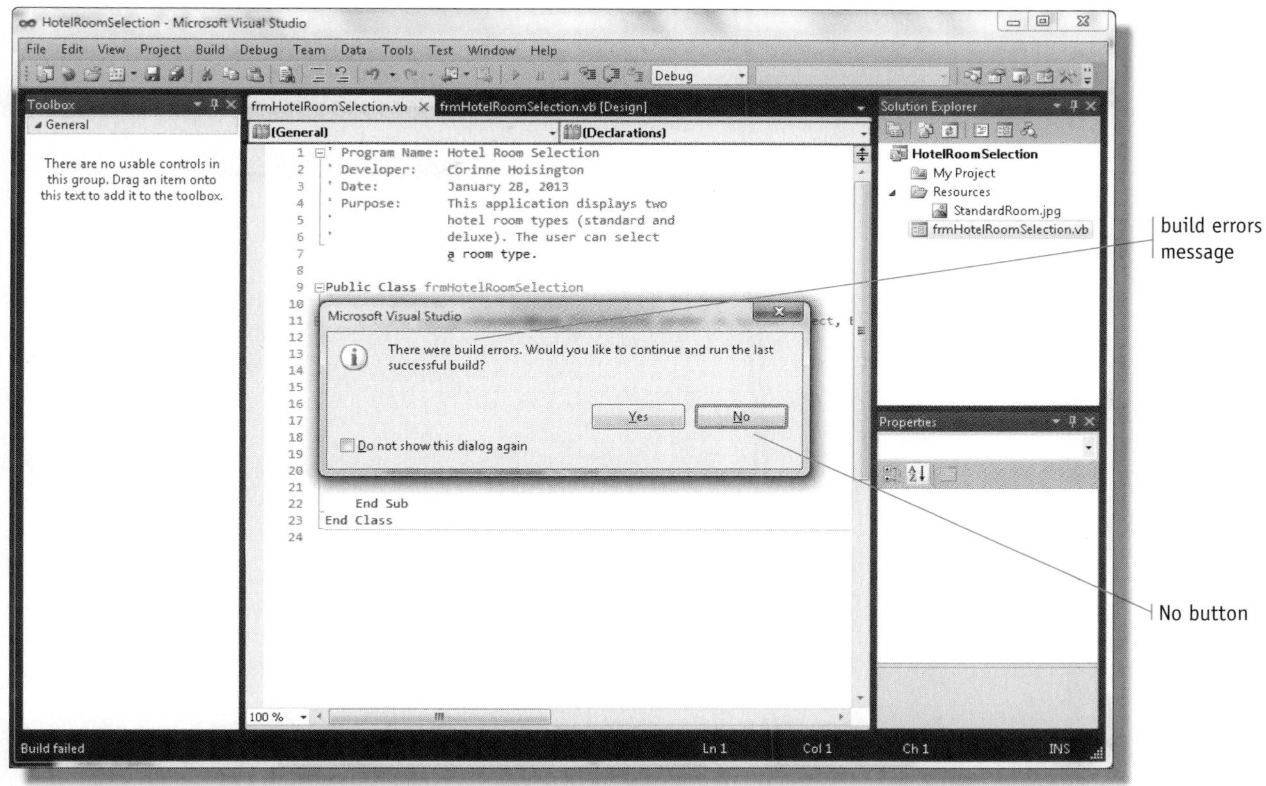

FIGURE 3-57

The **build errors message** means the Visual Basic compiler detected a coding error in the program. An absolute requirement when programming Visual Basic programs is that when you see the build errors message, you *always click the No button.* Under no circumstances should you click the Yes button in the dialog box. When you click the No button, you can perform the steps on the next page to make corrections in your program:

STEP 1 Click the No button in the Microsoft Visual Studio dialog box that informs you of a build error (see Figure 3-57).

When you click the No button, Visual Studio displays the program code and the Error List window (Figure 3-58). The ***Error List window*** *identifies the number of errors that occurred and displays a description of the error detected. The description, Declaration expected, in Figure 3-58 means Visual Studio expected to find a different type of statement than it found. In addition, the window contains the file in which the error occurred (frmHotelRoomSelection.vb), the line number of the statement in error (7), and the vertical column within the statement where the error was detected (17). In the code editing window, the location of the error is noted by a blue squiggly line.*

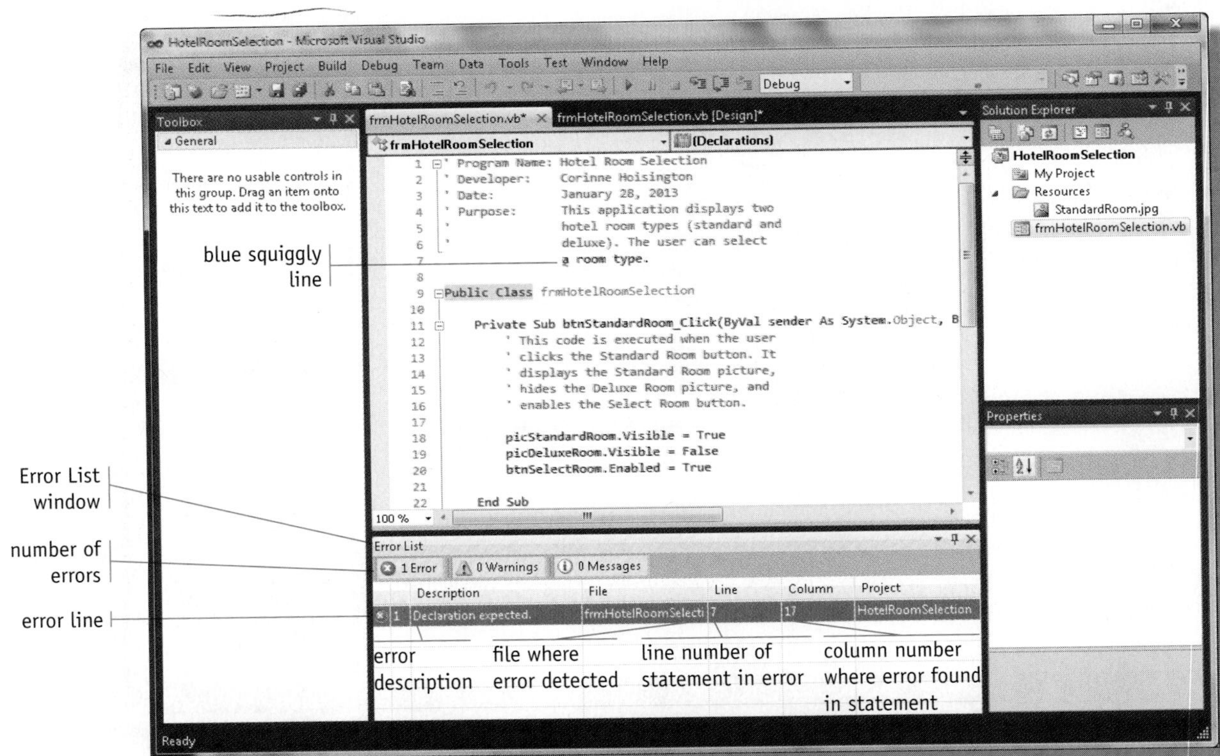

FIGURE 3-58

STEP 2 Double-click anywhere on the error line.

Visual Studio highlights the error in blue so the developer, if desired, can type and replace the highlighted text with the correct code (Figure 3-59). With the error highlighted, the developer must examine the statement to determine the error. By looking at line 7, column 17, where the letter a is highlighted, it is clear that a line intended to be a comment was not treated as a comment by Visual Studio. Further examination reveals the required apostrophe is missing.

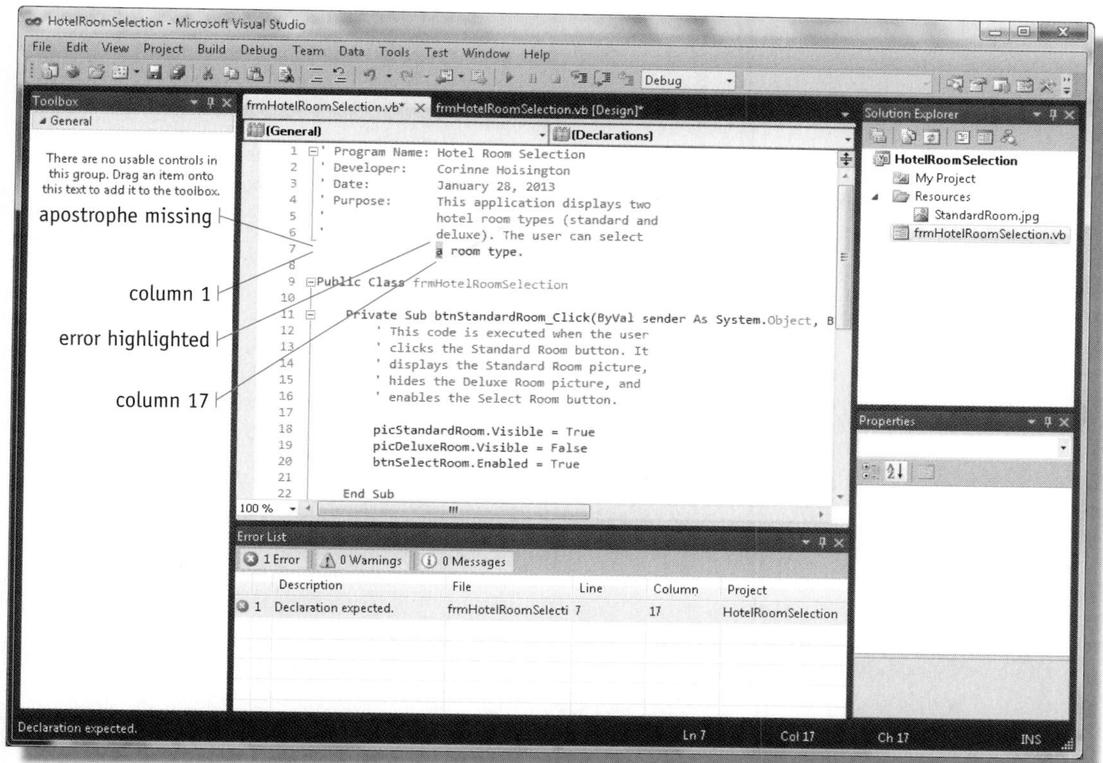

FIGURE 3-59

STEP 3 Click in the leftmost column on line 7 to place the insertion point at that location.

The insertion point is located in the leftmost column on line 7 of the program (Figure 3-60).

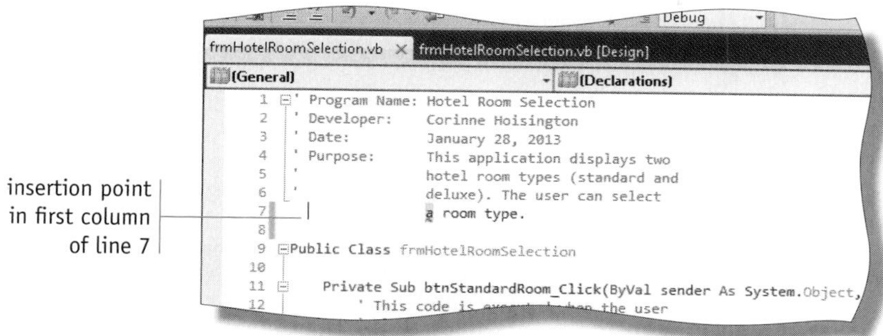

FIGURE 3-60

STEP 4 Type an apostrophe.

The apostrophe is located in the first column on line 7 of the program (Figure 3-61).

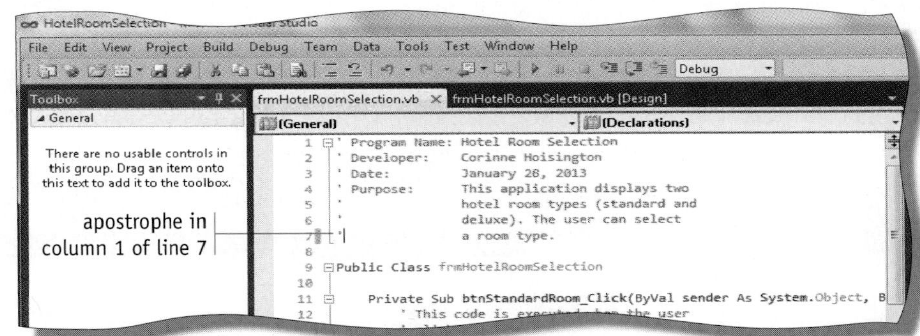

FIGURE 3-61

STEP 5 Click anywhere in the code editing window.

When you click anywhere in the window, the insertion point moves to that location (Figure 3-62). If the statement has been corrected, the error line is removed from the Error List window, and the number of errors is reduced by one. In Figure 3-62, the number of errors is zero because only one error was found in the program. It is possible to have multiple errors detected when the program is compiled.

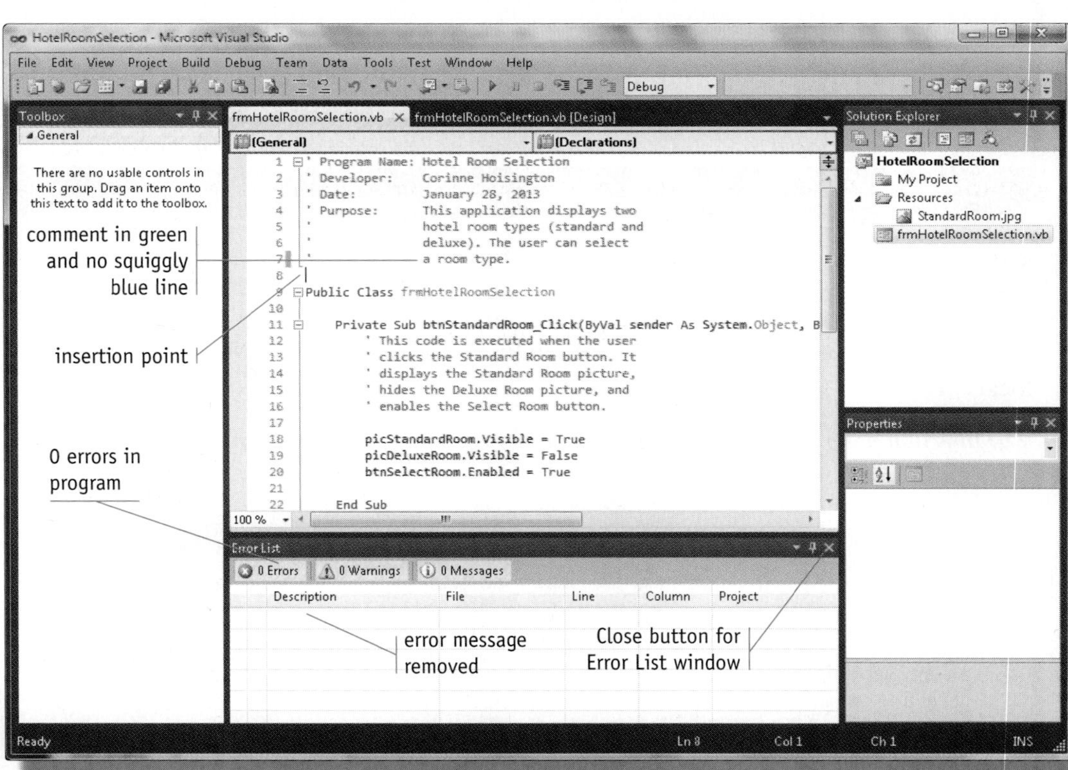

FIGURE 3-62

ONLINE REINFORCEMENT

To view a video of the process in the previous steps, visit scsite.com/vb2010/ch3 and then select Figure 3-58.

You can close the Error List window by clicking the Close button for the window (see Figure 3-62).

In Figure 3-57 on page 149, it was assumed the developer, after making the error, immediately ran the program. If, before running the program, the developer moved the insertion point to any other part of the program, or clicked any other element in the window, then Visual Studio would provide a visual cue that an error was made by displaying a blue squiggly line under the error. The line shown in Figure 3-58 is the type of line that Visual Studio would display. If you see a blue squiggly line in your code, it means you have made an error entering the code. You do not have to run the program to find coding errors. If a blue squiggly line appears in your code, an error has been made and you must correct it.

Additional Click Events

In the sample program in this chapter, multiple buttons can trigger events. For example, when the user clicks the Exit Window button, the program window should close and the program should terminate. To indicate that clicking the Exit Window button will trigger an event, and to prepare to write the code for the event, complete the same steps for the Exit Window button that you learned for the Standard Room button, as shown in the following figure:

STEP 1 On the frmHotelRoomSelection.vb [Design] tabbed page, double-click the Exit Window Button object.

Visual Studio opens the code editing window and displays the frmHotelRoomSelection.vb tabbed page (Figure 3-63). Visual Studio also inserts the event handler code for the click event on the btnExitWindow object. Two horizontal lines separate the event handler code for the btnExitWindow object from code for other event handlers that might be in the program. The developer must write the code that will be executed when the click event occurs. The insertion point is located in the proper place to begin writing code.

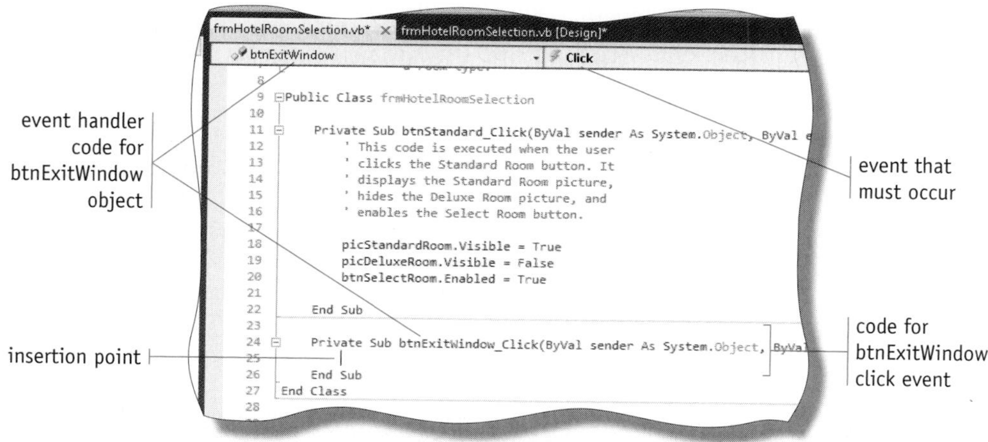

FIGURE 3-63

ONLINE REINFORCEMENT

To view a video of the process in the previous steps, visit scsite.com/vb2010/ch3 and then select Figure 3-63.

Entering Code

As you have seen, you can enter code in the code window using the IntelliSense tools you have learned. The first code written for an event, however, should be comment code that indicates what the event is and what processing will occur. The comment code for the Exit Window event handler is shown in Figure 3-64.

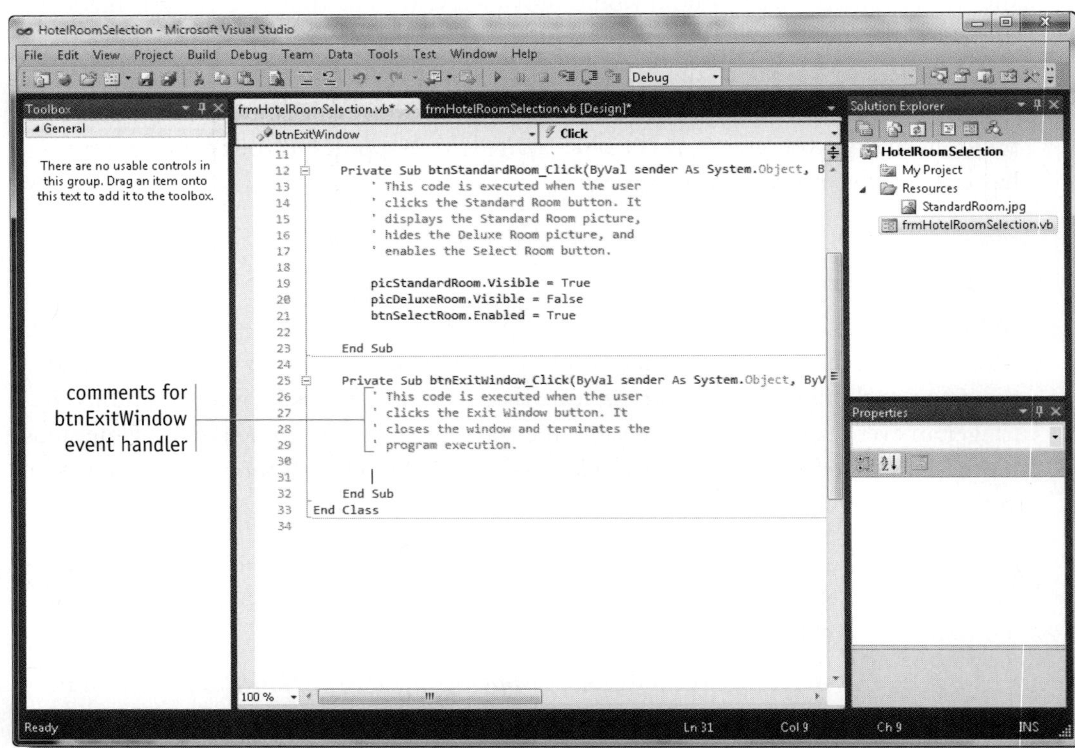

FIGURE 3-64

Close Procedure

The Visual Basic statement to close the window and terminate the program calls a procedure that performs the actual processing. A **procedure** is a set of prewritten code that can be called by a statement in the Visual Basic program. When the procedure is called, it performs its processing. The procedure used to close a window and terminate a program is the Close procedure.

You can use the statement in Figure 3-65 to call the Close procedure:

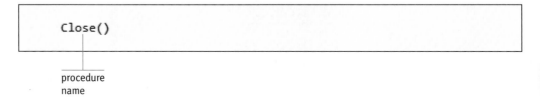

FIGURE 3-65

The word Close specifies the name of the procedure to be called. The left and right parentheses immediately following the name of the procedure identifies the Visual Basic statement as a **procedure call statement**.

When the statement in Figure 3-65 is executed, the Close procedure will be called and control will be given to the prewritten programming statements in the Close procedure. These statements will close the window and terminate the application.

To enter the Close statement into the program, you can type `clo` and then select Close in the IntelliSense list, as shown in the following steps.

STEP 1 With the insertion point positioned as shown in Figure 3-64 on page 154, type `clo` to highlight Close in the IntelliSense list.

When you type the letters clo IntelliSense highlights the word Close in the IntelliSense list (Figure 3-66).

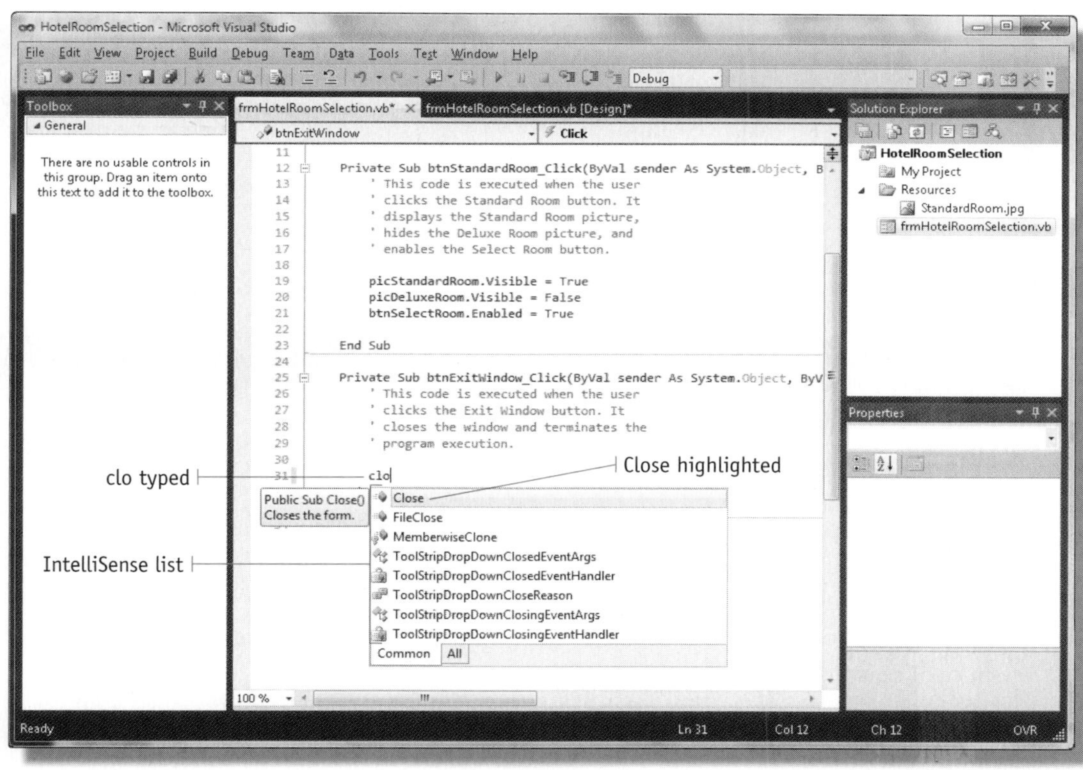

FIGURE 3-66

STEP 2 Press the ENTER key.

IntelliSense enters Close in the statement and, because it knows Close is a procedure call, automatically appends the open and closed parentheses to the statement (Figure 3-67). Then, Visual Studio returns the insertion point to the next line.

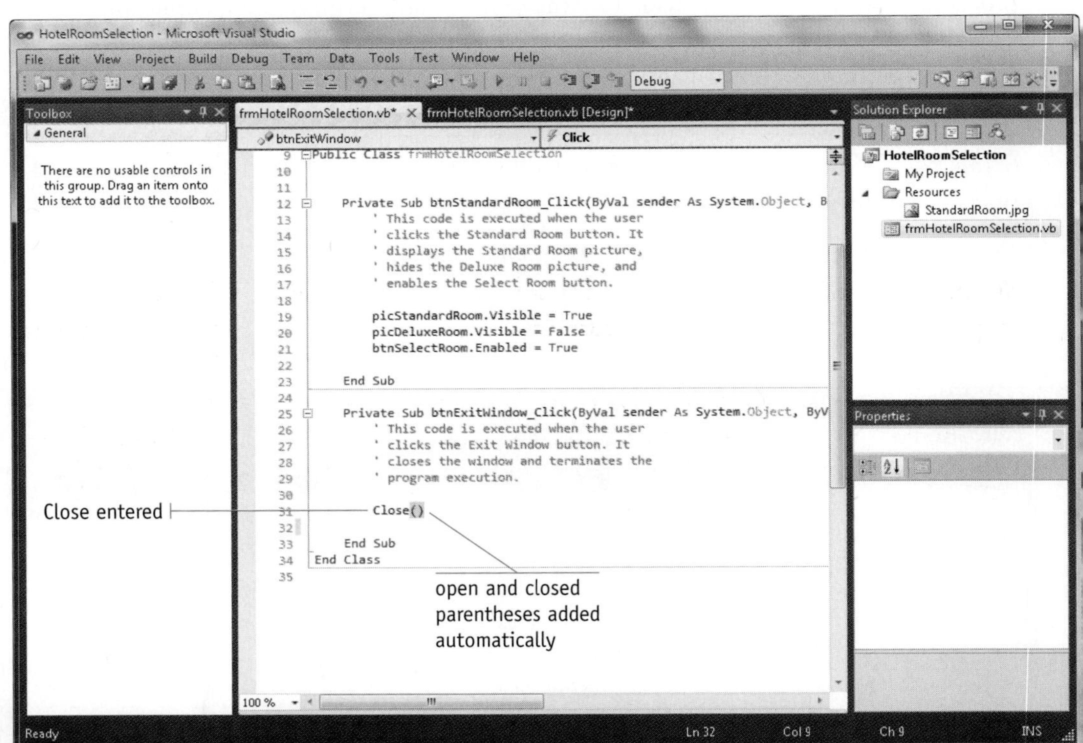

FIGURE 3-67

ONLINE REINFORCEMENT

To view a video of the process in the previous steps, visit scsite.com/vb2010/ch3 and then select Figure 3-66.

IN THE REAL WORLD

Developers can write their own procedures to perform required processing and then store the procedures in a library so they and other programmers can use the procedures. You will learn more about using procedures throughout this book.

Prewritten procedures available to Visual Basic developers through Visual Studio are an important element when using rapid application development because the developer is not required to write the procedure code. The developer merely writes a single statement to call the procedure. You will use many procedures in this book for a variety of reasons.

Printing Code

In some instances, you will find the need to print the code in the program. Sometimes as you review the code, you might find it easier to read and understand the code on a printed page rather than on your computer screen. In other cases, you might want to share the code with another developer and the printed page often is a better tool for this than a monitor screen. To print the code in a program, you can complete the following steps:

1. Click File on the menu bar to display the File menu.
2. Click Print on the File menu to display the Print dialog box.

3. Ensure that a check mark appears in the Include line numbers check box if you want line numbers on your printout. Most developers prefer line numbers on printouts.
4. Make any other selections you find necessary in the Print dialog box.
5. Click the OK button in the Print dialog box to print the code.

If you have a color printer, the code will be printed with correct color. Otherwise, shades of gray will represent the colors shown in the code editing window. If a line of code extends beyond one printed line, an arrow will appear at the end of the first printed line to indicate it continues to the next printed line.

HEADS UP

Visual Studio 2010 does not provide a tool to print the user interface designed on the frmHotelRoomSelection.vb [Design] tabbed page. You can implement a workaround to print the user interface using the following steps: 1) Open Microsoft Word; 2) Make Visual Studio 2010 the active program window; 3) With the user interface displayed on the frmHotelRoomSelection.vb [Design] tabbed page, hold down the ALT key and then press the PRINT SCREEN key; 4) Make Microsoft Word the active window; 5) Click the Paste button on the Word Standard Toolbar. The screen shot created in Step 3 will be pasted into the Word document; 6) Print the Word document.

Coding Summary

Writing code is the essence of programming in Visual Basic 2010. Much of the emphasis in this book will be on writing the code required to implement applications of all kinds.

Once you understand coding and the statements shown in this chapter, you are ready to continue the process of designing and implementing the Hotel Room Selection program.

Phase 3 — Design the Program Processing Objects

The next phase in the program development life cycle requires determining the processing objects for the program and creating the event planning document. In the Hotel Room Selection program and in programs of similar complexity, the designer need not be concerned about determining the processing objects. The only processing object required for the program is the Windows Form object. In later, more complex programs, this task will become important.

So, for the Hotel Room Selection program, the next task is to design the event planning document.

Event Planning Document

As you have learned, programs written using a graphical user interface normally are event-driven programs. An **event** means the user has initiated an action that causes the program to perform the type of processing called for by the user's action. Once the mock-up for the user interface has been created, the developer must document the events that can occur based on the user interface.

The **event planning document** consists of a table that specifies an object in the user interface that will cause an event, the action taken by the user to trigger the event, and the event processing that must occur. The event planning document for the Hotel Room Selection program is shown in Figure 3-68 on the next page.

EVENT PLANNING DOCUMENT

Program Name: Hotel Room Selection	**Developer:** Corinne Hoisington	**Object:** frmHotelRoomSelection	**Date:** January 28, 2013
OBJECT	**EVENT TRIGGER**	**EVENT PROCESSING**	
btnStandardRoom	Click	Display the standard room picture Hide the deluxe room picture Enable the Select Room button	
btnSelectRoom	Click	Disable the Standard Room button Disable the Select Room button Disable the Deluxe Room button Hide the Instructions label Display the Confirmation Message label Enable the Exit Window button	
btnDeluxeRoom	Click	Display the deluxe room picture Hide the standard room picture Enable the Select Room button	
btnExitWindow	Click	Close the window and terminate the program	

FIGURE 3-68

The leftmost column on the event planning document identifies the object in the graphical user interface that can be used to trigger an event. In the Hotel Room Selection program, the four Button objects each can be used to trigger an event, so each of the Button objects must be included in the event planning document. Notice each of the Button objects is identified by its name. Using this technique ensures that the documentation is precise, and provides little room for error when the developer creates the code to implement these events.

The middle column identifies the event trigger, which is the action a user takes to cause the event to occur. In all four event cases in Figure 3-68, clicking the button triggers the event. As you will learn in this book, a variety of acts by a user can trigger an event. For example, a user might point to an object, right-click the object, or double-click the object. Each of these event triggers could trigger a different event.

The rightmost column on the event planning document specifies the event processing that the program must accomplish when the event occurs. This list of tasks for each event is a critical element in the program design. It must be precise and accurate. No processing step that must occur should be left out of the event processing column. The tasks should be in the same sequence as they will be accomplished in the program.

For example, the first task for the btnStandardRoom_Click event is to display the standard room picture. This is the primary task for the Standard Room button. In addition, however, several other tasks must be completed. When the program begins, the deluxe room picture is not visible, but if the user clicks the Deluxe Room button, then the picture will be visible. When the user clicks the Standard Room button, however, the deluxe room picture should not be visible. Therefore, each time the user clicks the Standard Room button, the processing must hide the deluxe room picture.

You also will recall that when program execution begins, the Select Room button is dimmed (disabled) and, after the user clicks a room button, it should be enabled. Therefore, each time the user clicks the Standard Room button, the Select Room button must be enabled because it might be the first time the user clicked the Standard Room button.

As you review the event planning document in Figure 3-68 on page 158, be sure you understand the processing that must occur for each event.

You should note that the event processing tasks in the right column identify *what* processing must be done when the event occurs. The manner in which these tasks will be accomplished is not identified specifically, although the information in the event planning document must be precise enough that the developer easily can write the code to implement the tasks specified.

Phase 4 — Code the Program

After the events and tasks within the events have been identified, the developer is ready to code the program. As you have learned in this chapter, coding the program means entering Visual Basic statements to accomplish the tasks specified on the event planning document. As the developer enters the code, she also will implement the logic to carry out the required processing.

Guided Program Development

To fine-tune the user interface in the Hotel Room Selection program and enter the code required to process each event in the program, complete the following steps to create the program shown in Figure 3-1 on pages 112 and 113.

NOTE TO THE LEARNER

In the following activity, you should complete the tasks within the specified steps. Each of the tasks is accompanied by a Hint Screen. The purpose of the Hint Screen is to indicate where in the Visual Studio window you should perform the activity; it also serves as a reminder of the method that you should use to create the user interface or enter code. If you need further help completing the step, refer to the figure number identified by the term, ref:, in the step.

Guided Program Development

1

- **Open the Mock-Up File** Open Visual Studio and then open the mock-up file for the user interface you created in Chapter 2. (If you did not create a mock-up file in Chapter 2, consult with your instructor to obtain the file).

- **Show the Windows Form Object BackColor Property** To finish the user interface, the back color of the Windows Form object must be specified. Select the frmHotelRoomSelection Windows Form object. In the Properties window, scroll until the BackColor property is visible, click the BackColor property name in the left column, and then click the BackColor arrow in the right column. If necessary, click the Web tab *(ref: Figure 3-3)*.

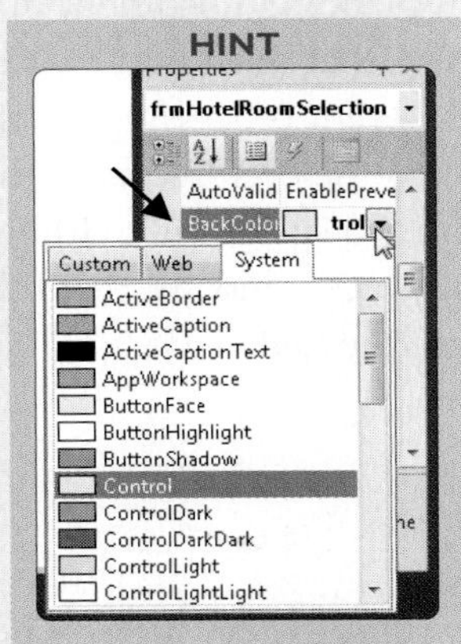

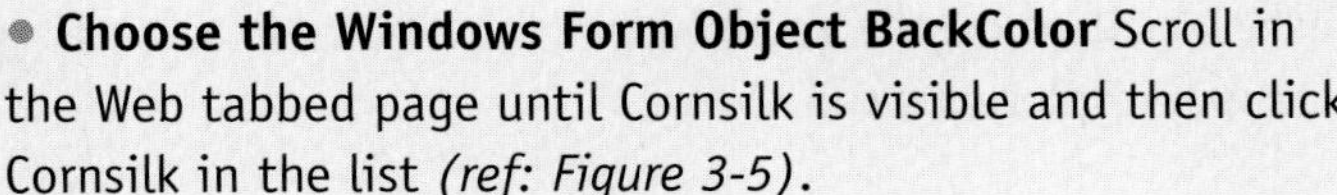

- **Choose the Windows Form Object BackColor** Scroll in the Web tabbed page until Cornsilk is visible and then click Cornsilk in the list *(ref: Figure 3-5)*.

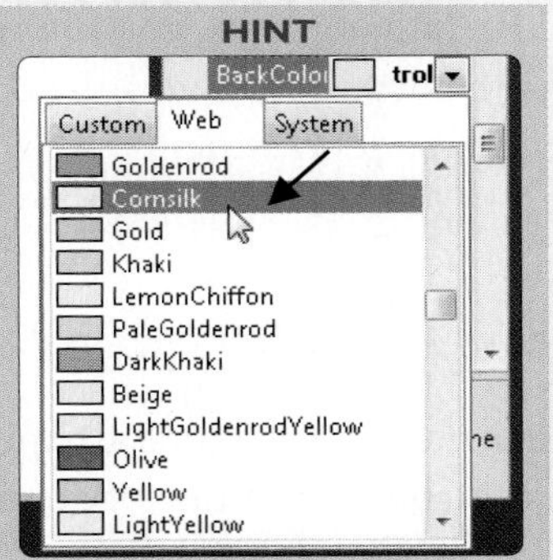

- **Select the Buttons** Next, you must specify the BackColor for the Button objects. Select the four buttons in the window using techniques you have learned previously.

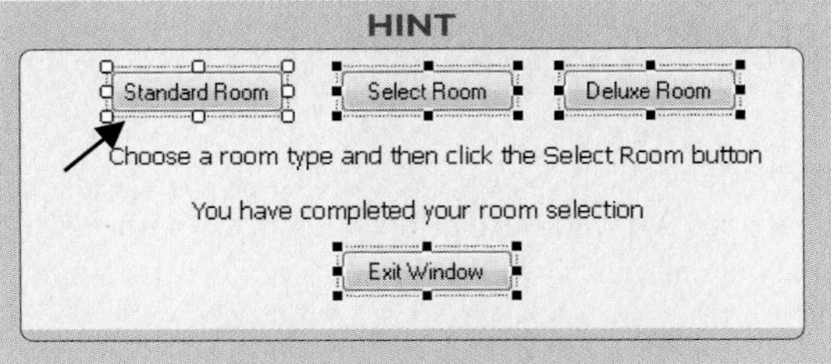

Guided Program Development *continued*

● **Choose the BackColor for the Buttons** Scroll in the Properties window until the BackColor property is visible. Click the BackColor property name in the left column, click the BackColor arrow in the right column, if necessary click the Web tab, scroll until the LightSalmon color is visible, and then click LightSalmon in the Web list. Click anywhere in the window to deselect the buttons *(ref: Figure 3-4)*.

HINT

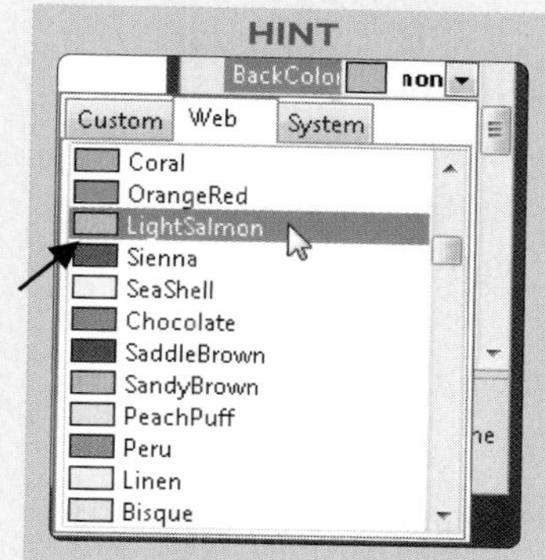

The BackColor for the Windows Form object is changed to Cornsilk and the BackColor for the buttons in the window is changed to LightSalmon (Figure 3-69).

RESULT OF STEP 1

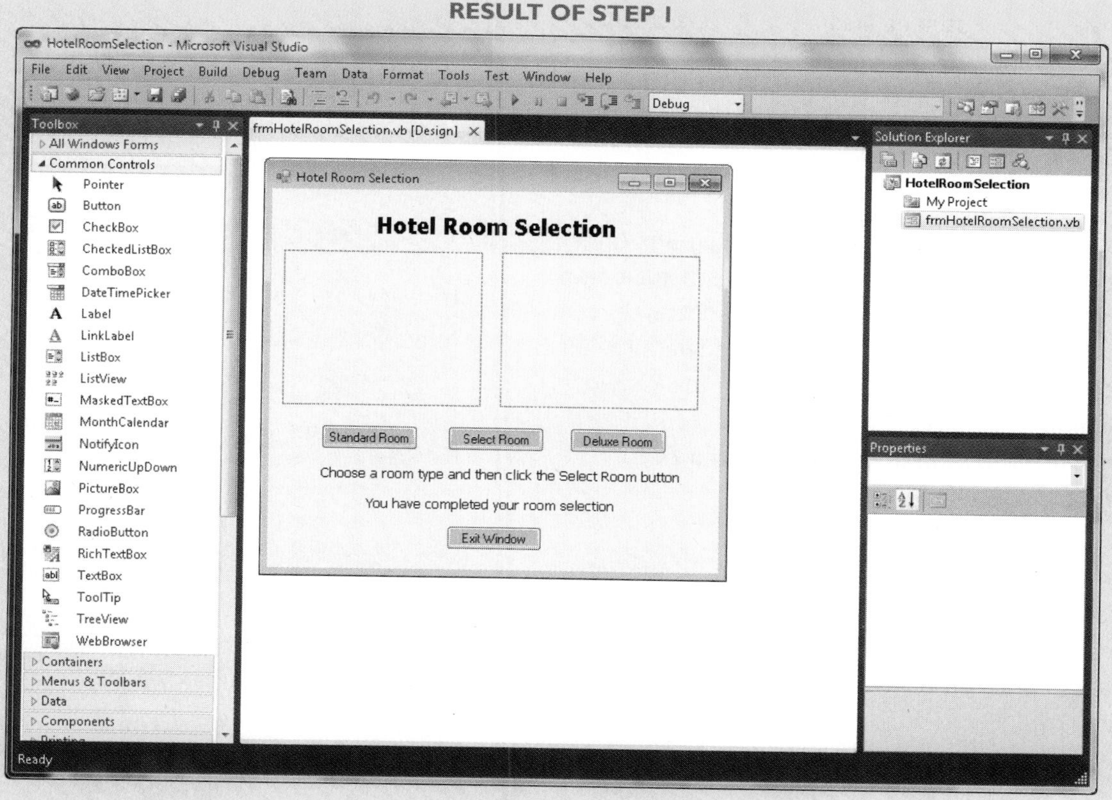

FIGURE 3-69

(continues)

Guided Program Development *continued*

2

- **Download the StandardRoom Image** To display the pictures in the PictureBox object, you must download the pictures from the Web and store them on your computer. Download the StandardRoom image from scsite.com/vb2010/ch3/images. Save the StandardRoom image on a USB drive or other storage media you have available on your computer *(ref: Figure 3-7)*.

- **Download the DeluxeRoom Image** Download the DeluxeRoom image from scsite.com/vb2010/ch3/images. Save the DeluxeRoom image on a USB drive or other storage media you have available on your computer *(ref: Figure 3-7)*.

3

- **Display the Select Resource Dialog Box** After acquiring the pictures, you must import them into the Resources folder and specify the PictureBox object where they will be displayed. Select the picStandardRoom PictureBox object. In the Properties window, click Image and then click the Ellipsis button in the right column *(ref: Figure 3-11)*.

HINT

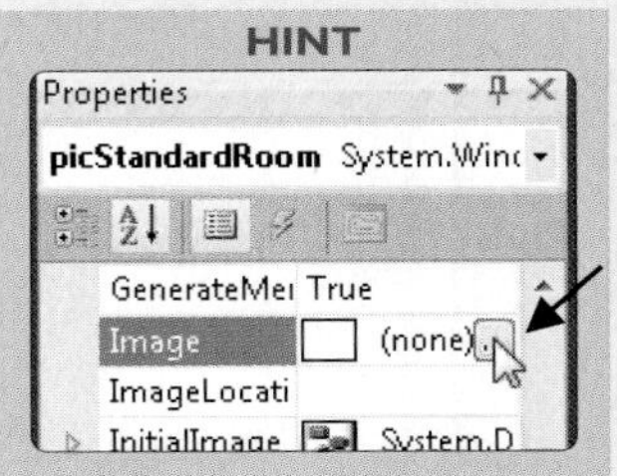

- **Import the StandardRoom Image** In the Select Resource dialog box, click the Import button, import the StandardRoom image from where you saved it in Step 2, and then click the OK button *(ref: Figure 3-14)*.

HINT

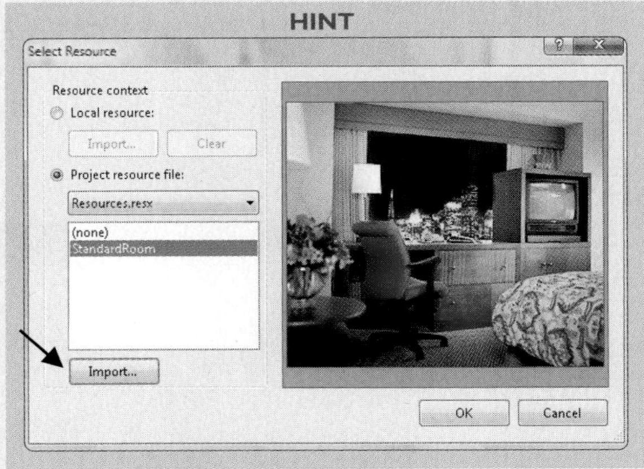

Guided Program Development *continued*

- **Import the DeluxeRoom Image** Using the Properties window and the same techniques, specify the DeluxeRoom image as the image for the picDeluxeRoom PictureBox object.

- **Set the SizeMode Property for the StandardRoom Image to StretchImage** When you import a picture, normally you must resize either the picture or the PictureBox object so the picture is displayed properly. To resize the StandardRoom image, select the picStandardRoom PictureBox object. In the Properties window for the picStandardRoom PictureBox object, click the SizeMode property name, click the SizeMode arrow, and then set the property to StretchImage *(ref: Figure 3-16)*.

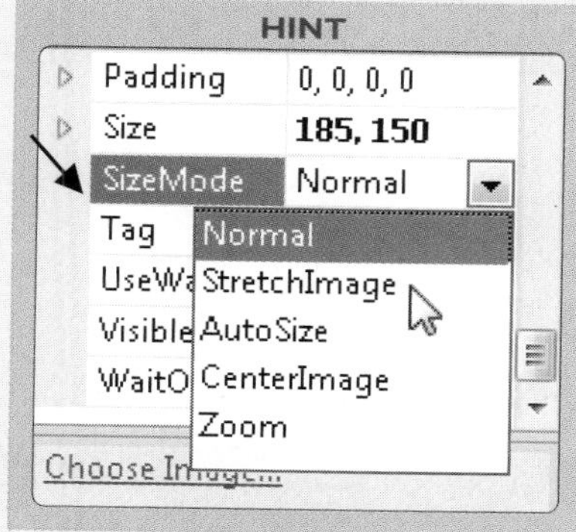

- **Set the SizeMode Property for the DeluxeRoom Image to StretchImage** Using the same technique, set the SizeMode property for the picDeluxeRoom PictureBox object to StretchImage.

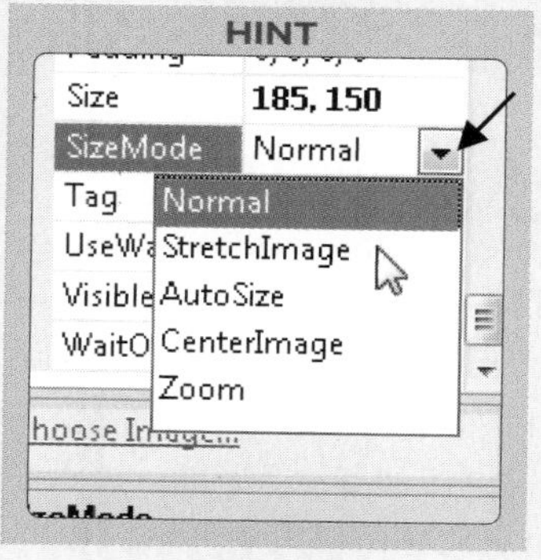

(continues)

Guided Program Development *continued*

The images are displayed in the correct PictureBox objects (Figure 3-70).

RESULT OF STEPS 2 & 3

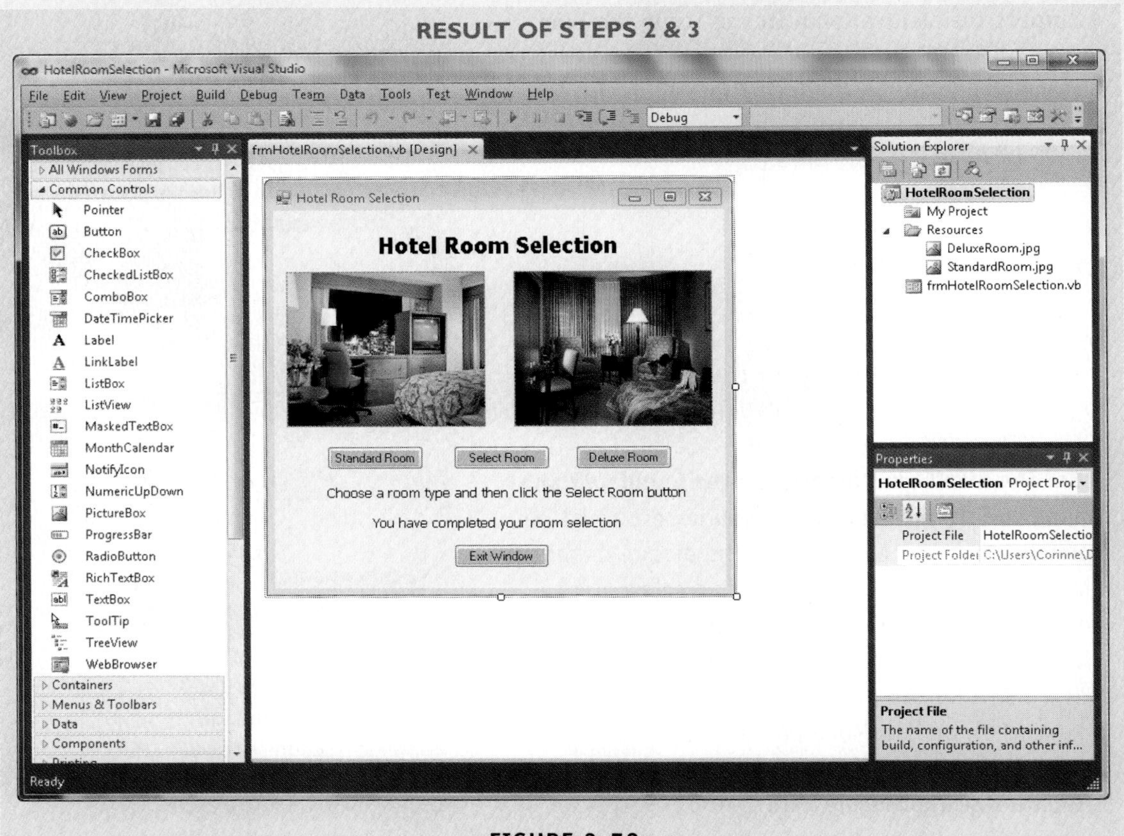

FIGURE 3-70

4

- **Set the Visible Property for the StandardRoom Image to False** When program execution begins, the pictures are not displayed in the window, so their Visible property must be set to False. In the Properties window for the picStandardRoom PictureBox object, click the Visible property name in the left column, click the Visible arrow for the Visible property, and then set the Visible property for the picStandardRoom PictureBox object to False *(ref: Figure 3-18)*.

HINT

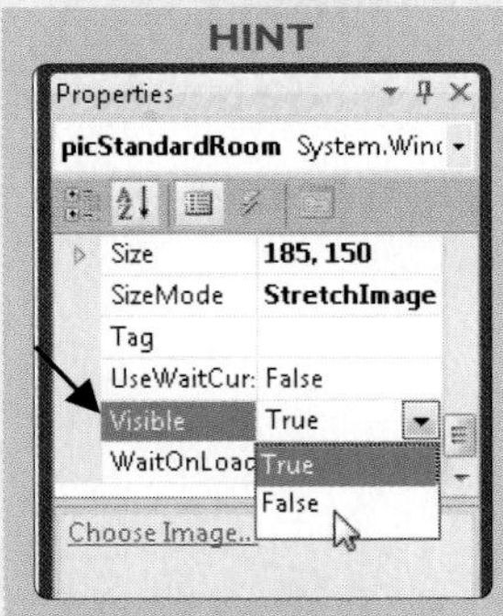

Guided Program Development *continued*

- **Set the Visible Property for the DeluxeRoom Image to False** Using the same technique, in the Properties window set the Visible property for the picDeluxeRoom PictureBox object to False *(ref: Figure 3-18)*.

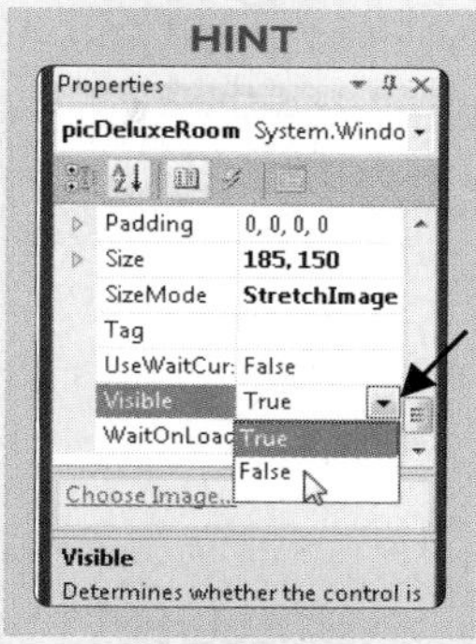

- **Set the Visible Property for the Confirmation Message to False** The confirmation message is not displayed when program execution begins. Therefore, using the same technique, in the Properties window set the Visible property for the lblConfirmationMessage Label object to False *(ref: Figure 3-18)*.

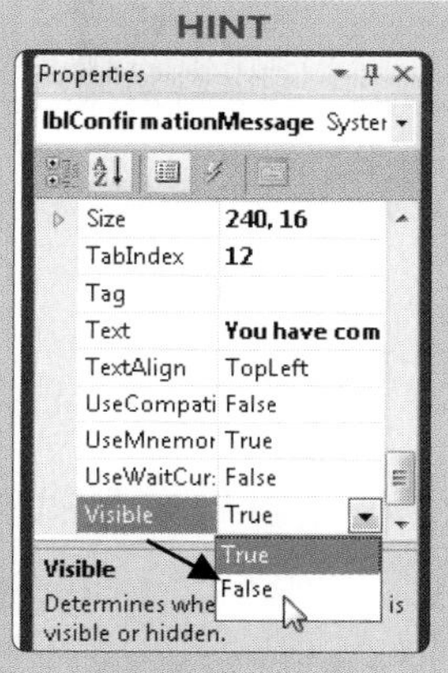

- **Run the Program** After you have made changes to a program, you should run it to ensure your changes work properly. Run the program to ensure the changes you have made are correct *(ref: Figure 3-22)*.

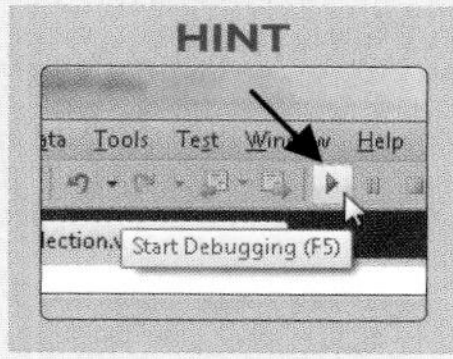

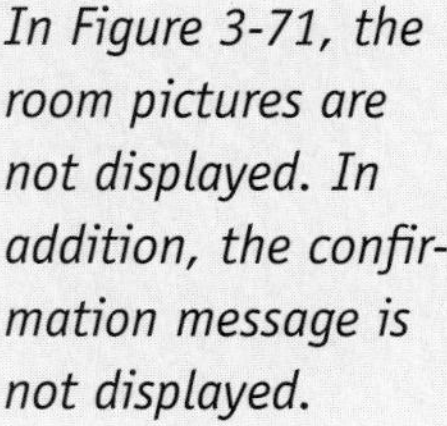

In Figure 3-71, the room pictures are not displayed. In addition, the confirmation message is not displayed.

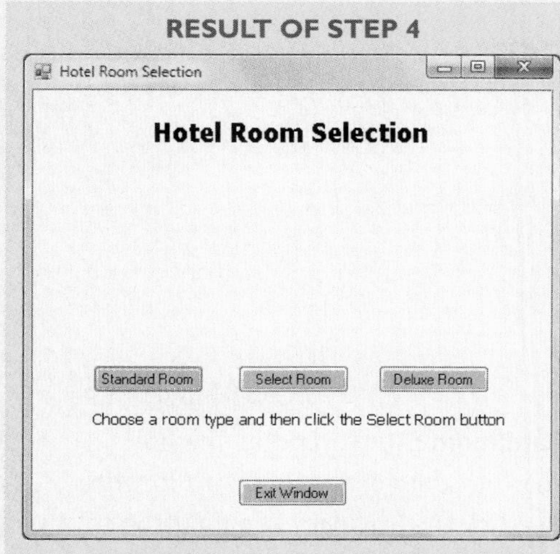

FIGURE 3-71

(continues)

Guided Program Development *continued*

5

- **Set the Select Room Button Enabled Property to False** Initially, the Select Room button and the Exit Window button must be dimmed. In the Properties window for the btnSelectRoom object, click the Enabled property name, click the Enabled arrow, and then set the Enabled property for the btnSelectRoom Button object to False *(ref: Figure 3-20)*.

HINT

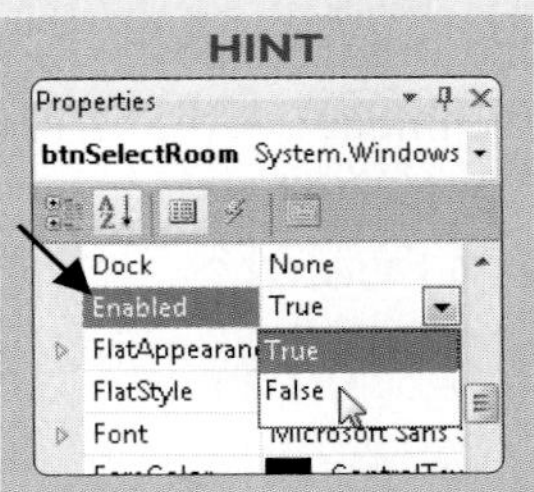

- **Set the Exit Window Button Enabled Property to False** Using the same technique, set the Enabled property for the btnExitWindow Button object to False *(ref: Figure 3-20)*.

HINT

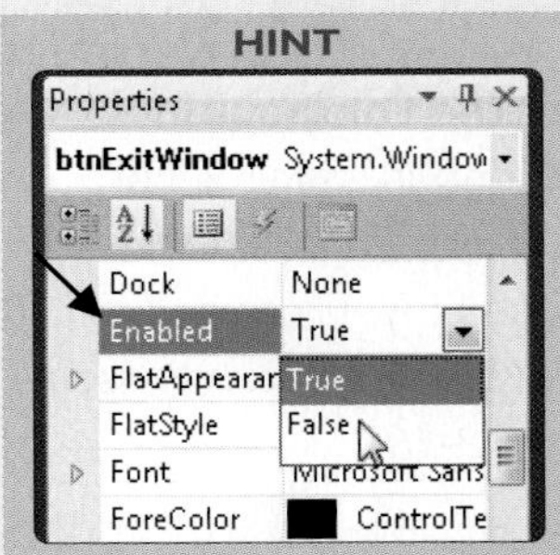

- **Run the Program** Once again, after you make changes always ensure the changes are correct. Run the program.

Both the Select Room button and the Exit Window button are dimmed, indicating the Enabled property for both buttons is False (Figure 3-72).

RESULT OF STEP 5

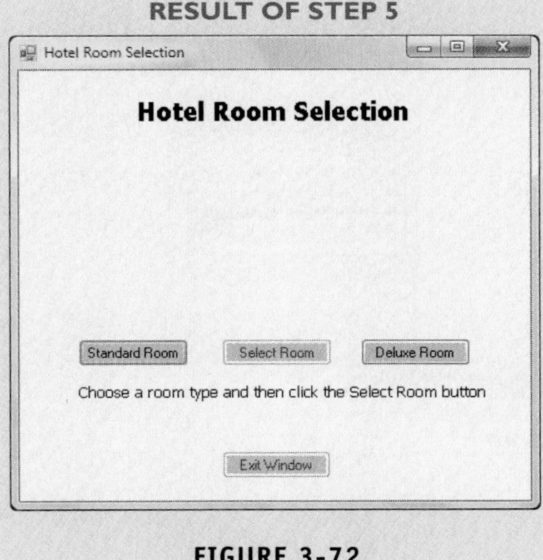

FIGURE 3-72

6

- **Open the Code Editing Window for the btnStandardRoom Event Handler** The user interface now is complete, so you should begin writing the code for the program. To write code, you must open the code editing window. Double-click the Standard Room button to open the code editing window for the btnStandardRoom_Click event *(ref: Figure 3-24)*.

HINT

Guided Program Development *continued*

- **Position the Insertion Point** When you begin writing the code for a program, the first step is to write the introductory comments. Click in the leftmost position of the first coding line (Public Class) *(ref: Figure 3-52)*.

HINT

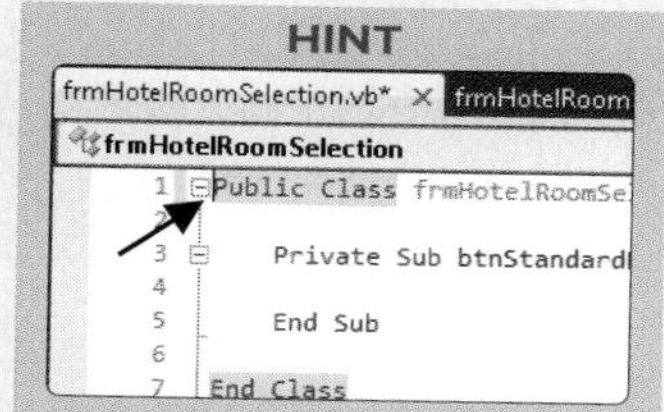

- **Create a Blank Line and Position the Insertion Point** Press the ENTER key and then press the UP ARROW key *(ref: Figure 3-53)*.

HINT

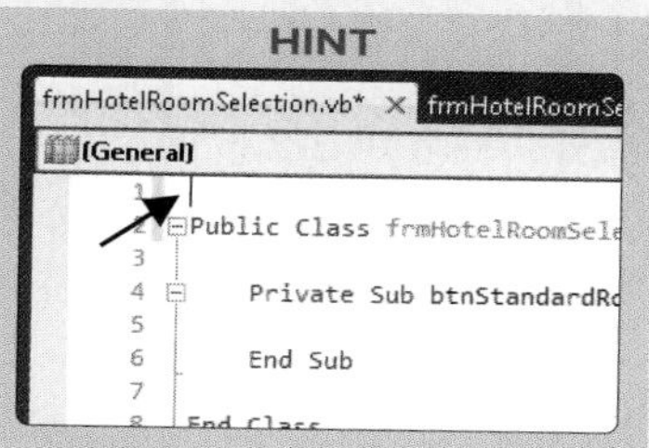

- **Enter the First Line of the Introductory Comments** The introductory comments provide the code reader with important information regarding the program. The first line normally specifies the name of the program. Type an apostrophe, press the SPACEBAR one time, type `Program Name:` on your keyboard, press the TAB key one time, type `Hotel Room Selection` and then press the ENTER key *(ref: Figure 3-54)*.

HINT

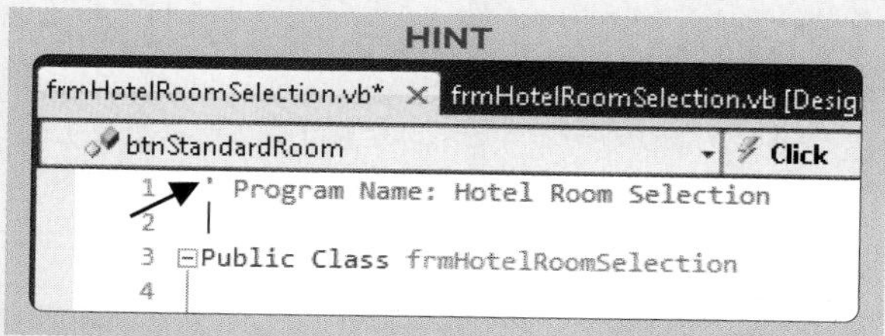

- **Enter the Developer Identification Comment Line** Type an apostrophe, press the SPACEBAR one time, type `Developer:` on your keyboard, press the TAB key one time, type your name and then press the ENTER key.

- **Enter the Date Comment Line** Type an apostrophe, press the SPACEBAR one time, type `Date:` on your keyboard, press the TAB key three times, enter the current date, and then press the ENTER key.

- **Enter the First Program Purpose Comment Line** Type an apostrophe, press the SPACEBAR one time, type `Purpose:` on your keyboard, press the TAB key two times, enter the first line of your own comments about the program, and then press the ENTER key.

- **Enter the Remaining Program Purpose Comment Lines** Insert additional lines of comments concerning the purpose of the program as you see fit.

(continues)

Guided Program Development *continued*

The comments appear at the top of the program (Figure 3-73).

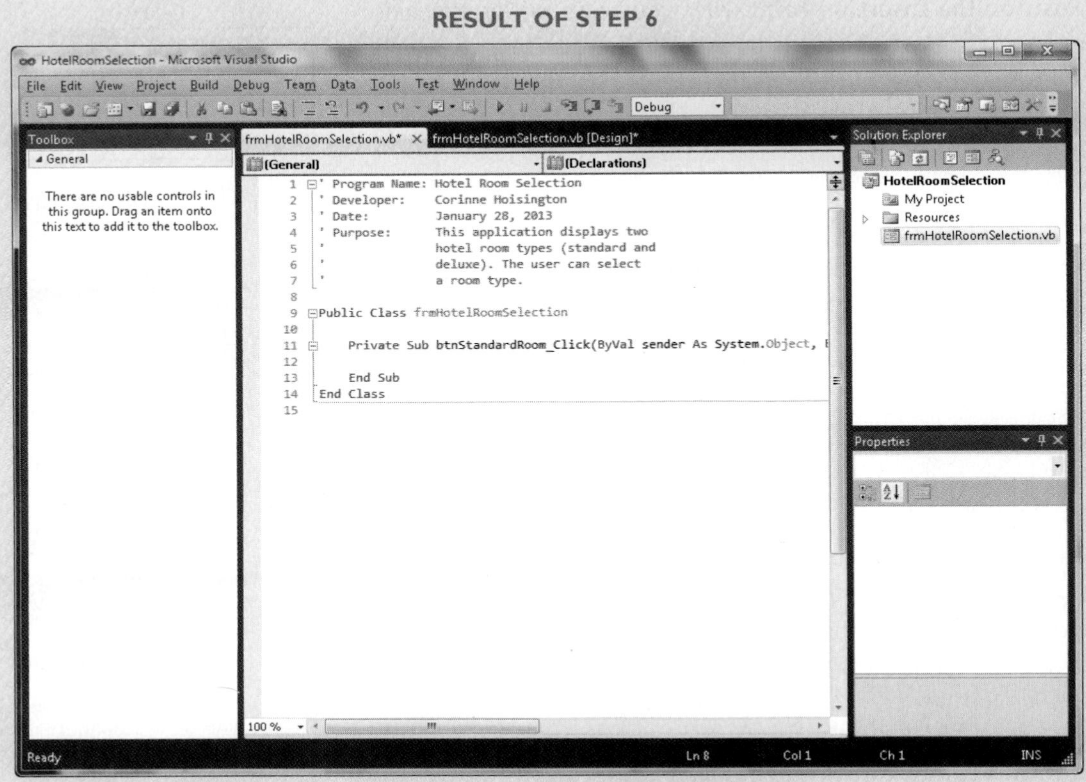

FIGURE 3-73

7

- **Position the Insertion Point Inside the Click Event Handler** With the insertion point located on the line above the line of code that begins with Public Class (see Figure 3-73), press the DOWN ARROW key four times and then press the TAB key two times to position the insertion point *(ref: Figure 3-48)*.

- **Enter the First Line of the Event Handler Comments** Each event handler should begin with comments describing what the event handler accomplishes. Type an apostrophe, press the SPACEBAR one time, and then enter the first line of comments for the btnStandardRoom_Click event handler. Press the ENTER key *(ref: Figure 3-49)*.

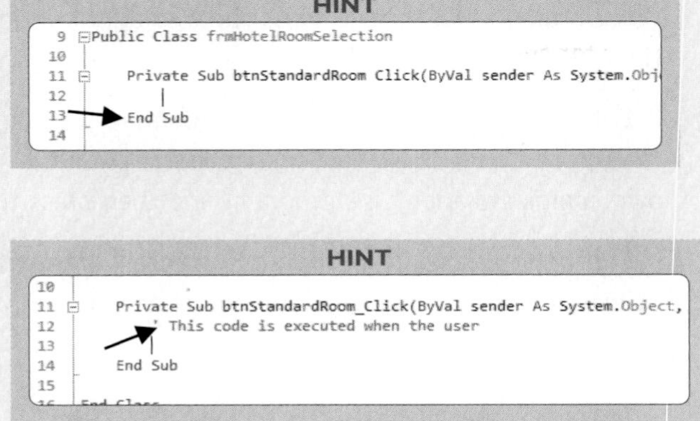

Guided Program Development *continued*

- **Enter the Remaining Event Handler Comments** Enter the remaining comments for the btnStandardRoom_Click event handler.

HINT

```
Public Class frmHotelRoomSelection

    Private Sub btnStandardRoom_Click(ByVal sender As System.Object, B
        ' This code is executed when the user
        ' clicks the Standard Room button. It
        ' displays the Standard Room picture,
        ' hides the Deluxe Room picture, and
        ' enables the Select Room button.

    End Sub
```

HEADS UP

As you enter executable code, you should refer to the event planning document to ensure the code you write implements the tasks identified. The event planning document is the guide to the code you write in each event handler.

- **Make the StandardRoom PictureBox Object Visible** The first executable line of code in the Standard Room Button object click event handler must make the StandardRoom PictureBox object visible. Using IntelliSense, enter the Visual Basic code statement to set the Visible property for the picStandardRoom PictureBox object to True *(ref: Figure 3-29)*.

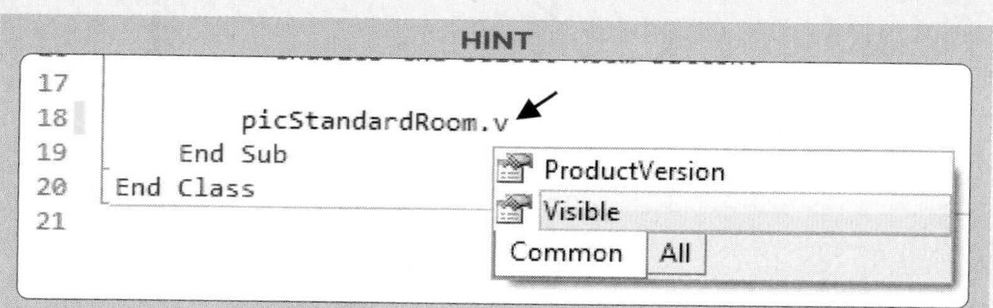

- **Make the DeluxeRoom Picture Box Object Not Visible** As documented in the event planning document, the next task is to make the Deluxe Room picture not visible in the window. Using IntelliSense, enter the Visual Basic code statement to set the Visible property for the picDeluxeRoom PictureBox object to False *(ref: Figure 3-37)*.

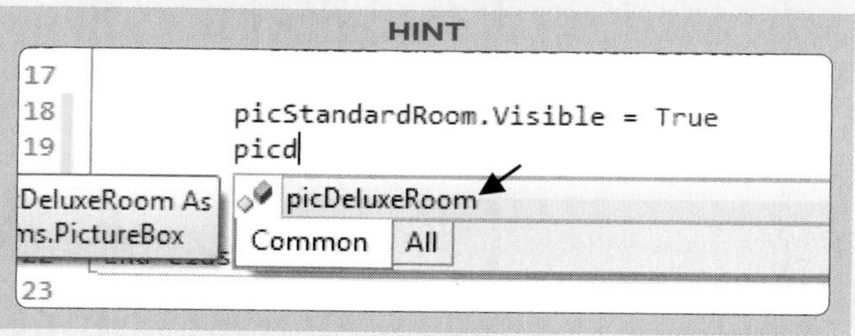

- **Enable the Select Room Button Object** The last task for the Standard Room button click event is to enable the Select Room button. Using IntelliSense, enter the Visual Basic code statement to set the Enabled property for the btnSelectRoom Button object to True *(ref: Figure 3-44)*.

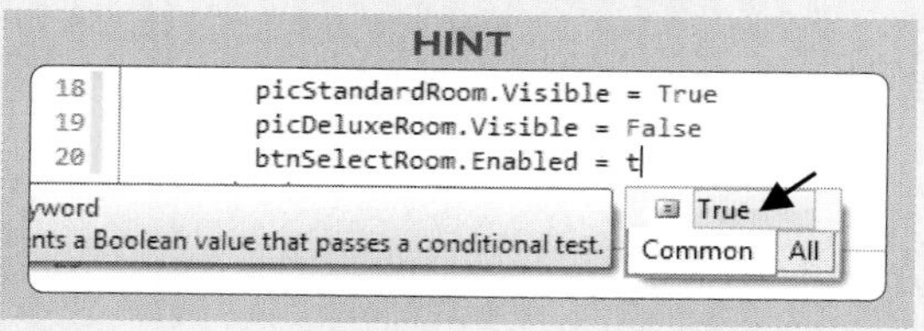

The lines of code are entered in the Standard Room Button object click event handler (Figure 3-74).

(continues)

Guided Program Development *continued*

The code will set the Visible property for the picStandardRoom PictureBox object to True, set the Visible property for the picDeluxeRoom PictureBox object to False, and set the Enabled property for the btnSelectRoom Button object to True.

RESULT OF STEP 7

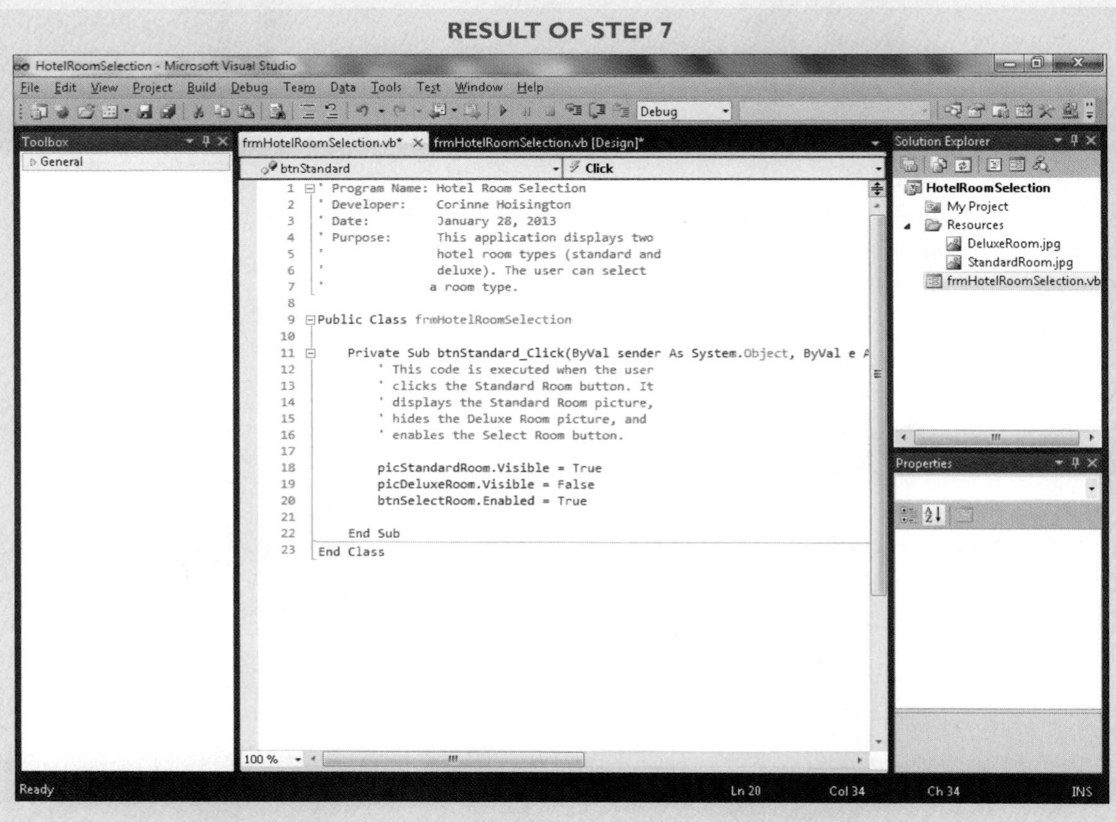

FIGURE 3-74

8

- **Run the Program** When the code for an event handler is complete, good practice dictates that you should run the program to ensure the event handler code works properly. Run the program. Click the Standard Room button.

Guided Program Development *continued*

When you click the Standard Room button, the Standard Room picture is displayed, the Deluxe Room picture is not displayed, and the Select Room button is enabled (Figure 3-75). These are the correct results. Note that if you click any of the other buttons in the window nothing happens. This is because you have not yet written the event handler code for these objects.

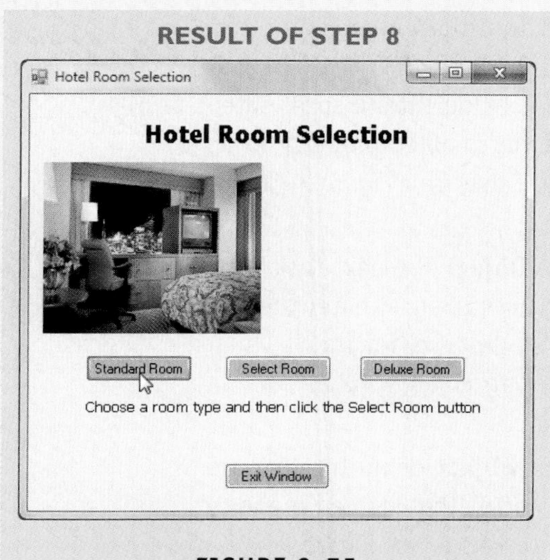

FIGURE 3-75

9

- **Display the Design Window** When the code for an event handler is completed, the next task is to write the code for another event handler. To do so, you must indicate the object for which the code will be written. You can do this on the Design tabbed page. Click the frmHotelRoomSelection.vb [Design] tab to return to the Design tabbed page.

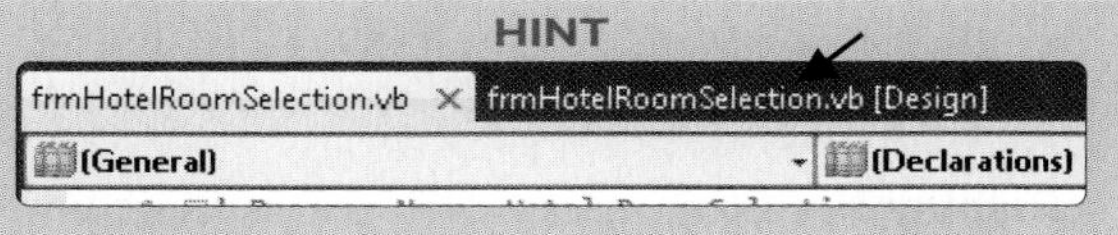

- **Open the Code Editing Window for the btnSelectRoom Event Handler** You must open the code editing window for the btnSelectRoom Button object to enter code for the event handler. Double-click the Select Room button to open the code editing window for the btnSelectRoom_Click event *(ref: Figure 3-24)*.

HINT

```
    Private Sub btnSelectRoom_Click(ByVal sender As Sys

    End Sub
End Class
```

- **Enter Event Handler Comments** When beginning the code for an event handler, the first step is to enter the event handler comments. Enter the comments that describe the processing in the btnSelectRoom_Click event handler.

HINT

```
    Private Sub btnSelectRoom_Click(ByVal sender As Syste
        ' This code is executed when the user
        ' clicks the Select Room button. It
        ' disables the Standard Room button,
        ' the Select Room button, and the
        ' Deluxe Room button. It hides the
        ' Instructios label, displays the
        ' Confirmation Message label, and
        ' enables the Exit Window button.


    End Sub
```

(continues)

Guided Program Development *continued*

- **Disable the btnStandardRoom Button Object** Referencing the event planning document (Figure 3-68 on page 158) the first task is to disable the Standard Room button. Using IntelliSense, enter the Visual Basic code statement to set the Enabled property for the btnStandardRoom Button object to False *(ref: Figure 3-42)*.

HINT

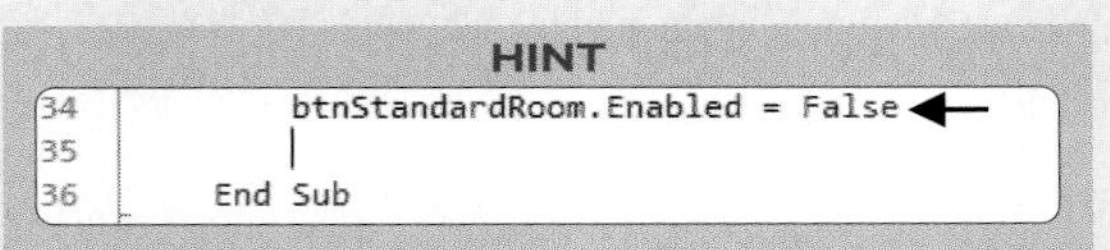

- **Disable the btnSelectRoom Button Object** The next task is to disable the Select Room button. Using IntelliSense, enter the Visual Basic code statement to set the Enabled property for the btnSelectRoom Button object to False *(ref: Figure 3-42)*.

HINT

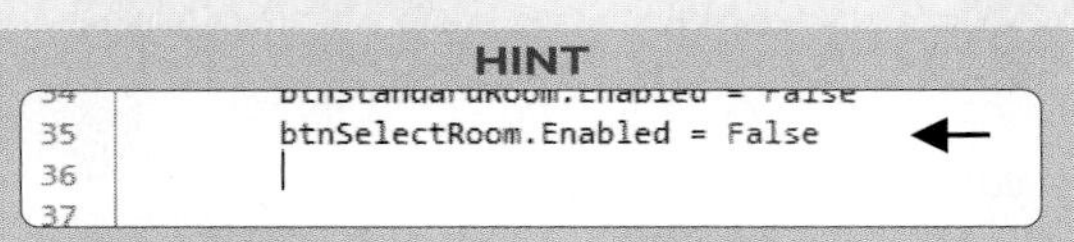

- **Disable the btnDeluxeRoom Button Object** Using IntelliSense, enter the Visual Basic code statement to set the Enabled property for the btnDeluxeRoom Button object to False *(ref: Figure 3-42)*.

- **Hide the Instructions Label Object** When the Select Room button is clicked, the instructions should not be displayed. Using IntelliSense, enter the Visual Basic code statement to set the Visible property for the lblInstructions Label object to False *(ref: Figure 3-29)*.

HINT

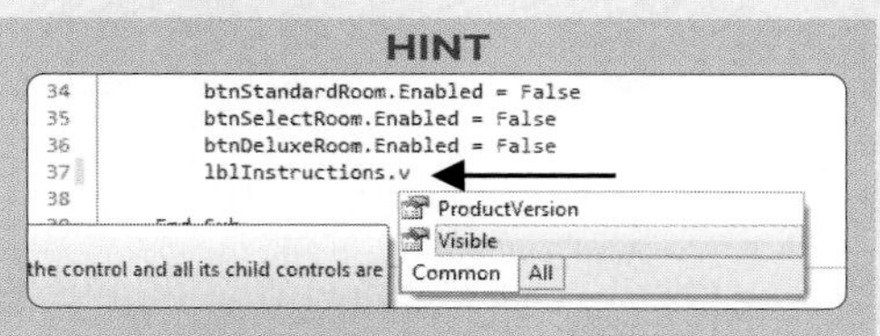

- **Display the Confirmation Message** The confirmation message must be displayed when the user clicks the Select Room button. Using IntelliSense, enter the Visual Basic code statement to set the Visible property for the lblConfirmationMessage Label object to True *(ref: Figure 3-29)*.

HINT

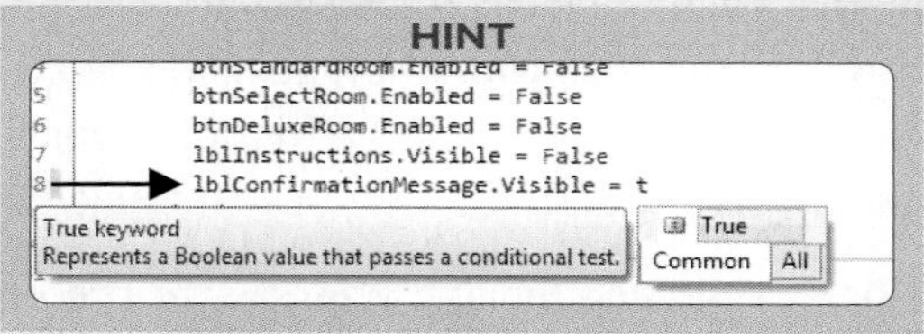

- **Enable the Exit Window Button** After the user clicks the Select Room button, the only allowable action is to click the Exit Window button and close the application. Therefore, the Exit Window button must be enabled. Using IntelliSense, enter the Visual Basic code statement to set the Enabled property for the btnExitWindow Button object to True *(ref: Figure 3-42)*.

HINT

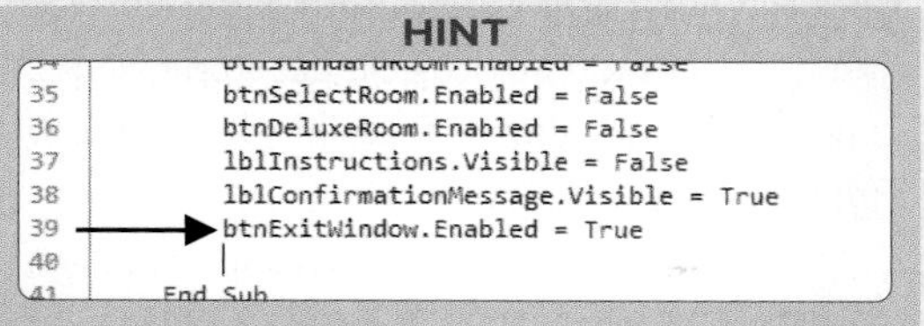

Guided Program Development *continued*

- **Run the Program** Run the program to ensure that it works correctly. Click the Standard Room button and then click the Select Room button.

After clicking the two buttons, the standard room picture is displayed; the Standard Room, Select Room, and Deluxe Room buttons are disabled; the Instructions label is not displayed; the Confirmation Message label is displayed; and the Exit Window button is enabled (Figure 3-76).

RESULT OF STEP 9

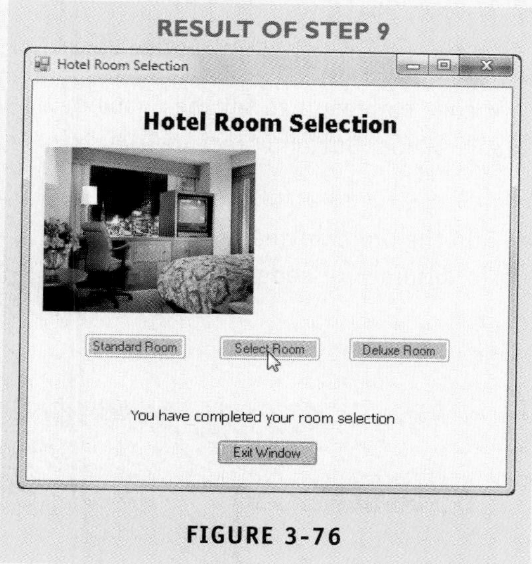

FIGURE 3-76

10

- **Display the Design Window** The next task is to write the code for the btnDeluxeRoom event handler. To return to the Design tabbed page so you can select the Deluxe Room button, click the frmHotelRoomSelection.vb [Design] tab.

HINT

- **Open the Code Editing Window for the btnDeluxeRoom Event Handler** Double-click the Deluxe Room button to open the code editing window for the btnDeluxeRoom_Click event *(ref: Figure 3-24)*.

HINT

- **Enter the Event Handler Comments** Using the techniques you have learned, enter the comments that describe the processing in the btnDeluxeRoom_Click event handler.

- **Make the DeluxeRoom PictureBox Object Visible** By referencing the event planning document, you can see the first task is to make the Deluxe Room picture visible. Using IntelliSense, enter the Visual Basic code statement to set the Visible property for the picDeluxeRoom PictureBox object to True *(ref: Figure 3-29)*.

(continues)

Guided Program Development *continued*

- **Make the Standard Room Picture Not Visible** Using IntelliSense, enter the Visual Basic code statement to set the Visible property for the picStandardRoom PictureBox object to False *(ref: Figure 3-29)*.
- **Enable the Select Room Button** Using IntelliSense, enter the Visual Basic code statement to set the Enabled property for the btnSelectRoom Button object to True *(ref: Figure 3-42)*.
- **Run the Program** Run the program and then click the Deluxe Room button to ensure your code works correctly.

The completed code for the Select Room button event handler and the Deluxe Room button event handler is shown in Figure 3-77.

RESULT OF STEP 10 (CODE)

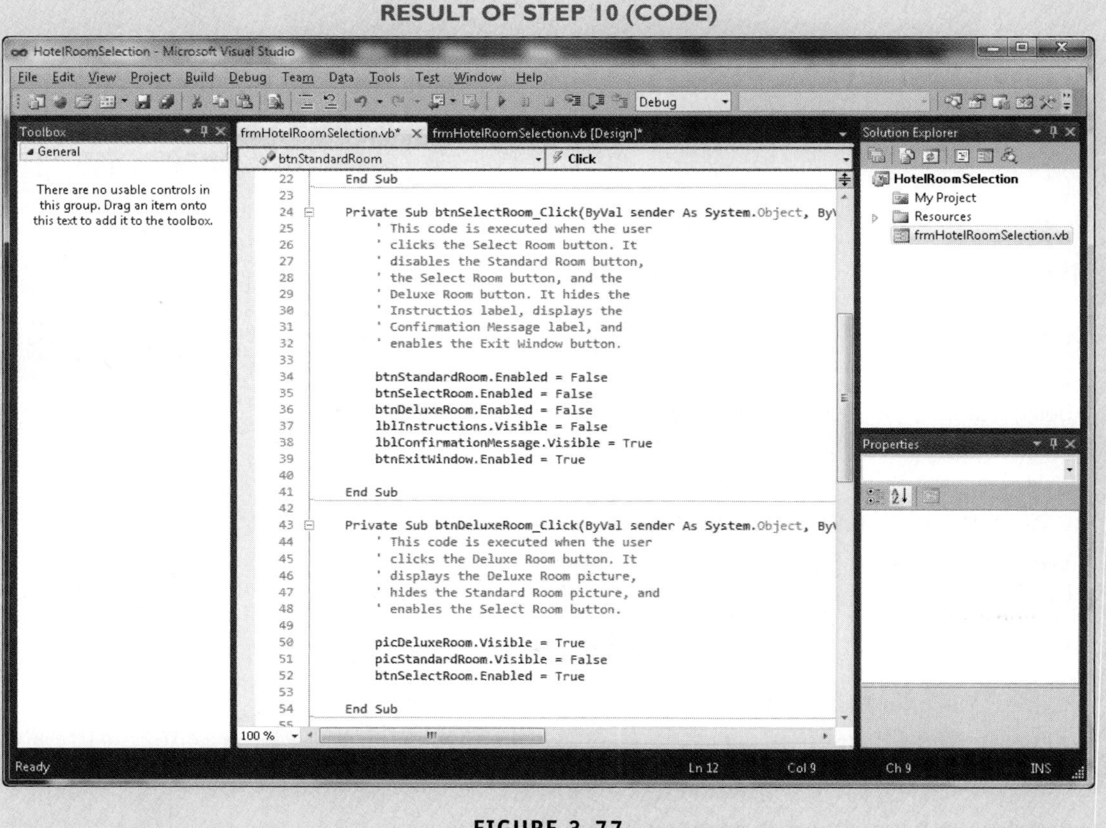

FIGURE 3-77

Guided Program Development *continued*

When you click the Deluxe Room button, the Deluxe Room picture is displayed, the Standard Room picture is not displayed, and the Select Room button is enabled (Figure 3-78). The program is working properly.

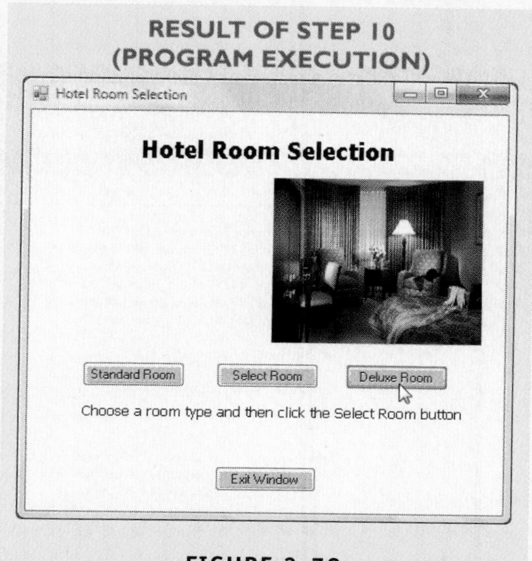

FIGURE 3-78

11

- **Display the Design Window** Click the frmHotelRoom-Selection.vb [Design] tab to return to the Design tabbed page.

- **Open the Code Editing Window for the btnExitWindow Event Handler** Double-click the Exit Window button to open the code editing window for the btnExitWindow_Click event *(ref: Figure 3-24)*.

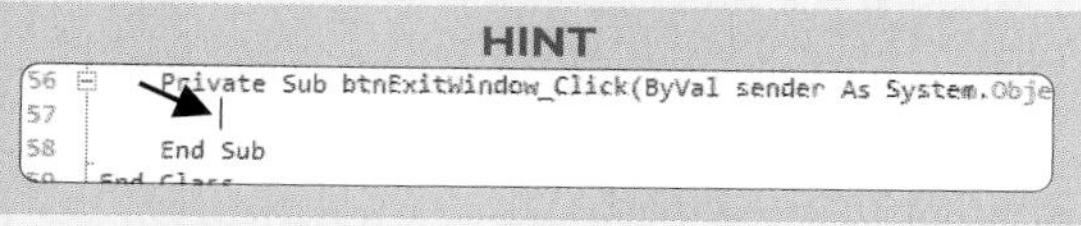

- **Enter the Event Handler Comments** Using the techniques you have learned, enter the comments that describe the processing in the btnExitWindow_Click event handler.

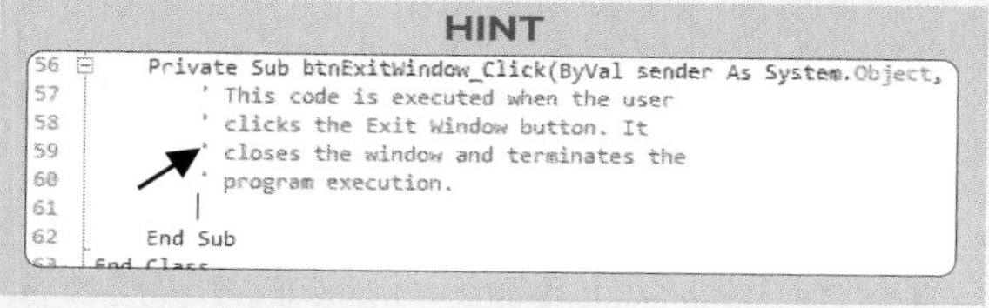

- **Enter the Close() Procedure Call** Using IntelliSense, enter the Visual Basic code statement to close the window and terminate the program *(ref: Figure 3-66)*.

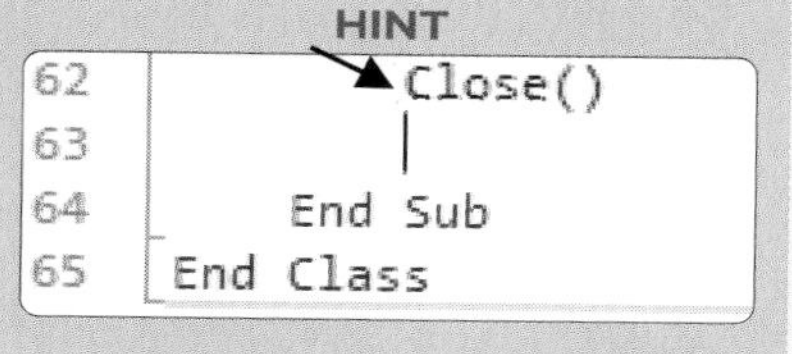

(continues)

Guided Program Development *continued*

The Close() procedure call statement is entered (Figure 3-79). When the procedure call is executed, the application will be closed.

RESULT OF STEP 11

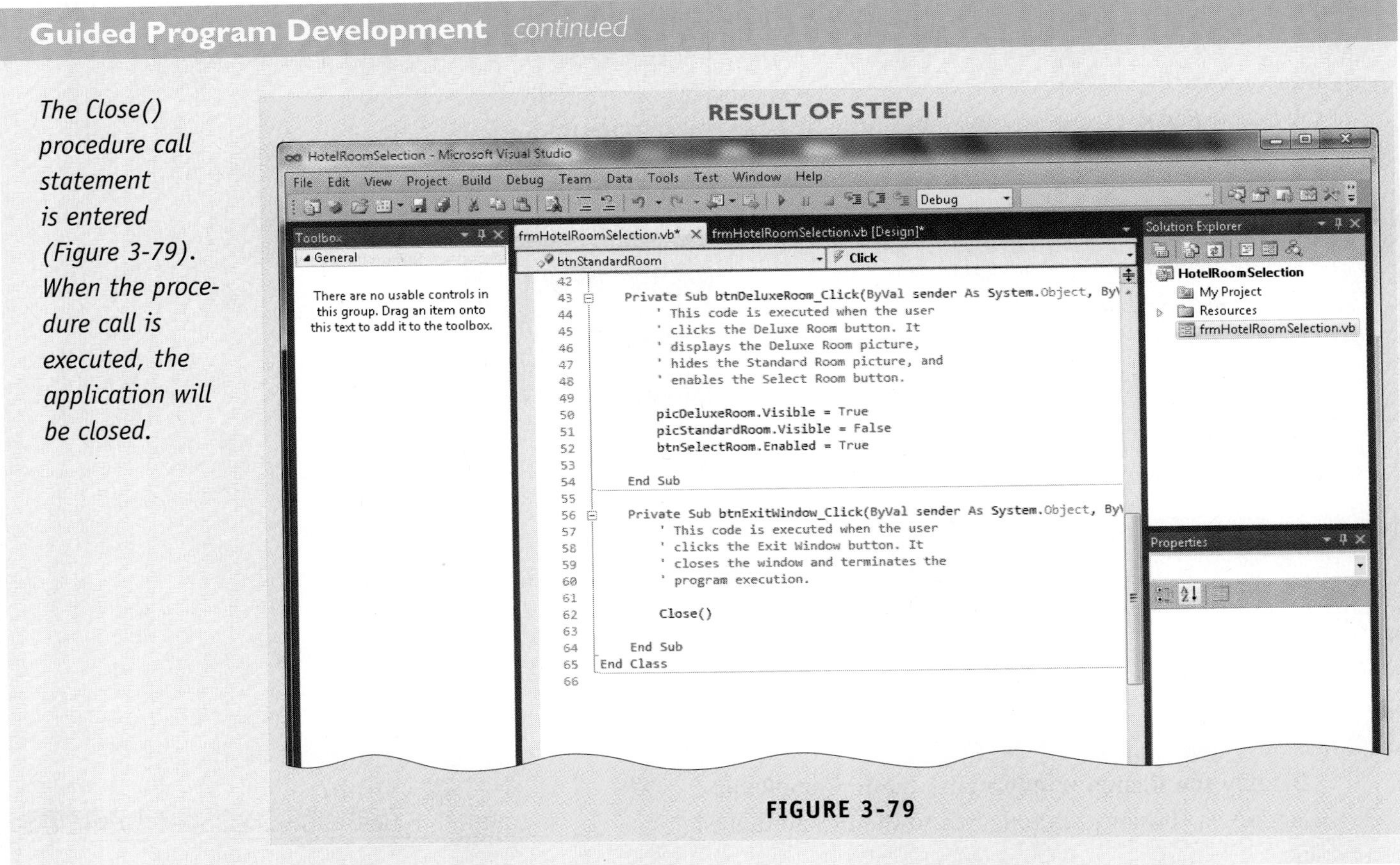

FIGURE 3-79

12

- **Run the Program** Run the program to ensure that it works correctly: 1. Click the Standard Room button; 2. Click the Deluxe Room button; 3. Click the Standard Room button; 4. Click the Select Room button; 5. Click the Exit Window button.

Code Listing

The complete code for the sample program is shown in Figure 3-80.

```
' Program Name: Hotel Room Selection
' Developer:    Corinne Hoisington
' Date:         January 28, 2013
' Purpose:      This application displays two
'               hotel room types (standard and
'               deluxe). The user can select
'               a room type.

Public Class frmHotelRoomSelection

    Private Sub btnStandardRoom_Click(ByVal sender As System.Object, ByVal e As System.EventArgs) Handles btnStandardRoom.Click
        ' This code is executed when the user
        ' clicks the Standard Room button. It
        ' displays the Standard Room picture,
        ' hides the Deluxe Room picture, and
        ' enables the Select Room button.

        picStandardRoom.Visible = True
        picDeluxeRoom.Visible = False
        btnSelectRoom.Enabled = True

    End Sub

    Private Sub btnSelectRoom_Click(ByVal sender As System.Object, ByVal e As System.EventArgs) Handles btnSelectRoom.Click
        ' This code is executed when the user
        ' clicks the Select Room button. It
        ' disables the Standard Room button,
        ' the Select Room button, and the
        ' Deluxe Room button. It hides the
        ' Instructios label, displays the
        ' Confirmation Message label, and
        ' enables the Exit Window button.

        btnStandardRoom.Enabled = False
        btnSelectRoom.Enabled = False
        btnDeluxeRoom.Enabled = False
        lblInstructions.Visible = False
        lblConfirmationMessage.Visible = True
        btnExitWindow.Enabled = True

    End Sub

    Private Sub btnDeluxeRoom_Click(ByVal sender As System.Object, ByVal e As System.EventArgs) Handles btnDeluxeRoom.Click
        ' This code is executed when the user
        ' clicks the Deluxe Room button. It
        ' displays the Deluxe Room picture,
        ' hides the Standard Room picture, and
        ' enables the Select Room button.

        picDeluxeRoom.Visible = True
        picStandardRoom.Visible = False
        btnSelectRoom.Enabled = True

    End Sub

    Private Sub btnExitWindow_Click(ByVal sender As System.Object, ByVal e As System.EventArgs) Handles btnExitWindow.Click
        ' This code is executed when the user
        ' clicks the Exit Window button. It
        ' closes the window and terminates the
        ' program execution.

        Close()

    End Sub
End Class
```

FIGURE 3-80

Summary

In this chapter you have learned to fine-tune a graphical user interface to maximize its usefulness and to enter code for object event handlers.

The items listed in the table in Figure 3-81 include all the new Visual Studio and Visual Basic skills you have learned in this chapter.

Visual Basic Skills

Skill	Figure Number	Web Address for Video
Set the BackColor property	Figure 3-2	scsite.com/vb2010/ch3/figure3-2
Locate and Save an Image from the World Wide Web	Figure 3-7	scsite.com/vb2010/ch3/figure3-7
Import an Image into the Program Resources Folder	Figure 3-11	scsite.com/vb2010/ch3/figure3-11
Size an Image	Figure 3-16	scsite.com/vb2010/ch3/figure3-16
Set the Visible Property in the Properties Window	Figure 3-18	scsite.com/vb2010/ch3/figure3-18
Set the Enabled Property in the Properties Window	Figure 3-20	scsite.com/vb2010/ch3/figure3-20
Run a Visual Basic 2010 Program	Figure 3-22	scsite.com/vb2010/ch3/figure3-22
Enter Visual Basic 2010 Code for Event Handling	Figure 3-24	scsite.com/vb2010/ch3/figure3-24
Enter a Visual Basic 2010 Statement using IntelliSense	Figure 3-29	scsite.com/vb2010/ch3/figure3-29
Enter a Visual Basic 2010 Statement to Set the Visible Property to True	Figure 3-29	scsite.com/vb2010/ch3/figure3-29
Enter a Visual Basic 2010 Statement to Set the Visible Property to False	Figure 3-37	scsite.com/vb2010/ch3/figure3-37
Enter a Visual Basic 2010 Statement to Set the Enabled Property to True	Figure 3-42	scsite.com/vb2010/ch3/figure3-42
Enter Comments in Visual Basic 2010 Code	Figure 3-47	scsite.com/vb2010/ch3/figure3-47
Enter Introductory Comments in Visual Basic 2010 Code	Figure 3-52	scsite.com/vb2010/ch3/figure3-52
Correct Errors in a Visual Basic 2010 Program	Figure 3-58	scsite.com/vb2010/ch3/figure3-58
Enter a Close() Statement into Visual Basic 2010 Code	Figure 3-66	scsite.com/vb2010/ch3/figure3-66
Print Code	Pages 156–157	

FIGURE 3-81

Learn It Online

Start your browser and visit scsite.com/vb2010/ch3. Follow the instructions in the exercises below.

1. **Chapter Reinforcement TF, MC, SA** Click one of the Chapter Reinforcement links for Multiple Choice, True/False, or Short Answer below the Learn It Online heading. Answer each question and submit to your instructor.
2. **Practice Test** Click the Practice Test link. Answer each question, enter your first and last name at the bottom of the page, and then click the Grade Test button. When the graded practice test is displayed on your screen, submit the graded practice test to your instructor. Continue to take the practice test until you are satisfied with your score.
3. **Crossword Puzzle Challenge** Click the Crossword Puzzle Challenge link below the Learn It Online heading. Read the instructions, and then click the Continue button. Work the crossword puzzle. When you are finished, click the Submit button. When the crossword puzzle is redisplayed, submit it to your instructor.

Knowledge Check

1. Which property controls the background color of the Form object?
2. Which property controls the background color of a Button object?
3. Which color palette is guaranteed to be displayed properly on every computer?
4. What is the use of the Image property for a PictureBox object?
5. To display an image in a PictureBox object in your application, you first must store the image in which folder within the application?
6. When you click the Ellipsis button for the Image property of a PictureBox object (Figure 3-82), what action does Visual Studio 2010 take?

FIGURE 3-82

7. What is the default setting of the PictureBox object SizeMode property?
8. Which option in the SizeMode property should be selected to make the image fit within the PictureBox object?
9. Which property has been set to False if a Button object in a window is dimmed when program execution begins?

(continues)

Knowledge Check *continued*

10. Which property has been set to False if a PictureBox object is not displayed when you run the application?
11. What two options can you select for the Visible property in the Properties window?
12. Write a line of code that would set the Visible property for a PictureBox object named picHomeTown to False.
13. Write a line of code that would set the Enabled property for a Button object named btnStart to True.
14. Write a line of code that would set the Visible property for a Label object named lblDisplayTuition to True.
15. Write a comment line of code that states, "The following code displays the image".
16. What color text is used to display comments in the code editing window of Visual Basic 2010?
17. Write a line of code that will close an application window and terminate the application.
18. What does a blue squiggly line mean in the code editing window?
19. Why is it best that you use IntelliSense when you enter code in the code editing window? List two reasons.
20. Which symbol is associated with the assignment statement?

Debugging Exercises

1. Fix the following line of code to set the Visible property for the picCompanyLogo PictureBox object to True.

   ```
   picCompanyLogo.Visible.True
   ```

2. Fix the following line of code to disable the btnExitProgram Button object.

   ```
   btnExitProgram.Enabled = No
   ```

3. Fix the following line of code to set the Visible property for the lblDirections Label object to False.

   ```
   lblDirections.Visible = ' False
   ```

Debugging Exercises *continued*

4. Fix the following comment line of code.

```
The ' following line of code makes the college logo visible
```

5. Fix the following line of code.

```
Close
```

6. Examine the code window and the Error List window in Figure 3-83. Then, write a line of code to replace the line of code in error.

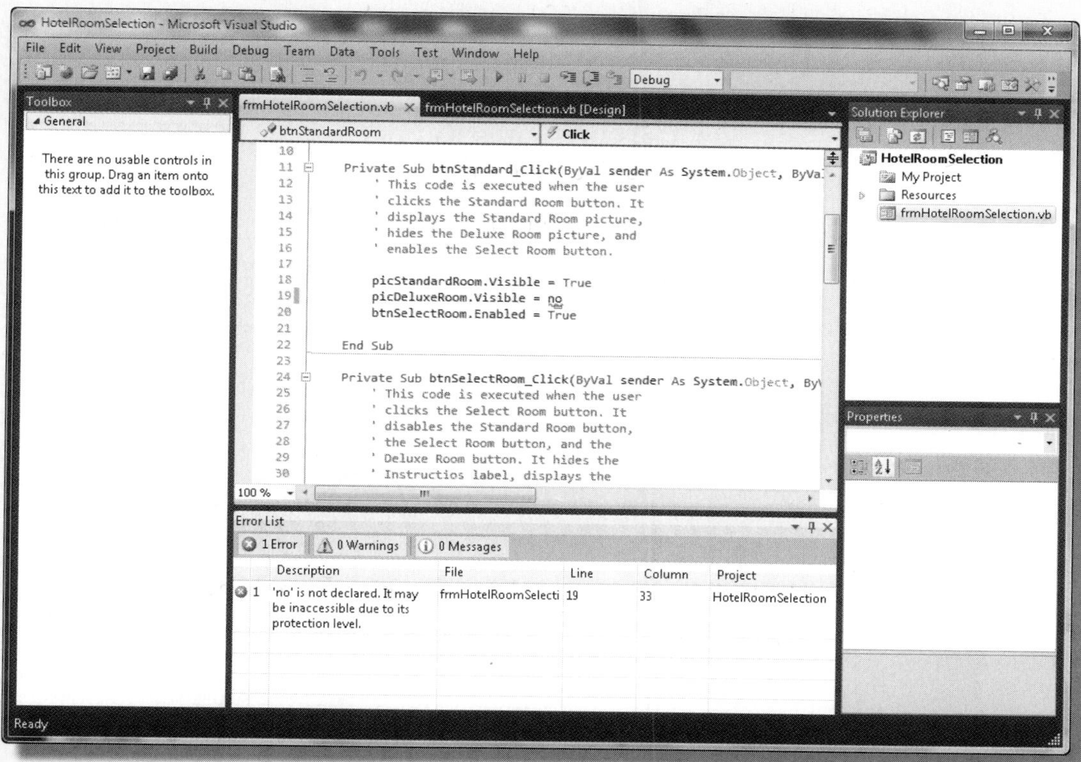

FIGURE 3-83

Program Analysis

1. For a bakery application shown in Figure 3-84, write the Visual Basic 2010 coding statement to view the cake picture when the user clicks the btnView button, assuming the Visible property for the picCake PictureBox object had been set to False in the Properties window.

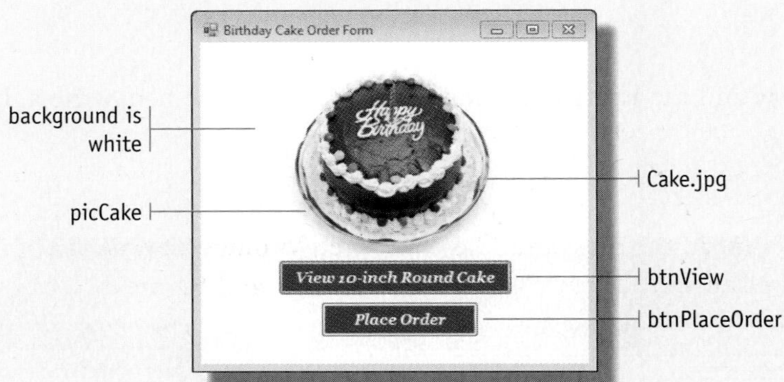

FIGURE 3-84

2. Which property in the Properties window controls whether the btnPlaceOrder button is dimmed when the program begins execution? Which option for the property would you select to cause the button to be dimmed when the program begins execution?

3. When you import the picture of the cake into the Resources folder and select the image for use in the picCake PictureBox object, which SizeMode property option would you select to view the complete picture?

4. Write the Visual Basic 2010 coding statement for the btnView click event that would cause the btnPlaceOrder button to be active (not dimmed).

5. To make the window background color White as shown in Figure 3-84, what property should you modify?

6. What property is used to cause the text, Birthday Cake Order Form, to be displayed in the window title bar?

7. What procedure should be used to close the window and terminate the application when the user clicks the Place Order button?

Case Programming Assignments

Complete one or more of the following case programming assignments. Submit the program and materials you create to your instructor. The level of difficulty is indicated for each case programming assignment.

● = Easiest
●● = Intermediate
●●● = Challenging

1 ●
EUROPEAN HOSTEL SELECTION

Based on the Windows form mock-up you created in Chapter 2, complete the Hostel Location Selection program by changing the window background color, downloading and adding the images, and writing the code that will execute according to the program requirements. Before writing the code, create an event planning document for each event in the program. The completed Windows Form object and the other objects in the user interface are shown in Figure 3-87a, Figure 3-87b, and Figure 3-87c.

REQUIREMENTS DOCUMENT

Date submitted: January 17, 2013

Application title: Vacation Hostel Location Selection

Purpose: The hostel selection application will allow a user to select the location in London or Dublin.

Program Procedures: From a window on the screen, the user should identify a hostel location (London or Dublin) and then indicate the location of the hostel.

Algorithms, Processing and Conditions:

1. The user must be able to identify the London or Dublin hostel, back and forth until the selection is made.
2. When the user identifies the hostel location, a picture of that hostel should appear in the window.
3. Only one picture should be displayed at a time. If a user identifies the London hostel, only the London hostel picture should be displayed; if a user identifies the Dublin hostel, only the Dublin hostel picture should be displayed.
4. When the user makes a hostel selection, a message stating that the selection of a hostel location has been made should be displayed. In addition, the user should be stopped from identifying a hostel location after the hostel selection has been made.
5. After the user makes a hostel selection, the only allowable action is to exit the window.

Notes and Restrictions:

1. A user cannot make a hostel selection until he or she has identified a hostel location.

Comments:

1. The pictures shown in the window can be found on scsite.com/vb2010/ch3/images. The names of the pictures are LondonHostel and DublinHostel.

FIGURE 3-85

(continues)

Case Programming Assignments

***European Hostel Selection** (continued)*

USE CASE DEFINITION

1. User clicks London hostel button or Dublin hostel button.
2. Program displays a picture of the hostel identified by the user and enables the hostel selection button.
3. User clicks hostel buttons to view hostel locations if desired. Program displays the picture of the identified hostel.
4. User clicks the Select Location button.
5. Program displays a hostel selection confirmation message, and disables both hostel buttons and the Select Location button. The Exit Window button becomes active.
6. User terminates the program by clicking the Exit Window button.

FIGURE 3-86

In Figure 3-87a, no button has been clicked. In Figure 3-87b, the user has clicked the Dublin Hostel button. In Figure 3-87c, the user has clicked the Select Location button.

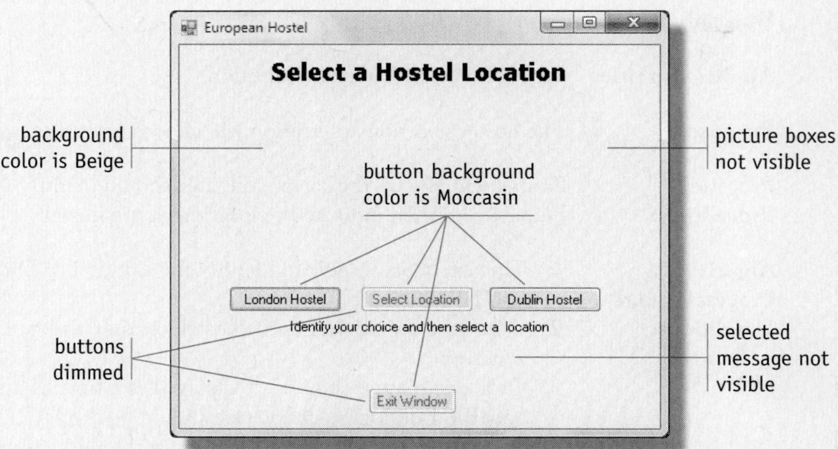

FIGURE 3-87a

FIGURE 3-87b

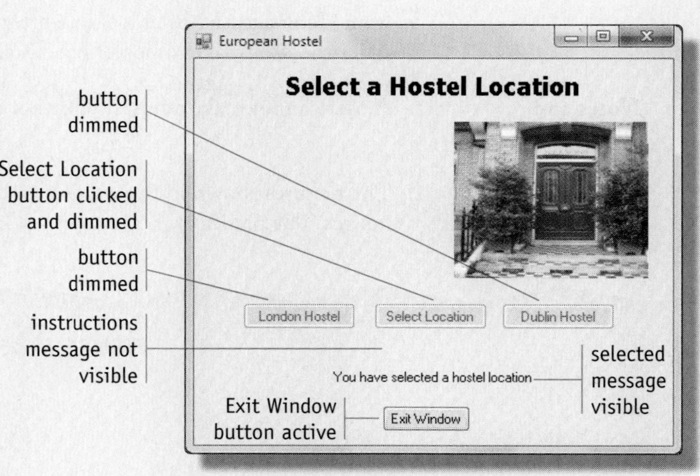

FIGURE 3-87c

Case Programming Assignments

2 • BANKING

Based on the Windows form mock-up you created in Chapter 2, complete the Banking program by changing the window background color, downloading and adding the image, and writing the code that will execute according to the program requirements. Before writing the code, create an event planning document for each event in the program. The completed Windows Form object and the other objects in the user interface are shown in Figure 3-90a and Figure 3-90b.

REQUIREMENTS DOCUMENT

Date submitted:	January 14, 2013
Application title:	Bank Welcome Screen with Banking Hours
Purpose:	This application displays a welcome screen for the First Corner National Bank. The user can choose an option to view the hours of the bank.
Program Procedures:	From a window on the screen, the user makes a request to see the bank's open hours.
Algorithms, Processing, and Conditions:	1. The user first views a welcome screen that displays the bank's name (First Corner National Bank), bank picture, and a phrase that states the bank is FDIC insured. 2. When the user opts to view the bank hours, the following hours are displayed: Monday–Thursday 9:00AM – 5:00PM Friday 9:00AM – 8:00PM Saturday 9:00AM – 1:00PM 3. After the user views the hours, the only allowable action is to exit the window.
Notes and Restrictions:	n/a
Comments:	1. The picture shown in the window can be found on scsite.com/vb2010/ch3/images. The name of the picture is BankBuilding.

FIGURE 3-88

(continues)

Case Programming Assignments

Banking *(continued)*

USE CASE DEFINITION

1. The window opens, displaying the title of the bank, the bank's picture, and a message that the bank is FDIC insured. The View Banking Hours button and the Exit Window button are enabled.
2. User clicks View Banking Hours button.
3. Program displays the banking hours above the buttons. The View Banking Hours button is disabled.
4. User clicks the Exit Window button to terminate the application.

FIGURE 3-89

In Figure 3-90a, no button has been clicked. In Figure 3-90b, the user has clicked the View Banking Hours button.

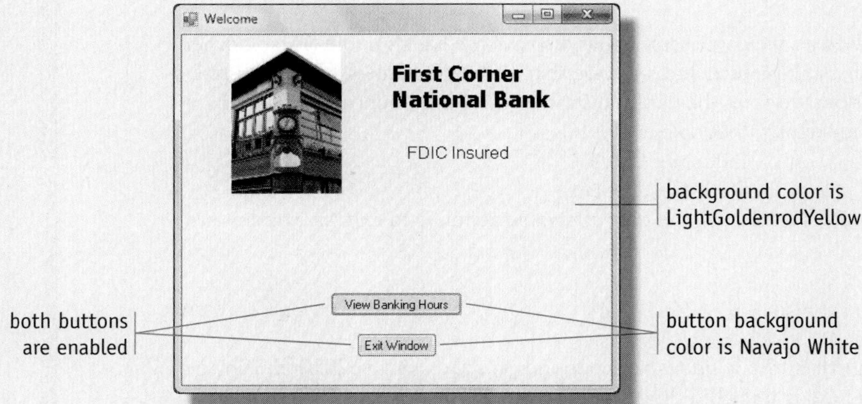

FIGURE 3-90a

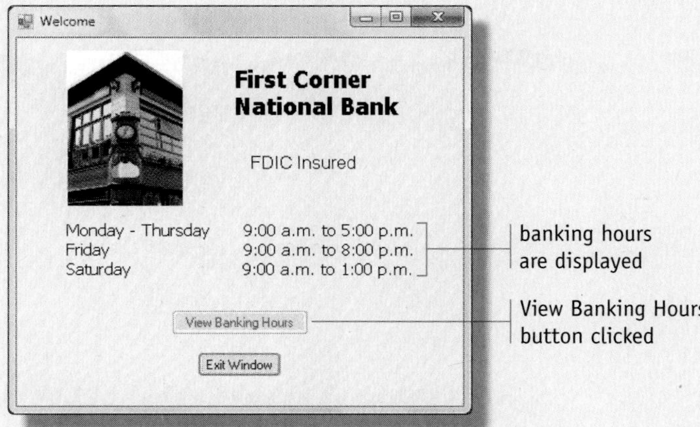

FIGURE 3-90b

Case Programming Assignments

3 • VISUAL BASIC 2010 TERMS

Based on the Windows form mock-up you created in Chapter 2, complete the Visual Basic 2010 Terms program by changing the window background color, downloading and adding the image, and writing the code that will execute according to the program requirements. Before writing the code, create an event planning document for each event in the program. The completed Windows Form object and the other objects in the user interface are shown in Figure 3-93a and Figure 3-93b.

REQUIREMENTS DOCUMENT

Date submitted: August 16, 2013

Application title: Visual Basic 2010 Terms

Purpose: This application displays the definitions of common Visual Basic terms. When the user chooses to view the definition, the term's definition is displayed.

Program Procedures: From a window on the screen, the user makes a request to see one of three VB definitions.

Algorithms, Processing, and Conditions:

1. The user first views a screen that displays three VB terms.
2. An image of a computer is displayed at the top of the window throughout the running of the application.
3. The user can select any of the three terms displayed on the buttons, and the definition appears after each selection is made.
4. The user can click any of the terminology buttons and the definition will appear. Any previous definitions will disappear.
5. An exit button is available at all times allowing the user to end the application.

Notes and Restrictions:

1. Only one definition should be displayed at a time, so if a user selects a second term, the second definition only should be displayed.

Comments:

1. The computer picture shown in the window can be found on scsite.com/vb2010/ch3/images. The name of the picture is Computer.

FIGURE 3-91

(continues)

Case Programming Assignments

Visual Basic 2010 Terms *(continued)*

USE CASE DEFINITION

1. The window opens and displays a computer image, the title (Visual Basic 2010 Terms), three buttons labeled with VB terms, and an Exit Window button. The Exit Window button is enabled.
2. User clicks each of the terminology buttons to review the definitions.
3. Program displays the definitions to the right of the buttons.
4. Only one definition shows at a time.
5. User clicks the Exit Window button to terminate the application.

FIGURE 3-92

In Figure 3-93a, no button has been clicked. In Figure 3-93b, the user has clicked the Developer button.

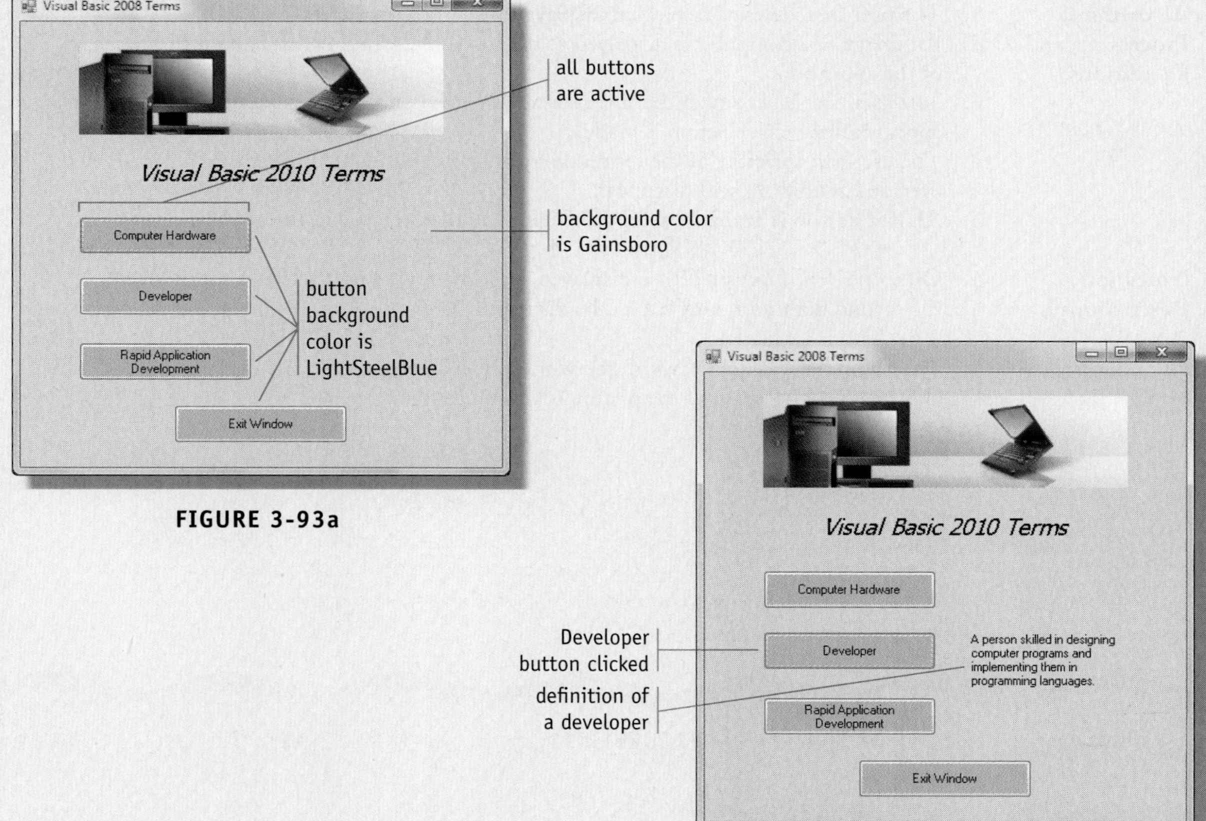

FIGURE 3-93a

FIGURE 3-93b

Case Programming Assignments

4 ●●

ONLINE STORE SPECIALS

Based on the Windows form mock-up you created in Chapter 2, complete the Online Store Specials program by finishing the user interface, downloading and adding the images, and writing the code that will execute according to the program requirements. Before writing the code, create an event planning document for each event in the program.

REQUIREMENTS DOCUMENT

Date submitted: January 6, 2014

Application title: Online Store Specials

Purpose: The online store specials program will display the daily, weekly, and holiday specials of the online store. The user can select the desired product and then add the product to the shopping cart.

Program Procedures: From a window on the screen, the user should select the daily special, the weekly special, or the holiday special. When a special is selected, the program should display a picture of the special product, the regular price of the product, and the special price of the product. The user should be able to select any special. Then, the user can add the product to the shopping cart.

Algorithms, Processing, and Conditions:

1. The user must select a special in order to display the special's product picture, regular price, and sales price.
2. The user cannot add a product to the shopping cart until a special is selected.
3. When a special is selected, only that special's picture and prices should be displayed in the window. No other special should be displayed.
4. After the user selects a special and adds it to the shopping cart, the only allowable user action is to exit the window.
5. A user should be able to exit the window at any time.

Notes and Restrictions: n/a

Comments:

1. The specials are: Daily Special: Cell Phone: Regular Price: $99.95; Special Price: $84.50
   Weekly Special: iPod Shuffle: Regular Price: $39.95: Special Price: $29.95
   Holiday Special: Digital Camera: Regular Price: $259.95; Special Price: $203.19
2. The pictures shown in the window can be found on scsite.com/vb2010/images. The names of the pictures are CellPhone, iPod, and DigitalCamera.

FIGURE 3-94

Case Programming Assignments

5 RAFFLE PRIZE SELECTION

Based on the Windows form mock-up you created in Chapter 2, complete the Raffle Prize Selection program by finishing the user interface, downloading and adding the images, and writing the code that will execute according to the program requirements. Before writing the code, create an event planning document for each event in the program.

REQUIREMENTS DOCUMENT

Date submitted: March 21, 2013

Application title: Raffle Prize Selection

Purpose: Your school has started selling raffle tickets for a scholarship fund that provides the winner a choice of raffle gifts. The winner can choose one of three prizes. So they can choose, the program must display each of the prizes upon request of the raffle winner. The winner then can make the choice of the prize he or she would like to receive.

Program Procedures: From a window on the screen, the user selects one of three raffle prizes. A picture of the prize is displayed in the window. The user then can choose the prize he or she wants to receive.

Algorithms, Processing, and Conditions:

1. The user selects a prize. Then, a picture of the prize is displayed in the window.
2. The user can select any of the three prizes. Only the picture for the selected prize should be displayed.
3. The user can select prizes back and forth to see the pictures for the prizes.
4. After the user finds a prize he or she wants, the user chooses that prize for delivery.
5. After the user chooses a prize, a message stating that a raffle prize has been chosen should be displayed.
6. After the user chooses a prize, the only allowable action is to exit the window.

Notes and Restrictions:

1. The user should not be able to choose a prize until they have viewed the picture of at least one raffle prize.

Comments:

1. The raffle prizes available are a gas grill, a flat-screen television, and a laptop.
2. The pictures shown in the window can be found on scsite.com/vb2010/ch3/images. The names of the pictures are Grill, TV, and Laptop.

FIGURE 3-95

Case Programming Assignments

6 ●● SONG VOTING

Based on the Windows form mock-up you created in Chapter 2, complete the Song Voting program by finishing the user interface, downloading and adding the images, and writing the code that will execute according to the program requirements. Before writing the code, create an event planning document for each event in the program.

REQUIREMENTS DOCUMENT

Date submitted: February 22, 2013

Application title: Song Voting

Purpose: In your mall, a music store named "Millennium Music" wants a program that shows the #1 song in each of three music genres and allows the user to vote for his or her overall favorite. The user should be able to select one of three genres and then be able to vote for that song/genre as the user's overall favorite.

Program Procedures: From a window on the screen, the user selects one of three music genres. The name of the #1 song in the selected genre is displayed together with a picture of the artist or band for the song. Then, the user can vote for that song/genre as their overall favorite.

Algorithms, Processing, and Conditions:

1. The user selects a music genre. Then, the #1 song title in the genre and picture of the artist or band is displayed in the window.
2. The user can select any of the three music genres. Only the name of the song and the picture for the selected genre should be displayed.
3. The user can select music genres back and forth to see the #1 song for each genre and the associated artist or band.
4. After the user selects a genre, the user should be able to vote for that genre/song as the favorite. The user cannot vote until the user has selected a genre.
5. After the user votes, a message stating that voting has occurred should be displayed.
6. After the user votes, the only allowable action is to exit the window.

Notes and Restrictions:

1. The user should not be able to vote until he or she has selected a music genre.

Comments:

1. You (the developer) should select the three music genres and the #1 song for each of the genres.
2. The pictures of the artist or the band will depend on your selection of both the music genres and the #1 song in each of the genres. You should download a picture of the artist or band from the World Wide Web. You can search anywhere on the Web for the pictures. You will find that www.google.com/images is a good source.

FIGURE 3-96

Case Programming Assignments

7 ●●● ENGLISH-TO-SPANISH TRANSLATOR

Based on the problem definition (Figure 3-97) and the Windows form mock-up you created in Chapter 2, complete the English-to-Spanish translator program by finishing the user interface, downloading and adding any required images, and writing the code that will execute according to the program requirements. Before writing the code, create an event planning document for each event in the program.

The Bonita Travel Agency would like to create an English-to-Spanish translator of the most commonly used Spanish words for those booking a trip to a Spanish-speaking destination. Develop a Windows application for the Bonita Travel Spanish Translator. The English phrase should be displayed in the window. When the user selects an English phrase, the corresponding Spanish translation is displayed. Only one Spanish translation should be displayed at any given time. The user should be able to exit the window at any time.

English	Spanish Translation
Good morning	Buenos días
Thank you	Gracias
Goodbye	Adiós
Money	Dinero

FIGURE 3-97

Case Programming Assignments

8 TRAVEL SPECIALS

Based on the problem definition (Figure 3-98) and the Windows form mock-up you created in Chapter 2, complete the Travel Specials program by finishing the user interface, downloading and adding any required images, and writing the code that will execute according to the program requirements. Before writing the code, create an event planning document for each event in the program.

Your local travel agent would like a computer application to advertise the travel specials of the week from your city. This week's flight specials are:

Destination	Price
Orlando	$199 round trip
Las Vegas	$219 round trip
New Orleans	$320 round trip
Aruba	$520 round trip
Hawaii	$728 round trip

Write an application that will allow the user to select any of the five vacation destinations. When the user selects a vacation destination, the corresponding price and a picture of the destination should be displayed. Clear each prior price and picture when the user selects a different vacation destination. In addition to a picture of the destination, include a Web page address that features the selected location. After the user has selected a destination, the user should be able to book the vacation and then exit the window.

FIGURE 3-98

Case Programming Assignments

9 ●●● FOOTBALL TICKETS

Based on the problem definition (Figure 3-99) and the Windows form mock-up you created in Chapter 2, complete the Football Tickets program by finishing the user interface, downloading and adding any required images, and writing the code that will execute according to the program requirements. Before writing the code, create an event planning document for each event in the program.

Your favorite university football team has asked you to develop a Windows application that allows the user to see the four types of seat ticket types offered, one at a time. Then, the user should be able to reserve a single game ticket for the seat type. The four types of stadium seating and their base prices are as follows:

Name of Service	Minimum Price
Upper Endzone Seating	$75.00
Lower Endzone Seating	$100.00
Sideline seating	$150.00
Club Seats	$500.00

For each type of seating, your program should display the base price and a picture depicting an example of the seating type. Clear each seating price and picture when the user selects a different seating type. After the user has selected a ticket, the user should be able to purchase the ticket and then exit the window.

FIGURE 3-99

CHAPTER 4

Variables and Arithmetic Operations

OBJECTIVES

You will have mastered the material in this chapter when you can:

- Create, modify, and program a TextBox object
- Use code to place data in the Text property of a Label object
- Use the AcceptButton and CancelButton properties
- Understand and declare String and Numeric variables
- Use assignments statements to place data in variables
- Use literals and constants in coding statements
- Understand scope rules for variables
- Convert string and numeric data
- Understand and use arithmetic operators and arithmetic operations
- Format and display numeric data as a string
- Create a form load event
- Create a concatenated string
- Debug a program

Introduction

In the Hotel Room Selection program developed in Chapter 2 and Chapter 3, when the user clicked buttons in the user interface, events were triggered; but the user did not enter data. In many applications, users must enter data and then the program uses the data in its processing.

When processing data entered by a user, a common requirement is to perform arithmetic operations on the data in order to generate useful output information. Arithmetic operations include adding, subtracting, multiplying, and dividing numeric data.

To illustrate the use of user data input and arithmetic operations, the application in this chapter allows the user to enter the number of songs to be downloaded from the World Wide Web. The application then calculates the total cost of the downloads. The user interface for the program is shown in Figure 4-1.

FIGURE 4-1

ONLINE REINFORCEMENT

To view a video of program execution, visit scsite.com/vb2010/ch4 and then select Figure 4-1. Turn on your speakers to listen to the audio walk-through of the steps.

In Figure 4-1, the user entered 5 as the number of songs to download. When the user clicked the Calculate Cost button, the program multiplied 5 times the cost per song (99 cents) and then displayed the result as the total cost of downloads. When the user clicks the Clear button, the values for the number of song downloads and the total cost of downloads are cleared so the next user can enter a value. Clicking the Exit button closes the window and terminates the program.

To create this application, the developer must understand how to perform the following processes, among others:

1. Define a text box for data entry.
2. Define a label to hold the results of arithmetic operations.
3. Convert data in a text box to data that can be used for arithmetic operations.
4. Perform arithmetic operations on data a user enters.

The following pages describe the tools and techniques required to create the program shown in Figure 4-1.

User Interface

As you have learned in Chapter 2 and Chapter 3, after the program requirements document for an application has been completed, the first step is to define the graphical user interface. In this chapter, three new elements are introduced:

1. TextBox objects
2. Labels intended for variable text property values
3. Accept buttons

Each of these elements is described in the following sections:

TextBox Objects

A **TextBox object** allows users to enter data into a program. In Figure 4-2, the user can enter a value into the text box.

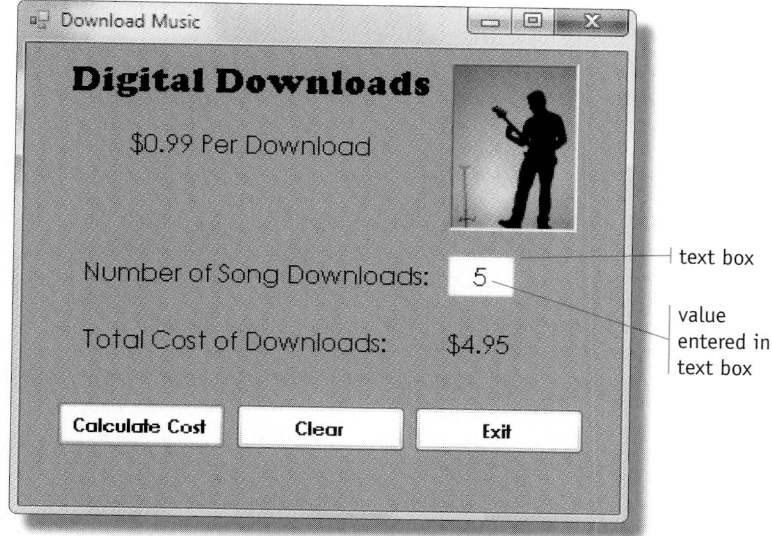

FIGURE 4-2

In Figure 4-2, the TextBox object is placed on the Windows Form object. A TextBox object automatically allows the user to enter data into the text box. To place a TextBox object on the Windows Form object, you can complete the steps on the following pages. (Note: The examples in this chapter illustrate new objects in the user interface. Portions of the user interface have already been completed. You should not expect to "click along" with these examples unless you create these elements or unless you follow the steps using an unformatted user interface.)

STEP 1 With Visual Studio open and the frmDigitalDownloads.vb [Design] tabbed page visible, point to the TextBox .NET component in the Toolbox.

The TextBox .NET component is highlighted in the Toolbox (Figure 4-3).

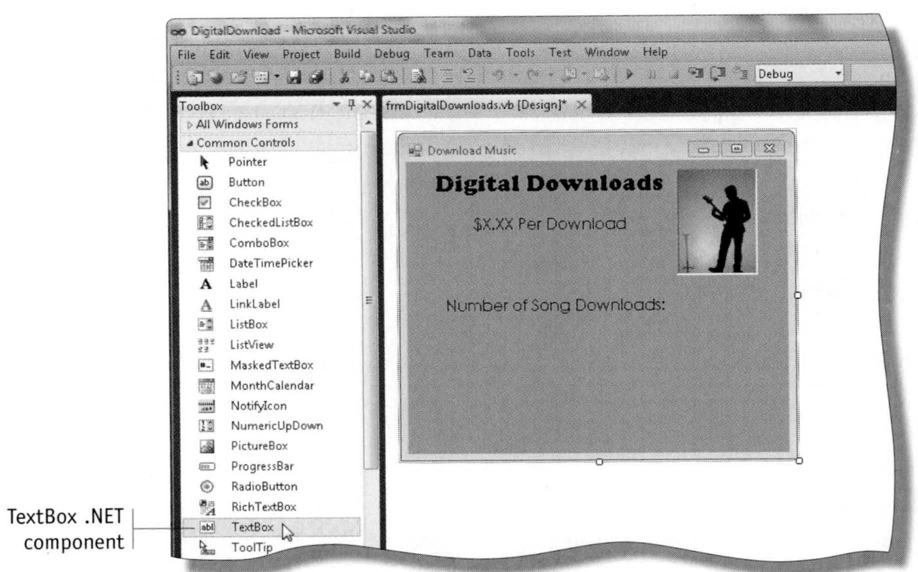

FIGURE 4-3

STEP 2 Drag the TextBox .NET component onto the Windows Form object at the desired location.

While you drag, the mouse pointer changes to indicate a TextBox object will be placed on the Windows Form object (Figure 4-4). Snap lines indicate where the TextBox object aligns with other objects on the Windows Form object. In Figure 4-4, the top of the TextBox object aligns with the top of the Label object. When adding a TextBox object to the Windows Form object, top alignment often provides a good beginning position.

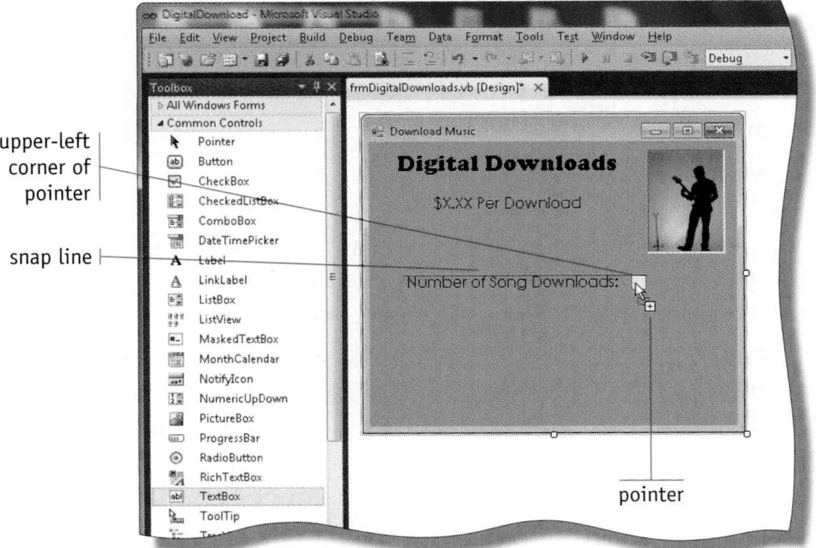

FIGURE 4-4

STEP 3 When the upper-left corner of the pointer is located where you want the TextBox object's upper-left corner, release the left mouse button.

Visual Studio places the TextBox object at the location identified by the mouse pointer (Figure 4-5). The default size of the TextBox object is 100 pixels wide by 20 pixels high. Notice that by default the TextBox object contains no text. You can change that by entering text in the Text property of the TextBox object.

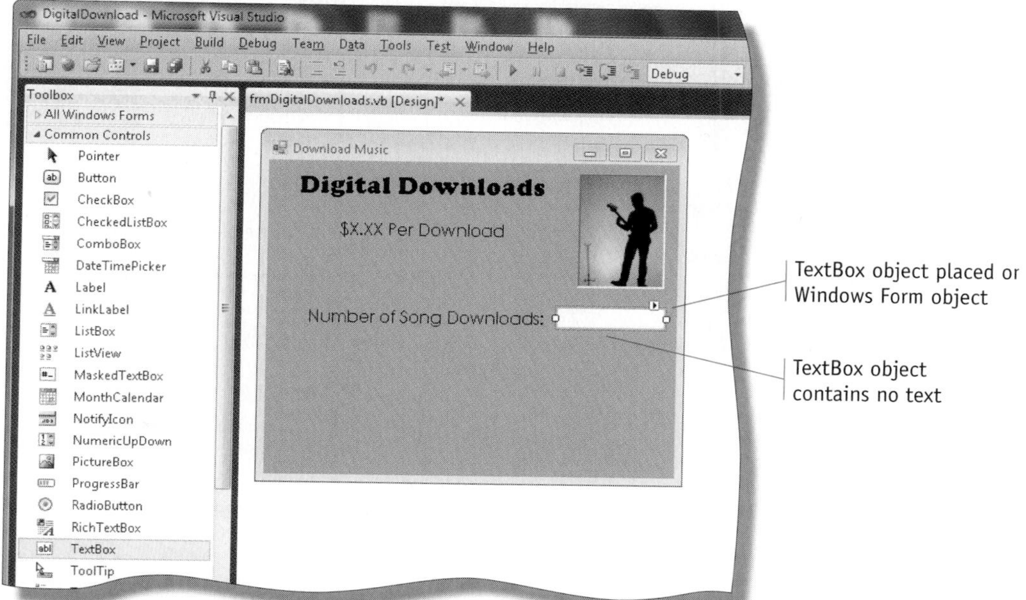

FIGURE 4-5

ONLINE REINFORCEMENT

To view a video of the process in the previous steps, visit scsite.com/vb2010/ch4 and then select Figure 4-3.

As you have learned, whenever you place an object on the Windows Form object, you must name the object. When naming a TextBox object, the prefix should be txt. Therefore, the name of the TextBox object in Figure 4-5 could be txtNumberOfDownloads.

Sizing and Positioning a TextBox Object

To properly place a TextBox object on the Windows Form object, you need to know the minimum and maximum size of the text box. The minimum size of the text box normally is determined by the maximum number of characters the user will enter into the text box. For example, if in the sample program the maximum number of downloads the user should order is 999, the minimum size of the text box must be large enough to display three numbers. Although it can be larger, it should not be smaller.

The maximum size of the text box often is determined by the design of the user interface; that is, the size should look and feel good in the user interface. To determine the minimum size of the text box, you can use the technique on the following pages:

STEP 1 Select the TextBox object. Select the (Name) property and name the TextBox object txtNumberOfDownloads. Scroll in the Properties window until the Text property is visible and then click the right column for the Text property.

The TextBox object is selected, as shown by the thick border and sizing handles (Figure 4-6). The Textbox object is named txtNumberOfDownloads. The Text property for the TextBox object is highlighted and the insertion point indicates you can enter text for the Text property.

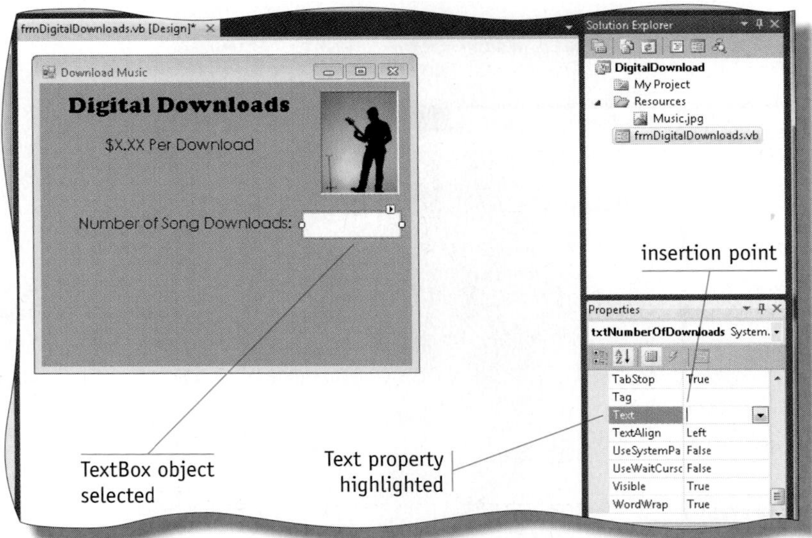

FIGURE 4-6

STEP 2 Type the maximum number of characters the user normally will enter into the text box and then press the ENTER key. When entering numbers, the digit 8 often is entered because it is wider than other digits. In this example, the value 888 is entered because three digits is the maximum number of digits the user normally will enter.

When the value is entered in the Text property of the TextBox object, the value is displayed in the TextBox object (Figure 4-7).

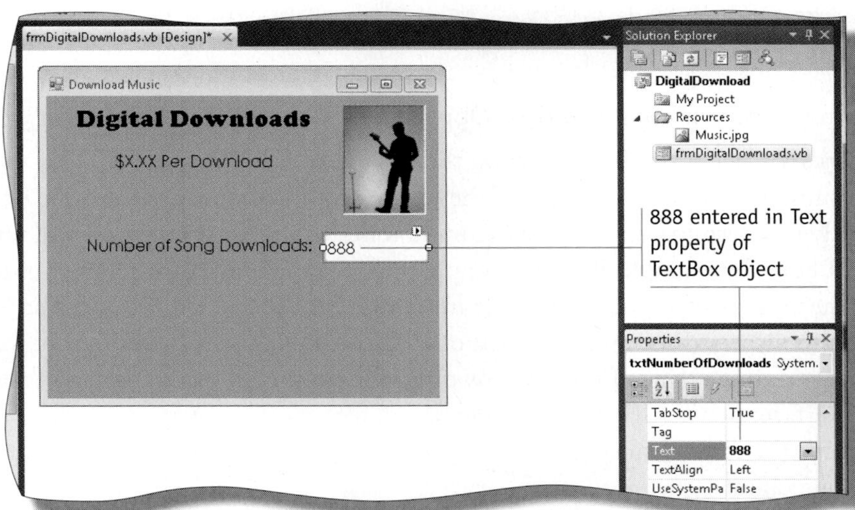

FIGURE 4-7

STEP 3 Using the Font property in the Properties window, change the Font property to the correct font and font size. For this application, change the font to Century Gothic and change the font size to 12. Then, drag the right edge of the TextBox object to resize the TextBox object so it is slightly wider than the 888 entry.

As you drag, the size of the TextBox object changes (Figure 4-8). When you release the left mouse button, the text box will be resized. When the font size is changed, the horizontal alignment of the text will change.

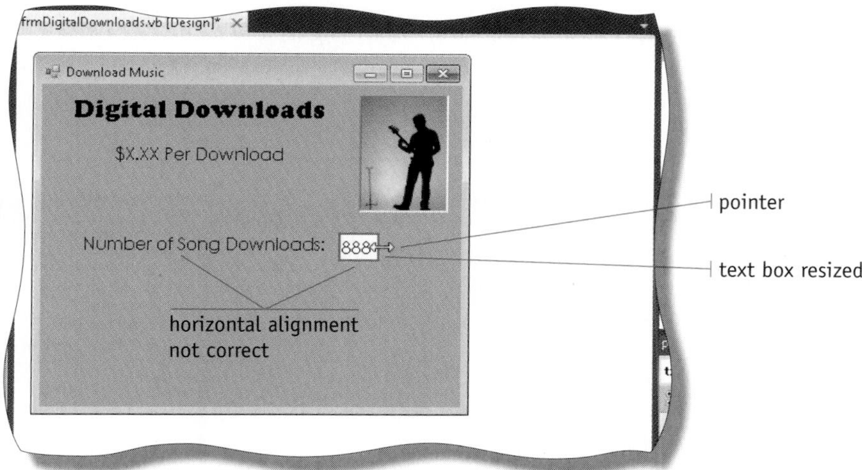

FIGURE 4-8

STEP 4 To horizontally align the text in the label and the text in the text box, drag the text box up until a red snap line indicates the bottoms of the text are aligned (Figure 4-9). Then, release the left mouse button.

When you drag the TextBox object, the red snap line indicates when the bottoms of the text are aligned (Figure 4-9). When you release the left mouse button, the TextBox object will be placed so the bottoms of the text are aligned.

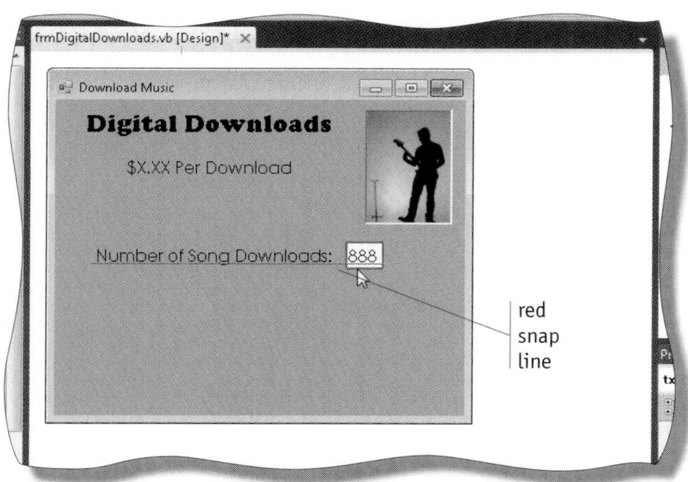

FIGURE 4-9

ONLINE REINFORCEMENT

To view a video of the process in the previous steps, visit scsite.com/vb2010/ch4 and then select Figure 4-6.

Aligning Text in a TextBox Object

In Figure 4-9, the numbers are left-aligned in the text box. Often, the user interface will be more useful if the value the user enters is centered in the text box. To align the text in a TextBox object, you can use the following method:

STEP 1 Select the TextBox object. In the Properties window, scroll until the TextAlign property is visible, click the TextAlign property in the left column, and then click the list arrow in the right column of the TextAlign property.

The TextAlign property list contains the values Left, Right, and Center (Figure 4-10).

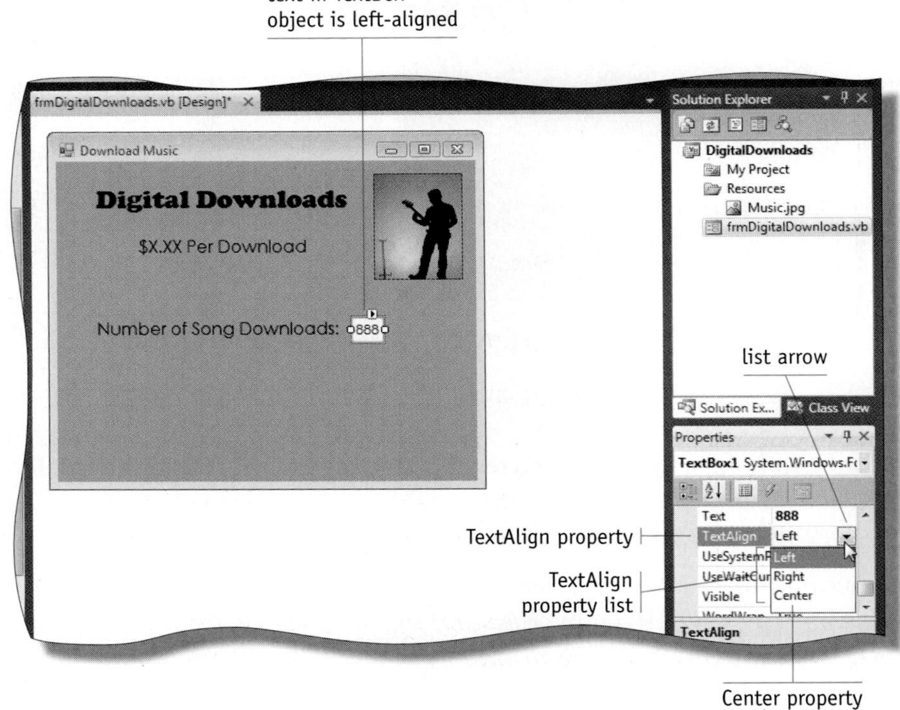

FIGURE 4-10

STEP 2 Click Center in the TextAlign property list.

The text in the TextBox object is centered (Figure 4-11). When a user enters data into the text box, the text also will be centered.

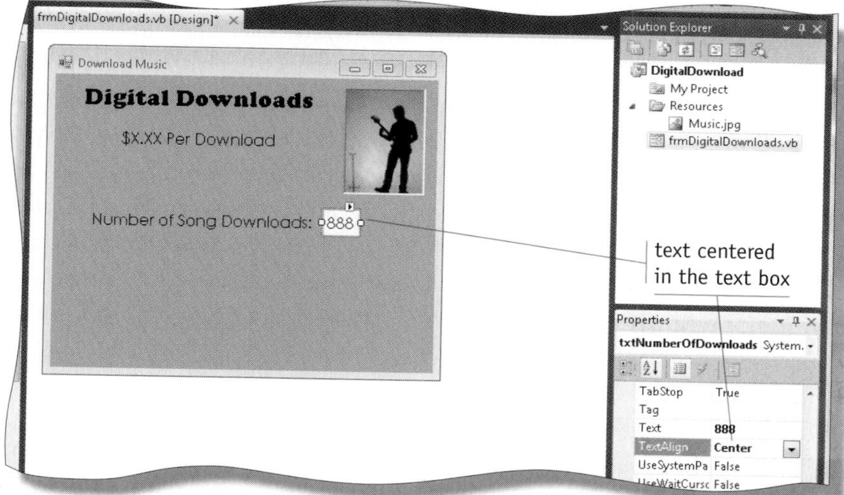

FIGURE 4-11

STEP 3 Because the TextBox object is sized properly, remove the digits in the TextBox object. Select the characters 888 in the Text property, press the DELETE key on your keyboard, and then press the ENTER key.

The TextBox object contains no text and is ready for use in the user interface (Figure 4-12).

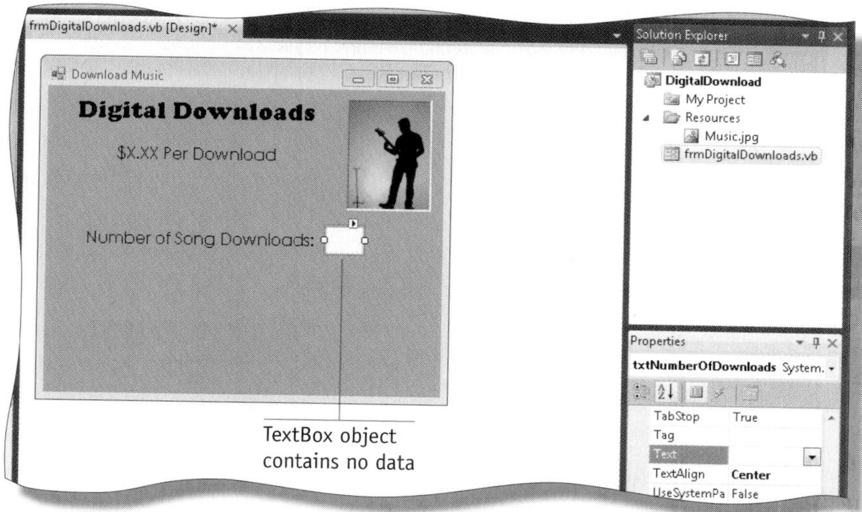

FIGURE 4-12

ONLINE REINFORCEMENT

To view a video of the process in the previous steps, visit scsite.com/vb2010/ch4 and then select Figure 4-10.

Entering Data in a TextBox Object

When the program is executed, the user can enter data in the text box. Users can enter both numbers and characters. In a text box, the user can enter many characters even though the program expects to find only a few. If the user enters more characters than can be displayed in the text box, the characters already entered scroll to the left and no longer are visible. A text box does not contain a scroll bar, so if a user enters more characters than can be visible in the text box, the user must move the insertion point left or right with the arrow keys on the keyboard to view the data in the text box. In most situations, a user should not enter more characters than are expected, and the text box should be designed to display all the characters that are expected.

In a default text box, only a single line of text can be entered regardless of the number of characters entered. A special option for a text box can be selected to allow the user to enter multiple lines of text. Additionally, the MaskedTextBox object can be used to control the format of the data a user enters. These types of text boxes are explained in the following sections.

Creating a MultiLine Text Box

A MultiLine text box allows the user to enter multiple lines in the text box. The TextBox object must be resized vertically to display the multiple lines. To create a TextBox object that can accept multiple lines, you can complete the following step:

STEP 1 Select the TextBox object, click the Action tag, and point to the MultiLine check box.

The TextBox Tasks list is displayed with the MultiLine check box (Figure 4-13). When you click the MultiLine check box, the TextBox object will be able to accept multiple lines.

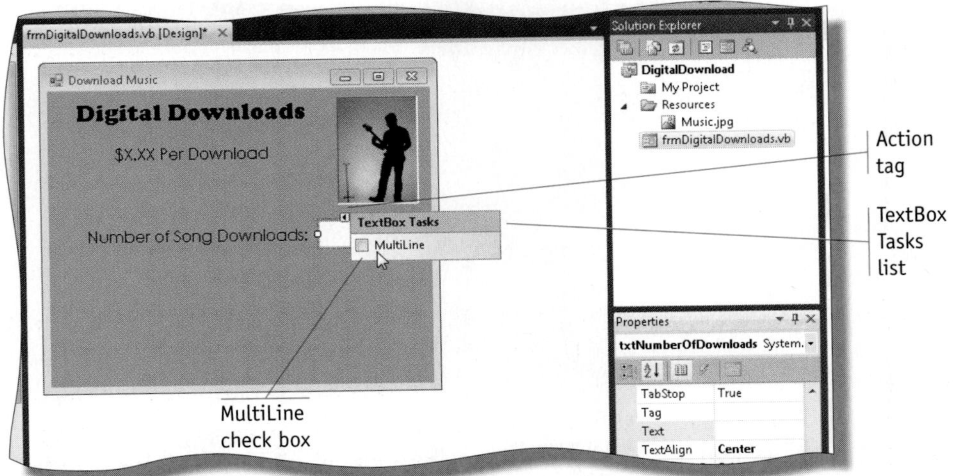

FIGURE 4-13

STEP 2 Click the MultiLine check box.

The text box is enabled to accept multiple lines.

In addition to enabling multiple lines, you should increase the vertical size of the TextBox object so the multiple lines will be visible when the user enters them.

ONLINE REINFORCEMENT

To view a video of the process in the previous steps, visit scsite.com/vb2010/ch4 and then select Figure 4-13.

Creating a MaskedTextBox Object

The MaskedTextBox object allows you to specify the data format of the value typed into the text box. Using the MaskedTextBox object removes confusion concerning what format should be used for the data the user enters. The term, mask, refers to a predefined layout for the data a user must enter. Figure 4-14 shows three examples of the use of the MaskedTextBox for the Short date input mask, the Phone number input mask, and the Social Security number input mask.

Prior to Data Entry

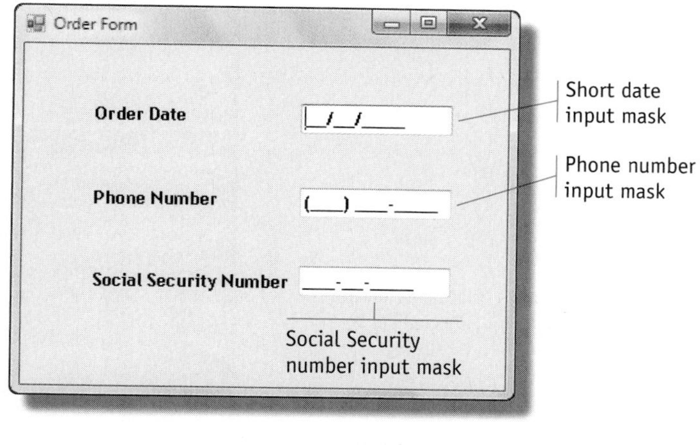

After Data Entry

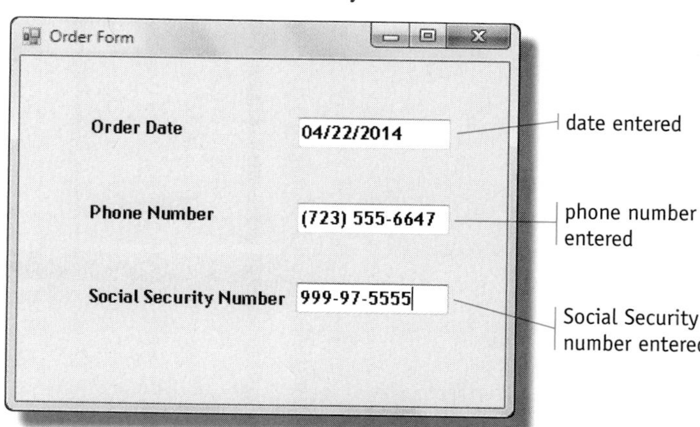

FIGURE 4-14

In Figure 4-14, before the user enters data the mask demonstrates to the user the format of the data to be entered. To enter data, the user merely selects the text box and then types data into the text box. The user need not enter any punctuation or any spacing. Therefore, to enter the date in the Order Date text box, the user typed 04222012, with no spaces, punctuation, or other keystrokes. Similarly, for the phone number, the user typed 7235556647, again with no spaces or other keystrokes. For the Social Security number, the user typed 999975555.

ONLINE REINFORCEMENT

To view a video of the process in the previous figure, visit scsite.com/vb2010/ch4 and then select Figure 4-14.

To place a MaskedTextBox object on the Windows Form object, you can complete the following steps:

STEP 1 Drag a MaskedTextBox .NET component from the Toolbox to the Windows Form object. Then, click the Action tag on the TextBox object and point to the Set Mask command.

The MaskedTextBox object is placed on the Windows Form object (Figure 4-15). When the Action button is clicked, the MaskedTextBoxTasks list is displayed. The Set Mask command is the only command in the list.

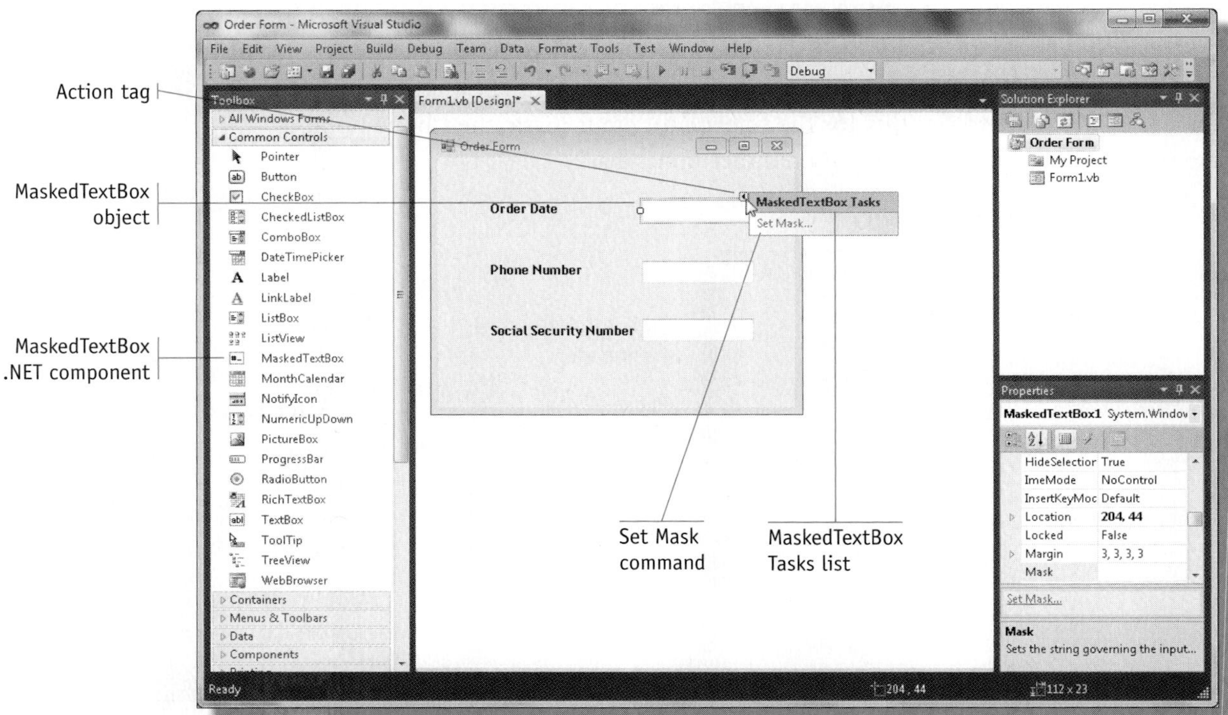

FIGURE 4-15

STEP 2 Click Set Mask on the MaskedTextBox Tasks list and then click the Short date mask description in the Input Mask dialog box.

Visual Studio displays the Input Mask dialog box (Figure 4-16). The Mask Description column contains all the masks that can be used for the MaskedTextBox object. The Short date mask description is highlighted. In the Preview box, you can type data to see how the mask will perform when it is used in the MaskedTextBox object. The Use Validating Type check box is selected so the object will verify the user entered valid numeric data.

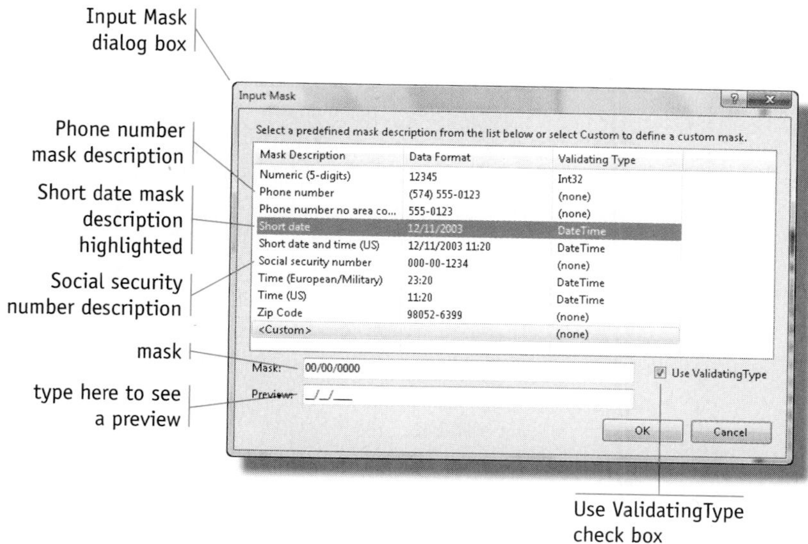

FIGURE 4-16

STEP 3 Click the OK button in the Input Mask dialog box and then click anywhere in the Windows Form object.

The mask is placed in the MaskedTextBox object (Figure 4-17).

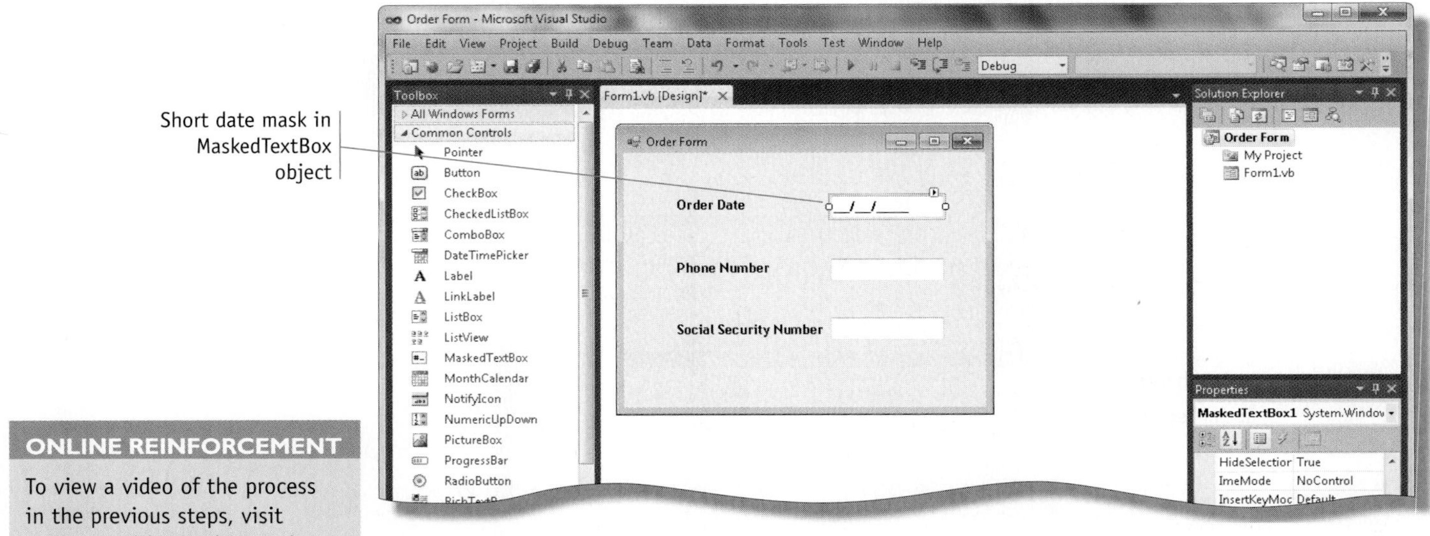

ONLINE REINFORCEMENT

To view a video of the process in the previous steps, visit scsite.com/vb2010/ch4 and then select Figure 4-15.

FIGURE 4-17

You can use the same technique to place the Phone number and Social Security number in the MaskedTextBox.

Label Objects

In the sample program, a Label object is used to display the total cost of downloads (see Figure 4-1 on page 196). The developer must accomplish two tasks to prepare the label for this purpose: a) Place the label on the Windows Form object at the correct location; b) Ensure that when the Label object contains its maximum value, its location on the Windows Form object will work within the user interface design.

To accomplish these two tasks, you can complete the steps on the following page:

STEP 1 Drag a Label object onto the Windows Form object to the correct location. Name the label lblTotalCostOfDownloads. Change the label to the appropriate font size (Century Gothic, 12 point). In the Text property for the Label object, enter the maximum number of characters ($888.88) that will appear in the label during execution of the program.

The properly sized characters appear in the label (Figure 4-18). The label is aligned vertically, but should be moved up to align horizontally with the Total Cost of Downloads label.

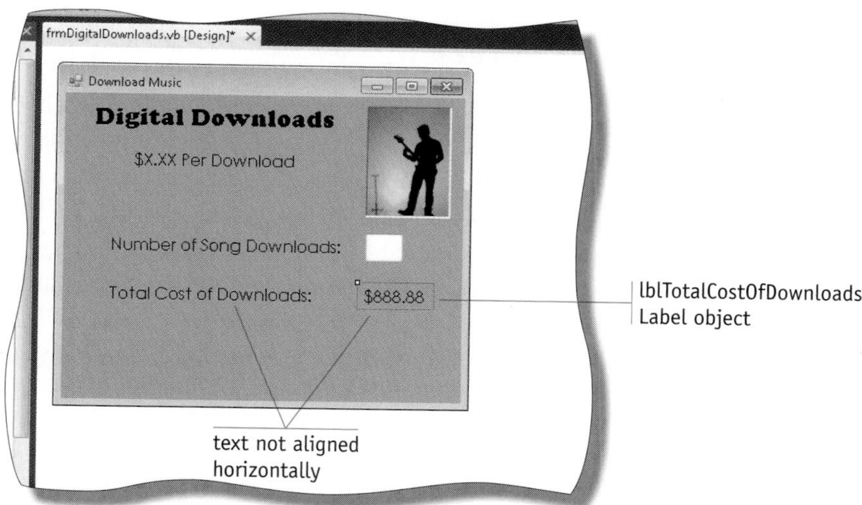

FIGURE 4-18

STEP 2 Drag the Label object up until the red snap line appears (Figure 4-19). Then release the left mouse button.

The label is aligned (Figure 4-19).

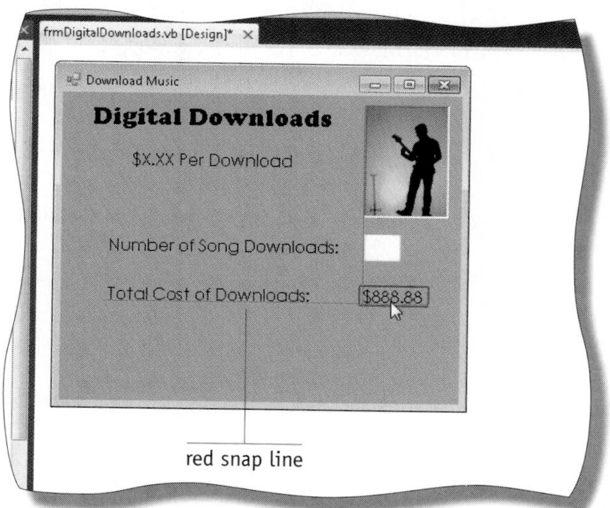

FIGURE 4-19

ONLINE REINFORCEMENT

To view a video of the process in the previous steps, visit scsite.com/vb2010/ch4 and then select Figure 4-18.

When program execution begins (see Figure 4-1 on page 196), the label that will contain the total cost of downloads should be blank. In Figure 4-19, however, it contains the value in the Text property of the Label object ($888.88). If the Text property in a Label object is set to no content, the Label object will not be displayed in the Windows Form object during design time, which makes the Label object difficult to work with in Design mode. Therefore, most designers place a value in the Text property of the Label object and leave it there during user interface design. Then, when program execution begins, the Label Text property will be set to blank. You will learn to do this later in this chapter.

Accept Button in Form Properties

Computer users often press the ENTER key to enter data into a text box and cause processing to occur. For example, in the sample program for this chapter, instead of typing the number of downloads and clicking the Calculate Cost button, users might prefer to have the option of typing the number of downloads and pressing the ENTER key.

You can assign a button in the user interface to be an Accept button, which means the program will carry out the event handler processing associated with the button if the user clicks the button or if the user presses the ENTER key. To assign the Calculate Cost button as the Accept button, you can complete the following steps:

STEP 1 Click a blank area in the Windows Form object to select it. Scroll in the Properties window until the AcceptButton property is visible. Click the AcceptButton property name in the left column and then click the AcceptButton property list arrow in the right column.

The AcceptButton property list displays the names of the Button objects on the selected Windows Form object (Figure 4-20). Any of these buttons can be chosen as the Accept button.

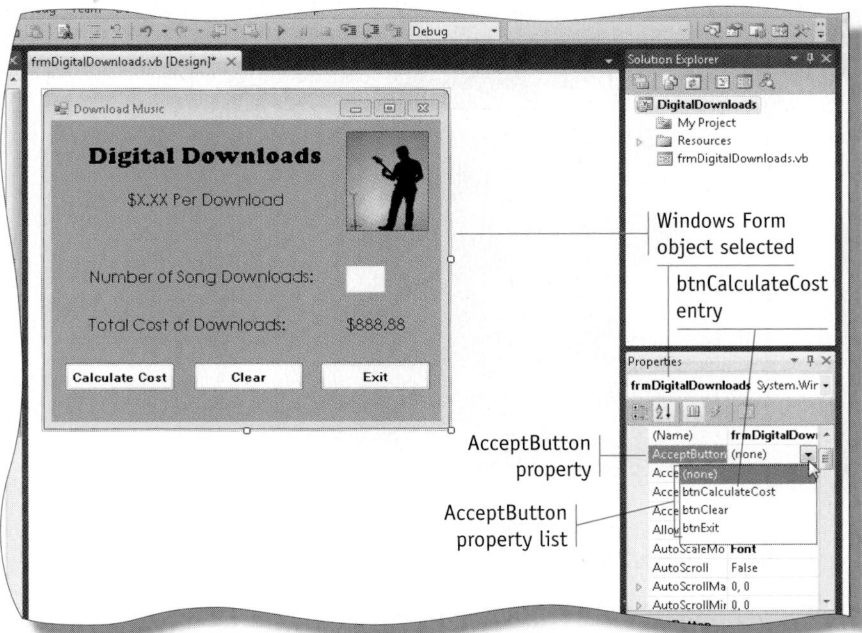

FIGURE 4-20

STEP 2 Click btnCalculateCost in the AcceptButton property list.

The btnCalculateCost Button object is designated as the Accept button. When the program is running, the user can press the ENTER key after entering data and the event handler processing for the Calculate Cost button will be executed.

ONLINE REINFORCEMENT

To view a video of the process in the previous steps, visit scsite.com/vb2010/ch4 and then select Figure 4-20.

Cancel Button in Form Properties

In the same manner as the Accept button, you can designate a Cancel button for the Windows Form object. When the user presses the ESC key, the event handler processing for the button identified as the Cancel button will be executed. In the sample program, the Cancel button will be used to clear the text box and the total cost of downloads, and place the insertion point in the text box. Thus, it performs the same activity as if the user clicks the Clear button. To specify the Cancel button for the sample program, you complete the following steps.

Step 1: Click a blank area in the Windows Form object to select it.
Step 2: Click the CancelButton property name in the left column in the Properties window for the Windows Form object, and then click the CancelButton list arrow.
Step 3: Click the button name (btnClear) in the CancelButton property list.

When the program is executed, the user can press the ESC key to perform the same processing as when the Clear button is clicked.

Visual Studio Preparation for Code Entry

When designing and creating the user interface, the Toolbox in Visual Studio 2010 provides the objects that you can place in the interface. When writing the code in the code editing window, however, the Toolbox is of little use. Therefore, many developers close the Toolbox when writing code in order to increase the space used for coding. To close the Toolbox, you can complete the step on the following page:

STEP 1 With the Toolbox visible (see Figure 4-21), click the Toolbox Close button. The Toolbox closes and the work area expands in size. To reshow the Toolbox after it has been closed, click the Toolbox button on the Standard toolbar.

Figure 4-21 illustrates the screen before the Toolbox is closed. The Toolbox Close button is visible. When the Toolbox is closed, clicking the Toolbox button on the Standard toolbar will open the Toolbox.

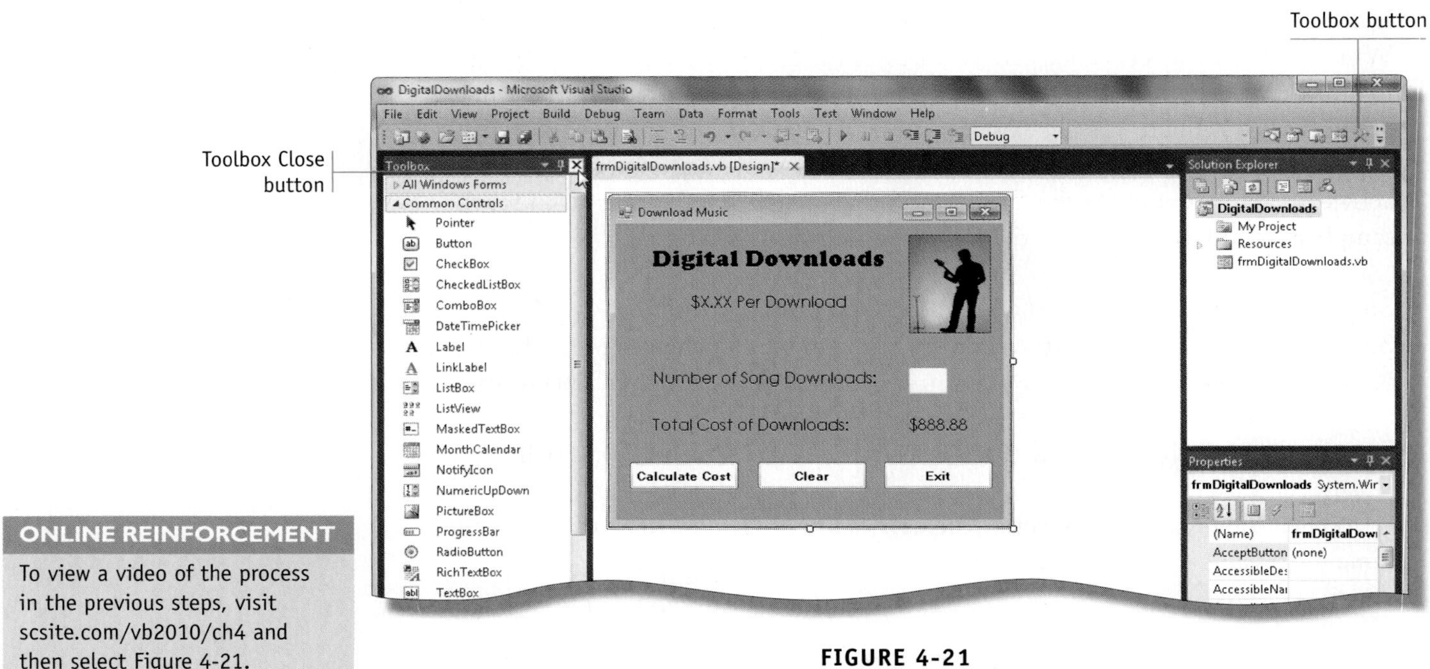

FIGURE 4-21

ONLINE REINFORCEMENT

To view a video of the process in the previous steps, visit scsite.com/vb2010/ch4 and then select Figure 4-21.

In the following sections, the Toolbox has been closed in the windows that show code.

Introduction to Data Entry and Data Types

As you have seen, the user can enter data into the program through the use of the TextBox object. When the user enters the data, the data becomes the value stored in the Text property of the object. For example, if the user enters the value 15 as the number of downloads, the Text property for the txtNumberOfDownloads TextBox object will contain the value 15.

String Data Type

Whenever data is stored in RAM, it is stored as a particular data type. Each data type allows data to be used in a specific manner. For example, to add two values together, the values must be stored in one of the numeric data types. The data type for the value the user enters in a TextBox object and that is stored in the Text property of the TextBox object is string. A **String** data type allows every character available on the computer to be stored in it.

When the user enters data into a TextBox object, often it is good programming style to copy the value entered from the Text property of the TextBox object to a String variable. A **variable** is a named location in RAM where data is stored. A **String variable** is a named location in RAM that can store a string value. Thus, a person's name, a dollar amount, a telephone number, or the number of song downloads can be stored in a String variable.

A variable is defined in the coding of the program. The statement in Figure 4-22 defines a string.

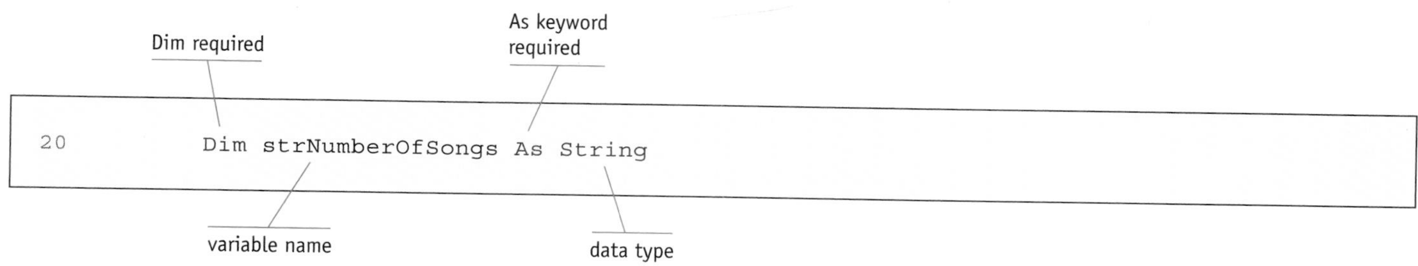

FIGURE 4-22

To begin the statement, the keyword Dim is required. This keyword stands for variable dimension. It indicates to the Visual Basic compiler that the entries that follow it are defining a variable.

The next entry is the variable name. Every variable must have a name so it can be referenced in other statements within the program. By convention, every String variable name begins with the letters, str, followed by a descriptive name. The name in Figure 4-22 (strNumberOfSongs) indicates the variable is a String variable that will contain the number of songs entered by the user.

The keyword As must follow the name of the variable as shown in Figure 4-22. If it is not included, a compilation error will occur. Following the word As is the declaration for the data type of variable being defined. In Figure 4-22, the data type is specified as String.

As a result of the statement in Figure 4-22, when the program is compiled, the Visual Basic compiler will allocate an area in RAM that is reserved to contain the value in the string.

VARIABLE NAME RULES

Variable names used in Visual Basic must follow a few simple rules: 1) The name must begin with a letter or an underline symbol (_); 2) The name can contain letters, numbers, and the underline symbol. It cannot contain spaces or other special characters; 3) No Visual Basic reserved words (words that appear in blue in the code editing window) can be used for variable names.

> **HEADS UP**
>
> When defining variables, good programming practice dictates that the variable names you use should reflect the actual values to be placed in the variable. That way, anyone reading the program code can easily understand the use of the variable. For example, a good variable name for a string variable that will contain an employee's last name would be strEmployeeLastName. Names you should not use include strXXX, strLN, strEmp, or strName. Each of these names is imprecise and potentially misleading. You should consider the people who will be reading your code when you name the variables in your program. Your goal must be to make the task of reading your code as clear and easy as possible.

The general format to define any variable is shown in Figure 4-23.

General Format: Define a Variable

```
Dim VariableName As DataType
```

EXAMPLE	*RESULT*
Dim strNumberOfSongs As String	String variable
Dim intNumberOfSongs As Integer	Integer variable
Dim decFinalCosts As Decimal	Decimal variable

FIGURE 4-23

The Integer and Decimal variables defined as examples in Figure 4-23 are numeric variables. You will learn about numeric variables shortly.

Assignment Statements

When a variable is defined as shown in Figure 4-22, the variable does not contain any data. One method to place data in the variable is to use an **assignment statement**. The assignment statement shown in Figure 4-24 will copy the data from the Text property of the txtNumberOfDownloads TextBox object into the strNumberOfSongs String variable.

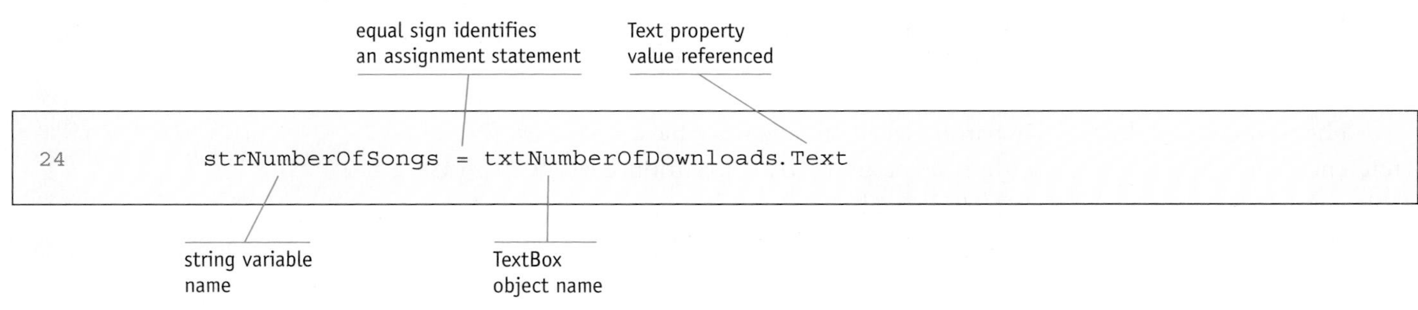

FIGURE 4-24

The variable name on the left of the assignment statement (strNumberOfSongs) identifies the variable to which a value will be copied. The equal sign indicates to the Visual Basic compiler that the statement is an assignment statement. It is required.

The value on the right of the equal sign is the value that will be copied to the variable on the left of the equal sign. In Figure 4-24, the value in the Text property of the txtNumberOfDownloads TextBox object will be copied to the strNumberOfSongs variable.

To enter the definition of the strNumberOfSongs variable and then enter the assignment statement in Figure 4-24 using IntelliSense, you can complete the following steps:

STEP 1 With Visual Studio displaying the code editing window and the insertion point located in the desired column, type `Dim` followed by a space. Then, type the name of the String variable you want to define, `strNumberOfSongs` on your keyboard.

The Dim keyword and the string name you typed are displayed in the code window (Figure 4-25). Notice the word, Dim, is blue to indicate it is a keyword.

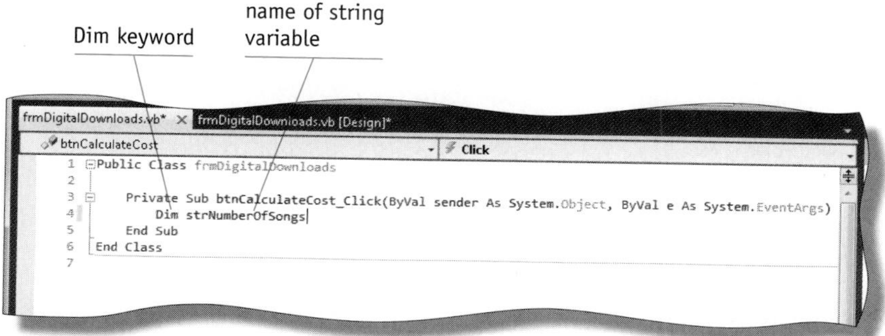

FIGURE 4-25

STEP 2 Press the SPACEBAR, type the word `As` and then press the SPACEBAR again.

The letters you typed are entered and when you typed the space following the word As, IntelliSense displayed a list (Figure 4-26). The IntelliSense list contains all the allowable entries that can follow the As keyword. To define a String variable, the entry should be String.

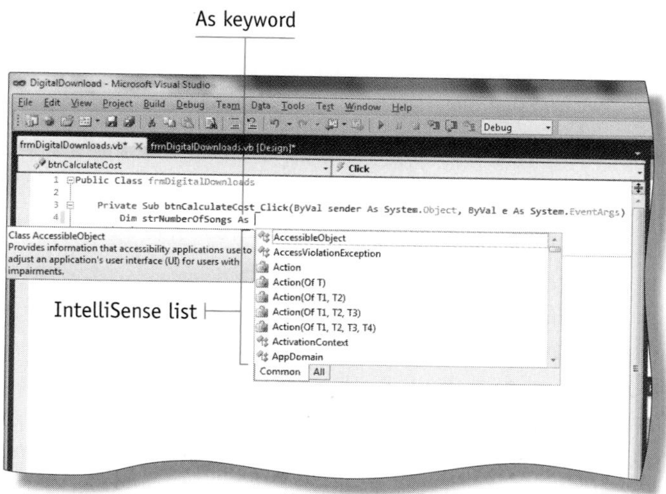

FIGURE 4-26

STEP 3 Because the entry should be String, type `str` on your keyboard.

IntelliSense highlights String in the IntelliSense list (Figure 4-27).

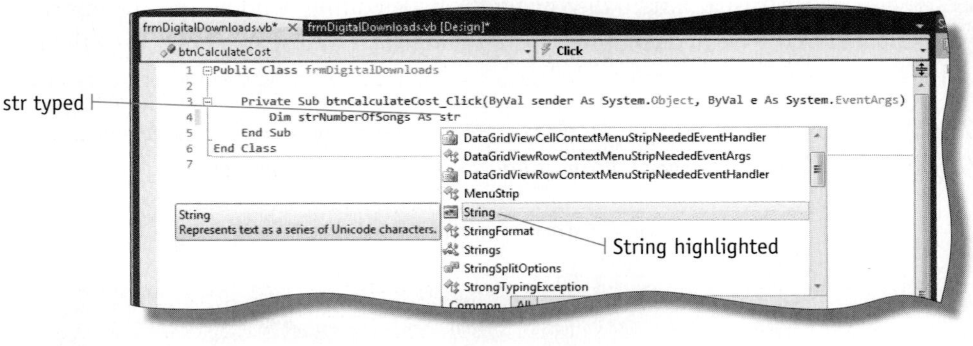

str typed

String highlighted

FIGURE 4-27

STEP 4 Press the ENTER key.

The Dim statement is entered (Figure 4-28). The green squiggly underline indicates the variable is not referenced within the program. Visual Studio will remove the line when the variable is used in an assignment statement or other statement.

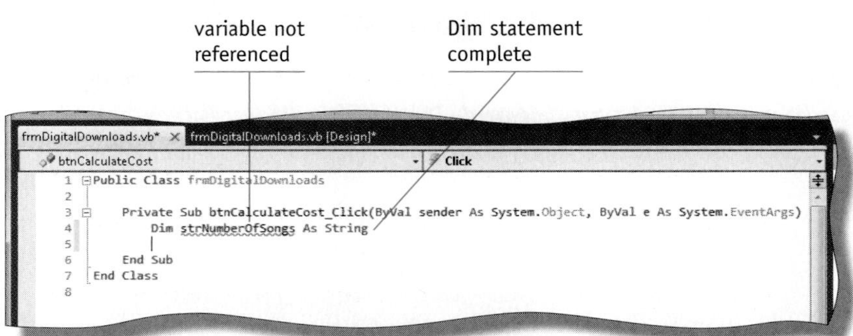
variable not referenced
Dim statement complete
frmDigitalDownloads.vb*
frmDigitalDownloads.vb [Design]*
btnCalculateCost
Click
Public Class frmDigitalDownloads
Private Sub btnCalculateCost_Click(ByVal sender As System.Object, ByVal e As System.EventArgs)
Dim strNumberOfSongs As String
End Sub
End Class

FIGURE 4-28

STEP 5 To begin the assignment statement, type `strn`. IntelliSense displays the only variable name that starts with the letters strn, the String variable strNumberOfDownloads.

IntelliSense displays a list of the entries that can be made in the statement (Figure 4-29). Whenever you want to reference a variable name in a statement, you can begin to type the first few letters of the variable name to have IntelliSense display a list of the allowable entries. The variable name strNumberOfSongs is highlighted because you typed strn.

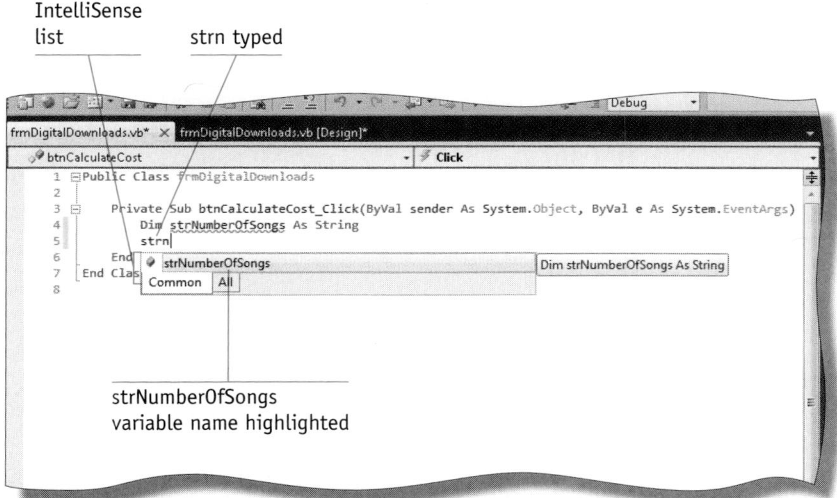

FIGURE 4-29

STEP 6 Press the SPACEBAR, press the EQUAL SIGN key, and then press the SPACEBAR.

IntelliSense enters the highlighted variable name, the spaces, and the equal sign you typed (Figure 4-30). The spaces are not required in Visual Basic but should be included in the statement for ease of reading. An IntelliSense listing automatically appears displaying the possible valid entries.

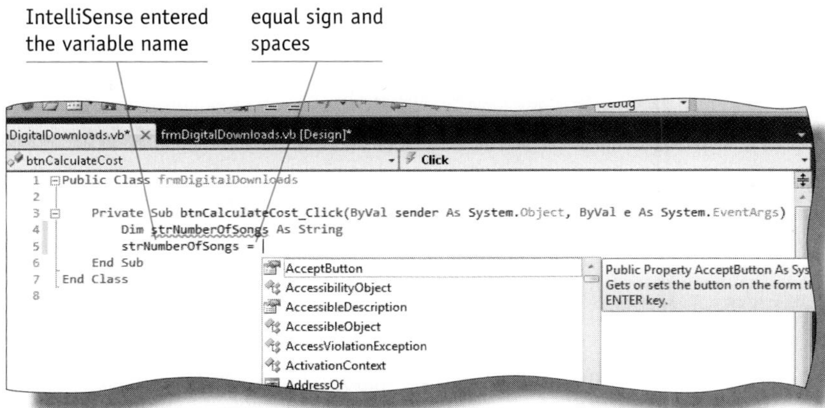

FIGURE 4-30

STEP 7 Type `txt` to display the IntelliSense list of the Form objects, and then type `n` to identify the txtNumberOfDownloads TextBox object in the IntelliSense list.

The IntelliSense list contains the valid entries for the statement; in this case only one object has the prefix of txt. The TextBox object txtNumberOfDownloads is highlighted in the list (Figure 4-31).

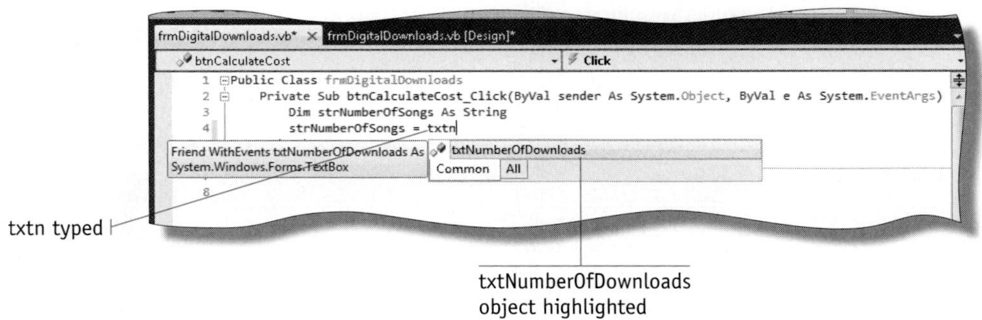

FIGURE 4-31

STEP 8 Press the PERIOD key and then, if necessary, type `te` to highlight the Text entry in the IntelliSense list.

After the dot operator (period) and the strNumberOfSongs object name are entered, Visual Studio displays the IntelliSense list (Figure 4-32). When you typed te, the Text entry was highlighted in the IntelliSense list.

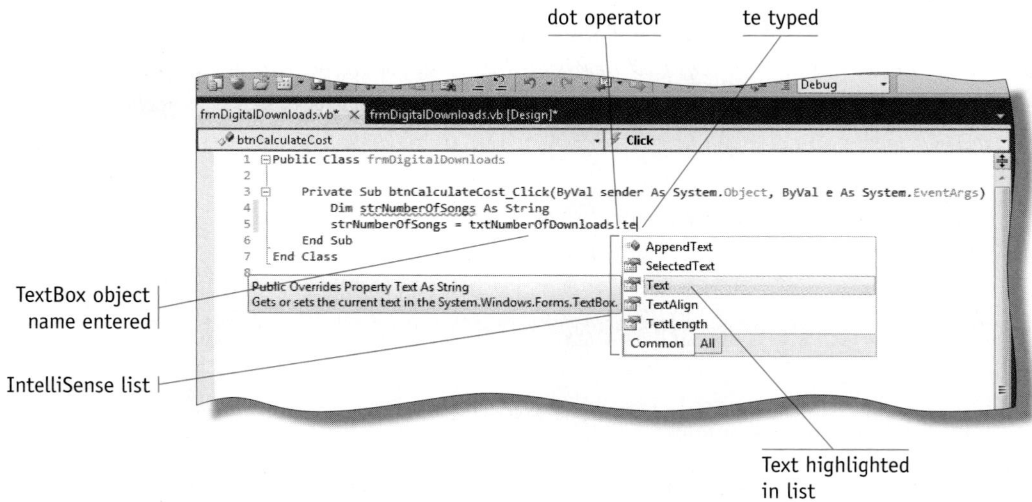

FIGURE 4-32

STEP 9 Press the ENTER key.

The assignment statement is entered (Figure 4-33). When the statement is executed, the value in the Text property of the txtNumberOfDownloads TextBox object will be copied to the location in memory identified by the strNumberOfSongs variable name. Notice also that the green squiggly lines in the Dim statement are removed because the variable now is referenced in a statement.

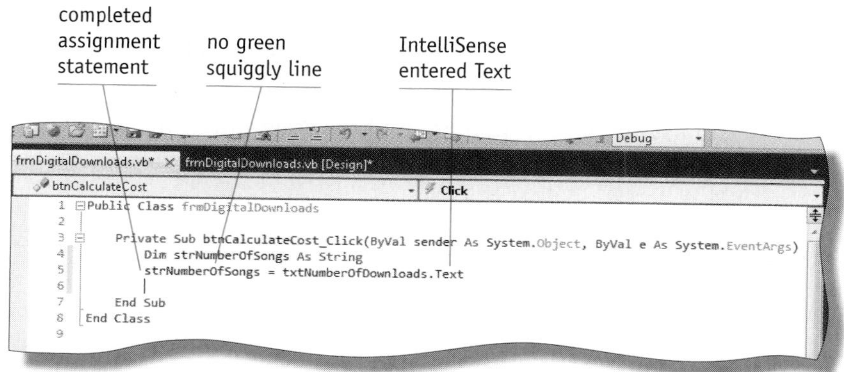
completed assignment statement
no green squiggly line
IntelliSense entered Text
Debug
frmDigitalDownloads.vb*
frmDigitalDownloads.vb [Design]*
btnCalculateCost
Click
Public Class frmDigitalDownloads
Private Sub btnCalculateCost_Click(ByVal sender As System.Object, ByVal e As System.EventArgs)
Dim strNumberOfSongs As String
strNumberOfSongs = txtNumberOfDownloads.Text
End Sub
End Class

FIGURE 4-33

> **ONLINE REINFORCEMENT**
>
> To view a video of the process in the previous steps, visit scsite.com/vb2010/ch4 and then select Figure 4-25.

You can use the method shown in the previous steps to declare a variable name and include it in assignment statements for all the variables you might define within a program. IntelliSense works the same with each variable name, regardless of the variable type.

> **HEADS UP**
>
> The rule for using IntelliSense to enter object names and variable names into a Visual Basic statement is: 1) To enter the name of an object that has been defined in the user interface, type the prefix; 2) To enter a variable name you have declared in the program, type the first few letters of the variable name to display an IntelliSense listing of possible names. In each case, IntelliSense will display a list of the allowable entries.

Numeric Data Types

As you will recall, the String data type can contain any character that can be entered or stored on a computer. String data types, however, cannot be used in arithmetic operations. A **numeric data type** must be used in arithmetic operations. So, in order to multiply two values, the values must be stored in one of the numeric data types.

Visual Basic allows a variety of numeric data types, depending on the need of the application. Each numeric data type requires a different amount of RAM in which the numeric value is stored, can contain a different type of numeric data, and can contain a different maximum range of values. The table in Figure 4-34 illustrates three widely used numeric data types. The data types are explained in the following sections.

Data Type	Sample Value	Memory Allocation	Range of Values
Integer	48	4 bytes	−2,147,483,648 to +2,147,483,647
Decimal	3.14519	16 bytes	Decimal values that may have up to 28 significant digits
Double	5.3452307 or 673.6529	8 bytes	−1.79769313486232e308 to +1.79769313486232e308

FIGURE 4-34

HEADS UP

Visual Basic 2010 now allows you to omit the data type without error. For example, entering Dim intValue = 1 does not produce an error because the compiler infers that the value of intValue is an Integer data type. This is called type inference. While you are learning beginning programming, it is best to use the data types to understand the changes as you convert one data type to another.

Integer Data Type

An **Integer data type** holds a nondecimal whole number in Visual Basic. As you can see from Figure 4-34, an Integer data type can store a value greater or less than 2 billion. Examples of an integer would be the number of songs to download, the number of credit hours you are taking in a semester, and the number of points your favorite football team scored. Notice that each of these examples is a whole number.

Normally, an Integer data type is stored in an Integer variable. An **Integer variable** identifies a location in RAM where an integer value is stored. To define an Integer variable and place a value in the variable through the use of an assignment statement, you can use the Dim statement and the assignment statement, as shown in Figure 4-35.

```
Dim intNumberOfSongs As Integer
intNumberOfSongs = 34
```

FIGURE 4-35

The Dim statement in Figure 4-35 is the similar to the Dim statement used to define the String variable (Figure 4-28 on page 216) except that the variable name begins with the prefix int; and the word Integer follows the word As. Four bytes of RAM will be reserved for any value that is stored in the intNumberOfSongs Integer variable as a result of the Dim statement in Figure 4-35.

The definition in Figure 4-35 will not place a value in the intNumberOfSongs variable. To place a value in the variable, you can use an assignment statement. The variable into which the value is to be placed (intNumberOfSongs) is entered on the left side of the equal sign, and the value to be placed in the variable (34) is entered on the right side of the equal sign. When the statement is executed, the value 34 will be copied to the RAM location identified by the variable name intNumberOfSongs.

You also can place an initial value in the variable. For example, to define an Integer variable to hold the number of credit hours you are taking, and to place the value 12 in that variable, you could write the Dim statement in Figure 4-36.


```
Dim intCreditHours As Integer = 12
```

FIGURE 4-36

The statement in Figure 4-36 defines the Integer variable named intCreditHours. The equal sign following the word Integer indicates to the Visual Basic compiler that the value to its right should be placed in the variable. As a result, the value 12 will be placed in the intCreditHours Integer variable when the program is compiled.

Decimal Data Type

A **Decimal data type** can represent accurately large or very precise decimal numbers. It is ideal for use in the accounting and scientific fields to ensure numbers keep their precision and are not subject to rounding errors. The Decimal data type can be accurate to 28 significant digits. (Significant digits are those that contribute to the precision of a number.) Often, Decimal data types are used to store dollar amounts. For example, to define the cost of downloads Decimal variable for the sample program in this chapter, the statement in Figure 4-37 can be used.

```
Dim decTotalCostOfDownloads As Decimal
```

FIGURE 4-37

The Dim statement is used to define the Decimal variable. The dec prefix is used for all Decimal variable names. When the compiler processes the statement in Figure 4-37, 16 bytes of RAM will be reserved for a value to be placed in the decTotalCostOfDownloads variable. Initially, no value will be present in the variable unless you specify a value, as shown in Figure 4-36. You can use an assignment statement to place data into the decTotalCostOfDownloads variable.

HEADS UP

A Double data type represents numbers in such a way that the number might not be precisely correct. For example, the value 0.07875 might be represented in the Double data type as 0.078749999999. Therefore, when exact precision is required, the Decimal data type is preferred over the Double data type. The advantages of the Double data type are that it can store a much larger and a much smaller number than the Decimal data type, and it requires only 8 bytes of memory for each Double variable versus 16 bytes for each Decimal variable.

Double Data Type

A **Double data type** can represent huge positive and very small negative numbers that can include values to the right of the decimal point. Sometimes, a Double data type is said to represent floating-point numbers, which means the decimal point can be anywhere within the number. The Dim statement in Figure 4-38 declares a Double variable that could be used in a tax application.

```
Dim dblTaxRate As Double
dblTaxRate = 0.07875
```

FIGURE 4-38

In Figure 4-38, the dblTaxRate Double variable is declared and then the assignment statement places the value 0.07875 in the memory location identified by the variable name. Note that a Double variable begins with the dbl prefix.

Other Data Types

Visual Basic supports a number of other data types that are used for more specialized situations. The two most widely used other types are the Char data type and the Boolean data type. These data types are summarized in the table in Figure 4-39.

Data Type	Sample Value	Memory Allocation	Range of Values
Char	A single character such as ? or M	2 bytes	Any single character
Boolean	True or False	2 bytes	True or False

FIGURE 4-39

Char Data Type

The **Char data type** represents a single keystroke such as a letter of the alphabet, punctuation, or a symbol. The prefix for a Char variable name is chr. When you assign a value to a Char variable, you must place quotation marks around the value. This is shown in Figure 4-40, where the value A is assigned to the chrTopGrade Char variable.

```
        Dim chrTopGrade As Char
        chrTopGrade = "A"
```

FIGURE 4-40

The value A in the assignment statement has quotation marks around it. In addition, Visual Studio displays the letter and the quotation marks in red text, indicating they are not Visual Basic keywords nor are they variable or object names. In fact, the value is called a literal. You will learn more about literals in a few pages.

Visual Studio allows 65,534 different characters in a program. These characters consist of numbers, letters, and punctuation symbols. In addition, a wide variety of technical characters, mathematical symbols, and worldwide textual characters are available, allowing developers to work in almost every known language, such as the Korean shown in Figure 4-41. These characters are represented by a coding system called Unicode. To learn more about Unicode, visit www.unicode.org.

유니코드에 대해 ?

어떤 플랫폼,
어떤 프로그램,
어떤 언어에도 상관없이
유니코드는 모든 문자에 대해 고유 번호를 제공합니다.

FIGURE 4-41

Even though you can assign a number to a Char variable, a Char variable cannot be used in arithmetic operations. A number to be used in an arithmetic operation must be assigned to a numeric variable.

Boolean Data Type

A Boolean data variable, whose name begins with the bln prefix, can contain a value that Visual Basic interprets as either True or False. If a variable in your program is intended to represent whether a condition is true or a condition is not true, then the variable should be a Boolean variable. In Figure 4-42, a Boolean variable called blnFullTimeStudent is declared and then the assignment statement sets the Boolean variable to True.

```
        Dim blnFullTimeStudent As Boolean
        blnFullTimeStudent = True
```

FIGURE 4-42

In Figure 4-42, the Dim statement is used to declare the blnFullTimeStudent Boolean variable. The assignment sets the Boolean variable to True. This variable can be checked in the program to determine if it is true or false, and appropriate processing can occur based on the finding.

Miscellaneous Data Types

Visual Basic also has a number of other data types that are used less often than the ones you have seen. These data types are summarized in the table in Figure 4-43.

Data Type	Sample Value	Memory Allocation	Range of Values
Byte	A whole number such as 7	1 bytes	0 to 255
Date	April 22, 2014	8 bytes	Dates and times
Long	A whole number such as 342,534,538	8 bytes	−9,223,372,036,854,775,808 through +9,223,372,036,854,775,807
Object	Holds a reference	4 bytes	A memory address
Short	A whole number such as 16,546	2 bytes	−32,786 through 32,767
Single	A number such as 312,672.3274	4 bytes	−3.4028235E+38 through 1.401298E−45 for negative values; and from 1.401298E−45 through 3.4028235E+38 for positive values

FIGURE 4-43

As a review, the prefixes for each of the data type variable names are shown in Figure 4-44.

Data Type	Prefix
String	str
Integer	int
Decimal	dec
Double	dbl
Char	chr
Boolean	bln
Byte	byt
Date	dtm
Long	lng
Short	shr
Single	sng

FIGURE 4-44

Literals

When you include a value in an assignment statement, such as in Figure 4-38 on page 221 and Figure 4-40 on page 222, this value is called a **literal** because the value being used in the assignment statement is literally the value that is required. It is not a variable. The Visual Basic compiler determines the data type of the value you have used for a literal based on the value itself. For example, if you type "Chicago," the compiler treats the literal as a String data type, while if you type 49.327, the compiler treats the literal as a Double data type. The table in Figure 4-45 displays the default literal types as determined by the Visual Basic compiler.

Standard Literal Form	Default Data Type	Example
Numeric, no fractional part	Integer	104
Numeric, no fractional part, too large for Integer data type	Long	3987925494
Numeric, fractional part	Double	0.99 8.625
Enclosed within double quotes	String	"Brittany"
Enclosed within number signs	Date	#3/17/1990 3:30 PM#

FIGURE 4-45

Forced Literal Types

Sometimes you might want a literal to be a different data type than the Visual Basic default. For example, you may want to assign the number 0.99 to a Decimal data variable to take advantage of the precision characteristics of the Decimal data type. As you can see in Figure 4-45, Visual Basic will, by default, consider the value 0.99 to be a Double data type. To define the literal as a Decimal literal, you must use special literal-type characters to force the literal to assume a data type other than the one Visual Basic uses as the default. You do this by placing the literal-type character at the end of the literal value. The table in Figure 4-46 shows the available literal-type characters, together with examples of their usage.

Literal-Type Character	Data Type	Example
S	Short	Dim shoAge As Short shoAge = 40S
I	Integer	Dim intHeight as Integer intHeight = 76I
D	Decimal	Dim decPricePerSong As Decimal decPricePerSong = 0.99D
R	Double	Dim dblWeight As Double dblWeight = 8491R
C	Char	Dim chrNumberOfDays As Char chrNumberOfDays = "7"C

FIGURE 4-46

In the first example, the value 40 will be processed by Visual Basic as a Short data type literal even though the value would by default be considered a Integer value. In the second example, the literal-type character confirms the value should be treated as an Integer data type. In the third example, the value 0.99 will be processed as a Decimal data type even though it would by default be considered a Double data type. In the fourth example, the value 8491 would, by default, be considered an Integer data value but because the R literal-type character is used, Visual Basic will treat it as a Double data type. In example 5, the value 7 will be treated as a Char data type.

Constants

Recall that a variable identifies a location in memory where a value can be stored. By its nature, the value in a variable can be changed by statements within the program. For example, in the sample program in this chapter, if one user requested 5 downloads and another user requested 12 downloads, the value in the strNumberOfSongs variable would be changed based on the needs of the user. In some instances, however, you might not want the value to be changed. For example, the price per download in the sample program is $0.99 per song. This value will not change, regardless of how many songs the user wants to download.

When a value in a program will remain the same throughout the execution of the program, a special variable called a constant should be used. A **constant** variable will contain one permanent value throughout the execution of the program. It cannot be changed by any statement within the program. To define a constant variable, you can use the code in Figure 4-47.

```
Const cdecPricePerDownload As Decimal = 0.99D
```

FIGURE 4-47

The following rules apply to a constant:

1. The declaration of a constant variable begins with the letters Const, not the letters Dim.
2. You must assign the value to be contained in the constant on the same line as the definition of the constant. In Figure 4-47, the value 0.99D is assigned to the constant variable on the same line as the Const definition of the constant.
3. You cannot attempt to change the value in the constant variable anywhere in the program. If you attempt this, you will produce a compiler error.
4. The letter c often is placed before the prefix of the constant variable name to identify throughout the program that it is a constant variable and cannot be changed.
5. Other than the letter c constant variable names are formed using the same rules and techniques as nonconstant names.

Using a named constant variable instead of a literal provides several significant advantages and should be done whenever a constant value is required in a program. These advantages include:

1. The program becomes easier to read because the value is identified through the use of the name. For example, instead of using the value 0.99D in a literal, it is used in a constant called cdecPricePerDownload. This variable name describes the use of the value 0.99D and makes the program easier to read.
2. If the constant is used in more than one place in the program and it must be changed in the code, it is much easier and more reliable to change the value one time in the constant as opposed to changing every occurrence of the value in a literal.

Referencing a Variable

You learned earlier that when a variable is declared, it will be underlined with a green squiggly line until it is referenced in a statement. This feature of Visual Basic is intended to ensure that you do not declare a variable and then forget to use it. It also helps ensure you do not waste memory by declaring an unnecessary variable.

It is mandatory when using a variable in a program that the variable is defined prior to using the variable name in a statement. For example, the code in the statements in Figure 4-48 *will cause an error* because the variable is used in an assignment statement before it is declared.

```
25          strNumberOfSongs = txtNumberOfDownloads.Text
26          Dim strNumberOfSongs As String
```

FIGURE 4-48

In the code in Figure 4-48, the variable strNumberOfSongs is referenced in an assignment statement (line 25) before it is defined (line 26). This creates a compile error as indicated by the blue squiggly line beneath the variable name strNumberOfSongs on line 25. If you attempt to compile the statements on lines 25 and 26, you will receive a build error. Always define a variable before it is used in a statement.

Scope of Variables

When you declare a variable in Visual Basic, you not only declare the data type of the variable, you also, implicitly, define the scope of the variable. The **scope of a variable** specifies where within the program the variable can be referenced in a Visual Basic statement. In larger programs, with multiple classes and multiple forms, scope becomes critical, but it is important that you understand the concept at this point.

You declare a variable in a region within a program. For example, in the sample program in this chapter, you can declare a variable in the click event handler for the Calculate Cost button. You could declare another variable in the click event handler for the Clear button. Scope determines where each of these variables can be referenced and used in the Visual Basic program. **The rule is: A variable can be referenced only within the region of the program where it is defined.** A region in the programs you have seen thus far in the book is the code between the Sub statement and the End Sub statement in the event handlers. The code between the Sub statement and the End Sub statement is a **procedure**.

Therefore, if you declare a variable within the click event handler for the Calculate Cost button, that variable cannot be referenced in the click event handler for the Clear button, and vice versa. A variable that can only be referenced within the region of the program where it is defined is called a **local variable**. This means the value in a variable defined in one region of the program cannot be changed by a statement in another region of the program.

In addition, when a variable is defined in a procedure and the procedure ends, the values in the local variables defined in the procedure are destroyed. Thus, local variables have a certain **lifetime** in the program. They are only "alive" from the time the procedure begins executing until the procedure ends. If the procedure is executed again, whatever value the variable once contained no longer is present. One execution of the procedure is a variable's lifetime. Therefore, if a user clicks the Calculate Cost button, the values in the variables are valid until the click event execution is completed. When the user clicks the Calculate Cost button again, all values from the first click are gone.

It is possible in a Visual Basic program to define variables that can be used in multiple regions of a program. These variables are called **global variables**. In most programs, local variables should be used because they minimize the errors than can be generated when using global variables.

Understanding the scope of a variable is important when developing a program. You will learn more about the scope of variables later in this chapter and throughout this book.

Converting Variable Data

Variables used in arithmetic statements in a Visual Basic program must be numeric variables. String variables cannot be used in arithmetic statements. If you attempt to do so, you will create a compilation error.

A user often enters data in a text box. Data in the Text property of a TextBox object is treated as String data. Because String data cannot be used in an arithmetic statement, the String data entered by a user must be converted to numeric data before it can be used in an arithmetic statement.

For example, in the sample program in this chapter, before the number of songs to download a user enters can be used in an arithmetic statement to determine the total cost of the downloads, that value must be converted to an Integer data type.

Visual Basic includes several procedures that allow you to convert one data type to another data type. You will recall that a **procedure** is a prewritten set of code that can be called by a statement in the Visual Basic program. When the procedure is called, it performs a particular task. In this case, the task is to convert the String value the user entered into an Integer data type that can be used in an arithmetic operation. A procedure to convert a String data type to an Integer data type is named ToInt32. The number 32 in the procedure name identifies that the representation of the integer will require 32 bits or 4 bytes, which is the memory required for the Integer data type. The procedure is found in the Convert class, which is available in a Visual Studio 2010 class library.

Using a Procedure

When you require the use of a procedure to accomplish a task in your program, you need to understand what the procedure does and how to code the procedure call in a program statement. A procedure can operate in one of two ways: it can perform its task and return a value, or it can perform its task and not return a value. You will recall in the Chapter 3 program that the Close() procedure closed the window and terminated the program. This is an example of a procedure that performs its task but does not return a value. A procedure of this type is called a **Sub procedure**.

In the Song Download program in this chapter, the requirement is to convert the number of songs String value the user enters into an Integer data type. Then, it can be used in an arithmetic operation. Therefore the procedure must return a value (the Integer value for the number of songs). A procedure that returns a value is called a **Function procedure**, or a **function**.

In addition, a procedure might require data to be passed to it when it is called in order to carry out its processing. In the sample program in this chapter, the Function procedure to convert a String variable to an Integer variable must be able to access the String variable in order to convert it. Therefore, in the statement that calls the Function procedure, the variable name for the String variable to be converted must be passed to the procedure. A value is passed to a procedure through the use of an argument.

An **argument** identifies a value required by a procedure. It is passed to the procedure by including its name within parentheses following the name of the procedure in the calling statement. For example, to pass the value stored in the strNumberOfSongs variable to the ToInt32 procedure, the statement in Figure 4-49 could be used.

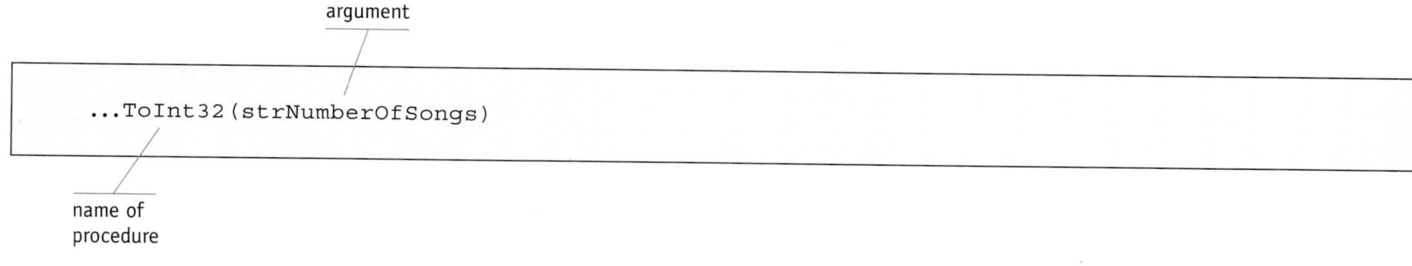

FIGURE 4-49

The name of the procedure is ToInt32. The argument is strNumberOfSongs, which is the String variable that contains the value to be converted to an Integer data type by the ToInt32 procedure. Notice that the argument is enclosed within parentheses.

Every procedure is a part of a class in Visual Basic. You will recall from Chapter 1 that a **class** is a named grouping of program code. When the calling statement must call a procedure, it first must identify the class that contains the procedure. Thus, in Figure 4-49 the calling statement is incomplete because the class name is not included in the statement. The class containing the ToInt32 procedure is the Convert class. To complete the procedure call statement, the class must be added, as shown in Figure 4-50.

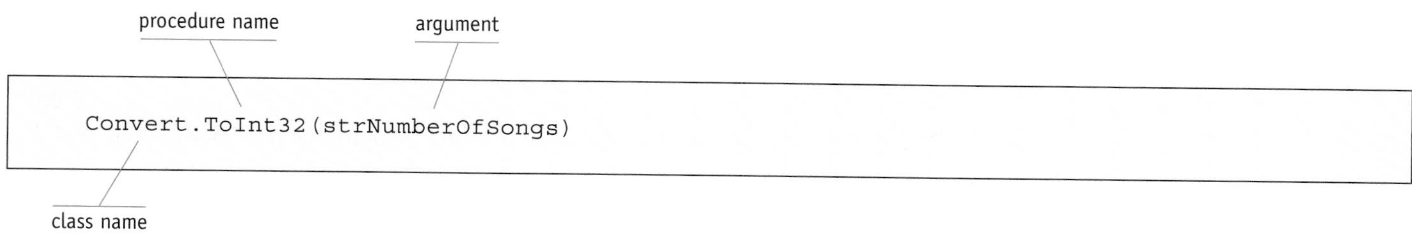

FIGURE 4-50

IN THE REAL WORLD

To review all the methods, or procedures, available with the Convert class, complete the following steps: 1) Click Help on the menu bar; 2) Click Index on the Help menu; 3) Type `convert.to` in the Look for text box; 4) Select the topic you want to review.

In Figure 4-50, the class name Convert begins the procedure call. A dot operator separates the class name from the procedure name (ToInt32). The argument (strNumberOfSongs) within the parentheses completes the procedure call.

When a Function procedure returns a value, such as the ToInt32 procedure that returns an integer value, in effect the returned value replaces the procedure call in the assignment statement containing the Function procedure call. So, in Figure 4-51, you can see that when the processing within the Function procedure is completed, the integer value is substituted for the procedure call in the assignment statement.

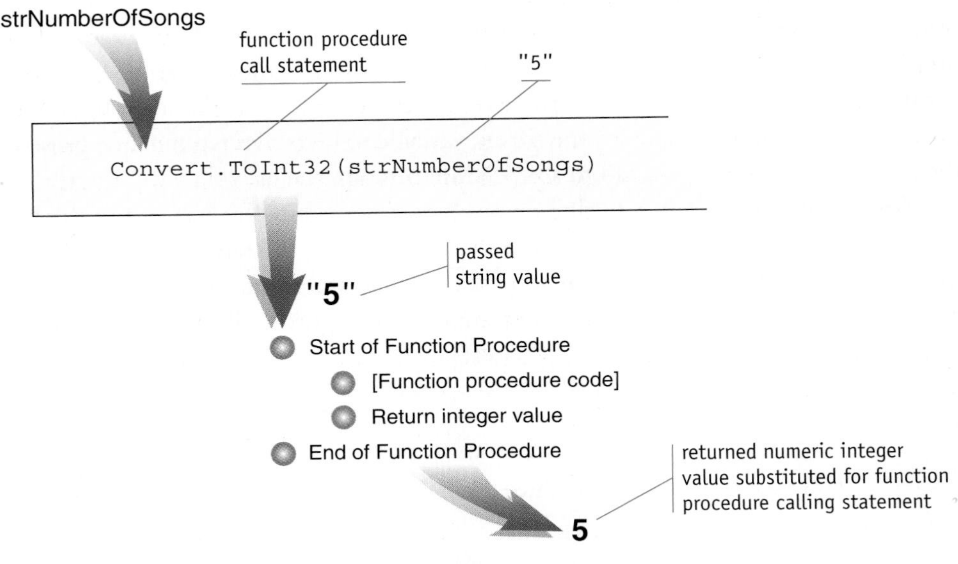

FIGURE 4-51

The complete assignment statement to convert the String data type in the strNumberOfSongs variable to an Integer data type and place it in the intNumberOfSongs variable is shown in Figure 4-52.

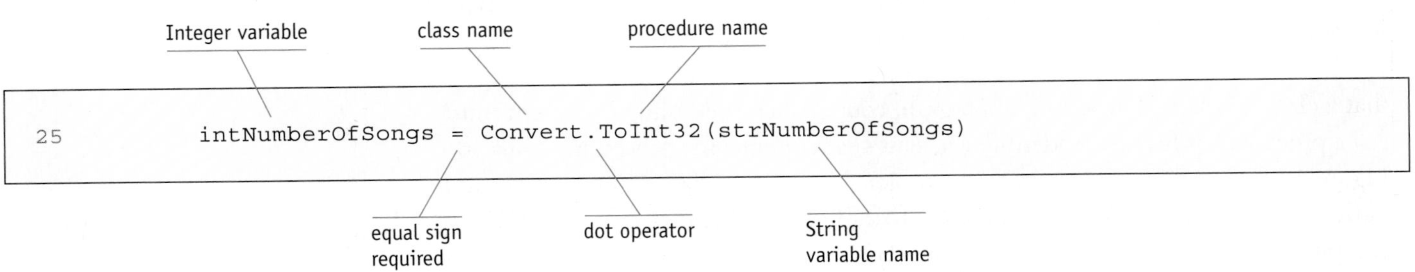

FIGURE 4-52

The intNumberOfSongs variable name on the left of the equal sign identifies the Integer variable where the converted value will be copied. The equal sign in the assignment statement is required. As a result of the assignment statement in Figure 4-52, the ToInt32 Function procedure found in the Convert class will convert the value in the strNumberOfSongs String variable to an integer value. The assignment statement will place that integer value in the intNumberOfSongs variable.

The use of Function procedures, and arguments with the procedure calls, is common when programming in Visual Basic. You will encounter many examples of Function procedure calls throughout this book.

Option Strict On

In the previous section, you saw an example of explicitly changing a value from one data type to another. Visual Basic will, by default, automatically convert data types if the data type on the right side of the equal sign in an assignment statement is different from the data type on the left side of the equal sign. Quite often, however, the automatic conversion can introduce errors and produce an incorrect converted value. Therefore, allowing automatic conversion normally is not good programming style.

To prevent automatic conversion of values, the developer must insert the Option Strict On statement in the program prior to any event handler code in the program. In Figure 4-53, the Option Strict On statement is shown just following the introductory comments in the sample program for this chapter.

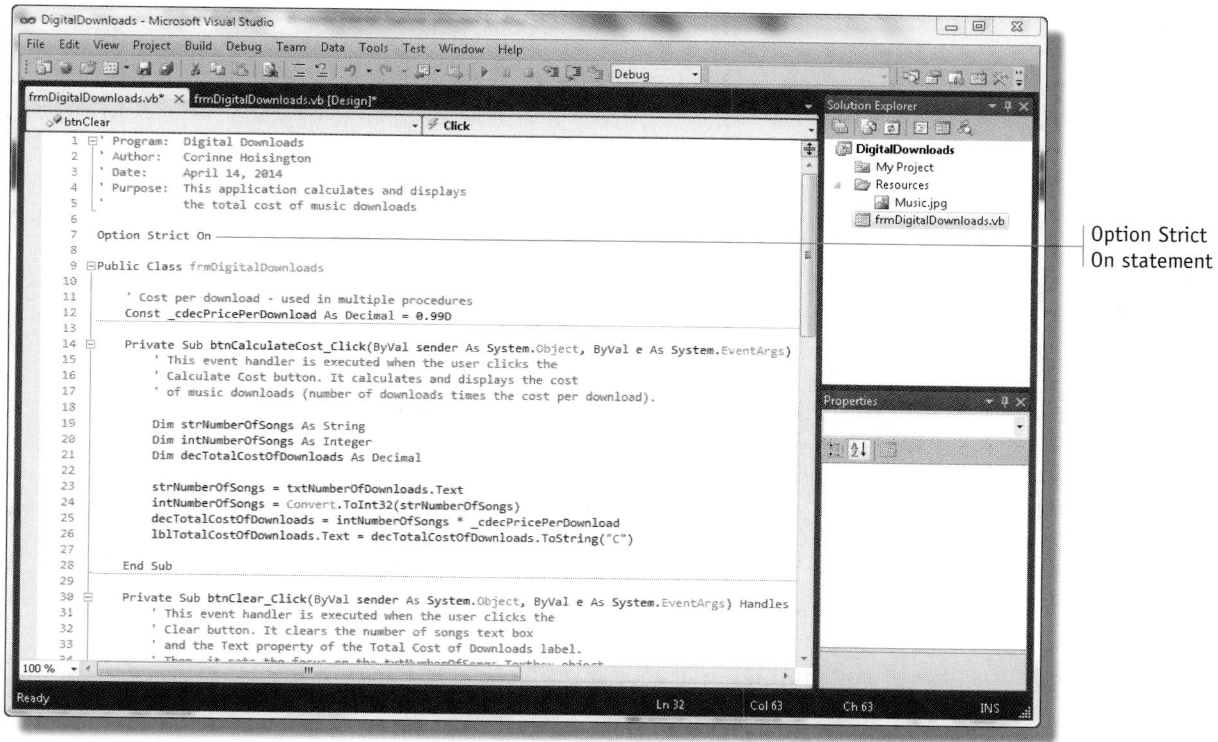
DigitalDownloads - Microsoft Visual Studio
File Edit View Project Build Debug Team Data Tools Test Window Help
Debug
frmDigitalDownloads.vb*
frmDigitalDownloads.vb [Design]*
btnClear
Click
' Program: Digital Downloads
' Author: Corinne Hoisington
' Date: April 14, 2014
' Purpose: This application calculates and displays
' the total cost of music downloads
Option Strict On
Public Class frmDigitalDownloads
' Cost per download - used in multiple procedures
Const _cdecPricePerDownload As Decimal = 0.99D
Private Sub btnCalculateCost_Click(ByVal sender As System.Object, ByVal e As System.EventArgs)
' This event handler is executed when the user clicks the
' Calculate Cost button. It calculates and displays the cost
' of music downloads (number of downloads times the cost per download).
Dim strNumberOfSongs As String
Dim intNumberOfSongs As Integer
Dim decTotalCostOfDownloads As Decimal
strNumberOfSongs = txtNumberOfDownloads.Text
intNumberOfSongs = Convert.ToInt32(strNumberOfSongs)
decTotalCostOfDownloads = intNumberOfSongs * _cdecPricePerDownload
lblTotalCostOfDownloads.Text = decTotalCostOfDownloads.ToString("C")
End Sub
Private Sub btnClear_Click(ByVal sender As System.Object, ByVal e As System.EventArgs) Handles
' This event handler is executed when the user clicks the
' Clear button. It clears the number of songs text box
' and the Text property of the Total Cost of Downloads label.
Solution Explorer
DigitalDownloads
My Project
Resources
Music.jpg
frmDigitalDownloads.vb
Properties
100 %
Ready
Ln 32
Col 63
Ch 63
INS
Option Strict On statement

FIGURE 4-53

The Option Strict On statement explicitly disallows any default data type conversions in which data loss would occur and any conversion between numeric types and strings. Therefore, you must write explicit conversion statements in order to convert from one data type to another. This approach minimizes potential errors that can occur from data conversion.

Arithmetic Operations

The ability to perform arithmetic operations on numeric data is fundamental to computer programs. Many programs require arithmetic operations to add, subtract, multiply, and divide numeric data. For example, in the Digital Downloads program in this chapter, the price per song downloaded must be multiplied by the number of songs to be downloaded in order to calculate the total cost of downloads. The formula is shown in Figure 4-54.

Total Cost of Downloads = Number of Song Downloads times Price per Download

FIGURE 4-54

An assignment statement is used in Visual Basic 2010 to perform the arithmetic operation shown in Figure 4-54. The statements used in the sample program and a depiction of the operation are shown in Figure 4-55.

```
20          Dim strNumberOfSongs As String
21          Dim intNumberOfSongs As Integer
22          Dim decTotalCostOfDownloads As Decimal
23          Const cdecPricePerDownload As Decimal = 0.99D
24
25          strNumberOfSongs = txtNumberOfDownloads.Text
26          intNumberOfSongs = Convert.ToInt32(strNumberOfSongs)
27          decTotalCostOfDownloads = intNumberOfSongs * cdecPricePerDownload
```

decTotalCostOfDownloads = intNumberOfSongs * cdecPricePerDownload

FIGURE 4-55

In the code in Figure 4-55, the variable strNumberOfSongs is assigned the value the user entered by the assignment statement on line 25 (see Figure 4-24 for a detailed explanation of this statement). The statement on line 26 converts the value in the strNumberOfSongs variable to an integer and copies it to the intNumberOfSongs variable (see Figure 4-52 for an explanation of this statement).

The statement on line 27 multiplies the integer value in the intNumberOfSongs variable times the constant value in the cdecPricePerDownload variable, and then copies the result to the decTotalCostOfDownloads variable. For example, if the user enters the value 5 as the number of downloads, as depicted in the diagram, the value 5 is multiplied by the value .99 (the value in the cdecPricePerDownload variable), and the result (4.95) is copied to the decTotalCostOfDownloads variable.

Arithmetic Operators

An important element on the right side of the equal sign in the assignment statement on line 27 is the multiply **arithmetic operator**, which is an asterisk (*). Whenever the compiler encounters the multiply arithmetic operator, the value on the left of the operator is multiplied by the value on the right of the operator and these values are replaced in the assignment statement by the product of the two numbers. Thus, in Figure 4-55 the arithmetic expression intNumberOfSongs * cdecPricePerDownload is replaced by the value 4.95. Then, the assignment statement places the value 4.95 in the decTotalCostOfDownloads variable.

The multiply arithmetic operator is only one of the arithmetic operators available in Visual Basic 2010. The table in Figure 4-56 lists the Visual Basic 2010 arithmetic operators, their use, and an example of an arithmetic expression showing their use.

Arithmetic Operator	Use	Assignment Statement Showing Their Use
+	Addition	decTotal = decPrice + decTax
–	Subtraction	decCost = decRegularPrice – decDiscount
*	Multiplication	decTax = decItemPrice * decTaxRate
/	Division	decClassAverage = decTotalScores / intNumberOfStudents
^	Exponentiation	intSquareArea = intSquareSide ^ 2
\	Integer Division	intResult = 13 \ 5
Mod	Modulus Arithmetic (remainder)	intRemainder = 13 Mod 5

FIGURE 4-56

The arithmetic operators shown in Figure 4-56 are explained in the following paragraphs.

Addition

The **addition arithmetic operator** (+) causes the numeric values immediately to the left and immediately to the right of the operator to be added together and to replace the arithmetic expression in the assignment statement. For example, in Figure 4-57, the value in the decPrice variable is added to the value in the decTax variable.

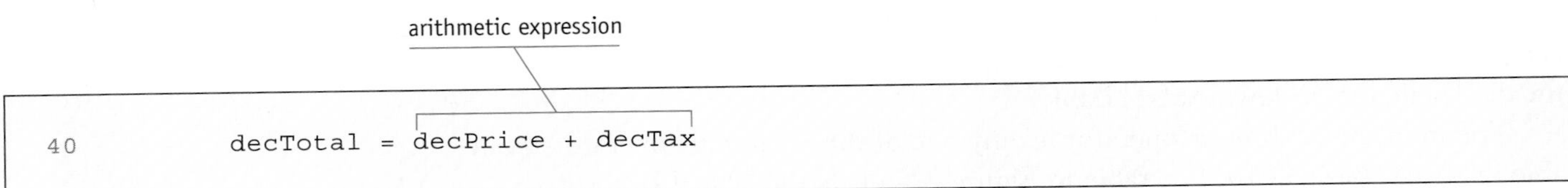

FIGURE 4-57

In Figure 4-57, the arithmetic expression (decPrice + decTax) is evaluated by adding the value in the decPrice variable to the value in the decTax variable. Then, the assignment statement copies the sum to the decTotal variable in RAM.

An arithmetic expression that uses the addition operator can contain more than two numeric values to be added. For example, in Figure 4-58, three variables are used in the arithmetic expression.

```
decTotalPay = decRegularPay + decOvertimePay + decBonusPay
```

FIGURE 4-58

In Figure 4-58, the value in decRegularPay is added to the value in decOvertimePay. The result then is added to decBonusPay. That sum is copied to the decTotalPay variable. Visual Basic imposes no limit on the number of variables that can be used in an arithmetic expression.

In addition to variables, arithmetic expressions can contain literals. The assignment statement in Figure 4-59 uses a literal.

```
decTicketCost = decInternetTicketCost + 10.25
```

FIGURE 4-59

In Figure 4-59, the value 10.25 is added to the value in the decInternetTicketCost variable and that sum is placed in the decTicketCost variable. Generally, literals should not be used in arithmetic expressions unless it is known that the value will not change. For example, if the extra cost for the ticket could change in the future, good program design would dictate that the value be placed in a variable (perhaps even a constant).

Subtraction

In order to subtract one value from another in an assignment statement, the **subtraction arithmetic operator** (−) is used, as shown in Figure 4-60.

```
decNetProfit = decRevenue - decCosts
```

FIGURE 4-60

In Figure 4-60, the value in the decCosts variable is subtracted from the value in the decRevenue variable. The result then is copied into the decNetProfit variable. If the value in decCosts is greater than the value in decRevenue, the value placed in the decNetProfit variable will be negative.

Using Arithmetic Results

After an arithmetic operation has been performed using an assignment statement, the values used in the arithmetic operation together with the answer obtained can be used in subsequent arithmetic operations or for other purposes within the program. For example, the result of one operation can be used in a subsequent calculation (Figure 4-61).

```
67        decComputerCost = decMonitorCost + decSystemUnitCost
68        decNetComputerCost = decComputerCost - decSystemDiscount
```

FIGURE 4-61

In Figure 4-61, the statement on line 67 determines the computer cost by adding the cost of the monitor and the cost of the system unit. The statement on line 68 calculates the net computer cost by subtracting the system discount from the computer cost that is calculated on line 67. Whenever a value is stored in a variable, it can be used in other statements within the program.

Multiplication

Multiplication is accomplished through the use of an assignment statement and the multiplication operator (*), as shown in Figure 4-62.

```
intLandPlotArea = intLandPlotLength * intLandPlotWidth
```

FIGURE 4-62

In Figure 4-62, the value in the intLandPlotLength variable is multiplied by the value in the intLandPlotWidth variable. The product of the multiplication is placed in the intLandPlotArea variable.

When multiplication takes place, the signs of the numbers are considered. If two positive numbers are multiplied, the answer is positive. If two negative numbers are multiplied, the answer is positive. If one positive number and one negative number are multiplied, the answer is negative.

When two numbers are multiplied, you must be aware of the size of the result. The largest number of digits that can appear in the product of two numbers is the sum of the number of digits in each of the values being multiplied. If the product is greater than the value that can be stored in the variable on the left of the assignment statement, an overflow error can occur and the program will be terminated.

Division

Visual Basic 2010 provides three arithmetic operators for division and related calculations. These operators are the slash (/), the backslash (\), and the entry MOD.

You use the slash for normal division. For example, in Figure 4-63, the value in the decTestScores variable is divided by 3 in order to obtain the average test score.

```
decAverageTestScore = decTestScores / 3
```

FIGURE 4-63

WATCH OUT FOR

Be sure that the divisor (the number on the right of the division operator) is not zero. If you attempt to divide by zero, your program will be terminated with an error.

You use the backslash (\) for integer division. With integer division, the quotient returned from the division operation is an integer. If the division operation produces a quotient with a remainder, the remainder is dropped, or truncated. The examples in Figure 4-64 illustrate the use of the integer division arithmetic operator.

Division Operation	Result
12\5	2
25\4	6
30\7	4

FIGURE 4-64

Notice in each example in Figure 4-64 that the result is a whole number with the remainder truncated.

The MOD operator divides the number on the left of the operator by the number on the right of the operator and returns an integer value that is the remainder of division operation. Integer division and the MOD operator often are used together, as shown in Figure 4-65.

```
86        intHours = intTotalNumberOfMinutes \ 60
87        intMinutes = intTotalNumberOfMinutes Mod 60
```

FIGURE 4-65

In Figure 4-65, the operation on line 86 will return only the integer value of the division. For example, if the intTotalNumberOfMinutes variable contains 150, a result of 2 (2 = 150\60) will be placed in the intHours variable. The operation on line 87 will place the remainder in the intMinutes variable. The remainder in the example is 30 (150 divided by 60 is 2, with a remainder of 30).

Exponentiation

Exponentiation means raising a number to a power. Exponentiation is accomplished by using the exponentiation arithmetic operator (^), as shown in Figure 4-66.

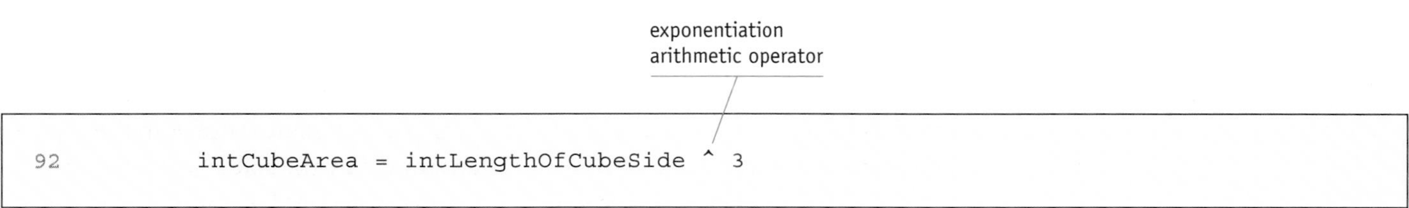

FIGURE 4-66

In Figure 4-66, the arithmetic expression is the same as intLengthOfCubeSide * intLengthOfCubeSide * intLengthOfCubeSide. So the value is cubed and copied to the intCubeArea variable.

The exponent used in the exponentiation operation can be a fraction. If the exponent is a fraction, the root is taken (Figure 4-67).

```
intLengthOfCubeSide = intCubeArea ^ (1 / 3)
```

FIGURE 4-67

In Figure 4-67, the cube root of the value in the intCubeArea variable is calculated and the result is copied to the intLengthOfCubeSide variable. Thus, if the area of the cube is 64, the value calculated for the length of the cube side would be 4 (4 * 4 * 4 = 64). The fractional exponent can never be negative, and it must be placed within parentheses.

Multiple Operations

A single assignment statement can contain multiple arithmetic operations. In Figure 4-68, the addition and subtraction operators are used to calculate the new balance in a savings account by adding the deposits to the old balance and subtracting withdrawals.

```
decNewBalance = decOldBalance + decDeposits - decWithdrawals
```

FIGURE 4-68

When the assignment statement in Figure 4-68 is executed, the value in the decOldBalance variable is added to the value in the decDeposits variable. Then, the value in the decWithdrawals variable is subtracted from that sum and the result is copied to the decNewBalance variable.

Notice in Figure 4-68 that the calculations proceed from the left to the right through the arithmetic expression.

Hierarchy of Operations

When multiple operations are included in a single assignment statement, the sequence of performing the calculations is determined by the following rules:

1. Exponentiation (^) is performed first.
2. Multiplication (*) and division (/) are performed next.
3. Integer division (\) is next.
4. MOD then occurs.
5. Addition (+) and subtraction (−) are performed last.
6. Within each of these five steps, calculations are performed left to right.

As a result of this predetermined sequence, an arithmetic expression such as decBonus + decHours * decHourlyRate would result in the product of decHours * decHourlyRate being added to decBonus.

An arithmetic expression such as decGrade1 + decGrade2 / 2 would result in the value in the decGrade2 variable being divided by 2, and then the quotient being added to the value in decGrade1 because division is performed before addition. It is likely that this is not the intended calculation to be performed. Instead, the intent was to add the value in decGrade1 to the value in decGrade2 and then divide the sum by 2. To force certain operations to be performed before others, you can use parentheses. Any arithmetic expression within parentheses is evaluated before expressions outside the parentheses, as shown in Figure 4-69.

```
        decAverageGrade = (decGrade1 + decGrade2) / 2
```

FIGURE 4-69

In Figure 4-69, because it is inside the parentheses, the addition operation will be completed before the division operation. Therefore, the result of the arithmetic expression is that the value in decGrade1 is added to the value in decGrade2. That sum then is divided by the value 2 and the quotient is copied to the decAverageGrade variable.

It is advisable to use parentheses around multiple arithmetic operations in an arithmetic expression even if the predetermined sequence of operations will produce the correct answer because then the sequence of operations is explicitly clear.

Displaying Numeric Output Data

As you have learned, the result of an arithmetic expression is a numeric value that normally is stored in a numeric variable. In most cases, to display the numeric data as information in a graphical user interface, the numeric data must be placed in the Text property of a Label object or a TextBox object. The Text property of these objects, however, requires that this data be a String data type. Therefore, to display a numeric value in a label or a text box, the numeric data must be converted to a String data type.

Each of the numeric data types provides a function called the ToString function that converts data from the numeric data type to the String data type. The general format of the function call for a Decimal numeric variable is shown in Figure 4-70.

IN THE REAL WORLD

You know that a procedure is a group of code that a program can call to perform a particular function, such as converting data stored in a numeric data type to data stored as a String data type. In some programming languages, a procedure is called a method. Therefore, in Visual Studio Help, as you search the index or other areas, you might find the word method used. Just remember that the terms method and procedure (both a Sub procedure and a function) are virtually synonymous.

General Format: ToString Function

```
decimalvariable.ToString()
```

FIGURE 4-70

The statement shown in Figure 4-70 consists of the name of the decimal variable containing data to be converted, the dot operator (.), and the name of the function (ToString). Notice that the function name is followed immediately by closed parentheses, which indicates to the Visual Basic compiler that ToString is a procedure name. When the function call is executed, the value returned by the ToString function replaces the call.

The function call normally is contained within an assignment statement to assign the returned string value to the Text property of a Label or TextBox object. The example in Figure 4-71 shows the assignment statement to convert the numeric value in the decTemperature variable to a String value that then is placed in the Text property of the lblTemperature Label object.

name of decimal variable

ToString function call

```
118          lblTemperature.Text = decTemperature.ToString()
```

FIGURE 4-71

In Figure 4-71, the name of the decimal variable (decTemperature) is followed by the dot operator and then the name of the function (ToString) with the required parentheses. When the statement on line 118 is executed, the ToString function is called. It converts the numeric value in the decTemperature variable to a String data type and returns the String data. The assignment statement then copies the returned String data to the Text property of the Temperature Label object.

HEADS UP

An important consideration when determining the formatting of a number is rounding. When using the ToString function, all values are rounded based on the digit following the last digit to be displayed. For example, if the value being converted to a Currency string from a numeric format is 729.837, the returned result will be rounded up ($729.84). If the value to be converted is 575.371, the returned result will be rounded down ($575.37). This feature is true when the precision specifier is used as well.

Format Specifications for the ToString Function

In the example in Figure 4-71, the conversion from numeric value to String value is a straight conversion, which means the value is returned but it is not formatted in any manner. For example, if the numeric value in the Decimal variable was 47.235, then this same value was returned as a String value.

The ToString function, however, can convert numeric data to String data using a specified format. For example, the value 2317.49 could be returned as $2,317.49. Notice that the returned value is in the form of dollars and cents, or currency. To identify the format for the numeric data to be returned by the ToString function, the **format specifier** must be included as an argument in the parentheses following the ToString function name. The table in Figure 4-72 identifies the commonly used format specifiers (assume the value in the numeric field is 8976.43561).

Format Specifier	Format	Description	Output from the Function
General(G)	ToString("G")	Displays the numbers as is	8976.43561
Currency(C)	ToString("C")	Displays the number with a dollar sign, a thousands separator (comma), two digits to the right of the decimal and negative numbers in parentheses	$8,976.44
Fixed(F)	ToString("F")	Displays the number with 2 digits to the right of the decimal and a minus sign for negative numbers	8976.44
Number(N)	ToString("N")	Displays a number with a thousands separator, 2 digits to the right of the decimal and a minus sign for negative numbers	8,976.44
Percent(P)	ToString("P")	Displays the number multiplied by 100 with a % sign, a thousands separator, 2 digits to the right of the decimal and a minus sign for negative numbers	897,643.56%
Scientific(E)	ToString("E")	Displays the number in E-notation and a minus sign for negative numbers	8.976436E+03

FIGURE 4-72

In Figure 4-72, each format specifier is used as an argument within parentheses. The argument must be included in the quotation marks (" ") on each side of the format specifier, as shown. The letter for the format specifier can either be uppercase or lowercase.

Precision Specifier

Each format specifier has a default number of digits to the right of the decimal point that will be returned. You can use a precision specifier, however, to override the default number of positions to the right of the decimal point. The **precision specifier** is a number that is included within the quotation marks in the function call to identify the number of positions to the right of the decimal point that should be returned. The examples in Figure 4-73 illustrate the use of the precision specifier (assume the value in the decNumericValue variable is 8976.43561):

Statement	Copied to Text Property of lblOutput Label Object
lblOutput = decNumericValue.ToString("C2")	$8,976.44
lblOutput = decNumericValue.ToString("C3")	$8,976.436
lblOutput = decNumericValue.ToString("F1")	8976.4
lblOutput = decNumericValue.ToString("N4")	8,976.4356
lblOutput = decNumericValue.ToString("P0")	897,644%

FIGURE 4-73

As you can see, the precision specifier identifies the number of digits to the right of the decimal point that should be displayed in the string returned from the ToString function. Notice that if the precision specifier is 0, no digits to the right of the decimal point are returned.

As with all conversions, when the number of positions to the right of the decimal point in the returned string is less than the number of digits to the right of the decimal point in the numeric value being converted, the returned value is rounded to the specified number of decimal places.

Clearing the Form — Clear Procedure and Focus Procedure

You will recall from the explanation of the Digital Downloads program in this chapter that when the user clicks the Clear button (see Figure 4-1 on page 196), the event handler for the Clear button must clear the results from window, allowing the user to enter the next value for the number of downloads. To perform this task, the Clear button event handler must complete the following tasks: 1) Clear the Text property of the TextBox object; 2) Clear the Text property of the Label object that displays the total cost of the downloads; 3) Set the focus on the TextBox object, which means place the insertion point in the text box. You will learn to accomplish these tasks in the following sections.

Clear Procedure

The Clear procedure clears any data currently placed in the Text property of a TextBox object. The general format of the Clear procedure is shown in Figure 4-74.

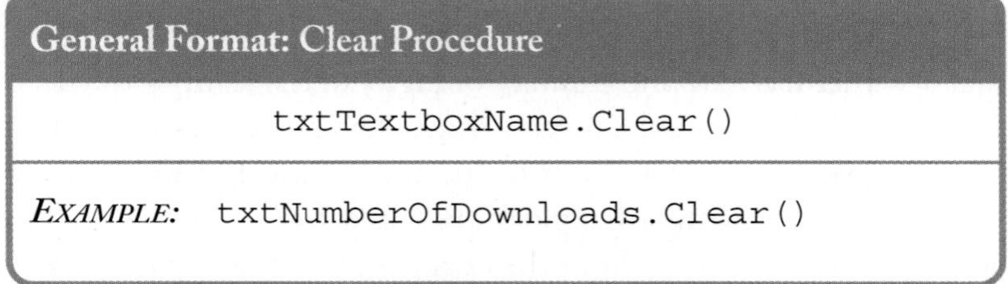

General Format: Clear Procedure
txtTextboxName.Clear()
EXAMPLE: txtNumberOfDownloads.Clear()

FIGURE 4-74

When the Clear procedure is executed, the Text property is cleared of any data. As with every procedure call, the name of the procedure must be followed by parentheses.

The process that occurs on the right of the equal sign is illustrated in Figure 4-81.

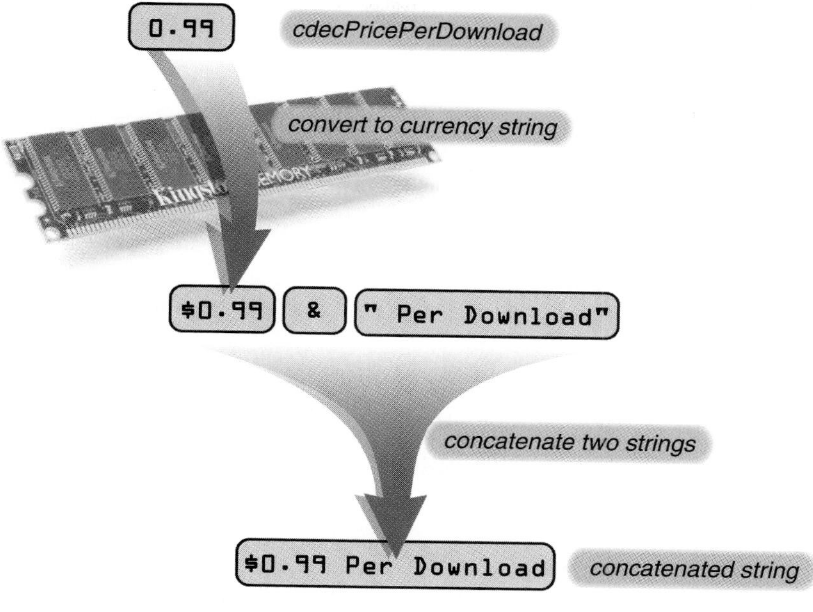

FIGURE 4-81

In Figure 4-81 you can see that to obtain the concatenated string, the Decimal value in the cdecPricePerDownload decimal variable is converted to a currency String data type. Then, that value is concatenated with the string literal to create the concatenated string. In the assignment statement in Figure 4-80, the concatenated string is assigned to the Text property of the lblCostHeading Label object.

Class Scope

You will recall from earlier in this chapter that when you declare a variable you also define the scope of the variable. The scope of a variable identifies where within the program the variable can be referenced. For example, if a variable is declared within an event handler procedure, the variable can be referenced only within that procedure.

Sometimes, a variable must be referenced in multiple event handlers. In the Digital Downloads program, the value in the cdecPricePerDownload variable is referenced in the Calculate button event handler when the total cost is calculated (see Figure 4-55 on page 232). The value also is referenced in the form load event when the heading is displayed (see Figure 4-80 on page 246). Because the variable is referenced in two different event handling procedures, it must be defined at the class level instead of the procedure (event handler) level. This means that the variable must be declared in the code prior to the first procedure, or event handler, in the program.

As you can see in Figure 4-82, the declaration of the cdecPricePerDownload variable follows the class definition statement but appears before the first event handler procedure.

beginning of program

class definition statement

```
' Program:   Digital Downloads
' Author:    Corinne Hoisington
' Date:      April 14, 2014
' Purpose:   This application calculates and displays
'            the total cost of music downloads

Option Strict On

Public Class frmDigitalDownloads

    ' Cost per download - used in multiple procedures
    Const _cdecPricePerDownload As Decimal = 0.99D

    Private Sub btnCalculateCost_Click(ByVal sender As System.Object, ByVal e As System
    .EventArgs) Handles btnCalculateCost.Click
        ' This event handler is executed when the user clicks the
        ' Calculate Cost button. It calculates and displays the cost
        ' of music downloads (number of downloads times the cost per download).
```

first event handler

declaration of Price Per Download variable

FIGURE 4-82

IN THE REAL WORLD

When a variable is declared for use throughout a class, the naming convention specifies that the name should begin with an underscore character (_). So, whenever you see a variable name that begins with the underscore character, you know that variable has class scope.

As a result of the code in Figure 4-82, the scope of the _cdecPricePerDownload variable will be all procedures within the class; that is, code within any event handler procedure within the class can reference the variable. Because the variable is declared as a constant, the value in the variable cannot be changed by code within the class; however, the value in the class can be referenced to calculate the total cost and to create the cost heading.

Debugging Your Program

When your program processes numeric data entered by a user, you should be aware of several errors that can occur when users enter data that the program does not expect. The three errors that occur most often are: 1) Format Exception; 2) Overflow Exception; 3) Divide By Zero Exception.

A **Format Exception** occurs when the user enters data that a statement within the program cannot process properly. In the Digital Downloads program, you will recall that the user is supposed to enter a numeric value for the number of song downloads desired. When the user clicks the Calculate Cost button, the program converts the value entered to an integer and then uses the numeric value in the calculation (see Figure 4-52 on page 230). If the user enters a nonnumeric value, such as abc shown in Figure 4-83a, the conversion process cannot take place because the argument passed to the Convert class is not a numeric value. When this occurs, a Format Exception error is recognized and the error box shown in Figure 4-83b is displayed.

FIGURE 4-83a

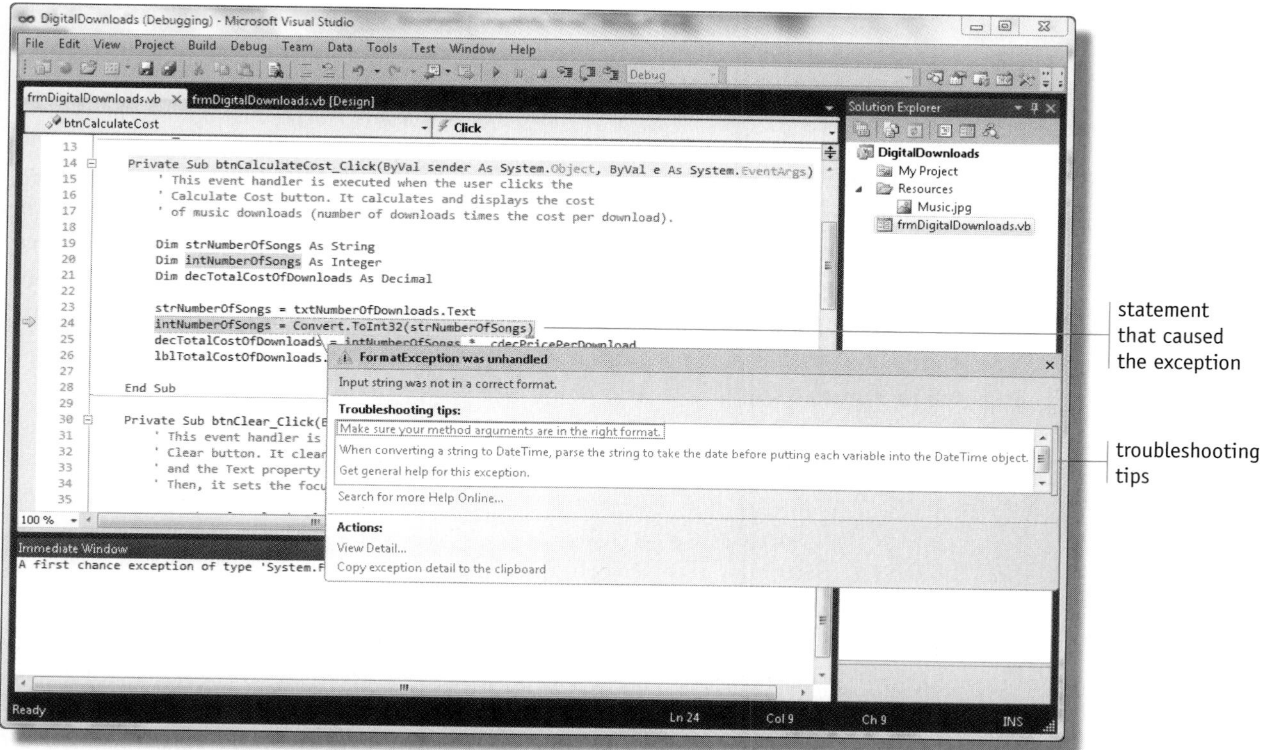

FIGURE 4-83b

In Figure 4-83a, the user entered the value abc and then clicked the Calculate Cost button. When control was passed to the ToInt32 procedure to convert the value from the String value entered in the text box to an Integer, the Format Exception was triggered because the value in the strNumberOfSongs was not numeric. When an exception occurs, the execution of the program is terminated. With Visual Studio running, click the Stop Debugging button on the Standard toolbar.

An **Overflow Exception** occurs when the user enters a value greater than the maximum value that can be processed by the statement. For example, in the Digital Downloads program, if the user enters a value in the text box that is greater than the value that can be converted by the ToInt32 procedure, an Overflow Exception occurs.

An Overflow Exception also can occur when a calculation creates a value larger than one that can be processed by a procedure. For example, if two large but valid numbers are multiplied, the product of the multiplication might be larger than can be processed.

The third type of common error is the **Divide By Zero Exception**. It is not possible to divide by zero, so if your program contains a division operation and the divisor is equal to zero, the Divide By Zero Exception will occur.

Whenever an exception occurs, a window similar to that shown in Figure 4-83b will be displayed.

To avoid exceptions, which should always be your goal, you can use certain techniques for editing the data and ensuring that the user has entered valid data that will not cause an exception. You will learn in Chapter 5 and Chapter 6 how to write code that checks user input to ensure exceptions do not occur because of the data users enter.

Program Design

As you have learned, the requirements document identifies the purpose of the program being developed, the application title, the procedures to be followed when using the program, any equations and calculations required in the program, any conditions within the program that must be tested, notes and restrictions that must be followed by the program, and any other comments that would be helpful to understanding the problem. The requirements document for the Digital Downloads application is shown in Figure 4-84.

REQUIREMENTS DOCUMENT

Date submitted: April 14, 2014

Application title: Digital Downloads

Purpose: The Digital Downloads program allows the user to enter the number of songs to be downloaded. The program calculates the total cost of the downloads based on a price of $0.99 per song.

Program Procedures: In a Windows application, the user enters the number of songs she wants to download. The program calculates the total cost of downloads. The user can clear the values on the screen and enter a new value for the number of downloads.

Algorithms, Processing, and Conditions:

1. The user must be able to enter the number of songs to be downloaded.
2. The user can initiate the calculation and display the total cost of the downloads.
3. The application computes the total cost of downloads by multiplying the number of downloads times the cost per download ($0.99).
4. The total cost of downloads is displayed as a currency value.
5. The user should be able to clear the value entered for the number of downloads and the total cost of downloads.
6. The user should be provided with a button to exit the program.

Notes and Restrictions: n/a

Comments:

1. A graphic should depict a musical image named Music. The graphic is available at scsite.com/vb2010/ch4/images.

FIGURE 4-84

The use case definition identifies the steps the user will take when using the program. The use case definition for the Digital Downloads program is shown in Figure 4-85.

USE CASE DEFINITION

1. The Windows application opens with a text box where the user can enter the number of song downloads. The user interface includes the text box, an area to display the total cost of downloads, a Calculate Cost button, a Clear button, and an Exit button.
2. The user enters the number of songs downloads.
3. The user clicks the Calculate Cost button.
4. The program displays the total cost of the song downloads.
5. The user clicks the Clear button to clear the Number of Song Downloads text box and erase the total cost of downloads amount.
6. The user repeats steps 2-5 if desired.
7. The user clicks the Exit button to terminate the application.

FIGURE 4-85

Event Planning Document

You will recall that the event planning document consists of a table that specifies an object in the user interface that will cause an event, the action taken by the user to trigger the event, and the event processing that must occur. The event planning document for the Digital Downloads program is shown in Figure 4-86.

EVENT PLANNING DOCUMENT

Program Name: Digital Downloads	**Developer:** Corinne Hoisington	**Object:** frmDigitalDownloads	**Date:** April 14, 2014
OBJECT	**EVENT TRIGGER**	**EVENT PROCESSING**	
btnCalculate	Click	Assign data entered in text box to a String variable Convert data entered to numeric integer Calculate total cost of downloads (number of downloads * price per download) Display total cost of downloads	
btnClear	Click	Clear number of song downloads text box Clear total cost of downloads label text Set focus on number of song downloads text box	
btnExit	Click	Close the window and terminate the program	
frmDigitalDownloads	Load	Display heading with price per download Clear the placement digits for total cost of downloads Label object Set focus on number of song downloads text box	

FIGURE 4-86

Code the Program

After identifying the events and tasks within the events, you are ready to code the program. As you have learned, coding the program means entering Visual Basic statements to accomplish the tasks specified on the event planning document. As you enter the code, you also will implement the logic to carry out the required processing.

Guided Program Development

To design the user interface for the Digital Downloads program and enter the code required to process each event in the program, complete the following steps:

NOTE TO THE LEARNER

As you will recall, in the following activity, you should complete the tasks within the specified steps. Each of the tasks is accompanied by a Hint Screen. The purpose of the Hint Screen is to indicate where in the Visual Studio window you should perform the activity; it also serves as a reminder of the method that you should use to create the user interface or enter code. If you need further help completing the step, refer to the figure number identified by the term ref: in the step.

Guided Program Development *continued*

Phase I: Create User Interface Mockup

1

- **Create a Windows Application** Open Visual Studio using the Start button on the Windows taskbar and the All Programs submenu. Close the Start page by clicking the Start Page Close button. To create a Windows application, click the New Project button on the Standard toolbar; if necessary, click Visual Basic in the Installed Templates pane; click Windows Forms Application in the center pane; double-click the term WindowsApplication1 in the Name text box and then type `DigitalDownload`. Click the OK button in the New Project dialog box.

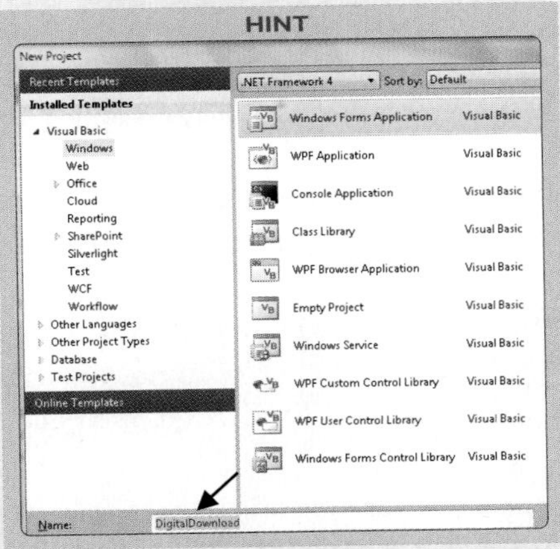

- **Display the Toolbox** Ensure the Toolbox is displayed in the Visual Studio window. If it is not, click the Toolbox button on the Standard toolbar. If necessary, click the plus sign next to the Common Controls category name in the Toolbox to display the tools *(ref: Figure 4-21)*.

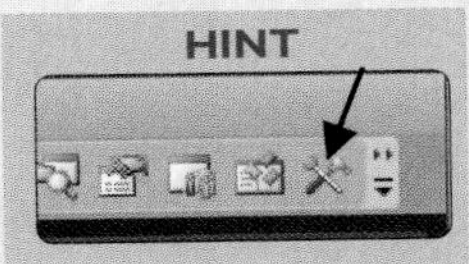

- **Name the Windows Form Object** In the Solution Explorer window, right-click the Form1.vb form file and select Rename. Type frmDigitalDownloads.vb and press the ENTER key.

- **Change the Title on the Title Bar** To change the title on the Windows Form object, click the form, scroll in the Properties window until the Text property is displayed, double-click in the right column of the Text property, type `Download Music`, and then press the ENTER key.

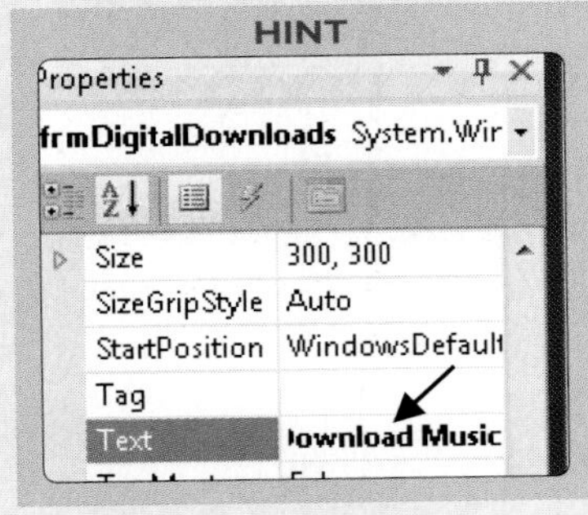

Guided Program Development *continued*

- **Resize the Windows Form Object** Drag the lower-right corner of the Windows Form object to resize it to approximately the size shown in Figure 4-87 on page 257. To match Figure 4-87 exactly, make the form size (397,338).

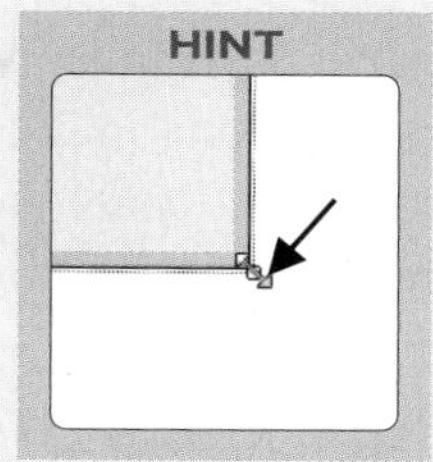

- **Add a PictureBox Object** Add a PictureBox object to the Windows Form object by dragging the PictureBox .NET component onto the Windows Form object. Place it in the upper-right corner of the Windows Form object.

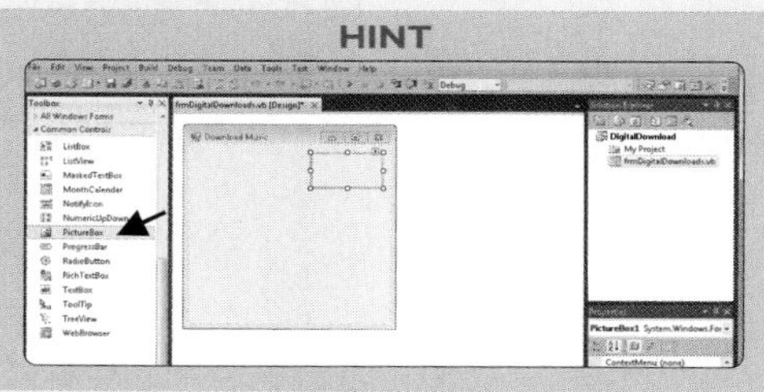

- **Name the PictureBox Object** With the PictureBox object selected, scroll in the Properties window until the (Name) property is visible. Double-click in the right column of the (Name) property, type `picDownloadHeading`, and then press the ENTER key.

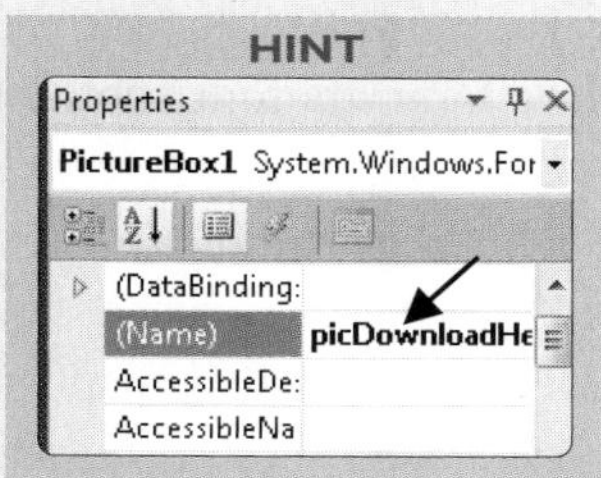

- **Resize the PictureBox Object** To resize the picDownloadHeading PictureBox object, if necessary select the PictureBox object. Click to the right of the Size property and change it to 81,110.

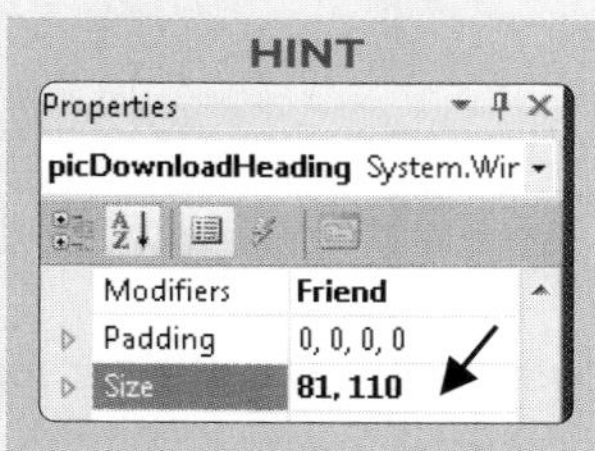

- **Add a Heading Label** To insert the Digital Downloads heading label, drag the Label .NET component from the Toolbox to the Windows Form object. Top-align the Label object and the PictureBox object through the use of blue snap lines. Position the PictureBox object and the Label object as shown in Figure 4-87.

(continues)

Guided Program Development *continued*

- **Name the Label Object** Give the name lblDigitalDownloads to the Label object by scrolling to the (Name) property in the Properties window, double-clicking in the right column of the (Name) property, typing `lblDigitalDownloads` and then pressing the ENTER key.

- **Change the Text of the Label Object** To change the text displayed in the Label object, scroll until the Text property is visible, double-click in the right column of the Text property, type `Digital Downloads` and then press the ENTER key.

- **Change the Heading Font, Font Style, and Size** To make the heading stand out on the Windows form, its font should be larger and more prominent. To change the font to Cooper, its style to Black, and its Size to 18, with the Label object selected, scroll in the Properties window until the Font property is visible. Click in the right column of the Font property, and then click the Ellipsis button that is displayed in the right column. In the Font dialog box that appears, scroll if necessary and then click Cooper (or a similar font) in the Font list, click Black in the Font style list, and click 18 in the Size list. Then click the OK button in the Font dialog box.

- **Horizontally Center the PictureBox Object and the Label Object** The PictureBox object and the Label object should be centered horizontally as a group. To complete this task, click the Windows Form object to unselect any object, click the PictureBox object to select it, hold down the CTRL key and then click the Label object. Click Format on the menu bar, point to Center in Form on the Format menu, and then click Horizontally on the Center in Form submenu.

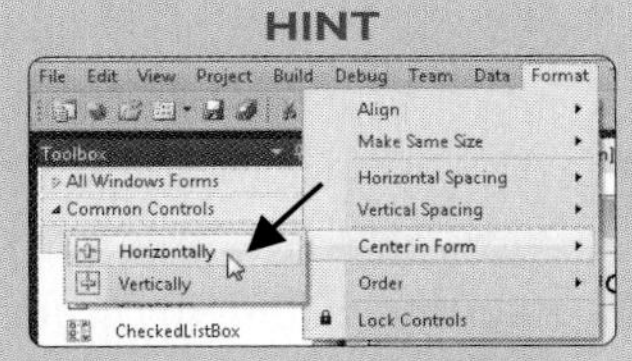

Guided Program Development *continued*

The PictureBox object and the Label object are placed on the re-sized Windows Form object (Figure 4-87). The font and font size for the Label object are appropriate for a heading in the window.

RESULT OF STEP 1

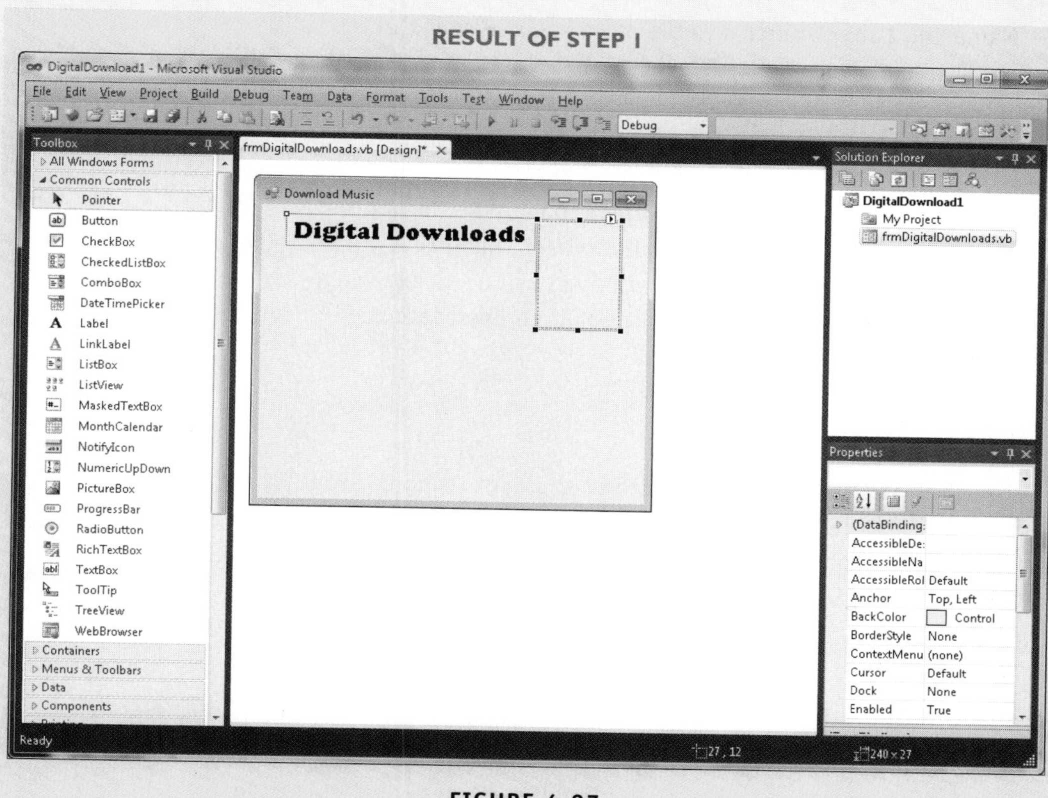

FIGURE 4-87

2

- **Add a Second Heading Label** To add the second heading label required for the Window, drag a Label .NET component from the Toolbox to the Windows Form object. Place the second Label object below the Digital Downloads Label object.

HINT

(continues)

Guided Program Development *continued*

- **Name the Label Object** Give the name lblCostHeading to the Label object you just placed on the Windows Form object.

- **Change the Text in the Label Object** Change the text in the lblCostHeading object to $X.XX Per Download. This text is a placeholder in the Label object so that the Label object will be visible when it is not selected, and so the Label object can be properly aligned.

- **Set the Font, Font style, and Size of the Font** Using the Font property and Ellipsis button in the Properties window to display the Font dialog box, change the font to Century Gothic, the Font style to Regular, and the Size to 12.

HINT

- **Center-Align the Two Label Objects** The lblCostHeading Label object should be centered under the lblDigitalDownloads Label object. To accomplish this, click the Windows Form object to unselect any other objects, select the lblDigitalDownloads Label object, hold down the CTRL key, and click the lblCostHeading Label object. Click Format on the menu bar, point to Align on the Format menu, and then click Centers on the Align submenu.

HINT

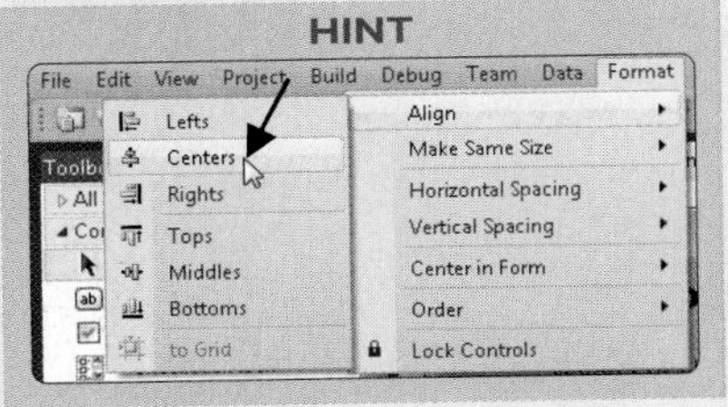

Guided Program Development *continued*

The PictureBox object and the Label objects are properly aligned in the Windows Form object (Figure 4-88).

RESULT OF STEP 2

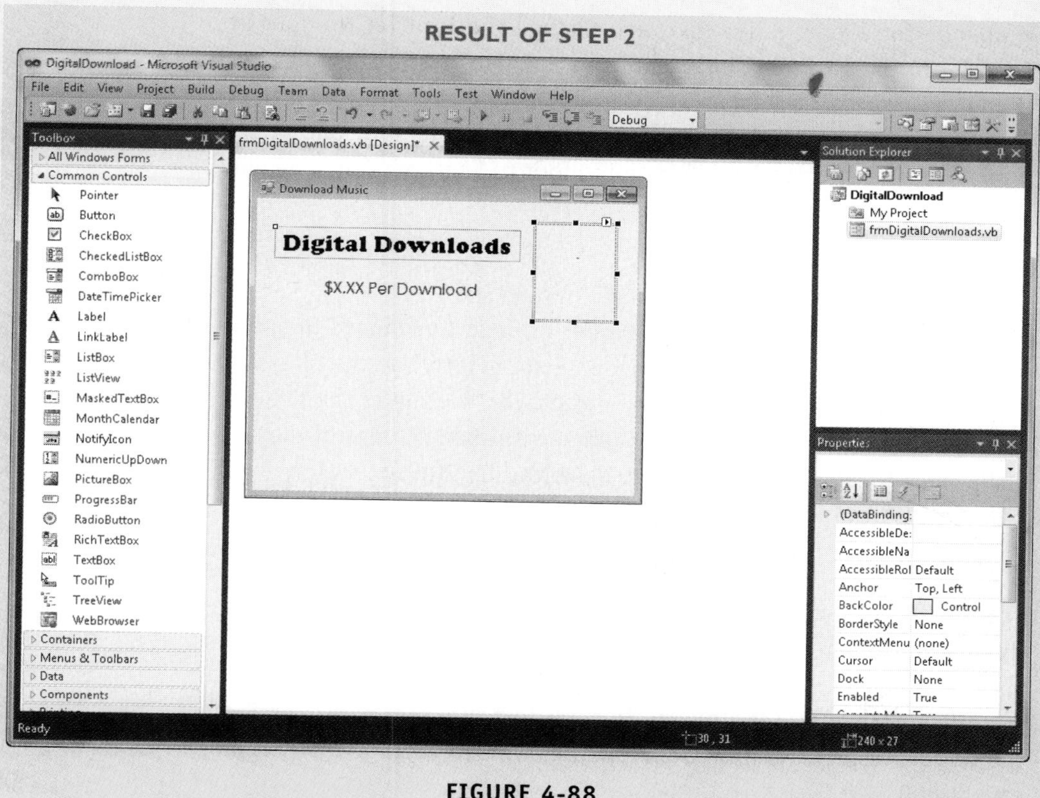

FIGURE 4-88

3

- **Add a Label for Number of Song Downloads** Add the Label object for the number of song downloads label by dragging it from the Toolbox. Place it below the lblDigitalDownloads object, and align the Label object using the blue snap lines.

HINT

HEADS UP

As you work through the development of your program, remember to save the program frequently. To save the program, you can click the Save All button on the Standard toolbar.

(continues)

Guided Program Development *continued*

- **Change the Name, Enter Text, and Change the Font for Number of Song Downloads Label** Using techniques you have learned previously, change the name of the Label object to lblNumberOfDownloads. In the Text property, enter Number of Song Downloads:. Using the Font property in the Properties dialog box, change the font to Century Gothic, Regular style, 12 point Size.

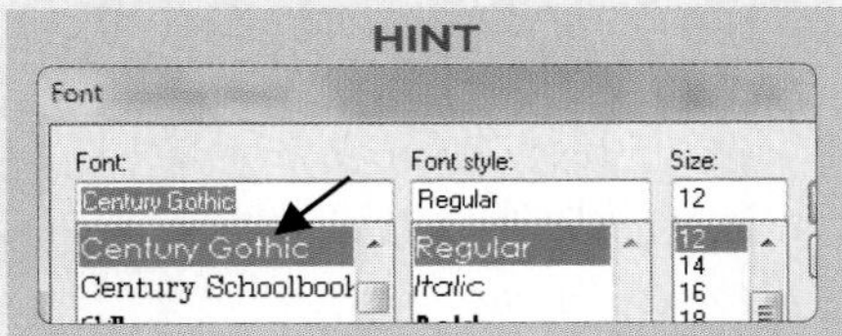

- **Add a TextBox Object for the Number of Song Downloads** Drag and drop a TextBox object onto the Windows Form object. Use the blue snap lines to align the top of the TextBox object with the top of the Number of Song Downloads Label object and align with the left edge of the picDownloadHeading Picture object. Name the TextBox object txtNumberOfDownloads *(ref: Figure 4-3)*.

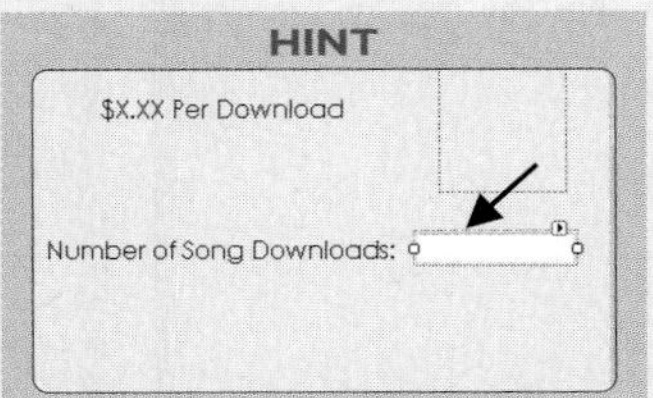

- **Enter Data into Text Property** As you learned in this chapter, even though the TextBox object will not contain text when the program begins execution, it still is necessary to enter text in the Text property of the TextBox object to size it properly. To enter text into the TextBox, select the TextBox object. Then, in the Properties window, change the Text property to 888 *(ref: Figure 4-6)*.

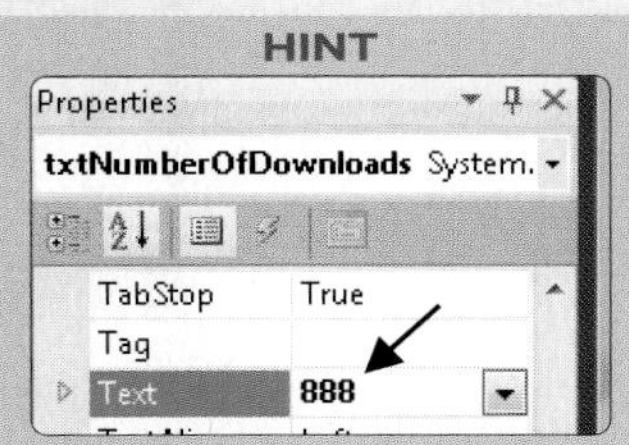

- **Change the Font and Size of the TextBox Object** Using the Properties dialog box, change the font for the TextBox object to Century Gothic, Regular style, 12 point Size. Drag the right border of the TextBox object so the numbers fit properly in the text box *(ref: Figure 4-8)*.

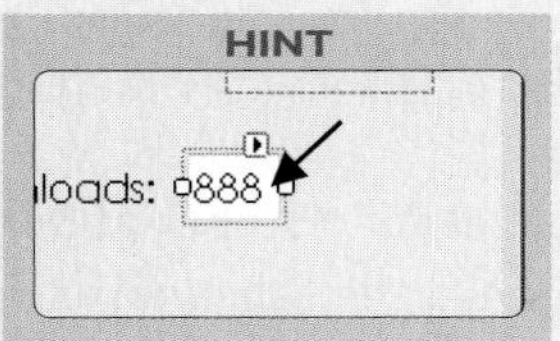

- **Align the Resized TextBox Object** To realign the resized TextBox object, drag it up until the red snap line indicates the text in the TextBox object is bottom-aligned with the label *(ref: Figure 4-9)*.

Guided Program Development *continued*

• **Center-Align Text in the TextBox Object** To center-align the text in the TextBox object, select the TextBox object, scroll in the Properties window until the TextAlign property is visible, click the list arrow in the right column of the TextAlign property, and then click Center on the TextAlign property list *(ref: Figure 4-10)*.

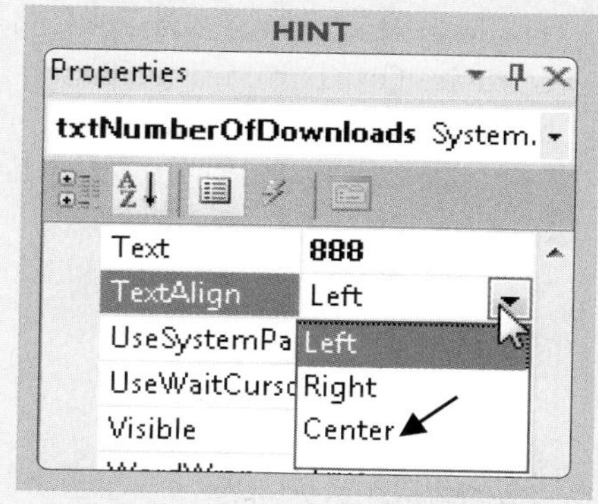

• **Remove Text from TextBox Object** Because the TextBox object is sized properly, remove the digits from the TextBox object by selecting the digits in the Text property of the object and pressing the DELETE key *(ref: Figure 4-12)*.

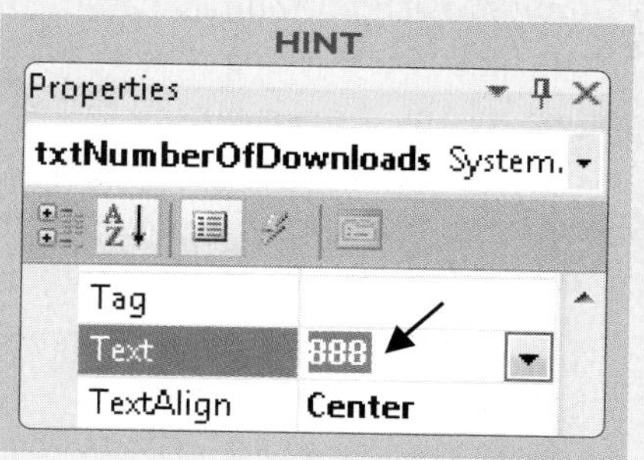

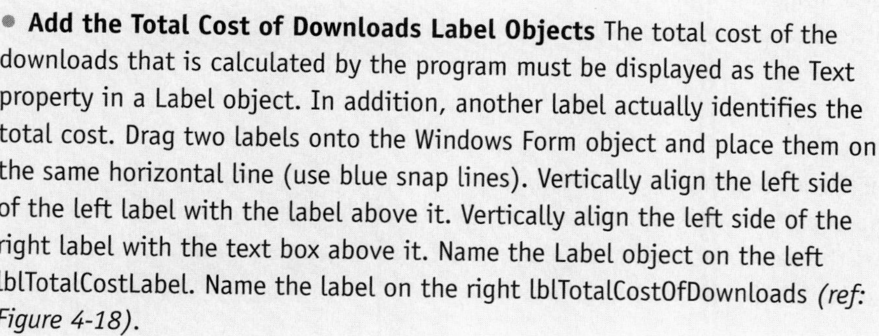

• **Add the Total Cost of Downloads Label Objects** The total cost of the downloads that is calculated by the program must be displayed as the Text property in a Label object. In addition, another label actually identifies the total cost. Drag two labels onto the Windows Form object and place them on the same horizontal line (use blue snap lines). Vertically align the left side of the left label with the label above it. Vertically align the left side of the right label with the text box above it. Name the Label object on the left lblTotalCostLabel. Name the label on the right lblTotalCostOfDownloads *(ref: Figure 4-18)*.

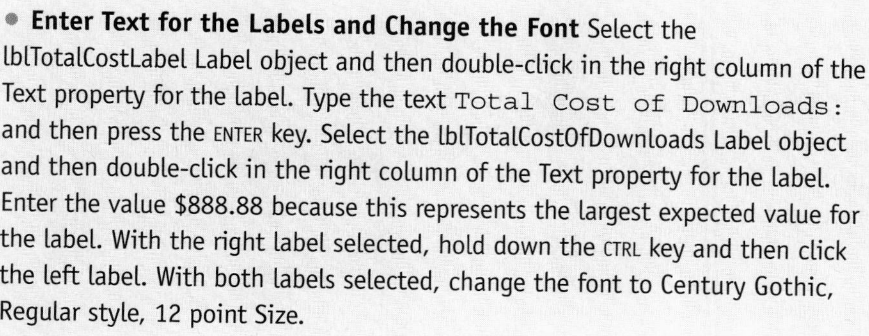

• **Enter Text for the Labels and Change the Font** Select the lblTotalCostLabel Label object and then double-click in the right column of the Text property for the label. Type the text `Total Cost of Downloads:` and then press the ENTER key. Select the lblTotalCostOfDownloads Label object and then double-click in the right column of the Text property for the label. Enter the value $888.88 because this represents the largest expected value for the label. With the right label selected, hold down the CTRL key and then click the left label. With both labels selected, change the font to Century Gothic, Regular style, 12 point Size.

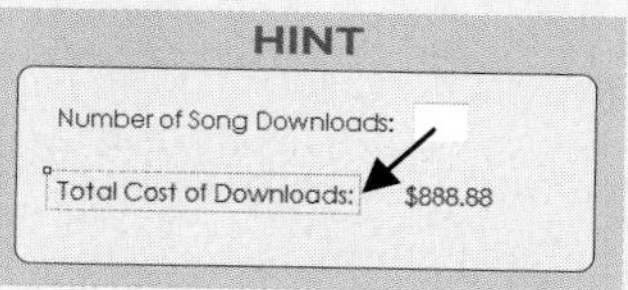

(continues)

Guided Program Development *continued*

- **Add Buttons** Three buttons are required for the user interface: the Calculate Cost button, the Clear button, and the Exit button. Drag three buttons onto the Windows Form object below the labels. Use blue snap lines to horizontally align the tops of the buttons. Using the (Name) property for each button, name the first button btnCalculateCost, name the second button btnClear, and name the third button btnExit.

- **Change the Button Text and Change the Font Style** Using the Text property for each button, change the text for the btnCalculateCost Button object to Calculate Cost. Change the text for the btnClear button to Clear. Change the text for the btnExit button to Exit. Select all three buttons (click the Calculate Cost button, hold down the CTRL key, and then click the other two buttons), click the Font property, click the Ellipsis button in the right column of the Font property, and in the Font dialog box, change the Font style to Bold.

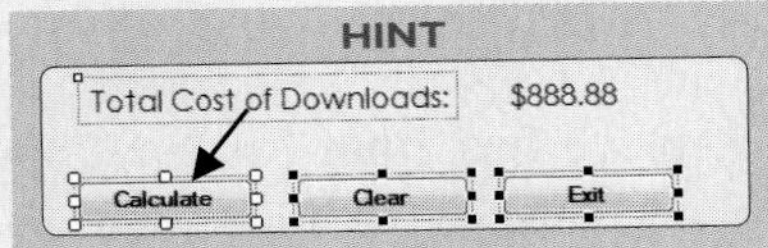

- **Change Button Size** The btnCalculateCost button does not display the entire Text property, so it must be enlarged. Drag the right border of the btnCalculateCost button until the entire Text property is visible.

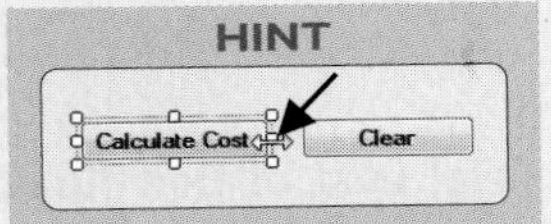

- **Change the Size of the Other Buttons** Click the btnCalculateCost button first, and then hold down the CTRL key and click the other two buttons to select all three buttons. Make these buttons the same size by clicking Format on the menu bar, pointing to Make Same Size on the Format menu, and clicking Both on the Make Same Size submenu.

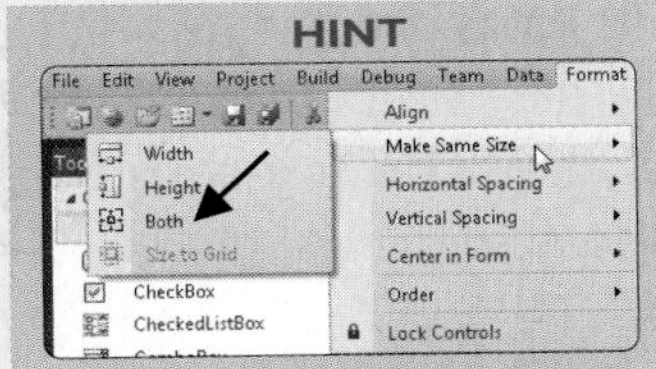

- **Space and Center the Buttons** With all three buttons selected, display the Format menu, point to Horizontal Spacing on the Format menu, and then click Make Equal on the Horizontal Spacing submenu. Display the Format menu, point to Center in Form on the Format menu, and then click Horizontally on the Center in Form submenu to center all three buttons horizontally in the Windows Form object.

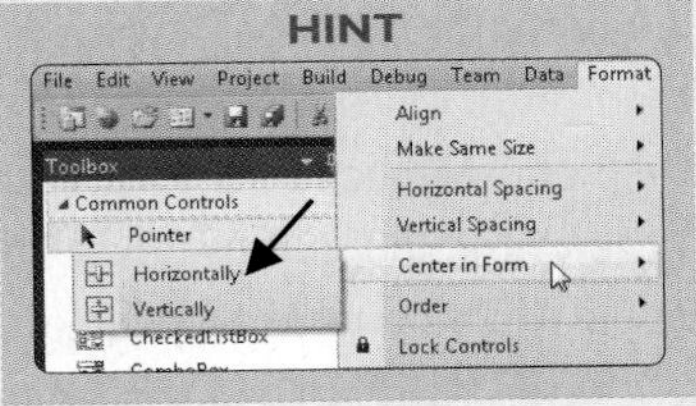

Guided Program Development *continued*

The mockup for the user interface is complete (Figure 4-89).

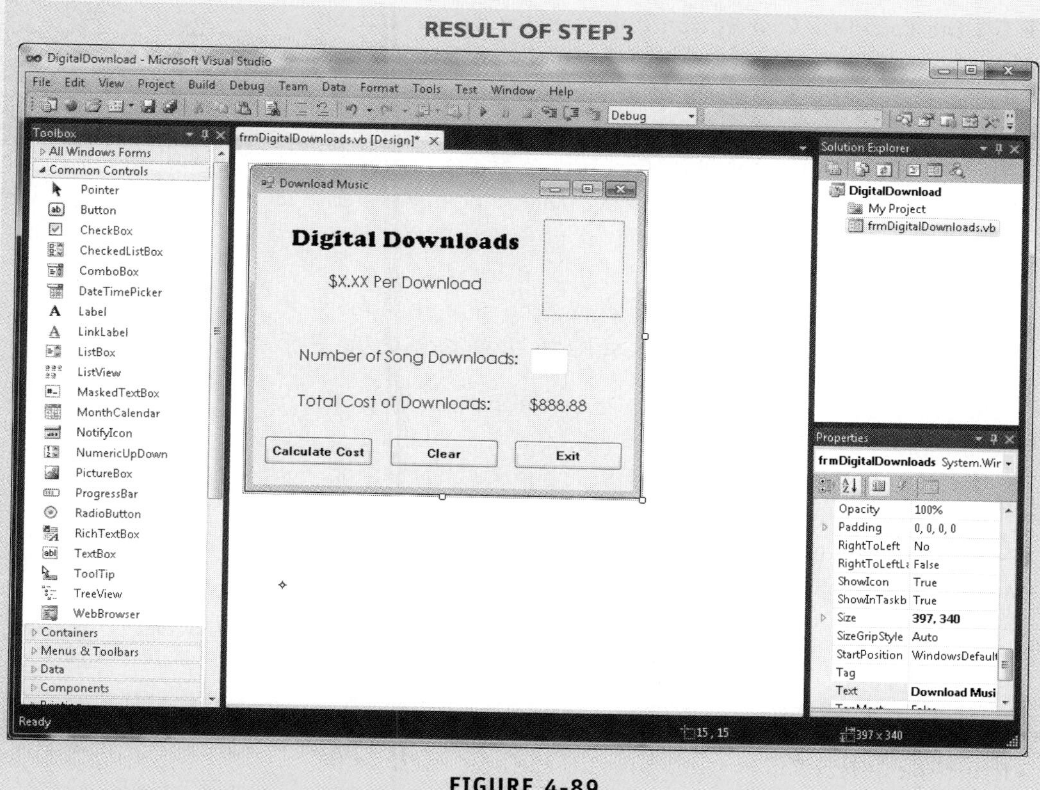

FIGURE 4-89

Phase 2: Fine-Tune the User Interface

4

- **Set the BackColor Property for the Windows Form Object** The user interface must be finished by setting the colors, adding images, and preparing the user interface for program execution. To set the BackColor property for the user interface to DarkSeaGreen, select the Windows Form object. In the Properties window, click the BackColor property; click the BackColor arrow in the right column of the BackColor property; if necessary, click the Web tab; scroll as required; and then click DarkSeaGreen in the BackColor list.

- **Set the BackColor for the Button Objects** To set the BackColor for the button objects to White, select all three buttons. Click the BackColor property in the Properties window; click the BackColor arrow in the right column of the BackColor property; if necessary, click the Web tab; scroll as required; and then click White in the BackColor list.

HINT

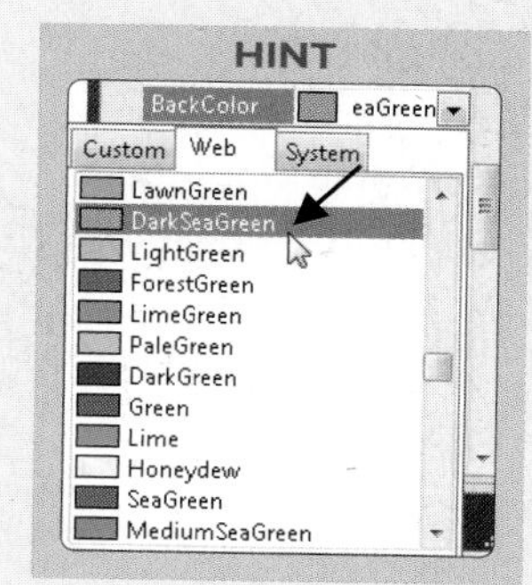

(continues)

Guided Program Development *continued*

- **Set the Calculate Cost Button Object as the Accept Button** When the user enters the number of song downloads, she should able to calculate the total cost of downloads by clicking the Calculate Cost button or by pressing the ENTER key on the keyboard. To assign the Calculate Cost button as the Accept button, select the Windows Form object by clicking anywhere in the window except on another object; scroll in the Properties window until the AcceptButton property is visible; click the AcceptButton property; click the AcceptButton property arrow; and then click btnCalculateCost in the list *(ref: Figure 4-20)*.

HINT

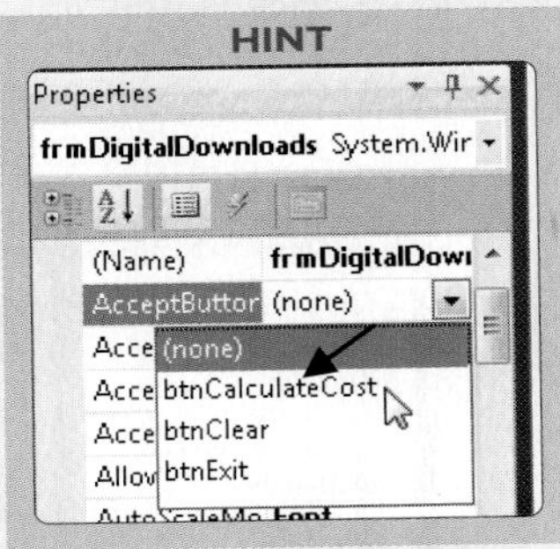

- **Set the Clear Button Object as the Cancel Button** When the user presses the ESC key on the keyboard, the same action as clicking the Clear button should occur. To set the Clear button as the Cancel button, click the Windows Form object, click the CancelButton property in the Properties window, click the CancelButton arrow, and then click btnClear in the list *(ref: Page 211)*.

HINT

- **Insert the Music Image into the picDownloadHeading PictureBox Object** The last step to ready the user interface for execution is to insert the image into the PictureBox object. To do so, if necessary download and save the Music image from scsite.com/vb2010/ch4/images. Then, with the picture box selected, click the ellipsis button of the Image property in the Properties window, click the Import button in the Select Resource dialog box, locate the image, and then import the image into the Resource folder. Click the OK button in the Select Resource dialog box.

HINT

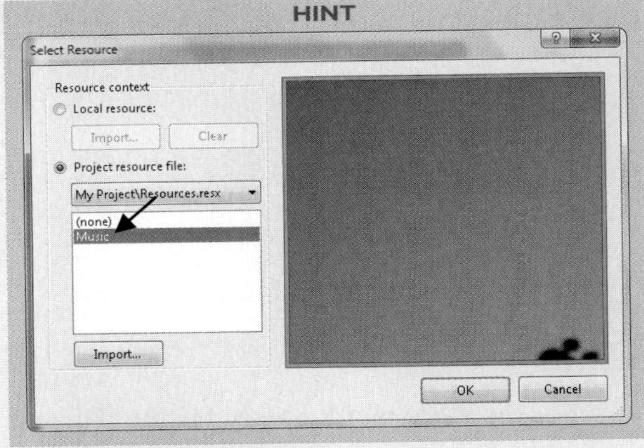

- **Resize the Image** To resize the Music image, with the picDownloadHeading PictureBox object selected, in the Properties window click the SizeMode property in the left column, click the SizeMode arrow in the right column, and then click StretchImage in the list.

HINT

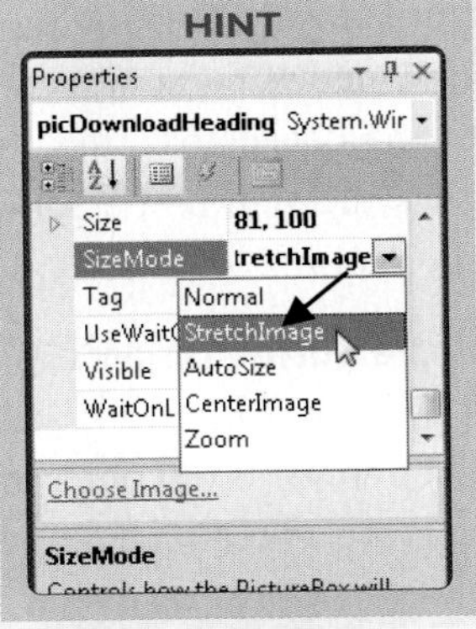

Guided Program Development *continued*

The user interface is complete (Figure 4-90).

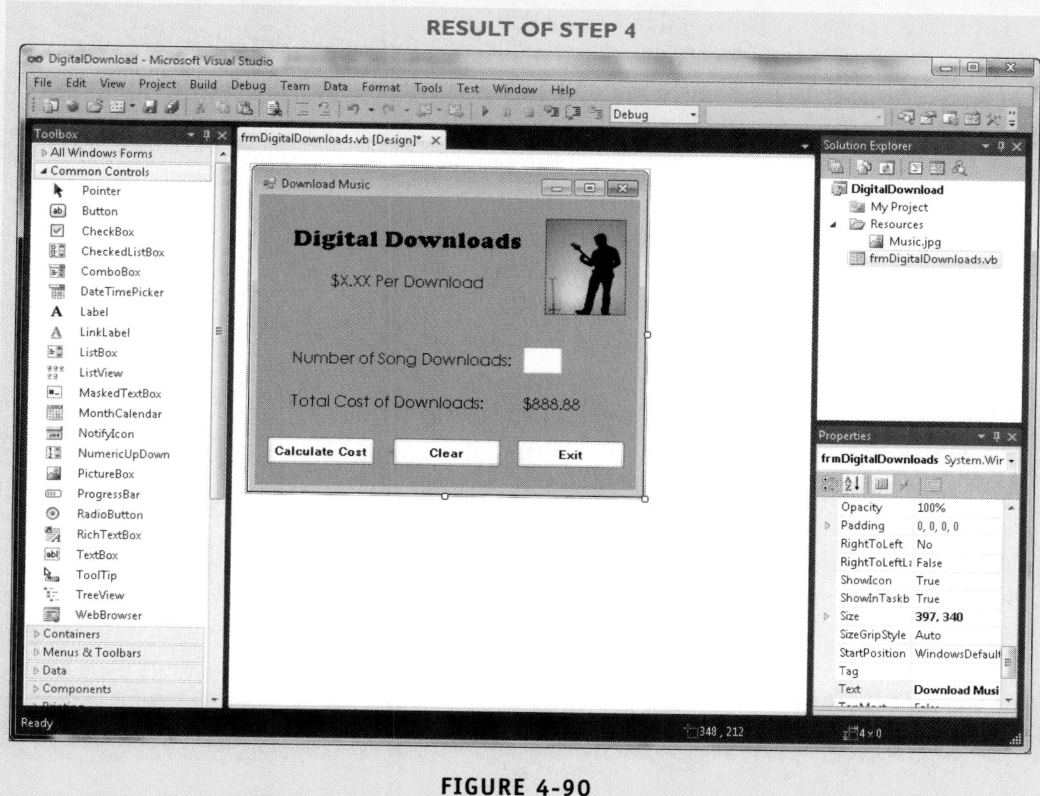

FIGURE 4-90

Phase 3: Code the Application

5

- **Code the Comments** Double-click the btnCalculateCost Button object on the frmDigitalDownloads Windows Form object to open the code editing window and create the btnCalculateCost_Click Event Handler. Click the Close button on the Toolbox title bar to close the Toolbox. Click in front of the first words, Public Class frmDigitalDownloads, and press the ENTER key to create a blank line. Press the UP ARROW key on your keyboard. Insert the first four standard comments. Insert the Option Strict On command at the beginning of the code to turn on strict type checking *(ref: Figure 4-53)*.

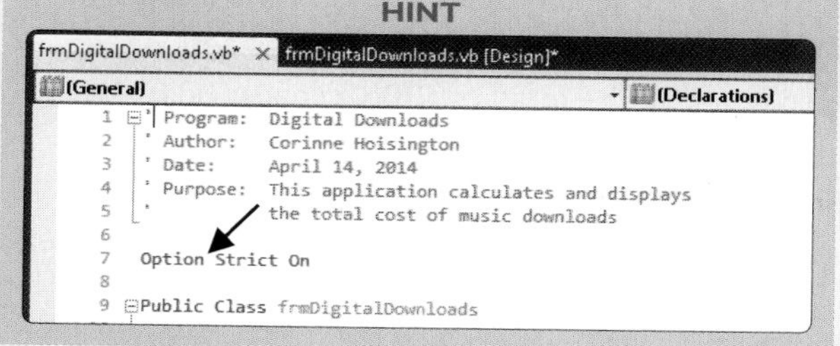

(continues)

Guided Program Development *continued*

- **Enter the _cdecPricePerDownload Class Variable** The next step is to enter the class variable that is referenced in more than one event handler within this program. This variable, which contains the price per download, is referenced for calculating the total cost and also for the heading. To enter this variable, press the DOWN ARROW key on your keyboard until the insertion point is on the blank line following the Public Class command (line 9). Press the ENTER key to add a blank line, then type the comment that identifies the variable. Press the ENTER key and then write the declaration for the _cdecPricePerDownload variable. The constant decimal variable should contain the value 0.99. The underline character (_) in the variable name indicates the variable is a class variable that is referenced in multiple procedures within the class *(ref: Figure 4-47)*.

HINT

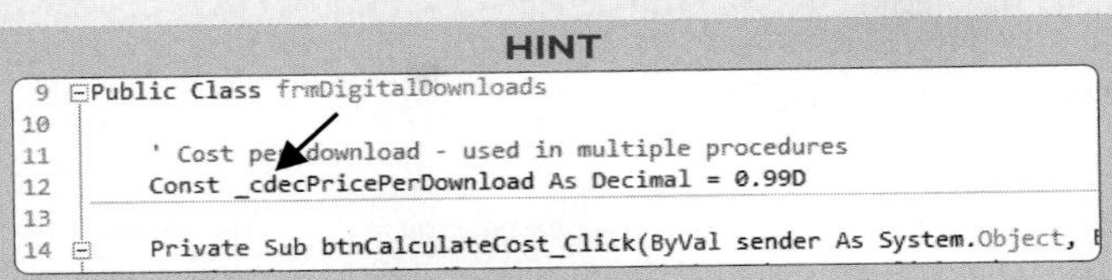

9 Public Class frmDigitalDownloads
10
11 ' Cost per download - used in multiple procedures
12 Const _cdecPricePerDownload As Decimal = 0.99D
13
14 Private Sub btnCalculateCost_Click(ByVal sender As System.Object,

- **Comment the btnCalculateCost_Click Event Handler** Following the Private statement for the btnCalculateCost_Click event handler, enter a comment to describe the purpose of the btnCalculateCost_Click event.

HINT

14 Private Sub btnCalculateCost_Click(ByVal sender As System.Object, ByVal e As Syste
15 ' This event handler is executed when the user clicks the
16 ' Calculate Cost button. It calculates and displays the cost
17 ' of music downloads (number of downloads times the cost per download).

- **Declare and Initialize the Variables** This event handler requires three variables: 1) strNumberOfSongs: Holds the number of song downloads entered by the user. 2) intNumberOfSongs: Holds the integer value for the number of song downloads entered by the user; 3) decTotalCostOfDownloads: Holds the calculated total cost of downloads. Declare these three variables *(ref: Figure 4-22, Figure 4-35, Figure 4-37)*.

HINT

```
19        Dim strNumberOfSongs As String
20        Dim intNumberOfSongs As Integer
21        Dim decTotalCostOfDownloads As Decimal
```

Guided Program Development *continued*

- **Write the Statements to Place the Number of Downloads in a Variable and Convert the Value to an Integer** The first steps in the event handler are to move the number of songs value from the Text property of the txtNumberOfDownloads TextBox object to a string variable and then convert that value to an integer value. Using IntelliSense, write the code to complete these steps *(ref: Figure 4-29, Figure 4-52)*.

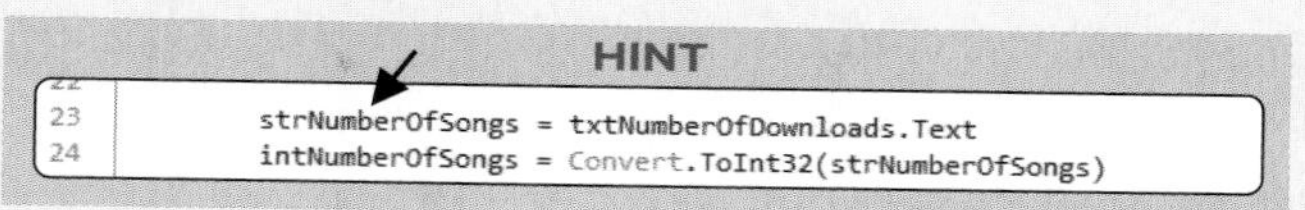
HINT
strNumberOfSongs = txtNumberOfDownloads.Text
intNumberOfSongs = Convert.ToInt32(strNumberOfSongs)

- **Calculate Total Cost of Downloads** To calculate the total cost of downloads and place the result in the decTotalCostOfDownloads variable, the number of songs is multiplied by the price per download. Using IntelliSense, write the statement to perform this calculation *(ref: Figure 4-55)*.

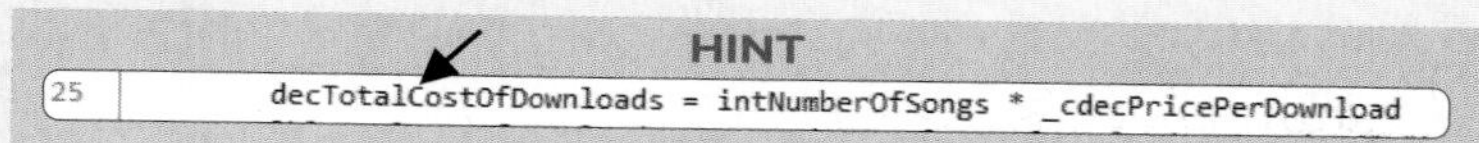
HINT
decTotalCostOfDownloads = intNumberOfSongs * _cdecPricePerDownload

- **Convert the Decimal Total Cost of Downloads to a String Currency Value and Place It in the Text Property of the lblTotalCostOfDownloads Label Object** Once the total cost of downloads has been calculated, it must be converted from a Decimal value to a currency String value so it can be displayed as the value in the Text property of a Label object. Write the statement to perform this conversion and place the converted value in the Text property of the lblTotalCostOfDownloads Label object *(ref: Figure 4-72)*.

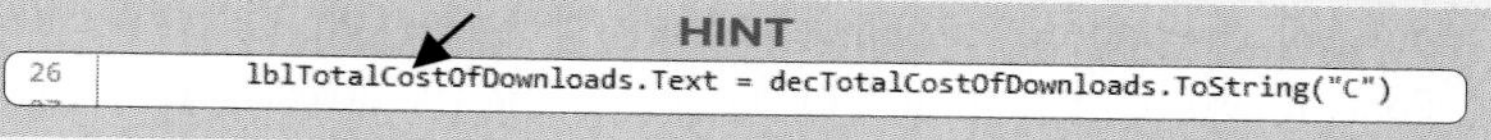
HINT
lblTotalCostOfDownloads.Text = decTotalCostOfDownloads.ToString("C")

(continues)

Guided Program Development *continued*

The coding for the btnCalculateCost_Click event handler is complete (Figure 4-91).

RESULT OF STEP 5

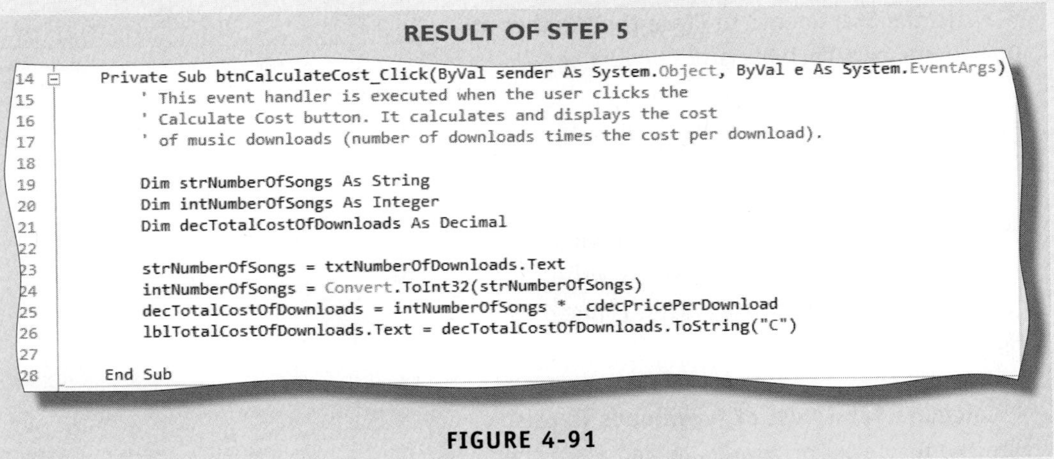

```
Private Sub btnCalculateCost_Click(ByVal sender As System.Object, ByVal e As System.EventArgs)
    ' This event handler is executed when the user clicks the
    ' Calculate Cost button. It calculates and displays the cost
    ' of music downloads (number of downloads times the cost per download).

    Dim strNumberOfSongs As String
    Dim intNumberOfSongs As Integer
    Dim decTotalCostOfDownloads As Decimal

    strNumberOfSongs = txtNumberOfDownloads.Text
    intNumberOfSongs = Convert.ToInt32(strNumberOfSongs)
    decTotalCostOfDownloads = intNumberOfSongs * _cdecPricePerDownload
    lblTotalCostOfDownloads.Text = decTotalCostOfDownloads.ToString("C")

End Sub
```

FIGURE 4-91

6

- **Run the Application** After you have entered code, you should run the application to ensure it is working properly. Run the Digital Downloads application by clicking the Start Debugging button on the Standard toolbar. Enter 10 for the number of song downloads and then click the Calculate Cost button. The Total Cost of Downloads should be $9.90. Enter 15 for the number of song downloads and then press the ENTER key on the keyboard.

When the number of downloads is 10 songs, the total cost of downloads is $9.90 (Figure 4-92).

RESULT OF STEP 6

FIGURE 4-92

Guided Program Development *continued*

7

• **Write the Code for the Clear Button Event Handler** Click the frmDigitalDownloads.vb [Design] tab in the coding window to return to the design window. Double-click the Clear button to create the event handler for the Clear button. The Clear button event handler must accomplish the following tasks: Clear the txtNumberOfDownloads text box; clear the value in the Text property of the lblTotalCostOfDownloads Label object; set the focus to the txtNumberOfDownloads text box. Write the comments for the event handler and then, using IntelliSense, write the code for the event handler *(ref: Figure 4-74, Figure 4-75, Figure 4-77).*

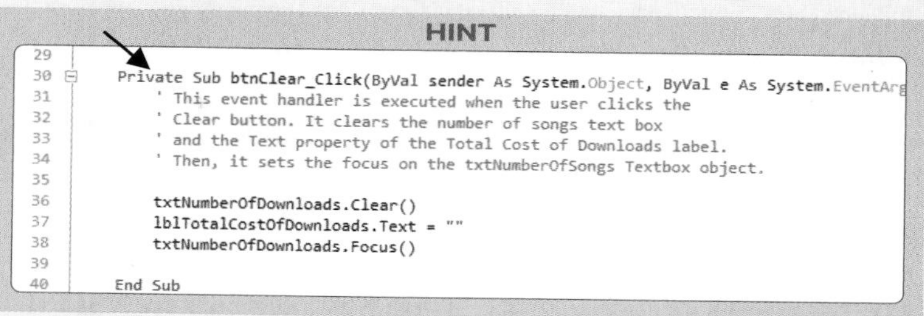
HINT
Private Sub btnClear_Click(ByVal sender As System.Object, ByVal e As System.EventAr
' This event handler is executed when the user clicks the
' Clear button. It clears the number of songs text box
' and the Text property of the Total Cost of Downloads label.
' Then, it sets the focus on the txtNumberOfSongs Textbox object.
txtNumberOfDownloads.Clear()
lblTotalCostOfDownloads.Text = ""
txtNumberOfDownloads.Focus()
End Sub

• **Write the Code for the Form Load Event Handler** Click the frmDigitalDownloads.vb [Design] tab in the coding window to return to the design window. Double-click the Windows Form object to create the event handler for the Form Load event. The Form Load event handler must accomplish the following tasks: Using concatenation, create and display the Price per Download heading in the Text property of the lblCostHeading Label object; clear the Text property of the lblTotalCostOfDownloads Label object; set the focus in the txtNumberOfDownloads TextBox object. Write the comments for the event handler and then, using IntelliSense, write the code for the event handler *(ref: Figure 4-75, Figure 4-77, Figure 4-80).*

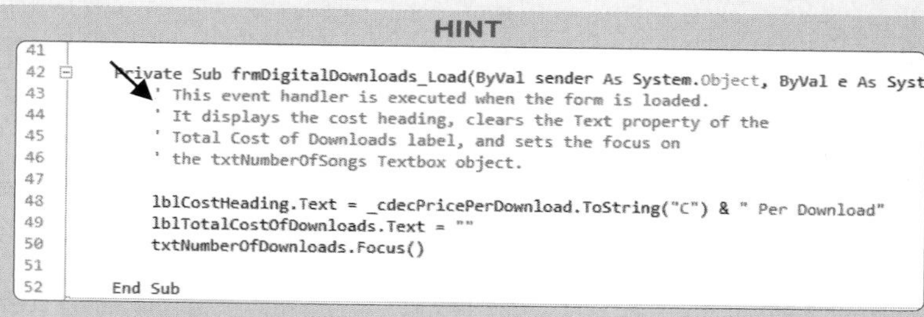
HINT
Private Sub frmDigitalDownloads_Load(ByVal sender As System.Object, ByVal e As Syst
' This event handler is executed when the form is loaded.
' It displays the cost heading, clears the Text property of the
' Total Cost of Downloads label, and sets the focus on
' the txtNumberOfSongs Textbox object.
lblCostHeading.Text = _cdecPricePerDownload.ToString("C") & " Per Download"
lblTotalCostOfDownloads.Text = ""
txtNumberOfDownloads.Focus()
End Sub

• **Write the Code for the Exit Button Event Handler** Click the frmDigitalDownloads.vb [Design] tab in the coding window to return to the design window. Double-click the Exit button to create the event handler for the Exit button. The Exit button event handler must close the window and terminate the application. Write the comments and code for this event handler.

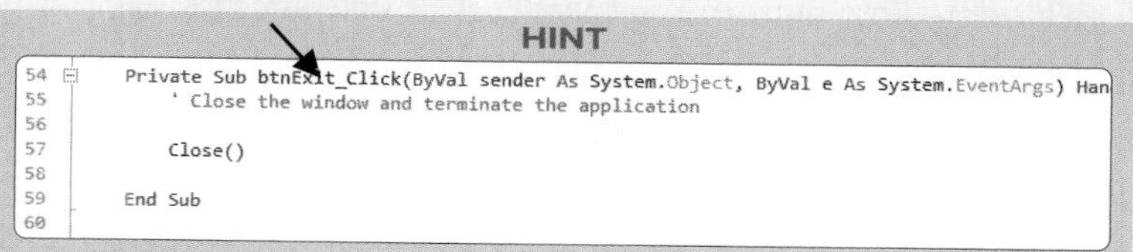
HINT
Private Sub btnExit_Click(ByVal sender As System.Object, ByVal e As System.EventArgs) Han
' Close the window and terminate the application
Close()
End Sub

(continues)

Guided Program Development *continued*

The coding is complete for the Clear button event handler, the Form load event handler, and the Exit button event handler (Figure 4-93).

RESULT OF STEP 7

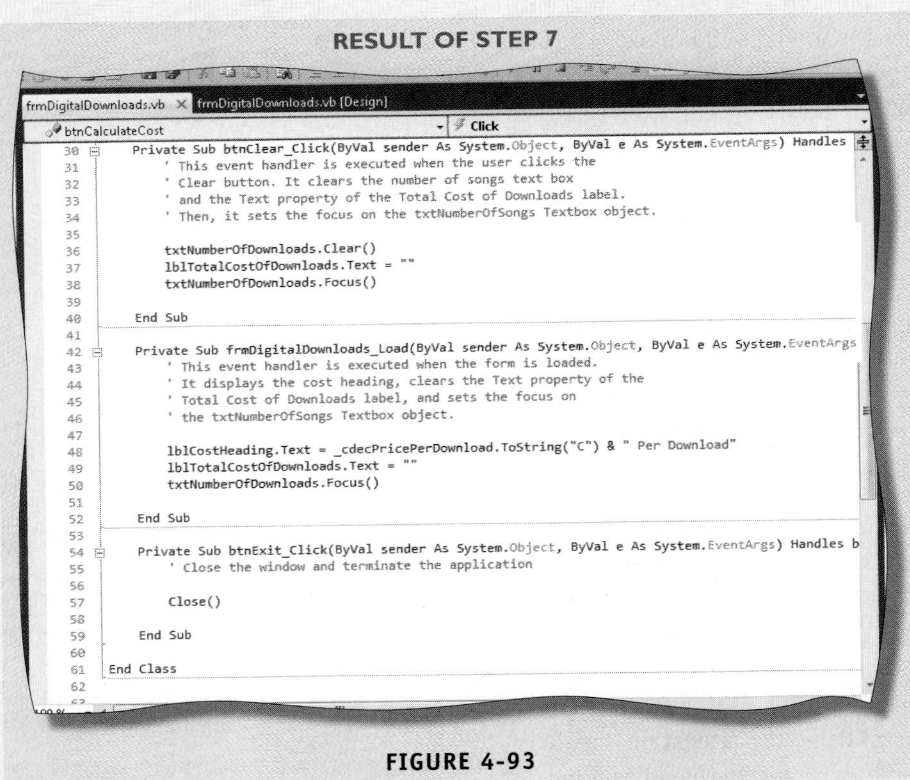
frmDigitalDownloads.vb
frmDigitalDownloads.vb [Design]
btnCalculateCost
Click
Private Sub btnClear_Click(ByVal sender As System.Object, ByVal e As System.EventArgs) Handles
' This event handler is executed when the user clicks the
' Clear button. It clears the number of songs text box
' and the Text property of the Total Cost of Downloads label.
' Then, it sets the focus on the txtNumberOfSongs Textbox object.
txtNumberOfDownloads.Clear()
lblTotalCostOfDownloads.Text = ""
txtNumberOfDownloads.Focus()
End Sub
Private Sub frmDigitalDownloads_Load(ByVal sender As System.Object, ByVal e As System.EventArgs
' This event handler is executed when the form is loaded.
' It displays the cost heading, clears the Text property of the
' Total Cost of Downloads label, and sets the focus on
' the txtNumberOfSongs Textbox object.
lblCostHeading.Text = _cdecPricePerDownload.ToString("C") & " Per Download"
lblTotalCostOfDownloads.Text = ""
txtNumberOfDownloads.Focus()
End Sub
Private Sub btnExit_Click(ByVal sender As System.Object, ByVal e As System.EventArgs) Handles b
' Close the window and terminate the application
Close()
End Sub
End Class

FIGURE 4-93

8

• **Test the Program** After finishing the coding, you should test the program to ensure it works properly. Run the Digital Downloads application by clicking the Start Debugging button on the Standard toolbar. Enter 20 for the number of song downloads and then click the Calculate Cost button. The Total Cost of Downloads should be $19.80. Click the Clear button to clear the text box and the label containing the total cost of downloads. Enter 5 for the number of song downloads and then press the ENTER key on the keyboard. The Total Cost of Downloads should be $4.95. Press the ESC key to clear the text box and the label containing the total cost of downloads. Enter other values to completely test the program.

The program runs properly (Figure 4-94).

RESULT OF STEP 8

Download Music
Digital Downloads
$0.99 Per Download
Number of Song Downloads:
20
Total Cost of Downloads:
$19.80
Calculate Cost
Clear
Exit

FIGURE 4-94

Code Listing

The complete code for the sample program is shown in Figure 4-95.

```
' Program:  Digital Downloads
' Author:   Corinne Hoisington
' Date:     April 14, 2014
' Purpose:  This application calculates and displays
'           the total cost of music downloads

Option Strict On

Public Class frmDigitalDownloads

    ' Cost per download - used in multiple procedures
    Const _cdecPricePerDownload As Decimal = 0.99D

    Private Sub btnCalculateCost_Click(ByVal sender As System.Object, ByVal e As System.EventArgs) Handles btnCalculateCost.Click
        ' This event handler is executed when the user clicks the
        ' Calculate Cost button. It calculates and displays the cost
        ' of music downloads (number of downloads times the cost per download).

        Dim strNumberOfSongs As String
        Dim intNumberOfSongs As Integer
        Dim decTotalCostOfDownloads As Decimal

        strNumberOfSongs = txtNumberOfDownloads.Text
        intNumberOfSongs = Convert.ToInt32(strNumberOfSongs)
        decTotalCostOfDownloads = intNumberOfSongs * _cdecPricePerDownload
        lblTotalCostOfDownloads.Text = decTotalCostOfDownloads.ToString("C")

    End Sub

    Private Sub btnClear_Click(ByVal sender As System.Object, ByVal e As System.EventArgs) Handles btnClear.Click
        ' This event handler is executed when the user clicks the
        ' Clear button. It clears the number of songs text box
        ' and the Text property of the Total Cost of Downloads label.
        ' Then, it sets the focus on the txtNumberOfSongs Textbox object.

        txtNumberOfDownloads.Clear()
        lblTotalCostOfDownloads.Text = ""
        txtNumberOfDownloads.Focus()

    End Sub

    Private Sub frmDigitalDownloads_Load(ByVal sender As System.Object, ByVal e As System.EventArgs) Handles MyBase.Load
        ' This event handler is executed when the form is loaded.
        ' It displays the cost heading, clears the Text property of the
        ' Total Cost of Downloads label, and sets the focus on
        ' the txtNumberOfSongs Textbox object.

        lblCostHeading.Text = _cdecPricePerDownload.ToString("C") & " Per Download"
        lblTotalCostOfDownloads.Text = ""
        txtNumberOfDownloads.Focus()

```

FIGURE 4-95 (continues)

```
    End Sub

    Private Sub btnExit_Click(ByVal sender As System.Object, ByVal e As System.EventArgs) Handles btnExit.Click
        ' Close the window and terminate the application

        Close()

    End Sub

End Class

```

FIGURE 4-95 (continued)

Summary

In this chapter you have learned to declare variables and write arithmetic operations. The items listed in the table in Figure 4-96 include all the new Visual Studio and Visual Basic skills you have learned in this chapter.

Visual Basic Skills

Skill	Figure Number	Web Address For Video
Place a TextBox object on the Windows Form object	Figure 4-3	scsite.com/vb2010/ch4/figure4-3
Size and position a TextBox object	Figure 4-6	scsite.com/vb2010/ch4/figure4-6
Align text in a TextBox object	Figure 4-10	scsite.com/vb2010/ch4/figure4-10
Create a MultiLine TextBox object	Figure 4-13	scsite.com/vb2010/ch4/figure4-13
Place a masked TextBox object on the Windows Form object	Figure 4-15	scsite.com/vb2010/ch4/figure4-15
Place and size a Label object on the Windows Form object	Figure 4-18	scsite.com/vb2010/ch4/figure4-18
Assign a Button object as the Accept button	Figure 4-20	scsite.com/vb2010/ch4/figure4-20
Assign a Button object as the Cancel button	Page 211	
Close the Toolbox	Figure 4-21	scsite.com/vb2010/ch4/figure4-21
Define a String variable	Figure 4-22	
Write an assignment statement	Figure 4-24	
Use IntelliSense to enter a variable and an assignment statement	Figure 4-25	scsite.com/vb2010/ch4/figure4-25
Declare an Integer data type	Figure 4-35	
Declare a Decimal data type	Figure 4-37	

Visual Basic Skills (continued)

Skill	Figure Number	Web Address For Video
Declare a Char data type	Figure 4-40	
Declare a Boolean data type	Figure 4-42	
Declare a constant variable	Figure 4-47	
Use an argument in a procedure call statement	Figure 4-49	
Write a procedure call statement for the ToInt32 procedure in the Convert class	Figure 4-52	
Enter the Option Strict On statement	Figure 4-53	
Perform arithmetic operations using arithmetic operators	Figure 4-56	
Display numeric output data	Figure 4-72	
Write a procedure call for the Clear procedure	Figure 4-74	
Write a procedure call for the Focus procedure	Figure 4-76	
Write a String concatenation statement	Figure 4-80	
Write a variable with class scope	Figure 4-82	
Understand a Format Exception	Figure 4-83	

FIGURE 4-96

Learn It Online

Start your browser and visit scsite.com/vb2010/ch4. Follow the instructions in the exercises below.

1. **Chapter Reinforcement TF, MC, SA** Click one of the Chapter Reinforcement links for Multiple Choice, True/False, or Short Answer below the Learn It Online heading. Answer each question and submit to your instructor.
2. **Practice Test** Click the Practice Test link below the Learn It Online heading. Answer each question, enter your first and last name at the bottom of the page, and then click the Grade Test button. When the graded practice test is displayed on your screen, submit the graded practice test to your instructor. Continue to take the practice test until you are satisfied with your score.
3. **Crossword Puzzle Challenge** Click the Crossword Puzzle Challenge link below the Learn It Online heading. Read the instructions, and then click the Continue button. Work the crossword puzzle. When you are finished, click the Submit button. When the crossword puzzle is redisplayed, submit it to your instructor.

Knowledge Check

1. Name three numeric data types that can contain a decimal point.
2. Write a Dim statement for each of the following variables using the variable type and variable name that would be best for each value.
   a. The population of the state of Alaska
   b. Your weekly pay
   c. The smallest data type you can use for your age
   d. A constant for the first initial of your first name
   e. The minimum wage
   f. The name of the city in which you live
   g. The answer to a true/false question
3. Determine if each of the following variable names is valid or invalid. Please state the error in the invalid variable names.
   a. _intRadian
   b. PercentOfSales#
   c. first_Input_Value
   d. R743-L56
   e. 3CPO
   f. Close
   g. Name Of Client

Knowledge Check *continued*

4. List the steps specifying how you would perfectly align a group of TextBox objects along their left edges.
5. Which data type would be best for currency amounts?
6. Explain the precedence for the order of operations.
7. What is the solution to each of the following arithmetic expressions?
   a. 3 + 4 * 2 + 6
   b. 16 / 2 * 4 – 3
   c. 40 – 6 ^ 2 / 3
   d. 68 Mod 9
   e. 9 \ 4 + 3
   f. 2 ^ 3 + (8 – 5)
   g. (15 Mod 2) – 1 + 4 * (16 \ 5)
8. What is the difference between a method and a procedure?
9. What is the difference between a variable and a literal?
10. Correct the following statements:
    a. `Dim itAge As Integr`
    b. `Dim dblDiscountRate As Dbl`
    c. `Constant cstrCollege As String = "CVCC"`
    d. `Dim strLastName As String`
       `strLastName = 'McNamara'`
    e. `1.5 * decHourlyPay = decOverTimePayRate`
11. Write a statement that sets the focus on the txtLastName TextBox object.
12. Write a statement that removes the contents of the txtAge TextBox object.
13. Write a statement that blanks the Text property of the lblEligibilityAge Label object.
14. Write a statement to convert the value in the String variable strWaistSize to an integer value and place the integer value in a variable named intWaistSize.
15. Write a statement to convert the value in the String variable strHourlyPay to a Decimal value and place the Decimal value in a variable named decWage.
16. Write a statement that closes the form that currently is open.
17. Write a statement that declares a constant named decInsuranceDeductible as a Decimal data type and set its value to 379.25.
18. Which Windows Form property allows the user to press the ENTER key while the form is active and activate a button's event handler?

(continues)

Knowledge Check *continued*

19. What is a local variable? How does its scope differ from that of a global variable?
20. When the following statements are executed, what would be displayed in the lblHourlyWage Label object?

```
decHourlyWage = 12.637
lblHourlyWage.Text = decHourlyWage.ToString("C")
```

Debugging Exercises

1. Fix the following code:

```
Option Strict On
Dim intDistance As Integer

intDistance = 17.5
```

2. Fix the following code:

```
Dim dblRegularPay As Double
Dim dblOvertimePay As Double

intRegularPay = 783.87
intOvertimePay = 105.92
lbl.TotalPay = (dblRegularPay + dblOvertimePay).ToString('C')
```

3. Analyze the following code and then correct it:

```
Public Class Form1

    Private Sub btnCalculate_Click(ByVal sender

        Dim strLengthOfSide As String
        Dim intArea As Integer

        strLengthOfSide = txtLengthOfSide.text
        intArea = strLengthOfSide ^ 2
        lblArea.text = intArea.ToString("C")
    End Sub

End Class
```

FIGURE 4-97

Program Analysis

1. What will occur when the user clicks the btnSlope Button?

```
Private Sub btnSlope_Click(ByVal sender As System.Object, ByVal e As
System.EventArgs) Handles btnSlope.Click
  Dim decRise As Decimal
  Dim decRun As Decimal
  Dim decSlope As Decimal

  decRise = 12.3D
  decRun = 2.1D
  decSlope = decRise / decRun
  lblSlope.Text = "The Line Slope is " & decSlope.ToString("F3")
 End Sub
```

2. How would the number .0256 be displayed if the format specifier ("P") is used in a Convert.ToString statement?
3. How would the number 3746.35555 be displayed if the format specifier ("F3") is used in a Convert.ToString statement?
4. If you want the user to enter her telephone number with the area code, which .NET component would be best to use on the Windows Form object?
5. Using the Format Specification with the ToString procedure, write the statement that would display:
   a. The value in the decDvdCost variable with a dollar sign and two places to the right of the decimal place in a label named lblDvd.
   b. The value in the decWithholdingTaxRate variable with a percent sign and one place to the right of the decimal point in a label named lblWithholdingTaxRate.
   c. The value in the decOilRevenue variable with commas as needed, two places to the right of the decimal place, and no dollar sign in a label called lblOilRevenue.
6. Write a single line of code to declare a variable decWindSpeed as a Decimal data type and assign it the value 25.47. Use a forced literal to ensure the compiler views this number as a Decimal data type.
7. What would the values of the following variables be at the end of the code that follows:
   a. intParts
   b. intBoxes
   c. intLeftovers

```
Dim intParts As Integer
Dim intBoxes As Integer
Dim intLeftovers As Integer

intParts = 77
intPartsPerBox = 9

intBoxes = intParts \ intPartsPerBox
intLeftovers = intParts Mod intBoxes
```

(continues)

Program Analysis *continued*

8. Are the following statements written correctly? If not, how should they be written?

```
Dim dblPay as Double
lblPay.Text = dblPay.ToString("C2")
```

9. For a Button object named btnCalories, write the click event handler to implement the following requirements to calculate the number of calories burned in a run:

   a. Declare variables named strMilesRan, decCaloriesConsumed, and decMilesRan.

   b. Declare a constant named cdecCaloriesBurnedPerHour and assign it the value 700 (assume you burn 700 calories for every mile you run).

   c. Allow the user to enter the number of miles she ran today.

   d. Convert the number of miles to a Decimal data type.

   e. Calculate the number of calories the user burned during her run.

   f. Display the result rounded to zero decimal places in a label named lblCaloriesBurned.

10. What would the output be when the user clicks the btnDrivingAge Button?

```
Private Sub btnDrivingAge_Click(ByVal sender As System.Object, ByVal e As
System.EventArgs) Handles btnDrivingAge.Click
    Dim intPresentAge As Integer
    Const cintDrivingAge As Integer = 16
    Dim intYearsToDrive As Integer

    intPresentAge = 13
    intYearsToDrive = cintDrivingAge - intPresentAge
    lblYearsLeft.Text = intYearsToDrive.ToString() & " year(s) until you
can drive."
  End Sub
```

Case Programming Assignments

Complete one or more of the following case programming assignments. Submit the program and materials you create to your instructor. The level of difficulty is indicated for each case programming assignment.

● = Easiest
●● = Intermediate
●●● = Challenging

1 ●

NEW YORK CITY BROADWAY TICKETS

Design a Windows application and write the code that will execute according to the program requirements in Figure 4-98 and the Use Case definition in Figure 4-99. Before writing the code, create an event planning document for each event in the program. The completed program is shown in Figure 4-100.

REQUIREMENTS DOCUMENT

Date submitted: January 31, 2014

Application title: New York City Broadway Tickets

Purpose: The Broadway tickets selection program allows a user to purchase tickets to a theatre production.

Program Procedures: From a window on the screen, the user chooses the number of tickets for her favorite artist/group and the total cost amount for the tickets will be displayed.

Algorithms, Processing, and Conditions:

1. The user must be able to enter the number of Broadway tickets for their favorite theatre production.
2. A picture of a Broadway theatre sign will be displayed throughout the entire process.
3. After the user enters the number of tickets needed, the user clicks the Display Cost button.
4. The total cost of the tickets at $153.50 per ticket will be displayed in currency format (total cost = number of tickets * 153.50).

Notes and Restrictions:

1. The user can clear the number of tickets entered and the total cost of the tickets with a clear button and enter another number of tickets.
2. An exit button should close the application.
3. The cost per ticket can vary, so the program should allow a different price to be placed in any headings and be used in any calculations.

Comments:

1. The picture is named Broadway and is found at scsite.com/vb2010/ch4/images.

FIGURE 4-98

(continues)

Case Programming Assignments

New York City Broadway Tickets *(continued)*

USE CASE DEFINITION

1. The Windows Application opens.
2. The user enters the number of Broadway tickets.
3. The user clicks the Display Cost button.
4. The program displays the total cost of the concert tickets.
5. The user can click the Clear button and repeat steps 2–4.
6. The user terminates the program by clicking the Exit button.

FIGURE 4-99

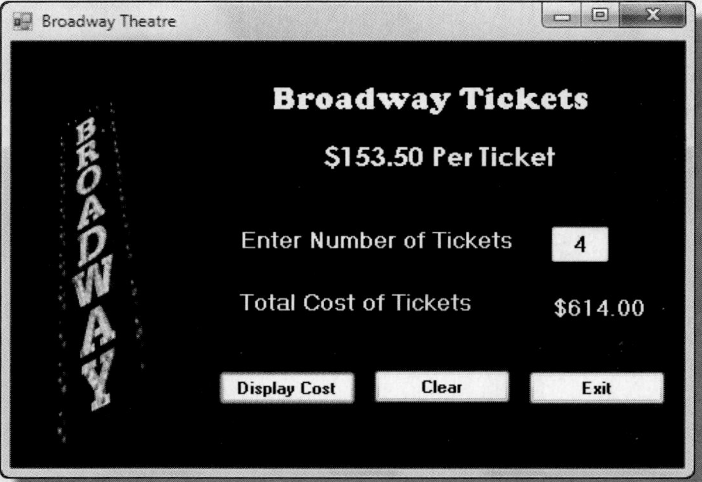

FIGURE 4-100

Case Programming Assignments

2 • TAXI METER

Design a Windows application and write the code that will execute according to the program requirements in Figure 4-101 and the Use Case definition in Figure 4-102. Before writing the code, create an event planning document for each event in the program. The completed program is shown in Figure 4-103.

REQUIREMENTS DOCUMENT

Date submitted: October 19, 2014

Application title: Taxi Fare

Purpose: The Taxi Fare Windows application computes the cost of a taxi fare.

Program Procedures: From a window on the screen, the user enters the number of miles traveled in the taxi. The program calculates and displays the cost of the total fare.

Algorithms, Processing, and Conditions:

1. The user must be able to enter the number of miles traveled in a taxi cab.
2. The title and a taxi logo (logo is named Taxi and is found at scsite.com/vb2010/ch4/images) will be displayed throughout the entire process.
3. After entering the number of miles traveled, the user clicks the Display Fare button.
4. The formula for calculating the fare is: Flat fee ($1.25) + (number of miles * $2.25 per mile).
5. The program displays the fare in currency format.

Notes and Restrictions:

1. The user can clear the number of miles and make another entry.
2. An exit button should close the application.

Comments: n/a

FIGURE 4-101

(continues)

Case Programming Assignments

Taxi Meter *(continued)*

USE CASE DEFINITION

1. The Windows Application opens.
2. The user enters the number of miles traveled.
3. The user clicks the Display Fare button.
4. The program displays the total fare.
5. The user can click the Clear button and repeat steps 2-4.
6. The user terminates the program by clicking the Exit button.

FIGURE 4-102

FIGURE 4-103

Case Programming Assignments

3 • WEEKLY PAY CALCULATOR

Design a Windows application and write the code that will execute according to the program requirements in Figure 4-104 and the Use Case definition in Figure 4-105. Before writing the code, create an event planning document for each event in the program. The completed program is shown in Figure 4-106.

REQUIREMENTS DOCUMENT

Date submitted:	May 11, 2014
Application title:	Weekly Pay Calculator
Purpose:	The Weekly Pay Calculator Windows application computes the weekly pay for an hourly employee.
Program Procedures:	From a window on the screen, a payroll clerk enters the total minutes an employee worked in a week and the hourly pay rate. The program displays the weekly pay for the employee.
Algorithms, Processing, and Conditions:	1. The payroll clerk must be able to enter the total minutes worked during the week and the hourly pay rate. 2. The company name (Western Distribution) and the picture (Payroll found at scsite.com/vb2010/ch4/images) will be displayed throughout the entire process. 3. After entering the total minutes worked and hourly pay rate, the payroll clerk clicks the weekly pay button. 4. The weekly pay is displayed in currency format together with the number of hours and minutes worked.
Notes and Restrictions:	1. The user can clear the total minutes worked, the hourly pay rate, the hours and minutes worked, and the weekly pay by clicking a clear button. He then can enter another employee's data. 2. An exit button should close the application. 3. In this application, if hours worked is greater than 40, the hourly pay rate still applies.
Comments:	n/a

FIGURE 4-104

(continues)

Case Programming Assignments

***Weekly Pay Calculator** (continued)*

USE CASE DEFINITION

1. The Windows Application opens.
2. The payroll clerk enters the total minutes worked by an employee and the employee's hourly pay rate.
3. The payroll clerk clicks the Weekly Pay button.
4. The program displays the hours worked, the minutes worked, and the employee's weekly pay.
5. The payroll clerk can click the Clear button and then repeat steps 2 through 4.
6. The user terminates the program by clicking the Exit button.

FIGURE 4-105

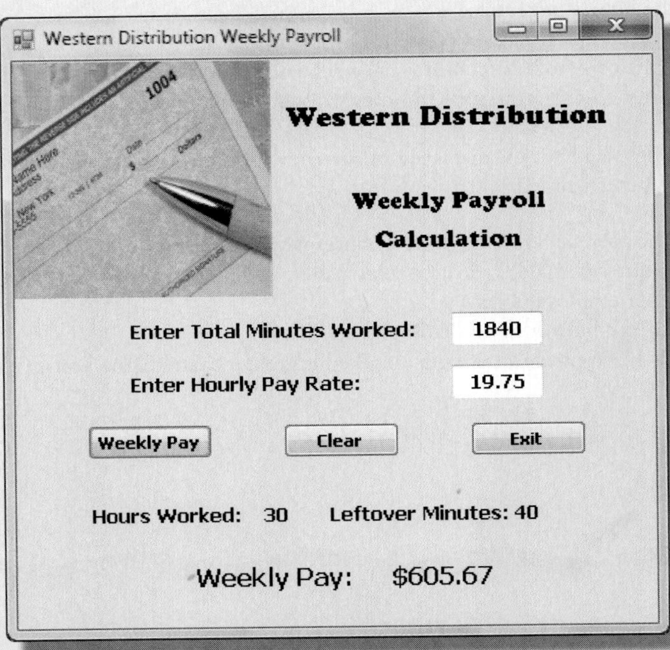

FIGURE 4-106

Case Programming Assignments

4 ●●

CASH REGISTER

Design a Windows application and write the code that will execute according to the program requirements in Figure 4-107. Before designing the user interface, create a Use Case definition. Before writing the code, create an event planning document for each event in the program.

REQUIREMENTS DOCUMENT

Date submitted: June 6, 2014

Application title: Cash Register

Purpose: The Cash Register Windows application will compute the tax and the final cost of a purchased item.

Program Procedures: From a window on the screen, the user enters the item name and amount of the item purchased. The program calculates the tax for the item and the final total, and then displays these values.

Algorithms, Processing, and Conditions:

1. The user must be able to enter the name of the item purchased and the cost of the item before tax.
2. The store name and store picture will be displayed throughout the entire process.
3. After the user enters the item name and the cost of the item, the user clicks the Display Cost button.
4. The program displays the item name with the cost, tax, and final total.
5. The cost, tax, and final total should appear in currency format.
6. The tax rate for all items is 7.75%.
7. The final total is calculated by adding the cost and the tax.

Notes and Restrictions:

1. The user can clear the item name, cost, tax, and final total with a clear button.
2. The user can click an exit button to close the application.

Comments:

1. The store picture shown in the window should be selected from the pictures available on the Web.

FIGURE 4-107

Case Programming Assignments

5 GRADE CALCULATOR

Design a Windows application and write the code that will execute according to the program requirements in Figure 4-108. Before designing the user interface, create a Use Case definition. Before writing the code, create an event planning document for each event in the program.

REQUIREMENTS DOCUMENT

Date submitted: January 4, 2014

Application title: Grade Calculator

Purpose: The Grade Calculator Windows application will compute and display the average of four numeric test grades.

Program Procedures: From a window on the screen, the user enters the Social Security number of a student and the four numeric scores from four tests taken by the student. The program determines the average of the four test scores and displays the result.

Algorithms, Processing, and Conditions:

1. The user must be able to enter the Social Security number of the student and the four test scores.
2. The Social Security number must be formatted properly with hyphens.
3. To determine the average test score, add the four entered test scores and divide by four.
4. The average score should be shown with one position to the right of the decimal point.

Notes and Restrictions:

1. The user can clear the Social Security number, test scores, and average score; and then enter new data.
2. The user can use an exit button to close the application.

Comments:

1. The designer should design the user interface, including all graphics and words used.

FIGURE 4-108

Case Programming Assignments

6 ●● CONVERT CURRENCY

Design a Windows application and write the code that will execute according to the program requirements in Figure 4-109. Before designing the user interface, create a Use Case definition. Before writing the code, create an event planning document for each event in the program.

REQUIREMENTS DOCUMENT

Date submitted: November 4, 2014

Application title: Convert Currency

Purpose: The Convert Currency Windows application will display the value of U.S. dollars in euros, English pounds, and Mexican pesos.

Program Procedures: From a window on the screen, the user should enter the number of U.S. dollars to be converted. The program will display the equivalent value in euros, British pounds, and Mexican pesos.

Algorithms, Processing, and Conditions:

1. The user must be able to enter the number of U.S. dollars to be converted.
2. After entering the number of U.S. dollars to be converted, the user clicks the Convert Currency button.
3. The program converts the number of U.S. dollars entered into the equivalent number of euros, English pounds, and Mexican pesos. The program displays all three currencies together with the U.S. dollars.
4. To find the conversion rates, the developer must consult the appropriate Web sites. A possible site is www.xe.com.
5. Because the currency rates change dynamically, the user should enter both the date and the time that the conversion rates were applied. The date and time should be displayed in U.S. format.
6. The user should be able to clear the date and time, the number of U.S. dollars entered, and the results of the calculations, and then enter new values.

Notes and Restrictions:

1. The user should be able to click an exit button to close the application.

Comments:

1. The designer must determine the design of the user interface, and the words and graphics used in the user interface.

FIGURE 4-109

Case Programming Assignments

7 ●●● SWIMMING POOL FILL

Create a requirements document and a Use Case Definition document, and then design a Windows application based on the following case project. Before writing the code, create an event planning document for each event in the program.

> Because filling a swimming pool with water requires much more water than normal usage, your local city charges a special rate of $0.77 per cubic foot of water to fill a swimming pool. In addition, it charges a one-time fee of $100.00 for pool filling. The city water works department has requested that you write a Windows application that allows the user to enter a swimming pool's length, width, and average depth to find the volume of the pool in cubic feet (volume = length * width * depth); and then display the pool's volume and the final cost of filling the pool, including the one-time fee. Allow the user to enter values with decimal places and compute the volume to one decimal place past the decimal point. The user should be able to clear all entries and then reenter data. To close the program, the user should be able to click a button.

FIGURE 4-110

Case Programming Assignments

8 ●●● HOT TUB DIMENSIONS

Create a requirements document and a Use Case Definition document, and then design a Windows application based on the following case project. Before writing the code, create an event planning document for each event in the program.

> You are interested in purchasing a hot tub. The hot tub listings on the Internet describe hot tubs that are all perfectly round in shape. Each ad states the diameter. Create a Windows application that computes the area and circumference of a hot tub by entering the diameter in feet and inches (example 7 feet and 4 inches). The area and circumference results should each go out two decimal places. You should be able to clear the entry, enter a new diameter, and exit the form.

FIGURE 4-111

Case Programming Assignments

9 ●●● HOURS AND YEARS SLEPT

Create a requirements document and a Use Case Definition document, and then design a Windows application based on the following case project. Before writing the code, create an event planning document for each event in the program.

The science museum has asked you to write a Windows application that children can use to find the total number of hours and years they have slept during their lifetime, assuming they sleep an average of 8 hours per night. The user should enter her first name, her birth date (ask for the month, day, and year separately in numeric form) and the current date (ask for the month, day, and year separately in numeric form). To calculate the number of hours slept, assume 360 days per year and 30 days per month. The program must display the user's name and the number of hours slept. Based on 360 days per year and 8 hours of sleep per day, the program also should show how many years, months, and days the user has slept in her lifetime. The user can click a Clear button to clear all entries and results. An Exit button must be available to close the application. Because children normally will use this program, the museum has asked you to develop a colorful and fun user interface.

FIGURE 4-112

CHAPTER 5

Decision Structures

OBJECTIVES

You will have mastered the material in this chapter when you can:

- Use the GroupBox object
- Place RadioButton objects in applications
- Display a message box
- Make decisions using If...Then statements
- Make decisions using If...Then...Else statements
- Make decisions using nested If statements
- Make decisions using logical operators
- Make decisions using Case statements
- Insert code snippets
- Test input to ensure a value is numeric

HEADS UP

This chapter in previous editions was written for mobile applications. As of the printing of this text, Microsoft has not included mobile applications for Phone 7 in Visual Basic 2010, only in C#. If this feature becomes available for Visual Basic, an online version of this chapter will be available at scsite.com/vb2010/ch5.

Introduction

Developers can code Visual Basic applications to make decisions based on the input of users or other conditions that occur. Decision-making is one of the fundamental activities of a computer program. In this chapter, you will learn to write decision-making statements in Visual Basic 2010.

Visual Basic allows you to test conditions and perform different operations depending on the results of that test. You can test for a condition being true or false and change the flow of what happens in a program based on the user's input.

Chapter Project

The sample program in this chapter is designed to be used by a carpenter or cabinetmaker to calculate an estimate for the wood needed for a job. The Wood Cabinet Estimate application is written for a cabinetmaker who wants a program on the job site that can provide a cost estimate for building wood cabinets.

The application requests that the user enter the number of linear feet of cabinetry required and the desired wood type. The Windows application then computes the cost of the cabinets based on the rate of $150.00 per linear foot for pine, $200.00 per linear foot for oak, and $350.00 per linear foot for cherry. Figure 5-1 shows the user interface for the application.

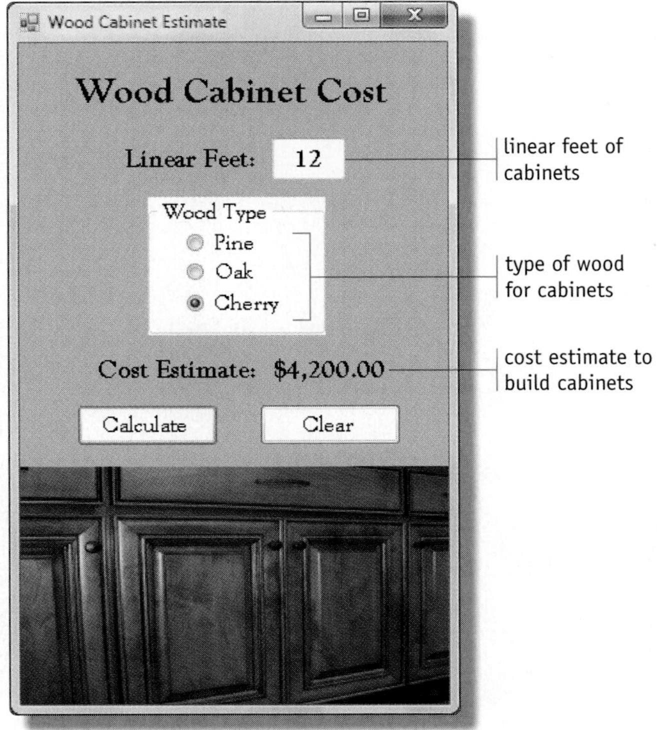

FIGURE 5-1

In Figure 5-1 on the previous page, the Wood Cabinet Estimate Windows application displays the title Wood Cabinet Estimate in the title bar. The linear footage the user enters in the TextBox object includes all cabinets for the job. The user chooses the wood type by selecting a RadioButton from the following list: Pine (the most common choice), Oak, or Cherry. After the user has entered the number of linear feet of cabinetry and selected a type of wood, the user clicks the Calculate button to obtain the cost estimate. The calculation is based on the linear feet multiplied by the cost of the selected wood. The cost estimate is displayed in currency format. In the example in Figure 5-1 on the previous page, the user entered 12 linear feet of cabinetry and selected cherry wood. After clicking the Calculate button, the application displayed a cost of $4,200.00 (12 × $350.00).

Clicking the Clear button will clear the linear footage, reset the RadioButton selection to Pine, which is the most common wood type, and clear the calculation result.

Checking the validity of data entered by the user is a requirement of this chapter project program. In Chapter 4, you learned that if you enter nonnumeric data and attempt to use it in a calculation, the program will be terminated. To check for invalid data, the Wood Cabinet Estimate program ensures that the user enters a numeric value greater than zero in the Linear Feet TextBox object. A warning dialog box appears if the user leaves the linear feet TextBox blank or does not enter a valid number. Figure 5-2 displays the Input Error warning dialog box, called a Message Box, which directs the user to enter the linear feet for the cabinets.

ONLINE REINFORCEMENT

To view a video of program execution, visit scsite.com/vb2010/ch5 and then select Figure 5-1.

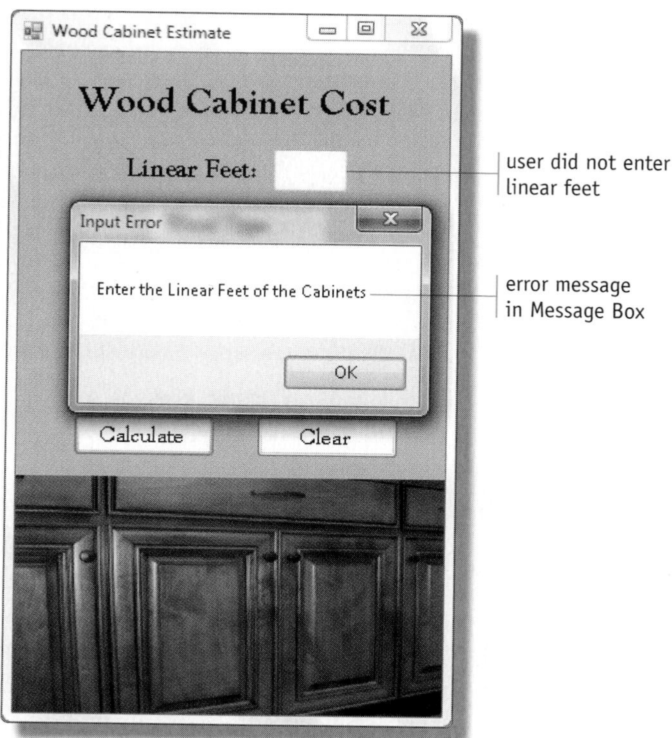

FIGURE 5-2

Checking input data for validity is an important task in Visual Basic programs. You will learn several data validation techniques in this chapter.

User Interface Design

The user interface for the Wood Cabinet Estimate Windows application includes three new objects: a GroupBox, RadioButtons, and Message Boxes. The Message Boxes appear when the user inputs a negative number or a nonnumeric value.

Using the GroupBox Object

The Wood Cabinet Estimate Form object requires a GroupBox object and RadioButton objects (Figure 5-3).

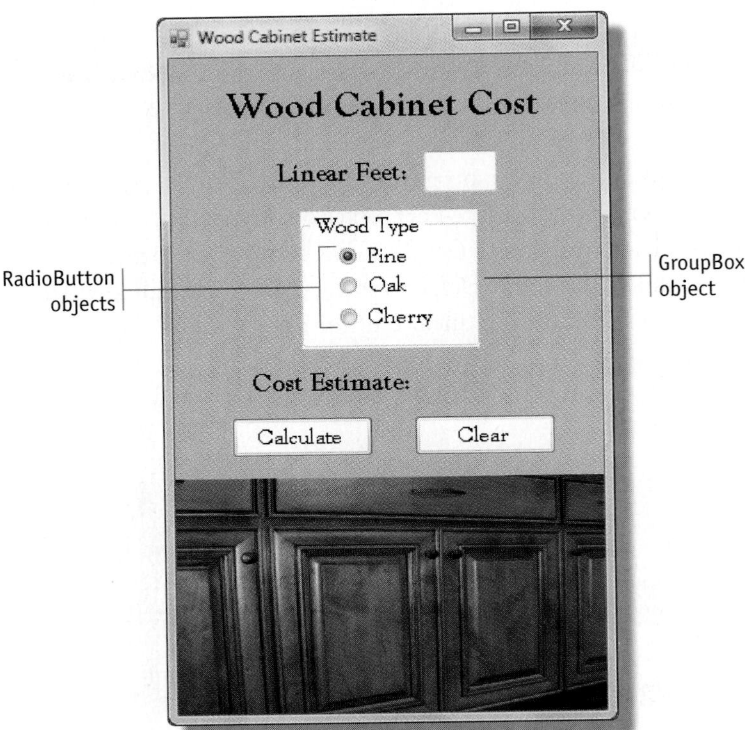

FIGURE 5-3

A GroupBox object associates items as a group, allowing the user to select one item from the group. It also includes caption text. RadioButton objects allow the user to make choices. In Figure 5-3, the GroupBox object groups the radio buttons for selecting the wood type. When RadioButton objects are contained in a group box, the user can select only one of the radio buttons. For example, in Figure 5-3 the Cherry radio button is selected. If the user clicks the Oak radio button, it will be selected and the Cherry radio button automatically will be deselected.

The GroupBox object shown in Figure 5-3 on the previous page is displayed with the Text property of Wood Type as the caption text. The prefix for the GroupBox object (Name) property is grp. To place a GroupBox object on the Form object, you can complete the following steps:

STEP 1 Drag the GroupBox object in the Containers category of the Toolbox over the Form object to the approximate location where you want to place the GroupBox object.

The mouse pointer changes when you place it over the Form object (Figure 5-4). The GroupBox object will be placed on the form at the location of the outline in the pointer.

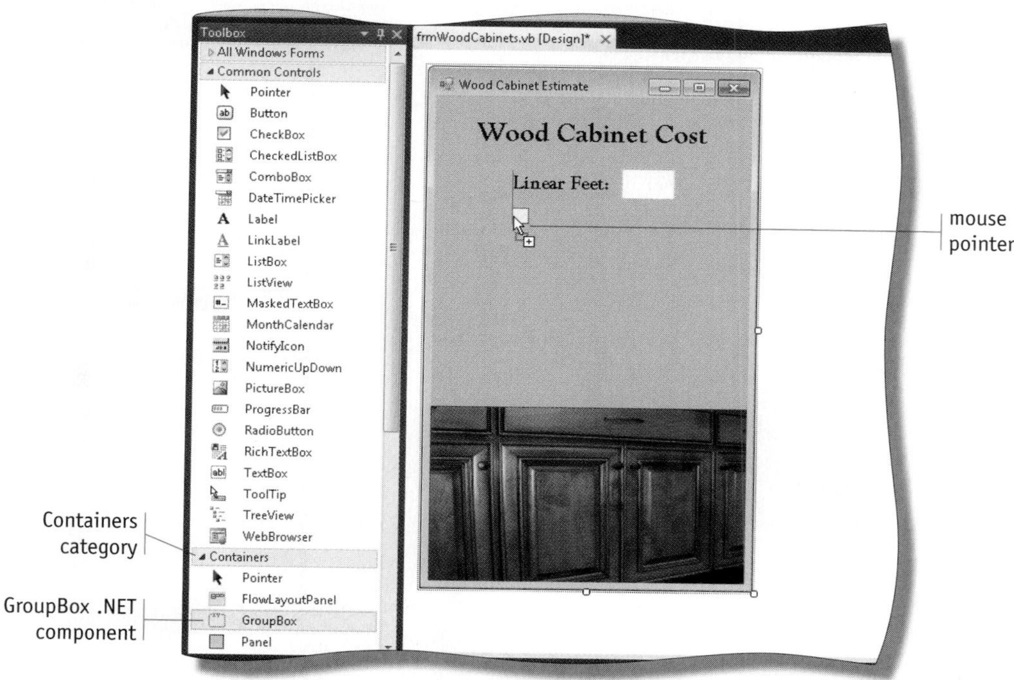

FIGURE 5-4

STEP 2 When the mouse pointer is in the correct location, release the mouse button. With the GroupBox object selected, scroll in the Properties window to the (Name) property. Double-click in the right column of the (Name) property and then enter the name `grpWoodType`. Double-click in the right column of the Text property to change the caption of the GroupBox object. Enter the text `Wood Type`.

The name you entered is displayed in the (Name) property in the Properties window, and the caption Wood Type is displayed in the caption (Figure 5-5).

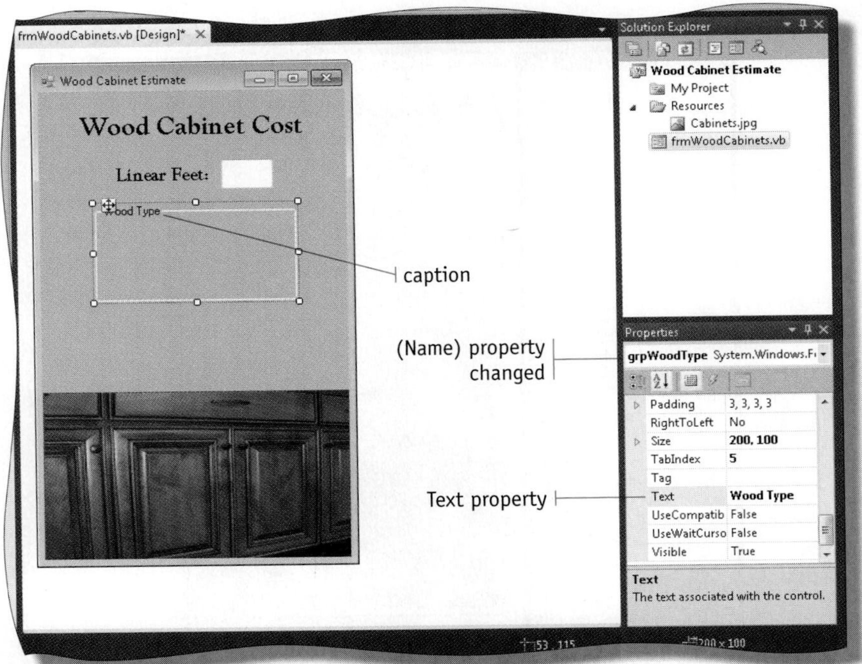

FIGURE 5-5

STEP 3 Click to the right of the Size property of the GroupBox object and enter `125,100` as the size. Change the Font property to Goudy Old Style, Regular, Size 12. Change the BackColor property to White.

The GroupBox object is sized on the form. If you want to move the panel to another location on the form, place the mouse pointer over the drag box on the border of the GroupBox object and then drag the GroupBox object to the desired location. The Font property is set to Goudy Old Style, and BackColor is white (Figure 5-6).

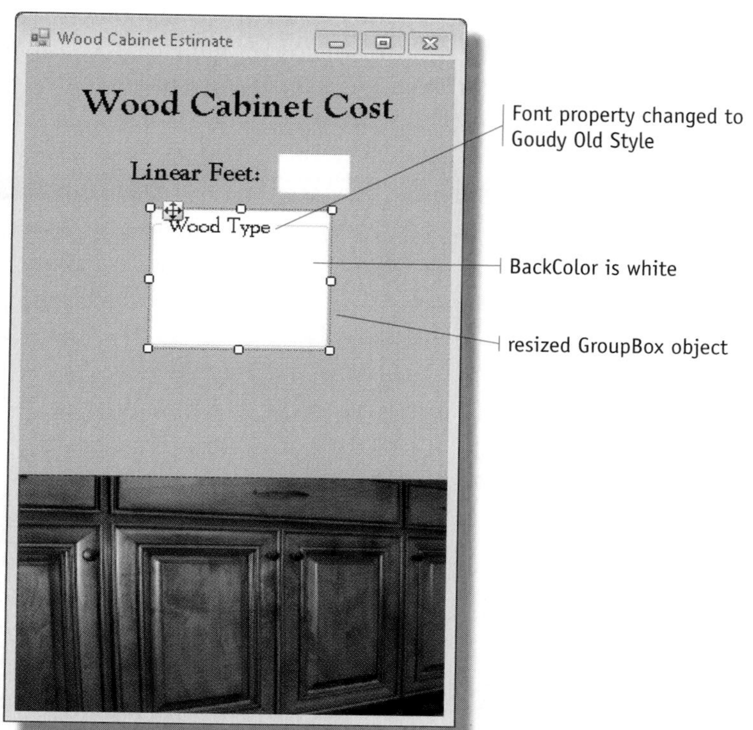

FIGURE 5-6

ONLINE REINFORCEMENT

To view a video of the process in the previous steps, visit scsite.com/vb2010/ch5 and then select Figure 5-4.

Grouping all options in a GroupBox object gives the user a logical visual cue. Also, when you move the GroupBox object, all its contained objects move as well.

Adding the RadioButton Objects

The GroupBox object in the Wood Cabinet Estimate application contains a set of RadioButton objects (see Figure 5-3 on page 294). The user may select only one type of wood: pine, oak, or cherry. To place RadioButton objects within the GroupBox object, you can complete the following steps:

STEP 1 Drag and drop one RadioButton object from the Toolbox into the GroupBox object on the Form object. Drag a second RadioButton object from the Toolbox into the GroupBox object, using blue snap lines to align and separate the RadioButton objects vertically.

The second RadioButton object is aligned vertically with a blue snap line, which separates it vertically from the first RadioButton object (Figure 5-7).

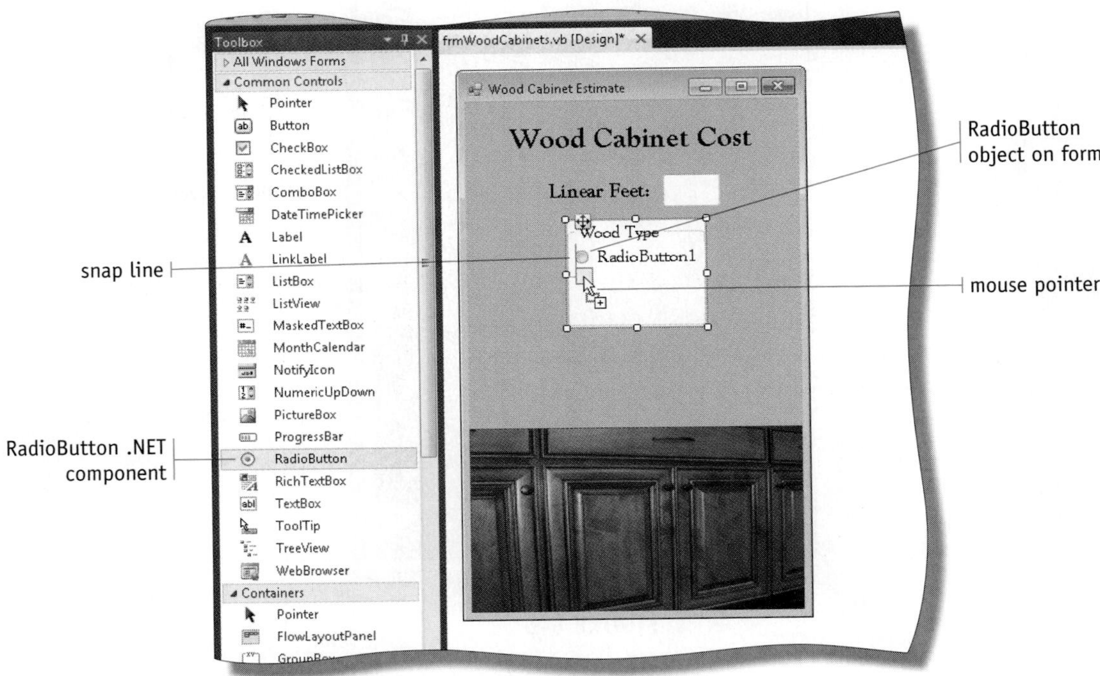

FIGURE 5-7

STEP 2 Release the mouse button to place the RadioButton object on the Form object within the GroupBox object. Using the same technique, add a third RadioButton object.

Three RadioButton objects are placed on the form and aligned within the GroupBox object (Figure 5-8).

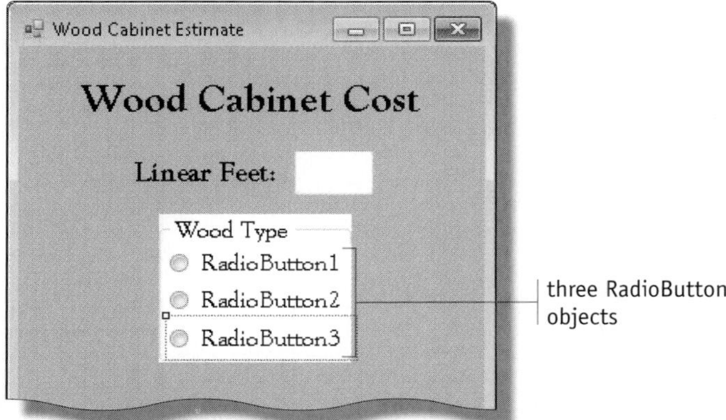

FIGURE 5-8

STEP 3 Name the RadioButton objects by selecting a RadioButton object, double-clicking in the right column of the (Name) property in the Properties window, and entering the name. The names for the radio buttons, from top to bottom, should be radPine, radOak, and radCherry.

The (Name) property is selected. The names radPine, radOak, and radCherry are entered (Figure 5-9).

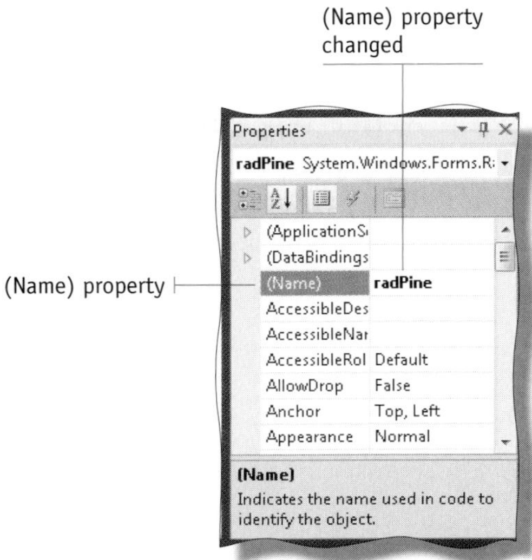

FIGURE 5-9

STEP 4 Change the Text property for each RadioButton by double-clicking in the right column of the Text property and typing `Pine` for the first RadioButton, `Oak` for the second RadioButton, and `Cherry` for the third RadioButton.

The Text property has been changed to the types of wood available: Pine, Oak, and Cherry (Figure 5-10).

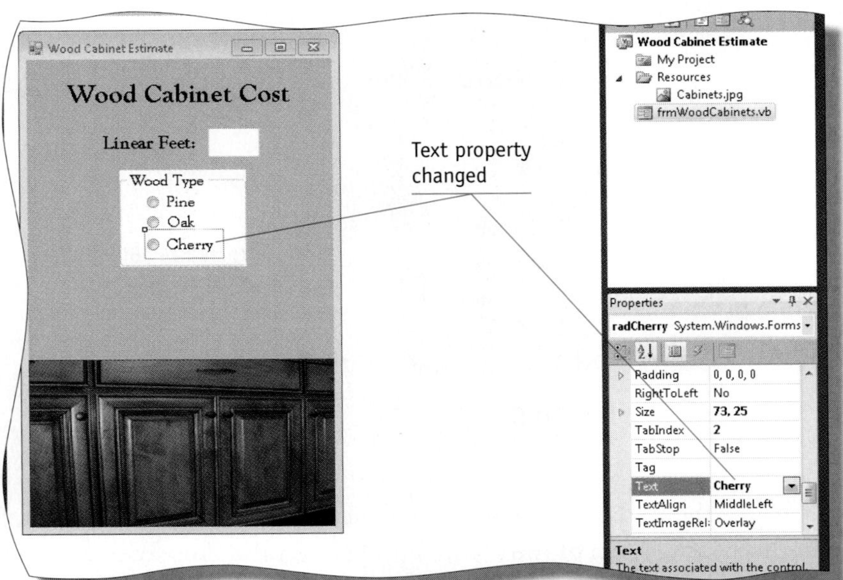

FIGURE 5-10

ONLINE REINFORCEMENT

To view a video of the process in the previous steps, visit scsite.com/vb2010/ch5 and then select Figure 5-7.

Using the Checked Property of RadioButton Objects

You will recall that the RadioButton objects in the Wood Cabinet Estimate application allow the user to select one wood type. When the user selects Cherry as the wood type, as shown in Figure 5-11 on the next page, the RadioButton is selected (the small circle in the radio button is shaded). When a RadioButton is selected, the Checked property of the Cherry RadioButton changes from False (unselected) to True (selected).

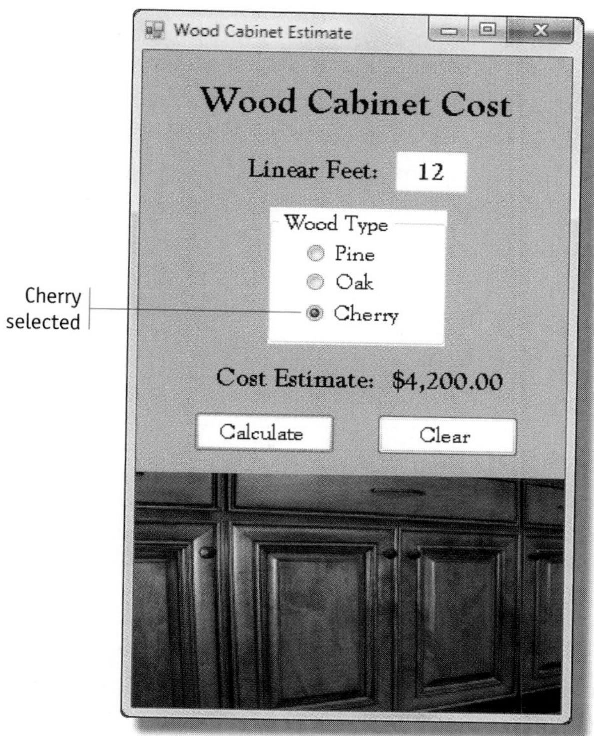

FIGURE 5-11

Often, during design time, you should set the Checked property to True for the most commonly selected RadioButton to save the user from having to select the most common choice. In the Wood Cabinet Estimate application, the cabinetmaker uses Pine most often. To cause the Pine RadioButton object named radPine to appear selected (shaded) when the program begins, you change the Checked property for the radPine RadioButton from False to True (Figure 5-12).

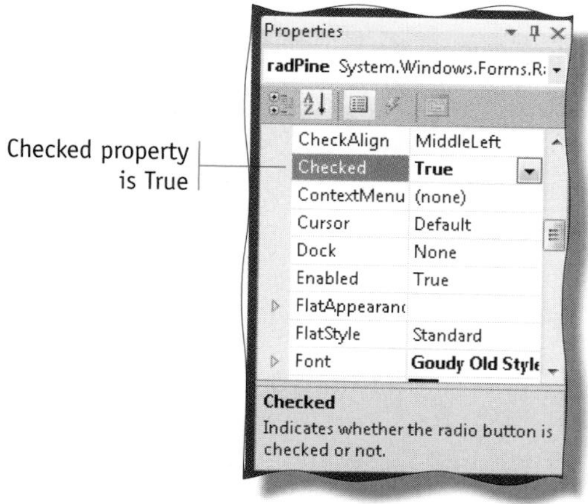

FIGURE 5-12

Windows Application Container Objects

The Panel object in a Windows application performs in the same manner as the GroupBox object. For Windows applications, Visual Basic provides four additional container objects: FlowLayoutPanel, SplitContainer, TabControl, and TableLayoutPanel. The GroupBox object is used most often; it provides several options not available with the Panel object. The table in Figure 5-13 shows the differences between the GroupBox and the Panel objects.

Option	GroupBox Object	Panel Object
Have a caption	Yes	No
Have scroll bars	Yes	No
Display a labeled border	Yes	No

FIGURE 5-13

Figure 5-14 shows the Windows application Toolbox, the Containers group of .NET components, and a GroupBox object and a Panel object in a Windows application. Notice in the Toolbox that the GroupBox and Panel objects are in a subcategory called Containers.

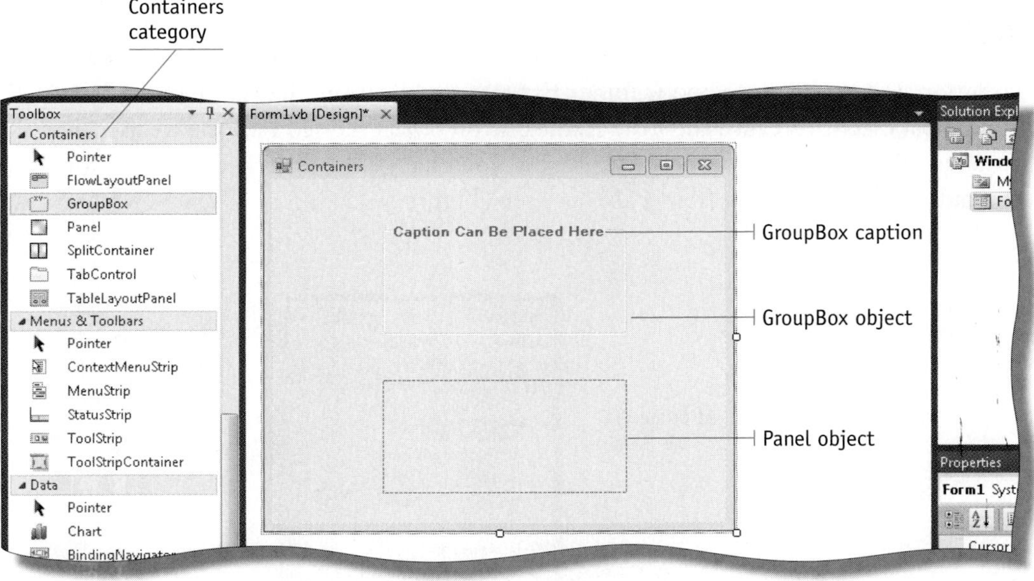

FIGURE 5-14

The GroupBox object in Figure 5-14 displays a border around the edges of the object, with a text area in the upper-left for a caption. The Panel object has a black dashed border that does not appear when the application is executed. GroupBox and Panel objects have the same purpose of grouping RadioButtons and other objects, but they differ in their appearance.

Related RadioButtons should be placed in a separate container object so that the user can select one radio button from each group. Always place the container object on the form first, and then drag the RadioButton objects into the container object.

The Course Sign-up example in Figure 5-15 displays a Windows application that allows the user to sign up for a Web Design course. Notice the two separate groups of RadioButton objects. In the Choose Course Level GroupBox object, the user should select a course level. In the Choose Semester GroupBox object, the user should identify the semester for the course. As you can see, the user selects one radio button from the left group and one radio button from the right group.

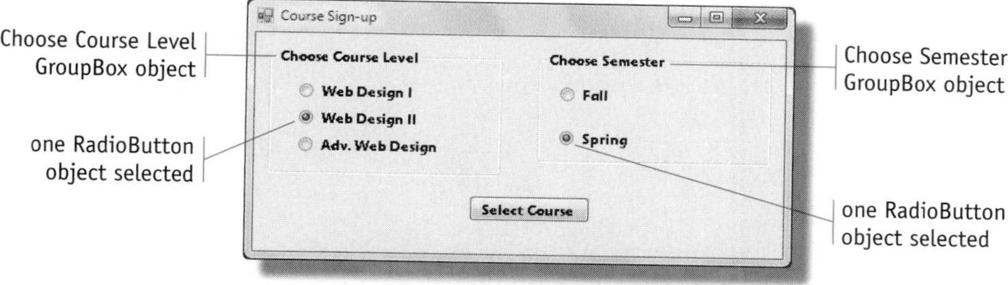

FIGURE 5-15

Displaying a Message Box

In the Wood Cabinet Estimate chapter project, a message box, also called a dialog box, opens if the user does not enter the length of the cabinets correctly. The dialog box displays an error message if the user omits the length or enters nonnumeric data (Figure 5-16).

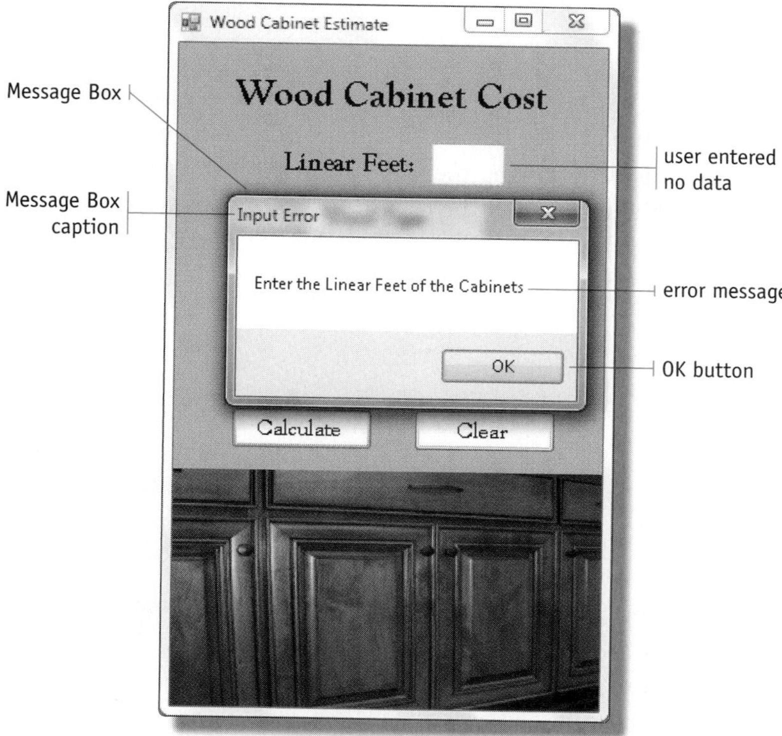

FIGURE 5-16

If the user enters a negative number for the length of the cabinets, a message box appears (Figure 5-17) stating that a positive number is necessary.

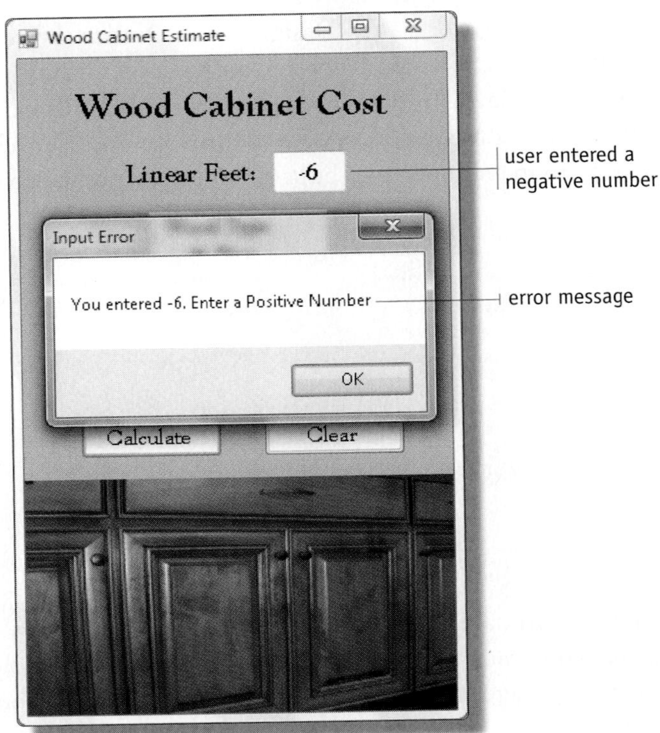

FIGURE 5-17

HEADS UP

You can create message boxes with two different commands: MessageBox.Show and MsgBox. This book focuses on the MsgBox command because it is shorter and easier to use.

This message box reminds the user to enter the linear feet of the cabinets. A message box window must be closed before the application can continue. The user can continue the application by clicking the OK button in the message box.

In Visual Basic, the message to the user in a message box window is displayed using a procedure named Show that is found in the MessageBox class. The syntax for the statement to display a message in a message box is shown in Figure 5-18 on the next page.

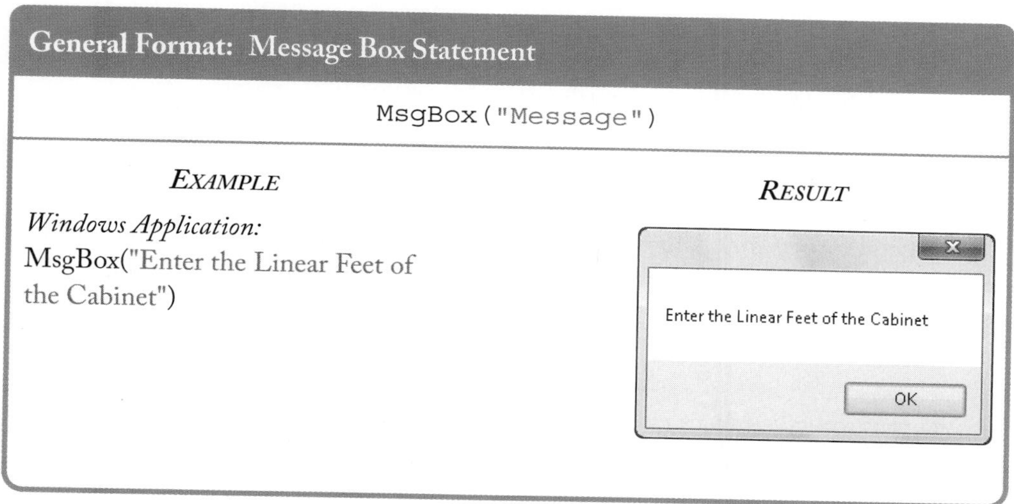

FIGURE 5-18

The string message shown in the parentheses will appear in the message box when the code is executed. The string message is considered an argument of the procedure. You will recall that an argument is a value that is passed to a procedure. The first argument for the MsgBox command contains the message to be printed in the message box window on top of the form during execution.

The example in Figure 5-19 illustrates the code that could be used in the Calculate button click event handler. This code could be executed if the user clicks the Calculate button without entering a numeric value in the Linear Feet text box (see Figure 5-17 on the previous page).

Displaying Message Box Captions

A message box can be displayed during execution with a variety of arguments. For example, a message box can display a message and a caption in the title bar (two arguments with two commas between the two arguments) using the syntax shown in Figure 5-19.

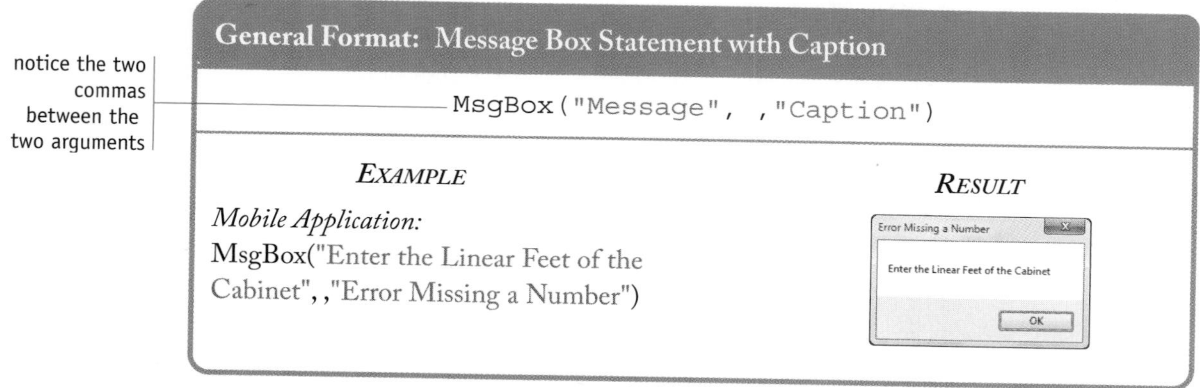

FIGURE 5-19

The title bar in the example in Figure 5-19 on the previous page displays a caption and the message box displays a message. In many applications, the caption is used to give further information to the user.

Message Box Buttons

The general format for changing the button command from OK to another button type is shown in Figure 5-20. The button entry can be a command or a value representing a command.

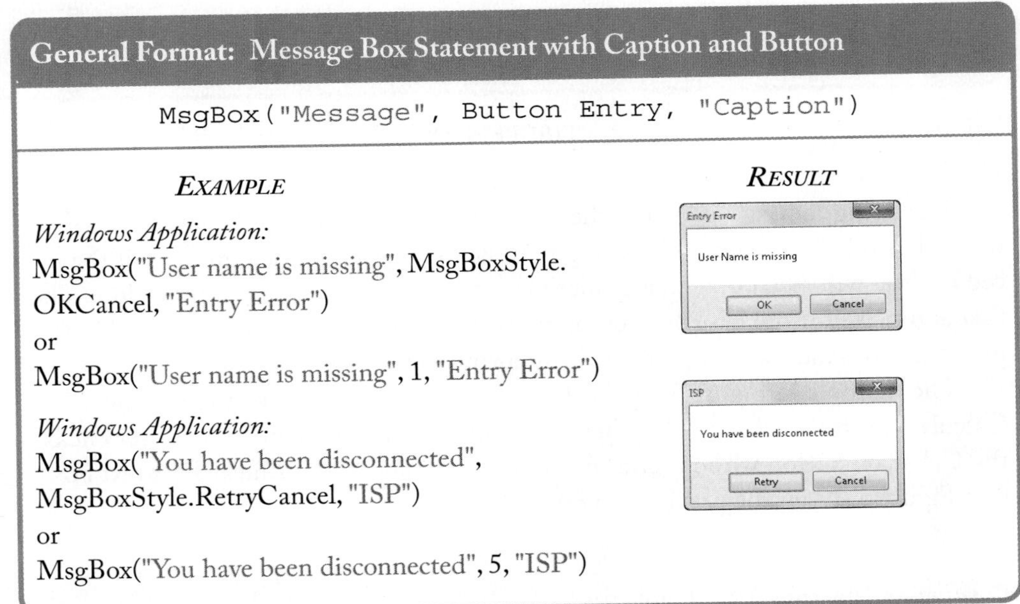

General Format: Message Box Statement with Caption and Button

```
MsgBox("Message", Button Entry, "Caption")
```

EXAMPLE

Windows Application:
MsgBox("User name is missing", MsgBoxStyle.
OKCancel, "Entry Error")
or
MsgBox("User name is missing", 1, "Entry Error")

Windows Application:
MsgBox("You have been disconnected",
MsgBoxStyle.RetryCancel, "ISP")
or
MsgBox("You have been disconnected", 5, "ISP")

RESULT

FIGURE 5-20

In the first example in Figure 5-20, the buttons specified are the OK button and the Cancel button. In the second example, the buttons shown are the Retry button and the Cancel button.

The table in Figure 5-21 shows all the possible entries that can be placed in the Button Entry portion of the argument passed to the Show procedure.

MsgBoxButtons Arguments	Value	Use
MsgBoxStyle.OKOnly	0	Displays an OK button — default setting
MsgBoxStyle.OKCancel	1	Displays an OK and Cancel button
MsgBoxStyle.AbortRetryIgnore	2	After a failing situation, the user can choose to Abort, Retry, or Ignore
MsgBoxStyle.YesNoCancel	3	Displays Yes, No, and Cancel buttons
MsgBoxStyle.YesNo	4	Displays Yes and No buttons
MsgBoxStyle.RetryCancel	5	After an error occurs, the user can choose to Retry or Cancel

FIGURE 5-21

Message Box Icons

In the button entry portion of the argument (the second argument), a message box icon can be added (Figure 5-22). The word "or" connects the button entry to the icon entry.

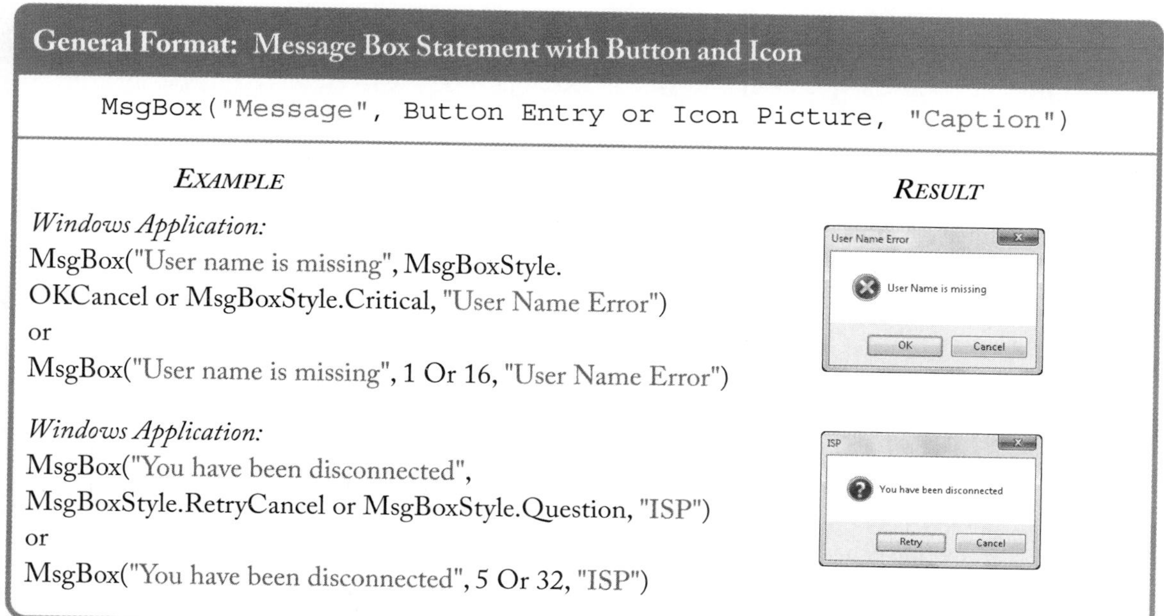

General Format: Message Box Statement with Button and Icon

```
MsgBox("Message", Button Entry or Icon Picture, "Caption")
```

EXAMPLE

Windows Application:
MsgBox("User name is missing", MsgBoxStyle.OKCancel or MsgBoxStyle.Critical, "User Name Error")
or
MsgBox("User name is missing", 1 Or 16, "User Name Error")

Windows Application:
MsgBox("You have been disconnected", MsgBoxStyle.RetryCancel or MsgBoxStyle.Question, "ISP")
or
MsgBox("You have been disconnected", 5 Or 32, "ISP")

RESULT

FIGURE 5-22

The picture icon represents the MsgBoxStyle that can be displayed as a graphic icon in the message box. Both examples in Figure 5-22 on the previous page show a graphic icon added to the message box.

The picture icon in the second argument can contain any of the entries shown in Figure 5-23.

MsgBoxStyle Icons	Value	Icon	Use
MsgBoxStyle.Critical	16		Alerts the user to an error
MsgBoxStyle.Question	32		Displays a question mark
MsgBoxStyle.Exclamation	48		Alerts the user to a possible problem
MsgBoxStyle.Information	64		Displays an information icon

FIGURE 5-23

In the general formats shown for a message box, you must follow the syntax of the statements exactly, which means the commas, quotation marks, and parentheses must be placed in the statement as shown in the general formats.

You can also add values to display both the buttons and a picture icon. In Figure 5-24, the value of the message button type AbortRetryIgnore is 2 and the value of the critical icon is 16. If you add 16 plus 2, the result is 18.

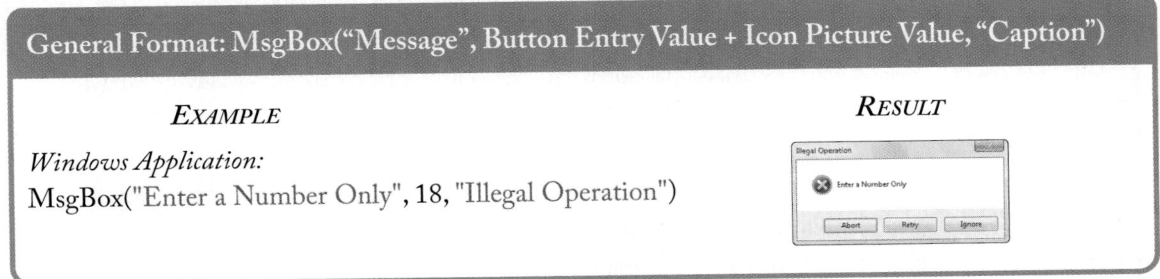

General Format: MsgBox("Message", Button Entry Value + Icon Picture Value, "Caption")

EXAMPLE

Windows Application:
MsgBox("Enter a Number Only", 18, "Illegal Operation")

RESULT

FIGURE 5-24

Message Box IntelliSense

When you enter the code for a message box, IntelliSense can assist you. To use IntelliSense to enter code for the message box shown in Figure 5-22 on the previous page that contains a message, caption, and button, you can complete the following steps:

STEP 1 In the code editing window, inside the event handler you are coding, type `msg` to display MsgBox in the IntelliSense list.

IntelliSense displays a list of the allowable entries (Figure 5-25). When you type `msg` *MsgBox is selected in the IntelliSense list.*

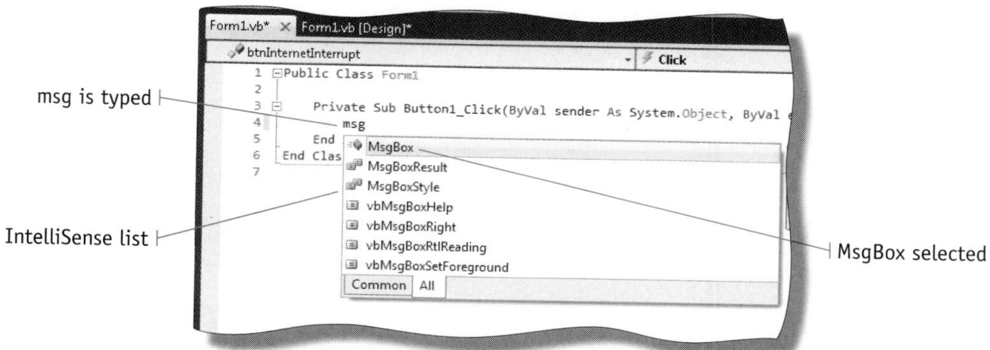

FIGURE 5-25

STEP 2 Press the Tab key to select MsgBox from the IntelliSense list. Type the following text: `("You have been disconnected from the Internet", m)`

The first argument for the message box is entered (Figure 5-26). IntelliSense displays a list of the allowable entries for the second argument.

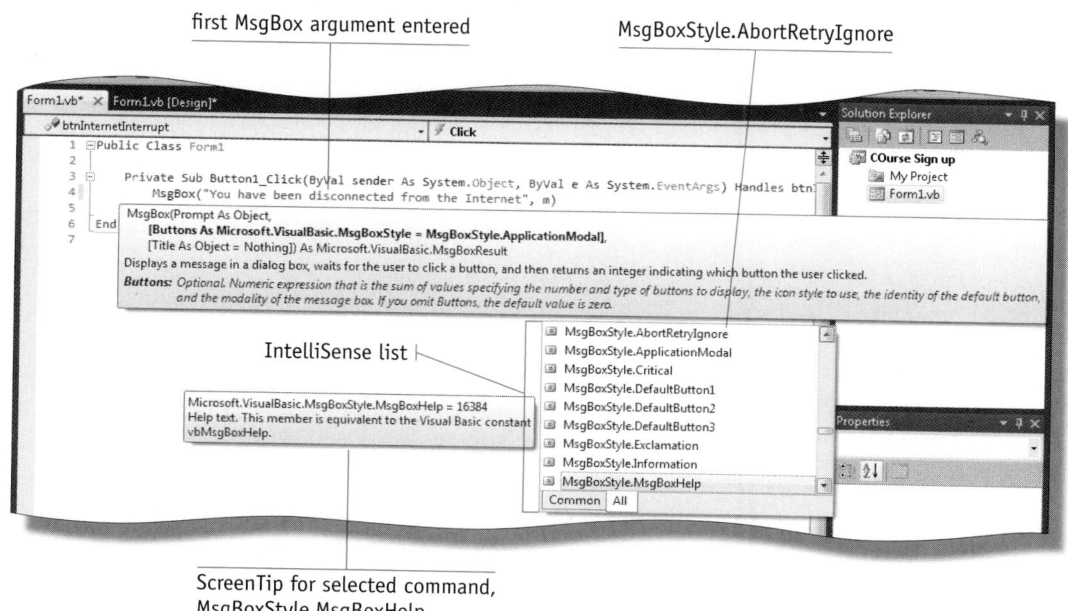

FIGURE 5-26

STEP 3 Select the MsgBoxStyle.AbortRetryIgnore argument by pressing the UP ARROW until the correct argument is highlighted. Type a comma. Then type "ISP" and a right parenthesis.

The MsgBoxStyle.AbortRetryIgnore argument is selected. After the comma is typed following the second argument, the caption "ISP" is typed with a right parenthesis (Figure 5-27).

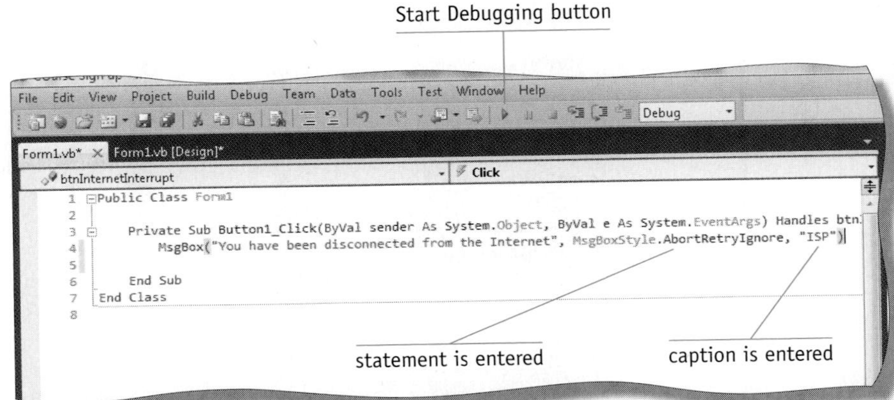

FIGURE 5-27

STEP 4 Click the Start Debugging button on the Standard toolbar.

The application runs, displaying the message box that shows the message, buttons, and caption (Figure 5-28).

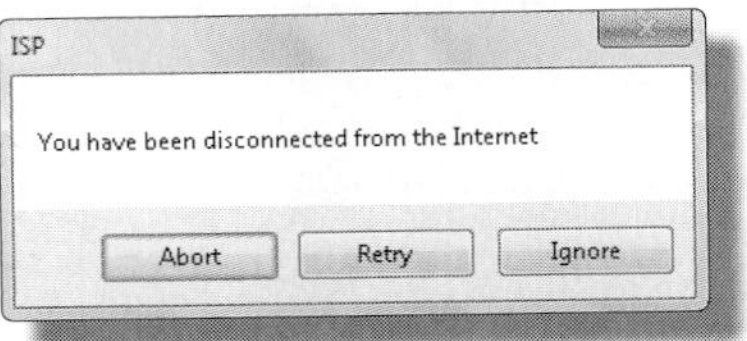

FIGURE 5-28

ONLINE REINFORCEMENT

To view a video of the process in the previous steps, visit scsite.com/vb2010/ch5 and then select Figure 5-25.

String Concatenation

Recall that when the Wood Cabinet Estimate application runs, the user enters the linear footage of the wood cabinets. If the user enters a number that is not greater than zero, such as −6, a message box appears that states "You entered –6. Enter a Positive Number", as shown in Figure 5-29.

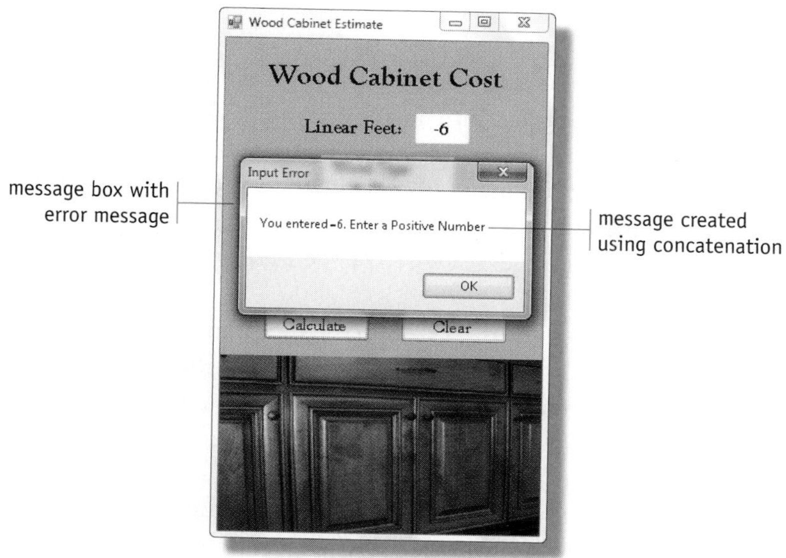

FIGURE 5-29

To create the message in the message box, you can use concatenation, which you learned about in Chapter 4. In Figure 5-29, the string message is constructed by joining a string ("You entered"), a variable named decFootage containing the linear footage entered (which must be converted to a string), and a string for the final part of the message (". Enter a Positive Number."). The code in Figure 5-30 creates the desired message box.

```
        MsgBox("You entered " & decFeet.ToString() & ". Enter a Positive Number", , "Input Error")
```

FIGURE 5-30

You will recall that the operator to concatenate strings is the ampersand (&). When the statement is executed, the three string elements are joined together (concatenated) to form the one string that is displayed in the message box.

HEADS UP

In older versions of Visual Basic, the plus (+) sign was used to concatenate strings instead of the ampersand (&) symbol. The + sign still functions for concatenation, but it can be confusing because it looks like the plus sign used in addition. You should always use the ampersand.

Making Decisions with Conditional Statements

In the Wood Cabinet Estimate chapter project, which calculates the cost of wood cabinets, the application allows the user to select one of three different types of wood: pine, oak, or cherry. The price per square foot is based on the user's choice of wood. To select the wood type, the user must click one of three radio buttons titled Pine, Oak, and Cherry. Then, based on the choice, the application uses a different wood cost.

Visual Basic uses decision structures to deal with the different conditions that occur based on the values entered into an application. A **decision structure** is one of the three fundamental control structures used in computer programming. For example, if the user clicks the Pine radio button, the wood cost is set to $150.00 per linear foot. The statement that tests the radio button is called a **conditional statement**. The condition checked is whether the Pine radio button is selected. If so, the wood cost is set to $150.00.

When a condition is tested in a Visual Basic program, the condition either is true or false. For example, when checking to determine if the Pine radio button is selected, the condition can either be true (the Pine radio button is checked) or false (the Pine radio button is not checked). All conditional statements result in the tested condition either being true or false.

To implement a conditional statement and the statements that are executed when a condition is true and statements executed when a condition is false, Visual Basic uses the If statement and its variety of formats. You will learn about the If statement in the following sections.

Using an If . . . Then Statement

In the sample program, an If . . . Then statement is used to determine the cost of the wood. The simplest form of the If . . . Then statement is shown in Figure 5-31.

```
5        If condition Then
6            Statement(s) executed when condition is true
7        End If
8
```

FIGURE 5-31

In Figure 5-31, when the condition tested in the If statement on line 5 is true, the statement(s) between the If and the End If keywords will be executed. If the condition is not true, no statements between the If and End If keywords will be executed, and program execution will continue with the statement(s) that follows the End If statement.

Visual Basic automatically indents statements to be executed when a condition is true or not true to indicate the lines of code are within the conditional If...Then structure. This is why the statement on line 6 in Figure 5-31 on the previous page is indented. The End If keyword terminates the If...Then block of code. After executing the If...Then block, execution continues with any statements that follow the closing End If statement.

HEADS UP

If Visual Basic does not automatically indent the code in an If . . . Then statement, follow these steps: 1) Click Tools on the menu bar at the top of the screen and then click Options; 2) if necessary, click the triangle next to Text Editor in the left panel; 3) if necessary, click the triangle next to Basic in the left panel; 4) if necessary, click VB Specific in the left panel; 5) ensure the Pretty listing (reformatting) of code check box contains a check mark; 6) click the OK button in the Options dialog box.

Relational Operators

In Figure 5-31 on the previous page, the condition portion of the If...Then statement means a condition is tested to determine if it is true or false. The conditions that can be tested are:

1. Is one value equal to another value?
2. Is one value not equal to another value?
3. Is one value greater than another value?
4. Is one value less than another value?
5. Is one value greater than or equal to another value?
6. Is one value less than or equal to another value?

To test these conditions, Visual Basic provides relational operators that are used within the conditional statement to express the relationship being tested. The table in Figure 5-32 shows these relational operators.

	Relational Operator	Meaning	Example	Resulting Condition
1	=	Equal to	8 = 8	True
2	<>	Not equal to	6 <> 6	False
3	>	Greater than	7 > 9	False
4	<	Less than	4 < 6	True
5	>=	Greater than or equal to	3 >= 3	True
6	<=	Less than or equal to	7 <= 5	False

FIGURE 5-32

A condition tested using a relational operator is evaluated as true or false. Example 1 tests whether 8 is equal to 8. Because it is, the resulting condition is true. Example 2 tests if 6 is not equal to 6. Because they are equal, the resulting condition is false. Similarly, Example 5 tests if 3 is greater than or equal to 3. Because they are equal, the resulting condition is true.

As an example of using a conditional operator, consider the following problem where an If statement is used to determine if someone is old enough to vote. If the value in the intAge variable is greater than or equal to 18, then the person is old enough to vote. If not, the person is not old enough to vote. The If...Then statement to test this condition is shown in Figure 5-33.

```
        If intAge >= 18 Then
                lblVotingEligibility.Text = "You are old enough to vote"
        End If
```

FIGURE 5-33

In Figure 5-33, if the value in the intAge variable is greater than or equal to 18, the string value "You are old enough to vote" is assigned to the Text property of the lblVotingEligibility Label object. If not, then no processing occurs based on the conditional statement and any statement(s) following the End If keyword will be executed.

You can see in Figure 5-33 that several keywords are required in an If...Then statement. The word If must be the first item. Next, the condition(s) to be tested are stated, followed by the word Then. This keyword is required in an If statement.

The End If keyword follows the statements to be executed when the condition is true. This entry also is required. It signals to the Visual Basic compiler that statements following it are to be executed regardless of the result of the conditional statement; that is, the End If keyword is the last element within the If block and no subsequent statements depend on it for execution.

To enter the If...Then statement shown in Figure 5-33, you can complete the following steps:

STEP 1 With the insertion point in the correct location in the code, type `if` and then press the SPACEBAR.

The statement begins with the word if (Figure 5-34). The If command is displayed in blue because it is a Visual Basic keyword. You can type uppercase or lowercase letters.

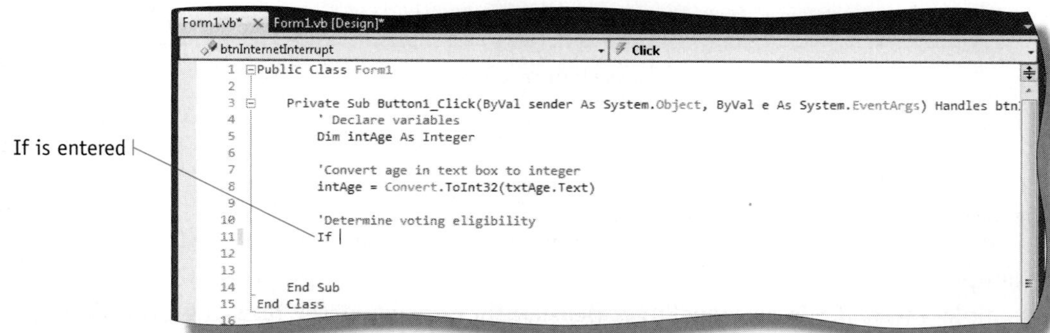

FIGURE 5-34

STEP 2 Type `inta` to select the variable named intAge in the IntelliSense list. Then, type `>=18` as the condition to be tested. Press the ENTER key.

The If . . . Then statement is entered in the code editing window (Figure 5-35). When the ENTER key is pressed, Visual Basic adds the keyword Then to the end of the If statement line of code and inserts spaces between the elements in the statement for ease of reading. In addition, Visual Basic inserts the End If keyword following a blank line. Notice the keywords Then and End If are capitalized and displayed in blue.

Form1.vb* × Form1.vb [Design]*

btnInternetInterrupt | Click

```
1  Public Class Form1
2
3      Private Sub Button1_Click(ByVal sender As System.Object, ByVal e As System.EventArgs) Handles btn
4          ' Declare variables
5          Dim intAge As Integer
6
7          'Convert age in text box to integer
8          intAge = Convert.ToInt32(txtAge.Text)
9
10         'Determine voting eligibility
11         If intAge >= 18 Then
12
13         End If
14
15     End Sub
16 End Class
17
```

condition being tested

keyword Then

blank line for statement(s) to be executed when condition is true

keywords End If

FIGURE 5-35

STEP 3 On the blank line (line 12 in Figure 5-35), enter the statement that should be executed when the condition is true. To place the message, "You are old enough to vote" in the Text property of the lblVotingEligibility Label object, insert the code shown in Figure 5-33 on the previous page. Remember to use IntelliSense to reference the lblVotingEligibility Label object.

The resulting statement is entered between the If and End If keywords (Figure 5-36). Notice that Visual Basic automatically indents the line for ease of reading. The blank line allows you to enter more statements. If you have no further statements, you can press the DELETE key to delete the blank line in the If . . . Then statement.

> **HEADS UP**
>
> Always place the words If and Then on the same programming line. If you use IntelliSense, this will be done automatically for you. The End If statement, which terminates the decision structure, also should be on a line by itself.

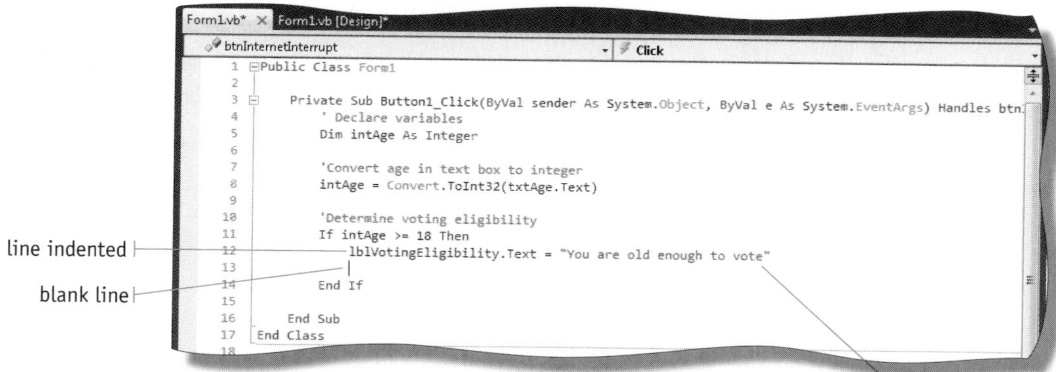

statement is executed when condition is true

FIGURE 5-36

> **ONLINE REINFORCEMENT**
>
> To view a video of the process in the previous steps, visit scsite.com/vb2010/ch5 and then select Figure 5-34.

Comparing Strings

You also can write an If . . . Then statement using the relational operators shown in Figure 5-32 on page 313 to compare string values. A string value comparison compares each character in two strings, starting with the first character in each string. For example, in the two strings in Figure 5-37, the comparison begins with the first character in each string, a. Because the characters are equal, the comparison continues with the second character in each string, b. Because these characters are equal, the comparison continues with the third characters in each string, c. Because all three characters are equal, the strings are considered equal and the resulting condition from the If statement is true.

```
        Dim String1 As String = "abc"
        Dim String2 As String = "abc"

        If String1 = String2 Then
            Me.lblStringTest.Text = "Equal"
        End If
```

FIGURE 5-37

All characters found in strings, including letters, numbers, and special characters, are in a sequence from low to high based on the manner in which the characters are coded internally on the computer. When using Visual Studio 2010, characters are stored and sequenced in Unicode, which is a coding methodology that can accommodate more than 60,000 characters. Appendix A in this book shows the Unicode sequence for the standard keyboard characters. You will find that the numbers are considered less than uppercase letters, and uppercase letters are considered less than lowercase letters.

Using the If . . . Then statement, the following comparisons produce the following resulting conditions:

Example 1:

```
Dim String1 As String = "Powder"
Dim String2 As String = "Power"

If String1 < String2 Then
```

Resulting Condition: True because in the fourth character position, the letter d is less than the letter e.

Example 2:

```
Dim String1 As String = "6"
Dim String2 As String = "T"

If String1 < String2 Then
```

Resulting Condition: True because in a string comparison, a number is less than an uppercase letter.

Example 3:

```
Dim String1 As String = "12"
Dim String2 As String = "9"

If String1 < String2 Then
```

Resulting Condition: True because in a string comparison, the characters in the first position of the string are compared first. Because the value 1 in String1 is less than the value 9 in String2, the entire value in String1 is considered less than the value in String2.

Example 4:

```
Dim String1 As String = "anchor"
Dim String2 As String = "Anchorline"

If String1 > String2 Then
```

Resulting Condition: True because a lowercase letter (the a in the first position of String1) is considered greater than an uppercase letter (the A in the first position of String2).

Comparing Different Data Types

Every type of data available in Visual Basic can be compared. Different numeric types can be compared to each other using an If statement. A single string character can be compared to a Char data type. The following examples illustrate some of the allowable comparisons.

Example 1: Decimal compared to Double

```
If decQuarterlySales > dblSalesQuota Then
```

If decQuarterlySales = 110,324.54 and dblSalesQuota = 112,435.54, the condition is false.

Example 2: Decimal compared to Integer

```
If decTirePressureReading > intTirePressureMaximum Then
```

If decTirePressureReading = 30.21 and intTirePressureMaximum = 30, the condition is true.

Example 3: Double compared to Integer

```
If dblCurrentTemperature >= intHeatDanger Then
```

If dblCurrentTemperature = 94.543 and intHeatDanger = 98, the condition is false.

Example 4: String compared to Char

```
If strChemistryGrade < chrPassingGrade Then
```

If strChemistryGrade = "B" and chrPassingGrade = "C", the condition is true.

Visual Basic allows comparisons between most data types. If you are unsure whether a comparison can be made, write an If statement to ensure the comparison is working properly.

Using the If . . . Then . . . Else Statement

An If . . . Then statement executes a set of instructions if a condition is true. If the condition is false, the instructions between the If statement and the End If statement are not executed and program execution continues with the statement(s) following the End If statement.

In many applications, the logic requires one set of instructions to be executed if a condition is true, and another set of instructions to be executed if a condition is false. For example, a requirement in a program could specify that if a student's test score is 70 or greater, a message stating "You passed the examination" should be displayed, while if the test score is less than 70, a message stating "You failed the examination" should be displayed.

To execute one set of instructions if a condition is true, and another set of instructions if the condition is false, you can use the If . . . Then . . . Else statement. Figure 5-38 illustrates the syntax of the If . . . Then . . . Else statement.

```
If condition Then
    Statement(s) executed if condition is true
Else
    Statement(s) executed if condition is false
End If
```

FIGURE 5-38

In the code in Figure 5-38, if the condition tested by the If statement is true, the statement(s) between the Then keyword and the Else keyword will be executed. If the condition tested is false, the statement(s) between the Else keyword and the End If keyword will be executed.

The example in Figure 5-39 on the next page shows the use of the If . . . Then . . . Else statement to calculate student fees by testing the student status.

statement is executed if student is a graduate

```
If strStudentStatus = "Graduate" Then
    decStudentFees = decGraduateFee * intNumberOfUnits
Else
    decStudentFees = decUndergraduateFee * intNumberOfUnits
End If
```

statement is executed if student is not a graduate

FIGURE 5-39

If the student is a graduate student, the student fees are calculated by multiplying the graduate fee times the number of units. If the student is not a graduate student, fees are calculated by multiplying the undergraduate fee times the number of units. Notice that a student cannot be both an undergraduate student and a graduate student, so either the statement following the Then keyword will be executed or the statement following the Else keyword will be executed.

HEADS UP

A condition cannot be true and false at the same time, so statements for a true condition and statements for a false condition cannot both be executed based on a single comparison.

Comparing to an Arithmetic Expression

An If statement can compare an arithmetic expression to a constant or other data type. For example, in Figure 5-40, the withdrawals from a bank account are compared to the value obtained by adding the current balance to deposits and then subtracting account charges.

```
If decWithdrawals > decCurrentBalance + decDeposits - decAccountCharges Then
    lblAccountStatus.Text = "Overdrawn"
Else
    lblAccountStatus.Text = "Balance is Positive"
End If
```

FIGURE 5-40

In Figure 5-40, if the value in the decWithdrawals variable is greater than the current balance plus the deposits minus the account charges, the Text property of the lblAccountStatus Label object is set to Overdrawn. If the value in decWithdrawals is less than or equal to the value from the arithmetic expression, the message Balance is Positive is placed in the Text property of the lblAccountStatus Label object. Notice that the arithmetic expression is evaluated prior to the comparison. If the condition is true, the statement between the Then and Else keywords is executed. If the condition is false, the statement between the Else and End If keywords is executed.

Using the If . . . Then . . . Elseif Statement

Complex logic problems might require a more complex structure than the If . . . Then . . . Else logic structure. For example, consider the following logical problem that must be solved in a computer program:

An online store charges a shipping amount based on the dollar amount of the order being shipped. The rules are: 1) If the order amount is above $500, the shipping cost is $30; 2) If the order amount is more than $400 and not greater than $500, the shipping cost is $25; 3) If the order amount is more than $200 and not greater than $400, the shipping cost is $20; 4) If the order amount is equal to or less than $200, the shipping cost is $15.

When one of the conditions is found to be true, the rest of the conditions are not tested because the correct condition has been found. To solve this problem, you should think this way:

1. If the order amount is greater than $500.00, then the shipping cost is $30.00 and no more processing must be done to determine the shipping cost.
2. If, however, the order amount is not greater than $500.00, I must check further to see if it is greater than $400.00 (400.01 through 500.00). If so, the shipping cost is $25.00.
3. If the order amount is not greater than $400.00, the next step is to check if it is greater than $200.00. Notice that if it is greater than $200.00 but not greater than $400.00, it must be in the range $201.00 to $400.00. If this is true, the shipping cost is $20.00.
4. If none of the above is true, then the order amount must be less than or equal to $200. In this case, the shipping cost is $15.00.

As you can see, a simple If . . . Then . . . Else statement could not solve this logic problem because the If . . . Then . . . Else structure tests only a single condition and specifies the processing based on whether the condition is true or false. For a problem where multiple conditions must be tested, the If . . . Then . . . ElseIf statement might be appropriate. The general format of the If . . . Then . . . ElseIf statement is shown in Figure 5-41.

```
If decOrderAmount > 500D Then
    Statement(s) executed if condition is true
ElseIf decOrderAmount > 400D Then
    Statement(s) executed if condition is true
ElseIf decOrderAmount > 200D Then
    Statement(s) executed if condition is true
ElseIf decOrderAmount > 0D Then
    Statement(s) executed if condition is true
End If
```

FIGURE 5-41

Once a condition in the code in Figure 5-41 on the previous page is true, Visual Basic bypasses the rest of the ElseIf statements. For example, assume the order amount is $455. The first condition tests if the order amount is greater than 500. The first condition would test false because 455 is not greater than 500.

Next, the ElseIf entry will test if 455 is greater than 400. Because the value 455 is greater than 400, the condition is true and the statement(s) on line 108 will be executed. The remaining ElseIf statements will not be evaluated because the true condition has been found.

Separate If . . . Then statements are not used in the example in Figure 5-41 on the previous page because each condition would have to be tested even though a condition had already been found to be true. When using an If . . . Then . . . ElseIf statement, after the condition is found to be true, the remaining conditions are not tested, making the process faster and more efficient.

HEADS UP

When testing conditions like those in the example in Figure 5-41 on page 320, make sure you do not leave a number out of the range of numbers being tested. For example, if one ElseIf statement tests decOrderAmount > 400.00 and the next ElseIf statement tests < 400.00, the value 400.00 has not been tested and the program will not properly process the value 400.00.

Trailing Else Statements

You may want to include a trailing Else statement at the end of an If . . . Then . . . ElseIf conditional statement to handle a condition that does not meet any of the conditions tested. In the example in Figure 5-42, the code is determining if the user is eligible for Social Security benefits. If the user's age is greater than or equal to 65, the user receives full benefits. If the user's age is between 0 and 65, the user is not eligible for benefits.

```
115         If intAge >= 65 Then
116             lblSocialSecurity.Text = "Full Benefits"
117         ElseIf intAge > 0 Then
118             lblSocialSecurity.Text = "Not Eligible for Benefits"
119         Else
120             lblSocialSecurity.Text = "Invalid Age"
121         End If
```

FIGURE 5-42

In Figure 5-42, the statement on line 120 that follows the trailing Else statement on line 119 is executed if the number in the intAge variable does not meet the conditions stated in the previous If statements. For example, if the intAge variable contains a negative value such as –12, the Text property of the lblSocialSecurity Label object will be set to "Invalid Age".

Nested If Statements

At times, more than one decision has to be made to determine what processing must occur. For example, if one condition is true, a second condition may need to be tested before the correct code is executed. To test a second condition only after determining that a first condition is true (or false), you must place an If statement within another If statement. When you place one If statement within another If statement, the inner If statement is said to be nested within the outer If Statement. The syntax of a nested If statement is shown in Figure 5-43.

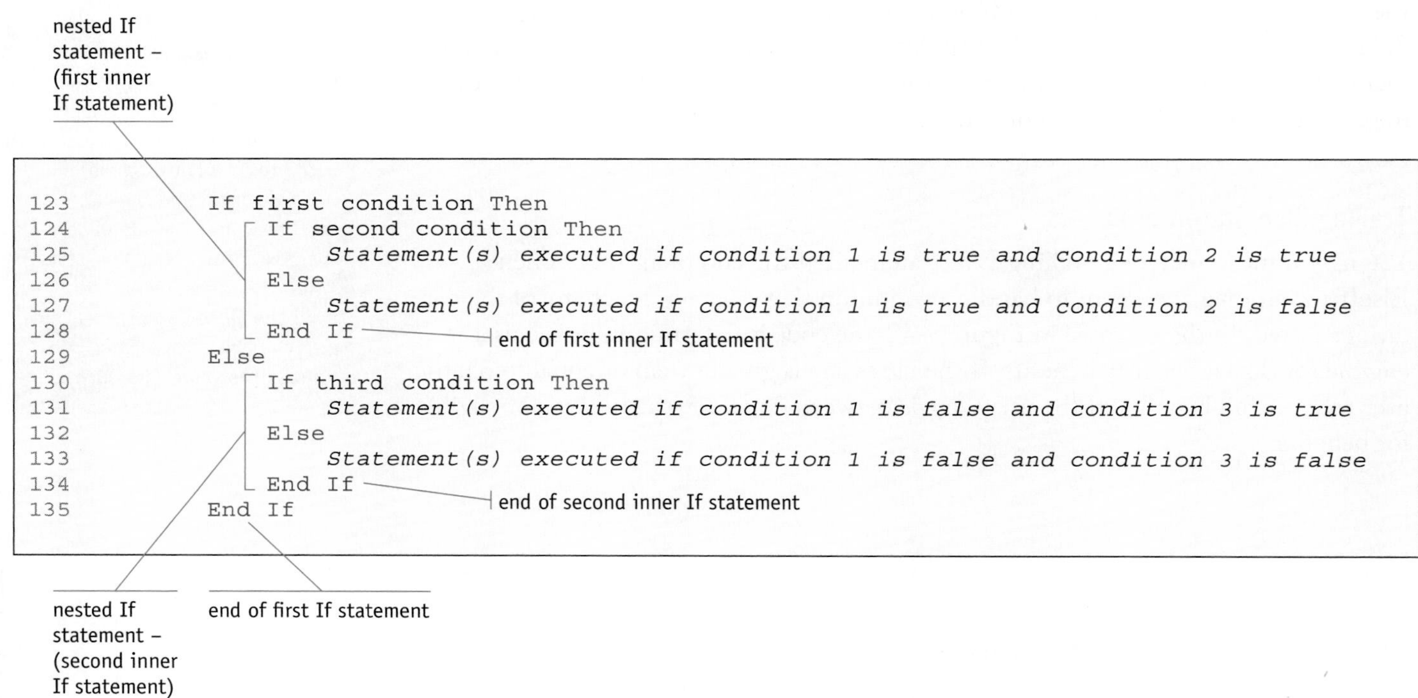

```
123  If first condition Then
124      If second condition Then
125          Statement(s) executed if condition 1 is true and condition 2 is true
126      Else
127          Statement(s) executed if condition 1 is true and condition 2 is false
128      End If
129  Else
130      If third condition Then
131          Statement(s) executed if condition 1 is false and condition 3 is true
132      Else
133          Statement(s) executed if condition 1 is false and condition 3 is false
134      End If
135  End If
```


FIGURE 5-43

In Figure 5-43, if the first condition tested is true, the statements following the keyword Then are executed. The statement to be executed when the first condition is true is another If statement (line 124) that tests the second condition. This second If statement is said to be a nested If statement or an inner If statement. If the second condition is true, the statement(s) on line 125 following the keyword Then for the first inner If statement are executed. If the second condition is not true, the statement(s) on line 127 following the keyword Else for the first inner If statement are executed. The End If entry (line 128) follows the first inner If statement, indicating the end of the effect of the first inner If statement.

If the first condition is not true, then the statements following the keyword Else on line 129 for the first If statement are executed. The statement to be executed when the first condition is not true is an If statement that tests the third condition (line 130). If the third condition is true, the statement(s) on line 131 following the Then keyword of the second inner If statement are executed. Finally, if the second inner If statement that tests the third condition is false, the statement(s) on line 133 are executed for the case when condition 1 is false and condition 3 is false.

To illustrate a nested If statement, assume a college has the following admissions policy: If an applying student has a GPA greater than 3.5 and an SAT score greater than 1000, then that student is granted admission. If an applying student has a GPA greater than 3.5 but an SAT score of 1000 or lower, the student is advised to retake the SAT exam. If an applying student has a GPA of 3.5 or lower but an SAT score greater than 1200, the student is granted a probationary admission, which means a 2.5 GPA must be achieved in the first semester of college. If an applying student has a GPA lower than 3.5 and an SAT score of 1200 or lower, the student is denied admission. The nested If statement to process this admission policy is shown in Figure 5-44.

```
140          If decGPA > 3.5D Then
141              If intSatScore > 1000 Then
142                  lblAdmissionStatus.Text = "You have earned admission"
143              Else
144                  lblAdmissionStatus.Text = "Retake the SAT exam"
145              End If
146          Else
147              If intSatScore > 1200 Then
148                  lblAdmissionStatus.Text = "You have earned probationary admission"
149              Else
150                  lblAdmissionStatus.Text = "You have been denied admission"
151              End If
152          End If
```

FIGURE 5-44

Notice in Figure 5-44 that the test for greater than 1000 on the SAT (line 141) must take place only after the test for a GPA greater than 3.5 (line 140), because the test for greater than 1000 is required only after it has been determined that the GPA is greater than 3.5. Therefore, a nested If statement is required. In addition, the test for greater than 1200 (line 147) should occur only after it has been determined that the GPA is less than 3.5. As you can see, you should use a nested If statement when a condition must be tested only after another condition has been tested.

Other Nested If Configurations

You can use nested If statements in a variety of forms. Assume, for example, that the admissions policy for a different school is as follows: If an applying student has a GPA greater than 3.5 and an SAT score greater than 1100, then that student is granted admission. If an applying student has a GPA greater than 3.5 but an SAT score of 1100 or lower, the student is advised to retake the SAT exam. If an applying student has a GPA of 3.5 or lower, the student is denied admission. The nested If statement in Figure 5-45 solves this logic problem.

```
154         If decGPA > 3.5D Then
155             If intSatScore > 1100 Then
156                 lblAdmissionStatus.Text = "You have earned admission"
157             Else
158                 lblAdmissionStatus.Text = "Retake the SAT exam"
159             End If
160         Else
161             lblAdmissionStatus.Text = "You have been denied admission"
162         End If
```

FIGURE 5-45

In Figure 5-45, if the GPA is greater than 3.5, then the first inner If statement on line 155 is executed to determine if the SAT score is greater than 1100. If so, the person has earned admission. If not, the person is advised to retake the SAT exam. If the GPA is not greater than 3.5, the student is denied admission. Notice that an If statement does not follow the Else keyword on line 160. An inner If statement need not follow both the If and the Else keywords.

Sometimes, after a condition is found to be true, a statement must be executed before the inner If statement is executed. For example, assume that if the GPA for a student is greater than 3.5, then the student should be informed that their GPA is acceptable for admission. The code in Figure 5-46 implements this condition.

```
If decGPA > 3.5D Then
    lblGPAStatus.Text = "Your GPA is acceptable"
    If intSatScore > 1100 Then
        lblAdmissionStatus.Text = "You have earned admission"
    Else
        lblAdmissionStatus.Text = "Retake the SAT exam"
    End If
Else
    lblGPAStatus.Text = "Your GPA is not acceptable"
    lblAdmissionStatus.Text = "You have been denied admission"
End If
```

FIGURE 5-46

In Figure 5-46 on the previous page, on line 165 the message "Your GPA is acceptable" is assigned to the Text property of the lblGPAStatus Label object prior to checking the SAT score. As you can see, after the first condition has been tested, one or more statements can be executed prior to executing the inner If statement. This holds true for the Else portion of the If statement as well.

Matching If, Else, and End If Entries

When you write a nested If statement, the inner If statement must be fully contained within the outer If statement. To accomplish this, you must ensure that each Else entry has a corresponding If entry, and an inner If statement must be terminated with an End If entry before either the Else entry or the End If entry for the outer If statement is encountered. If you code the statement incorrectly, one or more entries in the nested If statement will be identified with a blue squiggly line, indicating an error in the structure of the statement.

You also must place the correct statements with the correct If and Else statements within the nested If statement. For example, in Figure 5-47, the code is *incorrect* because the statement following the Else statements has been switched.

```
If decGPA > 3.5D Then
    lblGPAStatus.Text = "Your GPA is acceptable"
    If intSatScore > 1100 Then
        lblAdmissionStatus.Text = "You have earned admission"
    Else
        lblAdmissionStatus.Text = "You have been denied admission"
    End If
Else
    lblGPAStatus Text = "Your GPA is not acceptable"
    lblAdmissionStatus.Text = "Retake the SAT exam"
End If
```

incorrect statements

FIGURE 5-47

You must be precise when placing the executing statements in the nested If statement. It is easy to miscode a nested If statement.

Nesting Three or More Levels of If Statements

If statements are not limited to two levels of nesting. Three or more levels can be included in a nested If statement. When this is done, however, the nested If statement can become more difficult to understand and code. If more than two levels are required to solve a logic problem, great care must be taken to ensure errors such as the one shown in Figure 5-47 do not occur.

Testing the Status of a RadioButton Object in Code

In the Wood Cabinet Estimate chapter project, which finds the cost of wood cabinets, the user selects one RadioButton in the GroupBox object to select the wood type. The code must check each RadioButton to determine if that RadioButton has been selected by the user. When the user selects a radio button, the Checked property for that button is changed from False to True. In addition, the Checked property for other RadioButton objects in the GroupBox object is set to False. This Checked property can be tested in an If statement to determine if the RadioButton object has been selected.

To test the status of the Checked Property for a RadioButton object, the general statement shown in Figure 5-48 can be written.

```
        If radPine.Checked Then
            Statement(s) to be executed if radio button is checked
        End If
```

FIGURE 5-48

Notice in Figure 5-48 that the RadioButton property is not compared using a relational operator. Instead, when a property that can contain only True or False is tested, only the property must be specified in the If statement. When the property contains True, then the If statement is considered true, and when the property contains False, the If statement is considered false.

Testing RadioButtons with the If . . . Then . . . ElseIf Statement

When a program contains multiple RadioButton objects in a Panel object or a GroupBox object, only one of the radio buttons can be selected. The statement that can be used to check multiple radio buttons is the If . . . Then . . . ElseIf statement because once the checked radio button is detected, checking the remaining radio buttons is unnecessary.

In the Wood Cabinet Estimate application, the user will click one of three radio buttons (Pine, Oak, or Cherry) to select the type of wood to be used for cabinets. To use an If . . . Then . . . ElseIf statement to check the status of the radio buttons, the most likely choice should be checked first. By doing this, the fewest number of tests will have to be performed. Therefore, the first If statement should test the status of the Pine radio button (radPine). If the radPine button is checked, the Cost Per Foot should be set to the value in the decPineCost variable, which is 150.00. No further testing should be done (see Figure 5-49 on the next page).

```
        If radPine.Checked Then
            decCostPerFoot = decPineCost
        ElseIf radOak.Checked Then
            decCostPerFoot = decOakCost
        ElseIf radCherry.Checked Then
            decCostPerFoot = decCherryCost
        End If
```

FIGURE 5-49

If the radPine button is not checked, then the radOak button should be tested. If it is checked, the Cost Per Foot should be set to the value in the decOakCost variable (200.00) and no further testing should be done. If the radOak button is not checked, then the radCherry button should be tested. If the other two buttons are not checked, then the radCherry button must be checked because one of the three must be checked. The Cost Per Foot will be set to the value in the decCherryCost variable (350.00).

As you learned earlier, during design time you can set the Checked property to True for the most frequently selected RadioButton to save the user from having to select the most common choice. In the Wood Cabinet Estimate program, after the Cost Per Linear Foot has been determined and the Cost Estimate has been calculated, the user can click the Clear button to clear the Linear Feet text box, clear the Cost Estimate, and reset the radio buttons so that the Pine button is selected. The code to reset the radio buttons is shown in Figure 5-50.

```
        radPine.Checked = True
        radOak.Checked = False
        radCherry.Checked = False
```

FIGURE 5-50

In Figure 5-50, the Checked property for the radPine RadioButton object is set to True using the same method you have seen in previous chapters for setting an object property. Similarly, the Checked property for the other two RadioButton objects is set to False. As a result of these statements, the Pine radio button will be selected in the user interface, and the Oak and Cherry radio buttons will not be selected.

Block-Level Scope

In Chapter 4 you learned that the scope of a variable is defined by where it is declared within a program. For example, if a variable is declared within an event handler, then only code within that event handler can reference the variable. Code in one event handler within a program cannot reference a variable declared in another event handler.

Within an event handler, an If . . . Then . . . Else statement (the code beginning with the If keyword and ending with the corresponding Else keyword, or the code beginning with the Else keyword and ending with the End If keyword) is considered a block of code. Variables can be declared within the block of code. When this occurs, the variable can be referenced only within the block of code where it is declared. For example, variables defined within an If . . . Then block of code fall out of scope (cannot be referenced) outside that block of code. To illustrate this concept, the code in Figure 5-51 shows a variable, intYears, declared within an If . . . Then block of code.

```
11        If intAge < 18 Then
12            Dim intYears As Integer
13            intYears = 18 - intAge
14            lblMessage.Text = "You can vote in " & intYears & " years(s)."
15        Else
16            lblMessage.Text = "You can vote!"
17        End If
```

FIGURE 5-51

In Figure 5-51, on line 12 the variable intYears is declared as an Integer variable. On line 13, the variable is used in an arithmetic statement to receive the result of the calculation, 18 – intAge, which determines the number of years less than 18 that is stored in intAge. The result in intYears is concatenated with literals in the statement on line 14. The intYears variable can be referenced in any statements between the If keyword and the Else keyword. It cannot be referenced anywhere else in the program. Note that it cannot be referenced even in the Else portion of the If statement. When a statement referencing the intYears variable is written outside the area between the If keyword and the Else keyword, a compilation error will occur and the program will not be able to be compiled and executed.

Although the scope of the intYears variable in Figure 5-51 is between the If keyword on line 11 and the Else keyword on line 15, you should realize that the variable itself perseveres during the execution of the event handler procedure. Therefore, if the If statement in Figure 5-51 is executed a second time, the value in the intYears variable will be the same as when the If statement was completed the first time. To avoid unexpected results when the If statement is executed the second time, you should initialize block variables at the beginning of the block. In Figure 5-51, the statement on line 13 sets the value in the intYears variable immediately after the variable is declared, which is good programming technique.

Using Logical Operators

The If statements you have seen thus far test a single condition. In many cases, more than one condition must be true or one of several conditions must be true in order for the statements in the Then portion of the If . . . Then . . . Else statement to be executed. When more than one condition is included in an If . . . Then . . . Else statement, the conditions are called a **compound condition**. For example, consider the following business traveling rule: "If the flight costs less than $300.00 and the hotel is less than $120.00 per night, the business trip is approved." In this case, both conditions (flight less than $300.00 *and* hotel less than $120.00 per night) must be true in order for the trip to approved. If either condition is not true, then the business trip is not approved.

To create an If statement that processes the business traveling rule, you must use a **logical operator**. The most common set of logical operators are listed in Figure 5-52.

Logical Operator	Meaning
And	All conditions tested in the If statement must be true
Or	One condition tested in the If statement must be true
Not	Negates a condition

FIGURE 5-52

For the business traveling rule specified previously, you should use the And logical operator.

Using the And Logical Operator

The **And logical operator** allows you to combine two or more conditions into a compound condition that can be tested with an If statement. If any of the conditions stated in the compound condition is false, the compound condition is considered false and the statements following the Else portion of the If statement will be executed. The code in Figure 5-53 uses the And logical operator to implement the business traveling rule.

```
        If decFlightCost < 300D And decHotelCost < 120D Then
            lblTripMessage.Text = "Your business trip is approved"
        Else
            lblTripMessage.Text = "Your business trip is denied"
        End If
```

FIGURE 5-53

In Figure 5-53, both conditions in the compound condition (flight cost less than 300 and hotel cost less than 120) must be true in order for the business trip to be approved. If one of the conditions is false, then the compound condition is considered false and the If statement would return a false indication. For example, if the flight cost is 300 or more, the trip will not be approved regardless of the hotel cost. Similarly, if the hotel cost is 120 or more, the trip will not be approved regardless of the flight cost. This process is illustrated in the diagram in Figure 5-54 on the next page.

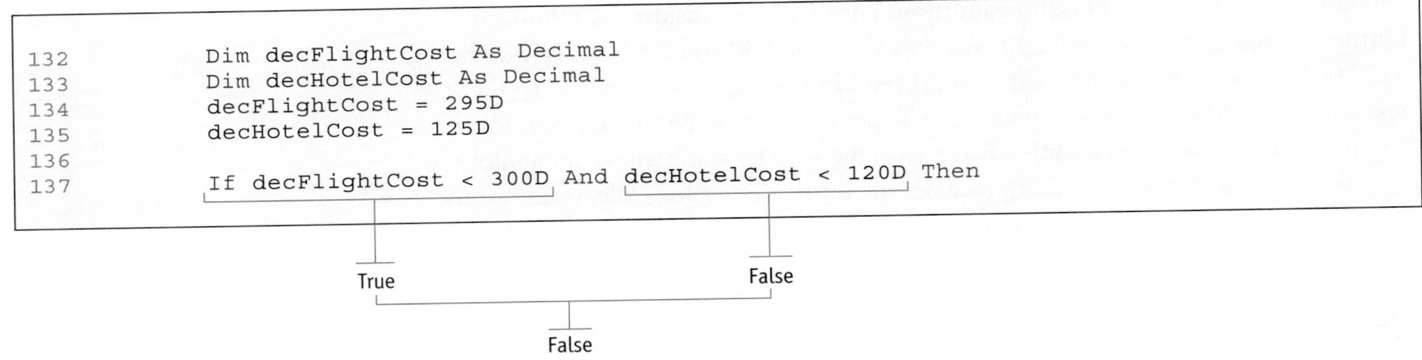

Dim decFlightCost As Decimal
Dim decHotelCost As Decimal
decFlightCost = 295D
decHotelCost = 125D
If decFlightCost < 300D And decHotelCost < 120D Then
True
False
False

FIGURE 5-54

In Figure 5-54, the flight cost is 295, so it is less than 300 and the first part of the compound condition is true. Following the And logical operator, the hotel cost (125) is not less than 120. Therefore, the second part of the compound condition is false. With the And logical operator, when either condition is false, the If statement considers the compound condition to be false. The result of the If statement in Figure 5-54 is that the compound condition is considered to be false.

Using the Or Logical Operator

When the **Or logical operator** is used to connect two or more conditions, the compound condition is true if any tested condition is true. Even if four conditional statements are included in the compound condition, if one conditional statement in the compound condition is true, the entire statement is considered true.

As an example, assume a college has an acceptance policy that states each student must either have a minimum of a 3.5 grade point average (GPA) or at least a 1080 score on the SAT college entrance exam to be accepted for enrollment. If the student meets one or both conditions, the student would be accepted. The If statement in Figure 5-55, which uses the Or logical operator, will solve this problem.

```
If decGPA >= 3.5D Or intSATScore >= 1080 Then
    lblAcceptance.Text = "You have been accepted"
Else
    lblAcceptance.Text = "You are not accepted"
End If
```

FIGURE 5-55

In Figure 5-55 if the GPA is 3.2, but the SAT score is 1130, the compound condition would be considered true because at least one of these conditions (SAT >= 1080) is true (Figure 5-56 on the next page).

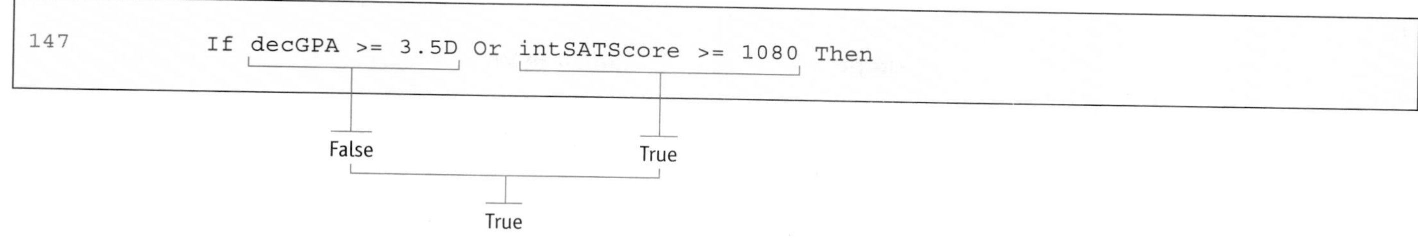

FIGURE 5-56

Using the Not Logical Operator

The **Not logical operator** allows you to state conditions that are best expressed in a negative way. In essence, the Not logical operator reverses the logical value of a condition on which it operates. For example, if a shoe store sells shoe sizes under size 14 from their showroom but requires special orders for larger sizes, the code could use the Not logical operator as shown in Figure 5-57 to negate the condition in the statement.

```
        If Not decShoeSize >= 14 Then
            lblOrderPolicy.Text = "Showroom shoe style available"
        Else
            lblOrderPolicy.Text = "Special order needed"
        End If
```

FIGURE 5-57

The statement in Figure 5-57 works, but the use of the Not logical operator makes the If statement somewhat difficult to understand. Generally, a statement that avoids the Not logical operator is more easily understood. For example, the code in Figure 5-58 accomplishes the same task as the code in Figure 5-57, but is easier to understand.

```
        If decShoeSize < 14 Then
            lblOrderPolicy.Text = "Showroom shoe style available"
        Else
            lblOrderPolicy.Text = "Special order needed"
        End If
```

FIGURE 5-58

IN THE REAL WORLD

Many developers avoid using the Not logical operator because it makes the code harder to understand. By removing the Not logical operator and reversing the relational operator, the statement becomes clearer.

Other Logical Operators

The Visual Basic programming language provides three other lesser used logical operators. These are shown in the table in Figure 5-59.

Logical Operator	Meaning
Xor	When one condition in the compound condition is true, but not both, the compound condition is true
AndAlso	As soon as a condition is found to be false, no further conditions are tested and the compound condition is false
OrElse	As soon as a condition is found to be true, no further conditions are tested and the compound condition is true

FIGURE 5-59

Order of Operations for Logical Operators

You can combine more than one logical operator in the same If . . . Then statement. In an If statement, arithmetic operators are evaluated first, relational operators are evaluated next, and logical operators are evaluated last. The order of operations for logical operators is shown in Figure 5-60.

Logical Operator	Order
Not	Highest Precedence
And, AndAlso	Next Precedence
Or, OrElse, Xor	Last Precedence

FIGURE 5-60

In most cases, if a developer uses multiple relational or logical operators in an If statement, the order of precedence should be established through the use of parentheses in order to clarify the sequence of evaluation. As in arithmetic expressions, conditional expressions within parentheses are evaluated before conditional expressions outside parentheses.

Select Case Statement

In some programming applications, different operations can occur based upon the value in a single field. For example, in Figure 5-61 on the next page, the user enters the number of the day in the week and the program displays the name of the day. The program must evaluate the number of the day value and display the correct name of the day.

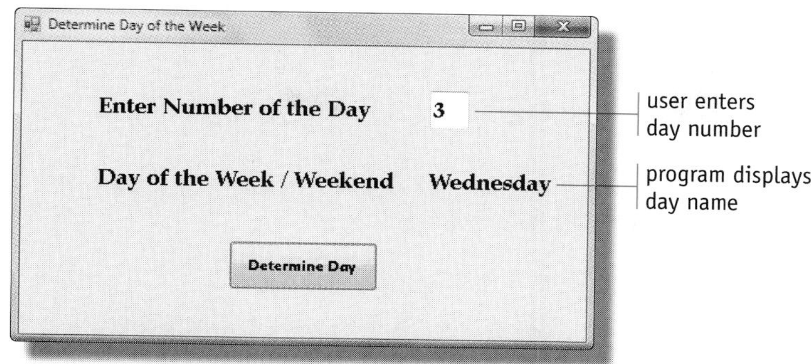

FIGURE 5-61

In Figure 5-61, if the number of the day is 1, then the value Monday should be displayed. If the number of the day is 2, then Tuesday should be displayed, and so on. If the number of the day is 6 or 7, then the value Weekend should be displayed. If the user does not enter a value of 1 through 7, the user should be told to enter a value between 1 and 7.

To solve this problem, a series of If . . . Then . . . ElseIf statements could be used. An easier and clearer way to solve the problem, however, is to use the Select Case statement.

When using a Select Case statement, the value in a single field, such as the day number, is evaluated and a different action, such as displaying the name of the day, is taken based on the value in the field.

A general example of the Select Case statement is shown in Figure 5-62.

The coding for the Determine Day of Week application is shown in Figure 5-63 on the next page.

```
        Select Case Test Expression
            Case First Expression
                Statement(s) for First Case
            Case Second Expression
                Statement(s) for Second Case
            Case Third Expression
                Statement(s) for Third Case
            Case Else
                Statement(s) for when the Case Conditions do not match the
                    test expressions above
        End Select
```

FIGURE 5-62

```
13          Select Case intDayNumber
14              Case 1
15                  lblDayOfWeek.Text = "Monday"
16              Case 2
17                  lblDayOfWeek.Text = "Tuesday"
18              Case 3
19                  lblDayOfWeek.Text = "Wednesday"
20              Case 4
21                  lblDayOfWeek.Text = "Thursday"
22              Case 5
23                  lblDayOfWeek.Text = "Friday"
24              Case 6
25                  lblDayOfWeek.Text = "Weekend"
26              Case 7
27                  lblDayOfWeek.Text = "Weekend"
28              Case Else
29                  lblDayOfWeek.Text = "Enter 1 through 7"
30          End Select
```

FIGURE 5-63

The Select Case statement begins with the Select Case command. The test expression entry is used to specify the value or variable that contains the value to be tested in the Select Case statement. In Figure 5-63, the variable is intDayNumber. So, when the Select Case statement is executed, each of the cases will be compared to the value in the intDayNumber variable.

Each Case statement specifies the value for which the test expression is checked. For example, the first Case statement on line 14 in Figure 5-63 specifies the value 1. If the value in the variable intDayNumber is equal to 1, the statement(s) following the first Case statement up to the second Case statement (line 16) are executed. In Figure 5-63, the assignment statement on line 15 that sets the Text property of the lblDayOfWeek to Monday is executed if the value in intDayNumber is equal to 1. More than one statement can follow a Case statement.

If the expression following the first Case statement is not true, then the next Case statement is evaluated. In Figure 5-63, the Case statement on line 16 checks if the value in intDayNumber is equal to 2. If so, the Text property of the lblDayOfWeek is set to Tuesday. This process continues through the remainder of the Case statements.

The Case Else statement on line 28 is an optional entry that includes all conditions not specifically tested for in the other Case statements. In Figure 5-63, if the value in the intDayNumber variable is not equal to 1 through 7, then the statement following the Case Else statement is executed. While not required, good programming practice dictates that the Case Else statement should be used so that all cases are accounted for and the program performs a specific action regardless of the value found in the test expression.

The End Select statement is required to end the Select Case statement. When you enter the Select Case statement in Visual Studio 2010, IntelliSense automatically includes the End Select statement.

Select Case Test Expressions

The example in Figure 5-63 on the previous page used an integer as the test expression value, but any data type can be used in the test expression. For example, the test expression in Figure 5-64 uses the Text property of the txtStudentMajor TextBox object as a string value.

```
Select Case Me.txtStudentMajor.Text
    Case "Accounting"
        lblDepartment.Text = "Business"
    Case "Marketing"
        lblDepartment.Text = "Business"
    Case "Electrical Engineering"
        lblDepartment.Text = "Engineering"
    Case "Biochemistry"
        lblDepartment.Text = "Chemistry"
    Case "Shakespearean Literature"
        lblDepartment.Text = "English"
    Case "Web Design and E-Commerce"
        lblDepartment.Text = "CIS"
    Case Else
        lblDepartment.Text = "Other"
End Select
```

FIGURE 5-64

In Figure 5-64, the Select Case statement is used to test the value in the Text property of the txtStudentMajor TextBox object and move the corresponding department name to the Text property of the lblDepartment object. The Case statements specify the values to be tested in the text box. The use of a string for the Select Case statement works in the same manner as other data types.

Using Relational Operators in a Select Case Statement

You can use relational operators in a Select Case statement. You must, however, use the keyword Is with the relational operator. For example, in Figure 5-41 on page 320, an If...Then...ElseIf statement was used to determine the shipping cost. That same processing could be accomplished using a Select Case statement, as shown in Figure 5-65.

HEADS UP

If you forget to type the Is keyword in the Case Is statement, Visual Studio will insert it for you.

```
Select Case decOrderAmount
    Case Is > 500D
        decShippingCost = 30D
    Case Is > 400D
        decShippingCost = 25D
    Case Is > 200D
        decShippingCost = 20D
    Case Is > 0D
        decShippingCost = 15D
    Case Else
        decShippingCost = 0D
End Select
```

FIGURE 5-65

Using Ranges in Select Case Statements

Another way to specify values in a Select Case statement is to use ranges. In Figure 5-66, the Case statements illustrate testing for six different conditions.

```
Select Case intGradeLevel
    Case 1 To 3
        lblGradeLevelExam.Text = "Early elementary"
    Case 4 To 6
        lblGradeLevelExam.Text = "Late elementary"
    Case 7 To 8
        lblGradeLevelExam.Text = "Middle school"
    Case 9 To 10
        lblGradeLevelExam.Text = "Early high school"
    Case 11
        lblGradeLevelExam.Text = "Late high school"
    Case 12
        lblGradeLevelExam.Text = "Final exam"
    Case Else
        lblGradeLevelExam.Text = "Invalid grade level"
End Select
```

FIGURE 5-66

As you can see, a range of values in a Case statement is specified by stating the beginning value, the word To, and then the ending value in the range. The Case statements will test the value in the intGradeLevel variable, and the appropriate statements will be executed.

You also can write Case statements with more than one distinct value being tested. In Figure 5-67, the Case statement tests the individual values of 1, 3, 8, 11, and 17 against the value specified in the intDepartmentNumber variable.

```
Select Case intDepartmentNumber
    Case 1, 3, 8, 11, 17
```

FIGURE 5-67

Notice in Figure 5-67 that each value in the Case statement is separated by a comma.

The code in Figure 5-68 shows a mixture of the two techniques, using both commas and a To statement.

```
Select Case intDepartmentNumber
    Case 2, 4, 7, 12 To 16, 22
```

FIGURE 5-68

Selecting Which Decision Structure to Use

In some instances, you might be faced with determining if you should use the Select Case statement or the If . . . Then . . . ElseIf statement to solve a problem. Generally, the Select Case statement is most useful when more than two or three values must be tested for a given variable. For example, in Figure 5-64 on page 335, six different values are checked in the Text property of the txtStudentMajor TextBox object. This is a perfect example of the use of the Select Case statement.

The If . . . Then . . . ElseIf statement is more flexible because more than one variable can be used in the comparison, and compound conditions with the And, Or, and Not logical operators can be used.

Code Snippets

Visual Basic includes a code library of almost five hundred pieces of code, called IntelliSense **code snippets**, that you can insert into an application. Each snippet consists of a complete programming task such as an If . . . Then . . . Else decision structure, sending an e-mail message, or drawing a circle. Inserting these commonly used pieces of code is an effective way to enhance productivity. You also can create your own snippets and add them to the library.

In addition to inserting snippets in your program, you can display a code snippet to ensure you understand the syntax and requirements for a given type of statement. To display and insert a code snippet for the If . . . Then . . . Else statement, you can complete the following steps:

STEP 1 Right-click the line in the code editing window where you want to insert the snippet.

Visual Studio displays a shortcut menu (Figure 5-69). It is important to right-click in the code editing window in the exact location where you want the code snippet to appear. If you right-click outside this location, the shortcut menu might list choices that are customized to that area of code and not include the code snippet for which you were searching. In addition, if you click in the wrong place, the snippet will be positioned in the incorrect location in your program.

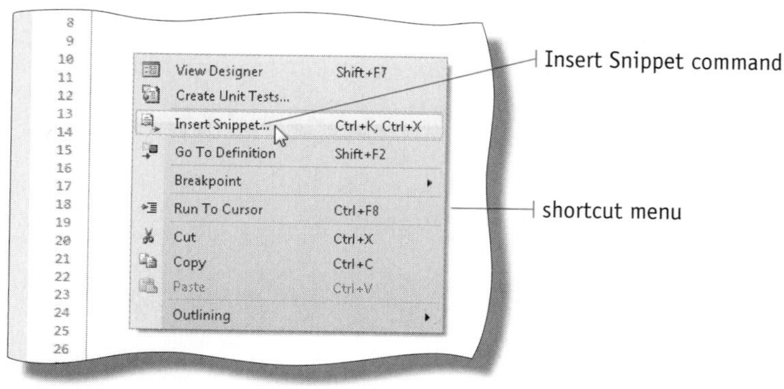

FIGURE 5-69

STEP 2 Click Insert Snippet on the shortcut menu.

Visual Studio displays a menu of folders containing snippets (Figure 5-70). The code snippets in each folder correspond to their folder titles.

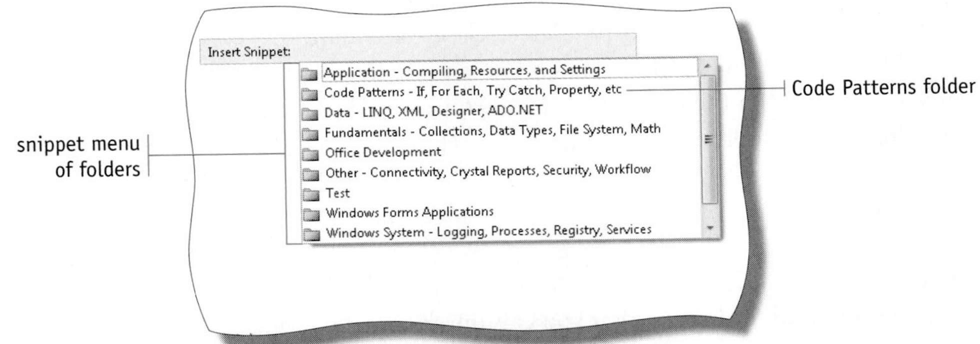

FIGURE 5-70

STEP 3 Double-click the folder Code Patterns - If, For Each, Try Catch, Property, etc, which contains commonly used code such as the If . . . Then . . . Else statement.

Visual Studio displays a menu of folders for code patterns (Figure 5-71).

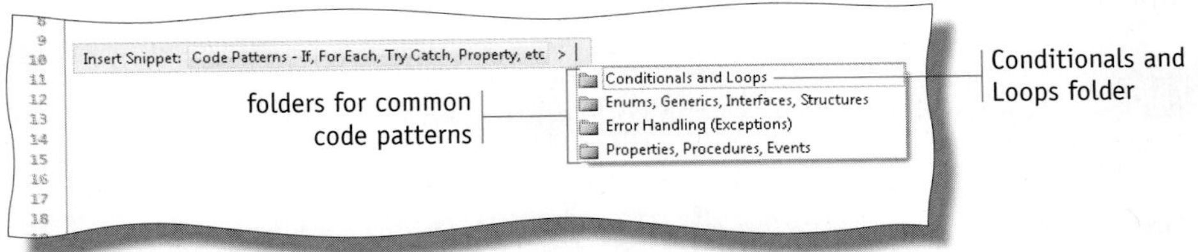

FIGURE 5-71

STEP 4 Double-click the Conditionals and Loops folder because an If . . . Then . . . Else statement is a conditional statement.

Visual Studio displays the list of Conditionals and Loops code snippets (Figure 5-72). Some of these statements will be unfamiliar until you complete Chapter 6, but you can see that the list of code snippets includes a number of different types of If statements.

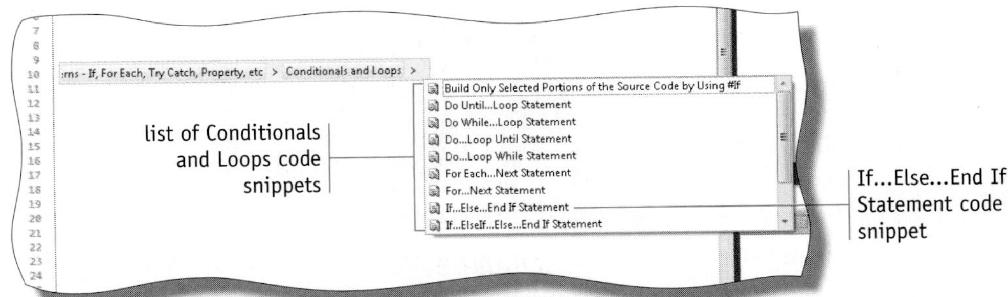

FIGURE 5-72

STEP 5 Double-click the If . . . Else . . . End If Statement code snippet.

The If . . . Else . . . End If Statement code snippet is inserted into the code on the line selected in step 1 (Figure 5-73). The highlighted text must be replaced by the condition(s) to be tested in the If statement. The code to be executed when the condition is true and the code to be executed when the condition is false must be added.

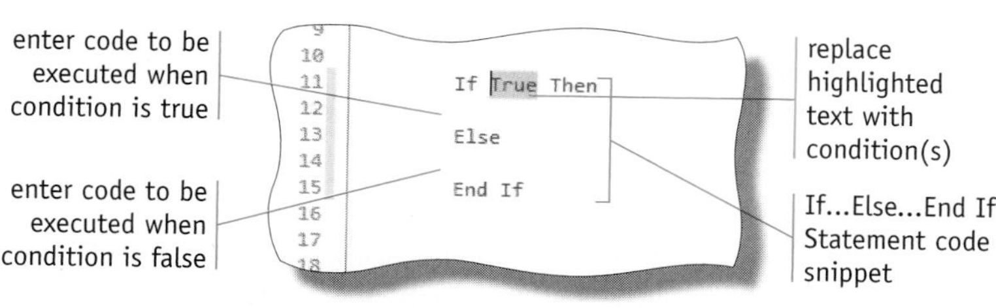

FIGURE 5-73

IN THE REAL WORLD

You might save time by inserting code snippets because you no longer need to search countless sources of code examples just to find a similar piece of code to copy and paste into your solution code.

ONLINE REINFORCEMENT

To view a video of the process in the previous steps, visit scsite.com/vb2010/ch5 and then select Figure 5-69.

You must modify the code snippet shown in Figure 5-73 in order for the code to work properly. You may find that modifying the code in the snippet, particularly in a complicated code snippet, is more work than using IntelliSense to enter the statement.

Code snippets are also helpful for learning or reviewing the format and syntax of a statement. For example, if you wanted to review the syntax of an If . . . Else If . . . Else . . . End If statement, you could insert the statement into the code editing window and examine it. You could then either click the Undo button to remove the statement or you could comment out the snippet code and keep it for your review. In many cases of checking syntax, reviewing a snippet is faster and clearer than consulting Visual Basic help.

Validating Data

Since the first days of computers, the phrase "garbage in, garbage out" has described the fact that allowing incorrect input data into a program produces incorrect output. Developers should anticipate that users will enter invalid data. Therefore, they must write code that will prevent the invalid data from being used in the program to produce invalid output.

For example, in the Wood Cabinet Estimate chapter project, the user is asked to enter the number of linear feet for the wood cabinets. If the user enters a negative number, a letter, or even leaves the text box blank, the program should inform the user of the input error and allow the user to reenter a proper value. If the program attempts to process invalid data, unexpected errors can occur, which is not the way a program should respond to invalid input data.

To properly check the linear feet value entered by the user, two checks must be performed. First, the program must check the value to ensure it is numeric. Second, the numeric value entered by the user must be checked to ensure it is greater than zero. These checks are explained in the following section.

Testing Input to Determine If the Value Is Numeric

In the Wood Cabinet Estimate program, if no check is performed on the input data and the user accidentally enters a nonnumeric character such as an "a" or fails to enter a value at all, the program will fail when Visual Basic attempts to convert that value to a number. An exception (error) screen will open and the program will be terminated. Therefore, the program must check the value entered by the user to ensure it is numeric. In addition, if the user enters a nonnumeric value, the program should inform the user of the error and request a valid numeric value.

The Visual Basic **IsNumeric function** can check the input value to determine if the value can be converted into a numeric value such as an Integer or Decimal data type. If so, it returns a True Boolean value. If the value is not recognized as a numeric value, the IsNumeric function returns a False Boolean value.

For example, the IsNumeric function can check the value in the Text property of the Linear Feet text box. If the user enters a letter such as "a" in the text box, the IsNumeric function would return a False Boolean value because the letter "a" is not numeric.

Because the IsNumeric function returns a Boolean value (True or False), it can be placed within an If statement as the condition to be tested. If the returned value is True, the condition in the If statement is considered true. If the returned value is False, the condition in the If statement is considered false. The code in Figure 5-74 uses an If statement to determine if the Text property of the txtLinearFeet TextBox object is numeric.

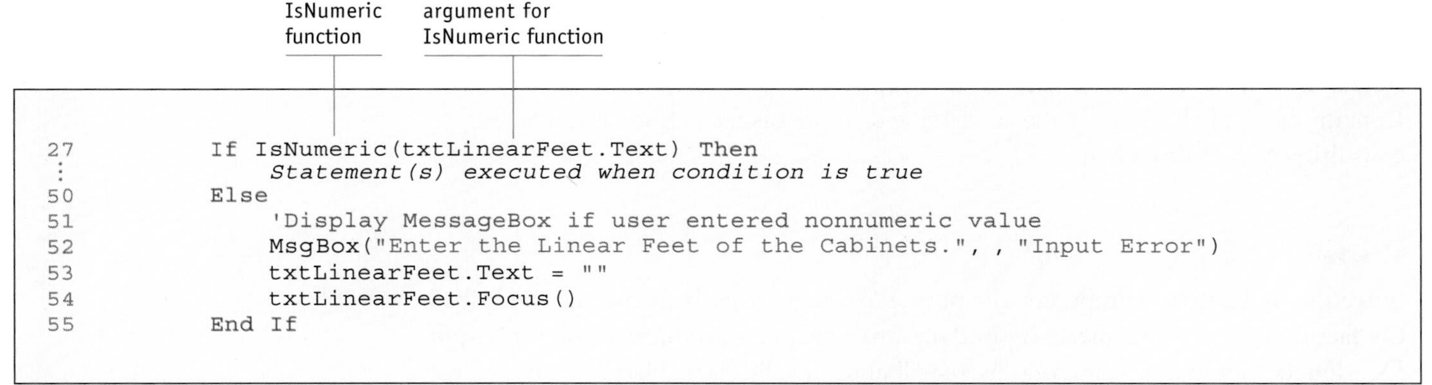


```
27          If IsNumeric(txtLinearFeet.Text) Then
 ⋮                Statement(s) executed when condition is true
50          Else
51                'Display MessageBox if user entered nonnumeric value
52                MsgBox("Enter the Linear Feet of the Cabinets.", , "Input Error")
53                txtLinearFeet.Text = ""
54                txtLinearFeet.Focus()
55          End If
```

FIGURE 5-74

In Figure 5-74, the If statement on line 27 calls the IsNumeric function. The Text property of the txtLinearFeet TextBox object is the argument for the IsNumeric function. As a result of this specification, the IsNumeric function will analyze the data in the Text property of the txtLinearFeet TextBox object. If the data can be converted to a numeric data type, then the function will return a Boolean value of True. If the data cannot be converted to a numeric data type, the function will return a Boolean value of False.

Once the function has returned a Boolean value, the If statement tests the Boolean value. If it is true, which means the value in the Text property of the txtLinearFeet TextBox object is numeric, the appropriate statements are executed. If the condition is false, meaning the value is not numeric, the statements on lines 51–55 are executed. The statement on line 52 displays a message box telling the user to enter the linear feet of the cabinet (see Figure 5-2 on page 293). The caption of the message box is "Input Error". The statement on line 53 clears the Text property. The statement on line 54 sets the focus on the text box so the user can reenter the value.

Checking for a Positive Number

If the condition in Figure 5-74 on the previous page is true, the value in the Text property must be converted to a Decimal data type. Then, the program checks to ensure the value entered is greater than zero. These statements are shown in Figure 5-75.

```
27          If IsNumeric(txtLinearFeet.Text) Then
28              decLinearFeet = Convert.ToDecimal(txtLinearFeet.Text)
29
30              ' Is linear feet greater than zero
31              If decLinearFeet > 0 Then
:                 Statement(s) executed when condition is true
33              Else
34                  ' Display error message if user entered a negative value
35                  MsgBox("You entered " & decLinearFeet.ToString() &
36                      ". Enter a Number Greater Than Zero.", , "Input Error")
37                  txtLinearFeet.Text = ""
38                  txtLinearFeet.Focus()
39              End If
40          Else
41              ' Display error message if user entered a nonnumeric value
42              MsgBox("Enter the Linear Feet of the Cabinets.", , "Input Error")
43              txtLinearFeet.Text = ""
44              txtLinearFeet.Focus()
45          End If
```

FIGURE 5-75

When the value in the Text property is numeric, it is converted to a decimal value (line 28). On line 31, the decimal value is compared to zero. If it is greater than zero, then the processing for a true statement is executed. If the value is not greater than zero, a message box is displayed informing the user an invalid entry was made (see Figure 5-29 on page 311). The user then can enter a valid value.

The process of validating input data is fundamental to programming when using a graphical user interface. A well-designed program must ensure the user enters valid data.

Program Design

As you have learned, the requirements document identifies the purpose of the program being developed; the application title; the procedures to be followed when using the program; any equations and calculations required in the program; any conditions within the program that must be tested; notes and restrictions that must be followed by the program; and any other comments that would be helpful to understanding the problem. The requirements document for the Wood Cabinet Estimate application is shown in Figure 5-76. The Use Case Definition document is shown in Figure 5-77 on the next page.

REQUIREMENTS DOCUMENT

Date submitted: January 29, 2014

Application title: Wood Cabinet Estimate

Purpose: This application calculates the estimated cost of wood cabinetry for a job bid.

Program Procedures: The user should enter the linear footage of cabinets needed and select the type of wood. The estimated cost for the cabinet job will be displayed.

Algorithms, Processing, and Conditions:

1. The user must be able to enter the number of linear feet of cabinetry.
2. The user must be able to select one of three wood types: pine, oak, or cherry.
3. The user can initiate the calculation and display the cost estimate for the wood cabinets.
4. The application computes the cost estimate of the cabinets based on the number of linear feet and the cost of the wood. Pine costs $150 per linear foot of cabinets, oak costs $200 per linear foot, and cherry costs $350 per linear foot.
5. The estimate calculation is: linear feet × cost per linear foot
6. The cost estimate is displayed in currency format.
7. The user should be able to clear the linear feet entered, reset the wood type to pine, and clear the cost estimate.

Notes and Restrictions:

1. If the user enters a nonnumeric value for the linear feet or if the TextBox object is empty, the user should be advised and asked for a valid entry.
2. If the user enters a negative number for the linear feet, the user should be advised and asked for a valid entry.

Comments:

1. The title of the Windows Form should be Wood Cabinet Estimate.

FIGURE 5-76

USE CASE DEFINITION

1. The window opens and displays the title, Estimate, a text box requesting the number of linear feet for the cabinets, radio buttons to select the wood type, and two buttons labeled Calculate and Clear.
2. The user enters the linear feet and selects one of the wood types.
3. The user clicks the Calculate button.
4. The user will be warned if a nonnumeric value is entered, the text box is left empty, or a negative number is entered.
5. The program displays the cost estimate for the cabinetry job.
6. The user clicks the Clear button to clear the Linear Feet text box, set the wood choice to Pine, and erase the cost estimate.
7. The user clicks the Close button to terminate the application.

FIGURE 5-77

Event Planning Document

You will recall that the event planning document consists of a table that specifies an object in the user interface that will cause an event, the action taken by the user to trigger the event, and the event processing that must occur. The event planning document for the Wood Cabinet Estimate program is shown in Figure 5-78.

EVENT PLANNING DOCUMENT

Program Name: Wood Cabinet Estimate	**Developer:** Corinne Hoisington	**Object:** frmWoodCabinets	**Date:** January 29, 2014
OBJECT	EVENT TRIGGER	EVENT PROCESSING	
btnCalculate	Click	Ensure data entered is numeric Display error message if data is not numeric or text box is empty Convert data entered to numeric Ensure data entered is greater than zero Display error message if data is not greater than zero Assign wood cost per foot based on type of wood selection Calculate cost (linear feet × cost per foot) Display cost	
btnClear	Click	Clear input text box Clear cost estimate Set the Pine radio button to checked Clear the Oak radio button Clear the Cherry radio button Set focus on input text box	
frmWoodCabinets	Load	Set focus on input text box Clear the placement zeros for cost	

FIGURE 5-78

Design and Code the Program

After the events and the tasks within the events have been identified, the developer is ready to create the program. As you have learned, creating the program means designing the user interface and then entering Visual Basic statements to accomplish the tasks specified on the event planning document. As the developer enters the code, she also will implement the logic to carry out the required processing.

NOTE TO THE LEARNER

As you will recall, in the following activity you should complete the tasks within the specified steps. Each task is accompanied by a Hint Screen. The Hint Screen indicates where in the Visual Studio window you should perform the activity and reminds you of the method to use to create the user interface or enter code. If you need further help completing the step, refer to the figure number identified by the term ref: in the step.

Guided Program Development

To design the user interface for the Wood Cabinet Estimate program and enter the code required to process each event in the program, complete the steps on the following pages.

Guided Program Development

Phase I: Design the Form

1

- **Create a Windows Application** Open Visual Studio using the Start button on the Windows taskbar and the All Programs submenu. Create a new Visual Basic Windows Application project by completing the following: Click the New Project button on the Standard toolbar; select and expand Visual Basic in the left pane; select Windows Application; name the project Wood Cabinet Estimate in the Name text box; then click the OK button in the New Project dialog box.

- **Name the Form** In the Solution Explorer pane, right-click Form1.vb and then click Rename. Type `frmWoodCabinets.vb`, and then press the ENTER key. Click the Yes button to automatically change the form (Name) in the Properties window.

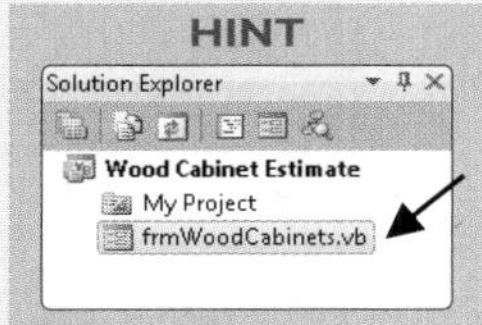

- **Change the Size Property** In the Properties window, change the Size property to 318,518.

- **Change the BackColor Property** In the the Properties window, change the BackColor property to Burly Wood.

- **Change the Title on the Title Bar** To change the title on the title bar, click the form, scroll down the Properties window until the Text property is displayed, double-click in the right column of the Text property, type Wood Cabinet Estimate, and then press the ENTER key.

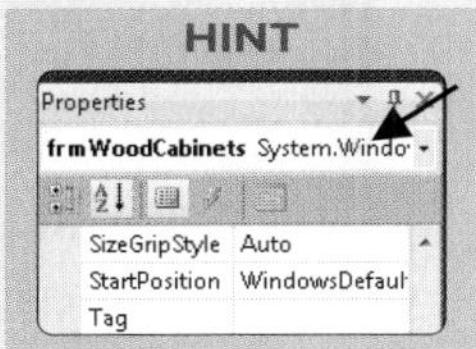

(continues)

...rogram Development *continued*

- **Add a Heading Title** Drag the first label onto the form and name the label lblHeading. Set the Text property for the Label object to Wood Cabinet Cost. Set the font to Goudy Old Style, Bold, Size 20. Position the label horizontally in the center of the form.

- **Add a Label** Drag the second label onto the frmWoodCabinets Form object and name the label lblLinearFeet. Set the Text property for the Label object to Linear Feet:. Set the font to Goudy Old Style, Bold, Size 14. Position the label to resemble Figure 5-79.

- **Add a TextBox Object** Drag a TextBox object onto the form. Using snap lines, align the top of the TextBox object with the top of the Label object. Name the TextBox object txtFeet. Change the TextAlign property to Center. Change the font to Goudy Old Style, Bold, Size 14. Reduce the width of the TextBox object to closely resemble Figure 5-79. Center the Label object and the TextBox object horizontally in the frmWoodCabinets Form object.

A title Label object is displayed on the first line of the form. A Label object and TextBox object occupy the second line of the frmWoodCabinets Form object (Figure 5-79). They are centered horizontally in the form.

RESULT OF STEP 1

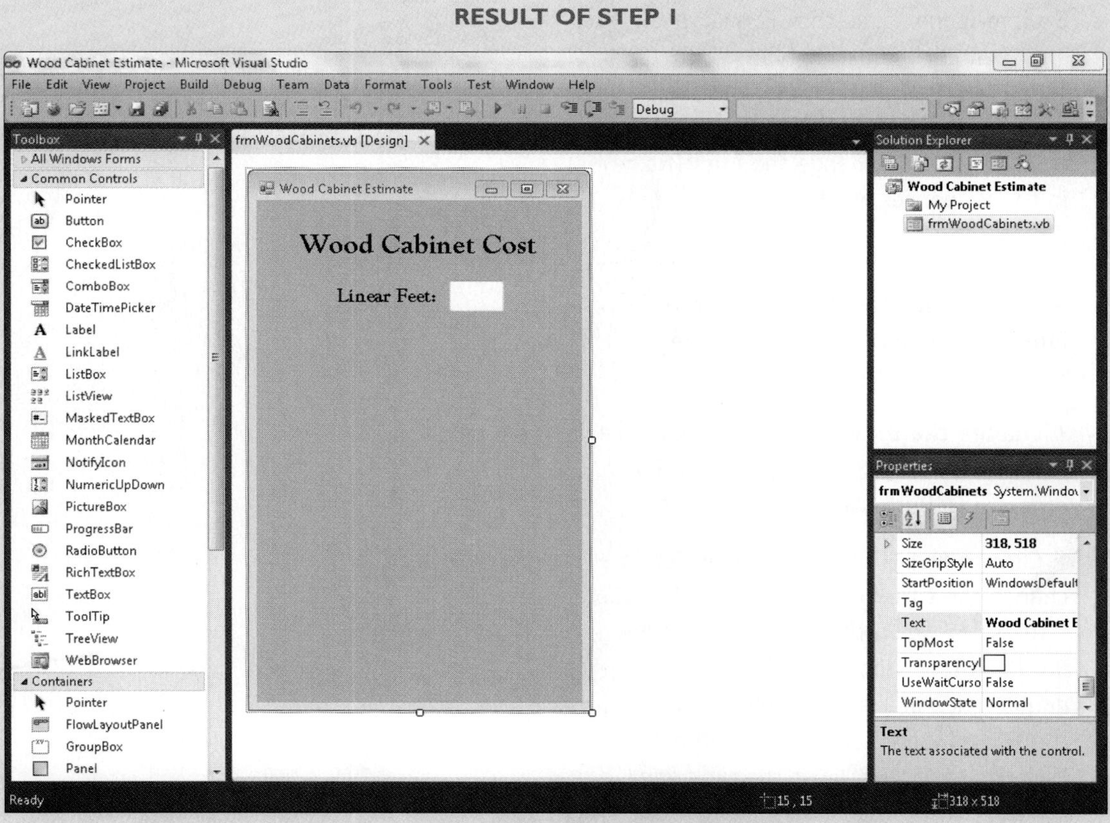

FIGURE 5-79

Guided Program Development *continued*

2

- **Add a GroupBox** Drag a GroupBox object onto the frmWoodCabinets Form object. Name the GroupBox grpWoodType. Change the Text property to Wood Type. Set the Size of the GroupBox object to 125,100. Change the BackColor of the GroupBox object to White. Center the GroupBox object horizontally in the frmWoodCabinets Form object, and change the font to Goudy Old Style, Regular, Size 12 *(ref: Figure 5-4)*.

- **Add Radio Buttons** Place three RadioButton objects on the GroupBox object. Name the first RadioButton radPine and change its Text property to Pine. Name the second RadioButton radOak and change its Text property to Oak. Name the third RadioButton radCherry and change its Text property to Cherry. Select the three RadioButtons and change the font to Goudy Old Style, Regular, Size 12 *(ref: Figure 5-7)*.

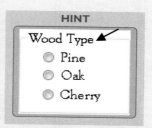

- **Set Radio Button Properties** Click the radPine RadioButton object and change its Checked property from False to True. Pine is the wood most commonly used by this cabinetmaker *(ref: Figure 5-11)*.

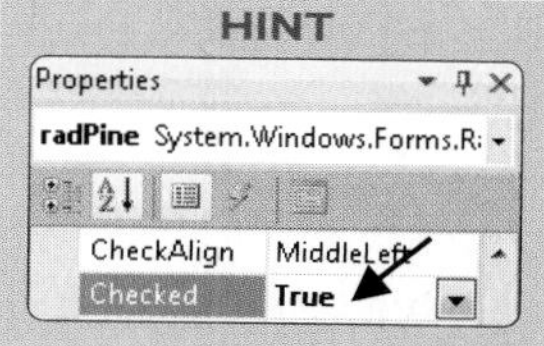

(continues)

Guided Program Development *continued*

The group box and radio buttons are included on the frmWoodCabinets Form object (Figure 5-80). The radPine radio button is selected because it is the most widely used wood type.

RESULT OF STEP 2

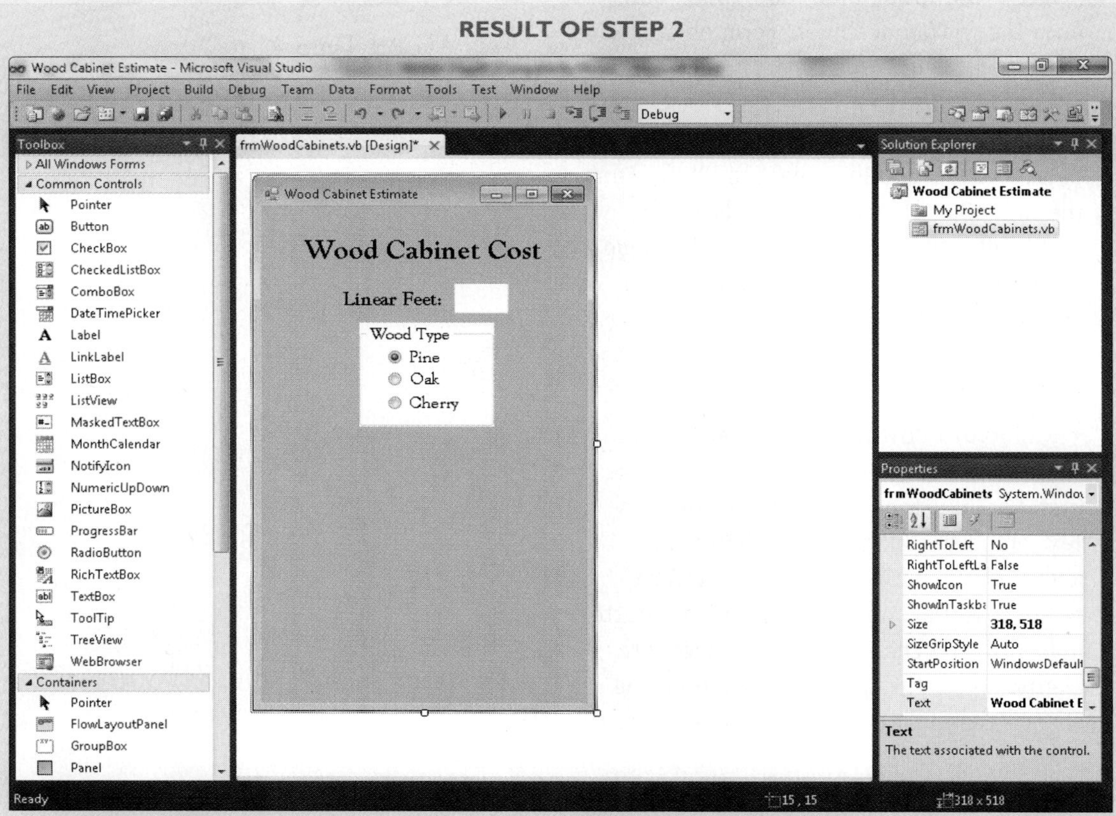

FIGURE 5-80

3

• **Add Estimate and Cost Labels** Drag two more Label objects below the GroupBox object. Align these labels by their tops using snap lines. Name the first label lblCost, change its Text property to Cost Estimate:, and resize the Label object to view the text. Name the second label lblCostEstimate and set its Text property to $0000.00. These placement zeros allow you to view the Label object when it is not selected. The placement zeros will be cleared using code when the form is loaded. Change the font for both Label objects to Goudy Old Style, Bold, Size 14. Horizontally center the labels as a unit on the frmWoodCabinets Form object.

HINT

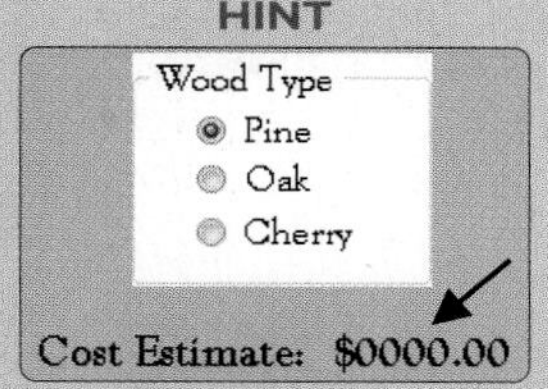

Guided Program Development *continued*

- **Add Calculate and Clear Buttons** Drag two Button objects onto the form. Align the tops of the Button objects using snap lines. Name the first Button object on the left btnCalculate and change its Text property to Calculate. Name the second Button object on the right btnClear and change its Text property to Clear. Change the font for these two buttons to Goudy Old Style, Regular, Size 12. Change the size of each button to 100,30. Change the BackColor property for each button to White.

- **Add a Picture to the Windows Form** Download the Cabinets.jpg picture from http://scsite.com/vb2010/ch5/images. Drag a PictureBox object to the bottom of the Windows Form. Name the picture picCabinets. Change the Size property of the PictureBox object to 310,175. Change the SizeMode property to StretchImage.

The user interface is complete (Figure 5-81).

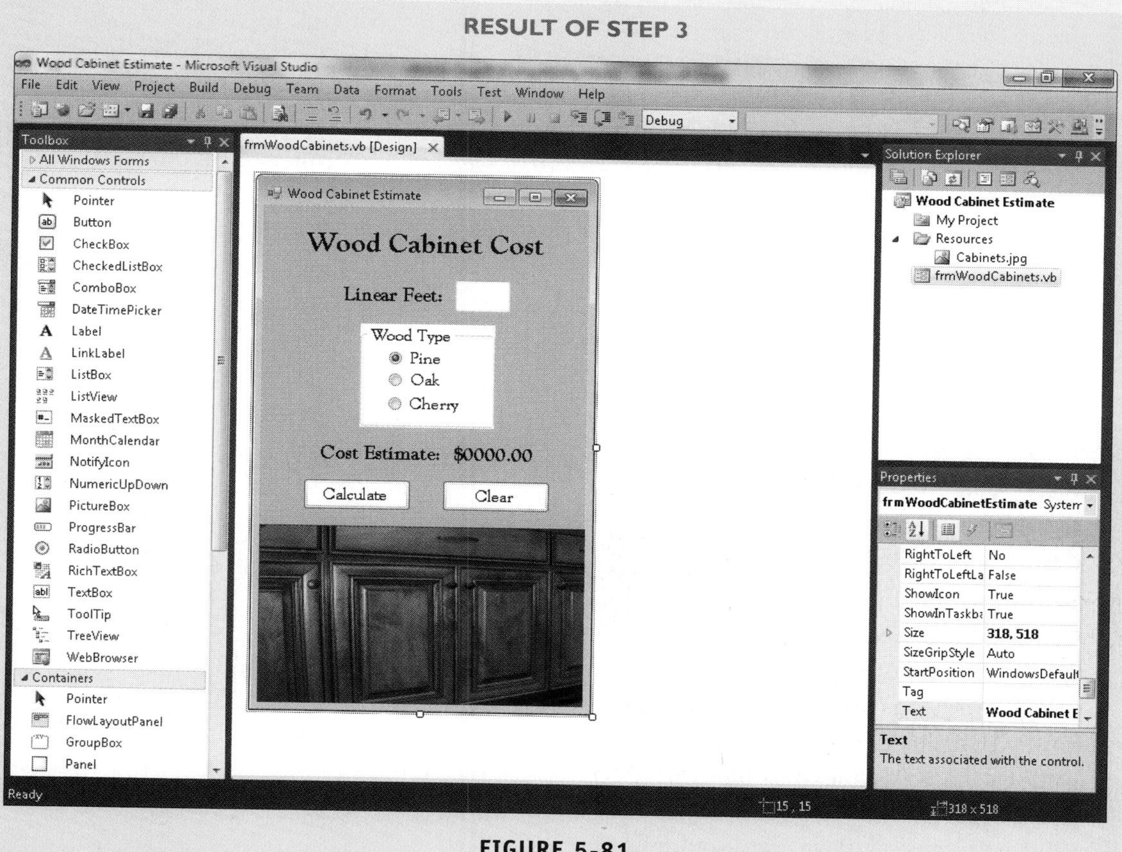

FIGURE 5-81

(continues)

Guided Program Development *continued*

Phase 2: Code the Application

4

- **Code the Comments** Double-click the btnCalculate Button object on the frmWoodCabinets Form object to open the code editing window and create the btnCalculate_Click event handler. Close the Toolbox. Click in front of the first words, Public Class frmWoodCabinetEstimate, and press the ENTER key to create a blank line. Insert the first four standard comments. Insert the Option Strict On command at the beginning of the code to turn on strict type checking.

HINT

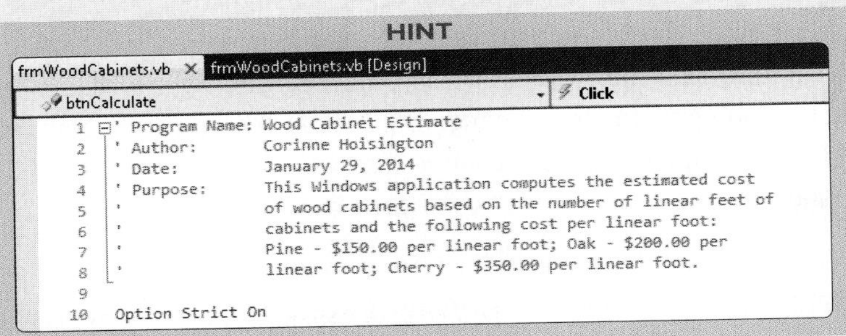

- **Comment the btnCalculate_Click Event Handler** Enter a comment to describe the purpose of the btnCalculate_Click event.

HINT

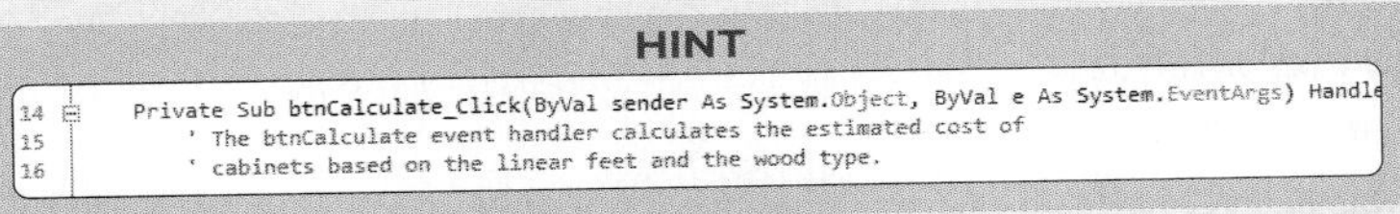

- **Declare and Initialize the Variables** This application requires six variables: 1) decFeet: Holds the estimated linear footage of the cabinets. 2) decCostPerFoot: Holds the cost per linear foot based on the wood type; 3) decCostEstimate: Is assigned the calculated final estimated cost; 4) decPineCost: Is assigned the value 150.00; 5) decOakCost: Is assigned the value 200.00; 6) decCherryCost: Is assigned the value 350.00. Declare and initialize these six variables.

HINT

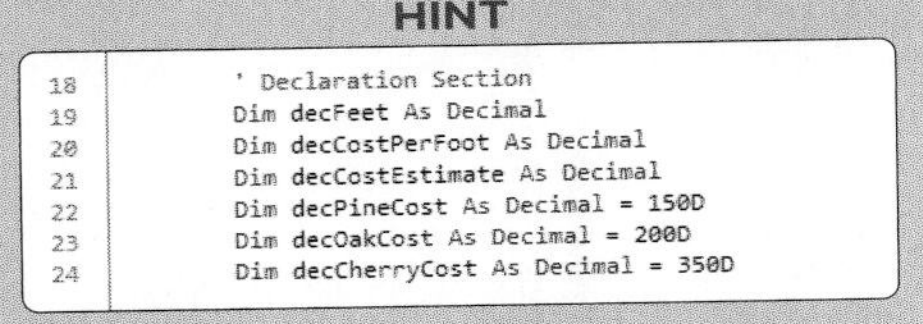

- **Write the If Statement to Test for Numeric Data** When the user clicks the Calculate button, the program must first ensure that the user entered a valid numeric value in the txtFeet TextBox object. If the user has entered a valid numeric value, the value must be converted from a string value into a decimal data type. Write the If statement and conversion statement required for this process *(ref: Figure 5-74)*.

HINT

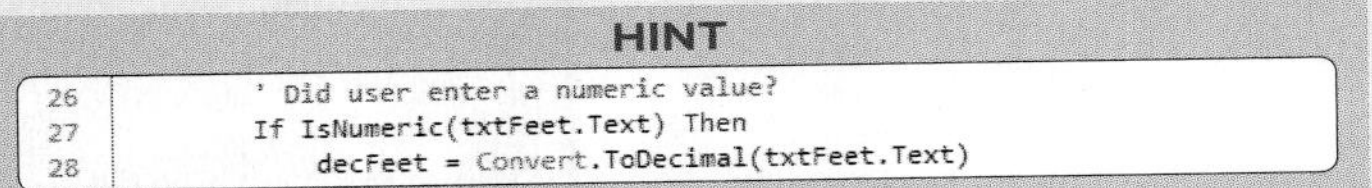

Guided Program Development *continued*

- **Write the If Statement to Test for a Positive Number** If the value is numeric, then the converted numeric value must be checked to ensure it is a positive number. Write the If statement to check if the converted numeric value is greater than zero *(ref: Figure 5-75)*.

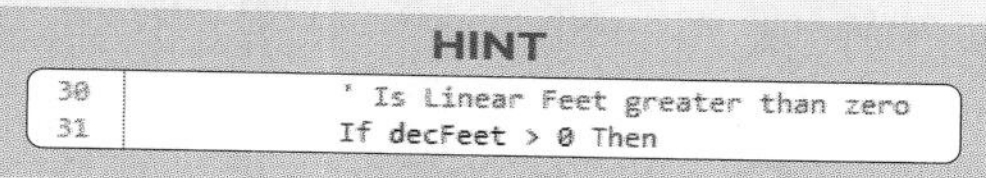

HINT

```
' Is Linear Feet greater than zero
If decFeet > 0 Then
```

- **Write the If Statements to Determine Cost Per Linear Foot** When the value is greater than zero, the cost per linear foot is determined by checking the status of the RadioButton objects and placing the appropriate cost per linear foot in the decCostPerFoot variable. Using the If . . . Then . . . ElseIf structure, write the statements to identify the checked radio button and place the appropriate cost in the decCostPerFoot variable *(ref: Figure 5-49)*.

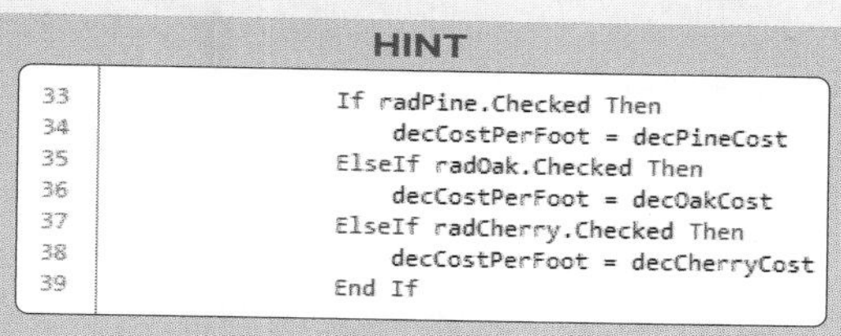

HINT

```
If radPine.Checked Then
    decCostPerFoot = decPineCost
ElseIf radOak.Checked Then
    decCostPerFoot = decOakCost
ElseIf radCherry.Checked Then
    decCostPerFoot = decCherryCost
End If
```

- **Calculate and Display the Cost Estimate** The next step is to calculate the cost estimate by multiplying the value in the decCostPerFoot variable times the linear feet. Then you should display the cost estimate in the cost estimate label. Write the statements to calculate and display the cost estimate in the currency format.

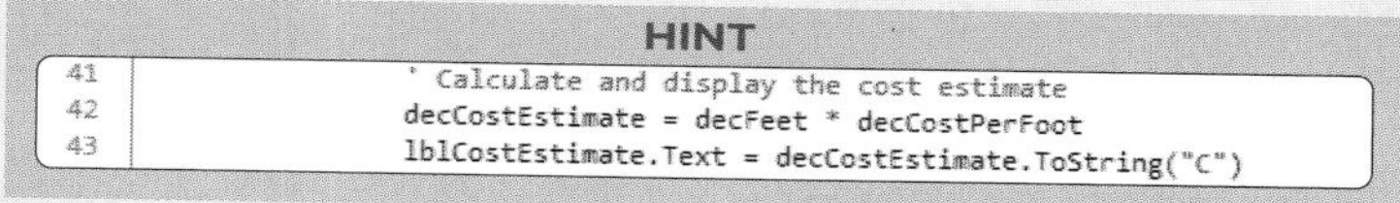

HINT

```
' Calculate and display the cost estimate
decCostEstimate = decFeet * decCostPerFoot
lblCostEstimate.Text = decCostEstimate.ToString("C")
```

- **Display Message Box If Value Entered Is Not Greater Than Zero** After the processing is finished for the true portion of the If statements, the Else portion of the If statements must be written. Write the code to display the message box containing the error message when the value entered by the user is not greater than zero *(ref: Figure 5–24)*.

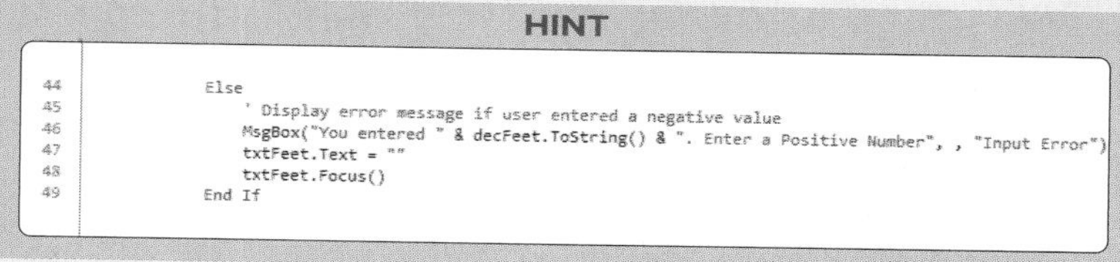

HINT

```
Else
    ' Display error message if user entered a negative value
    MsgBox("You entered " & decFeet.ToString() & ". Enter a Positive Number", , "Input Error")
    txtFeet.Text = ""
    txtFeet.Focus()
End If
```

(continues)

Guided Program Development *continued*

- **Display Error Message If Value Entered Is Not Numeric** Write the Else portion of the If statement if the value entered by the user is not numeric *(ref: Figure 5-24)*.

HINT

```
        Else
            ' Display error message if user entered a nonnumeric value
            MsgBox("Enter the Linear Feet of the Cabinets", , "Input Error")
            txtFeet.Text = ""
            txtFeet.Focus()
        End If
```

The code for the click event of the Calculate button is completed (Figure 5-82).

RESULT OF STEP 4

```
' Program Name: Wood Cabinet Estimate
' Author:       Corinne Hoisington
' Date:         January 29, 2014
' Purpose:      This Windows application computes the estimated cost
'               of wood cabinets based on the number of linear feet of
'               cabinets and the following cost per linear foot:
'               Pine - $150.00 per linear foot; Oak - $200.00 per
'               linear foot; Cherry - $350.00 per linear foot.

Option Strict On

Public Class frmWoodCabinetEstimate

    Private Sub btnCalculate_Click(ByVal sender As System.Object, ByVal e As System.EventArgs) Handles btnCalculate.Click
        ' The btnCalculate event handler calculates the estimated cost of
        ' cabinets based on the linear feet and the wood type.

        ' Declaration Section
        Dim decFeet As Decimal
        Dim decCostPerFoot As Decimal
        Dim decCostEstimate As Decimal
        Dim decPineCost As Decimal = 150D
        Dim decOakCost As Decimal = 200D
        Dim decCherryCost As Decimal = 350D

        ' Did user enter a numeric value?
        If IsNumeric(txtFeet.Text) Then
            decFeet = Convert.ToDecimal(txtFeet.Text)

            ' Is Linear Feet greater than zero
            If decFeet > 0 Then
                ' Determine cost per foot of wood
                If radPine.Checked Then
                    decCostPerFoot = decPineCost
                ElseIf radOak.Checked Then
                    decCostPerFoot = decOakCost
                ElseIf radCherry.Checked Then
                    decCostPerFoot = decCherryCost
                End If
```

FIGURE 5-82 (continues)

Guided Program Development *continued*

```
            ' Calculate and display the cost estimate
            decCostEstimate = decFeet * decCostPerFoot
            lblCostEstimate.Text = decCostEstimate.ToString("C")
        Else
            ' Display error message if user entered a negative value
            MsgBox("You entered " & decFeet.ToString() & ". Enter a Positive Number", , "Input Error")
            txtFeet.Text = ""
            txtFeet.Focus()
        End If
    Else
        ' Display error message if user entered a nonnumeric value
        MsgBox("Enter the Linear Feet of the Cabinets", , "Input Error")
        txtFeet.Text = ""
        txtFeet.Focus()
    End If
End Sub
```

FIGURE 5-82 (continued)

5

- **Create the Clear Button Click Event Handler** The Clear Button click event includes the following processing: 1) Clear the txtFeet Text property; 2) Clear the lblCostEstimate Text property; 3) Set the radPine Checked property to True; 4) Set the radOak and radCherry Checked properties to False; 5) Set the focus in the txtFeet text box. To enter this code, click the frmWoodCabinets.vb [Design] tab and then double-click the Clear button. Using IntelliSense, enter the required code.

HINT

```
Private Sub btnClear_Click(ByVal sender As System.Object, ByVal e As System.EventArgs) Handles btnClear.Click
    ' This event handler is executed when
    ' the user clicks the Clear button. It
    ' clears the Linear Feet text box and the
    ' cost estimate label, resets the radio
    ' buttons with Pine selected, and sets  the
    ' focus to the Linear Feet text box.

    txtFeet.Clear()
    lblCostEstimate.Text = ""
    radPine.Checked = True
    radOak.Checked = False
    radCherry.Checked = False
    txtFeet.Focus()
End Sub
```

(continues)

Guided Program Development *continued*

• **Create the Form Load Event Handler** When the frmWoodCabinets Form object loads, the following processing should occur: 1) The focus is in the txtFeet text box; 2) The lblCostEstimate Text property is set to null. Click the frmWoodCabinets.vb [Design] tab to return to Design view and then double-click the form. Enter the code for the form load event handler.

HINT

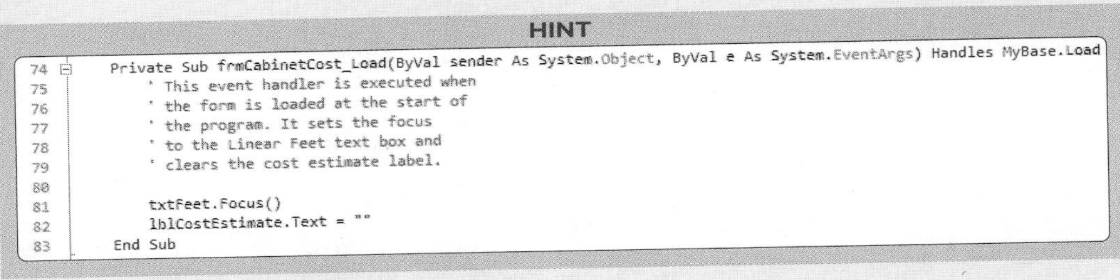

```
Private Sub frmCabinetCost_Load(ByVal sender As System.Object, ByVal e As System.EventArgs) Handles MyBase.Load
    ' This event handler is executed when
    ' the form is loaded at the start of
    ' the program. It sets the focus
    ' to the Linear Feet text box and
    ' clears the cost estimate label.

    txtFeet.Focus()
    lblCostEstimate.Text = ""
End Sub
```

6

• **Run the Application** After you have completed the code, you should run the application to ensure it works properly.

• **Test the Application** Test the application with the following data: 1) Linear feet: 25, wood type Oak; 2) Linear feet: 9, wood type Cherry; 3) Linear feet 100, wood type Pine; 4) Linear feet: Fifteen (use this word), wood type Cherry; 5) Linear feet: −21, wood type Oak; 6) Use other values to thoroughly test the program. After each test, click the Clear button before entering new data.

• **Close the Program** After testing the application, close the window by clicking the Close button (X) in the title bar of the window.

HINT

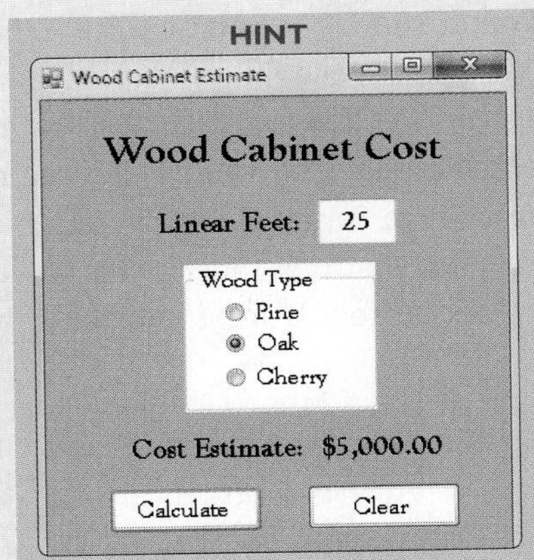

Debugging Exercises *continued*

5. The If...Then ... Else statement shown in Figure 5-90 contains one or more errors. Identify the error(s) and rewrite the statements correctly.

```
If strShippingMethod = "Overnite" Then
    If strDeliveryTime = "Morning"
        decDeliveryCost = 29.00D
    Else
        decDeliveryCost = 24.00D
Else
    If strShippingMethod = "Two Days" Then
        decDeliveryCost = 14.00D
    Else
        decDeliveryCost = 4.00D
End If
```

FIGURE 5-90

Program Analysis

1. Write an If...Then ... Else decision structure to compare the two numbers in the intPay1 and intPay2 variables. Display a message box stating intPay1 is greater than intPay2, or intPay1 is less than or equal to intPay2.
2. Write an If statement that displays the message box "Snow is possible" if the value in the variable decTemp is within the range 0 to 32.
3. Write an If...Then ... Else statement that checks the value in the variable chrGender for the value M (Male) or F (Female) and assigns the information shown in Figure 5-91 to lblCollegeExpectation.Text based on the gender. If the variable chrGender contains a value other than M or F, assign the message "Invalid Gender" to lblCollegeExpectation.Text.

Gender	College Expectation
Male	75% plan to graduate from college
Female	85% plan to graduate from college

FIGURE 5-91

(continues)

Program Analysis *continued*

4. Write a Select Case statement that tests the user's age in a variable named intAge and assigns the name of the favorite snack of that age group to the variable strSnack, according to the preferences shown in Figure 5-92.

Age	Favorite Snack
Under age 7	Yogurt
Age 7 to 12	Potato Chips
Age 13 to 18	Chocolate
Over Age 18	Gum

FIGURE 5-92

5. Rewrite the Select Case statement shown in Figure 5-93 as an If . . . Then . . . Else statement.

```
Select Case chrDepartment
    Case "B", "b"
        strDept = "Baby / Infant Clothing"
    Case "T", "t"
        strDept = "Technology"
End Select
```

FIGURE 5-93

6. Rewrite the If . . . Then . . . Else statement shown in Figure 5-94 as a Select Case statement.

```
If intGrade >= 9 And intGrade <= 12 Then
    lblSchool.Text = "High School"
ElseIf intGrade >= 7 Then
    lblSchool.Text = "Middle School"
ElseIf intGrade >= 1 Then
    lblSchool.Text = "Elementary School"
Else
    lblSchool.Text = "Invalid Grade"
End If
```

FIGURE 5-94

7. What is the output of the code shown in Figure 5-95 on the next page if the word Black is entered in the txtSkiSlope text box?

Program Analysis *continued*

```
Select Case Me.txtSkiSlope.Text
    Case "Green"
        MsgBox("Beginner Slope")
    Case "Blue"
        MsgBox("Intermediate Slope")
    Case "Black"
        MsgBox("Expert Slope")
    Case Else
        MsgBox("Invalid Entry")
End Select
```

FIGURE 5-95

8. After the execution of the Select Case structure in Figure 5-96, what value will be found in the Text property of lblFemaleHeight if the user enters the number 74 into the txtEnterHeight text box? If the number 81 is entered? If the number 59 is entered?

```
Dim intHeightInches As Integer
intHeightInches = Convert.ToInt32(txtEnterHeight.Text)
Select Case intHeightInches
    Case Is < 61
        lblFemaleHeight.Text = "Petite"
    Case 61 To 69
        lblFemaleHeight.Text = "Average"
    Case 70 To 80
        lblFemaleHeight.Text = "Tall"
    Case 80 To 120
        lblFemaleHeight.Text = "Towering"
    Case Else
        lblFemaleHeight.Text = "Not Possible"
End Select
```

FIGURE 5-96

9. In each of the following examples, is the condition True or False?

   a. "C" >= "C"

   b. "G" >= "g"

   c. "Amazed" < "Amaze"

   d. "Cool" < > "cool"

   e. "40" >= "Forty"

   f. ("Paris" < "Barcelona") And ("Amsterdam" <= "Prague")

   g. ("Ford" > "Chevrolet") Or ("Toyota" < "Honda")

   h. 3 ^ 2 <= 3 * 4

   i. Not ("CNN" >= "ABC")

   j. Not ("Tim" > "Tom") And Not ("Great" < > "great")

Case Programming Assignments

Complete one or more of the following case programming assignments. Submit the program and materials you create to your instructor. The level of difficulty is indicated for each case programming assignment.

●	= Easiest
●●	= Intermediate
●●●	= Challenging

1 ● PARKING TICKET FINES

Design a Windows application and write the code that will execute according to the program requirements in Figure 5-97. The data to use is shown in Figure 5-98 on the next page. Before writing the code, create an event planning document for each event in the program, as shown in Figure 5-99 on the next page. The completed Form object and other objects in the user interface are shown in Figure 5-100 on the next page.

REQUIREMENTS DOCUMENT

Date submitted: May 6, 2013

Application title: Parking Ticket Fines

Purpose: This Windows application calculates a parking ticket fine.

Program Procedures: The user selects the type of parking violation and indicates if the owner of the vehicle is a repeat offender. The user then requests that the program calculate and display the parking ticket fine.

Algorithms, Processing, and Conditions:

1. The user selects the type of parking violation.
2. If the owner of the vehicle has been ticketed previously for a parking offense in the city, the fine is doubled.
3. The user must be able to indicate the owner is a repeat offender.
4. The fine is calculated based on the chart in Figure 5-98.
5. The user must be able to initiate the display of the parking ticket fine.
6. The user should be able to clear the type of violation indicator, the repeat offender indicator, and the ticket fine.

Notes and Restrictions: n/a

Comments:

1. Obtain an image for this program from scsite.com/vb2010/ch5/images. The image file name is Parking.

FIGURE 5-97

Case Programming Assignments

Parking Ticket Fines *(continued)*

Parking Violation	Fine
Expired Meter	$35
No Parking Zone	$75
Blocking Driveway	$150
Illegal Handicap Parking	$500

FIGURE 5-98

USE CASE DEFINITION

1. The Windows application window opens.
2. The user selects the type of parking offense.
3. The user selects whether the user is a repeat offender.
4. The user clicks the Display Fine button to display the parking ticket fine.
5. The user clears the input and the result by clicking the Clear button.
6. If desired, the user repeats the process.

FIGURE 5-99

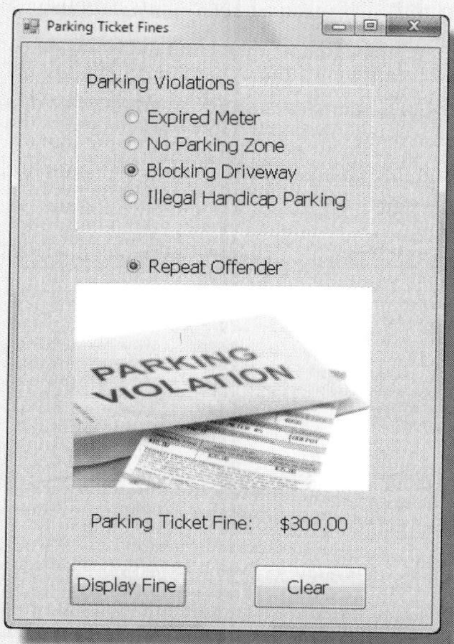

FIGURE 5-100

Case Programming Assignments

2 • AMUSEMENT PARK TICKETS

Design a Windows application and write the code that will execute according to the program requirements in Figure 5-101 and the Use Case Definition in Figure 5-102 on the next page. Before writing the code, create an event planning document for each event in the program. The completed Form object and other objects in the user interface are shown in Figure 5-103 on the next page.

REQUIREMENTS DOCUMENT

Date submitted: April 15, 2013

Application title: Amusement Park Tickets

Purpose: This Windows application calculates the cost of the amusement park tickets.

Program Procedures: The user should enter the number of single-day tickets for the amusement park. The park has a discount program for various club memberships. The user may use only one club membership. The user does not need to select a club membership. The park ticket costs $72 a day.

Algorithms, Processing, and Conditions:

1. The user enters the number of tickets.
2. The types of club memberships accepted are AAA (15% off full purchase cost), AARP (17.5% off full purchase cost), and Military ID (20% off full purchase price). The user can only select one type of membership.
3. The user must be able to initiate the calculation and display the total final cost of the tickets.
4. The user should be able to clear the number of tickets purchased, the types of membership, and the total cost.

Notes and Restrictions:

1. If a negative number is entered for tickets, the user should be advised and asked for a valid entry.
2. If a nonnumeric value is entered for the ticket number or if the input for the number of tickets is left blank, the user should be advised and asked for a valid entry.

Comments:

1. Obtain an image for this program from scsite.com/vb2010/ch5/images. The image file name is Amusement.

FIGURE 5-101

Case Programming Assignments

Amusement Park Tickets *(continued)*

USE CASE DEFINITION

1. The Windows application window opens.
2. The user enters the number of single-day tickets needed.
3. The user clicks the Display Cost button.
4. The program displays the total cost of the tickets after the discount is applied.
5. Using a MsgBox, the user is warned if a negative number is entered for the number of tickets.
6. Using the MsgBox, the user is warned if a nonnumeric value is entered for the number of tickets or if the value is left blank.
7. The user can clear the input and the results by clicking the Clear button.

FIGURE 5-102

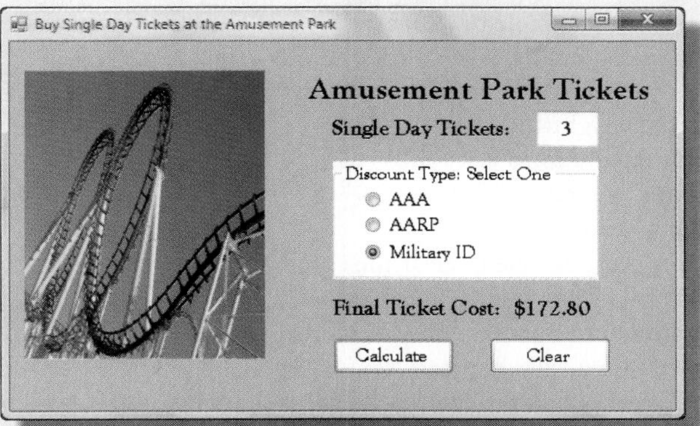

FIGURE 5-103

Case Programming Assignments

3 • PATIENT WEIGHT CONVERTER

Design a Windows application and write the code that will execute according to the program requirements in Figure 5-104 and the Use Case Definition in Figure 5-105 on the next page. Before writing the code, create an event planning document for each event in the program. The completed Form object and other objects in the user interface are shown in Figure 5-106 on the next page.

REQUIREMENTS DOCUMENT

Date submitted: May 11, 2013

Application title: Patient Weight Converter

Purpose: This Windows application converts the weight of the patient from pounds to kilograms and kilograms to pounds.

Program Procedures: The user enters the weight of the patient, selects the conversion type (pounds to kilograms or kilograms to pounds), and displays the converted weight of the patient.

Algorithms, Processing, and Conditions:

1. A user must be able to enter the weight of the patient in pounds or kilograms.
2. The user must be able to select the type of conversion: pounds to kilograms or kilograms to pounds.
3. The user must be able to initiate the weight conversion and the display of the patient's converted weight.
4. The conversion formulas are:
   kilograms = pounds / 2.2
   pounds = kilograms × 2.2
5. The user must be able to clear the entered weight, conversion choice, and results.

Notes and Restrictions:

1. If a nonnumeric value is entered or if the weight is left blank, the user should be advised and asked for a valid entry.
2. If a negative number is entered for the weight, the user should be advised and asked for a valid entry.
3. If the value entered is greater than 500 for the conversion from pounds to kilograms or greater than 225 for the conversion from kilograms to pounds, the user should be advised and asked for a valid entry.
4. The default conversion choice should be pounds to kilograms.
5. The converted weight should be displayed with one digit to the right of the decimal point.

Comments:

1. Obtain an image for this program from scsite.com/vb2010/ch5/images. The image file name is Scale.

FIGURE 5-104

Case Programming Assignments

Patient Weight Converter *(continued)*

USE CASE DEFINITION

1. The Windows application window opens.
2. The user enters the patient's weight.
3. The user selects the conversion type (pounds to kilograms or kilograms to pounds).
4. The user clicks the Display button to display the converted weight value.
5. The user clears the input and the result by clicking the Clear button.
6. If desired, the user repeats the process.

FIGURE 5-105

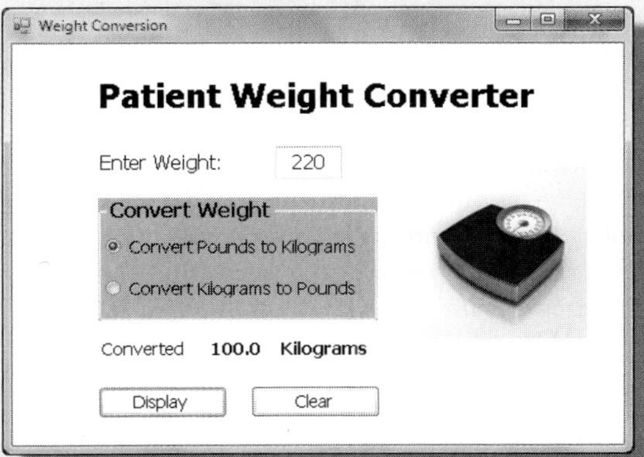

FIGURE 5-106

Case Programming Assignments

4 ●● HEALTH CLUB MEMBERSHIP

Design a Windows application and write the code that will execute according to the program requirements in Figure 5-107. Before designing the user interface, create a Use Case definition. Before writing the code, create an event planning document for each event in the program.

REQUIREMENTS DOCUMENT

Date submitted: April 22, 2013

Application title: Health Club Membership

Purpose: This Windows application calculates the prepayment amount for a new member of a health club.

Program Procedures: The user should enter the name of the new member, the number of months the new user would like to prepay, and the type of membership. The health club prepayment cost will be computed and displayed for the entered number of months. The per month costs for the three types of membership are:

Single Membership	$38 per month
Family Membership	$58 per month
Senior Membership	$27 per month

Algorithms, Processing, and Conditions:

1. The user must enter the name of the new member, the type of membership, and the number of months the new member would like to prepay.
2. Based on the type of membership, the prepayment cost is calculated using the following formula: number of prepay months × cost per month.
3. The user must be able to initiate the calculation and display the prepay amount for the health club membership.
4. The user should be able to clear the name of the new member, the number of prepay months, the type of membership, and the prepay amount for the new member.

Notes and Restrictions:

1. If the user enters a nonnumeric value for the number of months, the user should be advised and asked for a valid entry.
2. If the user enters a negative number for the number of months or if the user leaves the number of months input area blank, the user should be advised and asked for a valid entry.
3. If the user leaves the input area for the user name blank, the user should be advised and asked for a valid entry.
4. The default membership type is single membership.

FIGURE 5-107

Case Programming Assignments

5 ●● TWO-DAY PACKAGE SHIPPING

Design a Windows application and write the code that will execute according to the program requirements in Figure 5-108. Before designing the user interface, create a Use Case definition. Before writing the code, create an event planning document for each event in the program.

REQUIREMENTS DOCUMENT

Date submitted: May 6, 2013

Application title: Two-Day Package Shipping

Purpose: This Windows application calculates the cost of shipping a package with two-day delivery.

Program Procedures: The user enters the weight of the package (in pounds) and selects the destination of the package. The application will determine the cost of shipping. The destination of the package can be the continental U.S., Hawaii, or Alaska. If the package is going to Hawaii, a 20% surcharge is added to the shipping cost. If the package is going to Alaska, a 26% surcharge is added to the shipping cost.

Algorithms, Processing, and Conditions:

1. The user must be able to enter the number of pounds the package weighs and indicate that the package is being mailed to the continental U.S., Hawaii, or Alaska.
2. The shipping costs are calculated based on the rates in the table in Figure 5-109 on the next page. A 20% surcharge is added if the shipping destination is Hawaii. A 26% surcharge is added if the shipping destination is Alaska.
3. The user must be able to initiate the calculation and the display of the shipping cost.
4. The user must be able to clear the weight of the package and the shipping cost.

Notes and Restrictions:

1. If the entry for the shipping weight is blank or nonnumeric, the user should be advised and asked for a valid entry.
2. The maximum weight for a package is 30 pounds. If the weight is greater than 30 pounds, or if the value entered is not greater than zero, the user should be advised and asked for a valid entry.

FIGURE 5-108

(continues)

Case Programming Assignments

Two-Day Package Shipping *(continued)*

For Weight Not Over (Pounds)	2-Day Rate
2	$3.69
4	$4.86
6	$5.63
8	$5.98
10	$6.28
30	$15.72

FIGURE 5-109

Case Programming Assignments

6 ●● PAYROLL CALCULATOR

Design a Windows application and write the code that will execute according to the program requirements in Figure 5-110. Before designing the user interface, create a Use Case definition. Before writing the code, create an event planning document for each event in the program.

REQUIREMENTS DOCUMENT

Date submitted: May 11, 2013

Application title: Payroll Calculator

Purpose: This application calculates the payroll for employees of the Food For All local grocery store.

Program Procedures: In a Windows application, the user enters the employee's name, hours worked, and pay per hour. If the employee works more than 40 hours per week, the grocery store pays time-and-a-half for overtime. The tax rate can be the single rate (18%) or at the family rate (15%). The application should compute and display the gross pay, the tax based on the single or family rate, and the net pay.

Algorithms, Processing, and Conditions:

1. The user must be able to enter the employee's name, hours worked, and pay per hour.
2. The user must be able to indicate if the tax rate is at the single rate (18%) or the family rate (15%).
3. The user must be able to initiate the calculation and the display of the gross pay, the tax amount based on the single or family rate, and the net pay.
4. A Clear button will clear the user's input and final results.

Notes and Restrictions:

1. If the employee name, hours worked, or pay per hour are blank, the user should be advised and asked for a valid entry.
2. If the hours worked or pay per hour are nonnumeric, the user should be advised and asked for a valid entry.
3. The minimum value for hours worked is 5 hours. The maximum for hours worked is 60. If the user enters an hours worked value not within the range, the user should be advised and asked for a valid entry.
4. The minimum pay per hour is $8.00. The maximum pay per hour is $40.00 per hour. If the user enters a pay per hour value not within the range, the user should be advised and asked for a valid entry.
5. The user must be able to clear the employee's name, the hours worked, the pay per hour, and the pay information.

FIGURE 5-110

Case Programming Assignments

7 ●●● TECHNOLOGY CONFERENCE REGISTRATION

Based on the case project shown in Figure 5-111, create a requirements document and a Use Case Definition document, and then design a Windows application. Before writing the code, create an event planning document for each event in the program.

It is important that developers update their skills by attending developers' conferences. The Dynamic International Management Consortium (DIMC) runs and manages the ADSE (Active Developers Skill Enhancement) Conference two times per year. To encourage companies to send multiple employees to the conference, the cost per attendee is determined based on the number of attending developers from a given company. The table below specifies the cost per attendee.

Number of Conference Registrations per Company	Cost per Attendee
1	$695
2-4	$545
5-8	$480
8 or more	$395

DIMC has requested that you develop a Windows application that can determine and display the total cost per company for developers attending the conference. DIMC has a conference policy that states if any member of a company has attended a previous DIMC conference, the company receives a 15% discount from the total cost of its employees who attend. The policy also states that no more than 16 people from a single company can attend the conference. DIMC has asked that you design the program so that the user must enter valid data.

FIGURE 5-111

Case Programming Assignments

8 ●●● CAR RENTAL

Based on the case project shown in Figure 5-112, create a requirements document and a Use Case Definition document, and then design a Windows application. Before writing the code, create an event planning document for each event in the program.

The Adventure Car Rental Company has asked that you create a Windows application for the rental of an adventure vehicle. The user selects the number of rental days, up to 7 days. The user also can select one of three types of vehicles. The types of vehicles and the cost per day for each vehicle is shown in the table below.

Vehicle Model	Cost per Day
Jeep Wrangler	$55.00
Jeep Grand Cherokee	$85.00
Land Rover	$125.00

The customer has a choice of filling the gas tank themselves at the end of their use, or prepaying for a full tank of gas ($52 total). If the vehicle will be driven by more than one driver, a multiple driver cost of $22 per day is added to the cost of the vehicle. Adventure has asked that the Windows application determine and display the total rental cost of the vehicle for the amount of time and the options chosen by the user. Adventure also has requested that you include all appropriate checking for invalid data entry by the user.

FIGURE 5-112

Case Programming Assignments

9 ●●● TAKE-OUT SANDWICHES

Based on the case project shown in Figure 5-113, create a requirements document and a Use Case Definition document, and then design a Windows application. Before writing the code, create an event planning document for each event in the program.

Your local gas station chain has a made-to-order sandwich station. The station has asked you to create a Windows application that allows the customer to enter their order on a flat screen computer. Create an application that allows the user to select one of five sandwich choices (create your own list) with prices displayed, three types of bread choices at no additional cost, and four condiment choices at no additional cost. The station has a loyalty program that deducts 5% of the cost of an order for every 10 points a customer has earned. Allow the user to enter their total number of loyalty points and compute the cost of their order. A customer cannot receive money back if their loyalty points exceed the full cost of their sandwich.

FIGURE 5-113

CHAPTER 6

Loop Structures

OBJECTIVES

You will have mastered the material in this chapter when you can:

- Add a MenuStrip object
- Use the InputBox function
- Display data using the ListBox object
- Understand the use of counters and accumulators
- Understand the use of compound operators
- Repeat a process using a For...Next loop
- Repeat a process using a Do loop
- Avoid infinite loops
- Prime a loop
- Validate data
- Create a nested loop
- Select the best type of loop
- Debug using DataTips at breakpoints
- Publish a finished application using ClickOnce technology

Introduction

In Chapter 5, you learned about the decision structure, one of the major control structures used in computer programming. In this chapter you will learn another major structure called the **looping structure**, or the **iteration structure**.

A fundamental process in a computer program is to repeat a series of instructions either while a condition is true (or not true) or until a condition is true (or not true). For example, if a company is printing paychecks for its 5,000 employees, it can use the same set of instructions to print the check for each employee, varying only the name of the employee and amount paid for each check. This process would continue until all checks are printed. Unique check-printing instructions for each employee in the company are not required.

The process of repeating a set of instructions while a condition is true or until a condition is true is called **looping**, and when the program is executing those instructions, it is said to be in a loop. Another term for looping is **iteration**.

Chapter Project

The programming project in this chapter uses a loop to obtain input data and produce output information. A police department has requested a Windows application that determines the average speed for vehicles on a local highway. This application, called the Highway Radar Checkpoint application, computes the average speed for up to 10 vehicles that pass a checkpoint on a highway with a posted speed limit of 60 miles per hour (mph). The application uses a loop to request and display the speed for up to 10 vehicles. When the user has entered all vehicle speeds, the application displays the average speed of the vehicles (Figure 6-1).

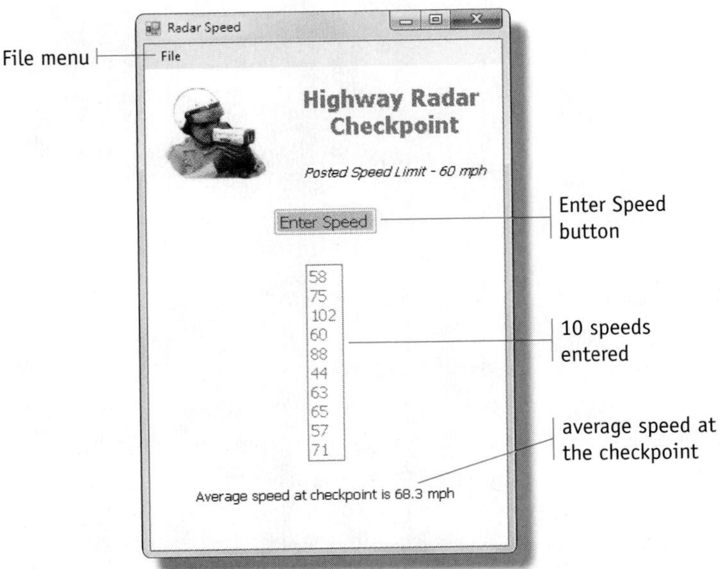

FIGURE 6-1

When assigning hot keys, you should be aware that menu item hot keys are not case-sensitive. Therefore, you should not assign "T" to one menu item and "t" to another.

Event Handlers for Menu Items

As you are aware, the design of the user interface occurs before you write the code for event handlers. When you are ready to write code, however, you must write an event handler for each menu item because clicking a menu item or using its hot key triggers an event. Writing a menu item event handler is the same as writing an event handler for a button click.

To code the event handler for the Exit menu item, you can complete the following steps:

STEP 1 In Design view, double-click the Exit menu item to open the code editing window.

The code editing window is displayed and the insertion point is located within the Exit item click event handler (Figure 6-12). When the user clicks the Exit item on the File menu, the code in the event handler will be executed. Note in Figure 6-12 that the Toolbox is closed.

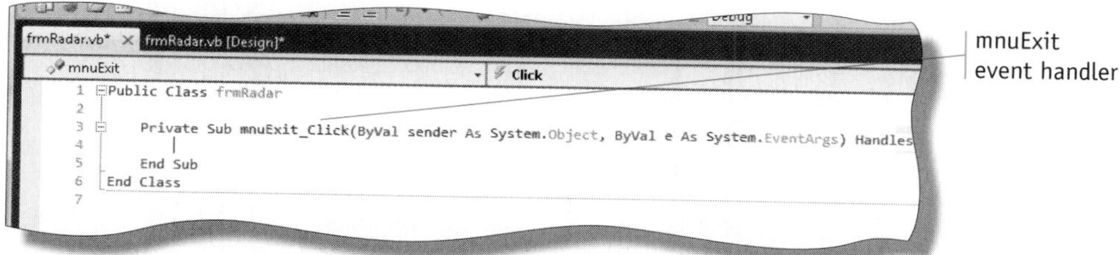

FIGURE 6-12

STEP 2 Using IntelliSense, enter the Close procedure call to close the window and terminate the application.

When executed, the Close procedure will close the window and terminate the program (Figure 6-13).

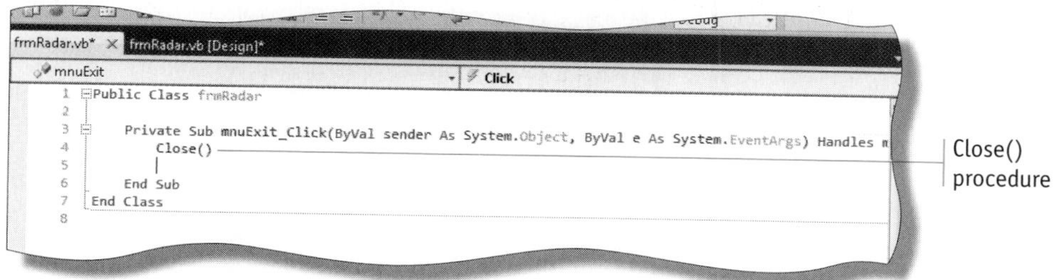

FIGURE 6-13

ONLINE REINFORCEMENT

To view a video of the process in the previous steps, visit scsite.com/vb2010/ch6 and then select Figure 6-12.

Standard Items for a Menu

Developers often customize the MenuStrip object for the specific needs of an application. In addition, Visual Basic 2010 contains an **Action Tag** that allows you to create a full standard menu bar commonly provided in Windows programs, with File, Edit, Tools, and Help menus. In Visual Basic 2010, an Action Tag (▶) appears in the upper-right corner of many objects, including a MenuStrip. Action Tags provide a way for you to specify a set of actions, called **smart actions**, for an object as you design a form. For example, to insert a full standard menu, you can complete the following steps:

STEP 1 With a new Windows Form object open, drag the MenuStrip .NET component onto the Windows Form object. Click the Action Tag on the MenuStrip object.

The MenuStrip Tasks menu opens (Figure 6-14).

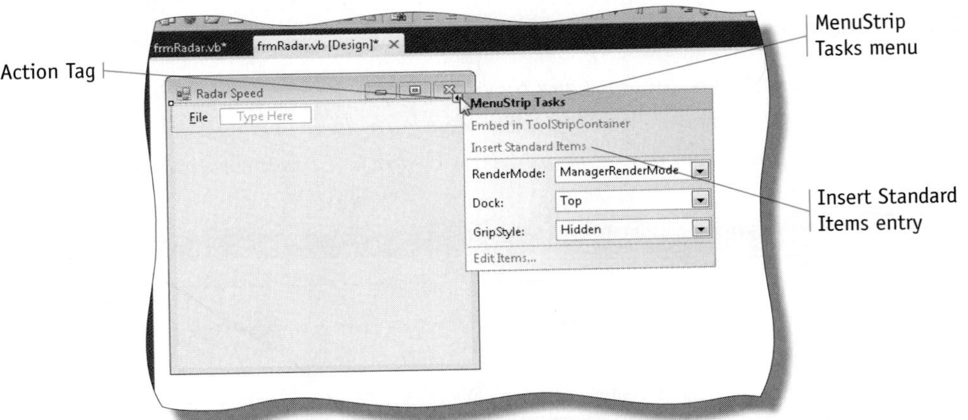

FIGURE 6-14

STEP 2 Click Insert Standard Items on the MenuStrip Tasks menu.

The MenuStrip object contains four menu names — File, Edit, Tools, and Help (Figure 6-15). These menus are the standard menus found on many Windows applications. Each menu contains the standard menu items normally found on the menus.

> **HEADS UP**
>
> In the new operating system, Windows 7, menus are de-emphasized as the focus switches to a more graphical layout such as the Ribbons used in Microsoft Office 2010, which uses more images for navigational control.

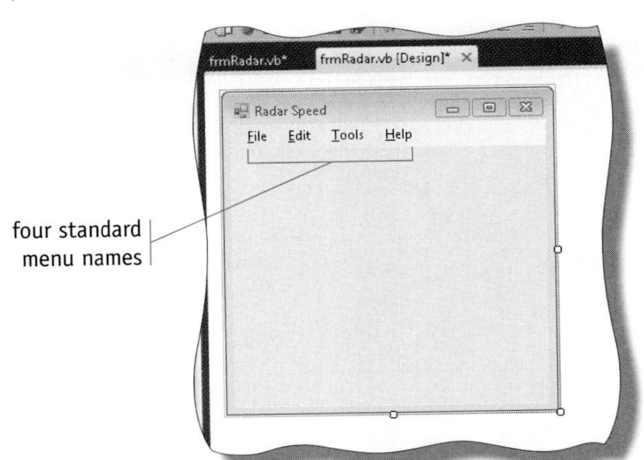

FIGURE 6-15

STEP 3 Click File on the menu bar to view the individual menu items and their associated icons on the File menu.

The standard File menu items (New, Open, Save, Save As, Print, Print Preview, and Exit) are displayed with their associated icons and shortcut keys (Figure 6-16). The other menus also contain standard items. You can code an event handler for each menu item by double-clicking the item.

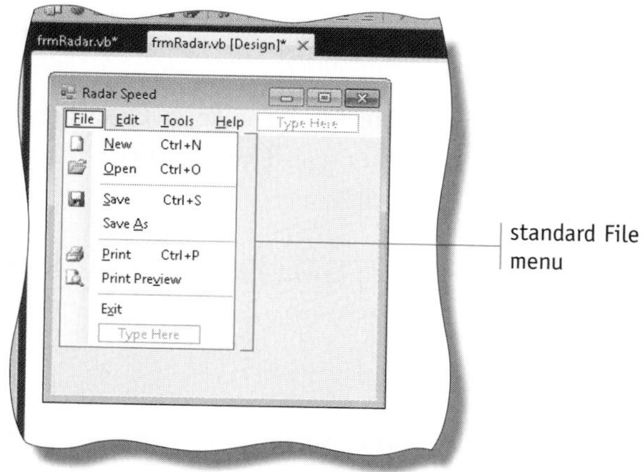

FIGURE 6-16

> **ONLINE REINFORCEMENT**
> To view a video of the process in the previous steps, visit scsite.com/vb2010/ch6 and then select Figure 6-14.

InputBox Function

To calculate the average vehicle speed, the Highway Radar Checkpoint application uses an InputBox object where users enter the speed for each vehicle. The InputBox object is a dialog box that prompts the user to enter a value. Similar to a MessageBox object, you code the InputBox function to specify when the InputBox object appears. The InputBox function displays a dialog box that consists of a message asking for input, an input area, a title, an OK button, and a Cancel button (see Figure 6-3 on page 379). When the user enters the text and clicks the OK button, the InputBox function returns this text as a string. If the user clicks the Cancel button, the function returns a null string (""). The code shown in Figure 6-17 demonstrates the syntax of the InputBox function:

General Format: InputBox Function

```
strVariableName = InputBox("Question to Prompt User", "Title Bar")
```

FIGURE 6-17

For example, the code in Figure 6-18 creates a dialog box that requests the user's age for a driver's license application. The string returned by the InputBox function is assigned to the strAge variable.

```
        Dim strAge As String

        strAge = InputBox("Please enter your age", "Driver's License Agency")
```

FIGURE 6-18

When the application is executed, the InputBox object in Figure 6-19 opens, requesting that the user enter her age. The InputBox function can be used to obtain input instead of a TextBox object.

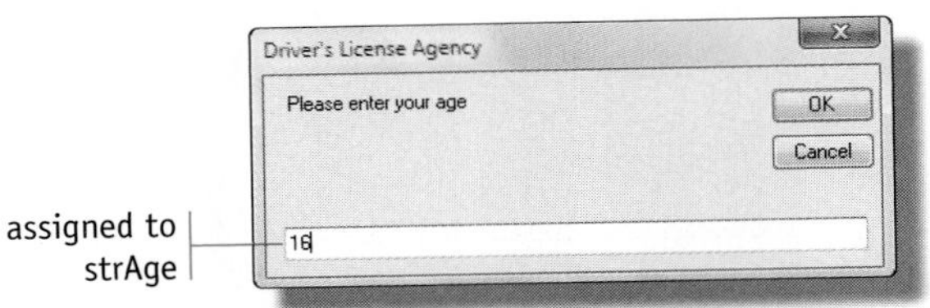

FIGURE 6-19

The InputBox object returns all entered data as a string, which then can be converted to the appropriate data type.

InputBox Object Default Value

The InputBox object can be assigned a default value. For example, if a college application for admission requests the student's home state and the college or university is located in Virginia, the most likely state, Virginia, can be the default value in the InputBox, as shown in Figure 6-20.

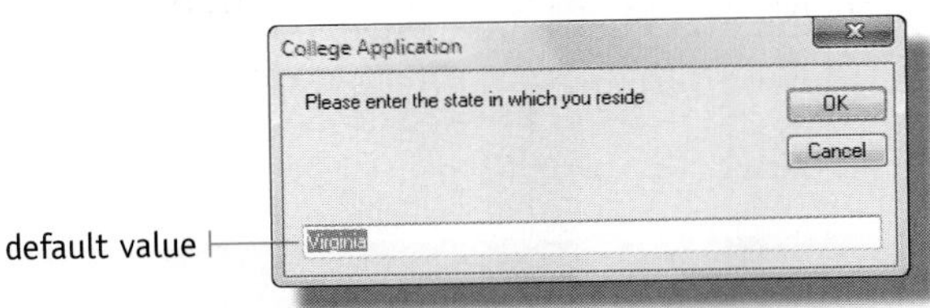

FIGURE 6-20

The code to produce this input box is shown in Figure 6-21.

```
        Dim strState As String

        strState = InputBox("Please enter the state in which you reside:", _
            "College Application", "Virginia")
```

FIGURE 6-21

As you can see, the third argument for the InputBox function call is the default value that is placed in the input box. It must be a string value and follow the syntax shown in Figure 6-21 on the previous page.

InputBox Object for Highway Radar Checkpoint Application

The Highway Radar Checkpoint application uses an InputBox object that requests the speed of vehicles numbered 1–10, as shown in Figure 6-22.

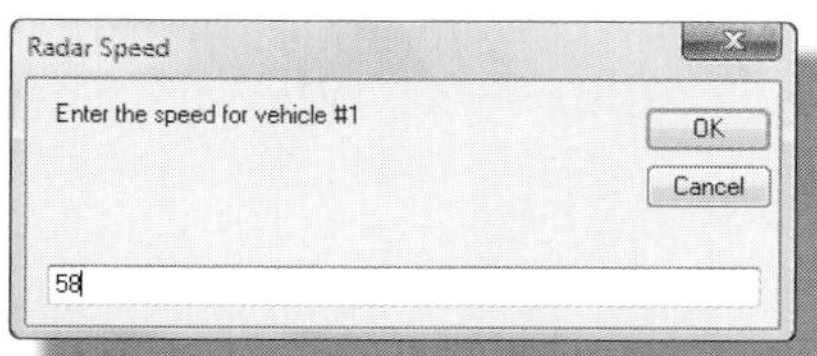

FIGURE 6-22

The code for the Radar Speed InputBox is shown in Figure 6-23. Notice that the prompt message for the user is assigned to the strInputBoxMessage variable, and the title bar text (Radar Speed) is assigned to the strInputBoxHeading variable.

```
        Dim strVehicleSpeed As String
        Dim strInputBoxMessage As String = "Enter the speed for vehicle #"
        Dim strInputBoxHeading As String = "Radar Speed"
        Dim intNumberOfEntries As Integer = 1

        strVehicleSpeed = InputBox(strInputBoxMessage _
            & intNumberOfEntries, strInputBoxHeading, " ")
```

FIGURE 6-23

The variable intNumberOfEntries identifies the vehicle number. It is included in the prompt message through the use of concatenation. The variable intNumberOfEntries is incremented later in the code so that it refers to the correct vehicle each time the InputBox function call is executed.

In Figure 6-23, the default value is specified as a space (" "). When the input box is displayed, a space will be selected in the input area. This space is required so that if a user clicks the OK button without entering any data, the InputBox will not return a null character (""), which indicates the user clicked the Cancel button. This normally is a good programming practice.

When the user clicks the Cancel button in an input box and the InputBox function returns a null character, the program can test for the null character to determine further processing.

HEADS UP

An InputBox object allows you to gather input without placing a TextBox for the requested value on the Windows Form object.

Displaying Data Using the ListBox Object

In the Highway Radar Checkpoint application, the user enters the speed of each vehicle into the InputBox object, and the program displays these speeds in a list box (see Figure 6-1 on page 378). To create such a list, you use the ListBox object provided in the Visual Basic Toolbox. A ListBox displays a group of values, called items, with one item per line. To add a ListBox object to a Windows Form object, you can complete the following steps:

STEP 1 Drag the ListBox object from the Toolbox to the Windows Form object where you want to place the ListBox object. When the pointer is in the correct location, release the left mouse button.

The ListBox object is placed on the form (Figure 6-24).

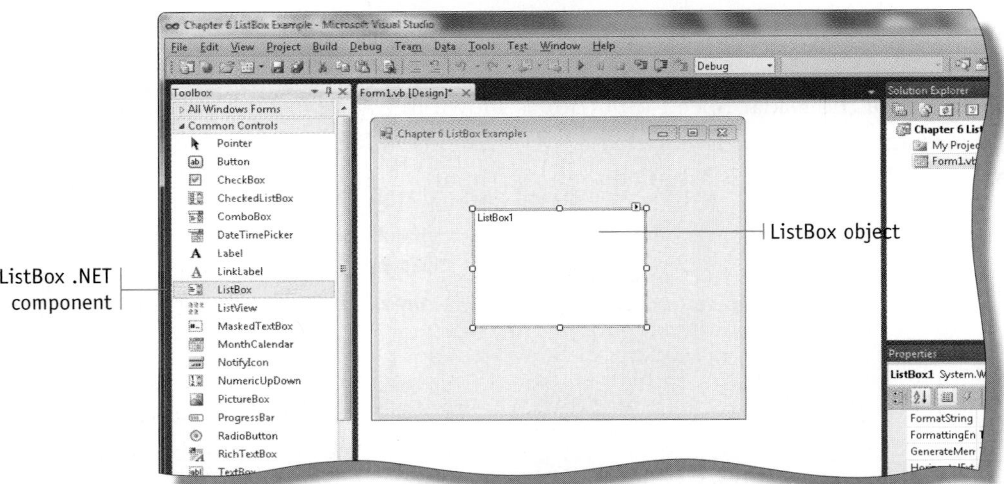

FIGURE 6-24

STEP 2 With the ListBox object selected, scroll in the Properties window to the (Name) property. Name the ListBox object `lstRadarSpeed`.

The name you entered is displayed in the (Name) property in the Properties window (Figure 6-25). Notice a ListBox object name begins with lst.

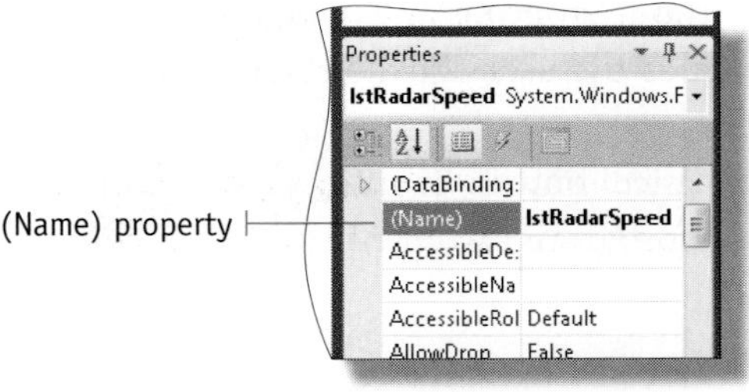

FIGURE 6-25

ONLINE REINFORCEMENT

To view a video of the process in the previous steps, visit scsite.com/vb2010/ch6 and then select Figure 6-24.

After placing a ListBox object on the Windows Form object, you can adjust the size as needed by dragging the size handles (see Figure 6-24 on the previous page). Be sure to resize the ListBox so that it is large enough to hold the application data. The ListBox object for the Highway Radar Checkpoint application is designed to be wide enough to hold three digits, and long enough to hold 10 numbers (Figure 6-26).

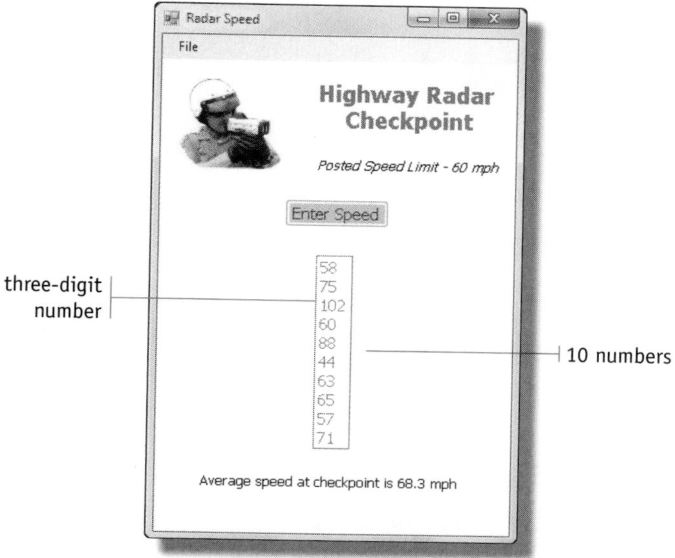

FIGURE 6-26

To display the speed of each vehicle in the list box, you must write code to add each item to the ListBox object. After an item is added, it is displayed in the list box. The general format of the statement to add an item to a ListBox object is shown in Figure 6-27.

General Format: Adding Items to a ListBox Object

```
lstListBoxName.Items.Add(Variable Name)
```

FIGURE 6-27

In Figure 6-27, the Add procedure will add the item contained in the variable identified by the Variable Name entry. The syntax for the statement must be followed precisely.

The code to add the vehicle speed to the lstRadarSpeed ListBox object and then display the speed of each vehicle (decVehicleSpeed) in the ListBox object is shown in Figure 6-28.

```
        lstRadarSpeed.Items.Add(decVehicleSpeed)
```

FIGURE 6-28

If the number of items exceeds the number that can be displayed in the designated space of the ListBox object, a scroll bar automatically is added to the right side of the ListBox object as shown in Figure 6-29.

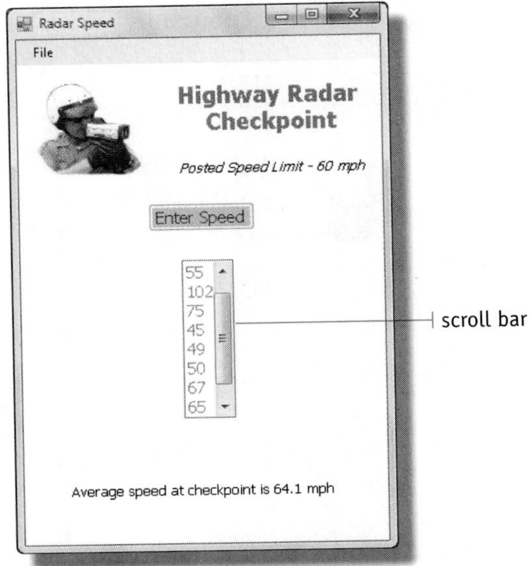

FIGURE 6-29

To clear the items in a ListBox object, the Clear method works as it does for the TextBox object. The syntax of the statement to clear the ListBox is shown in Figure 6-30.

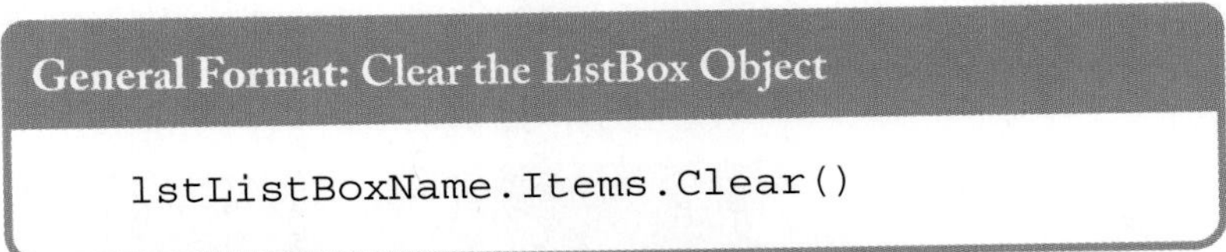

General Format: Clear the ListBox Object

```
lstListBoxName.Items.Clear()
```

FIGURE 6-30

In the Highway Radar Checkpoint application, the user can select the Clear menu item to clear the form. The code in Figure 6-31 removes the items from the lstRadarSpeed ListBox.

```
lstRadarSpeed.Items.Clear()
```

FIGURE 6-31

Add Items During Design

The Highway Radar Checkpoint application allows the user to add items to the ListBox object during program execution, but you also can add items to a ListBox object while designing the form. Adding items to the ListBox object during the design phase allows the user to select an item from the ListBox object during execution. For example, in an application to select a favorite clothing store, you can add items to a ListBox object named lstStores during the form design by completing the following steps:

STEP 1 Assume the lstStores ListBox object already has been placed and named on the Windows Form object. Select the ListBox object on the Windows Form object and then click the Items property in the Properties window.

The Items property in the Properties window is selected. An ellipsis button appears to the right of the (Collection) entry (Figure 6-32).

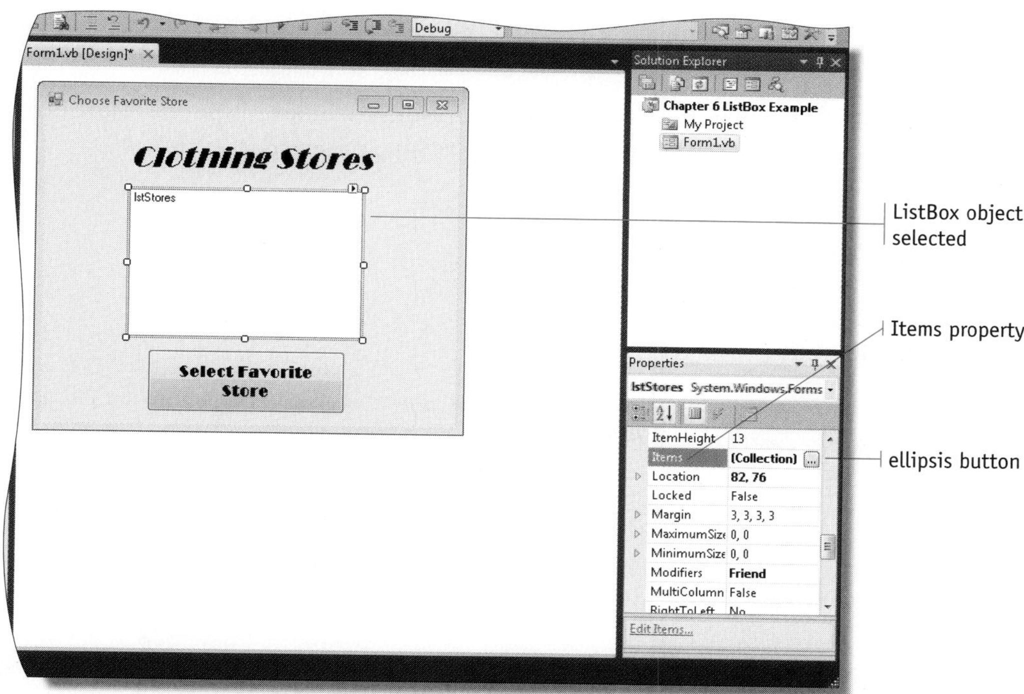

FIGURE 6-32

STEP 2 Click the ellipsis button in the right column of the Items property.

The String Collection Editor window opens, allowing you to enter items that will be displayed in the ListBox object named lstStores (Figure 6-33).

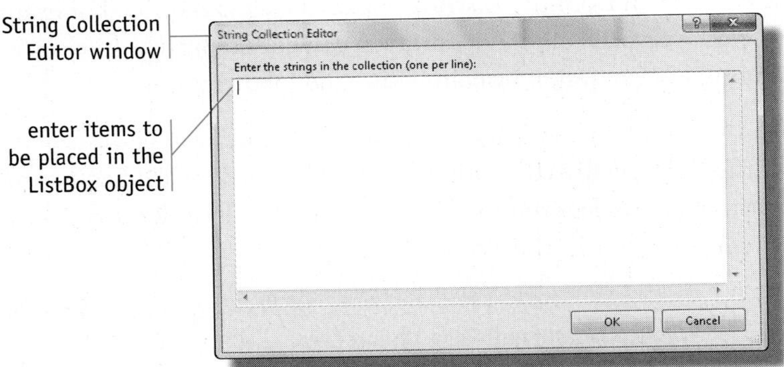

FIGURE 6-33

STEP 3 Click in the String Collection Editor window. Type the following items to represent popular retail stores, pressing ENTER at the end of each line:

```
Abercrombie & Fitch
Aeropostale
American Eagle
Express
Hollister
```

The items representing favorite retail stores appear in the String Collection Editor window on separate lines (Figure 6-34).

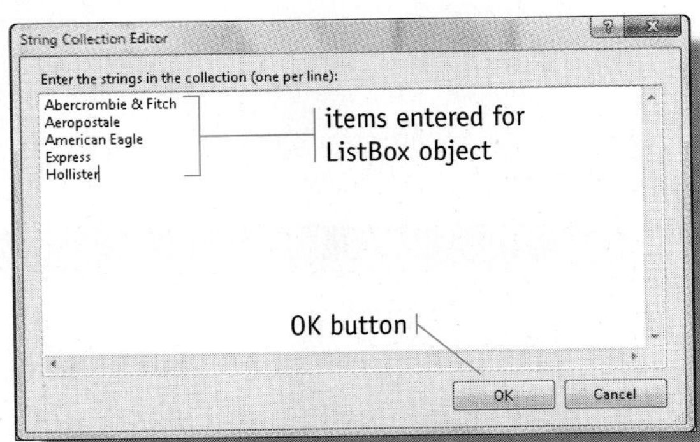

FIGURE 6-34

STEP 4 Click the OK button.

The Windows Form object displays the stores in the lstStores ListBox object (Figure 6-35). The user can select one of the items in the ListBox object during execution.

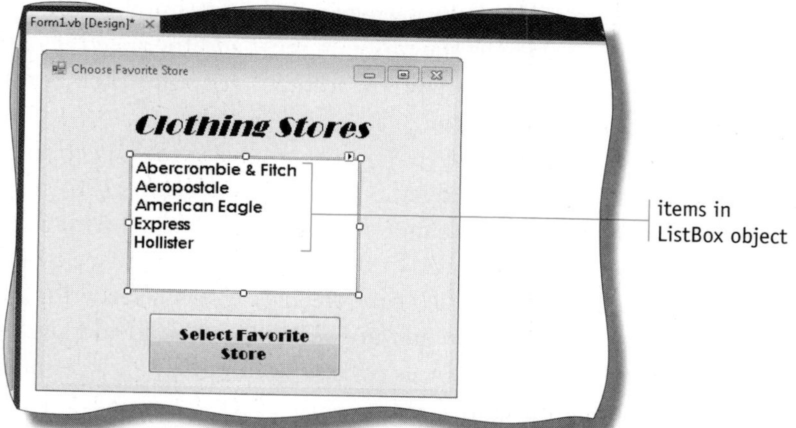

FIGURE 6-35

> **ONLINE REINFORCEMENT**
>
> To view a video of the process in the previous steps, visit scsite.com/vb2010/ch6 and then select Figure 6-32.

Selected Item Property

The SelectedItem property identifies which item in the ListBox is selected. An assignment statement is used to assign that property to a variable, as shown in Figure 6-36.

General Format: Assign the Selected Item in a ListBox Object

```
strVariableName = lstListBoxName.SelectedItem
```

FIGURE 6-36

The actual code to show the user's selection of their favorite store from the ListBox object named lstStores in a message box is shown in Figure 6-37.

```
        MsgBox("Your favorite store is "_
        &lstStores.SelectedItem & ".")
```

FIGURE 6-37

Accumulators, Counters, and Compound Operators

In the Highway Radar Checkpoint application, after the user enters the speeds of up to 10 vehicles, the application calculates the average speed (see Figure 6-1 on page 378). The formula to calculate the average speed is: (total of all speeds entered) / (number of vehicles). For example, if the total of all the speeds entered is 683 and 10 vehicle speeds were entered, the average speed is 68.3 mph.

To calculate the average, the program must add the speed of each vehicle to a variable. The variable that contains an accumulated value such as the total of all the speeds is called an **accumulator**.

To compute the average speed, the program also must keep track of how many vehicle speeds the user has entered. The variable that is used to keep track of this value is called a **counter**. A counter always is incremented with a constant value. This value can be positive or negative. In the Highway Radar Checkpoint program, the counter is incremented by 1 each time the user enters a speed for a vehicle.

You can use one of two techniques when you need to add a value to a variable and update the value in the variable, as with an accumulator or a counter. The first technique is shown in Figure 6-38.

```
26        decTotalVehicleSpeed = decTotalVehicleSpeed + decVehicleSpeedEntered
27        intNumberOfEntries = intNumberOfEntries + 1
```

FIGURE 6-38

In Figure 6-38, on line 26 the value in the decTotalVehicleSpeed variable is added to the value in the decVehicleSpeedEntered variable and the result is stored in the decTotalVehicleSpeed variable. This statement has the effect of accumulating the vehicle speed values in the decTotalVehicleSpeed accumulator. Similarly, the number of entries counter is incremented by 1 by the statement on line 27. The effect is that the value in the number of entries counter is increased by 1 each time the statement is executed.

A second method for accomplishing this task is to use a shortcut mathematical operator called a **compound operator** that allows you to add, subtract, multiply, divide, use modulus or exponents, or concatenate strings, storing the result in the same variable. An assignment statement that includes a compound operator begins with the variable that will contain the accumulated value, such as an accumulator or a counter, followed by the compound operator. A compound operator consists of an arithmetic operator and an equal sign. The last element in the assignment statement is the variable or literal containing the value to be used in the calculation.

This means that an assignment statement using a compound operator such as:

```
intNumberOfEntries += 1
```

which is an assignment statement using a compound operator, is the same as:

```
intNumberOfEntries = intNumberOfEntries + 1
```

The += compound operator adds the value of the right operand to the value of the left operand and stores the result in the left operand's variable. Similarly, the statement:

```
decTotalVehicleSpeed += decVehicleSpeedEntered
```

is the same as:

```
decTotalVehicleSpeed = decTotalVehicleSpeed + decVehicleSpeedEntered
```

The table in Figure 6-39 shows an example of compound operators used in code. Assume that intResult = 24, decResult = 24, and strSample = "tree".

Operation	Example with Single Operators	Example with Compound Operator	Result
Addition	intResult = intResult + 1	intResult += 1	intResult = 25
Subtraction	intResult = intResult − 3	intResult −= 3	intResult = 21
Multiplication	intResult = intResult * 2	intResult *= 2	intResult = 48
Decimal Division	decResult = decResult / 5	decResult /= 5	decResult = 4.8
Integer Division	intResult = intResult \ 5	intResult \ =5	intResult = 4
Exponents	intResult = intResult ^ 2	intResult ^= 2	intResult = 576
Concatenate	strSample = strSample & "house"	strSample &= "house"	strSample = "treehouse"

FIGURE 6-39

HEADS UP

The compound operators +=, −=, *=, /=, \=, ^=, and &= run faster than their regular longer equation counterparts because the statement is more compact.

Compound operators often are used by developers in Visual Basic coding. The coding example in Figure 6-40 uses several compound operators and a MsgBox object. When the following code is executed, the result shown in the MsgBox object is "Final Result = 2".

```
Dim intTotal As Integer
intTotal = 7
intTotal += 6
intTotal *= 2
intTotal /= 13
MsgBox("Final Result = " & intTotal.ToString(), , "Compound Operators")
```

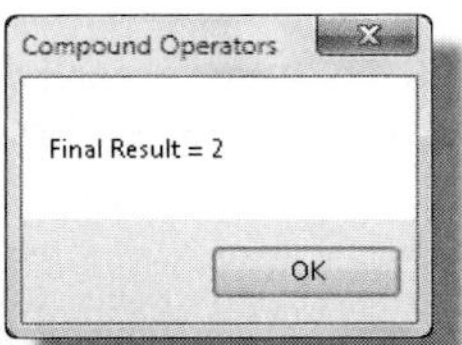

FIGURE 6-40

Compound operators also can be used to connect two strings using the concatenation operator (&). The code in Figure 6-41 creates the phrase, "To err is human!" in a MsgBox object by using compound operators to concatenate the strPhrase variable. Each compound operator joins another word to the end of the phrase assigned to the strPhrase variable.

```
Dim strPhrase As String
strPhrase = "To err"
strPhrase &= " is "
strPhrase &= "human!"
MsgBox(strPhrase, , "Compound Operators")
```

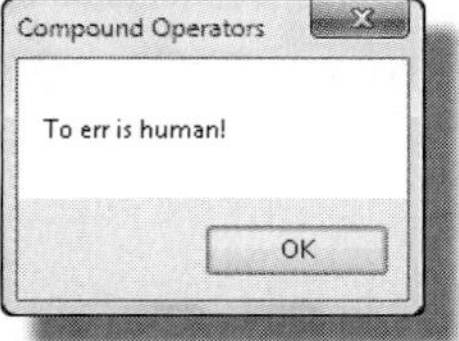

FIGURE 6-41

Using Loops to Perform Repetitive Tasks

In the Highway Radar Checkpoint application, the user enters up to 10 vehicle speeds using the InputBox function. The repetitive process of entering 10 vehicle speeds can be coded within a loop to simplify the task with fewer lines of code. Unlike If...Then statements that execute only once, loops repeat multiple times. Each repetition of the loop is called an **iteration**. An iteration is a single execution of a set of instructions that are to be repeated.

Loops are powerful structures used to repeat a section of code a certain number of times or until a particular condition is met. Visual Basic has two main types of loops: For...Next loops and Do loops.

Repeating a Process Using the For...Next Loop

You can use a For...Next loop when a section of code is to be executed an exact number of times. The syntax of a For...Next loop is shown in Figure 6-42.

General Format: For...Next loop

```
For Control Variable = Beginning Numeric Value To Ending Numeric Value

     ' Body of the Loop

Next
```

FIGURE 6-42

In Figure 6-42, the For...Next loop begins with the keyword For. Following this keyword is the control variable, which is the numeric variable that keeps track of the number of iterations the loop completes. To begin the loop, the For statement places the beginning numeric value in the control variable. The program then executes the code between the For and Next statements, which is called the body of the loop.

Upon reaching the Next statement, the program returns to the For statement and increments the value of the control variable. This process continues until the value in the control variable is greater than the ending numeric value. When this occurs, the statement(s) that follows the Next command are executed.

The first line of a For...Next loop that is supposed to execute four times is shown in Figure 6-43. The control value is a variable named intNumber.

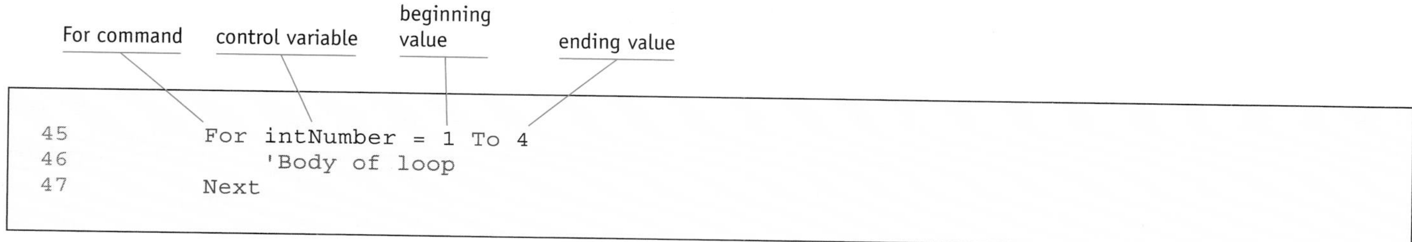

FIGURE 6-43

The first line in the For...Next loop in Figure 6-43 specifies that the control variable (intNumber) is assigned the value 1 because the literal 1 is the beginning value. Then the section of code between the For and Next statement, which is called the body of the loop, is executed. When the Next statement is encountered, control returns to the For statement where, by default, the value 1 is added to the control variable. The code in the body of the loop is executed again. This process continues until the value in the control value becomes greater than 4, which is the ending value. When this occurs, the statement(s) in the program that follow the Next command are executed. The table in Figure 6-44 illustrates this looping process.

Loop Iteration	Value of intNumber	Process
1	`intNumber = 1`	Executes the code inside the loop
2	`intNumber = 2`	Executes the code inside the loop
3	`intNumber = 3`	Executes the code inside the loop
4	`intNumber = 4`	Executes the code inside the loop
5 (exits the loop)	`intNumber = 5`	The control variable value exceeds the ending value, so the application exits the For...Next loop. This means the statement(s) following the Next command are executed.

FIGURE 6-44

Step Value in a For...Next Loop

A Step value is the value in a For...Next loop that is added to or subtracted from the beginning value on each iteration of the loop. If you do not include a Step value in the For statement, such as in Figure 6-43, by default the value in the control variable is incremented by 1 after each iteration of the loop.

You can include a Step value in a For statement. For example, in the For header statement in Figure 6-45, the Step value is 2. The control variable intNumber is set to the initial value of 1, and the lines of code in the body of the loop are executed. After the first iteration of the loop, the Step value is added to the control variable, changing the value in the control variable to 3 (1 + 2 = 3). The For loop will continue until the value in intNumber is greater than 99.

step value

```
For intNumber = 1 To 99 Step 2
    ' Body of loop
Next
```

FIGURE 6-45

The Step value can be negative. If so, the value in the control variable is decreased on each iteration of the loop. To exit the loop, you must specify an ending value that is less than the beginning value. This is illustrated in Figure 6-46.

negative Step value

```
        For intCount = 25 To -10 Step -5
            ' Body of loop
        Next
```

FIGURE 6-46

In the first iteration of the For...Next loop header in Figure 6-46, the control variable value is 25. The value in the control variable intCount is decreased by 5 each time the loop repeats. This repetition will continue until the value in the intCount control variable is less than −10. Then the loop exits.

The control variable in a For...Next loop can be assigned decimal values as well. The For loop header in Figure 6-47 has a starting value of 3.1. The loop ends when the value in the control variable is greater than 4.5. The Step value is 0.1, which means the value in decNumber increments by 0.1 each pass through the loop.

decimal Step value

```
        For decNumber = 3.1 To 4.5 Step 0.1
            ' Body of loop
        Next
```

FIGURE 6-47

A For...Next loop also can include variables and mathematical expressions as shown in Figure 6-48.

```
        For intNumber = intBegin To (intEnd * 2) Step intIncrement
            'Body of loop
        Next
```

FIGURE 6-48

In Figure 6-48, the control variable (intNumber) is initialized with the value in the intBegin variable. Each time the Next statement is encountered and control is returned to the For statement, the value in intNumber will be incremented by the value in the intIncrement variable. The loop will continue until the value in intNumber is greater than the product of the value in intEnd times 2.

Entering the For...Next Loop Code Using IntelliSense

To show the process for entering the For...Next loop code using IntelliSense, assume that an application is designed to show in a list box the population growth over the next six years for Alaska. Assume further that the current population of Alaska is 675,000 people and is expected to grow at 5% per year for the next six years. The code in Figure 6-49 will accomplish this processing.

```
        Dim intAlaskaPopulation As Integer = 675000
        Dim intYears As Integer

        For intYears = 1 To 6
            intAlaskaPopulation += (intAlaskaPopulation * 0.05)
            lstGrowth.Items.Add("Year " & intYears & " Population " & intAlaskaPopulation)

        Next
```

FIGURE 6-49

To use IntelliSense to enter the code shown in Figure 6-49, you can complete the following steps: (The following code assumes the lstGrowth ListBox object has been defined on the Windows Form object.)

STEP 1 In the code editing window, type `Dim intAlaskaPopulation As Integer = 675000` and then press the ENTER key. Type `Dim intYears As Integer` and then press the ENTER key two times. Type `for`, a space, and then an IntelliSense list opens.

The IntelliSense list shows all available entries (Figure 6-50).

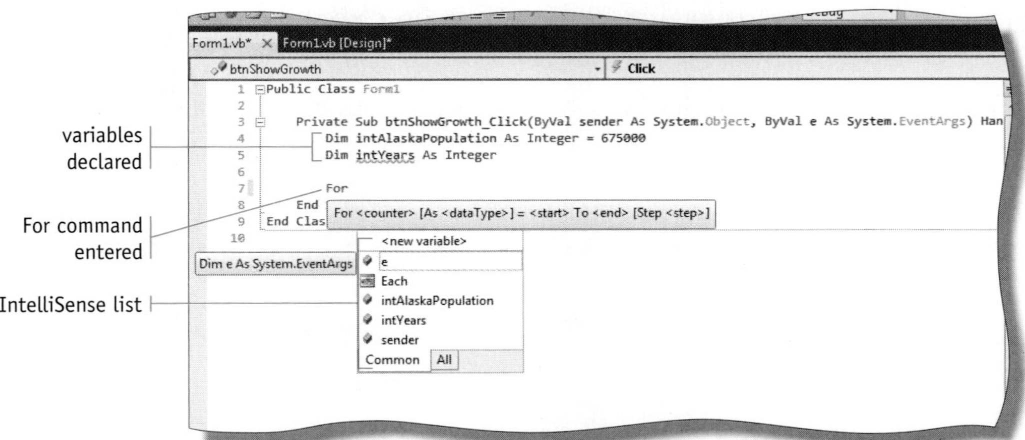

FIGURE 6-50

STEP 2 Type the first four letters of the intYears variable name (`intY`) to select intYears in the IntelliSense list. Type `= 1 to 6` and press the ENTER key to specify the beginning value and ending value for the loop.

Visual Basic automatically inserts the Next statement in the code (Figure 6-51). For, To, and Next are blue to indicate they are keywords.

IN THE REAL WORLD

It is best to indent the body of the loop to clearly display what is being repeated. When you use IntelliSense to enter the loop, Visual Basic automatically indents the code properly. When other developers read the code, it is easy to identify the indented portion as the loop body.

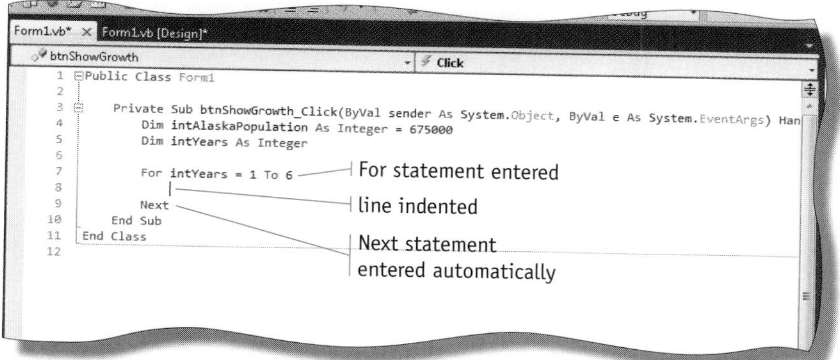

FIGURE 6-51

STEP 3 Use IntelliSense to select the appropriate variables. Enter the two new lines shown in Figure 6-52.

Each line of code automatically is indented between the For and Next statements (Figure 6-52).

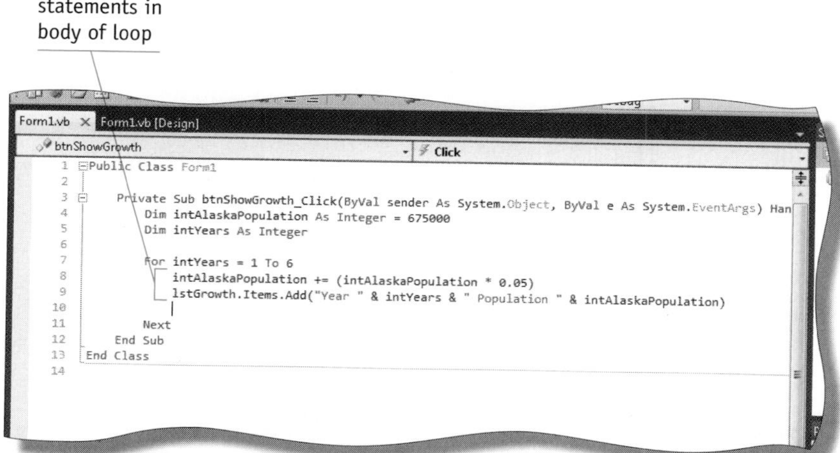

FIGURE 6-52

STEP 4 Run the program to see the results of the loop.

The loop calculates and displays the Alaskan population growth for six years based on 5% growth per year (Figure 6-53).

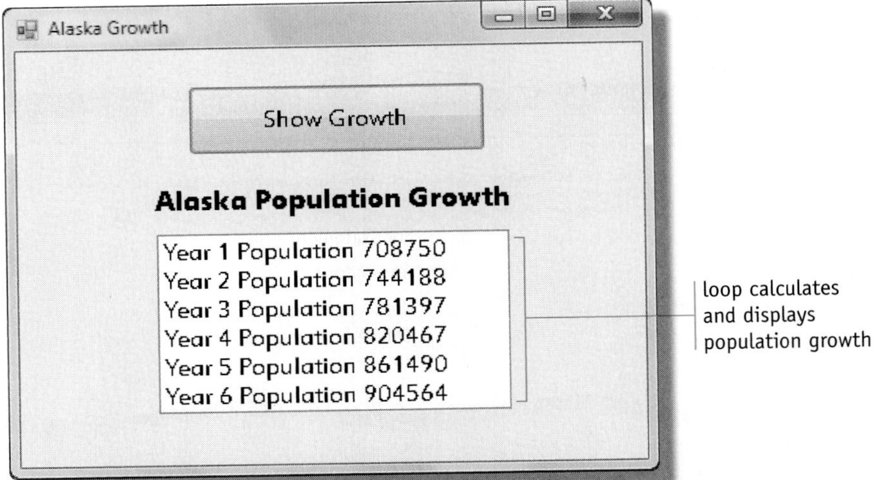

FIGURE 6-53

ONLINE REINFORCEMENT

To view a video of the process in the previous steps, visit scsite.com/vb2010/ch6 and then select Figure 6-50.

User Input and the For...Next Loop

The beginning, ending, and step values used in a For...Next loop can vary based on input from a user. For example, in Figure 6-54, the program displays the squared values of a range of numbers the user enters. The user enters the beginning (minimum) and ending (maximum) range of values, and then clicks the Calculate Values button to view the squares of the numbers in the range.

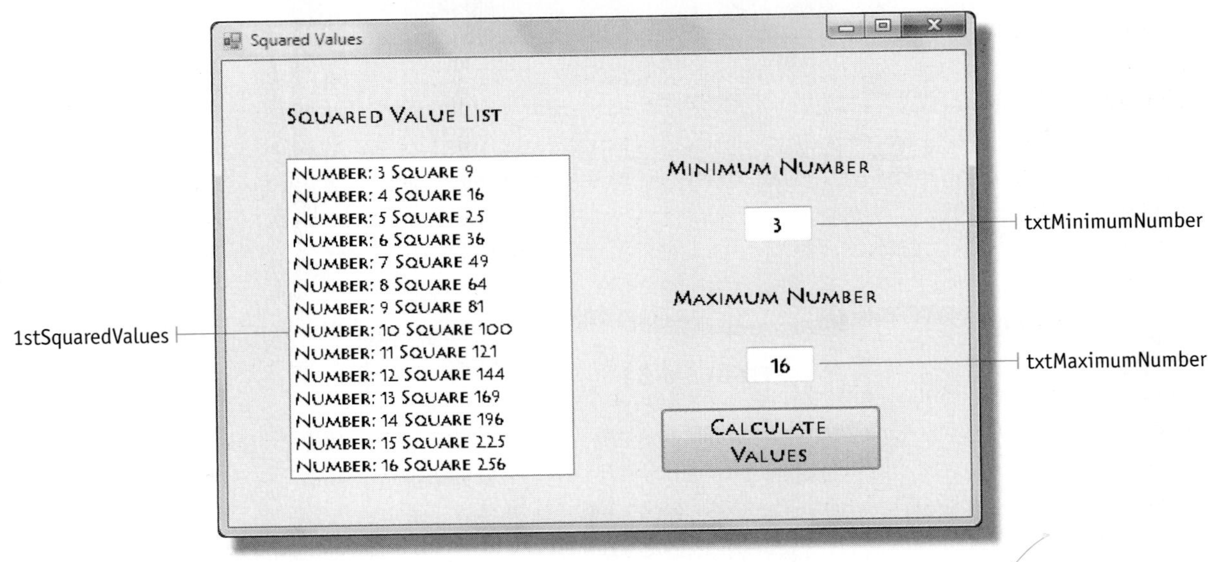

FIGURE 6-54

Bottom-Controlled Do While Loop

You can write a Do While loop where the condition is tested at the bottom of the loop. A bottom-controlled loop works the same way as the top-controlled Do While loop except that the body of the loop is executed before the condition is checked the first time, guaranteeing at least one iteration of a loop will be completed. The bottom-controlled Do While loop has the syntax shown in Figure 6-62.

General Format: Do While Loop (Bottom-Controlled)

```
Do

      ' Loop Body

Loop While condition
```

FIGURE 6-62

In the syntax shown in Figure 6-62, the word Do appears on its own line at the beginning of the loop. The loop body follows, and the Loop While statement is the last statement in the loop. The Loop While statement contains the condition that is tested to determine if the loop should be terminated. Because the While condition is in the last statement of the loop, the body of the loop is executed one time regardless of the status of the condition.

The code in Figure 6-63 is an example of a bottom-controlled Do While loop.

```
Dim intScore As Integer = 0
Do
    intScore = intScore + 1
Loop While intScore < 5
```

FIGURE 6-63

The body of the Do loop in Figure 6-63 is executed one time before the condition in the Loop While statement is checked. The variable intScore begins with the initial value of 0 and is incremented in the body of the loop, changing the value to 1.

The condition is then tested and found to be true because 1 < 5. The loop repeats and the value of intScore increases, as shown in Figure 6-64.

Loop Iteration	Value of intScore at Start of the Loop	Value of intScore When Checked	Result of Condition Tested
1	intScore = 0	intScore = 1	True
2	intScore = 1	intScore = 2	True
3	intScore = 2	intScore = 3	True
4	intScore = 3	intScore = 4	True
5	intScore = 4	intScore = 5	False

FIGURE 6-64

The body of the loop in Figure 6-63 on the previous page is executed five times because intScore is less than 5 during five iterations of the loop.

Do Until Loops

A loop similar to a Do While loop is called a Do Until loop. The Do Until loop allows you to specify that an action repeats until a condition becomes true. When the condition in a Do Until loop becomes true, the loop ends.

Top-Controlled Do Until Loop

A Do Until loop can be both top-controlled and bottom-controlled. The syntax of the top-controlled Do Until loop is shown in Figure 6-65.

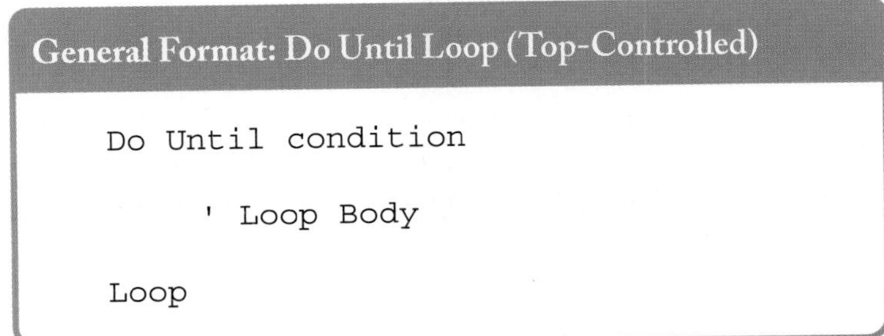

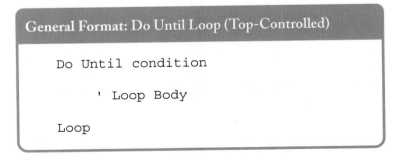

General Format: Do Until Loop (Top-Controlled)

```
Do Until condition

     ' Loop Body

Loop
```

FIGURE 6-65

A top-controlled Do Until loop begins with the keywords Do Until. Next, as with the Do While top-controlled loop, the condition is specified. The condition is expressed using the same relational operators that are available with If statements. Any condition that can be specified in an If statement can be specified in a Do Until condition. The condition can compare numeric values or string values.

The Do Until loop example shown in Figure 6-66 displays a parking meter application that computes the number of minutes a user can purchase based on the cost of 25 cents for each 15 minutes of parking. If the user only has 88 cents in pocket change, for example, the application computes how many minutes of parking time 88 cents will purchase.

```
        Dim decAmount As Decimal = 0.88
        Dim intQuarters As Integer = 0
        Dim intTime As Integer = 15
        Dim intParkingTime As Integer

        Do Until decAmount < 0.25
            intQuarters += 1
            decAmount -= 0.25
        Loop
        intParkingTime = intQuarters * intTime
        lblParkingTime.Text = "Parking Time: " &
                               intParkingTime.ToString() & " minutes"
```

FIGURE 6-66

In the code example in Figure 6-66, the Do Until loop condition is checked before the body of the loop executes. The first time the condition is tested, the expression decAmount < 0.25 is false because the decAmount variable contains 0.88. The body of the loop is executed because the Do Until will be executed until the value in decAmount is less than 0.25. When the body of the loop is executed, it adds 1 to intQuarters to count the number of quarters the user has for the parking meter and 0.25 is subtracted from decAmount because a quarter is worth 25 cents. Because decAmount is first assigned the value 0.88, the loop executes three times (decAmount = 0.88, decAmount = 0.63, and decAmount = 0.38) and stops when decAmount becomes less than 0.25. The lblParkingTime Label object displays the text "Parking Time: 45 minutes".

Bottom-Controlled Do Until Loop

The last of the four Do loops is the bottom-controlled Do Until loop. This Do Until loop checks the condition after the body of the loop is executed. The loop continues until the condition becomes true. The syntax of the bottom-controlled Do Until loop is shown in Figure 6-67.

General Format: Do Until Loop (Bottom-Controlled)

```
Do

    ' Loop Body

Loop Until condition
```

FIGURE 6-67

As shown in Figure 6-67 on the previous page, the bottom-controlled Do Until loop begins with the word Do. The body of the loop is executed one time regardless of the condition being tested. The Loop Until statement checks the condition. The loop will be repeated until the condition is true.

User Input Loops

Do loops often are written to end the loop when a certain value is entered by the user, or the user performs a certain action such as clicking the Cancel button in an input box. The value or action is predefined by the developer. For example, the loop in Figure 6-68 continues until the user clicks the Cancel button in the input box. If the user clicks the Cancel button, the InputBox function returns a null string that is assigned to the strTestGrade variable. The Do Until statement tests the string. If it contains a null character, the loop is terminated. The Do Until loop accumulates the total of all the entered test scores until the user clicks the Cancel button.

```
Do Until strTestGrade = ""
    strTestGrade = InputBox("Enter test grade", "Compute Average")
    If IsNumeric(strTestGrade) Then
        decGrade = Convert.ToDecimal(strTestGrade)
        decTotal += decGrade
    End If
Loop
```

FIGURE 6-68

Avoiding Infinite Loops

Recall that an **infinite loop** is a loop that never ends. It happens when the condition that will cause the end of a loop never occurs. If the loop does not end, it will continue to repeat until the program is interrupted. Figure 6-69 shows an example of an infinite loop.

```
Dim intProblem = 0
Do While intProblem <= 5
   Box.Show("This loop will not end", "Infinite Loop")
Loop
```

FIGURE 6-69

The Do While loop in Figure 6-69 never ends because the value in the variable intProblem is never changed from its initial value of zero. Because the value in intProblem never exceeds 5, the condition in the Do While loop (intProblem <= 5) never becomes false. The processing in a loop eventually must change the condition being tested in the Do While loop so the loop will terminate. When working in Visual Basic 2010, you can interrupt an infinite loop by clicking the Stop Debugging button on the Standard toolbar.

Priming the Loop

As you have learned, a top-controlled loop tests a condition prior to beginning the loop. In most cases, the value that is tested in that condition must be set before the condition is tested the first time in the Do While or Do Until statement. Starting a loop with a preset value in the variable(s) tested in the condition is called **priming the loop**. You have seen this in previous examples, such as in Figure 6-66 on page 411 where the value in decAmount is set before the condition is tested the first time.

In some applications, such as the Highway Radar Checkpoint application, the loop is primed with a value the user enters or an action the user takes. You will recall that the user enters the speed for a vehicle (up to 10 vehicles) or clicks the Cancel button in the input box to terminate the input operation. Prior to executing the Do Until statement the first time in the Do Until loop that processes the data the user enters, the InputBox function must be executed to obtain an initial value. Then, the Do Until statement can test the action taken by the user (enter a value or click the Cancel button). The coding to implement this processing is shown in Figure 6-70.

```
31    Dim strCancelClicked As String = ""
32    Dim intMaxNumberOfEntries As Integer = 10
33    Dim intNumberOfEntries As Integer = 1
 ⋮
39    strVehicleSpeed = InputBox(strInputMessage & intNumberOfEntries, strInputHeading, " ")
40
41
42    Do Until intNumberOfEntries > intMaxNumberOfEntries Or strVehicleSpeed = strCancelClicked
43
 ⋮
50                intNumberOfEntries += 1
 ⋮
59        If intNumberOfEntries <= intMaxNumberOfEntries Then
60            strVehicleSpeed = InputBox(strInputMessage & intNumberOfEntries, strInputHeading, " ")
61
62        End If
63
64    Loop
```

FIGURE 6-70

In the Do Until loop shown in Figure 6-70, you can see that the Do Until statement on line 42 tests two conditions: is the value in the intNumberOfEntries variable greater than the value in the intMaxNumberOfEntries variable, or is the value in the strVehicleSpeed variable equal to the value in the strCancelClicked variable, which is a null character (see line 31). If either of these conditions is true, the body of the loop will not be executed.

The Do Until loop must have two primed variables — the intNumberOfEntries variable and the strVehicleSpeed variable. The intNumberOfEntries variable is initialized to the value 1 on line 33. The strVehicleSpeed variable is initialized by the InputBox function call on line 39. In this function call, either the user has entered a value or clicked the Cancel button. If the user clicked the Cancel button, the body of the loop should not be entered.

To continue the loop, the processing within the body of the loop eventually must change one of the conditions being tested in the Do Until statement or the loop never terminates. In the sample program, the conditions being tested are whether the user has entered 10 vehicle speeds or whether the user has clicked the Cancel button. Therefore, within the loop, the variable containing the number of vehicle speeds entered (intNumberOfEntries) must be incremented when the user enters a valid speed, and the user must be able to enter more speeds or click the Cancel button. On line 50 in Figure 6-70 on the previous page, the value in the intNumberOfEntries is incremented by 1 each time the user enters a valid value. In addition, the statement on line 60 displays an input box that allows the user to enter a new value or click the Cancel button as long as the number of valid entries is not greater than the maximum number of entries.

Validating Data

As you learned in Chapter 5, you must test the data a user enters to ensure it is accurate and that its use in other programming statements, such as converting string data to numeric data, will not cause a program exception. When using an input box, the data should be checked using the IsNumeric function and If statements as discussed in Chapter 5. If the data is not valid, the user must be notified of the error and an input box displayed to allow the user to enter valid data.

For example, if the user enters non-numeric data, the input box in Figure 6-71 should be displayed.

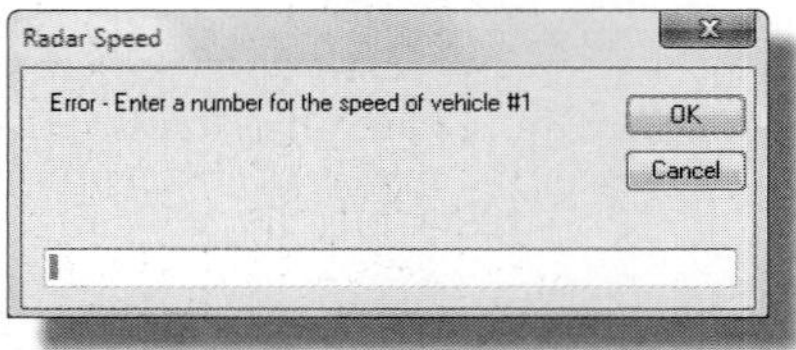

FIGURE 6-71

Similarly, if the user enters a negative number, the message in Figure 6-72 should be displayed in an input box.

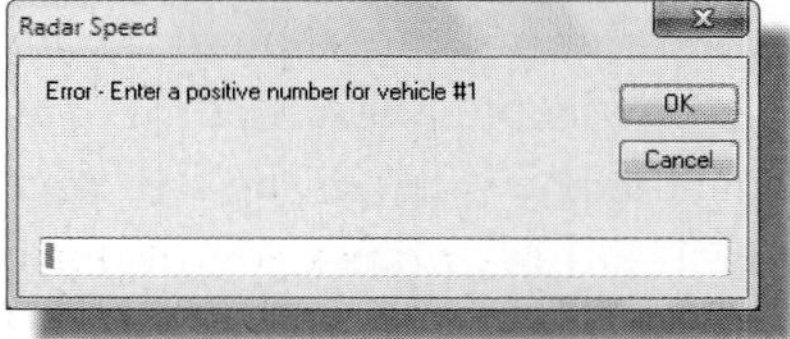

FIGURE 6-72

When error checking is performed within a loop and the user is asked to enter data through the use of an input box, the body of the loop must be executed each time the user enters data regardless of whether the data is valid or invalid. If the user enters valid data, then the data is processed according to the needs of the program.

The use of breakpoints and DataTips allows you to examine any variables during the execution of the program. By moving step by step through the program, normally you will be able to identify any errors that might occur in the program.

Publishing an Application with ClickOnce Deployment

After an application is completely debugged and working properly, you can deploy the project. Deploying a project means placing an executable version of the program on your hard disk (which then can be placed on CD or DVD), on a Web server, or on a network server.

You probably have purchased software on a CD or DVD. To install the application on your computer, you insert the CD or DVD into your computer and then follow the setup instructions. The version of the program you receive on the CD or DVD is the deployed version of the program.

When programming using Visual Basic 2010, you can create a deployed program by using **ClickOnce Deployment**. The deployed version of the program you create can be installed and executed on any computer that has the .NET framework installed. The computer does not need Visual Studio 2010 installed to run the program.

To publish the Highway Radar Checkpoint program using ClickOnce Deployment, you can complete the following steps:

> **HEADS UP**
>
> Your application should be complete, debugged, and working properly before you deploy it. Users expect a deployed program to be error-free. While you are debugging your program in Visual Studio 2010, you should run it in Debugging mode.

STEP 1 With the program open, click Build on the menu bar.

The Build menu is displayed (Figure 6-87).

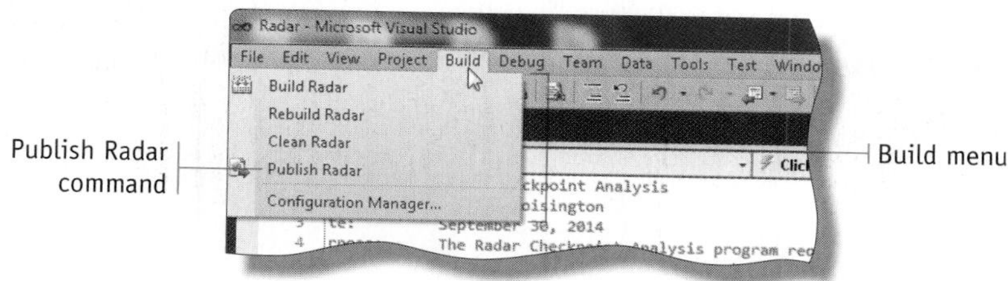

FIGURE 6-87

STEP 2 Click Publish Radar on the Build menu.

The Publish Wizard starts (Figure 6-88). The first Publish Wizard dialog box asks where you want to publish the application. The application can be published to a Web server, a network, or as a setup file on a hard disk or USB drive for burning on a CD or DVD. This dialog box includes publish\ as the default location, which you can change to a file location.

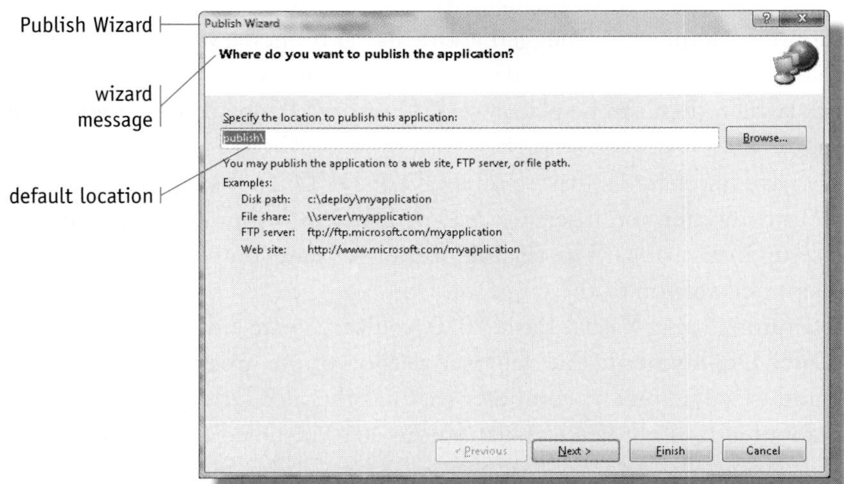

FIGURE 6-88

STEP 3 Change the default location from publish\ to a file location. To publish to a USB drive, type the drive letter. In this example, enter E: for a USB drive.

The Publish Wizard dialog box requests where the user intends to publish the application. The Radar application will be saved to the USB drive, which is drive E: in this example (Figure 6-89).

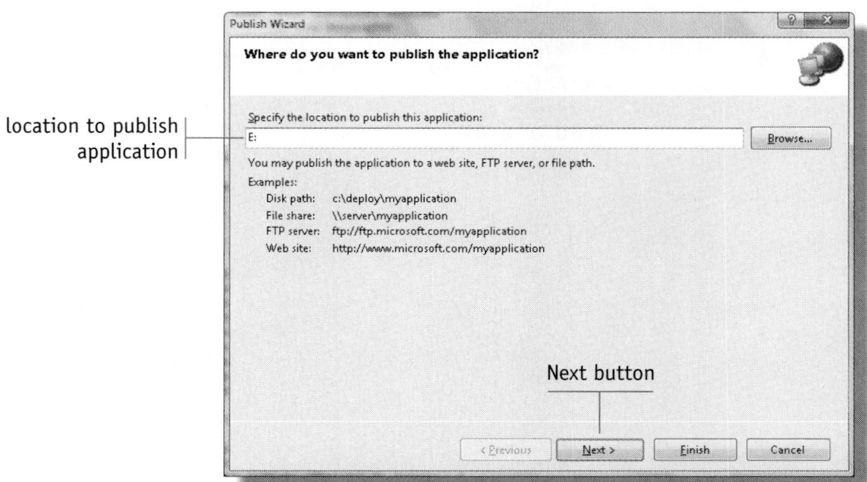

FIGURE 6-89

Guided Program Development *continued*

• **Add Menu Items** The next step is to add two menu items to the File menu. Click the Type Here box below the word File, and then enter `&Clear`. Name the Clear menu item mnuClearItem. Click the Type Here box below the Clear menu item, and then enter `E&xit` to make the "x" in Exit the hot key. Name the Exit menu item mnuExit (*ref: Figure 6-10*).

HINT

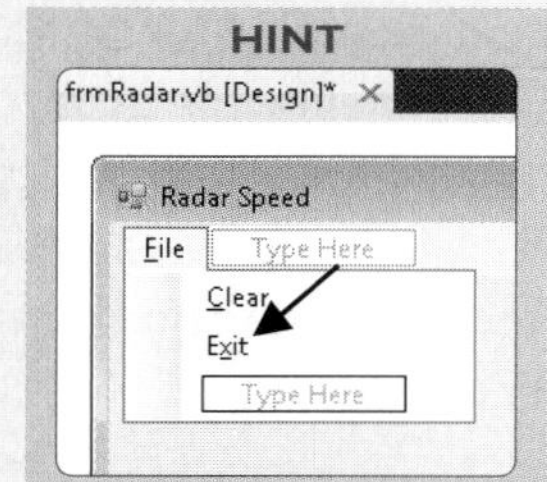

• **Add a PictureBox Object** Drag a PictureBox .NET component from the Toolbox to the left side of the Windows Form object. Name the PictureBox object picRadar. Change the Size property of the PictureBox object to 102, 89. Change the Location property of the PictureBox object to 13, 41.

HINT

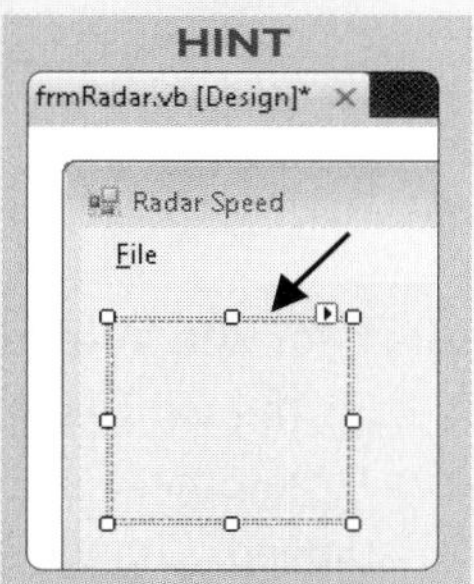

• **Add the Title Label Object** Drag a Label .NET component onto the Windows Form object. Name the label lblTitle. Enter the text for this label as Highway Radar Checkpoint on two lines (Hint: Click the Text property list arrow in the Properties window to enter a label with multiple lines. Press the ENTER key to move to a new line.) Choose the font Tahoma, Bold font style, and 18-point size. Change the TextAlign property to MiddleCenter by clicking the TextAlign list arrow and then clicking the Center block. Change the Location property of the lblTitle Label object to 133,41.

HINT

• **Add the Posted Speed Label** Place a Label object below the lblTitle Label object. Name the second Label lblPostedSpeed. In the Text property, enter `Posted Speed Limit - 60 mph`. Change the Font property to Tahoma, Italic font style, and 10-point size. Align the bottom of the lblPostedSpeed Label object with the bottom of the picRadar PictureBox object. Align the center of the lblPostedSpeed label with the center of the lblTitle Label object.

HINT

(continues)

Guided Program Development *continued*

- **Add the Enter Speed Button Object** Drag a Button object onto the Windows Form object below the picture box and labels. Name the Button btnEnterSpeed. Change the text of the button to Enter Speed. Change the font to 11-point Tahoma. Resize the Button object to view the complete text. Horizontally center the button in the Windows Form object.

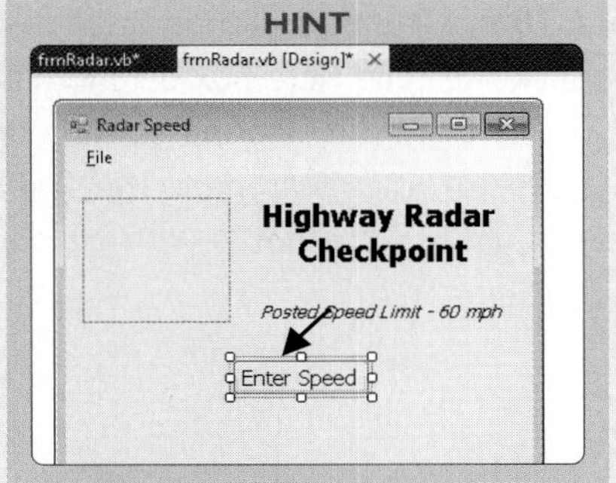

- **Add the ListBox Object for the Vehicle Speeds** To add the ListBox object that displays the vehicle speeds, drag a ListBox object onto the Windows Form object below the Button object. Name the ListBox lstRadarSpeed. Change the font for the text in the ListBox object to 11-point Tahoma. Resize the ListBox to the width of three characters because the top speed of a vehicle could reach speeds such as 102 mph. Lengthen the ListBox object to display 10 numbers. The Size property for the ListBox object in the sample program is 34, 184. Horizontally center the ListBox object in the Windows Form object (*ref: Figure 6-24*).

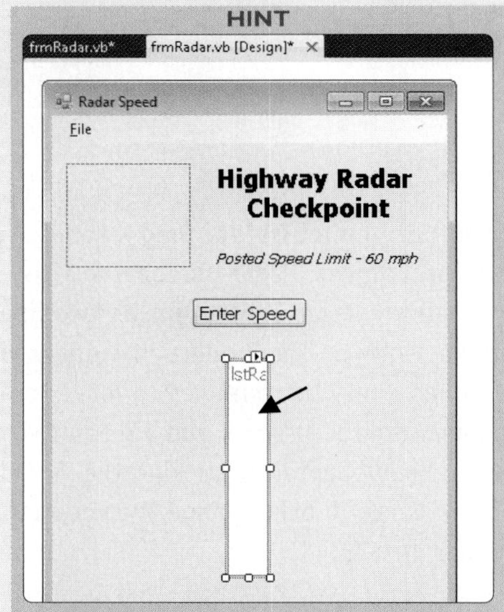

- **Add the Result Label** To add the label where the average speed message is displayed, drag a Label object onto the Windows Form object. Name the Label object lblAverageSpeed. Change the text to `Average speed at checkpoint is X.XX mph`. Change the font to Tahoma 10-point. Horizontally center the message in the Windows Form object.

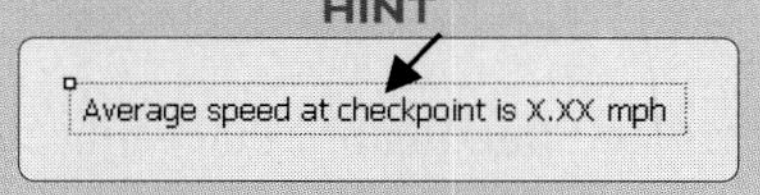

Guided Program Development *continued*

The user interface mockup is complete (Figure 6-99).

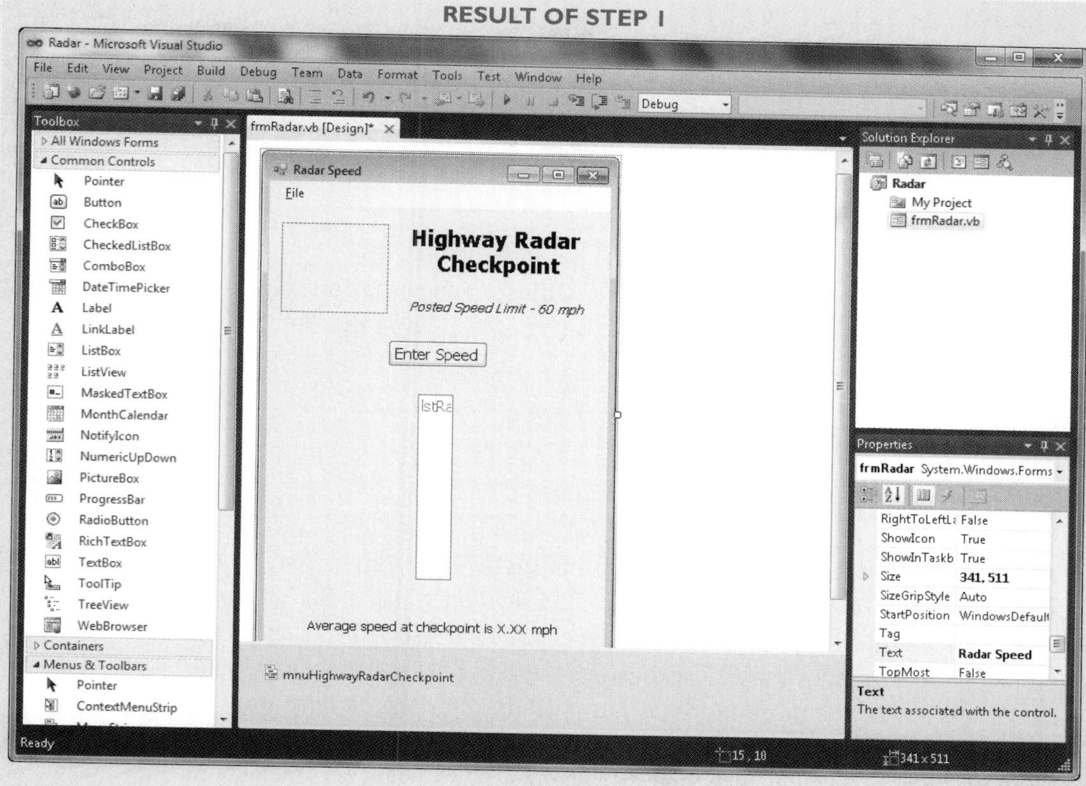

FIGURE 6-99

Phase 2: Fine-Tune the User Interface

2

- **Change the BackColor Property of the Windows Form Object** Select the Windows Form object and then change its BackColor property to White on the Web tab.

- **Change the Color for the Title Label** Change the ForeColor property for the lblTitle Label object to SteelBlue on the Web tab.

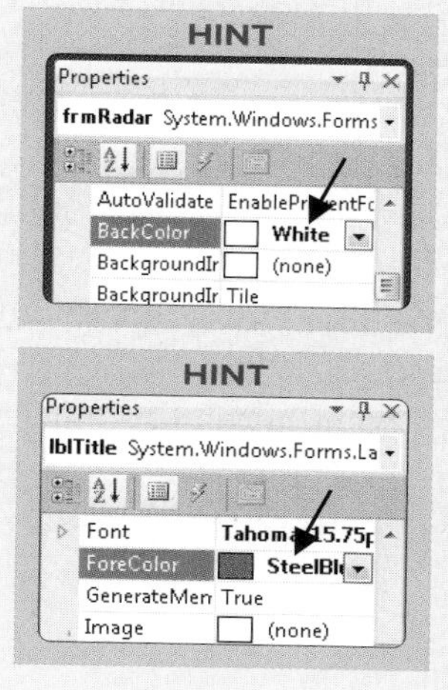

(continues)

Guided Program Development *continued*

- **Change the Button Color** Change the BackColor property of the btnEnterSpeed Button object to LightSteelBlue.

HINT

- **Change the Font Color for the List Box Object** Change the ForeColor property of the lstRadarSpeed ListBox object to SteelBlue on the Web tab.

HINT

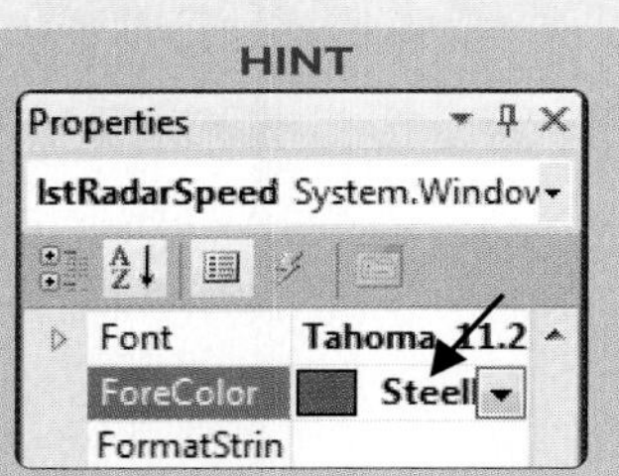

- **Insert and Size the Radar Image into the PictureBox Object** Visit scsite.com/vb2010/ch6/images and download the Radar image. Select the picRadar PictureBox object. In the Properties window, select the Image property and then click the ellipsis button in the right column. Import the Radar image from the location where you saved it. Click the OK button in the Select Resource dialog box. Select the SizeMode property, click the SizeMode arrow, and then click StretchImage.

HINT

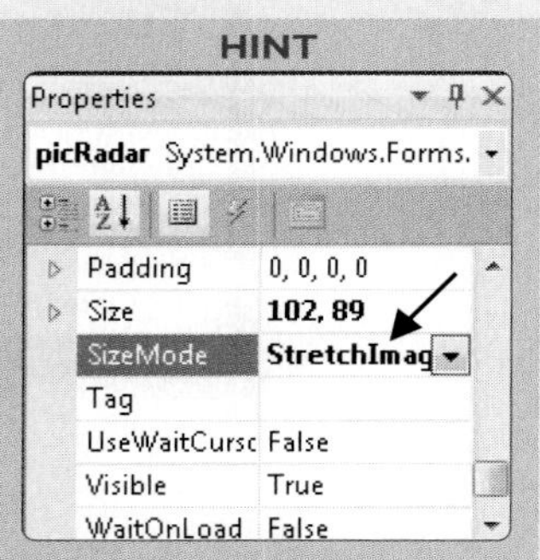

- **Change the Visible Property for the Average Speed Label** Select the lblAverageSpeed Label object and change its Visible property to False because the Label object is not displayed until the average for the speeds entered is calculated.

HEADS UP

As you work on your program, do not forget to save it from time to time. You can save the work you have done by clicking the Save All button on the Standard toolbar.

- **Make the Enter Speed Button the Accept Button** Click the background of the Windows Form object to select it. In the Properties window, click the AcceptButton list arrow to display the buttons in the user interface. Click btnEnterSpeed in the list. During program execution, when the user presses the ENTER key, the event handler for btnEnterSpeed executes.

HINT

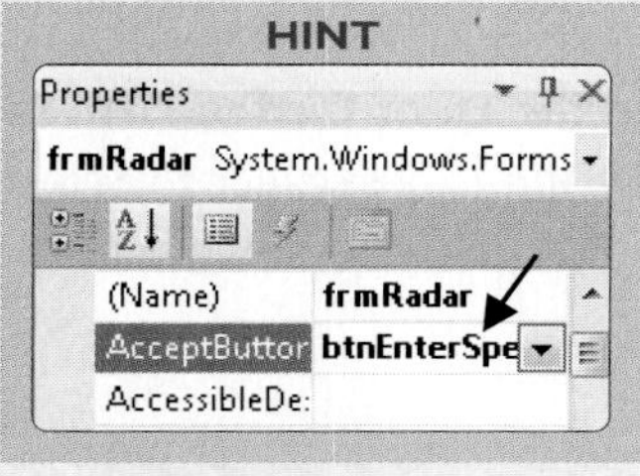

Guided Program Development *continued*

The user interface design is complete (Figure 6-100).

RESULT OF STEP 2

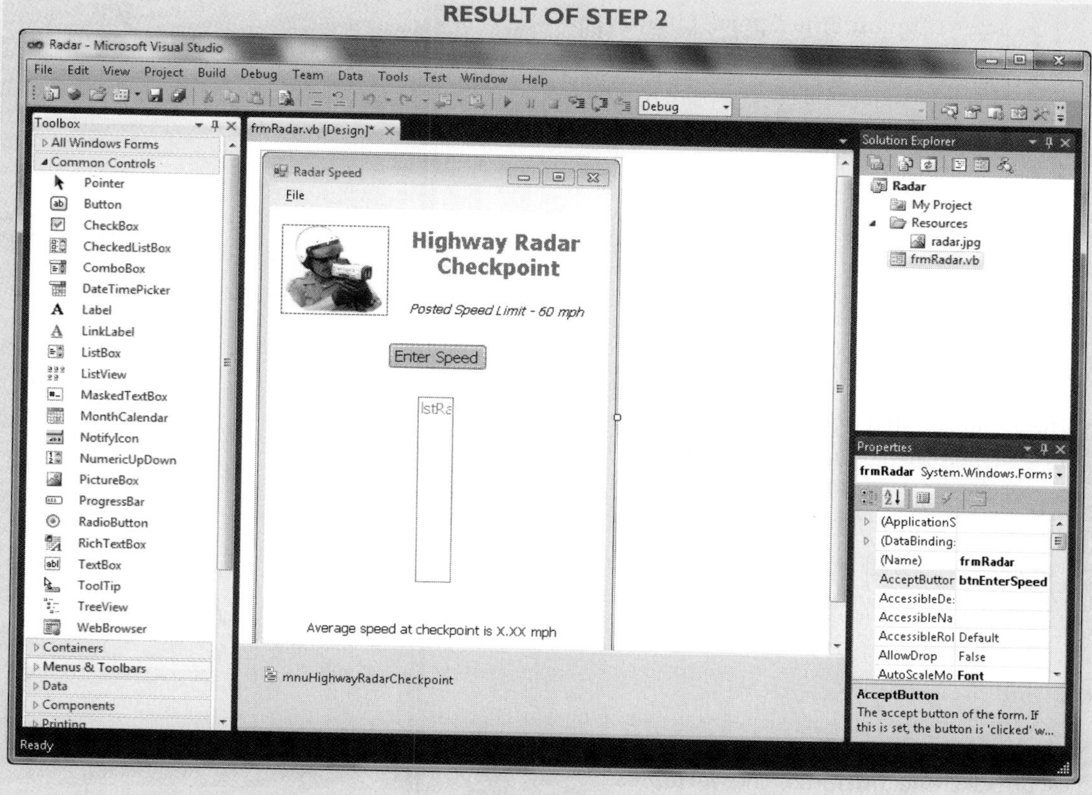

FIGURE 6-100

Phase 3: Code the Program

3

- **Enter the Comments for the Enter Speed Button Event Handler** Double-click the btnEnterSpeed Button object on the Windows Form object to open the button event handler. Insert the first four standard comments at the top of the code window. Insert the command Option Strict On at the beginning of the code to turn on strict type checking.

HINT

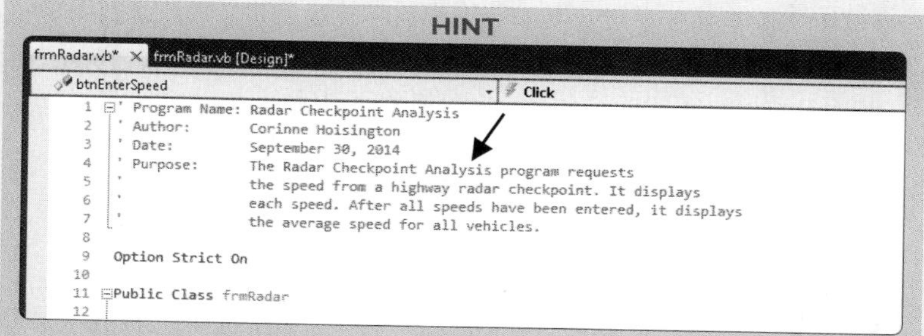

```
' Program Name: Radar Checkpoint Analysis
' Author:       Corinne Hoisington
' Date:         September 30, 2014
' Purpose:      The Radar Checkpoint Analysis program requests
'               the speed from a highway radar checkpoint. It displays
'               each speed. After all speeds have been entered, it displays
'               the average speed for all vehicles.

Option Strict On

Public Class frmRadar
```

(continues)

Guided Program Development *continued*

- **Comment the btnEnterSpeed_Click Event Handler** Enter a comment to describe the purpose of the btnEnterSpeed_Click event handler.

HINT

```
Private Sub btnEnterSpeed_Clic ByVal sender As System.Object, ByVal e As System.E
    ' The btnEnterSpeed click event accepts and displays up to ten speeds
    ' from the user, and then calculates and displays the average speed
```

- **Declare and Initialize the Variables to Calculate the Average Speed** Four variables are used to calculate the average speed (besides the vehicle count). These variables are: 1) strVehicleSpeed: Is assigned the value from the InputBox function call; 2) decVehicleSpeed: Is assigned the converted vehicle speed; 3) decAverageSpeed: Contains the calculated average speed; 4) decTotalOfAllSpeeds: The accumulator used to accumulate the total speeds entered by a user. Declare and initialize these four variables.

HINT

```
        ' Declare and initialize variables

        Dim strVehicleSpeed As String
        Dim decVehicleSpeed As Decimal
        Dim decAverageSpeed As Decimal
        Dim decTotalOfAllSpeeds As Decimal = 0D
```

- **Declare and Initialize the Variables Used with the InputBox Function Call** Five variables contain messages used in the input box to obtain the vehicle speeds. These variables are: 1) strInputMessage: Is used in the function call to contain the message displayed in the input box; 2) strInputHeading: Contains the message displayed in the title bar of the input box; 3) strNormalMessage: The normal message that appears in the input box when no error has occurred; 4) strNonNumericError: The message that appears in the input box when the user has entered a non-numeric value; 5) strNegativeError: The message that appears in the input box when the user has entered zero or a negative number. Declare and initialize these five variables.

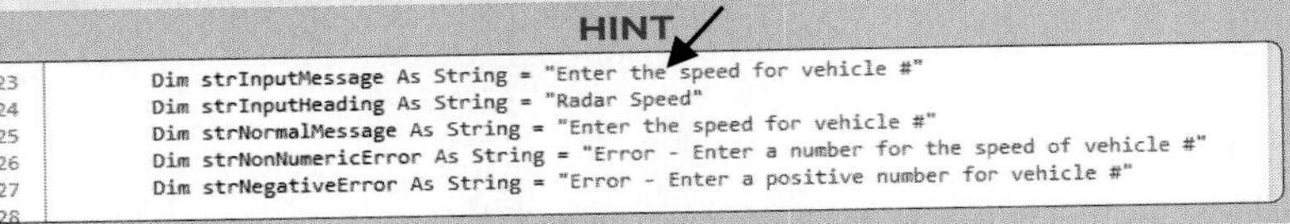

HINT
Dim strInputMessage As String = "Enter the speed for vehicle #"
Dim strInputHeading As String = "Radar Speed"
Dim strNormalMessage As String = "Enter the speed for vehicle #"
Dim strNonNumericError As String = "Error - Enter a number for the speed of vehicle #"
Dim strNegativeError As String = "Error - Enter a positive number for vehicle #"

Guided Program Development *continued*

- **Declare and Initialize Variables Used in the Loop Processing** Three variables are used for processing the loop in the program. These variables are: 1) strCancelClicked: This variable contains a null string. It is used to determine if the user clicked the Cancel button in the input box; 2) intMaxNumberOfEntries: Contains the maximum number of entries for vehicle speeds. Program requirements state the maximum number is 10; 3) intNumberOfEntries: The counter that counts the valid number of vehicle speeds entered by the user. This variable is used to determine when the maximum of entries has been made and to act as the divisor when calculating the average speed per vehicle.

HINT

```
        'Declare and initialize loop variables

        Dim strCancelClicked As String = ""
        Dim intMaxNumberOfEntries As Integer = 10
        Dim intNumberOfEntries As Integer = 1
```

- **Write Comments for the Do Until Loop and Write the Priming InputBox Function Call** You often can use comments to document a loop or other set of major processing statements. The comments here alert the reader to the role of the Do Until loop. The priming InputBox function call obtains the first vehicle speed, or allows the user to click the Cancel button. The normal message is displayed. The space at the end of the argument list places a space in the input box so if the user clicks the OK button without entering any data, it will not be treated the same as clicking the Cancel button *(ref: Figure 6-70)*.

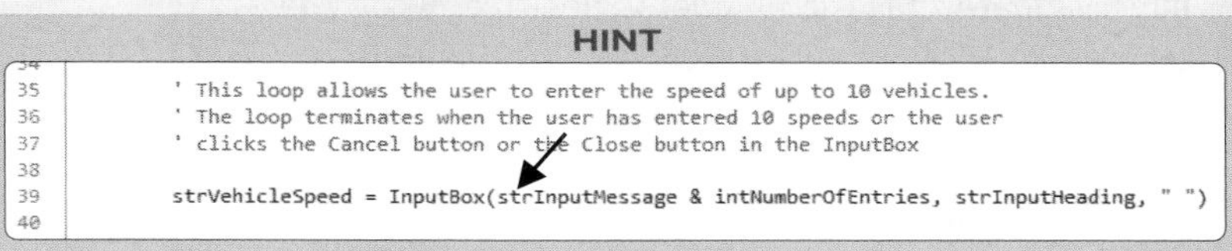
HINT

```
        ' This loop allows the user to enter the speed of up to 10 vehicles.
        ' The loop terminates when the user has entered 10 speeds or the user
        ' clicks the Cancel button or the Close button in the InputBox

        strVehicleSpeed = InputBox(strInputMessage & intNumberOfEntries, strInputHeading, " ")
```

- **Code the Do Until Loop** Because the application requests the speed of up to 10 vehicles, the Do Until loop should continue until 10 speeds are entered or until the user clicks the Cancel or Close Button in the input box. Enter the Do Until loop using IntelliSense *(ref: Figure 6-59, Figure 6-65, Figure 6-70)*.

HINT

```
        Do Until intNumberOfEntries > intMaxNumberOfEntries Or strVehicleSpeed = strCancelClicked
```

(continues)

Guided Program Development *continued*

- **Validate the Entry is a Number** The first process in the Do Until loop is to validate that the vehicle speed entered by the user is a numeric value. Enter the If...Then statement to test if the value in the strVehicleSpeed variable is numeric.

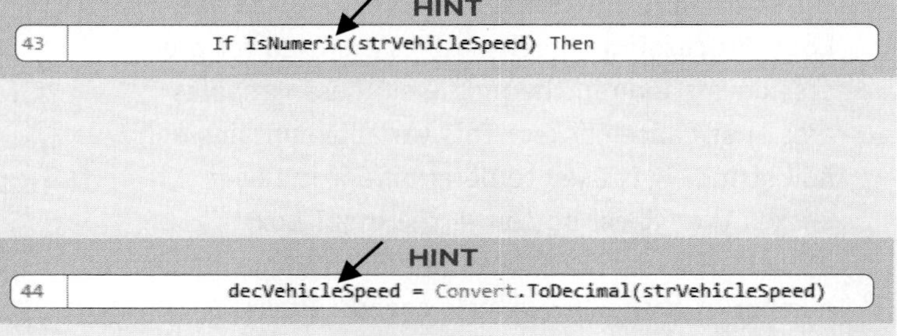


```
If IsNumeric(strVehicleSpeed) Then
```



```
decVehicleSpeed = Convert.ToDecimal(strVehicleSpeed)
```

- **Convert the Value Entered from String to Decimal Data Type** If the user entered a numeric value, the next step is to convert the string value the user entered to a Decimal data type. Using IntelliSense, enter the code to convert the value in the strVehicleSpeed variable from String to Decimal data type and place the result in the decVehicleSpeed variable.

- **Validate That the Entered Value is a Positive Number** After the value is converted, the program must validate that the number is positive. Write the If...Then statement to test whether the value in the decVehicleSpeed variable is greater than zero.

```
If decVehicleSpeed > 0 Then
```

- **Perform the Processing When the User Enters a Valid Speed** After ensuring the speed entered by the user is valid, the next steps are to perform the processing for valid speeds. Four steps are required: 1) Add the speed as an item to the lstRadarSpeed ListBox object *(ref: Figure 6-28)*; 2) Add the speed the user entered to the decTotalOfAllSpeeds accumulator *(ref: Figure 6-38)*. The accumulated speed is used to calculate the average speed; 3) Increment the intNumberOfEntries counter by 1 because the user entered a valid speed *(ref: Figure 6-38)*. This value is used as the divisor to determine the average speed, and also as one of the indicators that the loop should be terminated; 4) Because the user entered a valid speed, the normal message should be displayed in the input box the next time the input box is displayed. Therefore, the normal message should be moved to the strInputMessage variable. Using IntelliSense, enter the code for these four activities.

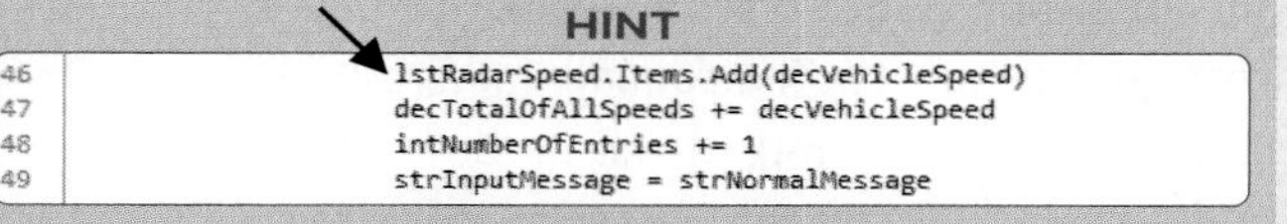


```
lstRadarSpeed.Items.Add(decVehicleSpeed)
decTotalOfAllSpeeds += decVehicleSpeed
intNumberOfEntries += 1
strInputMessage = strNormalMessage
```

Guided Program Development *continued*

- **Assign an Error Message if the User Entered a Negative Speed** If the user entered a negative speed, the next the input box that is displayed should show the negative number error message *(ref: Figure 6-73)*. Following the Else statement for the If statement that checks for a number greater than zero, enter the assignment statement that places the value in the strNegativeError variable in the strInputMessage variable.

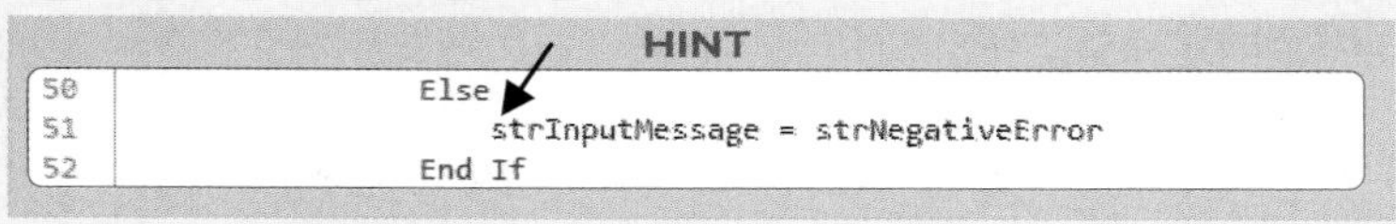
HINT
Else
strInputMessage = strNegativeError
End If

- **Assign an Error Message If the User Entered a Non-Numeric Speed** If the user entered a non-numeric speed, the next the input box that is displayed should show the non-numeric error message *(ref: Figure 6-73)*. Following the Else Statement for the If statement that checks for numeric data, enter the assignment statement that places the value in the strNonNumericError variable in the strInputMessage variable.

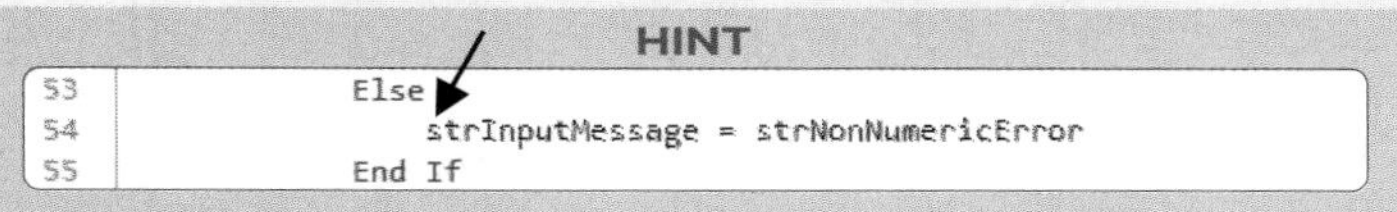
HINT
Else
strInputMessage = strNonNumericError
End If

- **Code the InputBox Function Call** The first InputBox function call was placed before the Do Until loop to prime the loop. To continue the process after the first value is entered, another InputBox function is needed as the last statement inside the loop to request subsequent values. This statement should be executed only if the maximum number of entries has not been exceeded. So, an If structure is required to determine if the maximum number of entries has been reached. If not, the InputBox function call is executed *(ref: Figure 6-73)*.

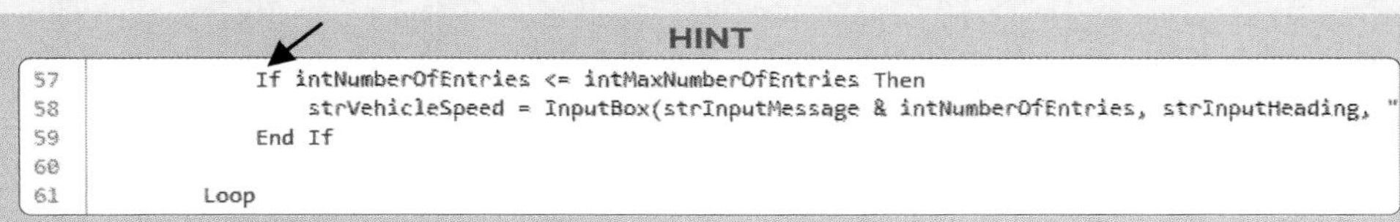
HINT
If intNumberOfEntries <= intMaxNumberOfEntries Then
strVehicleSpeed = InputBox(strInputMessage & intNumberOfEntries, strInputHeading, "
End If
Loop

(continues)

Guided Program Development *continued*

The coding for the variables and Do Until loop that processes the data in the program is complete (Figure 6-101). It is important that you examine the code in Figure 6-101 and understand the loop processing. The priming of the loop by both setting the value in the intNumberOfEntries value (line 33) and calling the InputBox function (line 39) is critical for proper execution of the loop. Increasing the loop counter when a valid entry is made (line 48) also is fundamental in the loop processing because testing this counter is one way the Do Until loop can be terminated. Also, using variables for messages instead literals in the actual code demonstrates how professional programs are coded. You should follow these examples in your programming.

RESULT OF STEP 3

```
18
19          Dim strVehicleSpeed As String
20          Dim decVehicleSpeed As Decimal
21          Dim decAverageSpeed As Decimal
22          Dim decTotalOfAllSpeeds As Decimal = 0D
23          Dim strInputMessage As String = "Enter the speed for vehicle #"
24          Dim strInputHeading As String = "Radar Speed"
25          Dim strNormalMessage As String = "Enter the speed for vehicle #"
26          Dim strNonNumericError As String = "Error - Enter a number for the speed of vehicle #"
27          Dim strNegativeError As String = "Error - Enter a positive number for vehicle #"
28
29          'Declare and initialize loop variables
30
31          Dim strCancelClicked As String = ""
32          Dim intMaxNumberOfEntries As Integer = 10
33          Dim intNumberOfEntries As Integer = 1
34
35          ' This loop allows the user to enter the speed of up to 10 vehicles.
36          ' The loop terminates when the user has entered 10 speeds or the user
37          ' clicks the Cancel button or the Close button in the InputBox
38
39          strVehicleSpeed = InputBox(strInputMessage & intNumberOfEntries, strInputHeading, " ")
40
41          Do Until intNumberOfEntries > intMaxNumberOfEntries Or strVehicleSpeed = strCancelClicked
42
43              If IsNumeric(strVehicleSpeed) Then
44                  decVehicleSpeed = Convert.ToDecimal(strVehicleSpeed)
45                  If decVehicleSpeed > 0 Then
46                      lstRadarSpeed.Items.Add(decVehicleSpeed)
47                      decTotalOfAllSpeeds += decVehicleSpeed
48                      intNumberOfEntries += 1
49                      strInputMessage = strNormalMessage
50                  Else
51                      strInputMessage = strNegativeError
52                  End If
53              Else
54                  strInputMessage = strNonNumericError
55              End If
```

FIGURE 6-101 (continues)

Guided Program Development *continued*

```
        If intNumberOfEntries <= intMaxNumberOfEntries Then
            strVehicleSpeed = InputBox(strInputMessage & intNumberOfEntries, strInputHeading, " ")
        End If

    Loop
```

FIGURE 6-101 (continued)

4

- **Set the Result Label's Visible Property** When you finish the Do Until loop, you must complete three tasks to finish the Enter Speed button click event handler: 1) The label that will contain the average speed must be made visible; 2) The average speed must be calculated and displayed; 3) The Enter Speed button must be disabled. Using IntelliSense, write the code to make the lblAverageSpeed label visible.

HINT

```
        ' Makes label visible
        lblAverageSpeed.Visible = True
```

- **Calculate the Average Speed** To calculate the average of the speeds the user entered, the value in the decTotalOfAllSpeeds variable must be divided by the number of vehicles for which speeds were entered. At the end of the loop shown in Figure 6-101, the value in the intNumberOfEntries variable always will be one greater than the actual number of vehicles entered, so the total of all speeds must be divided by the value in the intNumberOfEntries less 1. This calculation should occur only if one or more vehicle speeds were entered, so an If statement must be used to check if the value in the intNumberOfEntries variable is greater than 1. If so, the average speed is calculated; if not, the "No speed entered" message should be displayed. Using IntelliSense, write the code to perform this processing.

HINT

```
        'Calculates and displays average speed
        If intNumberOfEntries > 1 Then
            decAverageSpeed = decTotalOfAllSpeeds / (intNumberOfEntries - 1)
            lblAverageSpeed.Text = "Average speed at checkpoint is " & _
                decAverageSpeed.ToString("F1") & " mph"
        Else
            lblAverageSpeed.Text = "No speed entered"
        End If
```

(continues)

Guided Program Development *continued*

- **Change the Enter Speed Button Enabled Property to False** After the average speed is calculated and displayed, the Enabled property of the btnEnterSpeed button is set to False to dim the button. Using IntelliSense, write the code to accomplish this processing.

HINT

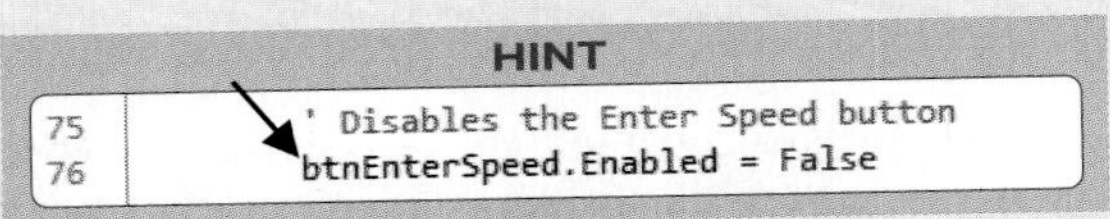

' Disables the Enter Speed button
btnEnterSpeed.Enabled = False

The code for the btnEnterSpeed button click event handler is completed (Figure 6-102).

RESULT OF STEP 4

```
Private Sub btnEnterSpeed_Click(ByVal sender As System.Object, ByVal e As System.EventArgs) Handles btnEnterSpeed.Click
    ' The btnEnterSpeed click event accepts and displays up to ten speeds
    ' from the user, and then calculates and displays the average speed

    ' Declare and initialize variables

    Dim strVehicleSpeed As String
    Dim decVehicleSpeed As Decimal
    Dim decAverageSpeed As Decimal
    Dim decTotalOfAllSpeeds As Decimal = 0D
    Dim strInputMessage As String = "Enter the speed for vehicle #"
    Dim strInputHeading As String = "Radar Speed"
    Dim strNormalMessage As String = "Enter the speed for vehicle #"
    Dim strNonNumericError As String = "Error - Enter a number for the speed of vehicle #"
    Dim strNegativeError As String = "Error - Enter a positive number for vehicle #"

    'Declare and initialize loop variables

    Dim strCancelClicked As String = ""
    Dim intMaxNumberOfEntries As Integer = 10
    Dim intNumberOfEntries As Integer = 1

    ' This loop allows the user to enter the speed of up to 10 vehicles.
    ' The loop terminates when the user has entered 10 speeds or the user
    ' clicks the Cancel button or the Close button in the InputBox

    strVehicleSpeed = InputBox(strInputMessage & intNumberOfEntries, strInputHeading, " ")

    Do Until intNumberOfEntries > intMaxNumberOfEntries Or strVehicleSpeed = strCancelClicked

        If IsNumeric(strVehicleSpeed) Then
            decVehicleSpeed = Convert.ToDecimal(strVehicleSpeed)
            If decVehicleSpeed > 0 Then
                lstRadarSpeed.Items.Add(decVehicleSpeed)
                decTotalOfAllSpeeds += decVehicleSpeed
                intNumberOfEntries += 1
                strInputMessage = strNormalMessage
            Else
                strInputMessage = strNegativeError
            End If
        Else
            strInputMessage = strNonNumericError
        End If
```

FIGURE 6-102 (continues)

Guided Program Development *continued*

```
            If intNumberOfEntries <= intMaxNumberOfEntries Then
                strVehicleSpeed = InputBox(strInputMessage & intNumberOfEntries, strInputHeading, " ")
            End If

        Loop

        ' Makes label visible
        lblAverageSpeed.Visible = True

        'Calculates and displays average speed
        If intNumberOfEntries > 1 Then
            decAverageSpeed = decTotalOfAllSpeeds / (intNumberOfEntries - 1)
            lblAverageSpeed.Text = "Average speed at checkpoint is " & _
                decAverageSpeed.ToString("F1") & " mph"
        Else
            lblAverageSpeed.Text = "No speed entered"
        End If

        ' Disables the Enter Speed button
        btnEnterSpeed.Enabled = False

    End Sub
```

FIGURE 6-102 (continued)

(continues)

Guided Program Development *continued*

5

- **Run the Program** After coding a major section of the program, you should run the program to ensure it is working properly. Click the Start Debugging button on the Standard toolbar to run the Highway Radar Checkpoint program. Click the Enter Speed button and then enter a vehicle speed 10 times. Verify the speeds are displayed properly and the average speed is correct. Close the program by clicking the Close button. Run the program again, click the Enter Speed button, enter four vehicle speeds, enter a non-numeric speed, enter a speed that is less than zero, and then click the Cancel button in the input box. Ensure the speeds are displayed properly, the average speed is correct, and the error messages are displayed properly in the input box. Close the program. Run the program again, click the Enter Speed button, and then click the Cancel button in the input box. Ensure the no speed entered message is displayed. Close the program and then run it as many times as necessary to ensure the program is working properly. If the program does not run properly, consider setting a breakpoint and checking the values in the variables *(ref: Figure 6-76)*.

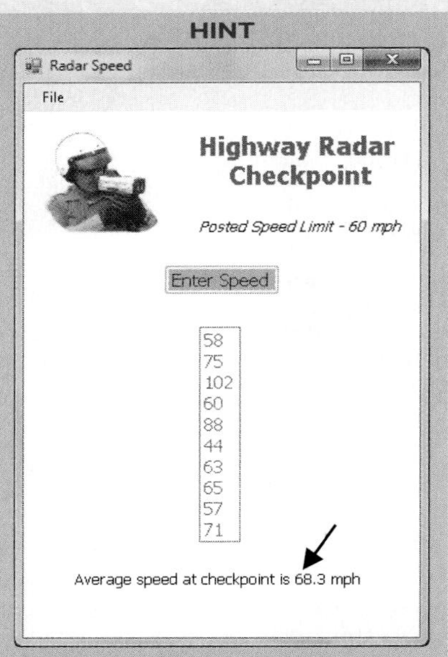

6

- **Enter the Code for the Clear Menu Item Click Event** Click the frmRadar.vb[Design]* tab in the code editing window to display the design window. Click File on the MenuStrip object, and then double-click the Clear menu item to open the Clear click event handler in the code editing window. The Clear click event handler must perform three tasks: 1) Clear the lstRadarSpeed list box; 2) Hide the average speed Label object; 3) Enable the Enter Speed Button object. Using IntelliSense, write the code for these three tasks.

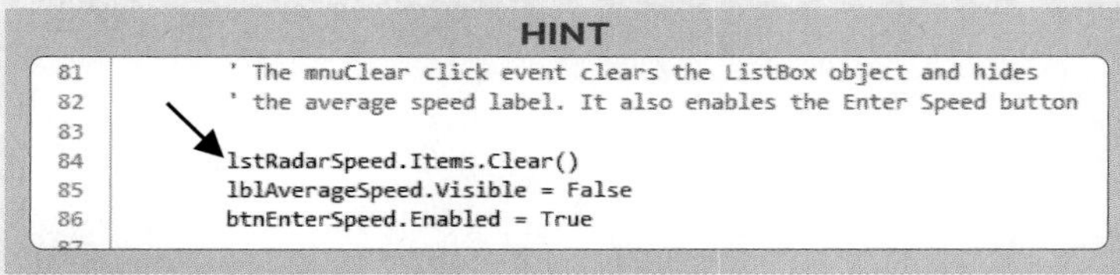
HINT

```
' The mnuClear click event clears the ListBox object and hides
' the average speed label. It also enables the Enter Speed button

lstRadarSpeed.Items.Clear()
lblAverageSpeed.Visible = False
btnEnterSpeed.Enabled = True
```

Guided Program Development *continued*

• **Enter the Code for the Exit Menu Item Click Event** Return to the design window. Double-click the Exit menu item. In the code window, enter a Close procedure call that will close the window and terminate the program.

HINT

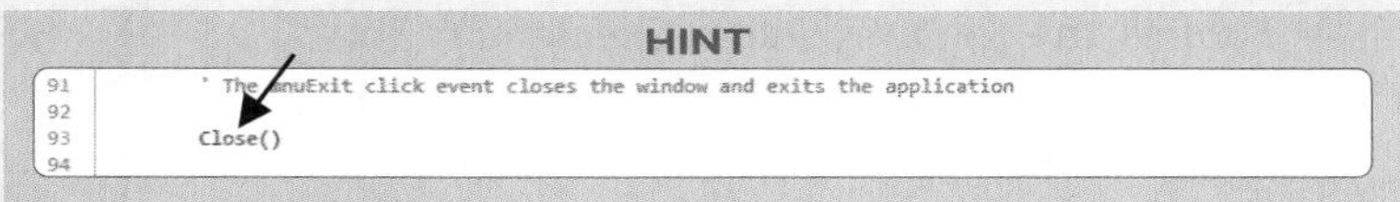

' The mnuExit click event closes the window and exits the application
Close()

The code for the Clear menu item click event and the Exit menu item click event is completed (Figure 6-103). The program code for the program is done.

RESULT OF STEP 6

```
    Private Sub mnuClear_Click(ByVal sender As System.Object, ByVal e As System.EventArgs) Handles mnuClearItem.Click
        ' The mnuClear click event clears the ListBox object and hides
        ' the average speed label. It also enables the Enter Speed button

        lstRadarSpeed.Items.Clear()
        lblAverageSpeed.Visible = False
        btnEnterSpeed.Enabled = True

    End Sub

    Private Sub mnuExit_Click(ByVal sender As System.Object, ByVal e As System.EventArgs) Handles mnuExitItem.Click
        ' The mnuExit click event closes the window and exits the application

        Close()

    End Sub

End Class
```

FIGURE 6-103

(continues)

Guided Program Development *continued*

7

- **Publish the Highway Radar Checkpoint Program Option** After completing the program, you can publish it using ClickOnce deployment so it can be installed on multiple computers. To open the Publish Wizard and begin the deployment process, click Build on the menu bar and then click Publish Radar on the Build menu *(ref: Figure 6-87)*.

HINT

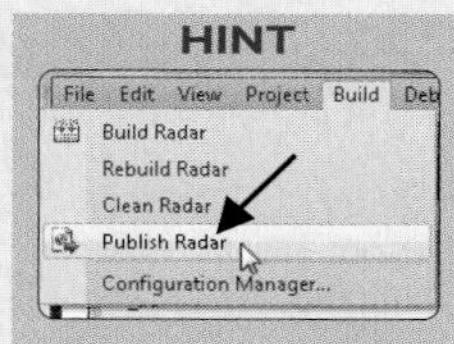

- **Select the Publish File Location** The Publish Wizard dialog box asks where you want to publish the application. Change the default location to the same file location that you used to save your Windows application by clicking the Browse button and then selecting the drive. For example, select the E: drive, a USB drive. After selecting the drive, click the Next button in the Publish Wizard dialog box *(ref: Figure 6-88)*.

HINT

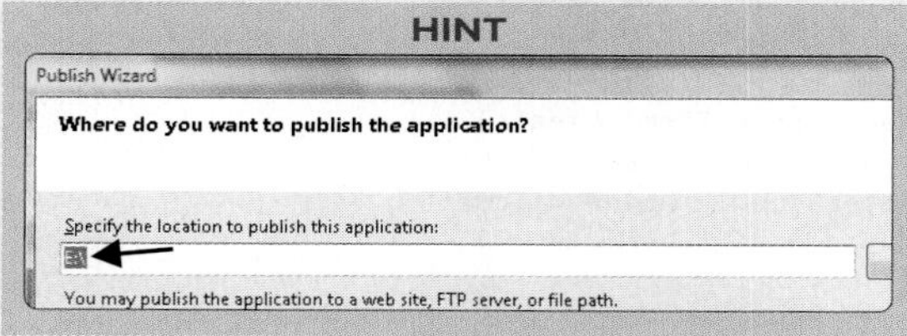

- **Select How the Users Will Install the Application** In the next Publish Wizard dialog box, select the option that lets users install the application from a CD-ROM or DVD-ROM. Then, click the Next button *(ref: Figure 6-90)*.

HINT

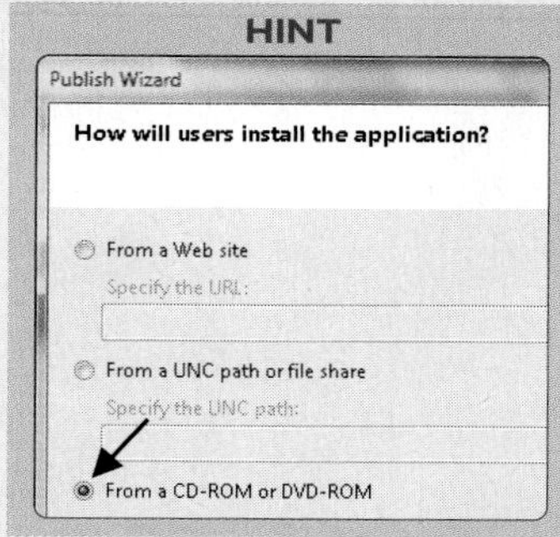

Guided Program Development *continued*

- **Indicate the Application Will Not Check for Updates** Click the The application will not check for updates radio button to indicate no updates will be checked. This is the normal selection when programs are placed on CDs or DVDs. Then, click the Next button in the Publish Wizard dialog box *(ref: Figure 6-91)*.

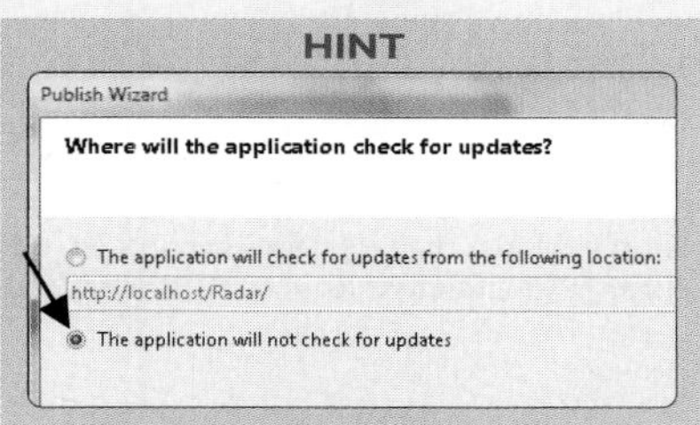
HINT
Publish Wizard
Where will the application check for updates?
The application will check for updates from the following location:
http://localhost/Radar/
The application will not check for updates

- **View the Summary Window** The Publish Wizard summary is displayed. Click the Finish button to publish the application *(ref: Figure 6-92)*.

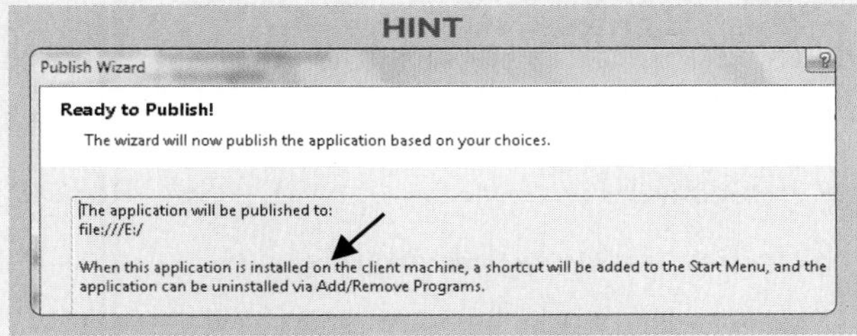
HINT
Publish Wizard
Ready to Publish!
The wizard will now publish the application based on your choices.
The application will be published to:
file:///E:/
When this application is installed on the client machine, a shortcut will be added to the Start Menu, and the application can be uninstalled via Add/Remove Programs.

- **View the Installation Files** After the publishing succeeds, a folder is created with the installation files that could be placed on a CD, DVD, or other computer (*ref: Figure 6-94*).

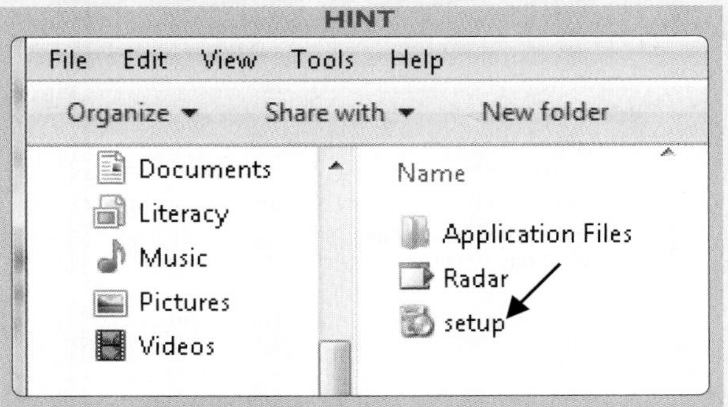
HINT
File Edit View Tools Help
Organize Share with New folder
Documents
Literacy
Music
Pictures
Videos
Name
Application Files
Radar
setup

(continues)

Code Listing

The complete code for the sample program is shown in Figure 6-104.

```
' Program Name: Radar Checkpoint Analysis
' Author:       Corinne Hoisington
' Date:         September 30, 2014
' Purpose:      The Radar Checkpoint Analysis program requests
'               the speed from a highway radar checkpoint. It displays
'               each speed. After all speeds have been entered, it displays
'               the average speed for all vehicles.

Option Strict On

Public Class frmRadar

    Private Sub btnEnterSpeed_Click(ByVal sender As System.Object, ByVal e As System.EventArgs) Handles btnEnterSpeed.Click
        ' The btnEnterSpeed click event accepts and displays up to ten speeds
        ' from the user, and then calculates and displays the average speed

        ' Declare and initialize variables

        Dim strVehicleSpeed As String
        Dim decVehicleSpeed As Decimal
        Dim decAverageSpeed As Decimal
        Dim decTotalOfAllSpeeds As Decimal = 0D
        Dim strInputMessage As String = "Enter the speed for vehicle #"
        Dim strInputHeading As String = "Radar Speed"
        Dim strNormalMessage As String = "Enter the speed for vehicle #"
        Dim strNonNumericError As String = "Error - Enter a number for the speed of vehicle #"
        Dim strNegativeError As String = "Error - Enter a positive number for vehicle #"

        'Declare and initialize loop variables

        Dim strCancelClicked As String = ""
        Dim intMaxNumberOfEntries As Integer = 10
        Dim intNumberOfEntries As Integer = 1

        ' This loop allows the user to enter the speed of up to 10 vehicles.
        ' The loop terminates when the user has entered 10 speeds or the user
        ' clicks the Cancel button or the Close button in the InputBox

        strVehicleSpeed = InputBox(strInputMessage & intNumberOfEntries, strInputHeading, " ")

        Do Until intNumberOfEntries > intMaxNumberOfEntries Or strVehicleSpeed = strCancelClicked

            If IsNumeric(strVehicleSpeed) Then
                decVehicleSpeed = Convert.ToDecimal(strVehicleSpeed)
                If decVehicleSpeed > 0 Then
                    lstRadarSpeed.Items.Add(decVehicleSpeed)
                    decTotalOfAllSpeeds += decVehicleSpeed
                    intNumberOfEntries += 1
                    strInputMessage = strNormalMessage
                Else
                    strInputMessage = strNegativeError
                End If
            Else
                strInputMessage = strNonNumericError
            End If

            If intNumberOfEntries <= intMaxNumberOfEntries Then
                strVehicleSpeed = InputBox(strInputMessage & intNumberOfEntries, strInputHeading, " ")
            End If

        Loop

        ' Makes label visible
```

FIGURE 6-104 (continues)

```
        lblAverageSpeed.Visible = True

        'Calculates and displays average speed
        If intNumberOfEntries > 1 Then
            decAverageSpeed = decTotalOfAllSpeeds / (intNumberOfEntries - 1)
            lblAverageSpeed.Text = "Average speed at checkpoint is " & _
                decAverageSpeed.ToString("F1") & " mph"
        Else
            lblAverageSpeed.Text = "No speed entered"
        End If

        ' Disables the Enter Speed button
        btnEnterSpeed.Enabled = False

    End Sub

    Private Sub mnuClear_Click(ByVal sender As System.Object, ByVal e As System.EventArgs) Handles mnuClearItem.Click
        ' The mnuClear click event clears the ListBox object and hides
        ' the average speed label. It also enables the Enter Speed button

        lstRadarSpeed.Items.Clear()
        lblAverageSpeed.Visible = False
        btnEnterSpeed.Enabled = True

    End Sub

    Private Sub mnuExit_Click(ByVal sender As System.Object, ByVal e As System.EventArgs) Handles mnuExitItem.Click
        ' The mnuExit click event closes the window and exits the application

        Close()

    End Sub

End Class
```

FIGURE 6-104 (continued)

Summary

In this chapter you have learned to design and write code to implement loops and to create menus, list boxes, and an input box. The items listed in the following table include all the new Visual Studio and Visual Basic skills you have learned in this chapter.

Visual Basic Skills

Skill	Figure Number	Web Address for Video
Place a MenuStrip object on the Windows Form object	Figure 6-5	scsite.com/vb2010/ch6/figure6-5
Code the Exit menu item event	Figure 6-12	scsite.com/vb2010/ch6/figure6-12
Insert a full standard menu	Figure 6-14	scsite.com/vb2010/ch6/figure6-14
Code the InputBox function	Figure 6-17	
Add a ListBox object	Figure 6-24	scsite.com/vb2010/ch6/figure6-24
Add an item to a ListBox object	Figure 6-27	
Add items to a ListBox object during design	Figure 6-32	scsite.com/vb2010/ch6/figure6-32
Assign a selected item from a ListBox object	Figure 6-36	
Write code using compound operators	Figure 6-39	
Write the code for a For...Next loop	Figure 6-42	
Use IntelliSense to enter the code for a For...Next loop	Figure 6-50	scsite.com/vb2010/ch6/figure6-50
Write code for a top-controlled Do While loop	Figure 6-56	
Use IntelliSense to code a Do While loop	Figure 6-59	scsite.com/vb2010/ch6/figure6-59
Write code for a bottom-controlled Do While loop	Figure 6-62	
Write code for a top-controlled Do Until loop	Figure 6-65	
Write code for a bottom-controlled Do Until loop	Figure 6-67	
Avoid infinite loops	Figure 6-69	
Prime a loop	Figure 6-70	
Validate data	Figure 6-73	
Create a nested loop	Figure 6-74	
Set a breakpoint and use a DataTip	Figure 6-76	scsite.com/vb2010/ch6/figure6-76
Publish an application with ClickOnce deployment	Figure 6-87	scsite.com/vb2010/ch6/figure6-87

FIGURE 6-105

CHAPTER 7

Creating Web Applications

OBJECTIVES

You will have mastered the material in this chapter when you can:

- Create a Web application
- Build a Web form using ASP.NET 4.0
- Set Web form properties
- Use the full screen view
- Add objects to a Web form
- Add a DropDownList object
- Add a Calendar object
- Add a custom table for layout
- Validate data on Web forms
- Use the <br> tag in Visual Basic code
- Use string manipulation methods in the String class

Introduction

Visual Studio allows you to create applications that can execute on the World Wide Web. Visual Basic 2010 includes ASP.NET 4.0 technology, with which you can create a user interface and a form for a Web application. A **Web form** is a page displayed in a Web browser, such as Internet Explorer and Firefox, that requests data from the user. The Visual Basic tools and techniques you use are familiar to you from what you have learned thus far in this course.

A practical example of a Web application developed using Visual Basic 2010 that can be delivered over the Internet is the project developed in this chapter — a bed-and-breakfast Web site that includes a Home page and Reservations page. This chapter project is based on a request from an inn called the Mystic Bed and Breakfast to create a Web application for guests who want to reserve rooms online. The application displays a Web form that requests the guest's first and last names, e-mail address, suite selection(s), the number of nights they want to stay, and the check-in date, as shown in Figure 7-1.

> **IN THE REAL WORLD**
>
> When you create an ASP.NET 4.0 Web application, you do not need IIS (Internet Information Services) or FrontPage Server extensions installed on the computer to execute and test the Web page.

FIGURE 7-1

After the Web page is displayed in a browser, the user can click the Reservations navigation button to complete the form by entering the requested information, and then click the Submit button on the form. The application validates the information the user entered by confirming that the guest entered a name, provided an e-mail address in the correct format, and selected a valid check-in date. If the user makes an error, a message identifies the error, as shown in Figure 7-2.

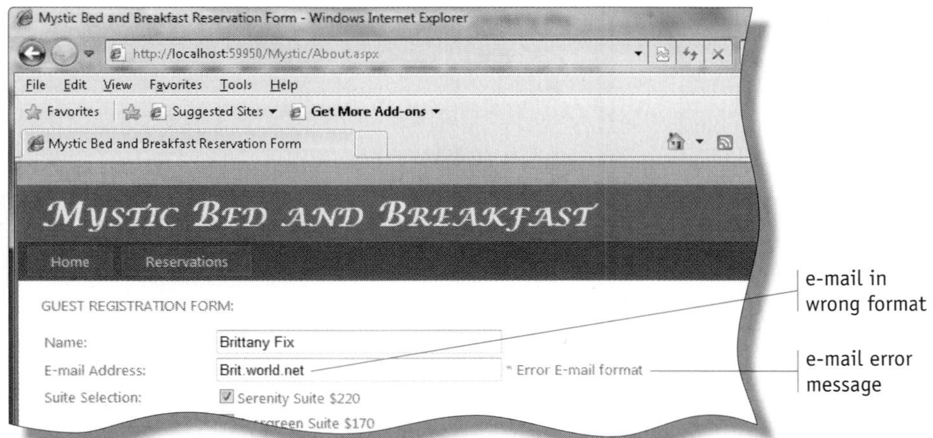

FIGURE 7-2

ONLINE REINFORCEMENT

To view a video of program execution, visit scsite.com/vb2010/ch7 and then select Figure 7-1.

When the validation is complete, the total cost of the stay is calculated and the reservation information is confirmed, as shown in Figure 7-3.

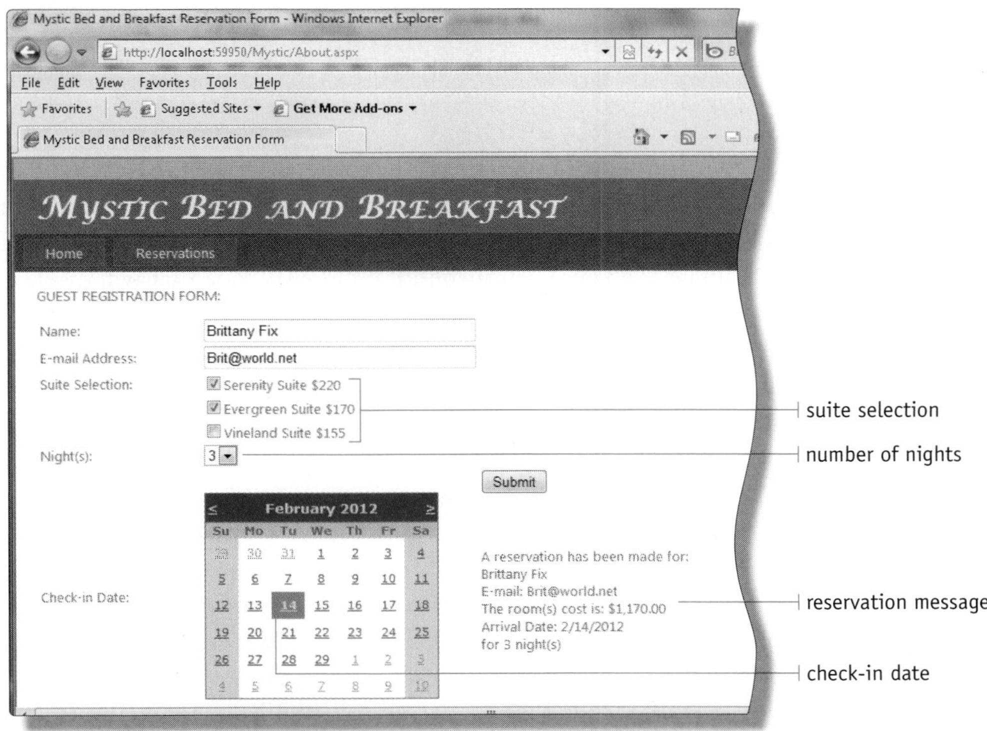

FIGURE 7-3

Creating a Web Application

To develop a form such as the one shown in Figure 7-3 on the previous page using Visual Basic, you create a Web application, which is similar to creating a Windows application. When completed, a Visual Basic Web application is displayed as a Web page(s) in a browser.

A Web page that allows users to enter information on a Web form, like the Mystic Bed and Breakfast page in this chapter, is considered a **dynamic** Web page because the user enters data and the Web page reacts to the data. In contrast, a Web page that displays information such as text and pictures with no interactivity is called a **static** Web page.

After a Web page is created, the Web page is hosted (placed) on a Web server. A **Web server** is a computer that stores Web documents and makes them available to people on the Internet. When you test your Web application created using Visual Basic 2010, Visual Studio 2010 creates a temporary Web server on your computer so you can view your Web page in a browser. When your Web page is ready for the world to see, it must be placed on an actual Web server.

Understanding the Active Server Page (ASP.NET 4.0) Platform

The ASP.NET 4.0 technology used with Visual Basic 2010 creates an **active server page** (**ASP**). When describing an active server page, developers speak of the server-side computer and the client-side computer. The server-side computer is the Web server that contains the actual active-server page and that will deliver the page to the client-side computer via the Internet. The client-side computer (often referred to as the client) runs the Web browser that requests a Web page from the Web server and displays the page.

An active server page has two primary components: the generated code component that executes on the Web server, and the HTML component that is interpreted and executed by a Web browser.

When Visual Basic compiles an active server page using ASP.NET 4.0 technology, the page contains both the server-side code that will operate on data entered by the user, such as computing the total cost of a reservation in the Mystic Bed and Breakfast Web application, and the HTML code that will display the page in a Web browser on the client-side computer. When the page is requested by a browser, ASP sends the HTML code to the client requesting the Web page, where the page is displayed. The user can interact with the page by entering data or making selections, such as selecting the check-in date. When, in the Mystic Bed and Breakfast application for example, the user clicks the Submit button, the data is sent to the Web server, where the coding within the application is executed. For example, the coding can calculate the total room cost and then display it on the Web form.

When you develop an ASP page in Visual Basic, the work you do on the design page to create the user interface will generate the HTML code for the active server page. This code includes the HTML to format and display the page, and might include JavaScript code to perform certain processing, such as ensuring that a text box contains data.

The event handler code that you write in Visual Basic for an event, such as clicking the Submit button, is executed on the Web server. So, in the Mystic Bed and Breakfast dynamic Web page, when the user clicks the Submit button, the control returns to the Web server and the event handler code written by the developer is executed. This code can perform calculations and other processing as you have seen in previous chapters. When the event handler code changes an object displayed in the Web page, such as changing the Label object that contains the reservation message, that change immediately is displayed on the Web page.

Creating a Web Site with Visual Studio 2010

Visual Studio 2010 introduces a technology for creating Web pages that makes Web page design faster and simpler. A new Web component is now part of ASP.NET 4.0 that dramatically improves designing HTML layout. Microsoft Expression Web, the Web site software that replaces FrontPage, is built into the design portion of ASP.NET, making it easier for designers to open a Visual Basic 2010 Web page in Expression Web without any conversion issues. You can also open an Expression Web page directly in Visual Basic 2010. You do not need Expression Web to work with its Web pages in Visual Basic 2010, but Expression Web has many tools to enhance Web design.

Creating a Dynamic Web Site Using Visual Basic

Using Visual Basic 2010 to create a dynamic Web site is similar to creating an interactive Windows application — you drag objects from the Toolbox and place them in a design window to build a form. Some of the Web form objects are different from Windows objects because they are designed for use online. To create a Visual Basic Web project for the Mystic Bed and Breakfast application, you can complete the following steps:

HEADS UP

To reopen a saved Visual Basic Web application, open Visual Studio and then click Open Web Site on the File menu. Browse to the main project folder to open the Web site.

STEP 1 Start Visual Studio. Click the New Web Site button on the Standard toolbar.

The New Web Site dialog box opens (Figure 7-4).

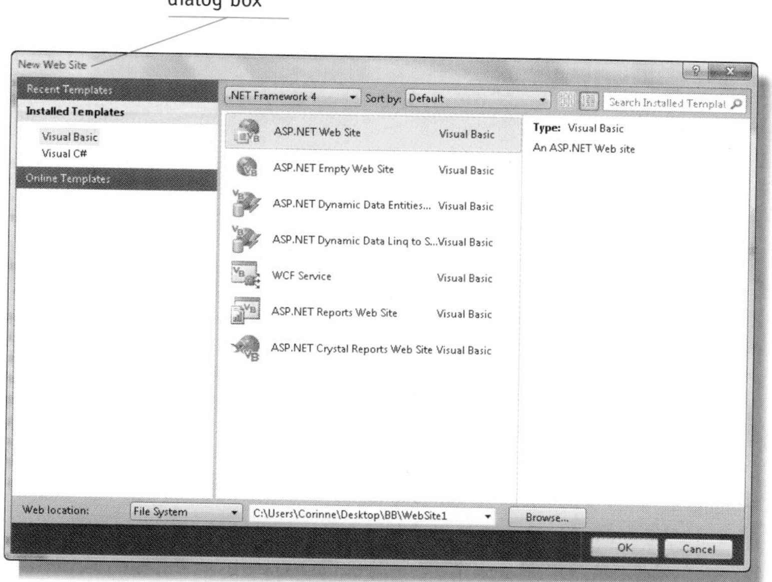

FIGURE 7-4

STEP 2 In the center pane, click ASP.NET Web Site, if necessary. Name the chapter project application Mystic in the Location text box. In Figure 7-5, the Web Site is placed on the e: drive.

The ASP.NET Web Site will be stored on the e: drive (Figure 7-5).

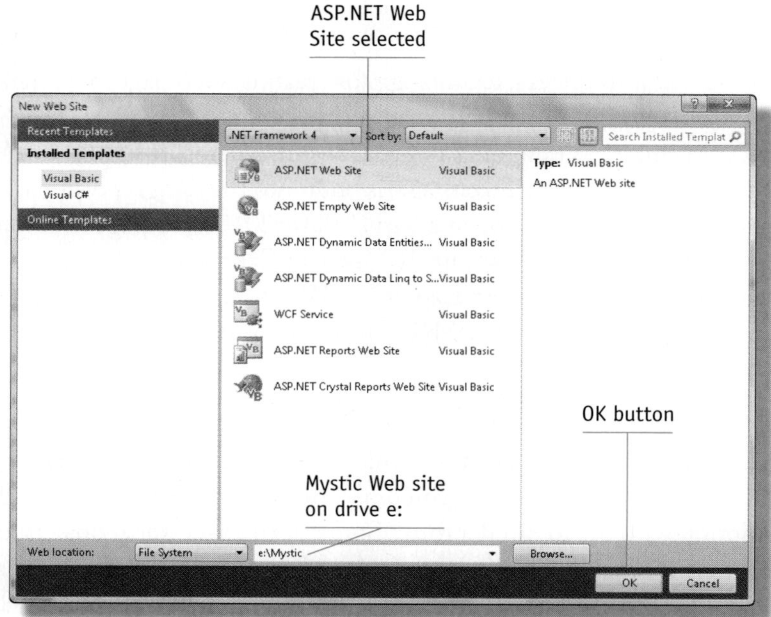

FIGURE 7-5

STEP 3 Click the OK button in the New Web Site dialog box.

The Web application Design window opens (Figure 7-6). The Default.aspx page is displayed. On the scroll bar at the bottom of the page, the Design button is selected, showing that the design window is displayed.

HEADS UP

Be sure you do not use blank spaces in the Web application filename because browsers do not support a blank space in any Web page address.

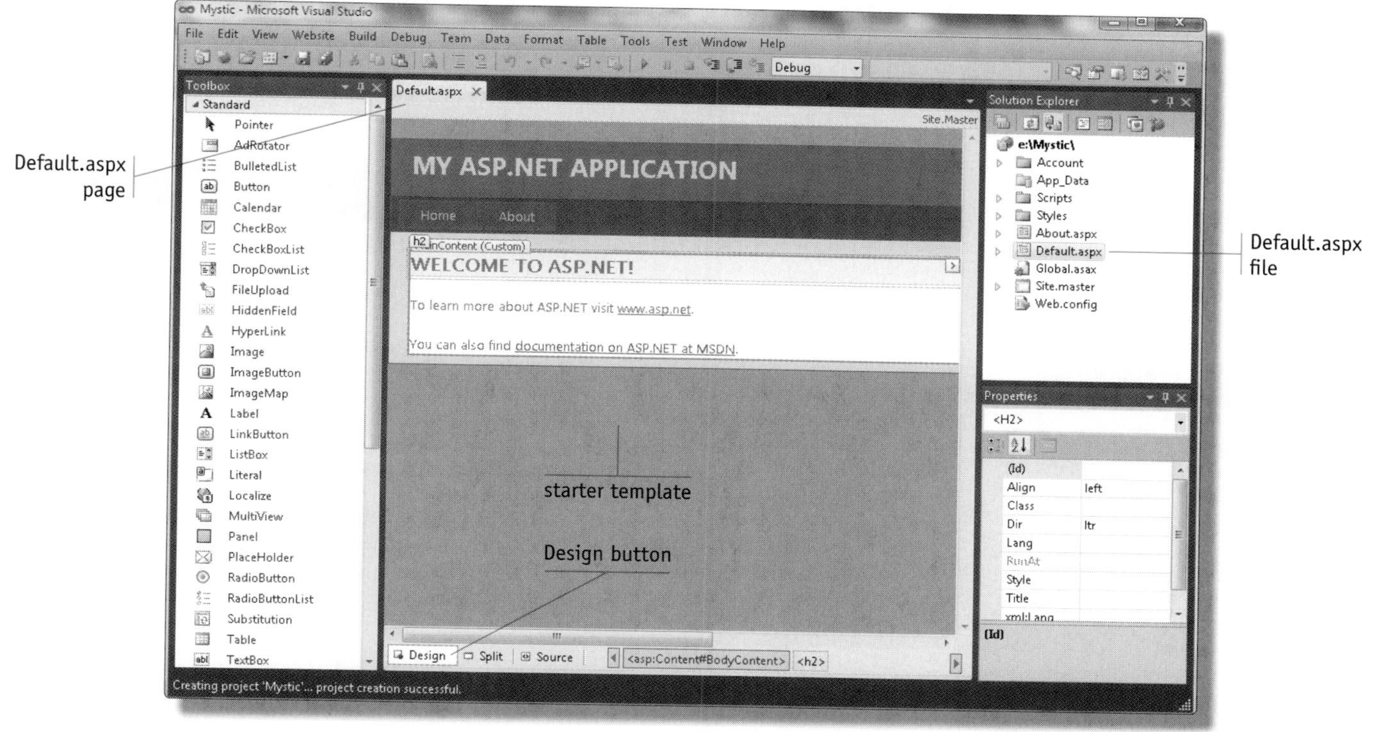

FIGURE 7-6

ONLINE REINFORCEMENT

To view a video of the process in the previous steps, visit scsite.com/vb2010/ch7 and then select Figure 7-4.

Using a Multi-Page Starter Template

Visual Basic 2010 provides a starter template to assist you in designing a Web page. The starter template allows you to create a new ASP.NET application with some layout and structure already implemented within it. Figure 7-7 on the next page shows the file named Site.master in the Solution Explorer. The Site.master file is a master page file that provides an overall layout for the site with headers, buttons, and footers. A master page is designed to create a consistent layout for the pages in your application. It defines the look and feel and standard behavior that you want for all of the pages in your Web site. If you change the color or title of the master page, all the pages in the site will reflect that same color and title. First design the master page and then customize the actual pages on the Web site. The Web site in this project has two pages. The default page (default.aspx) serves as the Home page, which gives the traveler information about the Mystic Bed and Breakfast Inn. The Reservations page (About.aspx) provides a reservation form that a traveler can use to make reservations.

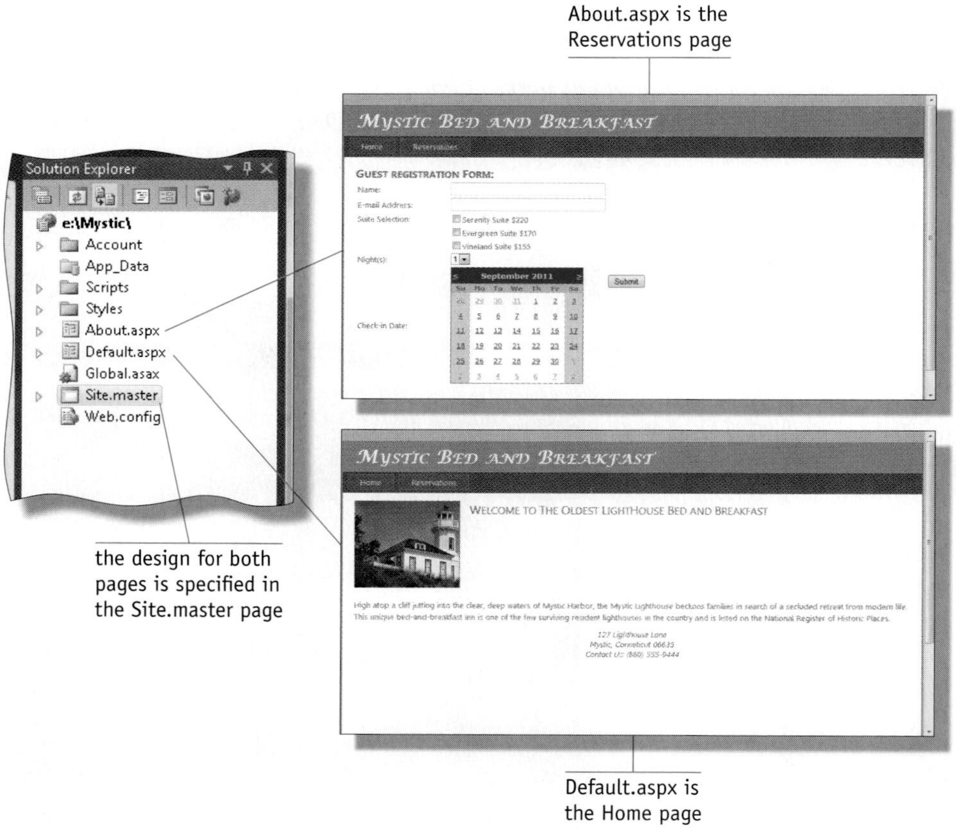

About.aspx is the Reservations page

the design for both pages is specified in the Site.master page

Default.aspx is the Home page

FIGURE 7-7

> **HEADS UP**
>
> If you prefer to design a Web page without using the starter templates, select ASP.NET Empty Web Site before you name the project when you create a new Web Site project.

Customizing the Master Page

The master page specifies the layout, color, and text that are repeated on the actual Web pages that are displayed by the browser. A master page is basically defined as a nondisplaying page. It contains the information about the layout of the page, which will be used in the creation of body pages. It enables the users to create the layouts of the pages quickly and conveniently across the entire Web site. To change the text on the master page, you can complete the following steps:

STEP 1 In the Solution Explorer window, double-click Site.master to open the page.

The Site.master page opens (Figure 7-8).

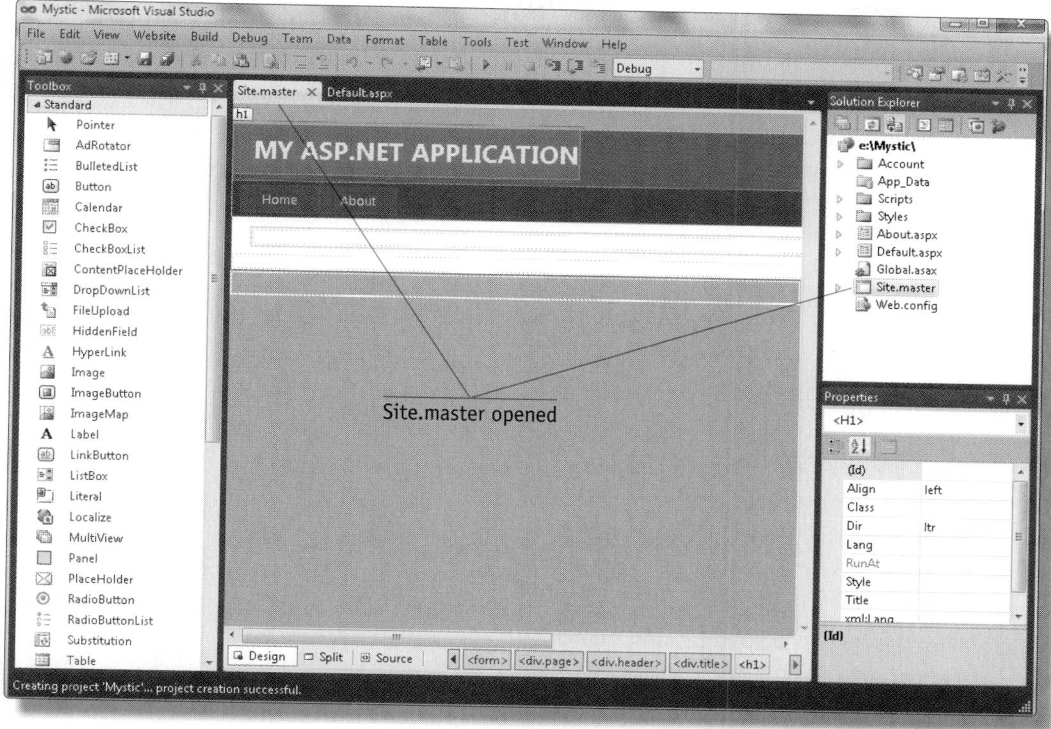

FIGURE 7-8

STEP 2 Click View on the menu bar, point to Toolbars, and then click Formatting. Select the text at the top of the Site.master page MY ASP.NET APPLICATION. Type `MYSTIC BED AND BREAKFAST` to replace the original title. On the Formatting toolbar, click the Font Name tool, select Lucida Calligraphy, click the Font Size tool, and then select xx-large.

The title on the Master page changes to MYSTIC BED AND BREAKFAST. The font and size are changed (Figure 7-9).

HEADS UP

You can also change the color of the page by selecting the background color and foreground color tools on the Formatting toolbar.

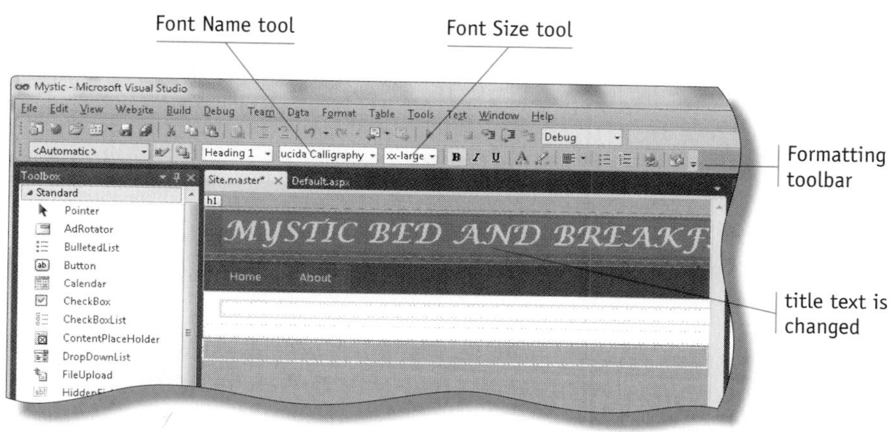

FIGURE 7-9

ONLINE REINFORCEMENT

To view a video of the process in the previous steps, visit scsite.com/vb2010/ch7 and then select Figure 7-8.

Customizing Navigation Buttons on the Master Template

The Master page has navigation buttons that play an integral role in making your site easy to use and navigate. By default, the Master site has two buttons: Home, which connects to the Default.aspx page when clicked, and About, which connects to the About.aspx page when clicked. It would make more sense for the About button to be named Reservations. To rename the second navigation button to the word Reservations, follow these steps:

STEP 1 On the Site.master page, point to the two navigation buttons. Click the Smart Tag and then click Edit Menu Items.

The Menu Item Editor window opens (Figure 7-10).

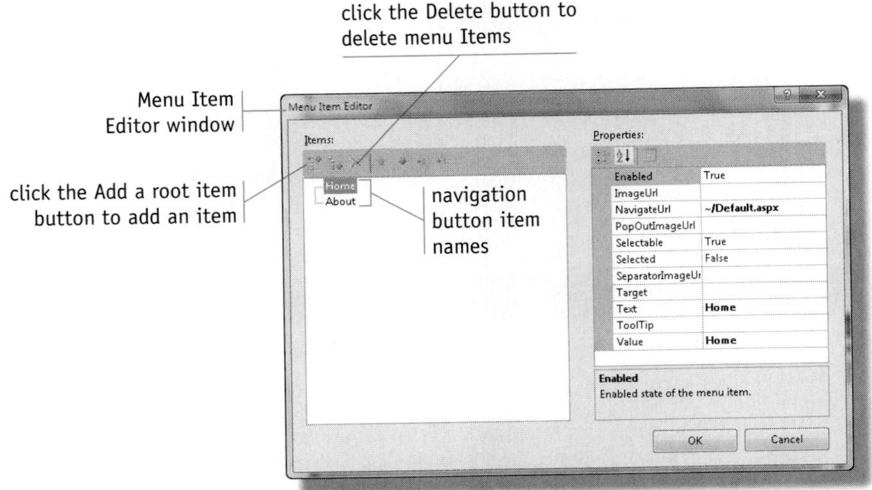

FIGURE 7-10

STEP 2 Click the About item in the list. In the Properties pane, change the Text property from About to Reservations.

The Text property on the About item is changed to Reservations (Figure 7-11).

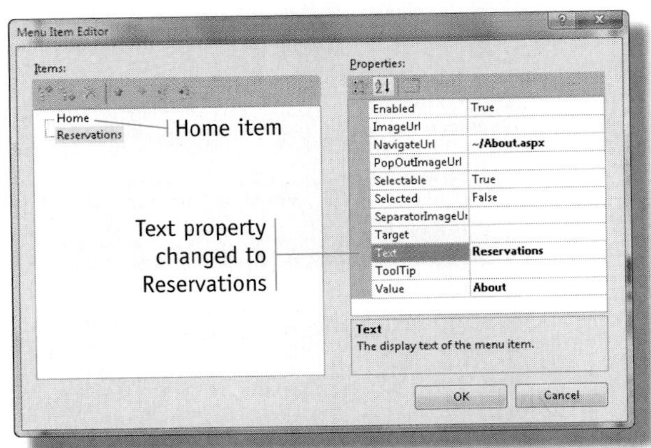

FIGURE 7-11

STEP 3 Click the OK button, and then click a blank spot on the form to close the Menu Tasks menu.

The second navigation button changes to Reservations (Figure 7-12).

FIGURE 7-12

ONLINE REINFORCEMENT

To view a video of the process in the previous steps, visit scsite.com/vb2010/ch7 and then select Figure 7-10.

Customizing the Default Page

After the Site.master is designed, the content pages in this Web site automatically inherit the changes in the page style and navigation buttons. For example, the Default.aspx page, which serves as the Home page to the Mystic Bed and Breakfast site, inherits the font and button changes made when the Master page was customized.

Adding Objects to the Web Page

Using Visual Studio's ASP.NET 4.0 objects and code, you can create interactive Web forms. You place objects on the Web page using a Toolbox similar to the one used for Windows applications, though the ASP.NET 4.0 categories of tools are different. The Mystic Bed and Breakfast chapter project uses objects in the Standard and Validation categories of the Toolbox shown in Figure 7-13.

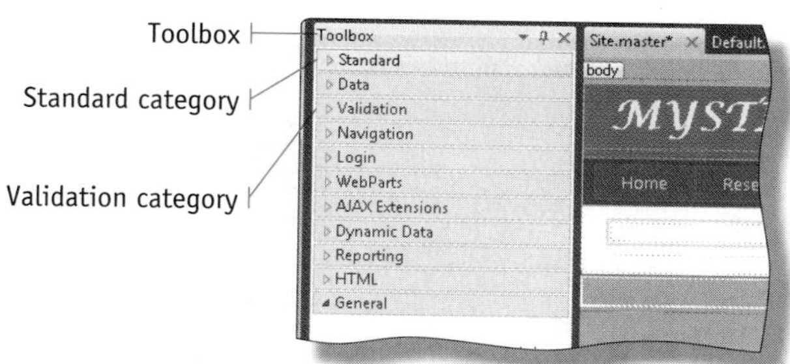

FIGURE 7-13

Toolbox objects unique to Web application objects include Login objects for allowing user access, Navigation objects for creating site maps, and Validation objects for checking Web form input. Some Windows application objects work the same way, but have different object names in the Web environment. For example, in a Windows application you use a PictureBox object to display a picture, but in an ASP.NET 4.0 Web page, you use an Image object. Both the PictureBox object and the Image object place an image into the application, but the Image object needs a URL to specify where the picture resides. The Home page displays a picture, a description, and the address of the Mystic Bed and Breakfast Inn.

Adding an Image Object to the Default Page

On the Mystic Bed and Breakfast Home page (Default.aspx), an image of the Mystic Bed and Breakfast Inn is displayed in an Image object on the left side of the page below the navigation buttons. The **Image** object is similar to the PictureBox object in a Windows application. The major difference is where the Image object is stored. Most Web pages reference a picture stored on a Web server connected to the Internet. On an ASP.NET Web form, you do this by specifying the entire URL (Web address) in the ImageUrl property of an Image object. To add an Image object that displays an image stored on a Web server, you can complete the following steps:

STEP 1 In the Solution Explorer, double-click Default.aspx. Notice that the Default.aspx page has inherited the title and Reservations navigation page from the Site.master. Select the three lines starting with WELCOME TO ASP.NET! in the MainContent area and press the DELETE key.

The Default.aspx page opens and the MainContent area is cleared (Figure 7-14).

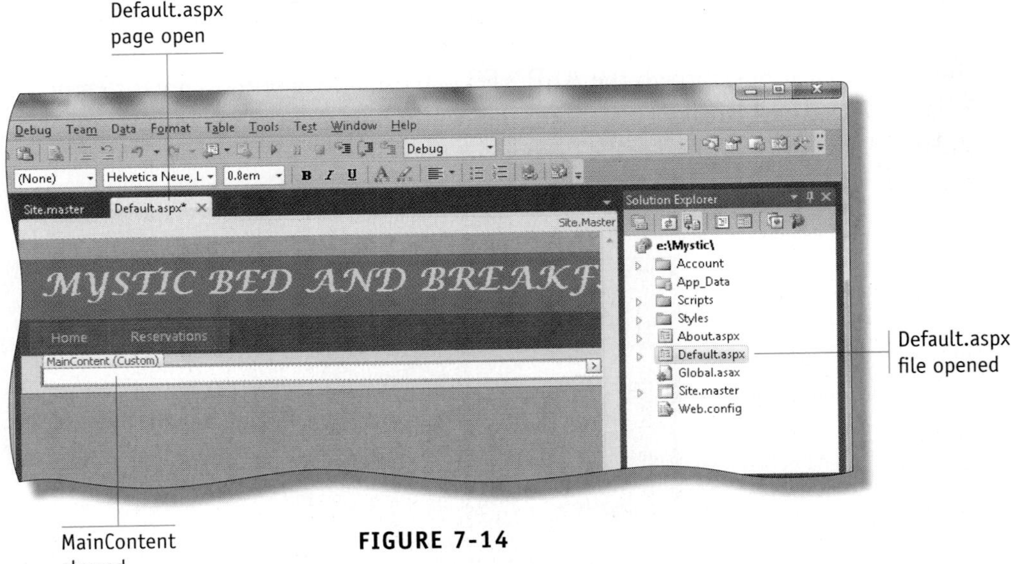

FIGURE 7-14

STEP 2 Drag the Image object from the Standard category in the Toolbox to the Web page under the navigation buttons. Resize the object so that it is 175 pixels by 150 pixels (px).

The Image object appears below the navigation buttons of the Default.aspx page and is resized (Figure 7-15). A placeholder appears in the Image object until you specify a URL or path to an image file.

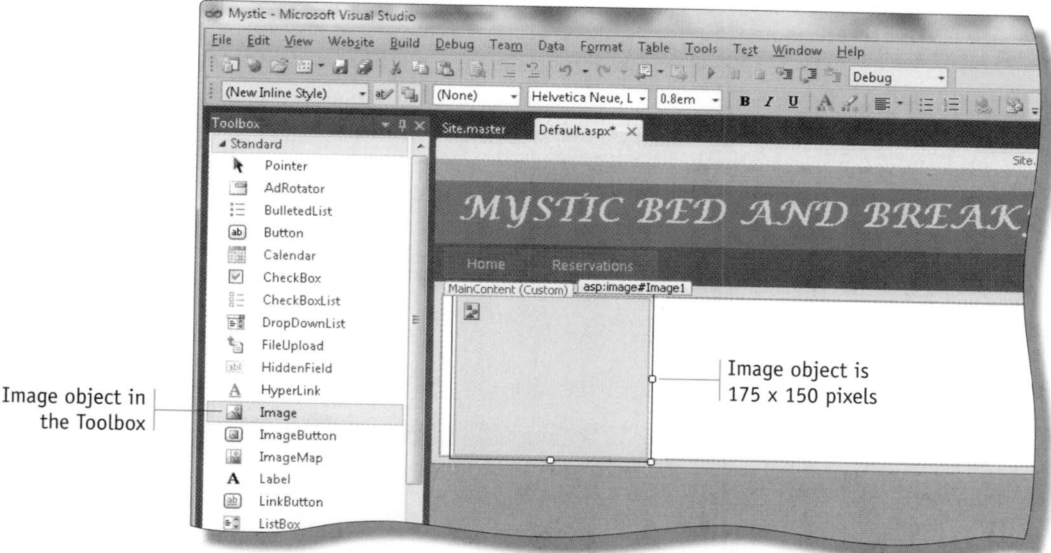

FIGURE 7-15

STEP 3 In the Properties window, name the Image object by entering `picMystic` in its (ID) property. Specify which image to display by entering the Web address `http://scsite.com/vb2010/ch7/images/bb.jpg` as the ImageUrl property. You need Internet connectivity to view the image.

The bb.jpg image appears in the Image object, replacing the placeholder (Figure 7-16).

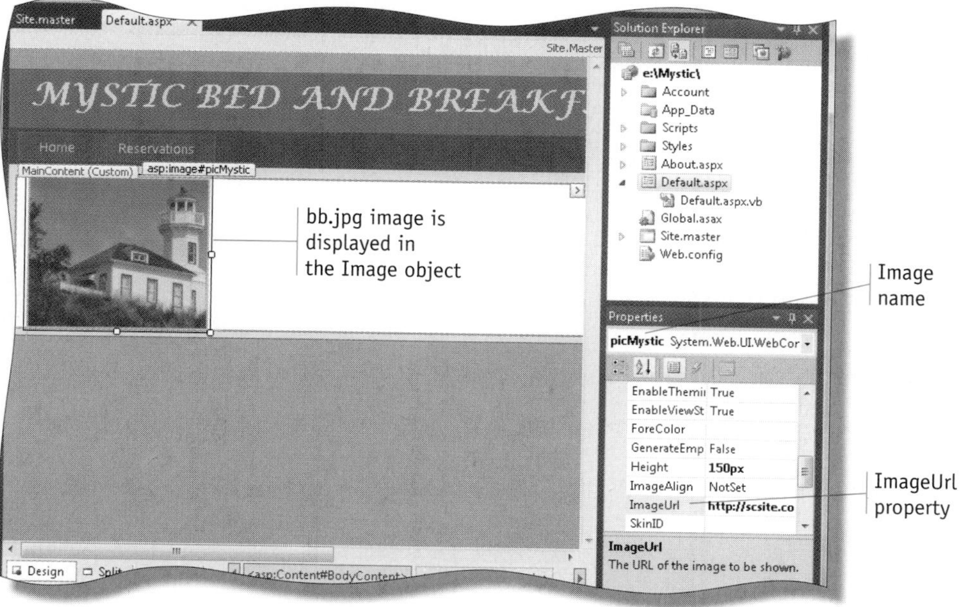

FIGURE 7-16

ONLINE REINFORCEMENT

To view a video of the process in the previous steps, visit scsite.com/vb2010/ch7 and then select Figure 7-14.

Entering Text Directly on the Web Page

ASP.NET 4.0 allows you to enter text directly on the Web page without creating labels. You should enter text directly on the page only if the text will not be changed by coded statements. Label objects are useful if you intend to change their contents after the user makes a selection on the Web page and the Web application needs to display a result. If the text is not going to change, type it directly on the page. As you type, use the SPACEBAR to add spaces and align text, and use the ENTER key to start a new line. To enter text directly on a Web page, follow these steps:

STEP 1 Click to the right of the Image object and type in all caps `WELCOME TO THE OLDEST LIGHTHOUSE BED AND BREAKFAST` directly on the Default.aspx page. Select the typed text and change the font size on the Formatting toolbar to x-large. Click a blank spot on the form to deselect the text.

The text WELCOME TO THE OLDEST LIGHTHOUSE BED AND BREAKFAST appears to the right of the picture, and the font size is changed to x-large (Figure 7-17).

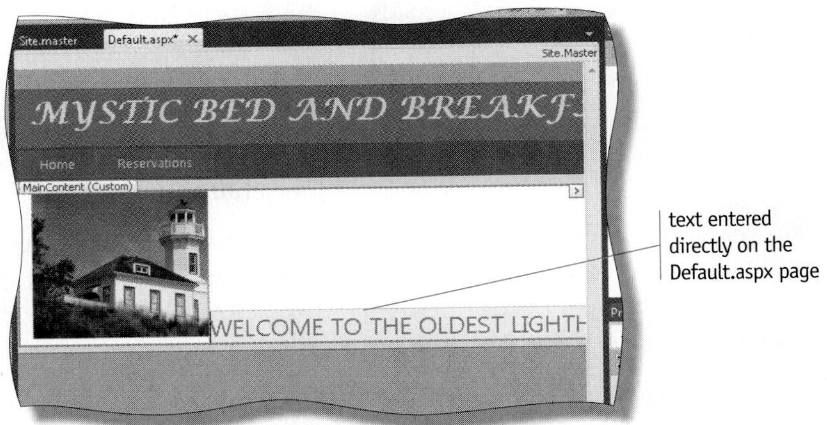

FIGURE 7-17

STEP 2 To change the vertical alignment, select the text, click the Style property, and then click the ellipsis button to the right of the Style property in the Properties window. In the Category pane of the Modify Style dialog box, click Block. In the vertical-align drop box, select top.

The Style property is changed to top vertical alignment in the Modify Style dialog box (Figure 7-18).

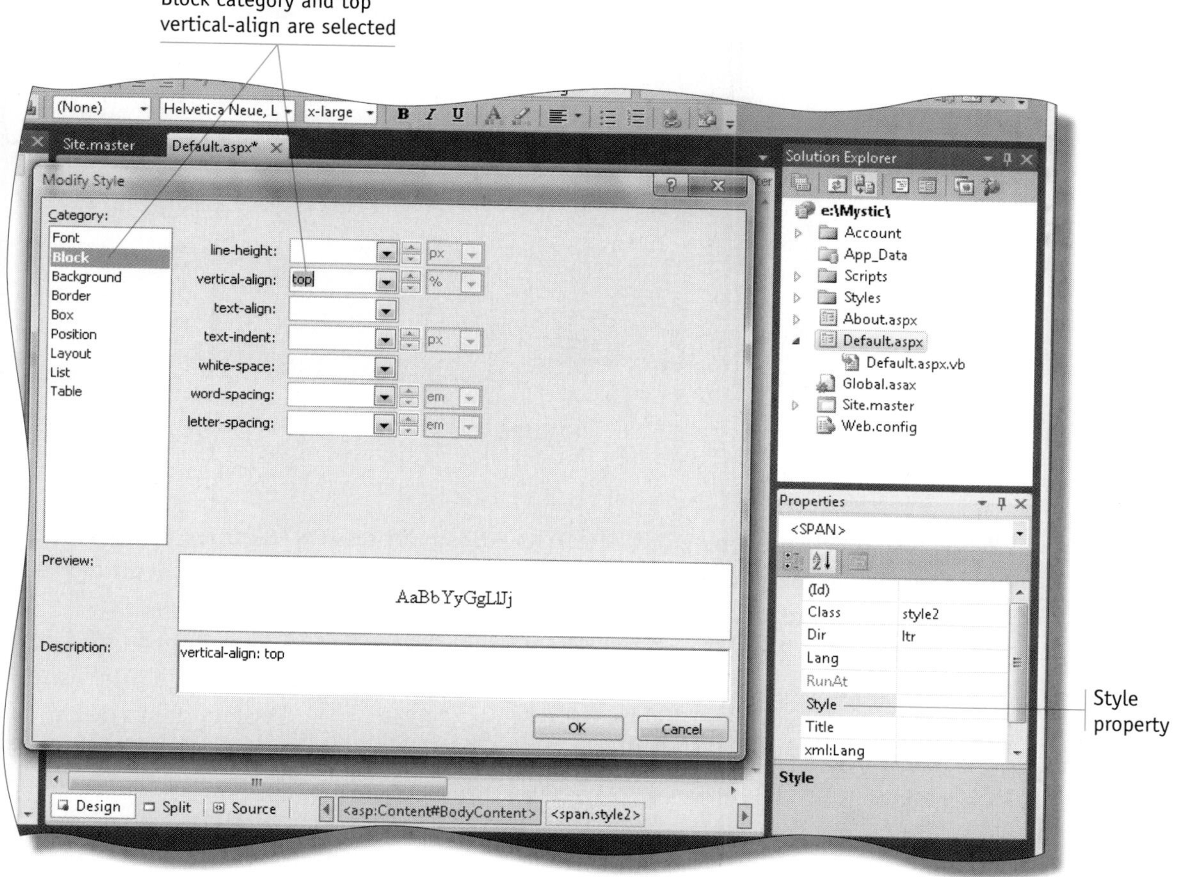

FIGURE 7-18

STEP 3 Click the OK button, and then click a blank spot to deselect the text.

The typed text is vertically aligned to the top of the MainContent area (Figure 7-19).

FIGURE 7-19

STEP 4 Click after the word BREAKFAST and press ENTER three times. Change the font size to medium in the Formatting toolbar. Enter the text `High atop a cliff jutting into the clear, deep waters of Mystic Harbor, the Mystic Lighthouse beckons families in search of a secluded retreat from modern life. This unique bed and breakfast inn is one of the few surviving resident lighthouses in the country and is listed on the National Register of Historic Places.`

The text describing the Mystic Bed and Breakfast is displayed on the page (Figure 7-20).

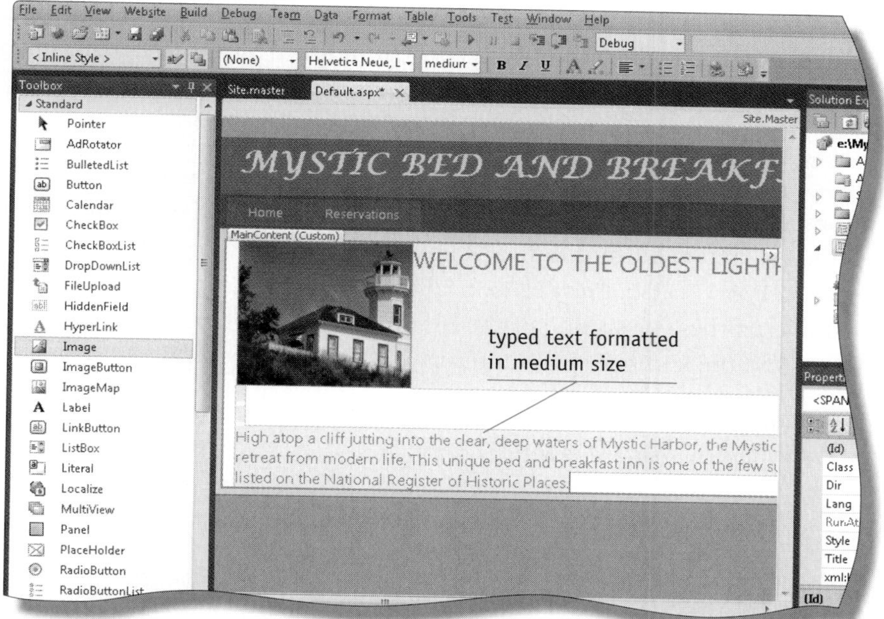

FIGURE 7-20

ONLINE REINFORCEMENT

To view a video of program execution, visit scsite.com/vb2010/ch7 and then select Figure 7-17.

Creating an ASP Web Form for the Reservations Page

Web pages are often interactive. For example, an online college application has text boxes that can be validated to be sure the information is correct. The Reservations ASP form in the Mystic Web application will request the name, e-mail address, the number of suites needed, the number of nights, and the date of arrival.

Adding a Table for Alignment on a Web Form

A table is often used to organize Web site content into columns. On the Reservations page (About.aspx), a table is used to simplify object placement. The Mystic Bed and Breakfast reservation form includes a table with seven rows and three columns filled with TextBox objects, CheckBox objects, a DropDownList object, and a Calendar object. To add a table to the Reservations page, follow these steps:

STEP 1 In the Solution Explorer window, double-click About.aspx to create a Web form for the Reservations page. Delete the text in the MainContent area. Click below the navigation buttons in the MainContent area and type `GUEST RESERVATION FORM:`. Press ENTER. Click Table on the menu bar, and then click Insert Table. In the Size section of the Insert Table dialog box, change the number of Rows to 7 and the number of Columns to 3.

The Insert Table dialog box opens and the number of rows is changed to seven and the number of columns is changed to three (Figure 7-21).

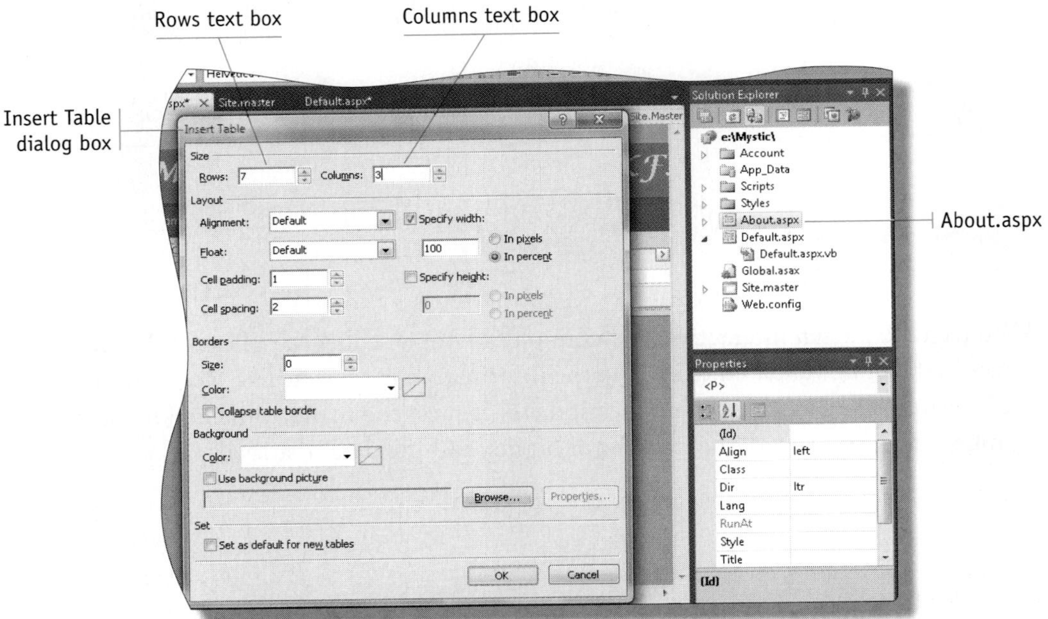

FIGURE 7-21

STEP 2 Click the OK button. To resize the columns, point to a column divider until a two-sided arrow appears. Drag the divider to change the column width. As you drag, a ScreenTip shows the width of the column in pixels. Resize the first column until it is 150 px wide. Resize the second column to 250 px wide.

The table is displayed in the About.aspx page. The column width of the first column is changed to 150 px and the second column is changed to 250 px (Figure 7-22).

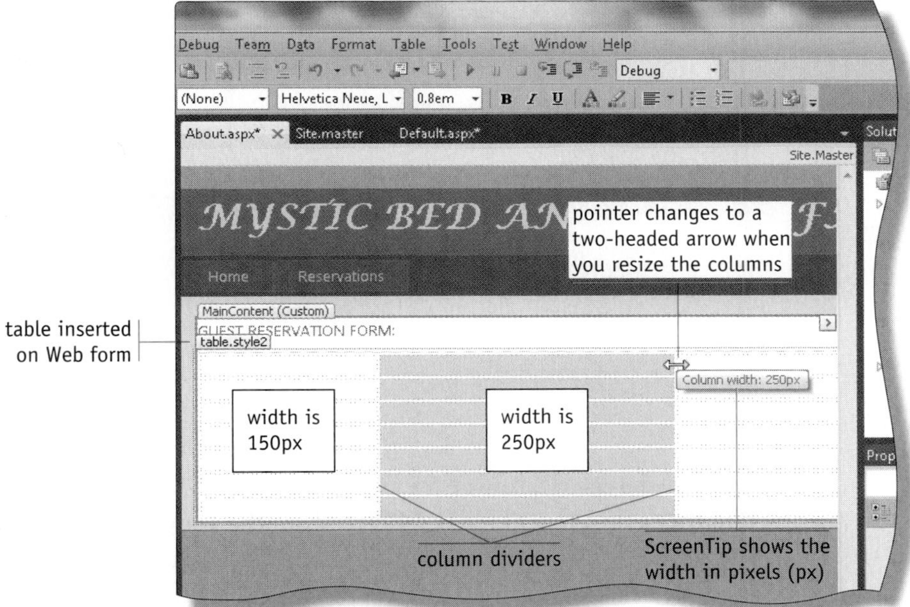

FIGURE 7-22

ONLINE REINFORCEMENT

To view a video of program execution, visit scsite.com/vb2010/ch7 and then select Figure 7-21.

Adding TextBox and Button Objects

Like other Web form objects, TextBox and Button objects are similar to their Windows counterparts apart from a few exceptions. A TextBox object on a Web page usually is provided for data entry, allowing a user to enter a name, address, e-mail address, or zip code, for example. The Text property of a TextBox object, therefore, is blank. A Button object on a Web form serves the same purpose as it does in Windows applications. Because the user generally clicks the Button object after completing the Web form, the Text property for a Button object on a Web form often is Submit. To name the TextBox and Button objects, you use the (ID) property. To add TextBox and Button objects, follow these steps:

STEP 1 On the About.aspx Web form, click in the first cell of the table and type `Name:` to enter text directly into the table. Open the Toolbox, drag a TextBox object from the Toolbox to the form, and then position the TextBox object in the second cell in the table. Resize the TextBox object to a width of 250 px. Name this TextBox object txtName using the (ID) property.

Text is typed into the first cell and a TextBox object is placed inside the second cell on the top row of the table (Figure 7-23).

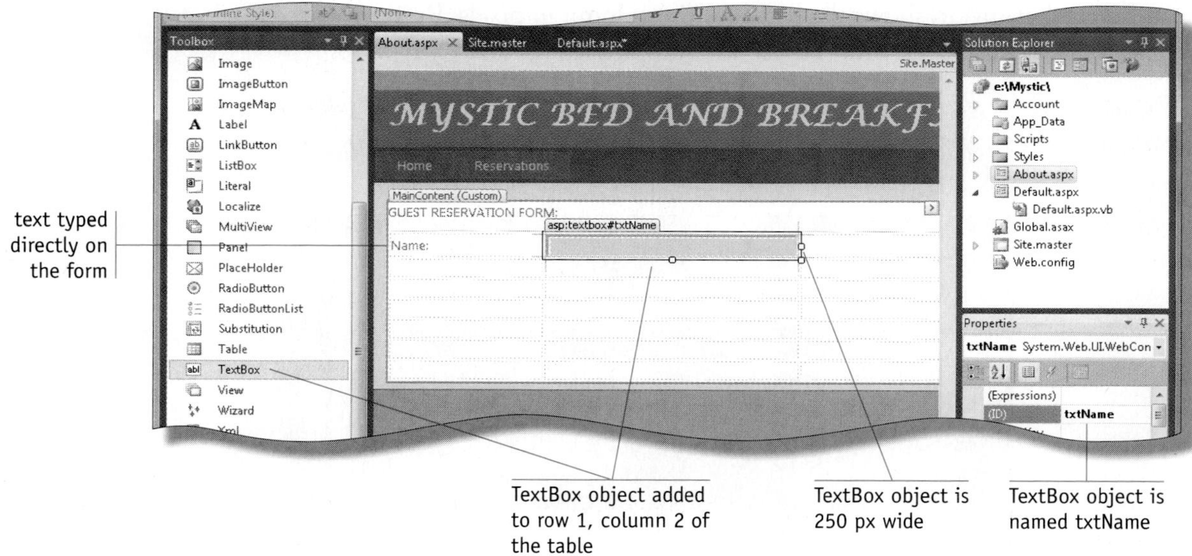

FIGURE 7-23

STEP 2 In the first cell in the second row of the table, type `E-mail Address:` to enter text directly into the table. Drag a TextBox object from the Toolbox to the form and then position the TextBox object in the second cell in the second row in the table. Resize the TextBox object to a width of 250 px. Name this TextBox object txtEmail using the (ID) property.

Text is typed into the first cell and a TextBox object is placed inside the second cell on the second row of the table (Figure 7-24).

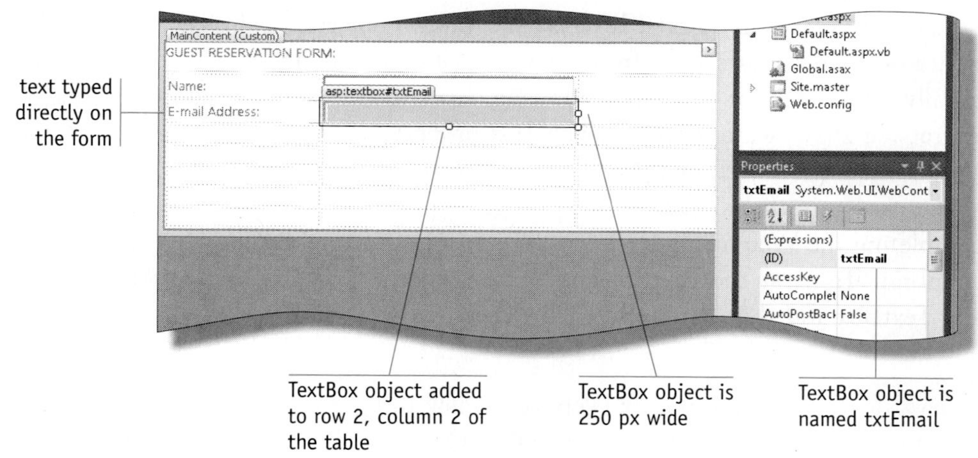

FIGURE 7-24

ONLINE REINFORCEMENT

To view a video of the process in the previous steps, visit scsite.com/vb2010/ch7 and then select Figure 7-23.

Adding CheckBox Objects

Three CheckBox objects are used in the Mystic Bed and Breakfast reservation form to determine which suite(s) the guest wants to reserve. The **CheckBox** object allows the user to choose from several options. It is similar to the RadioButton object, except the CheckBox object allows the user to pick more than one option. In contrast, the RadioButton object allows a user to choose only one option from a group of related options. The CheckBox and RadioButton objects work the same in Web, Windows, and Mobile applications

When you name a CheckBox object, you should include the chk prefix in its (ID) property. In addition, you can specify that a check box is selected by default when a form opens. For example, because the Serenity suite is the most popular suite choice at the Mystic Bed and Breakfast Inn, the check box for the Serenity suite should be selected when the page first is displayed. To specify this setting, change the Checked property of the CheckBox object from False to True.

In the Mystic Bed and Breakfast application, the user can select one or more suites based on an individual or group reservation. For example, as shown in Figure 7-25, a family might select the Serenity suite for the parents and the Evergreen suite for the children. RadioButton objects would not work in this example because only one RadioButton object can be selected at the same time within the same group.

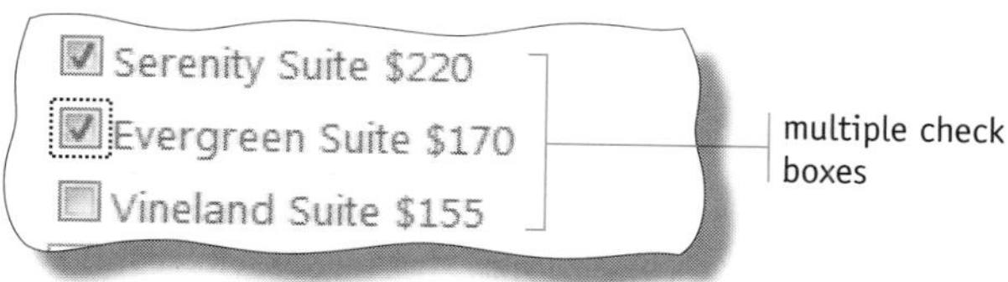

FIGURE 7-25

To place a CheckBox object on a Web form, you can complete the following steps:

STEP 1 On the third row, type `Suite Selection:` in the first cell. Drag the CheckBox object from the Toolbox to the Web form, and then position it on the third row, second cell.

The CheckBox object is placed on the Web form (Figure 7-26). The placeholder text will remain until you change the Text property. It does not, however, appear on the Web page when the page is displayed in a Web browser.

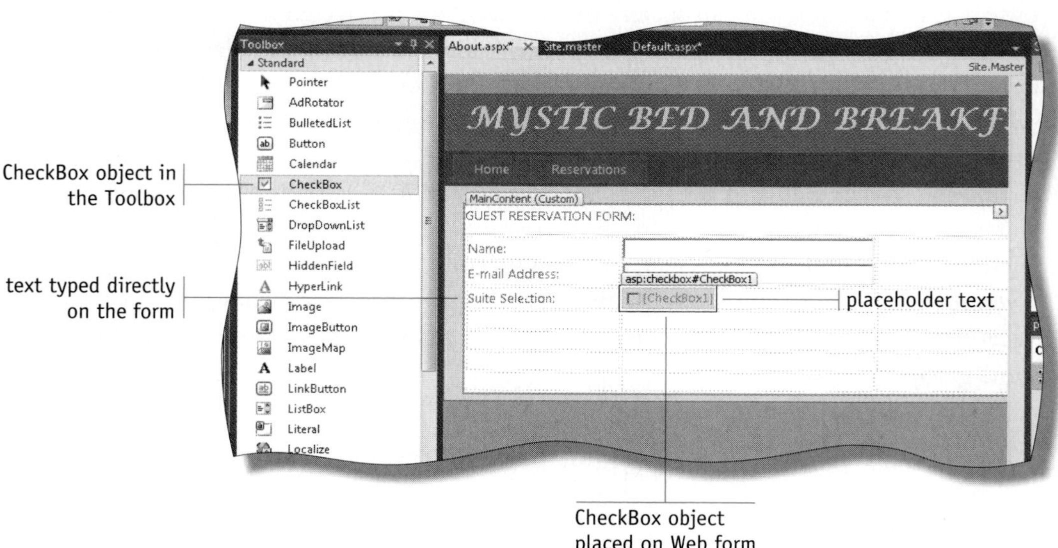

FIGURE 7-26

STEP 2 Name the CheckBox object by clicking to the right of its (ID) property in the Properties window and then entering `chkSerenity`. Change the Text property of the CheckBox object to Serenity Suite $220.

The CheckBox object is named chkSerenity in the (ID) property. After changing the Text property of chkSerenity, the CheckBox object on the form displays the new text (Figure 7-27).

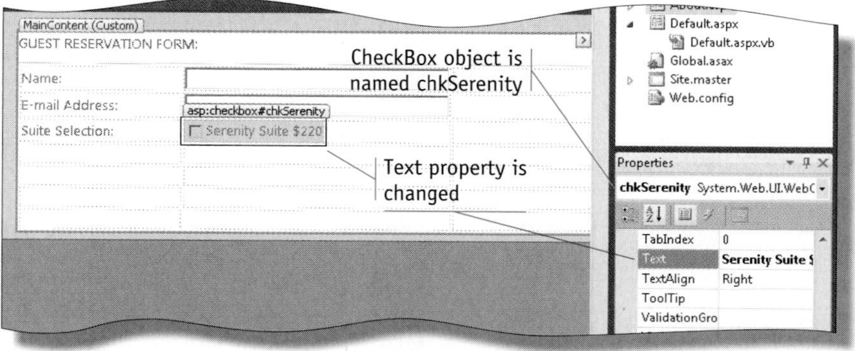

FIGURE 7-27

STEP 3 In the Mystic application, the Serenity suite is the most popular suite. This suite, therefore, should be checked when the form opens to save time for the user. To select the Serenity suite check box, change the Checked property for the object from False to True.

The Serenity Suite CheckBox object appears with a check mark on the form, and the Checked property is set to True (Figure 7-28).

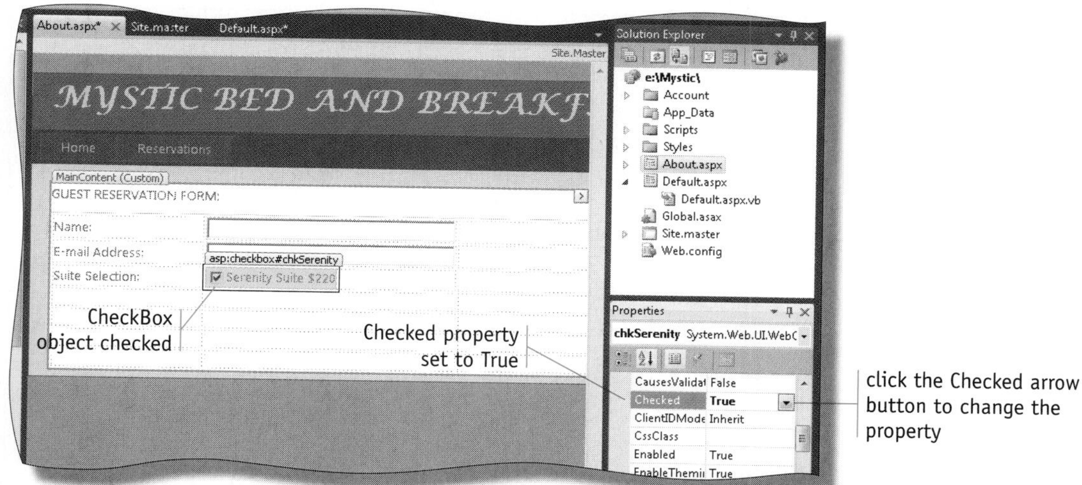

FIGURE 7-28

STEP 4 In the second column, fourth and fifth row of the table, add two more CheckBox objects named chkEvergreen and chkVineland, respectively. Change the Text property of the first CheckBox object to Evergreen Suite $170 and the second CheckBox object to Vineland Suite $155.

Two CheckBox objects are added to the form (Figure 7-29).

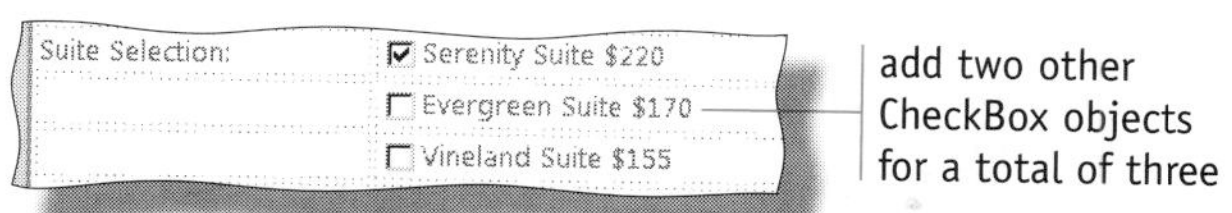

FIGURE 7-29

ONLINE REINFORCEMENT

To view a video of the process in the previous steps, visit scsite.com/vb2010/ch7 and then select Figure 7-25.

Coding for CheckBox Objects

After the user selects one or more CheckBox objects representing the suite selections and clicks the Submit button on the Web form, control returns to the Web server. On the Web server, the event handler for the Submit button can evaluate which CheckBox objects are selected. The code shown in Figure 7-30 determines which CheckBox objects are selected by referring to the Checked property, in the same manner as when RadioButton objects are checked.

```
42          If chkSerenity.Checked Then
43              decRoomCost += decSerenityCost
44          End If
45          If chkEvergreen.Checked Then
46              decRoomCost += decEvergreenCost
47          End If
48          If chkVineland.Checked Then
49              decRoomCost += decVinelandCost
50          End If
```

FIGURE 7-30

In Figure 7-30, the statement on line 42 checks the Checked property for the chkSerenity check box. If it is checked, the Serenity room cost is added to the value in the decRoomCost variable. Similarly, if the chkEvergreen check box is checked, its room cost is added to the value in the decRoomCost variable. The same is true for the chkVineland check box. If all three check boxes are checked, the value in the decRoomCost variable will be the sum of the individual room costs for all three rooms.

Adding a DropDownList Object

On the Mystic Bed and Breakfast Reservations Web form, guests can use a DropDownList object to specify the number of nights they plan to stay. The DropDownList object allows users to select one item from a predefined list. It is similar to the ListBox object used in Windows applications, except that for a DropDownList object, the list of items remains hidden until users click the list arrow button.

After adding a DropDownList object to a form and naming it, you can specify the items you want to display in the list. You often want to order these items alphabetically or numerically for ease of use. The first item in this list appears in the DropDownList object by default. The DropDownList object will not display the items in the list until you run the application and display the Web form in a browser. The user must click the list arrow to view the complete list of items during execution. The prefix for the name (ID) of the DropDownList object in Visual Basic is ddl.

In the Mystic application, a DropDownList object is used to determine the number of nights the guests plan to stay at the inn. To add a DropDownList object to the Web form, you can complete the following steps:

STEP 1 In the sixth row of the table, type `Night(s):` in the first column. Drag the DropDownList object to the second column of the sixth row. Name the DropDownList object by clicking to the right of the (ID) property in the object's Properties window and then typing `ddlNights`.

A DropDownList object appears on the Web form and is named ddlNights (Figure 7-31).

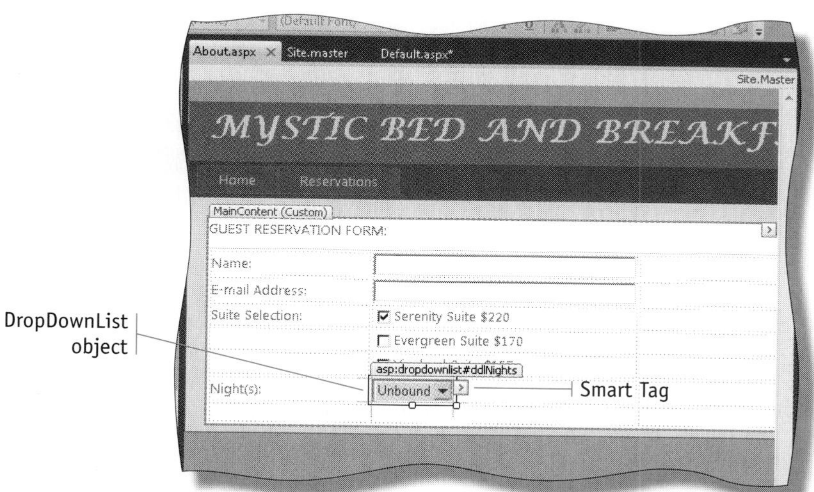

FIGURE 7-31

STEP 2 To fill the DropDownList object with list items, click the Smart Tag on the upper-right corner of the object.

The DropDownList Tasks menu opens (Figure 7-32).

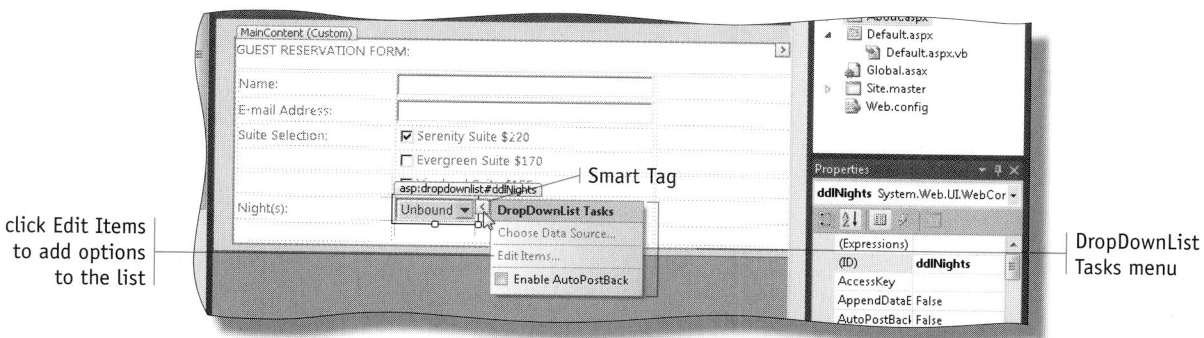

FIGURE 7-32

STEP 3 Click Edit Items on the DropDownList Tasks menu.

The ListItem Collection Editor dialog box opens (Figure 7-33).

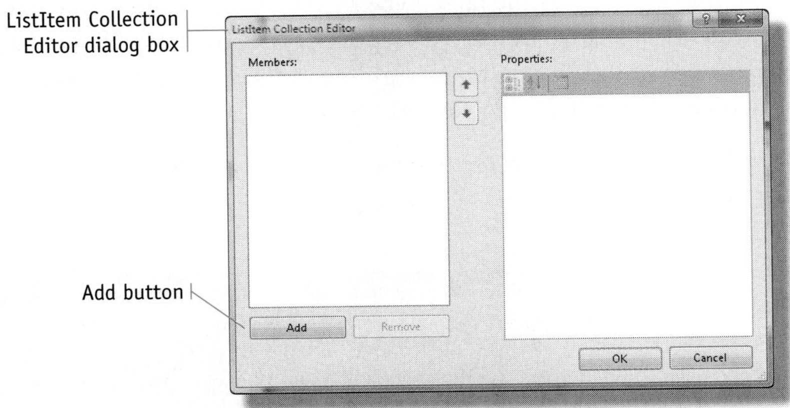

FIGURE 7-33

STEP 4 Click the Add button. In the ListItem Properties pane on the right side of the dialog box, click to the right of the Text property and enter `1` .

The number 1 is entered as the first item in the DropDownList object (Figure 7-34).

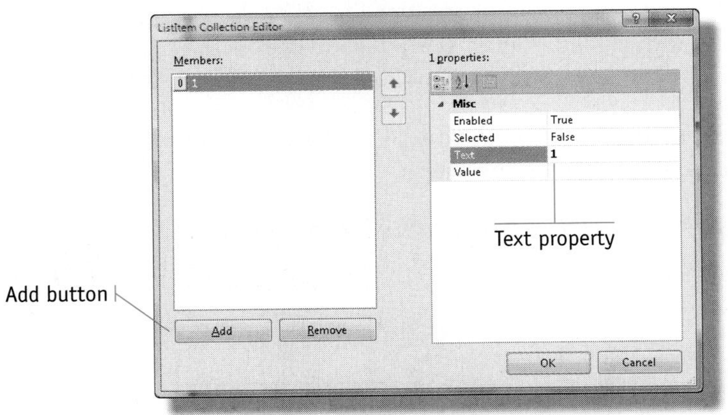

FIGURE 7-34

STEP 5 Click the Add button and enter 2 as its Text property. Repeat this step, entering the numbers 3 through 7 to specify the number of nights users can select in the DropDownList object. Click the OK button in the ListItem Collection Editor dialog box. Resize the DropDownList object to the width of a single digit, if necessary. To view the completed DropDownList object, run the application by clicking the Start Debugging button on the Standard toolbar. If necessary, click the Reservations navigation button to open the Reservations page in the browser. Click the list arrow on the DropDownList object in the Web page.

After clicking the Start Debugging button, the browser opens. After clicking the list arrow on the DropDownList object, the list item contents appear (Figure 7-35).

HEADS UP

The first time the ASP.NET application is executed, a Debugging Not Enabled dialog box may open. Select the first option to modify the Web.config file to enable debugging, and click the OK button.

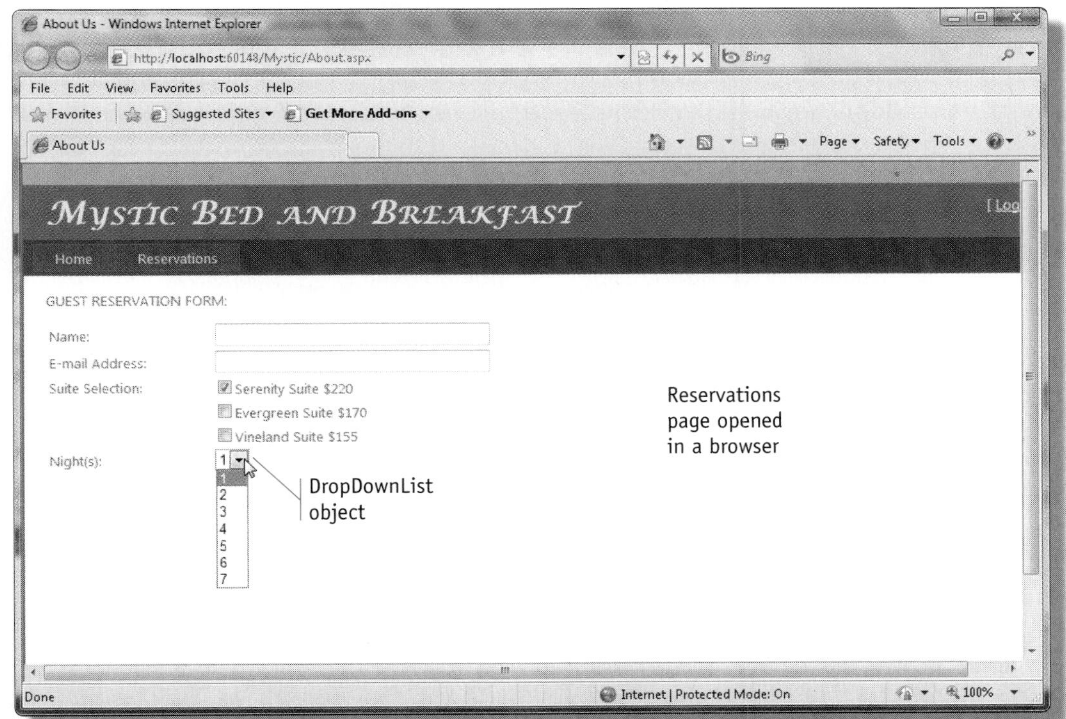

FIGURE 7-35

ONLINE REINFORCEMENT

To view a video of the process in the previous steps, visit scsite.com/vb2010/ch7 and then select Figure 7-31.

Adding a Calendar Object

The Mystic Bed and Breakfast Reservations form contains a calendar that allows guests to select their arrival date. Visual Basic provides an object to manipulate months, days, and years when specifying information such as reservations, anniversaries, or bill payments. The **Calendar** object is organized by month and displays the number of days in each month as appropriate for the year. For example, March has 31 days and February includes an extra day when the year is a leap year. By default, the Calendar object displays the current month according to the system date and selects the current day when the application is executed. You can use the Calendar object in any type of application, including Windows and Web applications. When creating a Calendar object, use the prefix cld in the name. To place the Calendar object on a Web form, you can complete the following steps:

STEP 1 Close the browser window. In the last row of the table, type `Check-in Date:`. Drag the Calendar object from the Toolbox to the Web form, and then position it on the form. In the (ID) property, name the Calendar object cldArrival.

The Calendar object is placed on the Windows form (Figure 7-36).

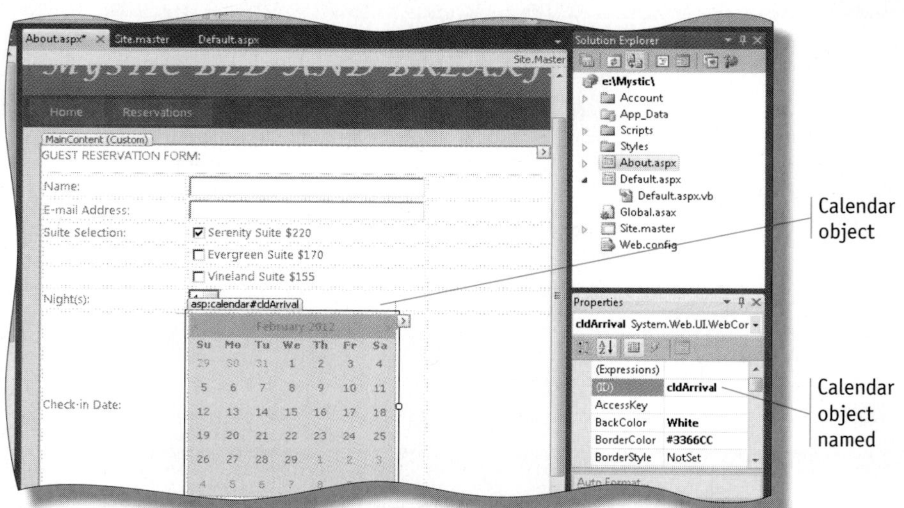

FIGURE 7-36

STEP 2 Select the Calendar object, if necessary, and then click the Smart Tag on the upper-right corner of the Calendar object.

The Calendar Tasks menu opens (Figure 7-37).

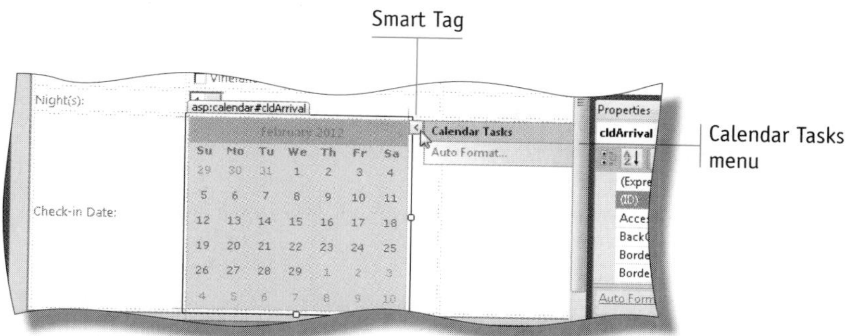

FIGURE 7-37

STEP 3 Click Auto Format on the Calendar Tasks menu. When the AutoFormat dialog box opens, click the Colorful 2 scheme in the Select a scheme list.

The AutoFormat dialog box previews the selected Colorful 2 scheme (Figure 7-38).

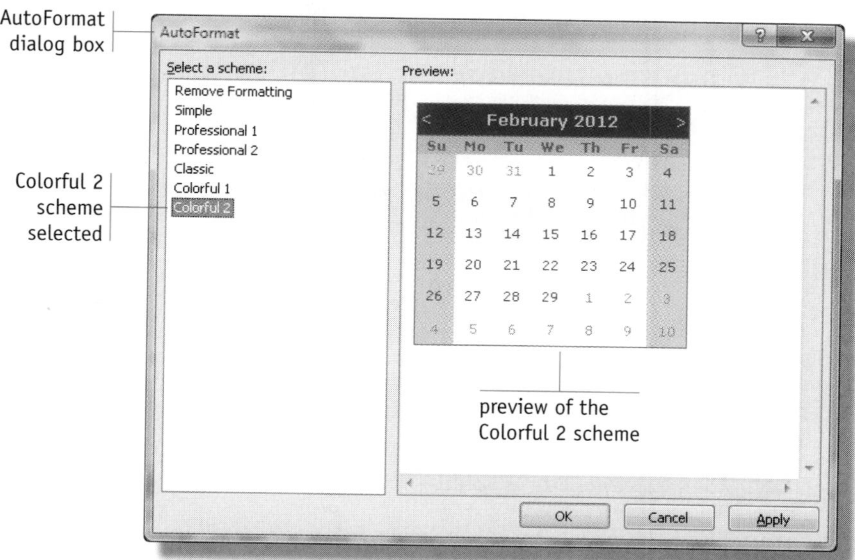

FIGURE 7-38

ONLINE REINFORCEMENT

To view a video of the process in the previous steps, visit scsite.com/vb2010/ch7 and then select Figure 7-36.

Specifying a Web Form Title

A Web form displays its title in the title bar of the browser used to view the form. You specify the title bar text for a Web form using the Title property. To change the browser Title property from its default of About Us on the Reservations page to the title, Mystic Bed and Breakfast Reservation Form, you can complete the following steps:

STEP 1 Click the OK button to close the AutoFormat dialog box. In the Properties window of the Reservations Web form, click the drop-down box at the top and select DOCUMENT.

DOCUMENT is selected in the Properties window (Figure 7-39).

FIGURE 7-39

STEP 2 In the Properties window, scroll until the Title property is visible, and then click in the right column of the Title property. Enter the title `Mystic Bed and Breakfast Reservation Form.`

The title Mystic Bed and Breakfast Reservation Form is entered in the Title property of the Properties window. This title will be displayed in the title bar of the browser for the Reservations page (Figure 7-40 on the next page).

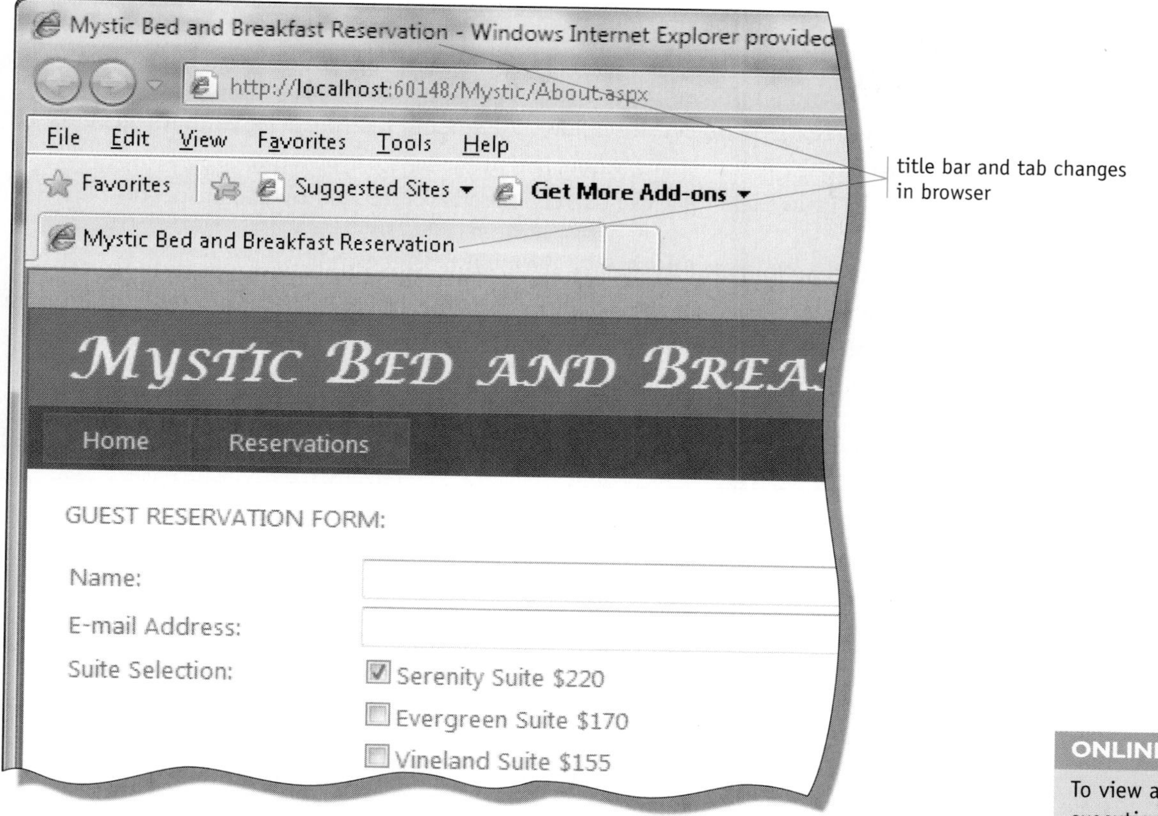

FIGURE 7-40

ONLINE REINFORCEMENT

To view a video of program execution, visit scsite.com/vb2010/ch7 and then select Figure 7-39.

Code for a Calendar Object

When using the Calendar object, two dates often are important: the selected date and the current date. In the Visual Basic code that you write in an event handler, you can include statements to reference both the selected date and the current date. The format of statements used to reference these two dates is shown in Figure 7-41.

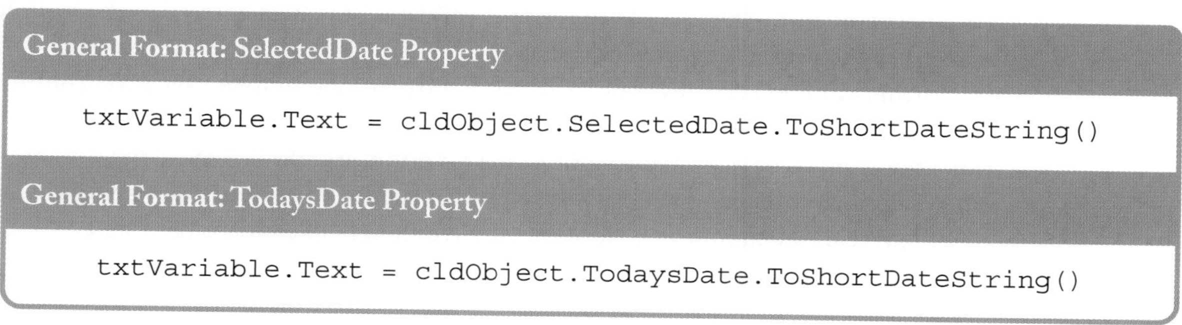

General Format: SelectedDate Property

```
txtVariable.Text = cldObject.SelectedDate.ToShortDateString()
```

General Format: TodaysDate Property

```
txtVariable.Text = cldObject.TodaysDate.ToShortDateString()
```

FIGURE 7-41

In Figure 7-41 on the previous page, the SelectedDate property references the date the user clicked in the Calendar object. In the general format, the ToShortDateString() procedure changes the date to a String format so it can be displayed in a TextBox object. If you are referencing just the selected date without the need to change it to a string value, the procedure is not required.

Similarly, in Figure 7-41, the current date is referenced by the property TodaysDate.

In the Mystic Bed and Breakfast application, it is important to ensure that the date the user selects is equal to or greater than the current date. For a reservation date, a user cannot select a date that has already passed. One of the If statements used in the sample program to test this condition is shown in Figure 7-42.

```
32        If cldArrival.SelectedDate < cldArrival.TodaysDate Then
33            lblCalendarError.Visible = True
34        Else
35            lblCalendarError.Visible = False
36        End If
```

FIGURE 7-42

In Figure 7-42, the selected date for the cldArrival Calendar object is compared to the current date (TodaysDate) for the cldArrival Calendar object. If the selected date is less than the current date, an error message is displayed; otherwise the error message is not displayed.

If the user does not click a date on the calendar prior to clicking the Submit button and running the event handler code, the Calendar object automatically returns a date that is less than the current date. Therefore, the If statement on line 32 will detect both the case when the user selects a date less than the current date, and the case when the user does not select a date.

Adding Validation Controls

An important part of creating Web forms is validating the data entered in the form to make sure the user has entered reasonable values. Instead of using a series of If statements or other complex code, ASP.NET 4.0 provides built-in validation control objects that compare a form's objects to a set rule using little or no code. The validation control objects check input forms for errors and display messages if users enter incorrect or incomplete responses. Built-in validation control objects include RequiredFieldValidator, which verifies that a required field contains data, and RangeValidator, which tests whether an entry falls within a given range.

Applying a Required Field Validator

The simplest validation control is the **RequiredFieldValidator** object, which finds a specified object to validate and determines whether the object is empty. For example, in the Mystic Bed and Breakfast application, the user must enter her first and last name. Otherwise, a reservation cannot be made. The RequiredFieldValidator object reminds the user to complete all required fields. You can customize this reminder by changing the ErrorMessage property, which often is helpful to let users know what they have done incorrectly. If the user enters a value in a field, the RequiredFieldValidator does not display an error message.

In the Mystic Bed and Breakfast reservation form, the first object to validate is the Name TextBox object, which is named txtName. You can add a RequiredFieldValidator object to the Web form that tests txtName to determine if it is empty. If it is, an error message appears reminding the user to enter a first name. After adding the RequiredFieldValidator object, you must specify that it validates the txtName TextBox object.

The prefix used for the RequiredFieldValidator is rfv. To validate a required TextBox object using a RequiredFieldValidator object, follow these steps:

STEP 1 In the Toolbox, hide the Standard tools by clicking the filled triangle icon next to Standard. Expand the Validation tools by clicking the open triangle icon next to Validation.

The seven Validation tools are displayed (Figure 7-43).

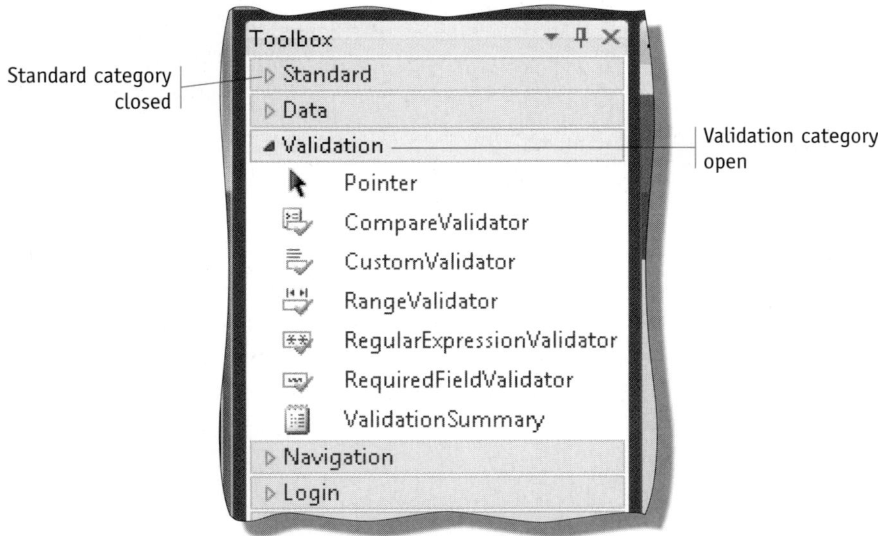

FIGURE 7-43

STEP 2 Drag the RequiredFieldValidator to the right of the Name TextBox object.

The RequiredFieldValidator object is placed to the right of txtName (Figure 7-44).

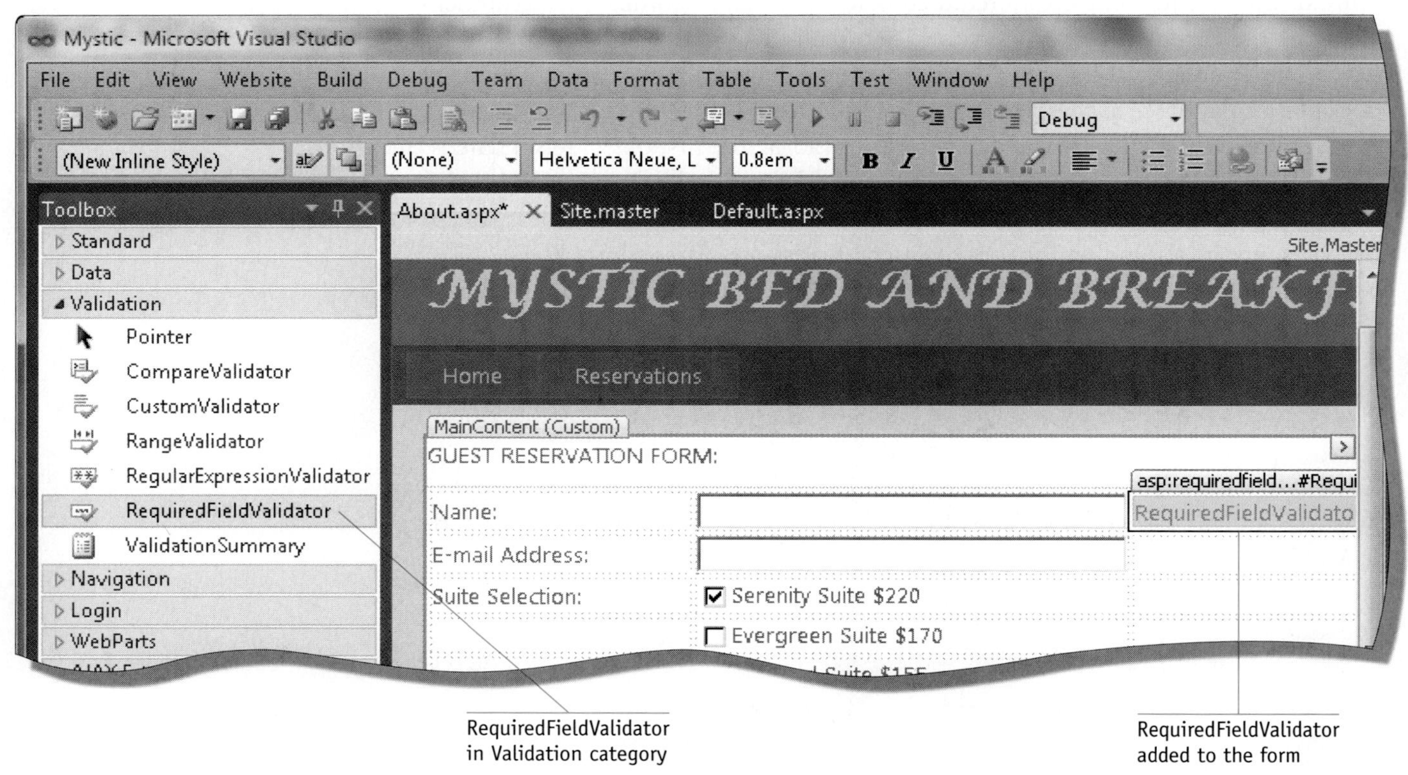

FIGURE 7-44

STEP 3 Name the RequiredFieldValidator by typing `rfvName` in its (ID) property.

The RequiredFieldValidator object is named rfvName (Figure 7-45).

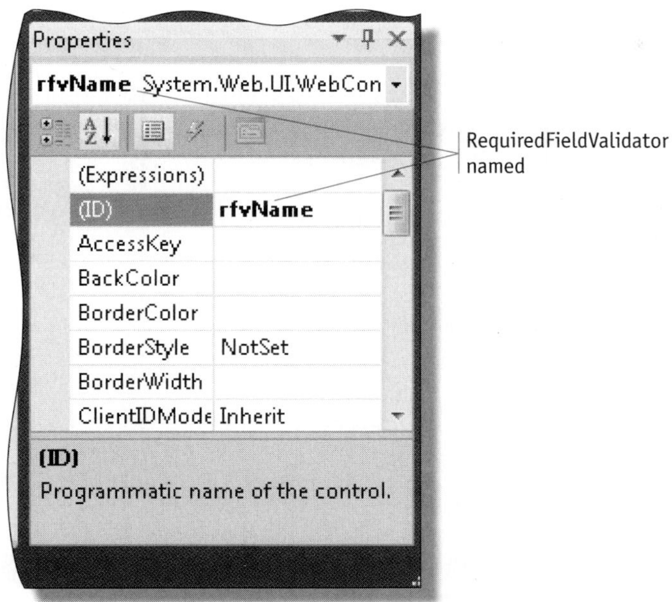

FIGURE 7-45

STEP 4 To specify that the rfvName RequiredFieldValidator object validates the txtName TextBox object, click to the right of the ControlToValidate property in the Properties window, click the list arrow, and then select txtName.

The ControlToValidate property is set to txtName (Figure 7-46).

FIGURE 7-46

STEP 5 In the Properties window for the RequiredFieldValidator, change the ErrorMessage property to *Enter Name.

*The ErrorMessage property is changed to * Enter Name (Figure 7-47).*

FIGURE 7-47

ONLINE REINFORCEMENT

To view a video of the process in the previous steps, visit scsite.com/vb2010/ch7 and then select Figure 7-43.

HEADS UP

Remember to change the data type of the RangeValidator control to compare values properly. If you forget to change the Type property from String to Integer for data such as high school grade level (9, 10, 11, or 12), the validation range will not work properly. If you set the minimum value to 9 and the maximum value to 12, the application would create an error message that states that 9 is greater than 12. The reason for the error is that the string "9" is compared to only the "1" in the number 12, and 9 comes after 1.

When the application is run on a Web browser with a Submit button, if the Submit button is clicked and no text has been entered in the txtName text box, the error message will be displayed.

Applying the Range Validator

Another validation control built into ASP.NET 4.0 is the **RangeValidator** control, which tests whether an input value falls within a given range. If you were testing whether a number entered on a Web page was a valid day in a month, the RangeValidator control could test if the day number is between 1 and 31. The RangeValidator control uses the prefix rgv in its name, and the following five properties to complete its validation:

- **ControlToValidate** property contains the name of the object you are validating.
- **MinimumValue** property contains the smallest value in the range.
- **MaximumValue** property contains the largest value in the range.
- **Type** property matches the data type of the value, such as Integer or String.
- **ErrorMessage** property explains to the user what value is requested.

Applying the Compare Validator

Another validation control is the **CompareValidator** object, which you use to compare an object's value with another object or a constant value. The CompareValidator control can also compare the value in one object to the value in another object. In the example shown in Figure 7-48, the user enters a password into a Web form, and re-enters the password to confirm that the two passwords are the same. You can use the CompareValidator control to verify that the passwords match.

FIGURE 7-48

The CompareValidator uses three properties to complete its validation:

- **ControlToValidate** property contains the name of the object that you are validating.
- **ControlToCompare** property contains the name of the object that you are comparing to the ControlToValidate property.
- **ErrorMessage** property contains a message stating that the value does not match.

In Figure 7-49, four properties are changed to apply the CompareValidator object to verify a password: (ID), ControlToCompare, ControlToValidate, and ErrorMessage. This figure also shows that the prefix for the CompareValidator object is cmv.

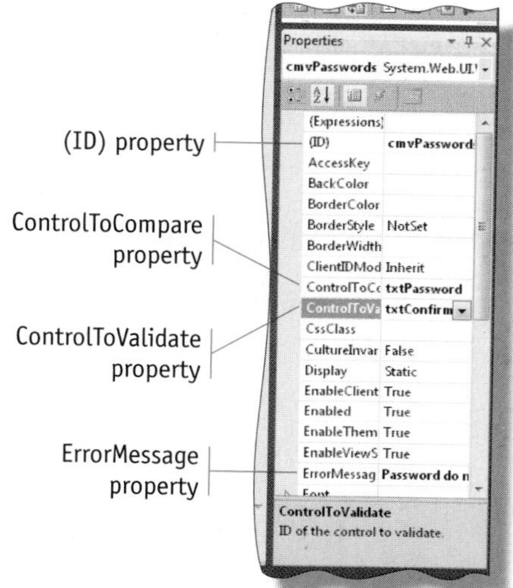

FIGURE 7-49

Applying the Regular Expression Validator

The **RegularExpressionValidator** control confirms whether the user entered data that matches standard formats such as a phone number, e-mail address, URL, zip code, or Social Security number. If the user does not enter the data in the proper format, an error message is displayed. The prefix rev is used for the RegularExpressionValidator control. The RegularExpressionValidator uses three properties to complete its validation:

- **ControlToValidate** property contains the name of the object that you are validating.
- **ErrorMessage** property contains a message stating that the value does not match the valid format.
- **ValidationExpression** property allows the user to select the format for the object.

In the Mystic Bed and Breakfast reservation form, the second TextBox object on the form requests the user's e-mail address. To confirm that the information entered is a possible e-mail address, a RegularExpressionValidator object can test the contents of the Text property of the txtEmail object and verify that it matches the format of a valid e-mail address, which follows the format of *name@isp.com.* To incorporate a RegularExpressionValidator object in a Web page, you can complete the following steps:

STEP 1 Drag the RegularExpressionValidator object from the Toolbox to the right of the E-mail Address TextBox object in the table.

The RegularExpressionValidator object is placed in the table to the right of txtEmail (Figure 7-50).

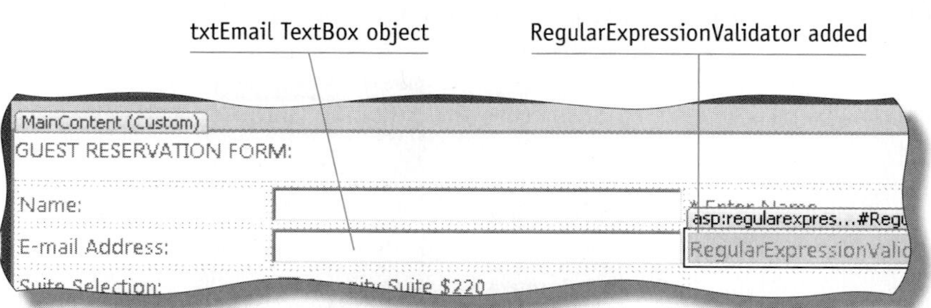

FIGURE 7-50

STEP 2 Name the RegularExpressionValidator by typing `revEmail` in its (ID) property.

The RegularExpressionValidator object is named revEmail (Figure 7-51).

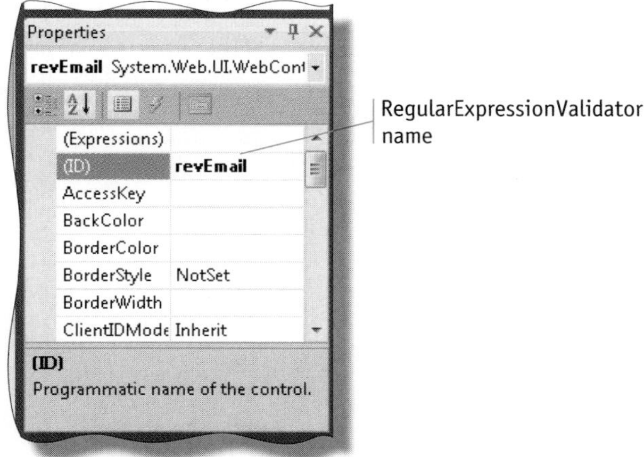

FIGURE 7-51

STEP 3 Click to the right of the ControlToValidate property, click the list arrow, and then click txtEmail.

The ControlToValidate property is set to txtEmail (Figure 7-52).

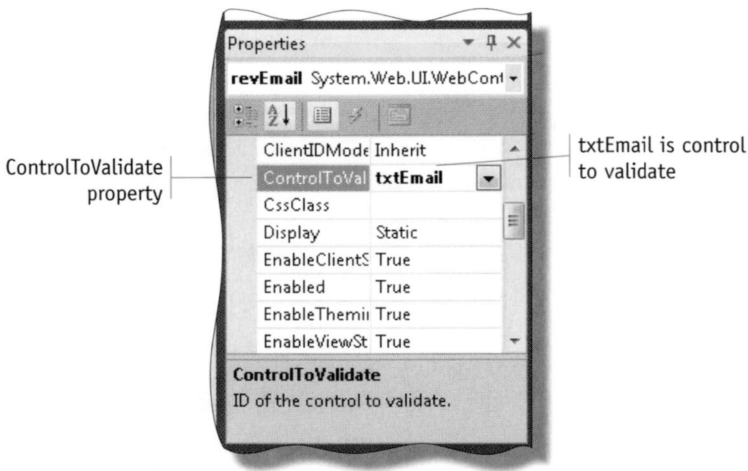

FIGURE 7-52

STEP 4 Change the ErrorMessage property to *Error E-mail Format.

*The ErrorMessage property is changed to * Error E-mail Format (Figure 7-53).*

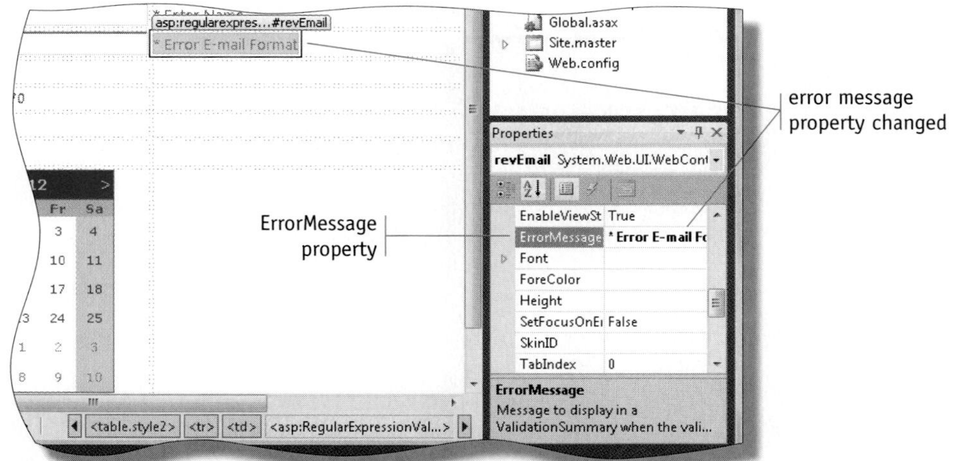

FIGURE 7-53

STEP 5 To set txtEmail to validate that it contains a standard e-mail address, click to the right of the ValidationExpression property, and then click its ellipsis button. In the Regular Expression Editor dialog box, select Internet e-mail address in the Standard expressions list.

The Internet e-mail address is selected as the standard expression to validate (Figure 7-54).

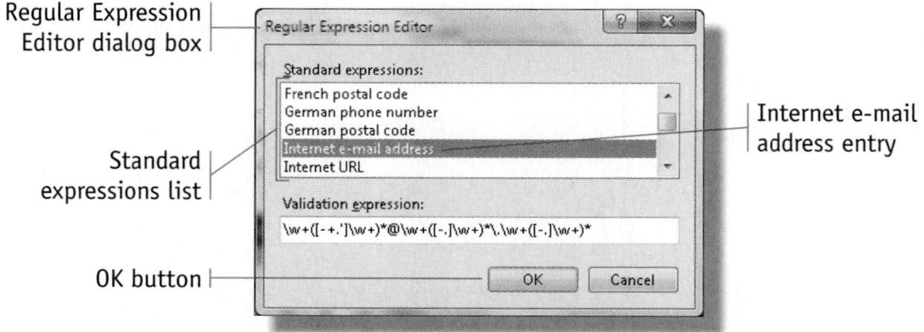

FIGURE 7-54

STEP 6 Click the OK button in the Regular Expression Editor dialog box. Run the application by clicking the Start Debugging button on the Standard toolbar. Enter a name and an e-mail address without an @ symbol, such as Brit.world.net, and then press the ENTER key.

An error message appears to the right of the E-mail Address TextBox object (Figure 7-55). When a valid e-mail address is entered and the ENTER key is pressed again, the error message is removed.

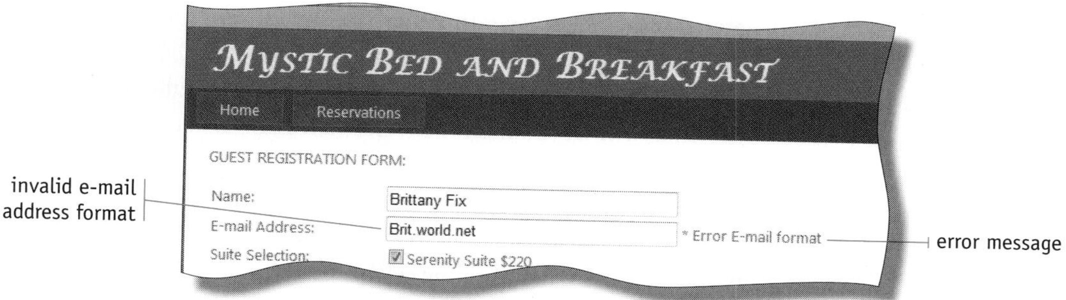

FIGURE 7-55

ONLINE REINFORCEMENT

To view a video of program execution, visit scsite.com/vb2010/ch7 and then select Figure 7-50.

Applying Multiple Validations

You can apply more than one type of validation control on an object to validate more than one aspect of the data. Often you may want to make a certain control required using the RequiredFieldValidator object, and to check the range using the RangeValidator object. In Figure 7-56, a RequiredFieldValidator confirms that the number of hours worked is not left blank, and the RangeValidator verifies that the number entered is between 1 and 60. Each validation control displays an error message if the object does not meet the specified criteria.

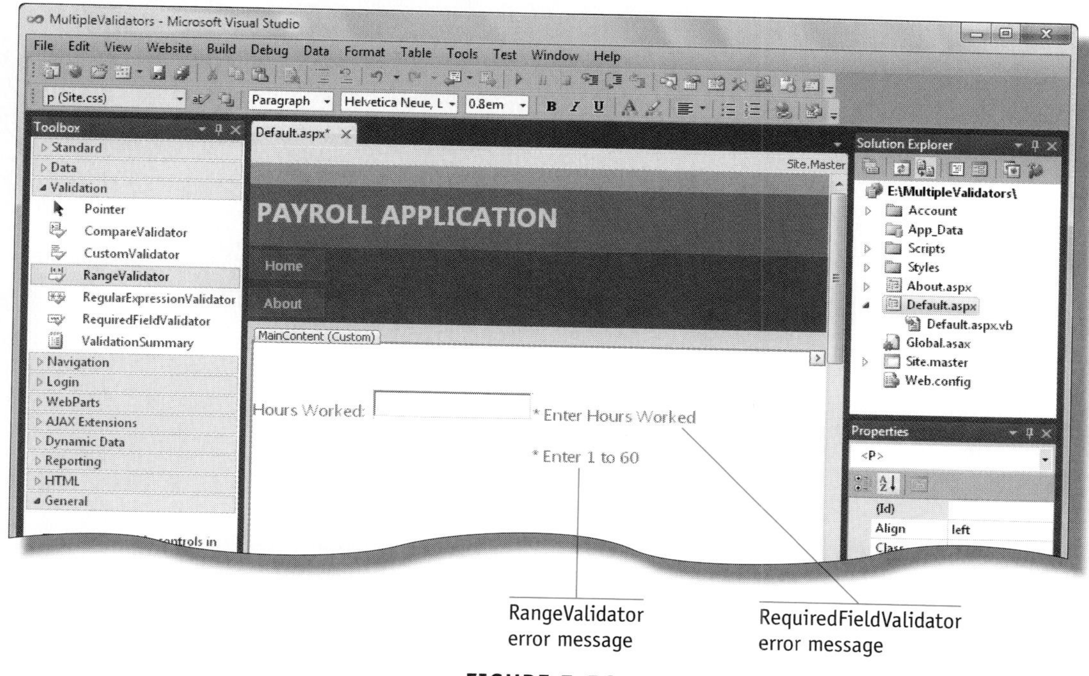

FIGURE 7-56

Displaying a ValidationSummary Control

Instead of validating data, the **ValidationSummary** control lets you display validation error messages in a single location, creating a clean layout for the Web form. By default, each validation control displays an error message next to the object it validates. On a large or complex form, however, the error messages might interfere with data or other objects. You can use the ValidationSummary object to display all of the error messages in a different place, listing them in a blank area at the top or bottom of the form, for example, where they will appear together when the validation criteria for any control is not met.

To use a ValidationSummary object, drag the object to the location on the Web page where you want the summary to appear. The prefix used for naming the ValidationSummary object is vsm. You do not have to set any properties, such as ControlToValidate, because the summary displays the error messages for all the other validation objects.

Using the
 Tag in Visual Basic Code

One HTML tag often used when creating Web pages is the **
** tag, which stands for break; it breaks the text by starting a new line. When you are creating a Web form in Visual Basic, you can use the <br> tag to skip a line before starting a new one in a Label object.

In the Mystic Bed and Breakfast chapter project, after the user enters reservation information, a confirmation message is displayed that includes details about the reservation such as the name, e-mail address, cost of the rooms, date, and number of nights (Figure 7-57).

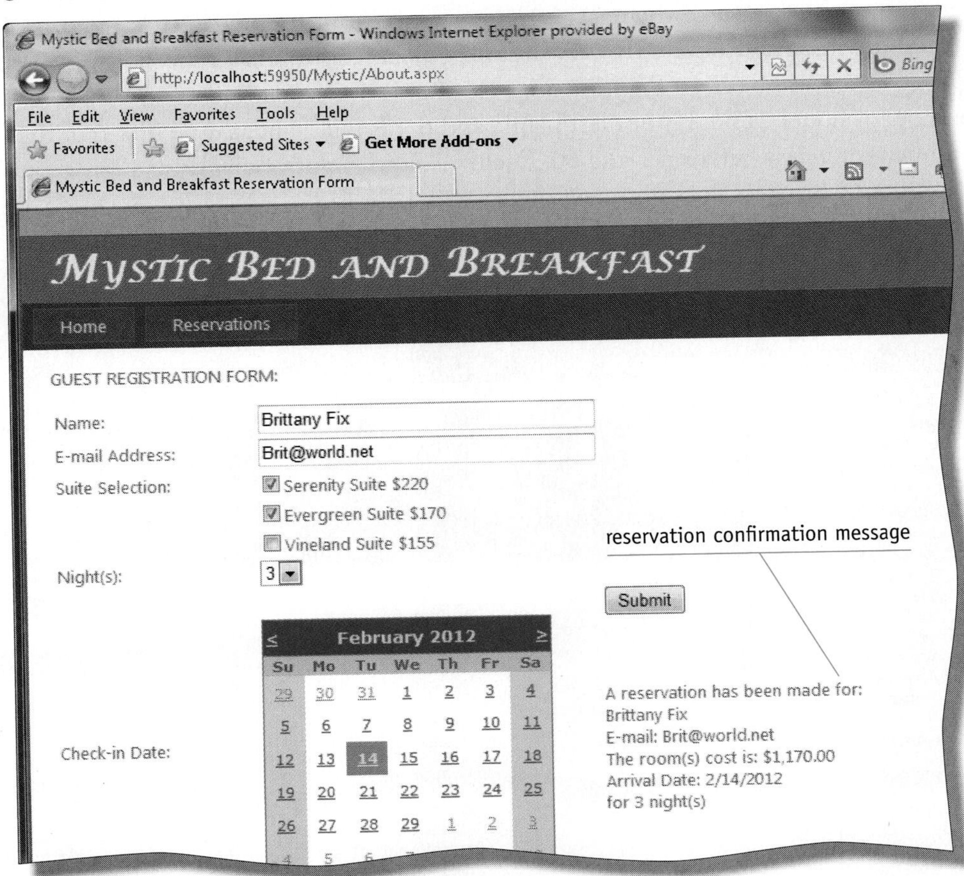

FIGURE 7-57

In Figure 7-57 on the previous page, the message consists of four lines. Each of the lines except the last line ends with the <br> tag so that the text that follows will be on the next line. The code to create the message is shown in Figure 7-58.

```
53    strMessage = "A reservation has been made for: " & "<br>" _
54        & strName & "<br>" & "E-mail: " & strEmail & "<br>"
55    strMessage &= "The room(s) cost is: " _
56        & decRoomCost.ToString("C") & "<br>"
57    strMessage &= "Arrival Date: " _
58        & cldArrival.SelectedDate.ToShortDateString() _
59        & "<br>" & " for " & intNumberOfNights & " night(s)"
60    lblReservation.Text = strMessage
```

FIGURE 7-58

In Figure 7-58, the message to be displayed is built in the strMessage String variable. On line 53, the first line of the message is placed in the variable. The last item in the string is the <br> tag, which will cause the text that follows to be on the next line. Notice that the tag must be within double quotation marks because it is a string.

The statements on lines 54 and 56 also end with the <**br**> tag. As a result of the statements in Figure 7-58, a five-line message will be created.

Using String Manipulation Properties and Procedures in the String Class

The String class in Visual Basic has many properties and procedures that allow you to manipulate strings, which you often need to do when developing Web forms. For example, you might want to find the length of the string that the user entered or convert lowercase text to uppercase. The commands discussed in this section work with ASP.NET 4.0 as well as in any Windows or mobile application.

Finding String Length

You can use the **Length** property to determine the number of characters in a particular string. The syntax for determining string length is shown in Figure 7-59.

General Format: Determine String Length

```
intValue = strName.Length
```

FIGURE 7-59

In the statement intLength = "Visual Basic".Length, the value placed in the intLength Integer variable would be 12 because the Length property counts spaces as well as characters. The code shown in Figure 7-60 determines if the zip code entered in the txtZipCode TextBox object has a length of five characters.

```
        Dim intCount As Integer

        intCount = txtZipCode.Text.Length
        If intCount <> 5 Then
            lblError.Text = "You must enter 5 digits"
        End If

```

FIGURE 7-60

If you enter only four digits in the zip code, as shown in Figure 7-61, a message appears reminding you to enter five digits.

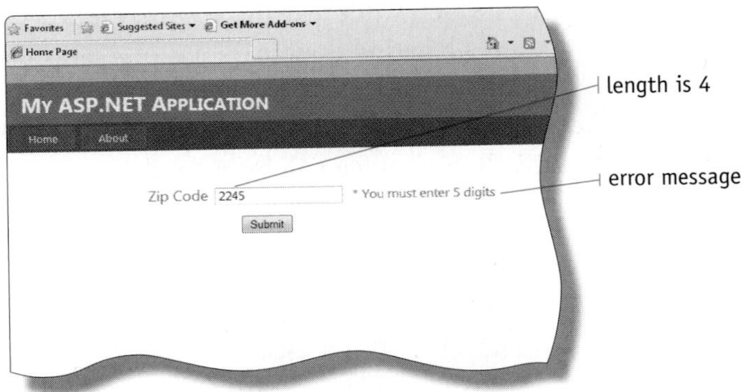

FIGURE 7-61

Using the Trim Procedure

When entering information into a TextBox object, the user might accidentally add extra spaces before or after the input string. When that string is used later, the extra spaces might distort the format of the output. To prevent this, Visual Basic provides a procedure named **Trim** to remove spaces from the beginning and end of a string. The syntax for the Trim procedure is shown in Figure 7-62.

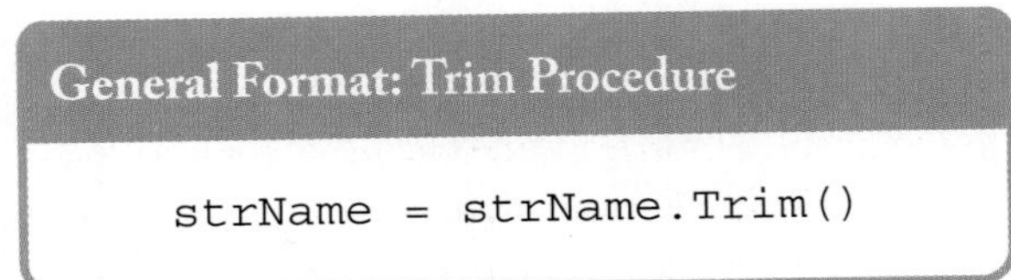

FIGURE 7-62

In the Mystic Bed and Breakfast reservation form, the user enters their name and an e-mail address. If the user includes spaces before or after the entries, the spaces will appear in the final output. The Trim procedure shown in Figure 7-63 removes extra spaces.

```
        ' Trim additional spaces that are entered by the user
        strName = txtName.Text.Trim
        strEmail = txtEmail.Text.Trim
```

FIGURE 7-63

Converting Uppercase and Lowercase Text

The **ToUpper** and **ToLower** procedures convert a string to all uppercase or all lowercase, respectively. The following syntax in Figure 7-64 shows how to use the ToUpper and ToLower procedures:

General Format: UpperCase and LowerCase Procedures

```
strName = strName.ToUpper()

strName = strName.ToLower()
```

FIGURE 7-64

When you compare a string, Visual Basic checks if you entered the word as specified. For example, if you enter YES in response to a question, but the code accepts only yes, the If statement as shown in Figure 7-65 would convert the response of YES to yes. The ToUpper() and ToLower() methods save coding time because all the possible ways to enter a response do not have to be compared.

```
        If strAnswer.ToLower() = "yes" Then
```

FIGURE 7-65

Program Design

As you have learned, the requirements document identifies the purpose of the program being developed, the application title, the procedures to be followed when using the program, any equations and calculations required in the program, any conditions within the program that must be tested, notes and restrictions that must be followed by the program, and any other comments that would be helpful to understanding the problem. The requirements document for the Mystic Bed and Breakfast Web application is shown in Figure 7-66 and the Use Case Definition is shown in Figure 7-67 on the next page.

REQUIREMENTS DOCUMENT

Date submitted: January 30, 2012

Application title: Mystic Bed and Breakfast Web Application

Purpose: This application allows the user to book a reservation at the Mystic Bed and Breakfast Inn using a Web form.

Program Procedures: From a Web application, the user should complete an online reservation form to enter the guest's name, e-mail address, starting date, number of nights, and room preference. The total cost of the stay should be calculated and displayed.

Algorithms, Processing, and Conditions:

1. The user must be able to enter the requested reservation information on a Web form. The information should include the guest's name, e-mail address, starting date of the stay, number of nights, and which rooms they prefer. The user can select one or more rooms from the following choices: Serenity Suite $220 a night, Evergreen Suite $170 a night, and Vineland Suite $155 a night.
2. After entering the reservation information, the user clicks the Submit button.
3. The information entered is validated.
4. The application displays the final cost of the stay.

Notes and Restrictions:

1. Data in the Name TextBox object is required. The data in the E-mail TextBox object is validated to confirm that it is in an e-mail address format. The Calendar object is checked to confirm that a date is selected and that the selected date is not before the current date. The maximum length of stay is 7 nights.

Comments:

1. Display a picture of the Mystic Bed and Breakfast Inn on the Web form.

FIGURE 7-66

USE CASE DEFINITION

1. The Web page opens, displaying the title Mystic Bed and Breakfast with a picture as well as TextBox objects to enter the guest's name and e-mail address. A Calendar object is used to select the beginning date of the reservation. A DropDownList object is used to enter the number of nights. The room preferences are entered with CheckBox objects.
2. User clicks the Submit button.
3. The data entered is checked and validated.
4. If necessary, the user makes corrections and resubmits the data.
5. The application confirms the reservation and displays the final cost of the stay.

FIGURE 7-67

Event Planning Document

You will recall that the event planning document consists of a table that specifies an object in the user interface that will cause an event, the action taken by the user to trigger the event, and the event processing that must occur. The event planning document for the Mystic Bed and Breakfast Web program is shown in Figure 7-68.

EVENT PLANNING DOCUMENT

Program Name: Mystic Bed and Breakfast Web Application	**Developer:** Corinne Hoisington	**Object:** Default.aspx	**Date:** January 30, 2012
OBJECT	**EVENT TRIGGER**	**EVENT PROCESSING**	

btnSubmit	Click	Validate the name to confirm it is not empty
		Validate e-mail address to confirm it is in the e-mail address format
		Trim extra spaces from name and e-mail data
		Blank the reservation message
		If a suite has not been selected
		  Display a suite error message
		  If arrival date is not valid
		    Display a calendar error message
		  Else
		    Hide the calendar error message
		Else
		  Hide suite error message
		  If arrival date is valid
		    Accumulate room costs
		    Convert number of nights to Integer
		    Calculate cost of room (total room costs * number of nights)
		    Create the reservation message
		    Display the reservation message
		  Else
		    Display calendar error message	

FIGURE 7-68

Code the Program

After identifying the events and tasks within the events, you are ready to create the program. As you have learned, creating the program means designing the user interface and then entering Visual Basic statements to accomplish the tasks specified on the event planning document. As you enter the code, you also will implement the logic to carry out the required processing.

Guided Program Development

To design the user interface for the mystic bed and breakfast web application and enter the code required to process each event in the program, complete the following steps:

NOTE TO THE LEARNER

As you will recall, in the following activity, you should complete the tasks within the specified steps. Each of the tasks is accompanied by a Hint Screen. The purpose of the Hint Screen is to indicate where in the Visual Studio window you should perform the activity; it also serves as a reminder of the method that you should use to create the user interface or enter code. If you need further help completing the step, refer to the figure number identified by the term ref: in the step.

Guided Program Development

Phase 1: Customize the Master and Home Pages

1

- **Begin the Web Application** Start Visual Studio, and then create a Visual Basic Web Site Application project by clicking the New Web Site button on the Standard toolbar. In the center pane, click ASP.NET Web Site, if necessary. Enter the project name `Mystic` and store the program on the e: drive (or a network or USB drive of your choice). Click the OK button *(ref: Figure 7-4)*.

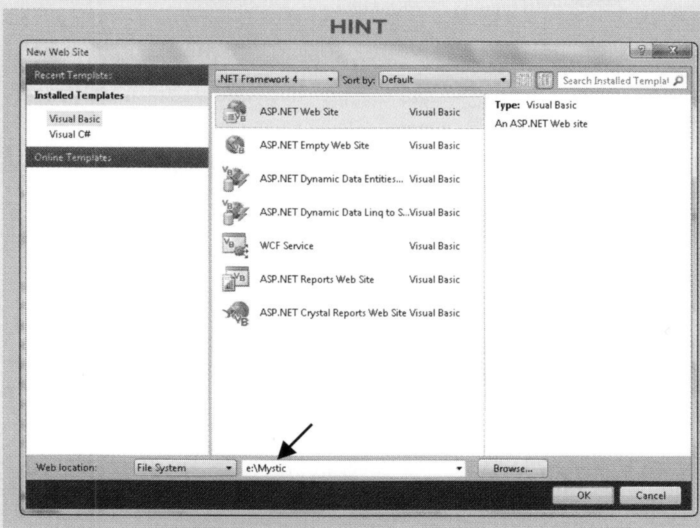

- **Change the Heading on the Site Master page** In the Solution Explorer window, double-click the Site.master page. On the page, select the heading MY ASP.NET APPLICATION. Type `MYSTIC BED AND BREAKFAST`. Select the typed title. On the Formatting toolbar, change the font to Lucida Calligraphy and the font size to xx-large.

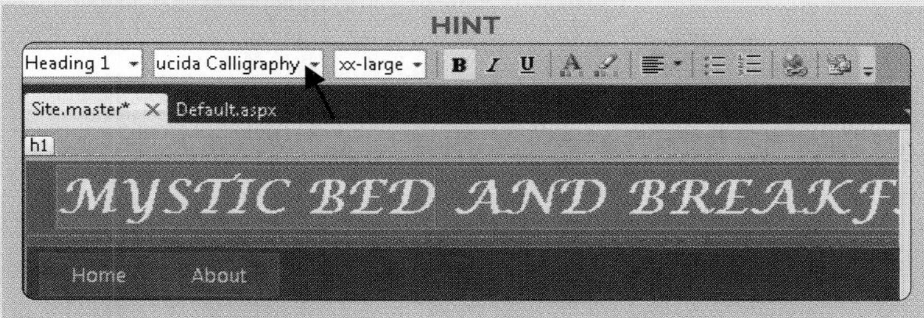

- **Change the Second Navigation Button** Point to the navigation buttons and then click the Smart Tag. Click Edit Menu Items. Click the About item. In the Properties window, change the Text property to Reservations and then click OK *(ref: Figure 7-11)*.

- **Add an Image Object** Double-click the Default.aspx page. Delete the three lines of text in MainContent area. Drag an Image object below the navigation buttons in the MainContent area of the Default.aspx page. Name the Image object picMystic. Resize the Image object to the size 175,150. Change its ImageUrl property to http://scsite.com/vb2010/ch7/images/bb.jpg *(ref: Figure 7-15)*.

- **Display the Formatting Toolbar** Click View on the menu bar, point to Toolbars, and then click Formatting.

(continues)

Guided Program Development *continued*

- **Type Directly on the Page** Click to the right of the Image object and type `WELCOME TO THE OLDEST LIGHTHOUSE BED AND BREAKFAST`. Highlight the text and change the font size to x-large. Click the ellipsis button of the Style property in the Properties window. In the Modify Style dialog box, select the Block category and then select top in the vertical-align box. Click the OK button. Press ENTER three times and change the font size to medium. Type the text `High atop a cliff jutting into the clear, deep waters of Mystic Harbor, the Mystic Lighthouse beckons families in search of a secluded retreat from modern life. This unique bed and breakfast inn is one of the few surviving resident lighthouses in the country and is listed on the National Register of Historic Places.` *(ref: Figure 7-17)*.

HINT

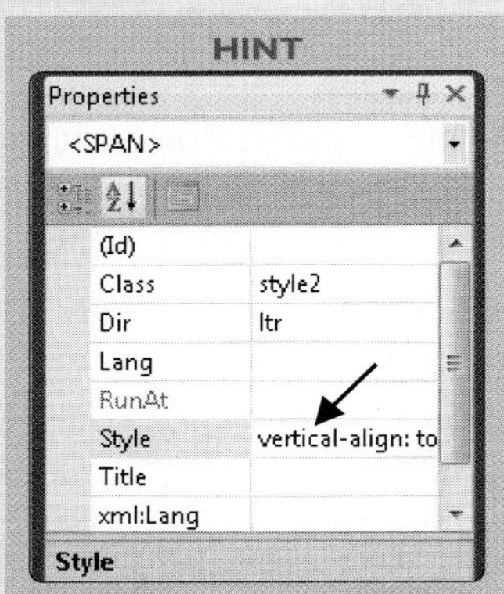

The Default.aspx Web page includes an image and typed text (Figure 7-69).

RESULT OF STEP 1

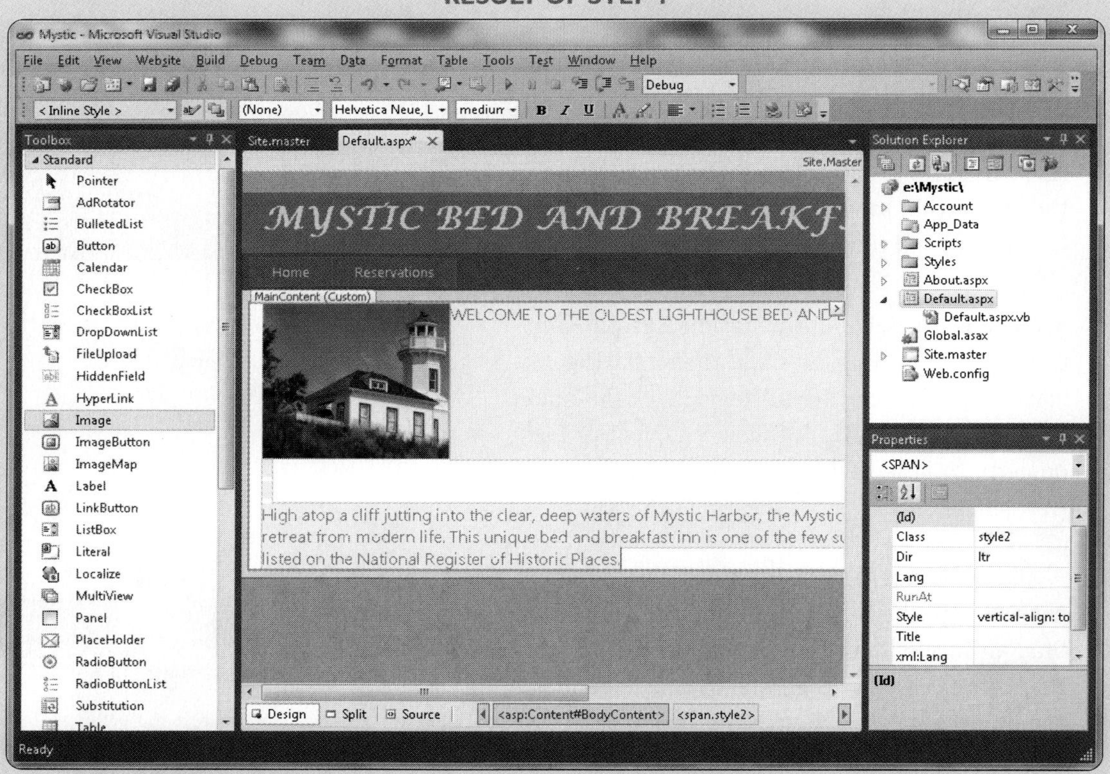

FIGURE 7-69

Guided Program Development *continued*

Phase 2: Build the Reservations Web Form

2

- **Insert a Table in the Web Form** In the Solution Explorer, double-click the About.aspx file. Delete the text in the MainContent area. Type `GUEST REGISTRATION FORM:` in the MainContent area. Press ENTER. Click Table on the menu bar, and then click Insert Table. In the Insert Table dialog box, enter 7 in the Rows text box and 3 in the Columns text box, and then click the OK button to create a table with seven columns and three rows *(ref: Figure 7-21)*.

HINT

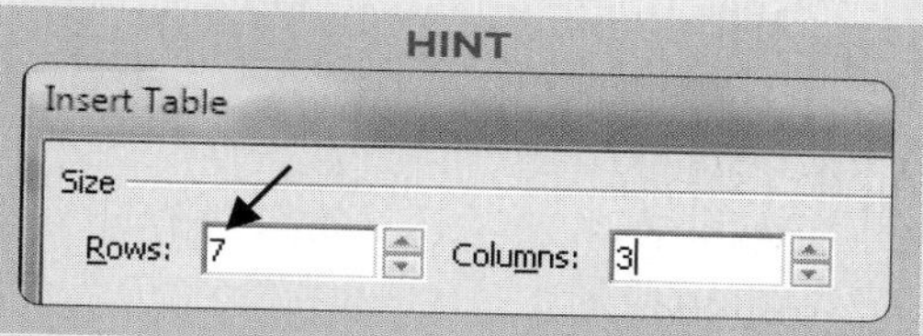

- **Change the Column Size of the Table** Point to the divider between the first and second columns of the table, and then drag to resize the first column to 150 pixels. Resize the second column to 250 pixels *(ref: Figure 7-22)*.

HINT

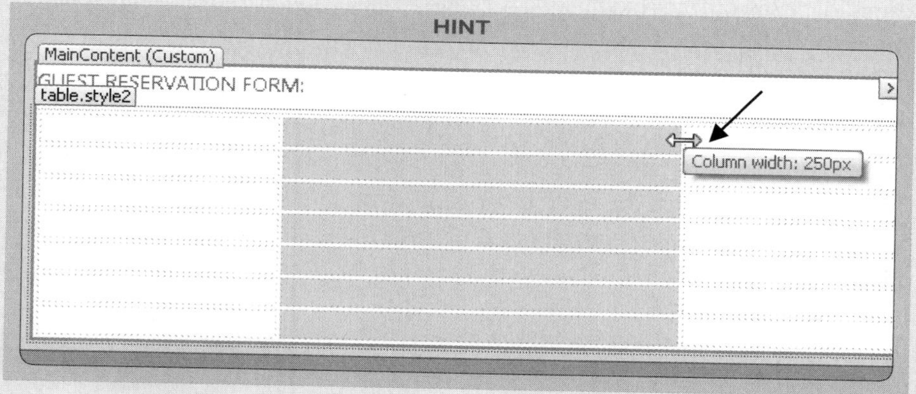

(continues)

Guided Program Development *continued*

Enter Text and Objects in the Table

- Enter the title for the text boxes as shown in the hint in the first column. In the second column, drag the first TextBox object to the right of the Name title, and then name the TextBox object txtName. Resize the object to 250 pixels wide *(ref: Figure 7-23)*.
- Drag the second TextBox object to the right of the E-mail Address title, and then name the TextBox object txtEmail. Resize the object to 250 pixels wide *(ref: Figure 7-24)*.
- Drag a CheckBox object to the right of the Suite Selection text. Name the CheckBox object `chkSerenity`. Change the Text property to Serenity Suite $220. Change the Checked property to True *(ref: Figure 7-27)*.
- Drag the second CheckBox object below the first CheckBox object, and then name the CheckBox object chkEvergreen. Change its Text property to Evergreen Suite $170. Drag the third CheckBox object below the second CheckBox object, and then name the third CheckBox object chkVineland. Change its Text property to Vineland Suite $155 *(ref: Figure 7-29)*.
- Type `Night(s):` in the next row. Drag a DropDownList object to the right of the Night(s) title. Change the name of the DropDownList object to ddlNights. Click the Smart Tag on the DropDownList object, and then click Edit Items. The ListItem Collection Editor dialog box opens. Click the Add button, and then enter the number 1 as the Text property. Click the Add button as necessary to add the numbers 2 through 7. After adding number 7, click the Remove button to remove the entry in the Members list, if necessary. Click the OK button *(ref: Figure 7-31)*.
- Type `Check-in Date:` and then drag a Calendar object to the next cell on the page. Name the Calendar object cldArrival. Click the Smart Tag on the Calendar object, and then click Auto Format. Select Colorful 2, and then click OK. Resize the Calendar object and move it as needed *(ref: Figure 7-36)*.

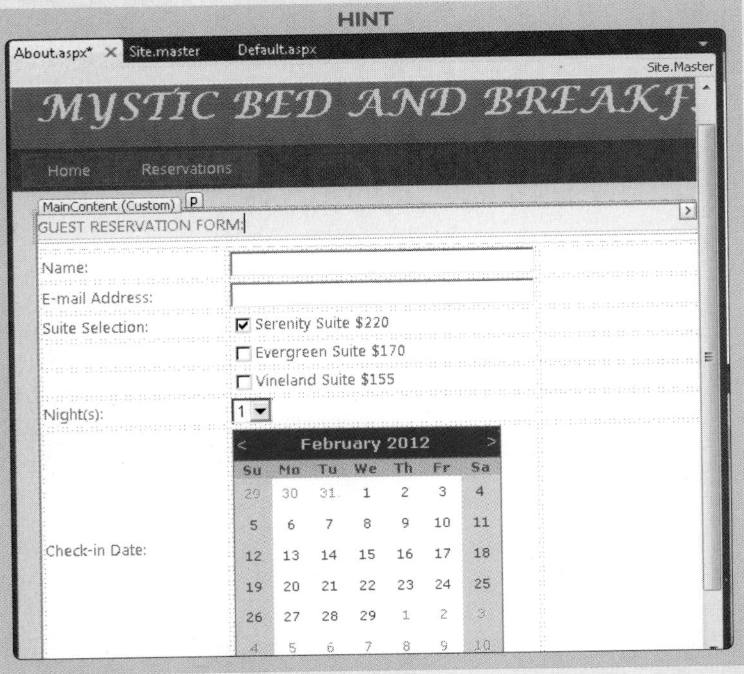

Guided Program Development *continued*

The Guest Reservation Form (About.aspx) includes typed text, text boxes, check boxes, a drop-down list, and a calendar (Figure 7-70).

RESULT OF STEP 2

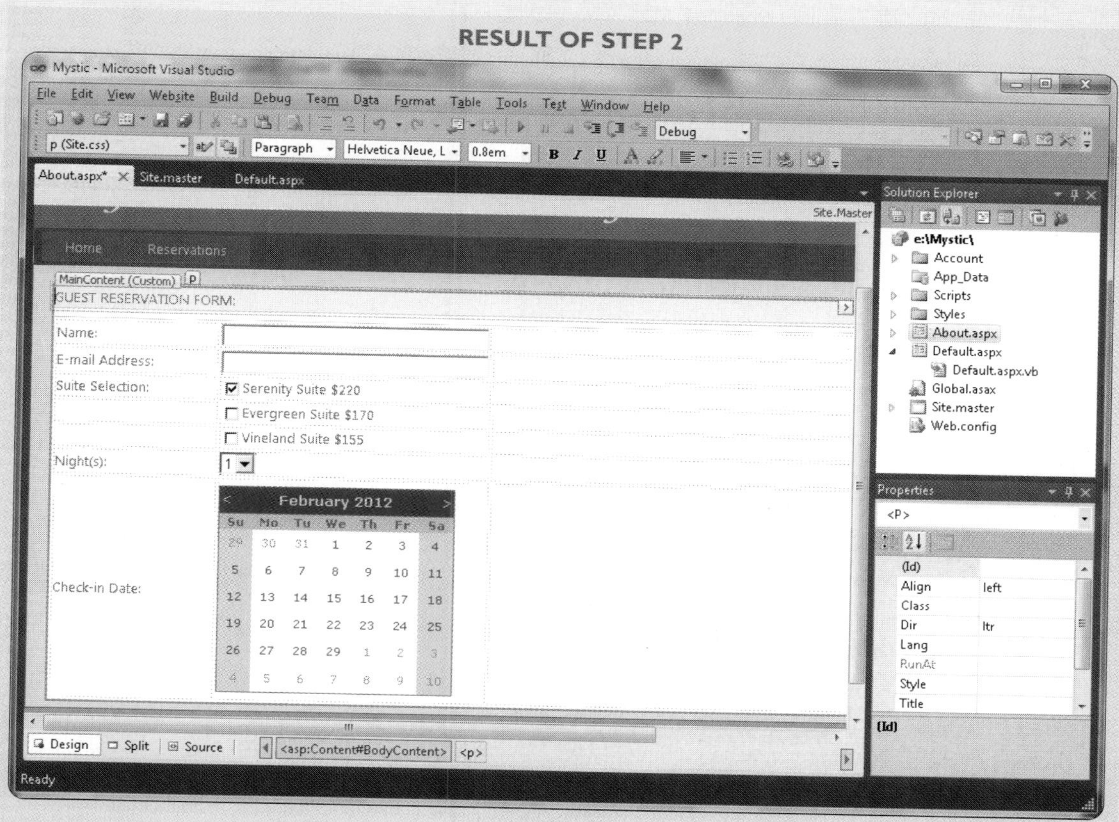

FIGURE 7-70

(continues)

Guided Program Development *continued*

Phase 3: Add Validation Objects

3

- **Add the Required Validation Objects** In the Toolbox, expand the Validation controls by clicking the expand icon next to Validation *(ref: Figure 7-44)*.

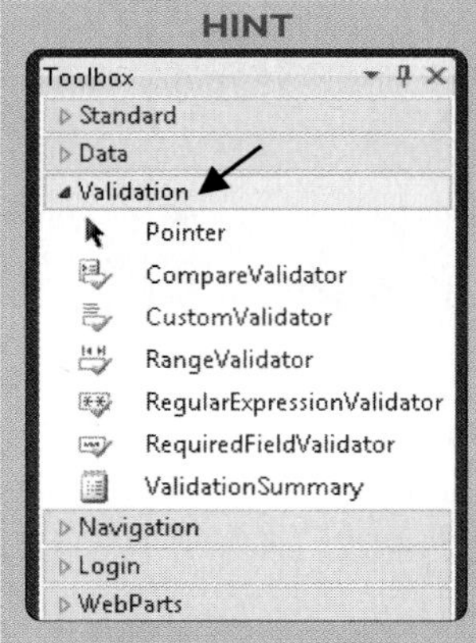

HEADS UP

When you run the Web application, a message may appear in a dialog box that states "Debugging Not Enabled." Select the "Modify the Web.config file to enable debugging" option button, and then click OK.

- **Validate the Name TextBox Object** Drag the RequiredFieldValidator object onto the Web form to the first row in the third column. Name the Validator Object rfvName. Change its ErrorMessage property to * Enter Name *(ref: Figure 7-45)*.

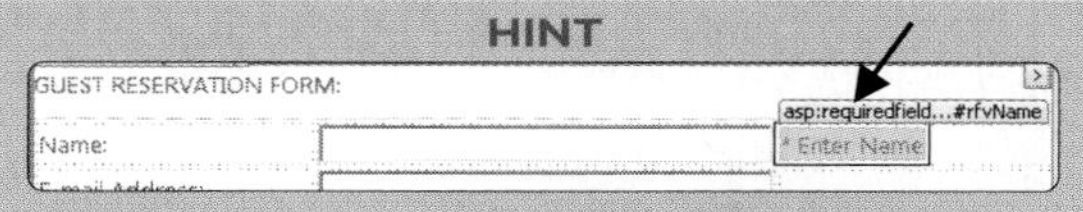

- **Select the TextBox Object to Validate** In the Properties window for the rfvName object, click the list arrow in the ControlToValidate property and then click txtName *(ref: Figure 7-46)*.

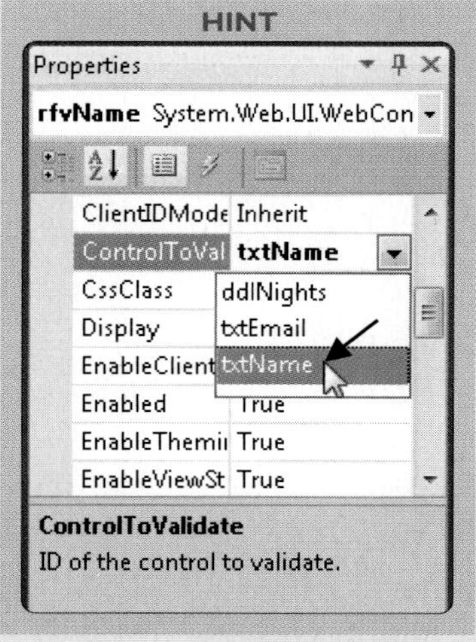

Guided Program Development *continued*

- **Validate the E-mail TextBox Object** Drag the RequiredFieldValidator object onto the Web form in the second row of the third column. Place the RequiredFieldValidator object to the right of the txtEmail TextBox object. Name the Validator object rfvEmail. Change its ErrorMessage property to * Enter a Valid E-mail. In the Properties window, click the list arrow in the ControlToValidate property and then click txtEmail.

- **Add Regular Expression Validator for E-Mail** Drag the RegularExpressionValidator object below the E-mail Address field. Name the Validator object revEmail. Change its ErrorMessage property to * Error E-mail format. Click the list arrow in the ControlToValidate property, and then click txtEmail. Click the ellipsis button in the ValidationExpression property. When the Regular Expression Editor dialog box opens, select Internet e-mail address. Click the OK button *(ref: Figure 7-54)*.

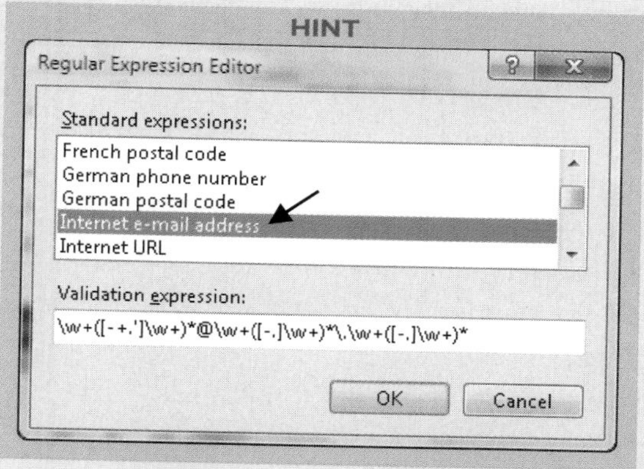

- **Add the Missing Suite Choice Message** Drag a Label object onto the Web form to the third row in the third column. Place the label in the same row as the Serenity check box. Name the label lblSuiteError. Change the Text property to * Select a Suite. Set the Visible property for the label to False.

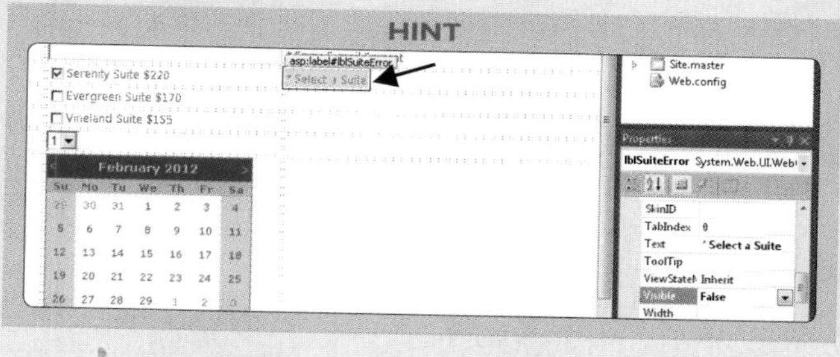

- **Add the Submit Button** Drag a Button object to the last row of the third column to the right of the Calendar object. Change the Button object (ID) property to btnSubmit. Change the Text property to Submit. Click after the Submit button and press Enter several times until the Submit button is at the top of the cell.

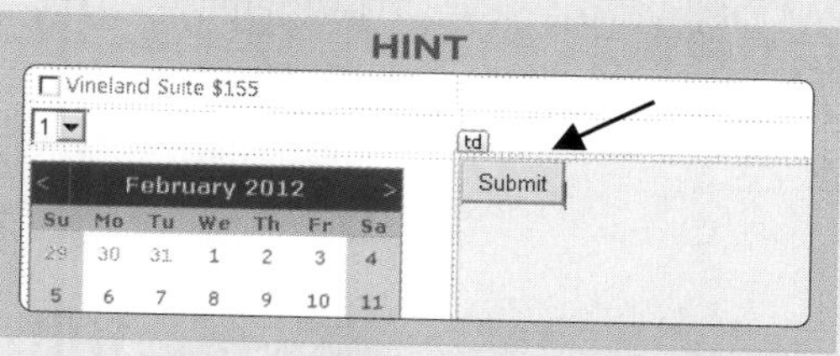

(continues)

Guided Program Development *continued*

• **Add a Calendar Warning Label** Drag a Label object to below the Submit button. Change the (ID) property of the Label object to lblCalendarError. Change the Text property to * Select a valid date and then click Submit. The warning message is displayed only if a valid date is not selected. Change the Visible property to False.

HINT

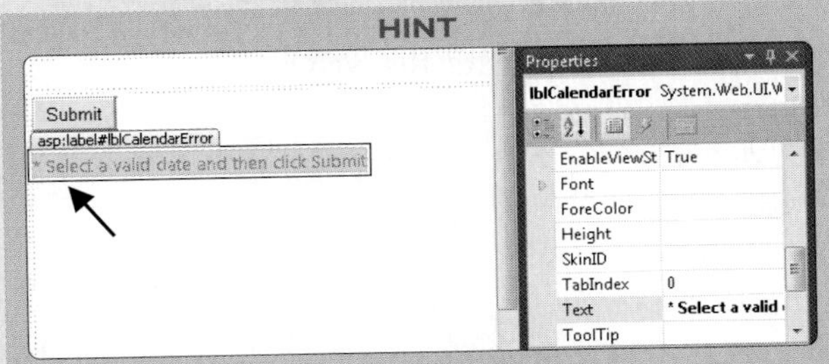

• **Add a Result Label** Drag a Label object below the Submit button and the calendar error Label object. Name the Label object lblReservation. Delete any value in the Text property. The lblReservation placeholder with the text [lblReservation] is displayed on the Web form, but will not appear in the actual Web page.

HINT

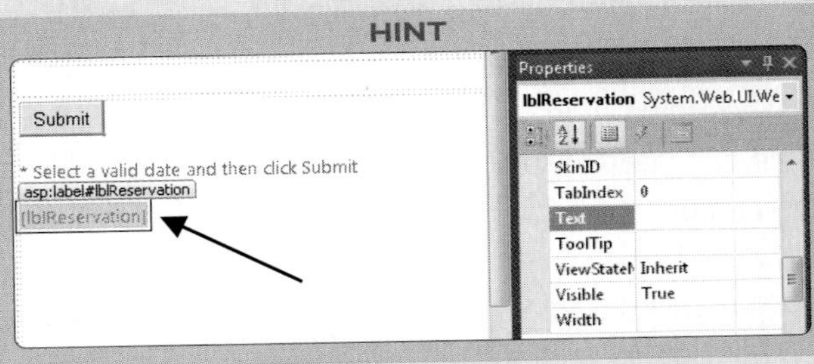

HEADS UP

When you run the Web application, you will notice a Log in link in the upper-right corner. This is for a password-protected site. You can delete the Log in link if you do not have a password-protected site.

The validation objects and messages are part of the Web form (Figure 7-71).

RESULT OF STEP 3

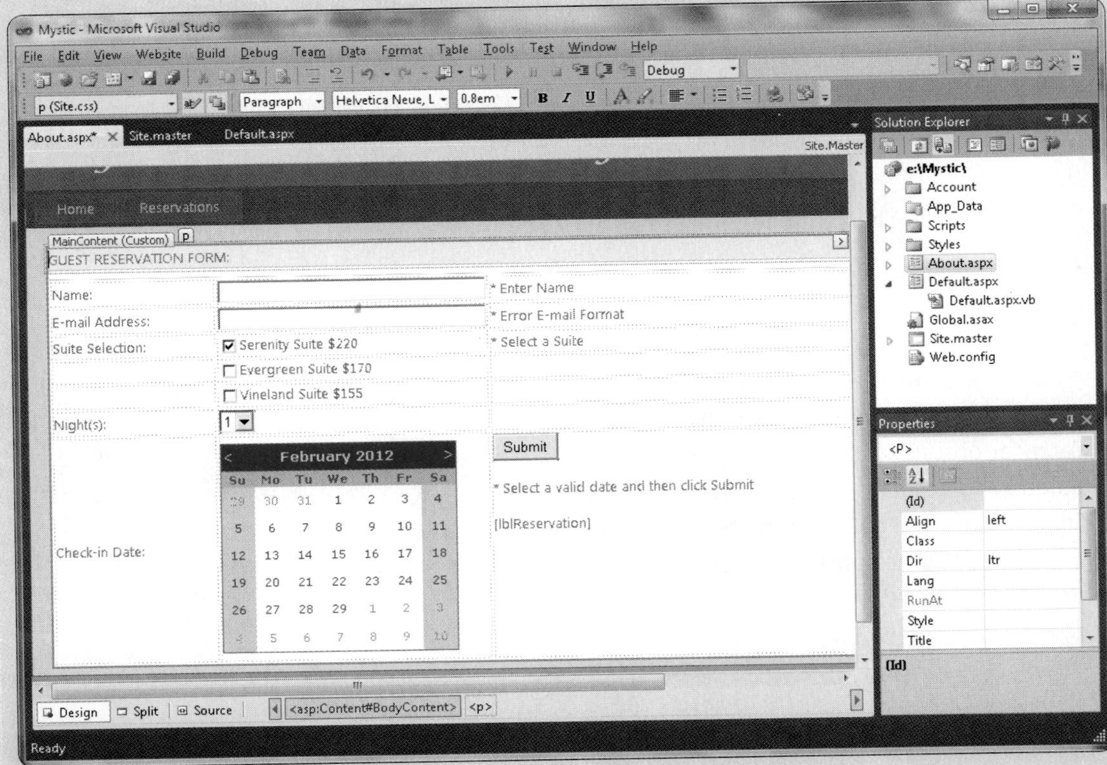

FIGURE 7-71

Guided Program Development *continued*

Phase 4: Code the Application

4

- **Code the Comments** Double-click the Submit button on the form to begin coding the btnSubmit_Click Event in the Web application. Insert the first four standard comments at the top of the Code window. Insert the command Option Strict On at the beginning of the code to turn on strict type checking.

HINT

```
' Project:  Bed and Breakast Online Reservation Form
' Author:   Corinne Hoisington
' Date:     March 30, 2013
' Purpose:  The following Web application will request reservation information
'           for the Mystic Bed and Breakfast. This web site will compute
'           the cost of the number of nights and room(s) selected.

Option Strict On
```

- **Comment on the btnSubmit Click Event** In the btnSubmit Click Event, enter a comment that explains the purpose of the Click Event.

HINT

```
    Protected Sub btnSubmit_Click(ByVal sender As Object, ByVal e As System.EventArgs) Handles
        ' The btnSubmit Click Event will calculate the cost of the cost of the room
        ' based on the type of suite selected and the number of nights reserved.
```

- **Initialize Variables** Click in the btnSubmit Click Event and enter the variables used in the application. These variables include String variables for the name and e-mail address; Decimal variables that will contain the room costs for the three rooms and the result of the room cost calculation; an Integer value for the number of nights the user selects from the drop-down list; and a String variable in which to compose the reservation message.

HINT

```
        ' Declare and initialize variables
        Dim decSerenityCost As Decimal = 220D
        Dim decEvergreenCost As Decimal = 170D
        Dim decVinelandCost As Decimal = 155D
        Dim strName As String
        Dim strEmail As String
        Dim decRoomCost As Decimal = 0D
        Dim intNumberOfNights As Integer
        Dim strMessage As String
```

(continues)

Guided Program Development *continued*

- **Trim the TextBox Object Data** Using the Trim procedure, write the code to remove excess spaces from the data the user entered. Place the trimmed Name from the TextBox object in the strName variable and the trimmed E-mail address in the strEmail variable *(ref: Figure 7-62)*.

HINT

```
        ' Trim additional spaces that are entered by the user
        strName = txtName.Text.Trim
        strEmail = txtEmail.Text.Trim
```

- **Clear the Reservation Message** Write a statement to clear the lblReservations label.

HINT

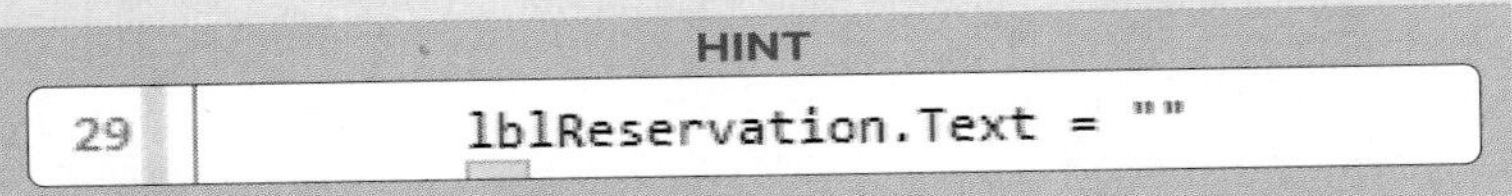

- **Ensure a Suite Type is Selected** Write an If statement that ensures a suite type has been selected. The Checked property of one or more of the CheckBox objects must be true. Use the Not operator to check for all three properties. If the suite type has not been selected, display the suite error message.

HINT

```
        If Not (chkVineland.Checked Or chkSerenity.Checked Or chkEvergreen.Checked) Then
            lblSuiteError.Visible = True
```

- **Ensure a Valid Date is Selected** Regardless of whether a valid suite was selected, the program must ensure a valid date was selected. Therefore, if a suite is not selected, write an If statement that ensures the date is valid (that is, the selected date is not less than the current date). If the date is invalid, display the calendar error message; otherwise, do not display the calendar error message.

HINT

```
        If Not (chkVineland.Checked Or chkSerenity.Checked Or chkEvergreen.Checked) Then
            lblSuiteError.Visible = True
            If cldArrival.SelectedDate < cldArrival.TodaysDate Then
                lblCalendarError.Visible = True
            Else
                lblCalendarError.Visible = False
            End If
```

Guided Program Development *continued*

- **Hide Suite Error Message When Suite is Selected** If a suite is selected, the suite error message must be hidden; that is, the suite error message Visible property must be set to False. Write the statement to set the Visible property to False.

HINT

```
        If Not (chkVineland.Checked Or chkSerenity.Checked Or chkEvergreen.Checked) Then
            lblSuiteError.Visible = True
            If cldArrival.SelectedDate < cldArrival.TodaysDate Then
                lblCalendarError.Visible = True
            Else
                lblCalendarError.Visible = False
            End If
        Else
            lblSuiteError.Visible = False
```

- **Ensure a Valid Date is Selected** When a suite has been selected, the program must ensure a valid date was selected. If a suite is selected and a valid date is selected, the data validity checking is complete and the room cost can be calculated. Write a statement to ensure that the selected date is greater than or equal to the current date, and if the date is valid, set the Visible property for the error message to False.

HINT

```
            If cldArrival.SelectedDate >= cldArrival.TodaysDate Then
                lblCalendarError.Visible = False
```

- **Determine Total of Room Costs** The user can select more than one suite type. For example, one room might be for parents and another room might be for their children. Therefore, the program must determine if each check box is checked, and if so, the room cost per night is accumulated. Write the statements to determine if a suite check box is checked and, if so, to accumulate the room costs in the decRoomCost variable.

HINT

```
                ' Calculate the cost of the room(s) selected by the user
                If chkSerenity.Checked Then
                    decRoomCost += decSerenityCost
                End If
                If chkEvergreen.Checked Then
                    decRoomCost += decEvergreenCost
                End If
                If chkVineland.Checked Then
                    decRoomCost += decVinelandCost
                End If
```

(continues)

Guided Program Development *continued*

- **Calculate Total Room Cost** To calculate the total room cost, the number of nights selected by the user from the drop-down list must be converted from a String to an Integer. Then, the calculation to determine the total room costs (number of nights x room cost) must occur. Write the statements to perform these activities.

HINT

```
                intNumberOfNights = Convert.ToInt32(ddlNights.SelectedItem.Text)
                decRoomCost = intNumberOfNights * decRoomCost
```

- **Create the Reservation Message** Write the code to create the reservation message, and place it in the strMessage String variable. Then, place the message stored in the strMessage variable in the Text property of the lblReservation Label object *(ref: Figure 7-58)*.

HINT

```
                strMessage = "A reservation has been made for: " & "<br>" _
                    & strName & "<br>" & "E-mail: " & strEmail & "<br>"
                strMessage &= "The room(s) cost is: " _
                    & decRoomCost.ToString("C") & "<br>"
                strMessage &= "Arrival Date: " _
                    & cldArrival.SelectedDate.ToShortDateString() _
                    & "<br>" & " for " & intNumberOfNights & " night(s)"
                lblReservation.Text = strMessage
```

- **Show Calendar Error Message** If the user did not select a valid date for the check-in date, display the calendar error message by changing the Visible property for the error message label to True.

HINT

```
            Else
                lblCalendarError.Visible = True
            End If
        End If
    End Sub
```

Code Listing

The complete code for the sample program is shown in Figure 7-72.

```
' Project:  Bed and Breakast Online Reservation Form
' Author:   Corinne Hoisington
' Date:     March 30, 2013
' Purpose:  The following Web application will request reservation information
'           for the Mystic Bed and Breakfast. This web site will compute
'           the cost of the number of nights and room(s) selected.
```

FIGURE 7-72 (continues)

```
Option Strict On
Partial Class About
    Inherits System.Web.UI.Page

    Protected Sub btnSubmit_Click(ByVal sender As Object, ByVal e As System.EventArgs) Handles btnSubmit.Click
        ' The btnSubmit Click Event will calculate the cost of the cost of the room
        ' based on the type of suite selected and the number of nights reserved.

        ' Declare and initialize variables
        Dim decSerenityCost As Decimal = 220D
        Dim decEvergreenCost As Decimal = 170D
        Dim decVinelandCost As Decimal = 155D
        Dim strName As String
        Dim strEmail As String
        Dim decRoomCost As Decimal = 0D
        Dim intNumberOfNights As Integer
        Dim strMessage As String

        ' Trim additional spaces that are entered by the user
        strName = txtName.Text.Trim
        strEmail = txtEmail.Text.Trim
        lblReservation.Text = ""
        If Not (chkVineland.Checked Or chkSerenity.Checked Or chkEvergreen.Checked) Then
            lblSuiteError.Visible = True
            If cldArrival.SelectedDate < cldArrival.TodaysDate Then
                lblCalendarError.Visible = True
            Else
                lblCalendarError.Visible = False
            End If
        Else
            lblSuiteError.Visible = False
            If cldArrival.SelectedDate >= cldArrival.TodaysDate Then
                lblCalendarError.Visible = False
                ' Calculate the cost of the room(s) selected by the user
                If chkSerenity.Checked Then
                    decRoomCost += decSerenityCost
                End If
                If chkEvergreen.Checked Then
                    decRoomCost += decEvergreenCost
                End If
                If chkVineland.Checked Then
                    decRoomCost += decVinelandCost
                End If
                intNumberOfNights = Convert.ToInt32(ddlNights.SelectedItem.Text)
                decRoomCost = intNumberOfNights * decRoomCost
                strMessage = "A reservation has been made for: " & "<br>" _
                    & strName & "<br>" & "E-mail: " & strEmail & "<br>"
                strMessage &= "The room(s) cost is: " _
                    & decRoomCost.ToString("C") & "<br>"
                strMessage &= "Arrival Date: " _
                    & cldArrival.SelectedDate.ToShortDateString() _
                    & "<br>" & " for " & intNumberOfNights & " night(s)"
                lblReservation.Text = strMessage
            Else
                lblCalendarError.Visible = True
            End If
        End If
    End Sub
End Class
```

FIGURE 7-72 (continued)

Summary

In this chapter you have learned to create an online Web application using ASP.NET 4.0. The items listed in the table shown in Figure 7-73 include all the new Visual Studio and Visual Basic skills you have learned in this chapter.

Visual Basic Skills

Skill	Figure Number	Web Address for Video
Examine the Mystic Bed and Breakfast chapter project application	Figure 7-1	scsite.com/vb2010/ch7/figure7-1
Create a Visual Basic Web project	Figure 7-4	scsite.com/vb2010/ch7/figure7-4
Change text on the Master page	Figure 7-8	scsite.com/vb2010/ch7/figure7-8
Rename navigation buttons	Figure 7-10	scsite.com/vb2010/ch7/figure7-10
Add an Image object on the Web page	Figure 7-14	scsite.com/vb2010/ch7/figure7-14
Enter text directly on the Web page	Figure 7-17	scsite.com/vb2010/ch7/figure7-17
Add a table for alignment on a Web form	Figure 7-21	scsite.com/vb2010/ch7/figure7-21
Add a TextBox object	Figure 7-23	scsite.com/vb2010/ch7/figure7-23
Add a CheckBox object	Figure 7-25	scsite.com/vb2010/ch7/figure7-25
Add a DropDownList object	Figure 7-31	scsite.com/vb2010/ch7/figure7-31
Add a Calendar object to a Web form	Figure 7-36	scsite.com/vb2010/ch7/figure7-36
Specify a Web form title	Figure 7-39	scsite.com/vb2010/ch7/figure7-39
Code a Check Box	Page 496	
Write code for a Calendar object	Page 503	
Validate TextBox object using a RequiredFieldValidator object	Figure 7-43	scsite.com/vb2010/ch7/figure7-43
Validate the range using a RangeValidator object	Page 508	
Validate two objects with the CompareValidator object	Page 509	
Validate data using a RegularExpressionValidator object	Figure 7-50	scsite.com/vb2010/ch7/figure7-50
Validate data using multiple validations	Page 513	
Display a ValidationSummary	Page 514	
Use the tag in Visual Basic	Page 514	
Use the String Length property	Page 515	
Use the Trim procedure	Page 516	
Convert uppercase and lowercase text	Page 517	

FIGURE 7-73

Learn It Online

Start your browser and visit scsite.com/vb2010/ch7. Follow the instructions in the exercises below.

1. **Chapter Reinforcement TF, MC, SA** Click one of the Chapter Reinforcement links for Multiple Choice, True/False, or Short Answer below the Learn It Online heading. Answer each question and submit to your instructor.
2. **Practice Test** Click the Practice Test link below Chapter 7. Answer each question, enter your first and last names at the bottom of the page, and then click the Grade Test button. When the graded practice test is displayed on your screen, submit the graded practice test to your instructor. Continue to take the practice test until you are satisfied with your score.
3. **Crossword Puzzle Challenge** Click the Crossword Puzzle Challenge link below the Learn It Online heading. Read the instructions, and then click the Continue button. Work the crossword puzzle. When you are finished, click the Submit button. When the crossword puzzle is redisplayed, submit it to your instructor.

Knowledge Check

1. Name five Web sites that incorporate Web forms and state the purpose of each Web form (such as to enter customer information for purchasing an item). Do not list any sites that were mentioned in this chapter.
2. What type of Web page does ASP.NET 4.0 create?
3. When you test a Web application, the page opens in a(n) ________.
4. A Web page or Web site is hosted on a(n) ________ ________.
5. A Web site that allows you to enter information is considered a(n) ________ Web page.
6. In an Active Server Page, what computer executes the event handler code you write in Visual Basic 2010?
7. In a Windows application, each object has a (Name) property. In a Web application, each object has a ________ property, which is similar to the (Name) property.
8. Write a line of code that would display the date selected by the user in the TextBox shown in Figure 7-74.

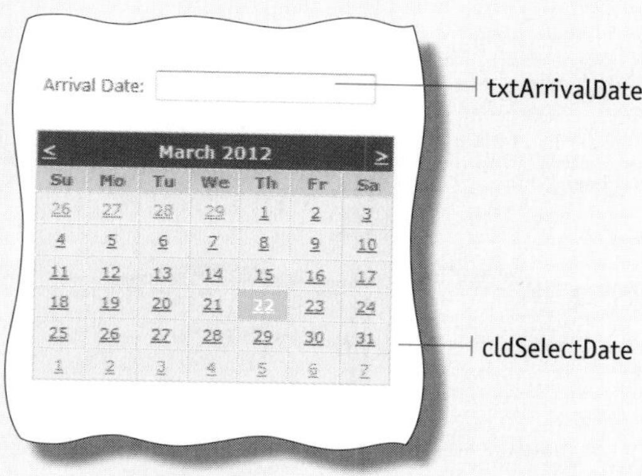

FIGURE 7-74

(continues)

Knowledge Check *continued*

9. In the ListBox object shown in Figure 7-75, write the lines of code that would display in a Label named lblSizeDisplay "You have selected size: Large" if the user selects "L".

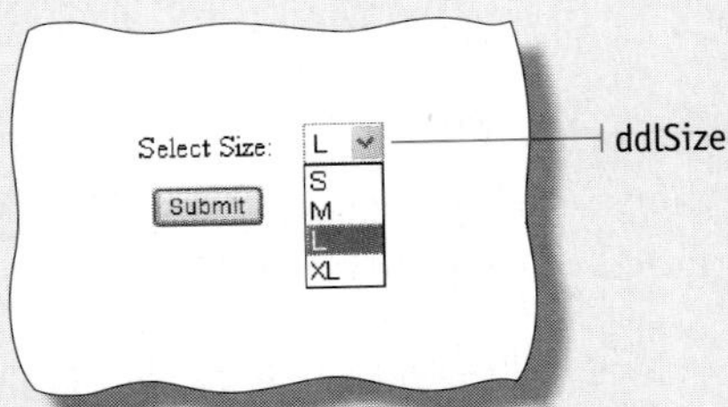

FIGURE 7-75

10. Explain the major difference between CheckBox and RadioButton objects.
11. What is the name of the property that assigns the object name to the validation control?
12. Which control validator confirms that the user enters the constant value of 9.0?
13. Which control validator checks if a value is between 10 and 30?
14. Which control validator confirms that a TextBox object is not left blank?
15. Write a line of code that would convert strResponse to all uppercase letters.
16. Write a line of code that would assign the length of a string named strCompany to the variable intSizeOfCompanyName.
17. Write a line of code that would display in a Label object named lblDisplayBirthday the date a user selected from a Calendar object named cldBirthdate.
18. How does the PictureBox object called an Image object in ASP.NET differ from an image in a Windows application?
19. In the browser window shown in Figure 7-76, name the type of validation and list any changes that were made in the Properties window.

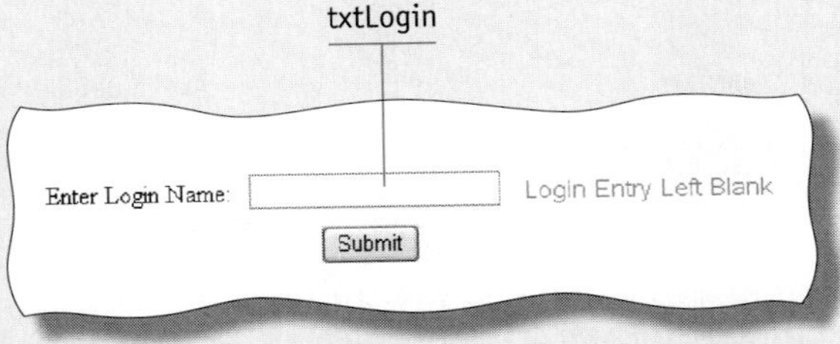

FIGURE 7-76

20. What is the name of the page that serves as a template for the pages that are actually displayed in the browser?

Debugging Exercises

1. Fix the error in the following line of code.

```
intFindLength = strHomeName(Length)
```

2. Fix the error in the following lines of code.

```
If (chkDormStudent.Checked)= True Then
decTuitionCost += 3400
End If
```

3. What will be contained in the Text property of the lblResult Label object after executing the following code?

```
Dim strPhrase As String
strPhrase = " On the Wings"
strPhrase += " of an Eagle! "
strPhrase = strPhrase.Trim()
lblResult.Text=strPhrase
```

4. What is the output of the following code?

```
Dim strPhrase As String
strPhrase = "Don't judge a book by its cover"
lblResult.Text= "Count =" & strPhrase.Length
```

5. Write the output that would be displayed in the Info label after the following statements are executed.

```
lblInfo.Text = "Home Address: " & "<br>" & "3506 Wards Rd" & "<br>" &
"Lynchburg, VA 24502"
```

Program Analysis

1. Name each of the property changes that are required in the Properties window for a Range Validator in order to validate that a TextBox named txtDeductibleRange contains a value in the range 250.00 up to and including 10,000.00. Display an error message that states "Please enter an acceptable deductible between 250 and 10,000".
2. Write a Visual Basic statement that displays the length of a variable named strSentence in a Label object named lblStringLength.
3. Write the section of code that would display a list of services in a Label object named lblService if the user selects any of the corresponding CheckBoxes shown in Figure 7-77.

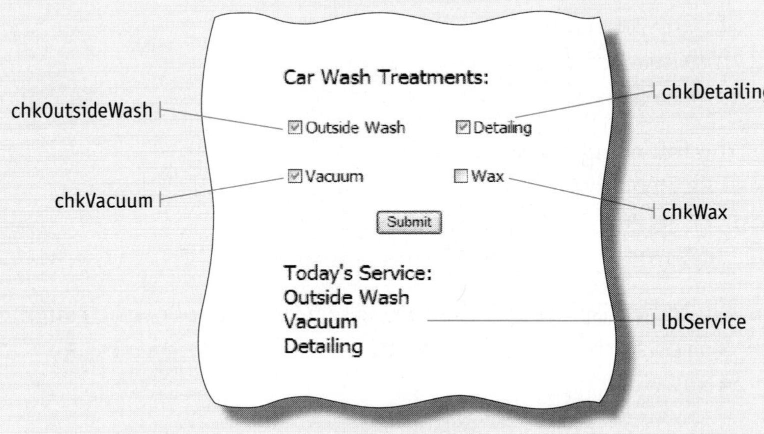

FIGURE 7-77

Case Programming Assignments

Complete one or more of the following case programming assignments. Submit the program and materials you create to your instructor. The level of difficulty is indicated for each case programming assignment.

● = Easiest
●● = Intermediate
●●● = Challenging

1 ● CRUISE RESERVATION WEB APPLICATION

Design a Web application for a cruise reservation application using the options shown in Figure 7-78. Write the code that will execute according to the program requirements shown in Figure 7-79 and the Use Case Definition document shown in Figure 7-80 on the next page. Before writing the code, create an event planning document for each event in the program. The completed Web page is shown in Figure 7-81 on the next page.

Cruise Option	Cost
First Three Nights Total for Inside Stateroom	$399
Each Additional Night for Inside Stateroom	$109
First Three Nights Total for Luxury Ocean View Cabin	$699
Each Additional Night for Luxury Ocean View Cabin	$159
Optional Shore Excursion to the Ancient Mayan Ruins in Mexico.	$179

FIGURE 7-78

REQUIREMENTS DOCUMENT

Date submitted: August 11, 2012

Application title: Cruise Reservation Web Application

Purpose: This application allows the user to book a reservation on a major cruise line.

Program Procedures: From a Web application, the user completes an online reservation form to select the type of room, the number of nights, sailing date, and optional shore excursion.

Algorithms, Processing, and Conditions:

1. The user must be able to enter the requested reservation information on a Web form. The information should include their name, whether the user wants an inside stateroom and/or a luxury ocean view cabin, the number of nights spent on the cruise line (3–7 nights), the initial sail date, and whether they want to book an optional shore excursion. The prices are displayed in Figure 7-78.
2. After entering the reservation information, the user clicks the Submit button.
3. The information entered is validated.
4. The application displays the final cost of the cruise that has been selected.

FIGURE 7-79 (continues)

(continues)

Case Programming Assignments

Cruise Reservation Web Application (continued)

Notes and Restrictions:

1. Data Validation controls should be used. The name is validated to confirm that it is not left blank.
2. The calendar object must have a date selected that is later than the current date.
3. The number of nights must be 3 to 7 nights.
4. A family may reserve both cabins.

Comments:

1. Display a picture of a cruise ship on the Web form. An image URL can be located on a search engine such as Bing or Google.
2. Place the image and title on the Site.master. Delete the second navigation button by selecting the Smart Tag and Edit Menu Items. Select About and then click the Remove button (red x).

FIGURE 7-79 (continued)

USE CASE DEFINITION

1. The Web page opens, displaying this week's cruise options, a picture of the cruise ship, one TextBox object to request name, two CheckBox objects to select cabins, a DropDownList object displaying the length of the cruise (3-7 Nights), a Calendar object to select the sail date, a CheckBox object indicating whether they want the optional shore excursion, and a Submit button.
2. The user enters the information, makes the appropriate selections, and clicks the Submit button.
3. Validation controls check the data.
4. The application displays the final cost of the cruise package.

FIGURE 7-80

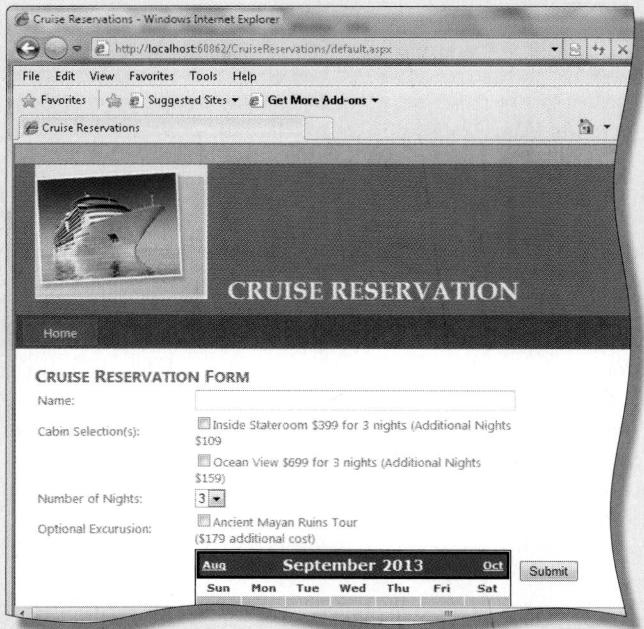

FIGURE 7-81

Case Programming Assignments

2 • NEW EMPLOYEE E-MAIL WEB APPLICATION

Design a Web application and write the code that will execute according to the program requirements shown in Figure 7-82 and the Use Case Definition document shown in Figure 7-83 on the next page. Before writing the code, create an event planning document for each event in the program. The completed Web page is shown in Figure 7-84 on the next page.

REQUIREMENTS DOCUMENT

Date submitted: July 31, 2013

Application title: New Employee E-mail Web Application

Purpose: This application allows a new employee to set up an e-mail address at the WebSide Company.

Program Procedures: From a Web application, the user should enter their first name and last name to create an e-mail address in the format: jim.bellweather@webside.com, with the first and last name in lowercase letters.

Algorithms, Processing, and Conditions:

1. The user must be able to enter their first name and their last name.
2. The user must select a department from a DropDownList object with the following choices: Accounting, Executive, Marketing, Sales, and Warehouse.
3. The user clicks the Submit button.
4. The information entered is validated.
5. The application displays the department and the new e-mail address in the format first name, dot, last name (all lowercase) @ sign, webside.com.

Notes and Restrictions:

1. Data Validation tools should be used. The first and last names are validated to confirm that they are not left blank.

Comments:

1. The e-mail address will be displayed in lowercase letters.
2. Place the title on the Site.master. Delete the second navigation button by selecting the Smart Tag and Edit Menu Items. Select About and then click the Remove button (red x).

FIGURE 7-82

Case Programming Assignments

New Employee E-Mail Web Application (continued)

USE CASE DEFINITION

1. The Web page opens, displaying the title WebSide New Employee E-mail Set-up, two TextBox objects to enter the user's name, a DropDownList object for selecting the department, and a Submit button.
2. User enters their first name and last name.
3. User selects the department.
4. User clicks the Submit button.
5. Validation controls check that the data was entered.
6. The application displays the department and the e-mail address.

FIGURE 7-83

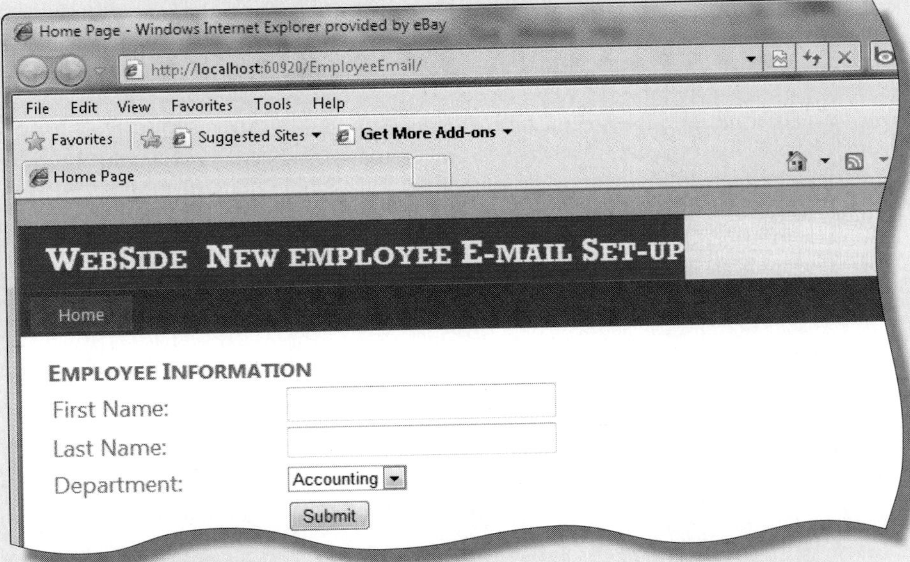

FIGURE 7-84

Case Programming Assignments

3 • ONLINE SERVICE

Design a Web application and write the code that will execute according to the program requirements shown in Figure 7-85 and the Use Case Definition document in Figure 7-86 on the next page. Before writing the code, create an event planning document for each event in the program. The completed Web page is shown in Figure 7-87 on the next page.

REQUIREMENTS DOCUMENT

Date submitted: January 4, 2015

Application title: Earth Connect Online Service Web Application

Purpose: This Web application allows the user to sign up for an Internet service provider for home connectivity.

Program Procedures: From a Web application, the user should select one of two types of home online service.

Algorithms, Processing, and Conditions:

1. The Web site has two pages. The Home page provides information about the Internet Service Provider. The second page is the sign-up for service page.
2. The user must be able to select information about the Internet service provider on a Web form. The information should include the first and last name of the user and whether they want options of hosting a personal Web site and renting a wireless router.
3. The cost for the service is as follows:

   Optional Services
   Host Personal Site: $2.99 per month
   Wireless Router: $3.99 per month

   Digital Subscriber Line (DSL)
   Initial Connection: $49.99
   Basic Monthly Service: $19.99

4. After the selection is entered, the user clicks the Sign Up for Internet Services button.
5. The information entered is validated.
6. The application displays the first month's cost (includes the initial connection fee), and the subsequent month's cost (does not include the initial connection fee).

Notes and Restrictions:

1. Data validation controls should be used. The first and last names are validated to confirm they are not left empty.
2. No optional service is required.

Comments:

1. Display a picture representing the World Wide Web on the Web form.

FIGURE 7-85

Case Programming Assignments

Online Service *(continued)*

USE CASE DEFINITION

1. The Home page opens, displaying a Home and Sign-Up button, an image representing the World Wide Web, and text that welcomes users to Earth Connect.
2. User clicks the Sign-Up button.
3. The Sign-up page opens, displaying an opening pricing page and an Internet service provider order form for a home connection, a picture representing the World Wide Web, two TextBox objects requesting the user's first and last names, a CheckBox object for selecting whether the user wants a personal site, a CheckBox object for indicating the user wants to rent a wireless router, and a Submit button.
4. User clicks the Submit button.
5. Validation controls check the data.
6. The application displays the first month's cost of connectivity to an Internet service provider with the services selected, and the subsequent month's cost for the service.

FIGURE 7-86

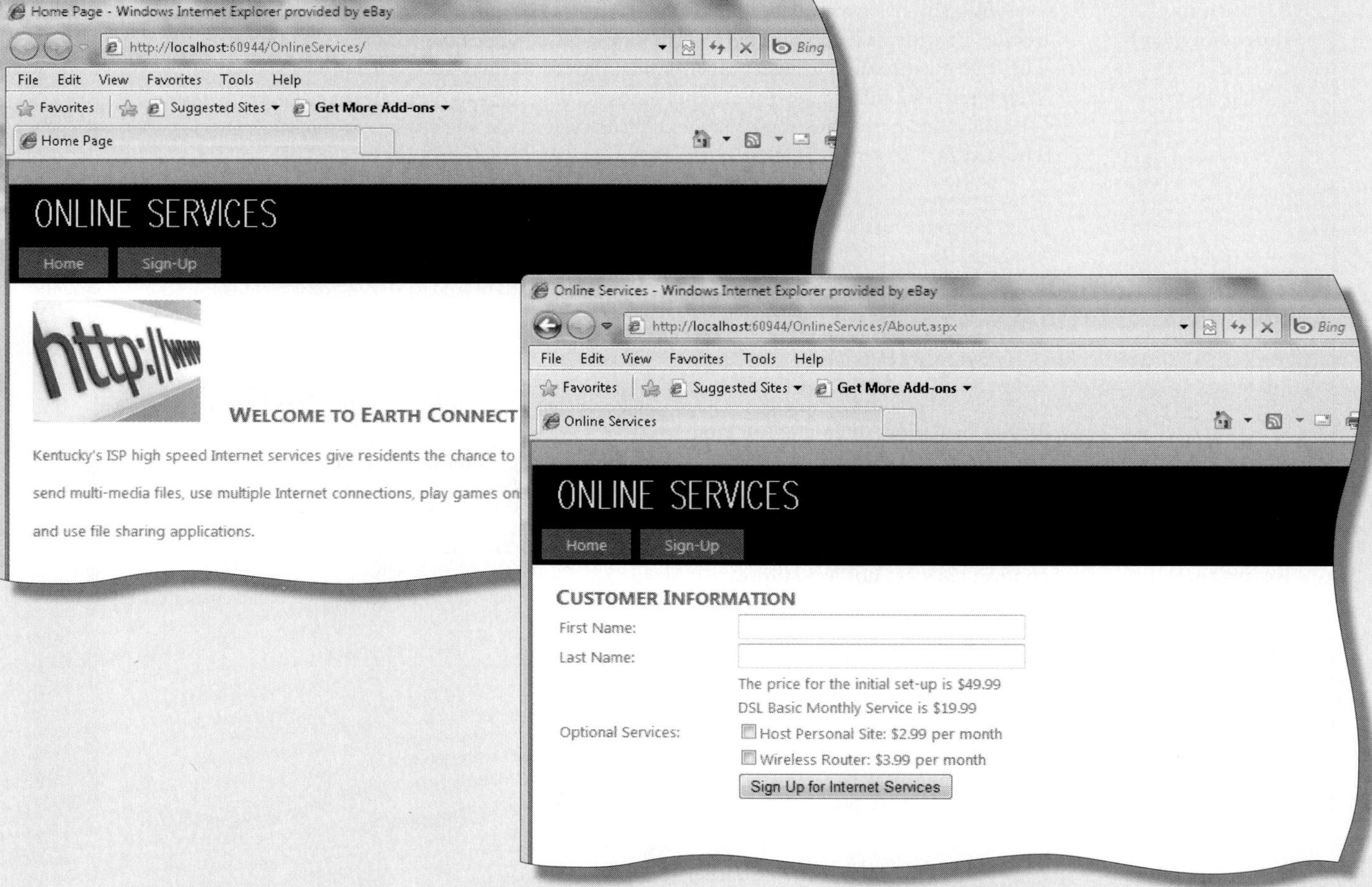

FIGURE 7-87

Case Programming Assignments

4 ●●

HELP DESK

Design a Web application and write the code that will execute according to the program requirements shown in Figure 7-88. Before writing the code, create an event planning document for each event in the program. Create a Use Case Definition document for the application.

REQUIREMENTS DOCUMENT

Date submitted: February 22, 2014

Application title: Help Desk Work Ticket Web Application

Purpose: This Web application allows college staff to fill in a Web form requesting help from a computer help desk.

Program Procedures: From a Web application, the user should enter their name, phone number, e-mail address, lab number (1–15), computer station number (1–30), the operating system (DropDownList object with 3 options), and a large TextBox object to describe the problem in order to create a work ticket for the help desk.

Algorithms, Processing, and Conditions:

1. The user must be able to enter information about the requested computer repair on a Web form. The user will enter their first and last name, e-mail address, telephone number, lab number (1–15), computer station number (1–30), the operating system (DropDownList object with the choices of Windows 7, Windows Vista, or Windows XP), and a large TextBox object to describe the problem in order to create a work ticket for the help desk.
2. After the information is entered, the user can click the Submit button.
3. The information entered is validated.
4. The application displays a help desk work ticket below the Submit button.

Notes and Restrictions:

1. Data validation tools should be used. The first and last names are validated to confirm that they are not left blank.
2. The e-mail address is checked to verify it is not blank and that it conforms to the proper e-mail format.
3. The phone number is checked to verify it is not blank and that it conforms to a U.S. phone number.
4. The lab number and computer number are to be validated to confirm they are within the proper ranges.

Comments: n/a

FIGURE 7-88

Case Programming Assignments

5 ●●

LIL CUCCI'S PIZZERIA ONLINE

Design a Web application that calculates the cost of pizza according to the prices listed in Figure 7-89. The Home page opens with a picture and information about the great homemade pizza pies. The Order page provides an order form and displays the final price. Write the code that will execute according to the program requirements shown in Figure 7-90 on the next page. Before writing the code, create an event planning document for each event in the program. Create a Use Case Definition document for the application.

Pizza Size	Cost
Small	$7.99
Medium	$9.99
Large	$12.99
Extra Large	$15.99
Each Extra Topping (Cheese Included)	$0.99

FIGURE 7-89

Case Programming Assignments

REQUIREMENTS DOCUMENT

Date submitted:	July 24, 2013
Application title:	Lil Cucci's Pizzeria Web Application
Purpose:	This Web application allows a customer to fill out a pizza order form.
Program Procedures:	From a Web application, the user should enter their name, address, and phone number. They also should select the size of pizza they would like to order and the toppings. The final cost of the order will be displayed.
Algorithms, Processing, and Conditions:	1. The Web site has two pages. The Home page promotes the pizzeria. The Order page displays an order form. 2. The user must be able to enter information to order a pizza using a Web form. The user will enter their first and last name, address, phone number, the size of the pizza from a DropDownList object and CheckBoxes displaying pizza topping choices (at least six kinds of toppings). 3. After the information is entered, the user clicks the Submit button. 4. The information entered will be validated. 5. The application displays the final cost of the pizza order and a message that the pizza will be delivered in 45 minutes.
Notes and Restrictions:	1. Data Validation tools should be used. The first and last names are validated to confirm that they are not left blank. 2. The phone number is checked to ensure it is not blank and that it conforms to a U.S. phone number.
Comments:	1. A picture of a pizza will be displayed on the Web form.

FIGURE 7-90

Case Programming Assignments

6 ●● THE VILLAGE BIKE SHOP

Design a Web application and write the code that will execute according to the program requirements shown in Figure 7-91. Before writing the code, create an event planning document for each event in the program. Create a Use Case Definition document for the application.

REQUIREMENTS DOCUMENT

Date submitted: January 4, 2014

Application title: The Village Bike Shop Reservation Form Web Application

Purpose: This Web application allows the user to reserve rental bikes online.

Program Procedures: From a Web application, the user should enter their name, address, and phone number. They also should select the type of bike, number of hours, date, and number of bicycles needed. The final cost of the order is displayed.

Algorithms, Processing, and Conditions:

1. The user must be able to view a graphic of a bicycle, a DropDownList object with the number of hours (1–8), a calendar requesting the date the bike is being reserved, the type of bike (beach cruiser, road, or mountain), and a TextBox object indicating the quantity (check to make sure the number is between 1 and 12).
2. After the information is entered, the user clicks the Submit button.
3. The information entered will be validated.
4. The application will display a summary of their reservation. Beach cruisers are $5 per hour, road bikes are $6 per hour, and mountain bikes are $7.50 per hour per bike. The total cost will be displayed for the total reservation with the date.

Notes and Restrictions:

1. Data Validation tools should be used. The range of the quantity ordered is to be 1–12.
2. The name, address, and phone number must be present.
3. The phone number must conform to a U.S. phone number.

Comments:

1. A picture of a bicycle will be shown on the Web form.

FIGURE 7-91

Case Programming Assignments

7 ●●● RE-CREATE AN ONLINE FORM

Create a requirements document and a Use Case Definition document, and design a Web application, based on the case project shown in Figure 7-92.

Find an online form on the Internet you would like to re-create that has varied objects such as a Label, RadioButton, CheckBox, TextBox, and DropDownList objects. Use a similar layout of the existing Web site and at least eight objects on the form to display your own version of the Web site for practice. Validate the form using validation objects as needed.

FIGURE 7-92

8 ●●● MOORE'S LAW

Create a requirements document and a Use Case Definition document, and then create a Web application, based on the case project shown in Figure 7-93.

Create a Web application that displays Moore's Law, which states that the computing power or the number of transistors within the same silicon processor doubles every 18 months. In other words, computing speed doubles every 18 months. As shown in the following table, allow the user to enter the current average speed in GHz and display the next 15 years of projected speed. Use the validation controls to make sure the entry is filled in and that the decimal entered is between 1.0 and 10.0.

Moore's Law

Enter the Speed of Computers Presently:

3.8

After 1.5 years 7.6 GHz
After 3.0 years 15.2 GHz
After 4.5 years 30.4 GHz
After 6.0 years 60.8 GHz
After 7.5 years 121.6 GHz
After 9.0 years 243.2 GHz
After 10.5 years 486.4 GHz
After 12.0 years 972.8 GHz
After 13.5 years 1945.6 GHz
After 15.0 years 3891.2 GHz

Display

FIGURE 7-93

Case Programming Assignments

9 JAVA SHOP

Create a requirements document and a Use Case Definition document, and then create a Web application, based on the case project shown in Figure 7-94.

To speed up the ordering process, a local coffee shop will allow customers to order their coffee on a touch screen while standing in line. The Web application will display the cost of the coffee. Allow the customer to enter their first name, display a DropDownList object with five coffee flavors, and allow the user to select the size of the coffee: Tall, Grande, and Vente. Prices for these sizes are shown in the table below. Use validation controls. The coffee shop also provides options such as a double shot, flavored syrups, whipped cream, and soy milk for 49 cents each. Display the person's name and order with the purchase price with a 6.5% sales tax.

Size	Price
Tall	$2.59
Grande	$3.09
Vente	$3.59

FIGURE 7-94

CHAPTER 8

Using Procedures and Exception Handling

OBJECTIVES

You will have mastered the material in this chapter when you can:

- Create a splash screen
- Pause the splash screen
- Add a ComboBox object to a Windows Form
- Write Code for a SelectedIndexChanged event
- Code a Sub procedure
- Pass an argument to a procedure by value
- Pass an argument to a procedure by reference
- Code a Function procedure to return a value
- Create a class-level variable
- Catch an exception using a Try-Catch block

Introduction

The programs you have written thus far in this course were relatively small applications. Most real-world software, however, solves more expansive problems. As an application grows, it is important to divide each facet of a problem into separate sections of code called **procedures**. By using the principle of divide and conquer to create procedures, the code becomes more manageable.

In previous programs you have learned about data verification to ensure the user enters valid data before the data is processed. To expand your knowledge of data verification, you need to understand exception handling using Try-Catch blocks, which can check for any error a user might commit. By managing exceptions using Try-Catch blocks, you build high-quality, robust applications.

Finally, one way to make your programs more professional is to display a splash screen while the full program loads. In this chapter, you will learn to design and write procedures, include Try-Catch blocks in your program, and create a splash screen.

Chapter Project

The sample program in this chapter displays two Windows forms and is more complex than previous applications. A travel agent has requested a Windows application that provides pricing information for an island water-sports company named Ocean Tours. The purpose of the Windows application is to display the pricing information for water sports at different island locations. Ocean Tours is located in Aruba, Jamaica, and Key West in the Caribbean. Each island specializes in different water sports activities. The table in Figure 8-1 shows the available tours for each island, the length of the tour, and the tour cost.

Location	Tour Type	Tour Length	Tour Cost
Aruba	Deep Sea Fishing	8 hours	$199
	Kayaking	2 hours	$89
	Scuba	3 hours	$119
	Snorkeling	4 hours	$89
Jamaica	Glass Bottom Boat	2 hours	$39
	Parasailing	2 hours	$119
	Snorkeling	3 hours	$59
Key West	Deep Sea Fishing	4 hours	$89
	Glass Bottom Boat	2 hours	$29
	Scuba	3 hours	$119
	Snorkeling	3 hours	$59

FIGURE 8-1

The program begins with an opening screen called a splash screen. Shown in Figure 8-2, this splash screen displays the company title and image logo for approximately five seconds.

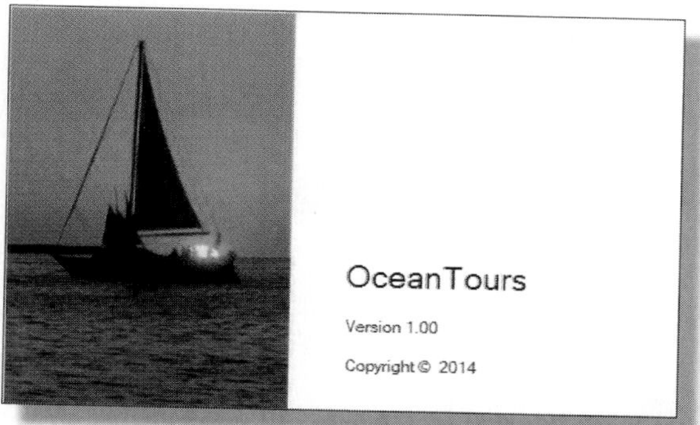

FIGURE 8-2

After the splash screen closes, the main form of the application opens requesting that the user select the island location. When the user clicks the ComboBox arrow, the three island locations of Aruba, Jamaica, and Key West appear in the drop-down list, as shown in Figure 8-3.

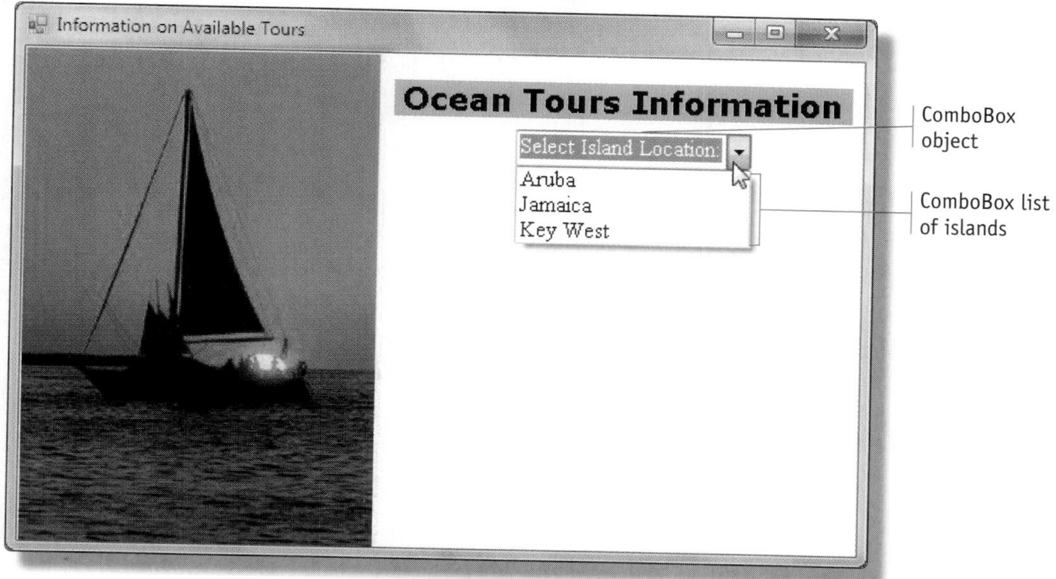

FIGURE 8-3

ONLINE REINFORCEMENT

To view a video of program execution, visit scsite.com/vb2010/ch8 and then select Figure 8-2.

After the user selects the island location, the Windows form displays form controls that request the number of guests in the party and the type of tour. The user enters the number of guests, selects the type of tour in which she will be traveling, and then clicks the Find Cost of Tour button. As shown in Figure 8-4, the program displays the cost and length of the tour.

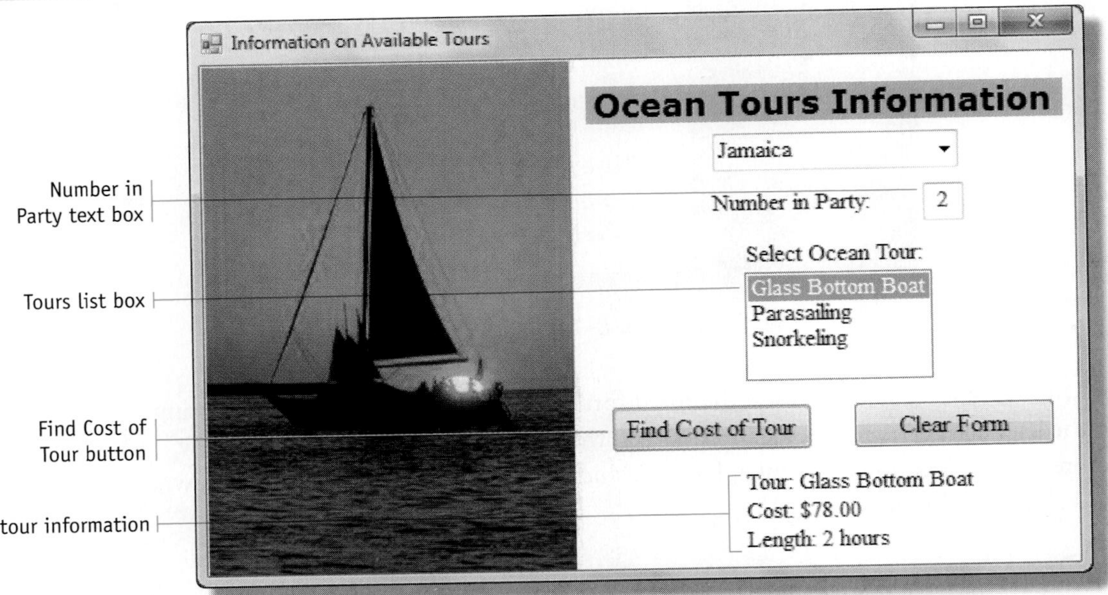

FIGURE 8-4

Creating a Splash Screen

A **splash screen** is an opening screen that appears as an application is loading, signaling that the program is about to start and displaying an image and information to engage the user. In the Ocean Tours chapter project, the splash screen displays a sailboat image and the title, the version, and the copyright information (see Figure 8-2 on the previous page).

Visual Basic provides a generic splash screen template you can add to your project with or without modification. You can change the generic graphic on the splash screen by changing the BackgroundImage property on the Properties window. To use the generic splash screen, you can complete the following steps:

STEP 1 Create a Windows application named Ocean Tours. Name the form frmTours. Click Project on the menu bar and then click Add New Item on the Project menu. Scroll down to view Splash Screen.

The Add New Item dialog box is displayed (Figure 8-5).

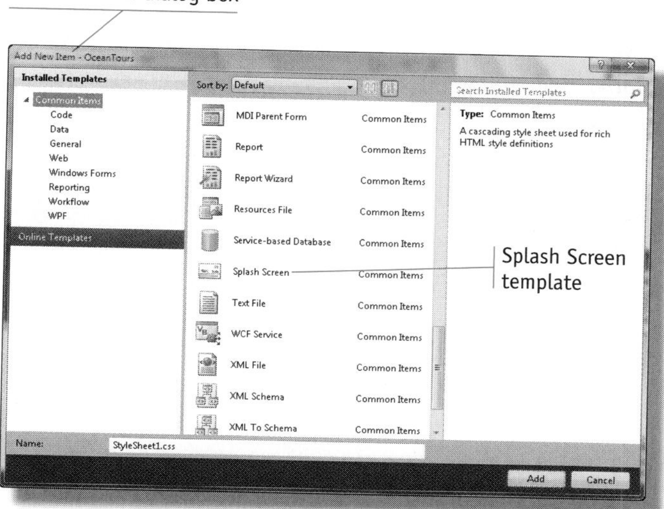

FIGURE 8-5

STEP 2 In the Add New Item dialog box, select Splash Screen in the center pane.

The Splash Screen template is selected (Figure 8-6).

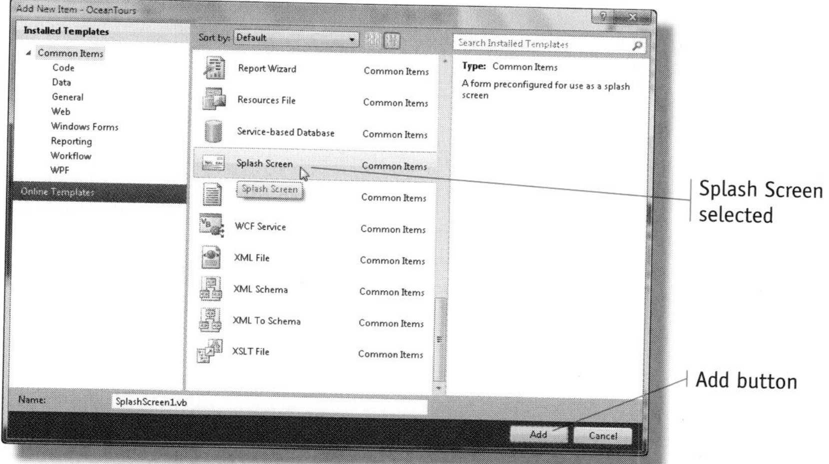

FIGURE 8-6

STEP 3 Click the Add button in the Add New Item dialog box.

A form preconfigured by Visual Studio as a splash screen opens as a new tab named SplashScreen1.vb[Design] in the Design window (Figure 8-7). The splash screen can be customized with different graphics and text to suit an application.

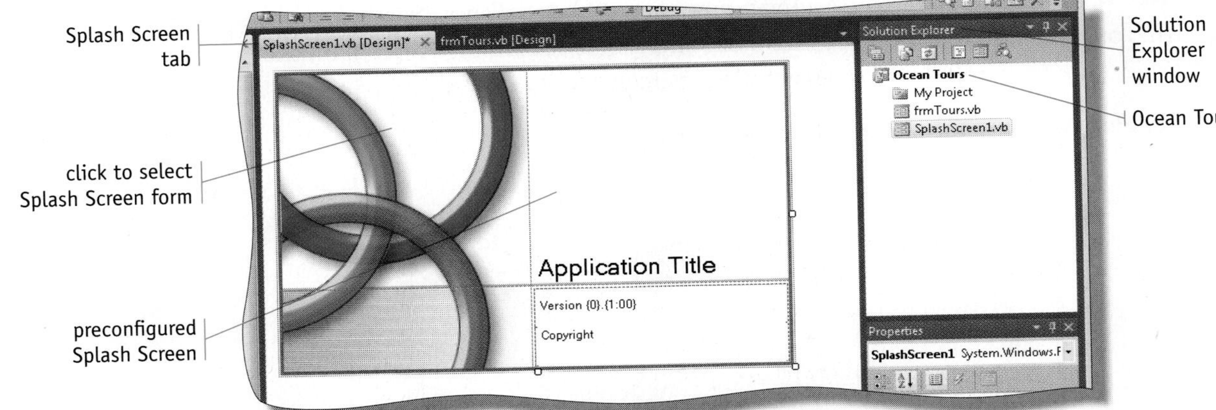

FIGURE 8-7

STEP 4 Click the splash screen form in the left side of the form to select the form. To set the application to display the splash screen first, right-click OceanTours in the Solution Explorer.

The splash screen form is selected (Figure 8-8). A shortcut menu opens.

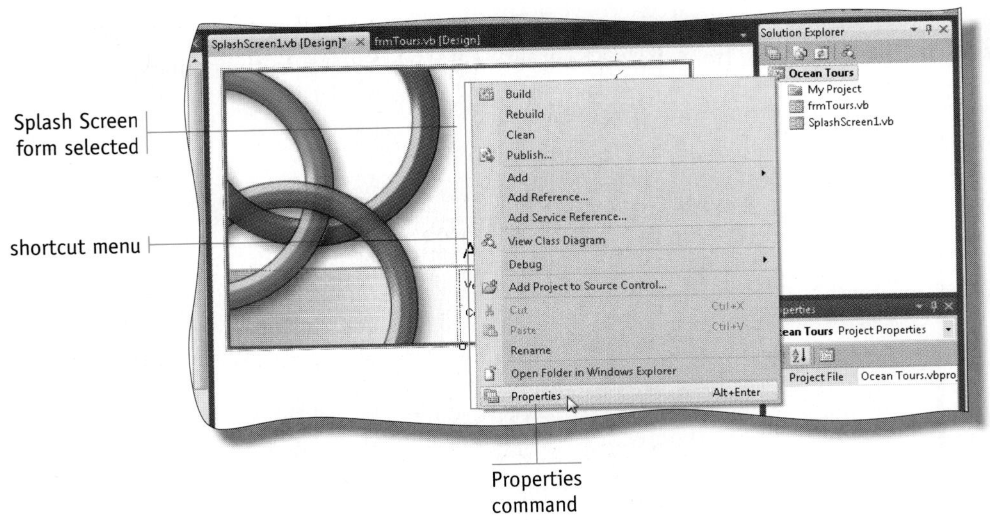

FIGURE 8-8

STEP 5 Click Properties on the shortcut menu.

The Project Designer opens displaying the Application tab (Figure 8-9). The Project Designer provides a central location for managing project properties, settings, and resources. The Project Designer appears as a single window in the Visual Studio IDE. It contains a number of pages that are accessed through tabs on the left.

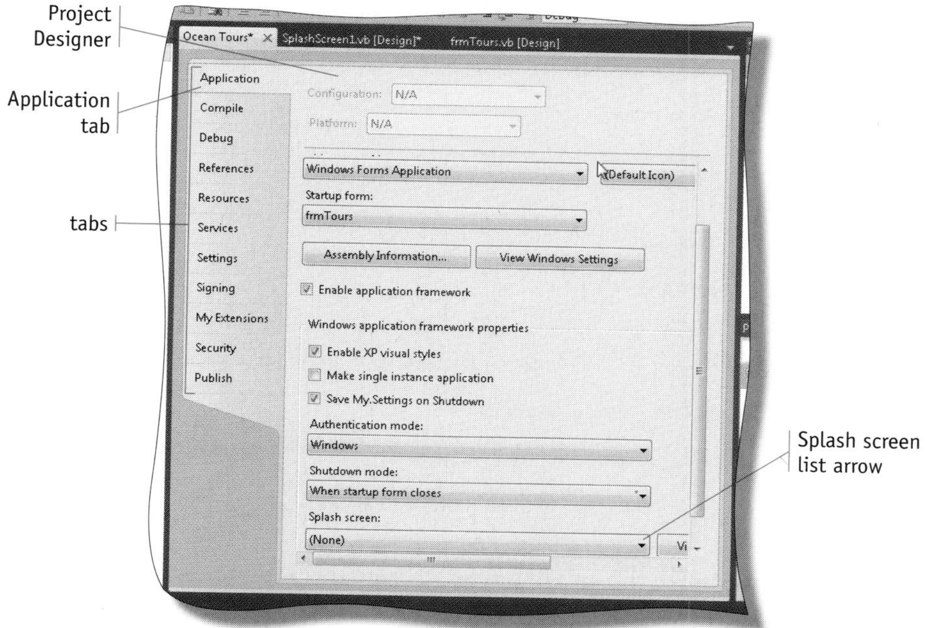

FIGURE 8-9

STEP 6 In the Windows application framework properties section, click the Splash screen list arrow, and then click SplashScreen1 to select the form as the splash screen used for project.

SplashScreen1 is selected in the Splash screen list (Figure 8-10).

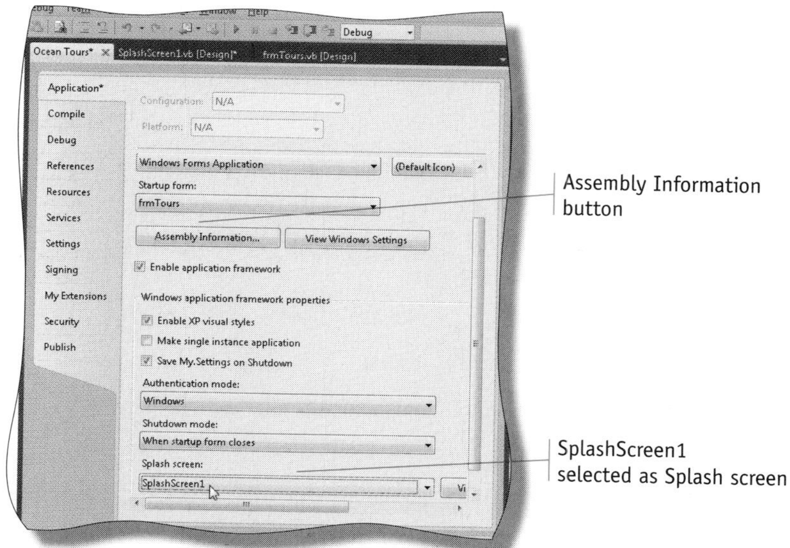

FIGURE 8-10

STEP 7 Click the Assembly Information button on the Properties Designer to open the Assembly Information dialog box.

The Assembly Information dialog box opens (Figure 8-11).

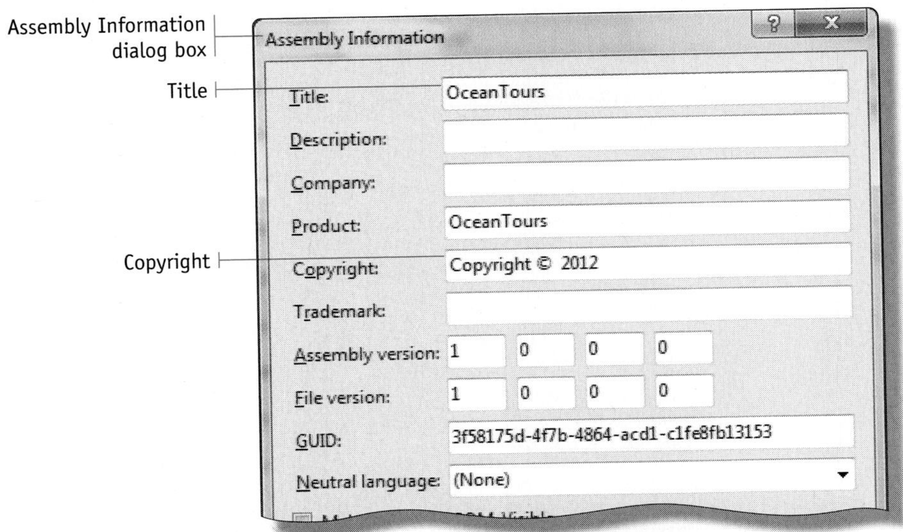

FIGURE 8-11

STEP 8 To customize the splash screen, change the Title to `Ocean Tours` and the Copyright to the present year. The File Version can be changed as you update the application.

The Title and Copyright year are changed. The text on the splash screen form will not change until the application runs (Figure 8-12).

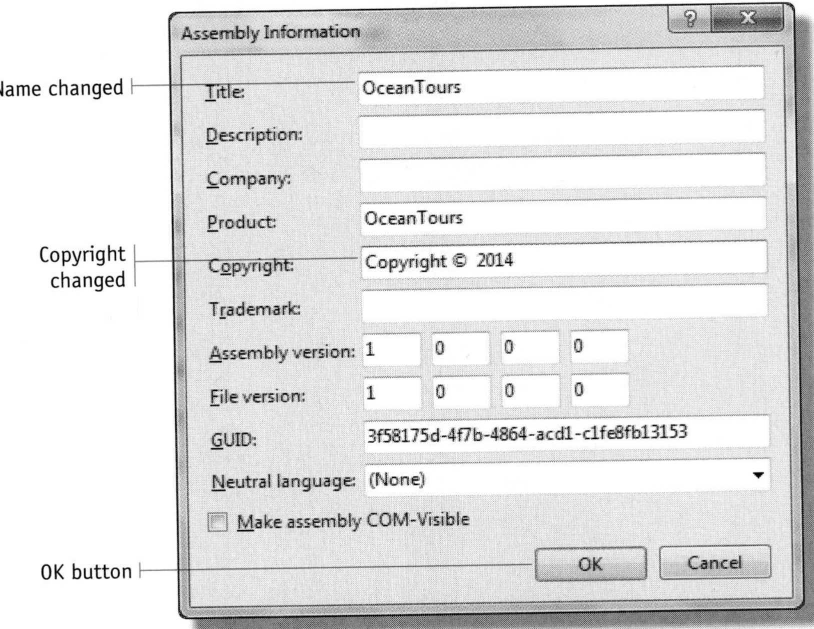

FIGURE 8-12

STEP 9 Click the OK button on the Assembly Information dialog box. Close the OceanTours* Project Designer window. To change the predefined image, first download the ocean.jpg picture from the scsite.com/vb2010/ch8/images Web site and store the image in a location you remember. Then, click the SplashScreen1.vb [Design] tab. Click the left side of the splash screen, making sure to select the entire splash screen form. The Properties window should identify MainLayoutPanel if you have selected the entire splash screen form. Click to the right of the Background Image property in the Properties window, and then click the ellipsis button. In the Select Resource dialog box, click the Project resource file radio button if necessary. Import the ocean.jpg picture by clicking the Import button in the Select Resource dialog box and selecting the ocean.jpg image from the location where you stored it. Click the OK button in the Select Resource dialog box.

The splash screen background image changes from the predefined image to the ocean.jpg image (Figure 8-13).

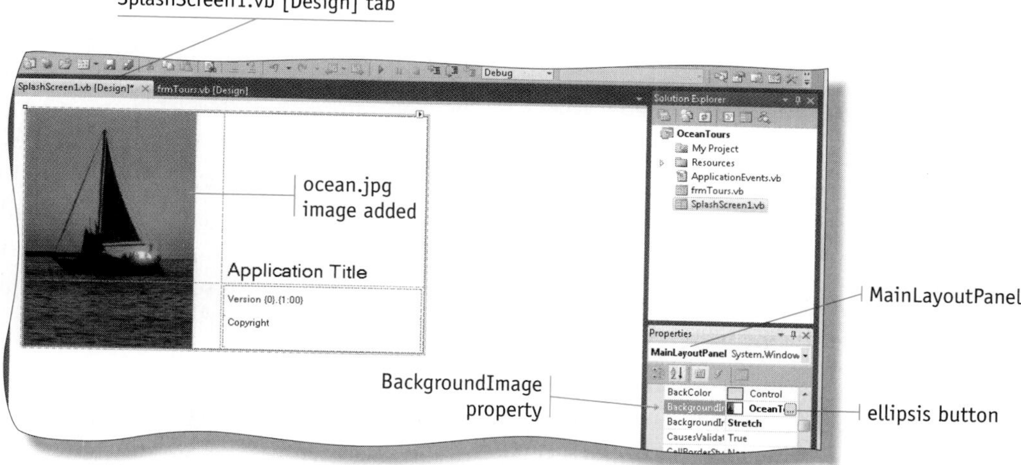

FIGURE 8-13

STEP 10 Run the application by clicking the Start Debugging button on the Standard toolbar.

The application begins to run. The splash screen appears for a moment and immediately closes (Figure 8-14). The amount of time the splash screen is displayed is based on the time needed to open the main form.

FIGURE 8-14

> **ONLINE REINFORCEMENT**
> To view a video of the process in the previous steps, visit scsite.com/vb2010/ch8 and then select Figure 8-5.

Pausing the Splash Screen

The user needs enough time to read the splash screen before it closes and the main form opens. To pause the splash screen for a specific time period, you can call the Sleep procedure. In fact, you can pause the execution of any application by calling the Thread.Sleep procedure. The Sleep procedure uses an integer value that determines how long the application should pause. To pause the splash screen, you can complete the following steps:

STEP 1 After the splash screen loads, the application executes any code in the form load event handler. To display the splash screen for five seconds, the code that calls the Sleep procedure should be in the form load event handler. To open the code editor window and the form load event handler, double-click the background of the frmTours Windows Form object in the Design window.

The frmTours_Load event handler opens in the code editor window (Figure 8-15).

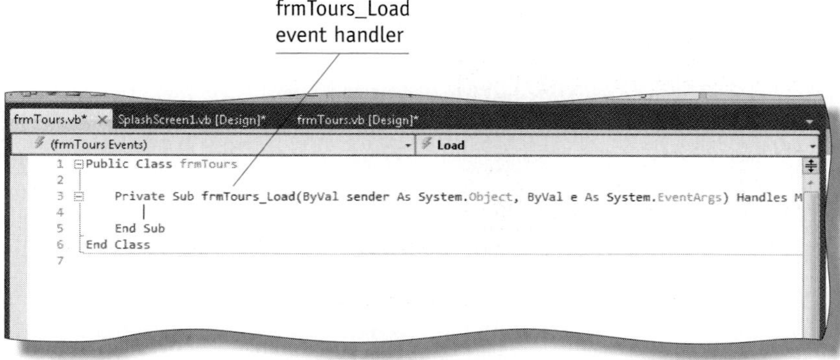

FIGURE 8-15

STEP 2 Click inside the frmTours_Load event handler. Type `Threading.` to cause IntelliSense to display a list of possible entries. If necessary, type `T` to select Thread from the IntelliSense list. Type `.S` to select Sleep from the IntelliSense list. Type `(5000)`.

The call for the Sleep procedure is entered (Figure 8-16). When the program executes and the frmTours_Load event is executed, the Sleep procedure suspends the execution of the application for 5000 milliseconds (5 seconds). This means that while the splash screen is displayed, the form will not be loaded for five seconds. You can increase the number of milliseconds if you want a longer pause.

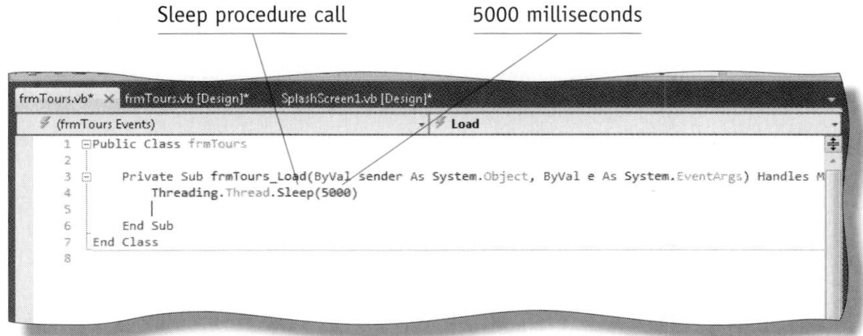

FIGURE 8-16

IN THE REAL WORLD

A splash screen is not crucial in all applications, but it can make an application look more complete. Using a splash screen properly makes a program appear to load much faster than it actually does. The user has something to look at almost immediately, even as the rest of a large program continues loading from a network or other medium.

ONLINE REINFORCEMENT

To view a video of the process in the previous steps, visit scsite.com/vb2010/ch8 and then select Figure 8-15.

Adding a ComboBox Object

The Ocean Tours sample program requires a new type of object, a ComboBox object, in the Windows form to determine which island the user will be touring (Figure 8-17).

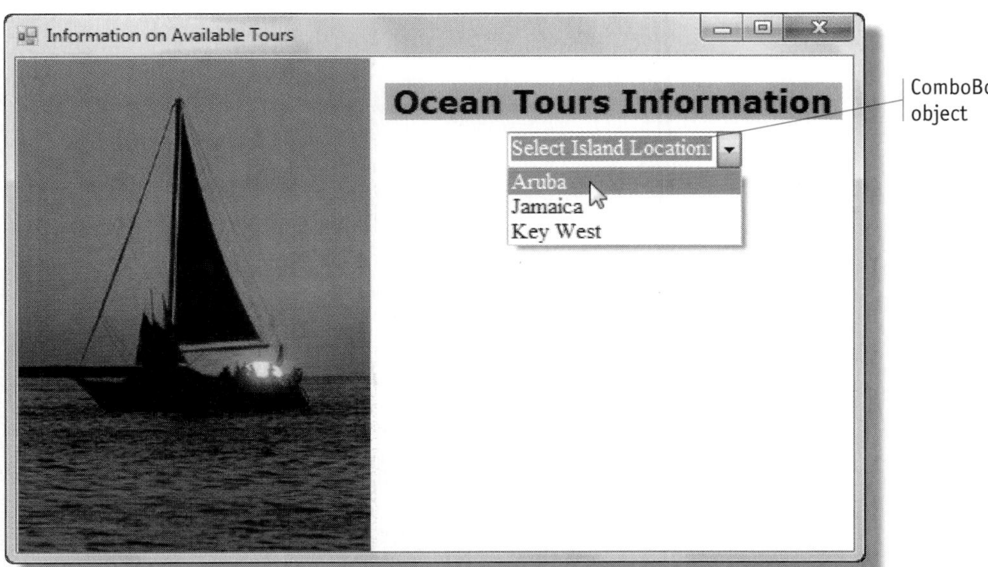

FIGURE 8-17

A ComboBox object consists of two parts. The top part is a text box that allows the user to enter text. The second part is a list box that, when the user clicks the box arrow, displays a list of items from which the user can select one item. To save space on a form, use a ComboBox object because the full list is not displayed until the user clicks the list arrow. The prefix for the ComboBox object (Name) property is cbo. To place a ComboBox object on a Windows Form object, you can complete the following steps:

STEP 1 Drag the ComboBox .NET component from the Common Controls category of the Toolbox to the approximate location where you want to place the ComboBox object.

The ComboBox object is placed on the Windows Form object (Figure 8-18).

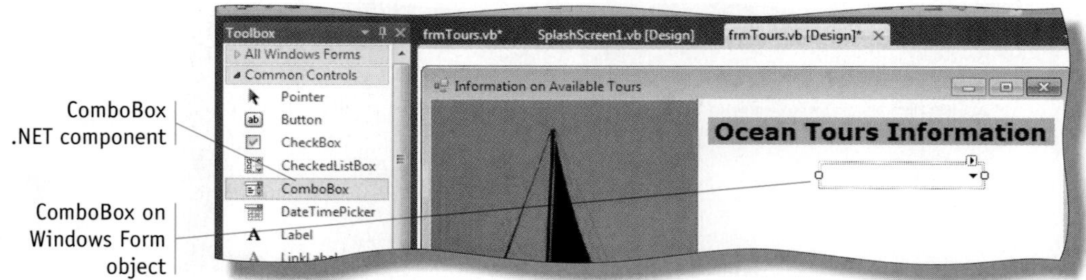

FIGURE 8-18

STEP 2 With the ComboBox object selected, scroll in the Properties window to the (Name) property. Double-click in the right column of the (Name) property and then enter the name `cboIsland`.

The name you entered is displayed in the (Name) property in the Properties window (Figure 8-19).

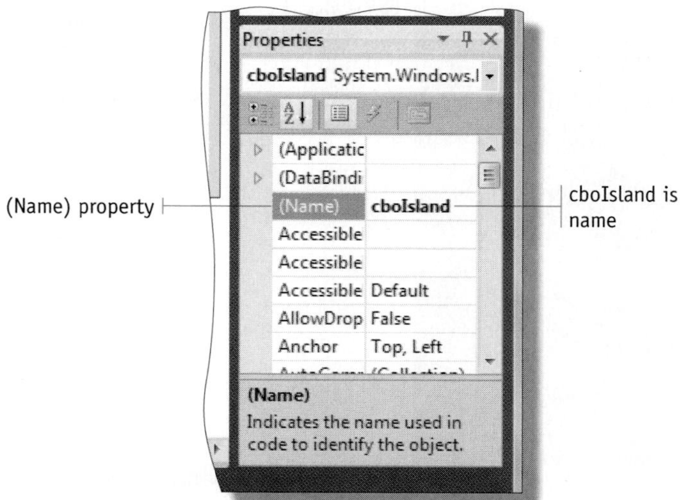

FIGURE 8-19

STEP 3 In the Properties window, scroll to the Text property. Click to the right of the Text property and enter `Select Island Location:` to specify the text that appears in the combo box. Resize the ComboBox object as needed to display the data in the box.

The Text property is changed to the instructions to select an island location (Figure 8-20).

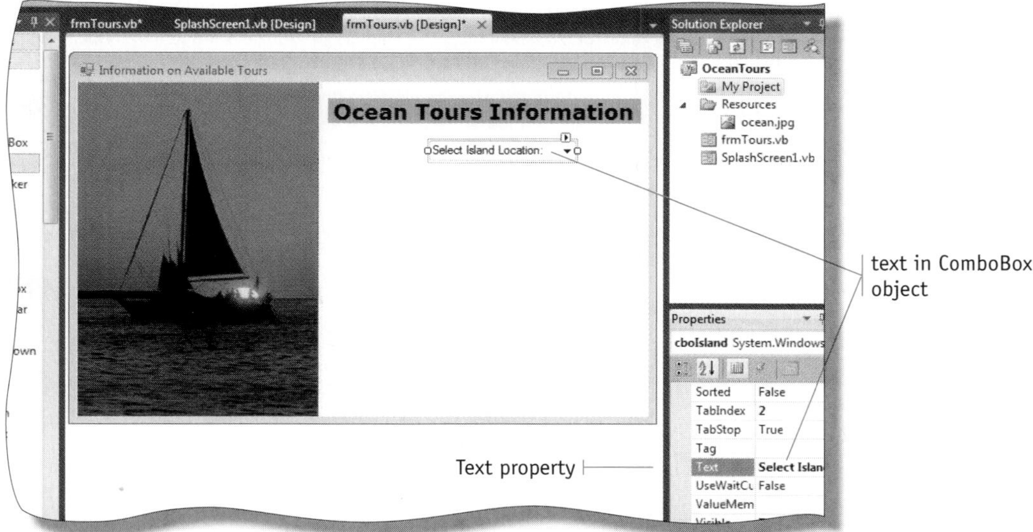

FIGURE 8-20

STEP 4 In the Properties window, scroll to the Items property, and click to the right of the Items property on the word (Collection). Click the ellipsis button. The String Collection Editor dialog box opens. Enter the island locations `Aruba` (press ENTER), `Jamaica` (press ENTER), and `Key West`.

The three items for the ComboBox list are shown in the String Collection Editor dialog box (Figure 8-21).

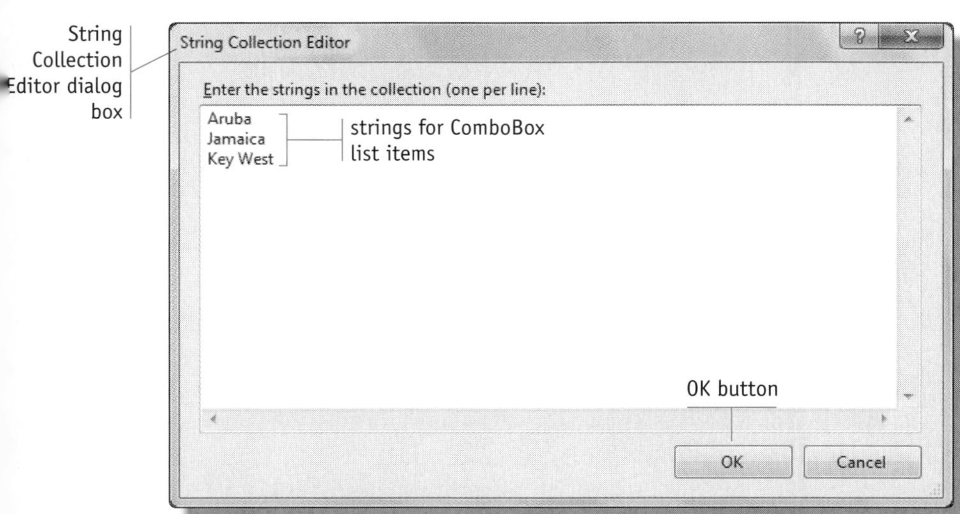

FIGURE 8-21

STEP 5 In the String Collection Editor dialog box, click the OK button. Click the Start Debugging button on the Standard toolbar to run the application. Click the list arrow on the right of the ComboBox object to view the contents. You can select a choice from the list.

The list in the ComboBox object contains the names previously entered in the String Collection Editor dialog box (Figure 8-22). The user can select one of the items in the list.

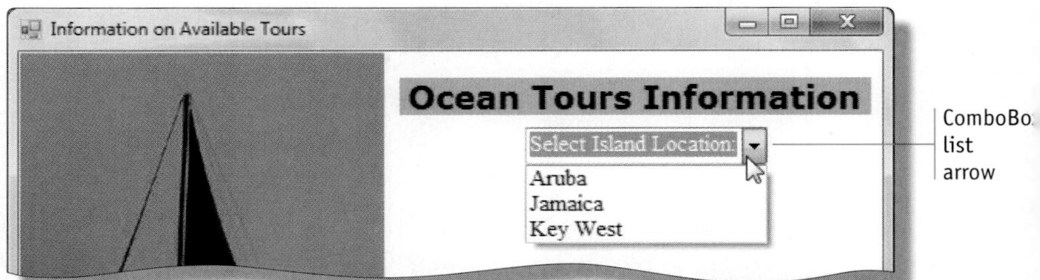

FIGURE 8-22

ONLINE REINFORCEMENT

To view a video of the process in the previous steps, visit scsite.com/vb2010/ch8 and then select Figure 8-18.

Determining the ComboBox Selected Index

To determine the cost of the tour selected in the Ocean Tours sample program, the user first selects the island location from the ComboBox object list. Code for the program must determine both that a value was selected and which one was selected. When the user selects an item in the ComboBox object list, the **SelectedIndex** property for the ComboBox object is assigned to the number that represents a zero-based index of the selected item. For example, if the user selects Aruba as shown in Figure 8-23, the index of 0 is the SelectedIndex for the ComboBox object, which can be assigned to an Integer data type variable.

HEADS UP

The ComboBox object also has a SelectedItem property, which returns a string value that represents the selected list item.

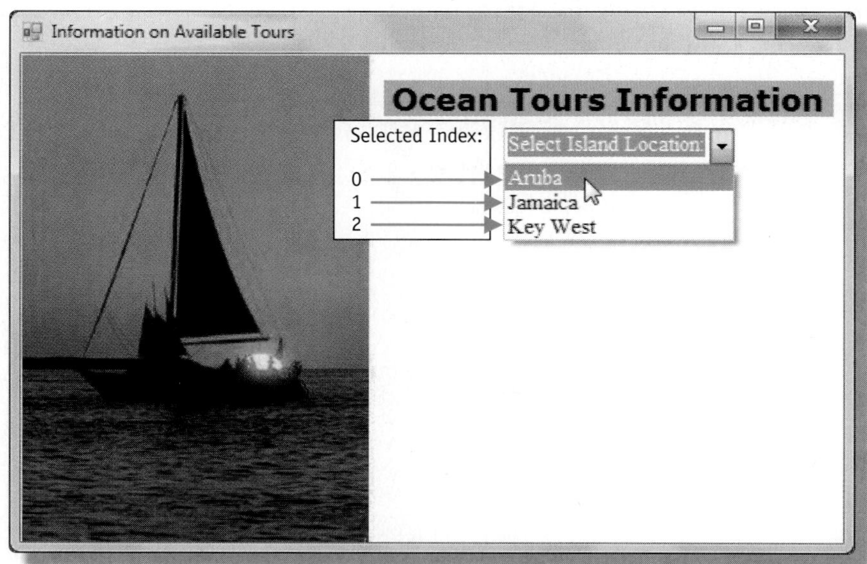

FIGURE 8-23

If the user has not made a selection, the SelectedIndex property is set to −1. To assign the item that the user selects using the SelectedIndex property, you can use a statement as shown in Figure 8-24.

```
intIslandChoice = cboIsland.SelectedIndex()
```

FIGURE 8-24

Handling SelectedIndexChanged Events

In the Ocean Tours chapter project, the user's first action is to select the vacation island location. When the Ocean Tours application opens, the user views the main title and a ComboBox object named cboIsland, as shown in Figure 8-25.

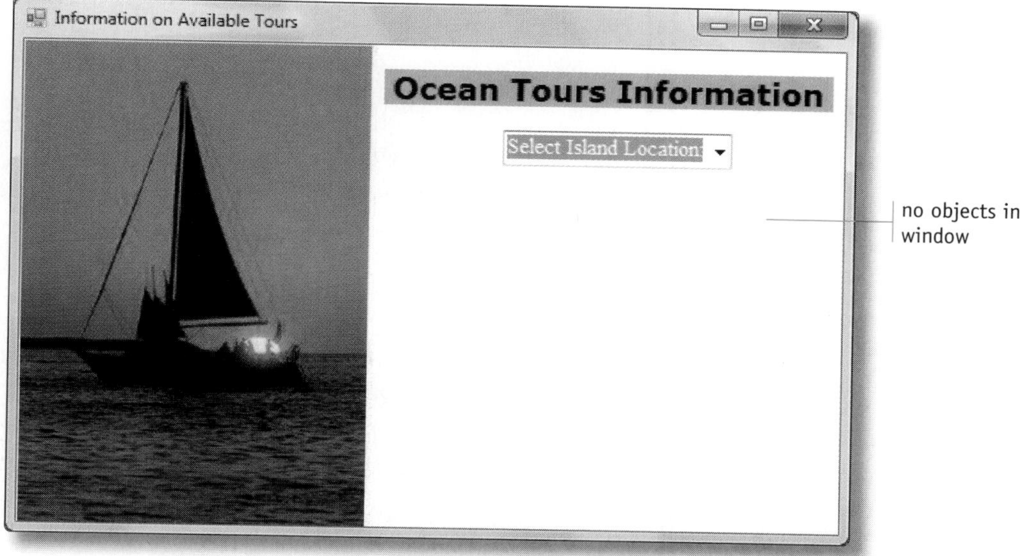

FIGURE 8-25

Notice that a Button object is not displayed in the window shown in Figure 8-25 on the previous page. When the user selects the island location, the application displays other objects on the form that request the number of people in the party, display the list of possible tour choices for that selected island, and request the month that the user is taking the tour. Instead of using a button click event to begin this process, another type of event handler called the **SelectedIndexChanged** event handler is executed when the user selects the island location of the tour. The SelectedIndexChanged event is triggered by the user selecting an item in the ComboBox object because the selected index in the ComboBox object is changed when the user makes a selection. To create a SelectedIndexChanged event, you can complete the following steps:

STEP 1 Select the ComboBox object named cboIsland on the Windows Form object.

The cboIsland ComboBox object is selected on the form (Figure 8-26).

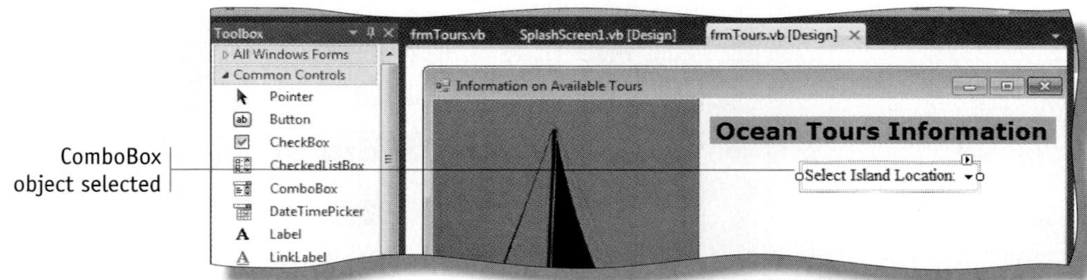

FIGURE 8-26

STEP 2 Double-click the ComboBox object. Close the Toolbox.

The code editing window is opened and the code generated by Visual Studio for the SelectedIndexChanged event handler is displayed (Figure 8-27). Within the event handler, you can write any code that should be executed when the user makes a selection in the cboIsland ComboBox object.

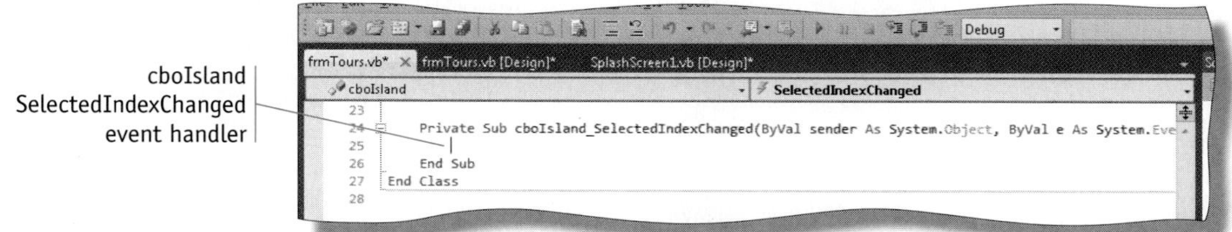

FIGURE 8-27

ONLINE REINFORCEMENT

To view a video of the process in the previous steps, visit scsite.com/vb2010/ch8 and then select Figure 8-26.

By executing an event handler when the user selects a particular item in the cboIsland ComboBox object, the program works efficiently without multiple user clicks. Many objects, such as the ListBox and DropDownList objects, can be used in the same manner as the ComboBox object with a SelectedIndexChanged event handler.

Procedures

The Ocean Tours application is a larger and more complex program than in previous chapters. Because the code for each event handler will be long, you should divide the code into smaller parts, each of which completes a specific task for the event handler. It is easier to deal with a larger program if you can focus on code that accomplishes a single task.

When a program is broken into manageable parts, each part is called a **procedure**. A procedure is a named set of code that performs a given task. In previous programs, you have called procedures, such as the Clear procedure and the ToString procedure, that have been written by the developers of Visual Studio. In the Ocean Tours program in this chapter, you will both write and call procedures.

Visual Basic provides two types of procedures: Sub procedures and Function procedures. The following sections explain these two type of procedures and how to code them.

Coding a Sub Procedure

A **Sub procedure** is a procedure that completes its task but does not return any data to the calling procedure. A Sub procedure in Visual Basic 2010 is defined by using the Sub keyword. A **Sub** procedure is the series of Visual Basic statements enclosed by the Sub and End Sub statements. Each time the Sub procedure is called, its statements are executed, starting with the first executable statement after the Sub statement and ending with the first End Sub statement. A Sub procedure is called with a statement consisting of the procedure name and a set of parentheses in the form of a **procedure call**, as shown in Figure 8-28.

HEADS UP

The word Private appearing before the Sub keyword specifies the Sub procedure can be called only by code within the class where the Sub procedure is located. For Sub procedures that perform tasks required only within the class, it should be used.

General Format: Procedure Call

The procedure call is made:

```
ProcedureName()
```

The **procedure declaration** that begins the Sub procedure has the form:

```
Private Sub ProcedureName()

    ' Line(s) of code

End Sub
```

FIGURE 8-28

IN THE REAL WORLD

You can create your own Sub procedures to perform specific or repeated tasks. Sub procedures are not triggered by clicking a button or in reaction to an event. Sub procedures must be called within the code.

In the Ocean Tours application, each island provides ocean tour selections. Based on the user's selection of an island location, the ListBox object in Figure 8-29 is filled with the various water tours available. For example, if the user selects Aruba, the tours Deep Sea Fishing, Kayaking, Scuba, and Snorkeling are displayed in the ListBox object.

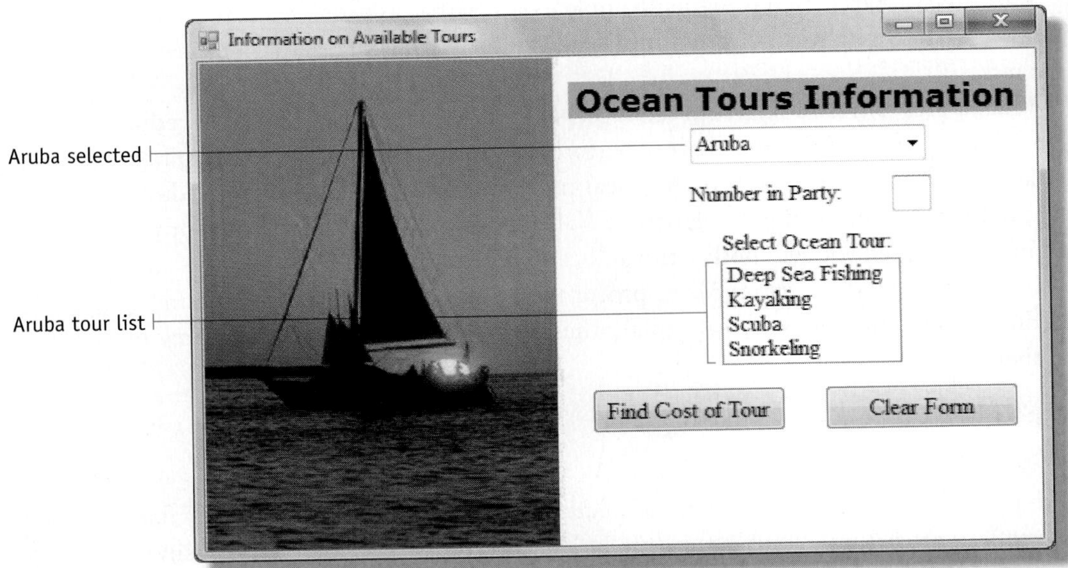

FIGURE 8-29

The items in the ListBox object are different based on the island selected. Figure 8-30 shows the code in the SelectedIndexChanged event handler that calls a Sub procedure to fill in the items in the ListBox object based on the island location selected by the user.

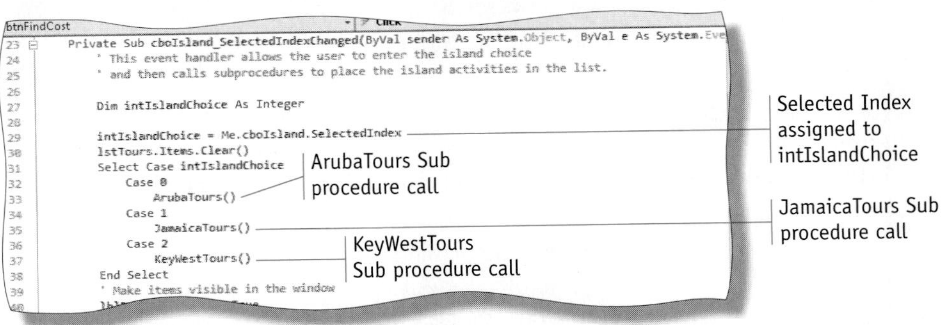

FIGURE 8-30

In Figure 8-30 on the previous page, the selected index for the cboIsland ComboBox is assigned to the Integer variable named intIslandChoice. Then, in the Case Select statement, the appropriate Sub procedure is called based on the island the user selected. When the selected index is equal to zero, the first item in the ComboBox list was selected, which is Aruba, so the ArubaTours Sub procedure is called. Notice that the name of the Sub procedure is specified followed by open and closed parentheses. As you learned previously, the Visual Basic compiler recognizes a procedure call by the parentheses.

The ArubaTours Sub procedure code is shown in Figure 8-31.

```
Private Sub ArubaTours()
    ' This procedure fills in the possible ocean tours for Aruba
    lstTours.Items.Add(_strDeepSeaFishing)
    lstTours.Items.Add(_strKayaking)
    lstTours.Items.Add(_strScuba)
    lstTours.Items.Add(_strSnorkeling)

End Sub
```

FIGURE 8-31

In the code in Figure 8-31, the string values for the types of tours available on Aruba are added as items in the lstTours ListBox object. Notice that the String variables contain an underscore as the first character. You will recall that this designation identifies the variables as class variables that can be referenced in any procedure within the class.

In Figure 8-30 on the previous page, if the SelectedIndex value is 1, the Jamaica Sub procedure is called, and if the SelectedIndex value is 2, the Key West Sub procedure is called. Each of those Sub procedures adds items to the lstTours ListBox object, depending on what tours are available on each island.

A Sub procedure call may be used within a loop, If statements, or even Select Case statements as shown in Figure 8-30 on the previous page. When a Sub procedure is called, the program gives control to the called Sub procedure and executes the lines of code within that Sub procedure. After the Sub procedure has completed its execution, program control returns to the calling procedure and program execution resumes in the calling procedure.

HEADS UP

A Sub procedure call is like a detour on the highway. After the Sub procedure is completed, control returns to the calling procedure.

Passing Arguments

Earlier chapters defined and used the term scope, and explained that variables declared within a procedure are limited in scope to their procedure. Code outside a procedure cannot interact with the variables declared within another procedure.

When a procedure is called, however, the call statement can pass an argument to the called procedure. You have experienced this in previous chapters when you passed a string value to the ToInt32 procedure to convert the string value to an integer value (Figure 8-32).

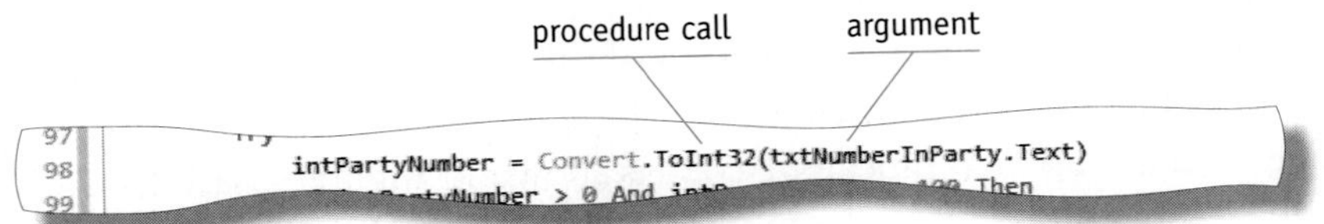

FIGURE 8-32

In Figure 8-32, the argument is contained within parentheses. In this example, the argument is the Text property of the txtNumberInParty TextBox object.

In many applications, passing variables to another procedure is essential because the called procedure requires the value(s) in order to complete its processing. For example, in Figure 8-33, the btnDaysOfWeek click event determines whether a certain day of the week is a weekday or a weekend day. When the Weekday Sub procedure is called, a variable named intNumericDayOfWeek is passed to the Weekday Sub procedure because the Sub procedure must know the numeric day in order to perform its processing.

```
    Private Sub btnDaysOfWeek_Click(ByVal sender As System.Object, ByVal e As System. ↙
    EventArgs) Handles btnDaysOfWeek.Click
        Dim intNumericDayOfWeek As Integer

        intNumericDayOfWeek = Convert.ToInt32(txtDay.Text)
        Weekday(intNumericDayOfWeek)
        MsgBox("Have a Great Week!", "Goodbye")
    End Sub

    Private Sub Weekday(ByVal intDay As Integer)
        If intDay = 1 Or intDay = 7 Then
            lblDisplayDay.Text = "Weekend"
        End If
        If intDay >= 2 And intDay <= 6 Then
            lblDisplayDay.Text = "Weekday"
        End If
    End Sub
```

FIGURE 8-33

In Figure 8-33 on the previous page, the variable named intNumericDayOfWeek is passed to the Weekday Sub procedure by the calling statement on line 24. The value in the intNumericDayOfWeek variable should be 1 for Sunday, 2 for Monday, 3 for Tuesday, 4 for Wednesday, 5 for Thursday, 6 for Friday, and 7 for Saturday.

When a value is passed to a Sub procedure, the Sub procedure declaration, which identifies the name of the Sub procedure, also must contain an entry that defines the argument for use within the Sub procedure. In the Weekday Sub procedure in Figure 8-33 on the previous page, the parentheses following the Sub procedure name -Weekday- on line 28 contain the command ByVal intDay as Integer within parentheses. This entry defines an Integer variable name (intDay) for use within the Sub procedure.

Visual Basic treats variables passed from a calling procedure to a called procedure in one of two ways: ByVal or ByRef. The following sections explain these two methods.

Passing Arguments by Value (ByVal)

When an argument is passed ByVal, it means the Sub procedure has access to the value of the passed argument, but does not actually reference the variable declared in the calling procedure. Instead, the value is copied into a variable whose name is specified in the Sub procedure declaration statement. Thus, in Figure 8-33 on the previous page, since the argument is passed ByVal, the value in the intNumericDayOfWeek is copied to the variable defined in the procedure declaration of the called Sub procedure (intDay).

The intDay variable contains the value passed from the calling procedure only so long as the called Sub procedure has processing control. When the Sub procedure has completed processing and passes control back to the calling procedure, the variable is lost. If the Sub procedure is called again, the variable is created again as a new variable with no preexisting value. So, you can consider the variable defined in the Sub procedure declaration as a temporary variable that exists only during processing within the Sub procedure when the argument is passed ByVal.

The temporary variable can be given any name, including the name of the variable in the calling procedure, but most developers use different names to avoid confusion. Notice that the name used in the calling procedure is intNumericDayOfWeek and the name used in the Sub procedure for the temporary variable is intDay.

When the argument is passed ByVal, the Sub procedure code can change the value in the temporary variable and use it in any manner required. The original value of the variable in the calling procedure is not affected because the value is copied into the temporary Sub procedure variable and the variable in the calling procedure is never referenced in the Sub procedure.

ByVal is the default for all passed arguments. The keyword ByVal is added automatically if you do not enter it when you code the Sub procedure declaration.

The code in Figure 8-34 illustrates the fact that the Sub procedure can change the passed value, but that value is not changed in the calling procedure when the value is passed ByVal.

```
    Private Sub btnShowMessages_Click(ByVal sender As System.Object, ByVal e As System.↙
    EventArgs) Handles btnShowMessages.Click
        Dim strMessage As String

        strMessage = "The Original Welcome Message"
        MsgBox(strMessage, ,"First Message")
        DisplayMessage(strMessage)
        MsgBox(strMessage, ,"Fourth Message")
    End Sub

    Private Sub DisplayMessage(ByVal strShowMessage As String)
        MsgBox(strShowMessage, ,"Second Message")
        strShowMessage = "The Changed Welcome Message"
        MsgBox(strShowMessage, ,"Third Message")
    End Sub
End Class
```

FIGURE 8-34

The output for the code in Figure 8-34 is shown in Figure 8-35.

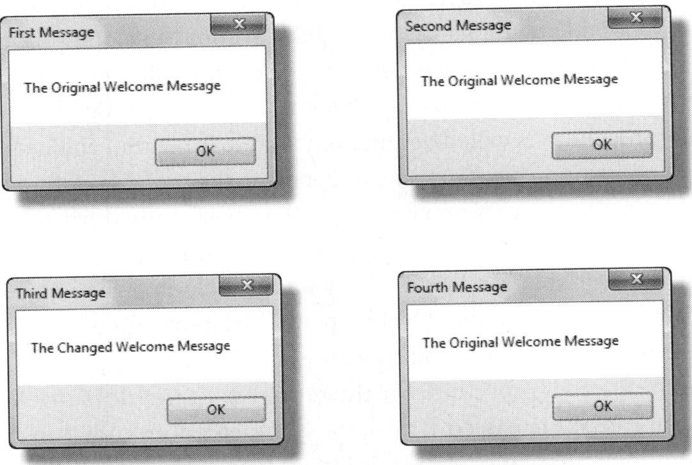

FIGURE 8-35

In Figure 8-35 you can see that the DisplayMessage Sub procedure in Figure 8-34 changed the message and the third message box displays this changed message, "The Changed Welcome Message". When the Sub procedure is finished and control is passed back to the calling procedure, however, the value in the strMessage variable, which was passed to the Sub procedure, was not changed, as shown in the Fourth Message window.

You can call the same Sub procedure repeatedly, as shown in Figure 8-36 on the next page. The Sub procedure DisplayMessage is called once and the Square Sub procedure is called three times. Notice that either literals or variables can be passed to a Sub procedure.

```
    Private Sub btnSquare_Click(ByVal sender As System.Object, ByVal e As System.
    EventArgs) Handles btnSquare.Click

        Dim decNum As Decimal

        decNum = 3.3
        DisplayMessage()
        Square(7.9)
        Square(4.0)
        Square(decNum)

    End Sub

    Private Sub Square(ByVal decValue As Decimal)
        lstResult.Items.Add("The square of " & decValue & " is " & _
         (decValue * decValue))

    End Sub

    Private Sub DisplayMessage()
        lstResult.Items.Add("Squares:")
    End Sub
```

FIGURE 8-36

After executing the code in Figure 8-36, the ListBox object in Figure 8-36 would contain the values shown in Figure 8-37.

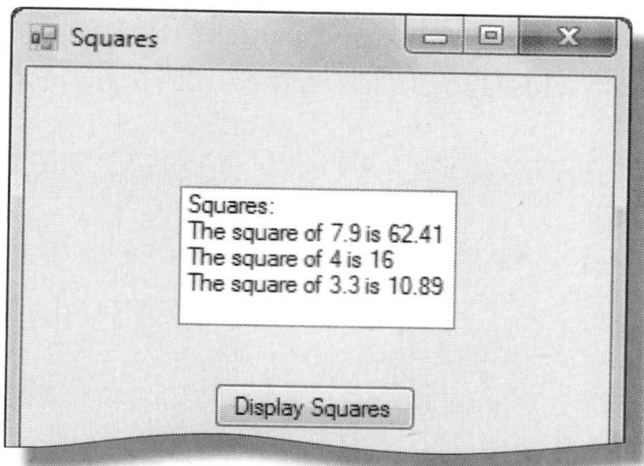

FIGURE 8-37

Passing Arguments by Reference (ByRef)

The second way in which to pass an argument from a calling procedure to a called Sub procedure is **by reference.** You specify you want to pass a value by reference by entering the keyword ByRef in the Sub procedure declaration.

Passing a value by reference allows code in the Sub procedure to modify the contents of the variable that is being passed because when you use ByRef, you are passing a reference to the variable that holds the value instead of the value as when you use ByVal. Thus, if a Sub procedure changes the value of a variable passed ByRef, the original variable in the calling procedure is changed. You should select the option to pass a variable by reference if you intend to change the original value when it is passed to the Sub procedure.

In the code example in Figure 8-38, the calling procedure assigns the value Vincent Van Gogh to the strFavoriteArtist variable (line 49) and then passes the variable ByRef (line 51).

```
46      Private Sub btnDisplayMessage_Click(ByVal sender As System.Object, ByVal e As
        System.EventArgs) Handles btnDisplayMessage.Click
47          Dim strFavoriteArtist As String
48
49          strFavoriteArtist = "Vincent Van Gogh"
50          MsgBox("Favorite Artist is " & strFavoriteArtist, , "First Message")
51          DisplayMessage(strFavoriteArtist)
52          MsgBox("Favorite Artist is now " & strFavoriteArtist, , "Fourth Message")
53      End Sub
54
55      Private Sub DisplayMessage(ByRef strshowArtist As String)
56          MsgBox("Favorite Artist is " & strshowArtist, , "Second Message")
57          ' The artist name is changed
58          strshowArtist = "Paul Cezanne "
59          MsgBox("Favorite Artist is " & strshowArtist, , "Third Message")
60      End Sub
61  End Class
```

FIGURE 8-38

The Sub procedure changes the value of the passed variable to Paul Cezanne (line 58). Because the variable is passed By Reference (ByRef), the value in the variable that is passed from the calling procedure is changed to Paul Cezanne. In the output shown in Figure 8-39, the changed value is displayed in the fourth message box when the btnDisplayMessage click event displays the last message box (line 52).

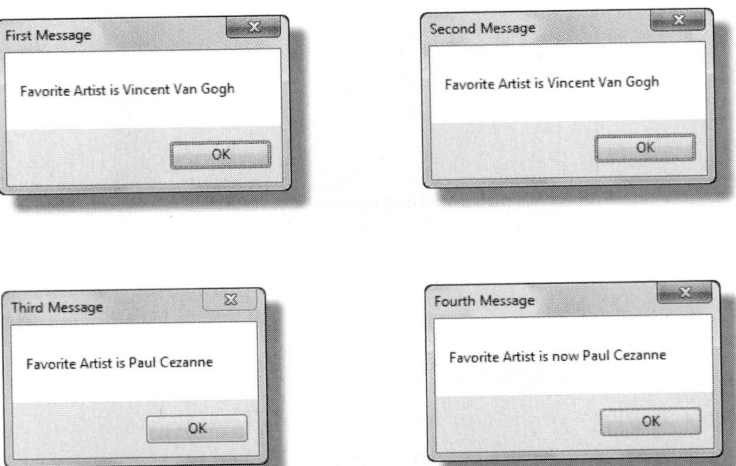

FIGURE 8-39

WATCH OUT FOR

Passing ByVal means the Sub procedure *cannot* change the original value. Passing ByRef means the Sub procedure *can* change the original value.

Passing Multiple Arguments

You can pass as many arguments as needed to a Sub procedure. If you have more than one argument, the variables are passed in the same order in which they appear in the procedure call statement.

Function Procedures

A **Function procedure** is similar to a Sub procedure except that a Function procedure returns a single value to the calling procedure. Just like a Sub procedure, you can pass variables to the Function procedure using ByVal and ByRef. A Function procedure uses the keyword Function (instead of the keyword Sub) in the procedure declaration. You also must specify a return data type in the procedure declaration to define the type of variable that is being returned to the calling procedure by the Function procedure. The Function procedure call has the syntax shown in Figure 8-40:

General Format: Function Procedure Call

The Function procedure call is made:

```
VariableName = FunctionProcedureName()
```

The **procedure declaration** that begins the Function procedure has the form:

```
Private Function FunctionProcedureName() as DataType

        ' Line(s) of code

        Return VariableName

End Function
```

FIGURE 8-40

The Private keyword is optional in the Function procedure declaration. If it is omitted, the default is Public, which means any code in any class can reference the Function procedure. In many instances, this is not desirable so the Private access modifier is used.

In the Function procedure call statement in Figure 8-40, the FunctionProcedureName on the right of the assignment statement is replaced by the value that is returned from the Function procedure. That value then is assigned to the variable on the left side of the equal sign.

HEADS UP

You can exclude the receiving variable in the procedure call if you use the value immediately, as in lblResult.Text = "Price: " & FindPrice(intValue).ToString().

The Function procedure is different in appearance from a Sub procedure in the following ways:

1. The Function procedure call has a receiving variable that is assigned the returned value from the Function procedure.
2. The data type of the return value is listed in the procedure declaration.
3. The keyword Return is used in the Function procedure to return a single value.

A Function procedure can pass only one value back to the calling procedure. The coding example in Figure 8-41 determines the gas mileage of a vehicle by dividing the number of miles driven by the number of gallons of gas used. The ComputeGasMileage Function procedure returns one value representing the gas mileage (Return statement on line 87). When the gas mileage value is returned, it is assigned to the receiving variable decMilesPerGallon (line 76 in the btnCompute click event).

```
69      Private Sub btnCompute Click(ByVal sender As System.Object, ByVal e As System.EventArgs) Handles btnCompute.Click
70          Dim decMiles As Decimal
71          Dim decGallons As Decimal
72          Dim decMilesPerGallon As Decimal
73
74          decMiles = Convert.ToDecimal(txtMiles.Text)
75          decGallons = Convert.ToDecimal(txtGallons.Text)
76          decMilesPerGallon = ComputeGasMileage(decMiles, decGallons)
77          MsgBox("You are getting " & decMilesPerGallon.ToString("F1") & " miles per gallon", ,"MPG")
78
79      End Sub
80
81      Function ComputeGasMileage(ByVal decMiles As Decimal, ByVal decGallons As Decimal) As Decimal
82          Dim decMileage As Decimal
83
84          decMileage = decMiles / decGallons
85          ' The following statement returns control to the calling
86          ' procedure and returns the value in the decMileage variable.
87          Return decMileage
88
89      End Function
```

FIGURE 8-41

When writing a Function procedure, do not place any lines of code after the Return statement because control returns to the calling procedure when the Return statement is executed.

It is best to use a Function procedure when you plan to return a value from a called procedure. In the Ocean Tours chapter project, a Function procedure returns the final cost of the selected tour as shown in Figure 8-42 on the next page.

Calling Procedure

```
105                 Select Case intIslandChoice
106                     Case 0
107                         decTotalCost = ArubaFindCost(intTourChoice, _
108                                               intGroupSize, intLengthOfTour)
```

Called Procedure

```
182     Private Function ArubaFindCost(ByVal intTourSelection As Integer, _
183      ByVal intGroupSize As Integer, ByRef intTourLength As Integer) As Decimal
184         ' This function calculates the cost of the tours to Aruba
185
186         Dim decTourCost As Decimal
187         Dim decFinalCost As Decimal
188         Dim decArubaDeepSeaCost As Decimal = 199D
189         Dim decArubaKayakCost As Decimal = 89D
190         Dim decArubaScubaCost As Decimal = 119D
191         Dim decArubaSnorkelCost As Decimal = 89D
192
193         Select Case intTourSelection
194             Case 0
195                 decTourCost = decArubaDeepSeaCost
196                 intTourLength = _intEightHours
197             Case 1
198                 decTourCost = decArubaKayakCost
199                 intTourLength = _intTwoHours
200             Case 2
201                 decTourCost = decArubaScubaCost
202                 intTourLength = _intThreeHours
203             Case 3
204                 decTourCost = decArubaSnorkelCost
205                 intTourLength = _intFourHours
206         End Select
207         decFinalCost = decTourCost * intGroupSize
208         Return decFinalCost
209
210     End Function
```

FIGURE 8-42

In Figure 8-42, the function call on line 107 calls the ArubaFindCost Function procedure. The arguments include the integer value of the user choice in the list box (intTourChoice), the integer value of the number in the party (intGroupSize), and a variable to contain the length of the chosen tour (intTourLength).

WATCH OUT FOR

If you need to return more than one variable to the calling procedure, use ByRef. You can only return one value using the Return keyword.

In the called Function procedure, the tour choice and group size are passed ByVal. The length of the tour is passed ByRef. Therefore, when the Function procedure changes a value in the length of tour a change is made in the passed variable.

You can use Sub procedures and Function procedures in any Visual Basic application including Windows applications, Web applications, and VSTO applications.

Creating a Private Class-Level Variable

In previous programs within this book you have defined class level variables for use in multiple procedures or event handlers within the class. In those programs, the variable was declared using the Dim statement (for an example, see the Chapter 7 program). You will recall that a class-level variable is defined within the class but outside any procedure. When a class-level variable is declared using the Dim statement, it can be referenced by any code within any procedure within the class.

It cannot, however, be referenced by any code outside the class (in larger projects, multiple classes can be created). When a class-level variable cannot be referenced outside the class in which it is declared, the variable is said to have Private access. Generally, it is a good programming practice to limit the scope of a class-level variable to the class in which it is declared.

By default, then, a class-level variable declared using the Dim statement has Private access. You also can declare class-level variables by using the Private keyword instead of the Dim keyword. The class-level variables used in the Ocean Tours program in this chapter are shown in Figure 8-43.

```
' Class variables
Private _intTwoHours As Integer = 2
Private _intThreeHours As Integer = 3
Private _intFourHours As Integer = 4
Private _intEightHours As Integer = 8
Private _strDeepSeaFishing As String = "Deep Sea Fishing"
Private _strKayaking As String = "Kayaking"
Private _strScuba As String = "Scuba"
Private _strSnorkeling As String = "Snorkeling"
Private _strGlassBottomBoat As String = "Glass Bottom Boat"
Private _strParasailing As String = "Parasailing"
```

FIGURE 8-43

As you can see in Figure 8-43 on the previous page, each of the variables is declared using the Private keyword. All of the variables will have Private access, which means code in any procedure within the class can reference the variables but code in another class cannot.

Exception Handling

In previous programs in this book, you have learned that ensuring users enter valid data is an essential task within the program. You have used loops and If statements to check the values entered by users to ensure that data they enter does not cause an exception within the program.

Visual Basic provides another tool you can use to detect exceptions and take corrective action. This tool is called the **Try-Catch** set of statements. The Try keyword means "Try to execute this code." The Catch keyword means "Catch errors here." A Try-Catch block includes a statement or statements that are executed in the Try block and the statements that are executed in the Catch block(s) when an exception occurs. The format of the Try-Catch block is shown in Figure 8-44.

General Format: Try-Catch block

```
Try
        'Try Block of Code – Executable statement(s) that may generate an exception.
Catch (filter for possible exceptions)
        ' Catch Block of Code for handling the exception
[Optional: Additional Catch blocks]
[Optional Finally]
        ' Optional statements that will always execute before finishing the Try block
End Try
```

FIGURE 8-44

To illustrate the use of a Try-Catch block, assume the value in one variable is being divided by the value in another variable. As you will recall, it is invalid to divide by zero. If an attempt is made to divide by zero, a DivideByZero exception will occur. Therefore, the divide operation should be placed in a Try block and the Catch block should be set for a divide by zero exception.

If the exception occurs, the code in Figure 8-45 will open a message box stating that an attempt was made to divide by zero.

```
91          Dim decNumerator As Decimal
92          Dim decDenominator As Decimal
93          Dim decDivision As Decimal
94
95          decNumerator = Convert.ToDecimal(txtNum.Text)
96          decDenominator = Convert.ToDecimal(txtDen.Text)
97          Try
98              decDivision = decNumerator / decDenominator
99          Catch Exception As DivideByZeroException
100             MsgBox("Attempt to divide by zero")
101         End Try
102
103     End Sub
104 End Class
```

FIGURE 8-45

In Figure 8-45, the divide operation occurs by the statement on line 98. Note that the divide operation is within the Try-Catch block, as defined by the Try keyword on line 97, the Catch keyword on line 99, and the End Try statement on line 101. You can define the particular class of exception in a Catch block by mentioning the name of the exception with the Catch keyword. In the OceanTours program (Figure 8-48 on page 582), DivideByZeroException is stated to catch that specific exception. If the value in decDenominator is zero when the divide operation occurs, the code in the Catch block will display a message box with an error message. More importantly, the program will not be terminated. A Try-Catch block allows the program to handle exceptions elegantly so that the program does not abruptly terminate.

Different types of exceptions can occur. The table shown in Figure 8-46 identifies some of the possible exceptions.

Exception Type	Condition when Exception Occurs	Code Example
ArgumentNullException	A variable that has no value is passed to a procedure	`Dim strTerm As String` `lstDisplay.Items.Add(strTerm)`
DivideByZeroException	A value is divided by zero	`intResult = intNum / 0`
FormatException	A variable is converted to another type that is not possible	`strTerm = "Code"` `intValue = Convert.ToInt32(strTerm)`
NullReferenceException	A procedure is called when the result is not possible	`Dim strTerm as String` `intValue = strTerm.Length`
OverflowException	A value exceeds its assigned data type	`Dim intCost as Integer` `intCost = 58 ^ 4000000000`
SystemException	Generic	`Catches all other exceptions`

FIGURE 8-46

In another example of a Try-Catch Block, in Figure 8-47 a very large number assigned to the variable intBaseValue is squared within a Try-Catch block. Notice that when the value intBaseValue is squared, the result will exceed the range for an Integer data type, causing an OverflowException. When the exception occurs within the Try block, the Catch block is called to deal with the OverflowException.

```
        Dim intBaseValue As Integer
        Dim intSquaredValue As Integer

        intBaseValue = 50000000
        Try
            intSquaredValue = intBaseValue ^ 2
        Catch Exception As OverflowException
            'This catch block detects an overflow of the range of the data type
            MsgBox("The value exceeds the range of the data type", , "Error")
        End Try
```

FIGURE 8-47

Multiple Catch blocks can be defined for a single Try block where each Catch block will catch a particular class of exception. This is useful when you want to state which type of error occurred, identifying to users the particular mistake that was made. It is best to order exceptions in Catch blocks from the most specific to the least specific. In other words, place the Catch block that is most likely to be needed for the most common exception first in a series of Catch statements. If an exception occurs during the execution of the Try block, Visual Basic examines each Catch statement within the Try-Catch block until it finds one whose condition matches that error. If a match is found, control transfers to the first line of code in the Catch block. If no matching Catch statement is found, the search proceeds to the next Catch statement in the Try-Catch block. This process continues through the entire code block until a matching Catch block is found in the current procedure. If no match is found, an exception that stops the program is produced.

In the Ocean Tours chapter project, the variable that is assigned the value of the number in the party needs to be validated. You want to make sure the user enters a number, not a letter or other symbol, and the number should be 1–99.

The code in Figure 8-48 displays a Try-Catch block used within a Function procedure named ValidateNumberInParty. It uses three Catch blocks.

```
124     Private Function ValidateNumberInParty() As Boolean
125         ' This procedure validates the value entered for the number in party
126 
127         Dim intPartyNumber As Integer
128         Dim blnValidityCheck As Boolean = False
129         Dim strNumberInPartyErrorMessage As String = _
130             "Please enter the number of people in your party (1-99)"
131         Dim strMessageBoxTitle As String = "Error"
132 
133         Try
134             intPartyNumber = Convert.ToInt32(txtNumberInParty.Text)
135             If intPartyNumber > 0 And intPartyNumber < 100 Then
136                 blnValidityCheck = True
137             Else
138                 MsgBox(strNumberInPartyErrorMessage, , strMessageBoxTitle)
139                 txtNumberInParty.Focus()
140                 txtNumberInParty.Clear()
141             End If
142         Catch Exception As FormatException
143             MsgBox(strNumberInPartyErrorMessage, , strMessageBoxTitle)
144             txtNumberInParty.Focus()
145             txtNumberInParty.Clear()
146         Catch Exception As OverflowException
147             MsgBox(strNumberInPartyErrorMessage, , strMessageBoxTitle)
148             txtNumberInParty.Focus()
149             txtNumberInParty.Clear()
150         Catch Exception As SystemException
151             MsgBox(strNumberInPartyErrorMessage, , strMessageBoxTitle)
152             txtNumberInParty.Focus()
153             txtNumberInParty.Clear()
154         End Try
155 
156         Return blnValidityCheck
157 
158     End Function
```

FIGURE 8-48

The Boolean variable, blnValidityCheck (line 128 in the code in Figure 8-48) is initially set to false, but it is set to true if an exception is not thrown (line 136); in other words, the Catch block was not executed because an exception was not thrown. This Boolean variable set to True then is returned to the calling procedure (line 156) and the calling procedure can continue its processing.

If an exception is thrown when the value in the Text property of the txtNumberInParty TextBox is converted to an integer (line 134), the statements below the Convert.ToInt32 statement will not be executed because control is passed to the appropriate Catch statement. The processing in each of the Catch blocks displays a message box with an error message, places the focus on the text box where the user enters the number in the party, and clears the text box.

When the processing in the Try-Catch block is complete, the Return statement on line 156 returns the value of the Boolean variable. If the data was valid, the Boolean variable contains the True value. If the data was not valid, it contains False because the variable initially was set to False (line 128) and its value was not changed by the Catch block processing.

An optional portion of the Try-Catch block is the Finally statement. The code in the Finally section always executes last regardless of whether the code in the Catch blocks has been executed. Place cleanup code, such as closing files, in the Finally section. Code in the Finally section always is executed, no matter what happens in the Try-Catch blocks.

Program Design

As you have learned, the requirements document identifies the purpose of the program being developed, the application title, the procedures to be followed when using the program, any equations and calculations required in the program, any conditions within the program that must be tested, notes and restrictions that must be followed by the program, and any other comments that would be helpful to understanding the problem. The requirements document for the Ocean Tours application is shown in Figure 8-49.

REQUIREMENTS DOCUMENT

Date submitted:	June 22, 2014
Application title:	Ocean Tours Trip Selection
Purpose:	This Windows application allows a customer to view ocean tours available in the Caribbean islands.
Program Procedures:	From a Windows application, the user can select ocean tours and find out pricing information.
Algorithms, Processing, and Conditions:	1. The user first selects the island location. No other objects are displayed at this time. 2. When the user selects an island, the following items are displayed in the window: Number in party text box and a custom list of the available tours on the chosen island. In addition, a button to find the cost of the tour and a button to clear the form are included. 3. The user enters the number of guests in their party. 4. From the custom list of tours that are available for the chosen island, the user selects the tour desired. 5. The total price for the ocean tour for the group is displayed.
Notes and Restrictions:	1. Validate numeric input with Try-Catch blocks. 2. Use multiple procedures to break the application into manageable sections.
Comments:	1. The ocean.jpg picture used in the Window is available at scsite/vb2010/ch8/images. 2. A splash screen is shown for approximately 5 seconds before the main window is displayed.

FIGURE 8-49

The use case definition for the application is shown in Figure 8-50.

USE CASE DEFINITION

1. A splash screen welcomes the user for approximately 5 seconds.
2 The user selects an island location.
3. The program displays a text box for the number of people in the party and a list of available ocean tours for the selected island.
4. The user enters the number of people in the party, selects a tour, and clicks the Find Cost of Tour button.
5. The program identifies the tour, calculates and displays the tour cost for the entire party, and specifies the length in hours of the tour.
6. The user can change any of the entries (island choice, number in party, and tour) and click the Find Cost of Tour button to recalculate the tour cost.
7. The user can clear the form by clicking the Clear Form button.

FIGURE 8-50

The table in Figure 8-51 contains the data for the tour type for each island, the tour length, and the tour cost.

Location	Tour Type	Tour Length	Tour Cost
Aruba	Deep Sea Fishing	8 hours	$199
	Kayaking	2 hours	$89
	Scuba	3 hours	$119
	Snorkeling	4 hours	$89
Jamaica	Glass Bottom Boat	2 hours	$39
	Parasailing	2 hours	$119
	Snorkeling	3 hours	$59
Key West	Deep Sea Fishing	4 hours	$89
	Glass Bottom Boat	2 hours	$29
	Scuba	3 hours	$119
	Snorkeling	3 hours	$59

FIGURE 8-51

Program Design When Using Sub and Function Procedures

As noted previously, when a program becomes larger, often it is advantageous to break the program into procedures, which perform specific tasks within the program. The goal of using procedures is to make the program easier to read and understand, and therefore make the program easier to debug. The final result is a program that is more reliable and easier to maintain.

The developer must determine what code should be placed in a procedure. Several rules are important to follow when creating procedures in a program; otherwise, the use of procedures might make the program more difficult and more confusing. These rules include:

1. The Sub procedure or the Function procedure should perform a single, defined task, such as checking the validity of a specific user input, or calculating the cost of a tour on an island. Procedures which perform multiple tasks tend to become large and difficult to design and code.
2. A Sub procedure or a Function procedure must perform reasonably substantial processing. It makes little sense to place a procedure call statement in a calling procedure and have the called procedure contain one or two program statements. It would be easier and clearer just to place the statements in the calling procedure.
3. When deciding whether a set of programming steps should be placed in a Sub procedure or a Function procedure, ask yourself the following questions: 1) Will the program be easier to read and understand if the code is placed in a separate procedure? 2) Does the proposed code perform a single task and does this task require more than three or four programming statements? 3) Can the Sub procedure or Function procedure perform its processing by receiving data as arguments, and by returning data either using the Return statement or by using ByRef arguments?

If the answers to these questions are yes, then the code is a good candidate for a procedure within your program.

In the Ocean Tours program developed in this chapter, four event handlers are required: 1) Selected Index Change: This event handler is executed when the user selects an island location from a combo box; 2) Find Cost Button: This event handler is executed when the user clicks the btnFindCost Button object; 3) Clear Button: This event handler is executed when the user clicks the btnClear Button object; 4) frmTours Load Event: This event handler is executed when the Windows Form object is loaded.

Within each event handler, the Event Planning Document is used to identify the tasks that must be accomplished. As each of the tasks is identified, you should ask the questions from above. If it appears the task should be accomplished in a procedure, the procedure must be included on the event planning document.

Event Planning Document

You will recall that the event planning document consists of a table that specifies an object in the user interface that will cause an event, the action taken by the user to trigger the event, and the event processing that must occur. The event planning document for the program in this chapter must specify two forms and the events that occur for objects on each form. In addition, the tasks that must be accomplished for each event must be identified and a decision made on whether that task will be accomplished in a Sub or Function procedure. The Event Planning Document for the Ocean Tours Trip Selection program is shown in Figure 8-52 and Figure 8-53.

EVENT PLANNING DOCUMENT

Program Name: Ocean Tours Trip Selection	**Developer:** Corinne Hoisington	**Object:** SplashScreen1	**Date:** June 22, 2014
OBJECT	**EVENT TRIGGER**	**EVENT PROCESSING**	
SplashScreen1_Load	Load	An opening splash screen opens with the company name, version number, and year	

FIGURE 8-52

EVENT PLANNING DOCUMENT

Program Name: Ocean Tours Trip Selection	**Developer:** Corinne Hoisington	**Object:** frmTours	**Date:** June 22, 2014
OBJECT	**EVENT TRIGGER**	**EVENT PROCESSING**	
cboIsland_SelectedIndexChanged	Select Index	Assign island choice selection to an Integer SUB (Aruba(), Jamaica(), KeyWest()): Based on the island selection, display a list of the available tours on the island. Change Visible property for all objects on the form to True Clear the labels that provide trip information Set the focus on the number in party text box	
ArubaTours()	Sub procedure call	Display list of available tours (deep sea fishing, kayaking, scuba, and snorkeling) in list box	
JamaicaTours()	Sub procedure call	Display list of available tours (glass bottom boat, parasailing, snorkeling) in list box	
KeyWestTours()	Sub procedure call	Display list of available tours (deep sea fishing, glass bottom boat, scuba, snorkeling) in list box	

FIGURE 8-53 (continues)

Program Name: Ocean Tours Trip Selection	**Developer:** Corinne Hoisington	**Object:** frmTours	**Date:** June 22, 2014
OBJECT	**EVENT TRIGGER**	**EVENT PROCESSING**	
btnFindCost	Click	SUB (ValidateNumberInParty): Validate the value in the number in party text box is valid FUNCTION (ValidateTourSelection): Ensure the user has selected a tour in the list box If the number in party is valid and a tour is selected: Convert number in party to an integer Set month to selected month +1 If the month is greater than zero Change selected island index to integer FUNCTION(ArubaFindCost, JamaicaFindCost, KeyWestFindCost): Calculate cost based on island choice Display tour, cost, and length Else display error message	
ValidateNumberInParty()	Function procedure call	Set Boolean indicator to False Convert number in party to integer If conversion valid If number >0 and <100 Set Boolean indicator to True for valid number If conversion not valid Catch format, overflow, and system exceptions Display error message boxes Place focus in number in party text box Clear number in party text box Return Boolean indicator	
ValidateTourSelection()	Function procedure call	Convert tour selection index to integer If conversion successful Place selected item string in ByRef variable Set Boolean validity indicator to True Else Display error message box Set Boolean validity indicator to False Return ocean tour selected index integer	
ArubaFindCost()	Function procedure call	If tour selected is deep sea fishing Set cost to Aruba deep sea cost for one person Set length to Aruba deep sea length If tour selected is kayaking Set cost to Aruba kayak for one person Set length to Aruba kayak If tour selected is scuba Set cost to Aruba scuba for one person Set length to Aruba scuba If tour selected is snorkel Set cost to Aruba snorkel for one person Set length to Aruba snorkel Calculate cost of trip: cost * number in party Return cost of trip	

FIGURE 8-53 (continues)

Program Name: Ocean Tours Trip Selection	**Developer:** Corinne Hoisington	**Object:** frmTours	**Date:** June 22, 2014
OBJECT	**EVENT TRIGGER**	**EVENT PROCESSING**	
JamaicaFindCost()	Function procedure call	If tour selected is glass bottom boat Set cost to Jamaica glass bottom boat cost for one person Set length to Jamaica glass bottom length If tour selected is parasail Set cost to Jamaica parasail for one person Set length to Jamaica parasail If tour selected is snorkel Set cost to Jamaica snorkel for one person Set length to Jamaica snorkel Calculate cost of trip: cost * number in party Return cost of trip	
KeyWestFindCost()	Function procedure call	If tour selected is deep sea fishing Set cost to Key West deep sea cost for one person Set length to Key West deep sea length If tour selected is glass bottom boat Set cost to Key West glass bottom boat for one person Set length to Key West glass bottom If tour selected is scuba Set cost to Key West scuba for one person Set length to Key West scuba If tour selected is snorkel Set cost to Key West snorkel for one person Set length to Key West snorkel Calculate cost of trip: cost * number in party Return cost of trip	
btnClear	Click	Set Select Item cbo text to "Select Island Location" Clear text boxes, list, and labels Hide all objects except Select Island cbo	
frmTours_Load	Load	Set sleeping period to 5000 milliseconds	

FIGURE 8-53 (continued)

Design and Code the Program

After identifying the events and tasks within the events, you are ready to create the program. As you have learned, creating the program means designing the user interface and then entering Visual Basic statements to accomplish the tasks specified on the event planning document. As you enter the code, you also will implement the logic to carry out the required processing.

Guided Program Development

To design the user interface for the Ocean Tours program and enter the code required to process each event in the program, complete the following steps:

NOTE TO THE LEARNER

As you will recall, in the following activity, you should complete the tasks within the specified steps. Each of the tasks is accompanied by a Hint Screen. The purpose of the Hint Screen is to indicate where in the Visual Studio window you should perform the activity; it also serves as a reminder of the method you should use to create the user interface or enter code. If you need further help completing the step, refer to the figure number identified by the term ref: in the step.

Guided Program Development

1

- **Create a New Windows Project** Open Visual Studio using the Start button on the Windows taskbar and the All Programs submenu. Close the Start page. Click the New Project button on the Standard toolbar. Begin a Windows Application project and title the project OceanTours. Name the Form object frmTours.vb.

- **Add a New Item to the Project** Click Project on the menu bar and then click Add New Item on the Project menu *(ref: Figure 8-5)*.

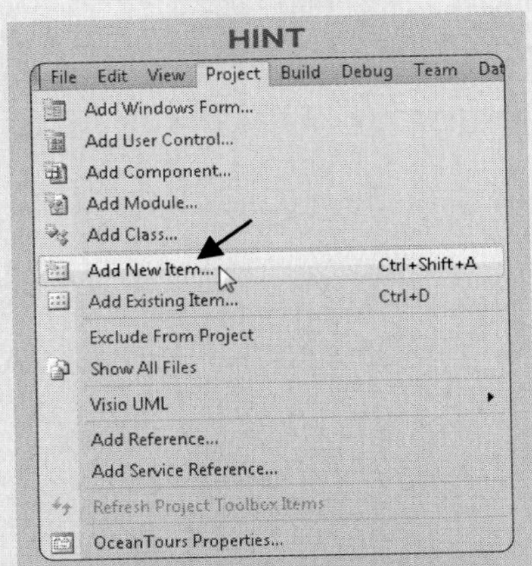

- **Select Splash Screen as the New Item** Select the Splash Screen Template. Click the Add button *(ref: Figure 8-6)*.

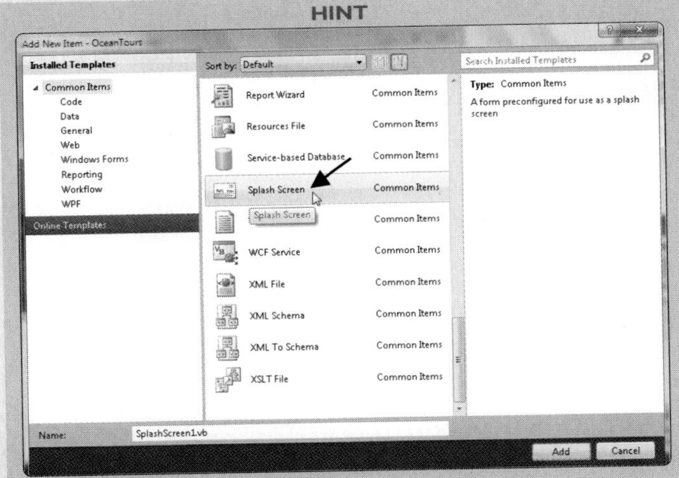

Guided Program Development *continued*

- **Select the Generic Splash Screen** When the generic splash screen opens, click the left side of the screen to select it *(ref: Figure 8-7)*.

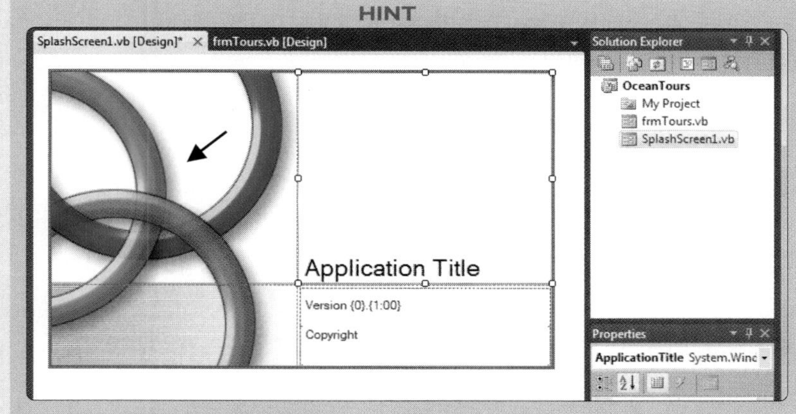

- **Prepare to Set the Contents of the Splash Screen** Right-click the application name OceanTours in Solution Explorer, and then click Properties on the shortcut menu to open the Project Designer window *(ref: Figure 8-8)*.

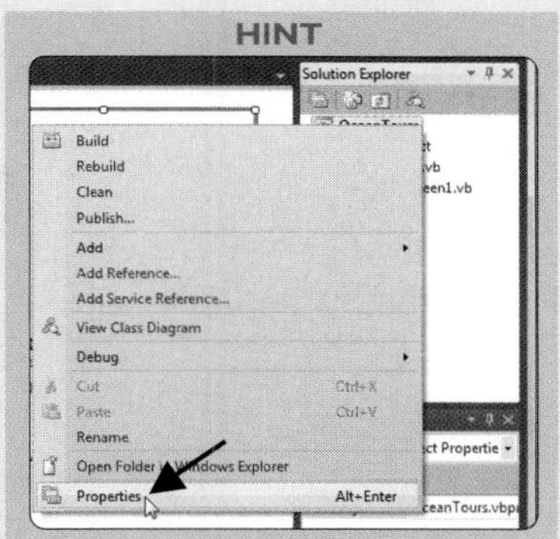

(continues)

Guided Program Development *continued*

- **Set the Splash Screen** On the Application tab, click the Splash screen list arrow to change the setting of (None) to SplashScreen1 *(ref: Figure 8-10)*.

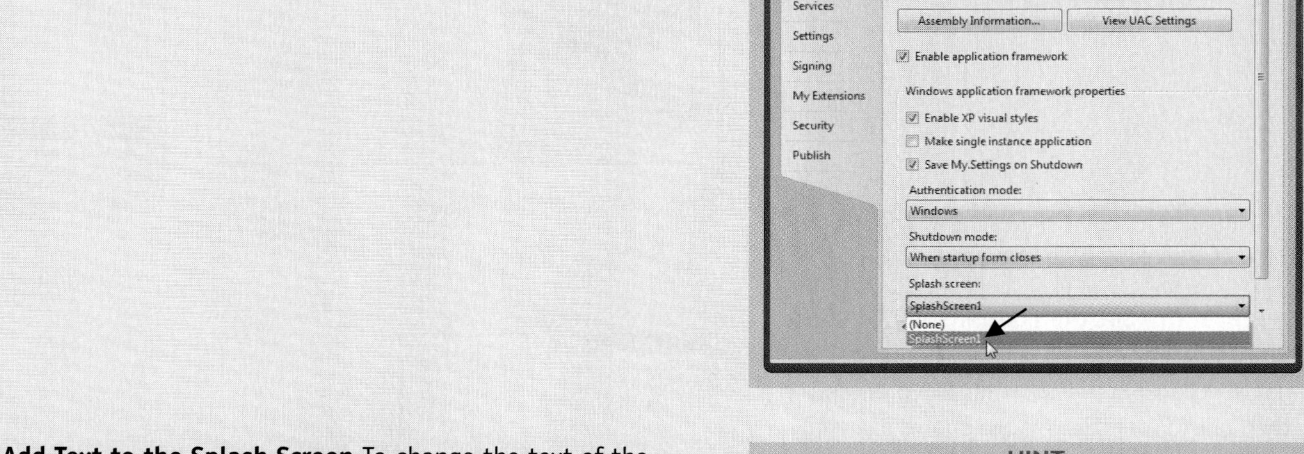

- **Add Text to the Splash Screen** To change the text of the splash screen, click the Assembly Information button in the Project Designer window *(ref: Figure 8-11)*.

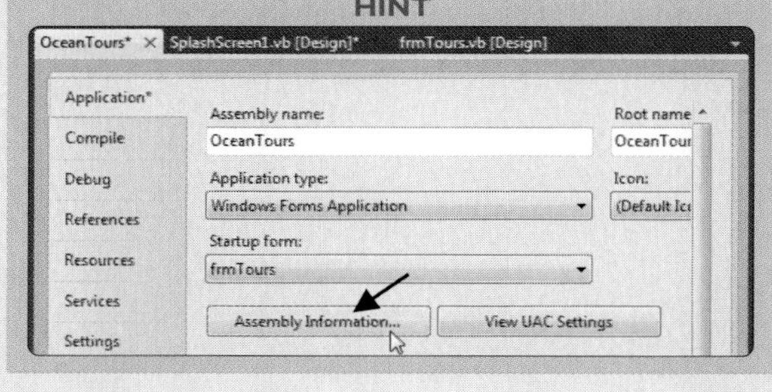

- **Set the Assembly Information** In the Assembly Information dialog box, change the title to `Ocean Tours` and change the copyright to the current year *(ref: Figure 8-12)*. Click the OK button to close the dialog box. Close the Properties window. The information on the Splash Screen form does not change. The changes appear when the application is executed.

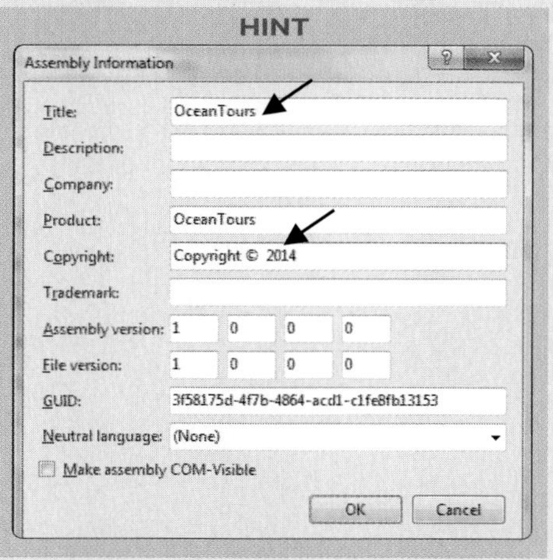

Guided Program Development *continued*

- **Change the Background Image** To customize the picture, click the background on the left side of the splash screen and select the BackgroundImage property in the Properties window. Click the ellipsis button *(ref: Figure 8-13)*.

HINT

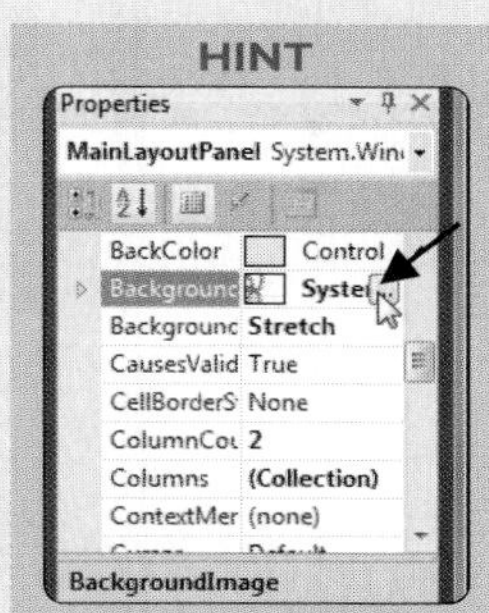

- **Select the Project Resource File** The Select Resource dialog box opens. Click the Project resource file option button, if necessary, and ensure the Resources.resx file is selected.

HINT

- **Select an Image File** Click Import and select the graphic image ocean.jpg. You can download and save the ocean image used in the Ocean Tours application from scsite.com/vb2010/ch8/images. Click the OK button in the Select Resource dialog box.

(continues)

Guided Program Development *continued*

The splash screen is designed (Figure 8-54).

RESULT OF STEP 1

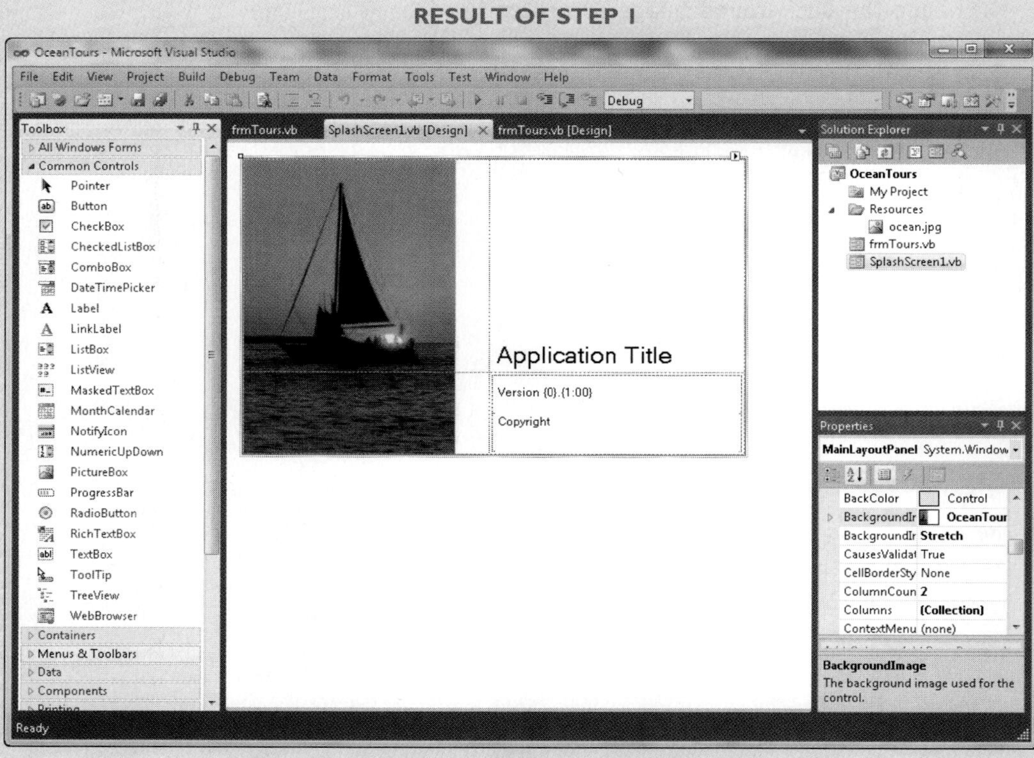

FIGURE 8-54

2

- **Title the Form Object** With the Windows Form object selected, change its Text property to `Information on Available Tours`.
- **Add a Background Image** With the Windows Form object selected, click the ellipsis button for the BackgroundImage property. Select the ocean image in the Select Resource dialog box. Click the OK button in the Select Resource dialog box.
- **Resize the Windows Form Object** Resize the Windows Form object to (574,376) to view the entire image.

Guided Program Development *continued*

- **Add a Panel Object** Drag a Panel object in the Containers category of the Toolbox to the portion of the Window object not covered by the image. Resize the Panel object so it covers the white space where no image is displayed.

- **Change Panel Object's BackColor to Transparent** In the BackColor property for the Panel object, click the BackColor property arrow, click the Web tab if necessary, and then click Transparent on the Web palette. Making the panel transparent allows all the objects placed on the Windows Form object to be visible but allows you to center and align objects within the Panel object instead of the entire Windows Form object.

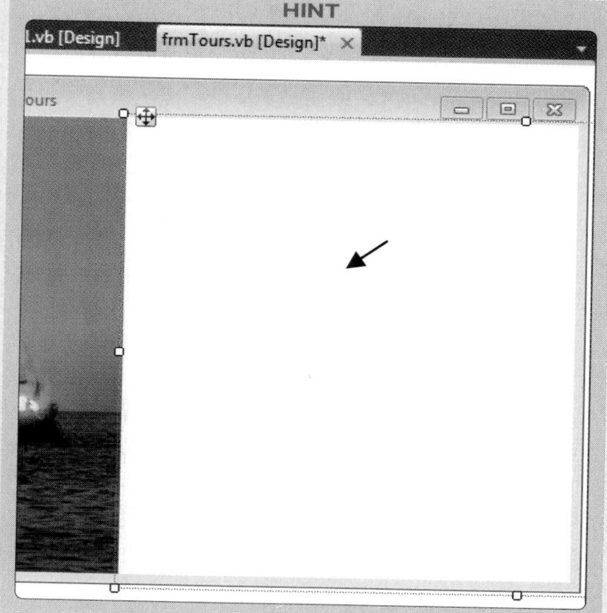

(continues)

Guided Program Development *continued*

- **Add a Label and a ComboBox Object** Add a Label object on the right side of the Form object. Change the Text property to `Ocean Tours Information.` Name the Label `lblTitle.` Change the font property to Verdana, Bold, 16pt. Change the BackColor property of the Label object to Dark Orange in the Web palette. The location of the Label object can be (10,18). Add a ComboBox object under the Label object. The location is (91,51). Name the ComboBox object `cboIsland.` Change the Text property to `Select Island Location:`. Resize the ComboBox object to see all the text *(ref: Figure 8-20)*. Change the font size to 11pt.

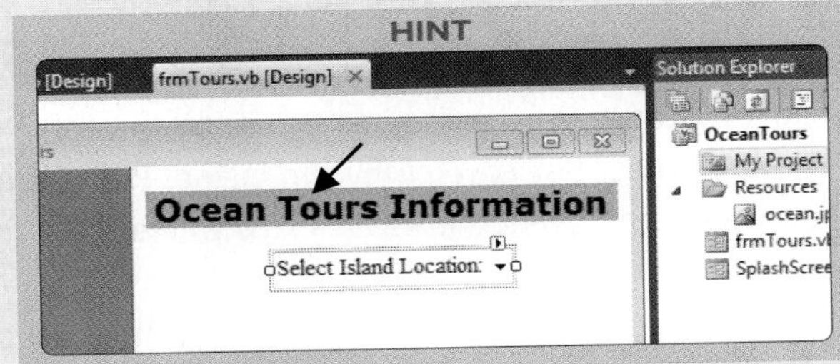

- **Add the Terms in the Items Property** Enter the following terms in the Items property of the ComboBox object: `Aruba`, `Jamaica`, and `Key West` on separate lines *(ref: Figure 8-21)*.

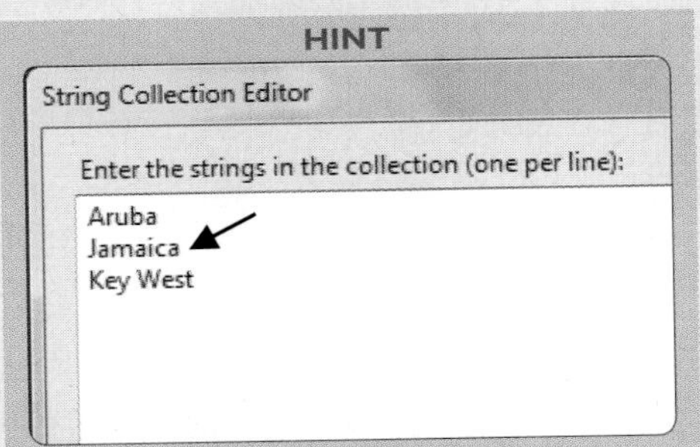

- **Add a Label Object** Drag a Label object from the Visual Basic Toolbox to the Form object. Place the Label object at location (87,89) within the Panel object. Change the Text property to `Number in Party:`. Name the Label object `lblParty`. Change the font size to 11pt.

- **Add a TextBox Object for the Number in Party** Drag a TextBox object from the Visual Basic Toolbox to the Panel object on the Windows Form object. Place the TextBox object at location (225,86). Resize the TextBox object to fit the length of approximately two numbers. Name the TextBox object `txtNumberInParty`. Change the font size to 11pt.

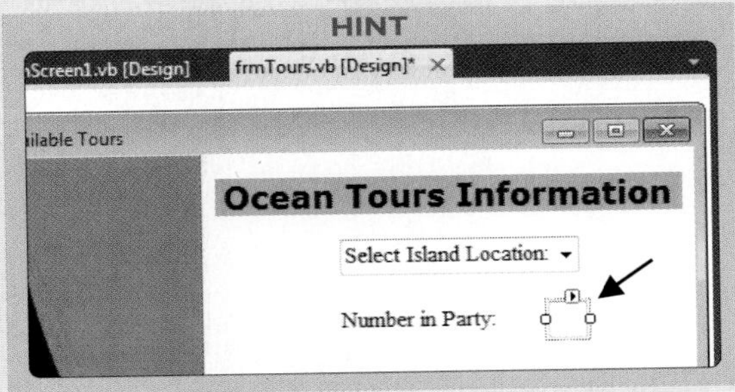

Guided Program Development *continued*

- **Add the Select Ocean Tour Label Object** Drag a Label object from the Visual Basic Toolbox to the Windows Form object. The location is (108,123). Change the Text property to `Select Ocean Tour:`. Name the Label Object `lblSelect`. Change the font size to 11pt.

- **Add the Tours ListBox Object** Drag a ListBox object from the Visual Basic Toolbox to the Windows Form object. The location is (110,143). Name the ListBox `lstTours`. Change the font size to 11pt.

HINT

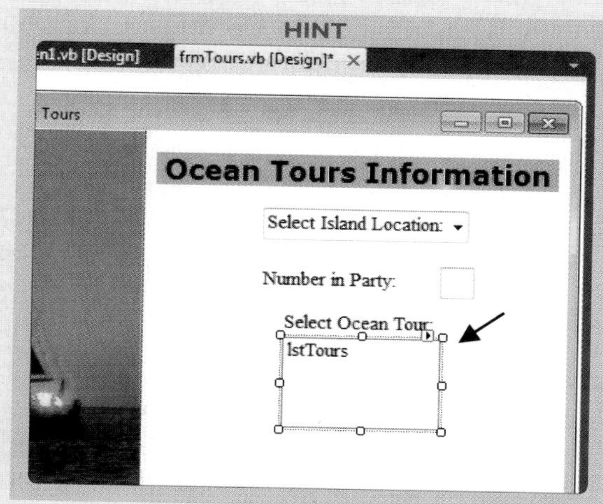

- **Add the Find Cost Button Object** Drag a Button object from the Visual Basic Toolbox to the Windows Form object. The location is (23,230). Name the Button Object `btnFindCost` and change the Text property to `Find Cost of Tour`. Resize the button until the Text is visible.

(continues)

Guided Program Development *continued*

- **Add the Clear Button Object** Drag a Button object from the Visual Basic Toolbox to the Windows Form object. The location is (178,230). Name the Button Object `btnClear` and change the Text property to `Clear Form`.

- **Add a Label Object for the Tour Type** Drag a Label object from the Visual Basic Toolbox to the Windows Form object. The location is (106,274). Name the Label object `lblTourType`. Enter 10 X's for the Text property.

- **Add a Label Object for the Cost** Drag a Label object from the Visual Basic Toolbox to the Windows Form object. The location is (106,293). Name this Label object `lblCost`. Enter 10 X's for the Text property.

- **Add a Label Object for the Tour Length** Drag a Label object from the Visual Basic Toolbox to the Windows Form object. The location is (106,312). Name this Label object `lblLength`. Enter 10 X's for the Text property.

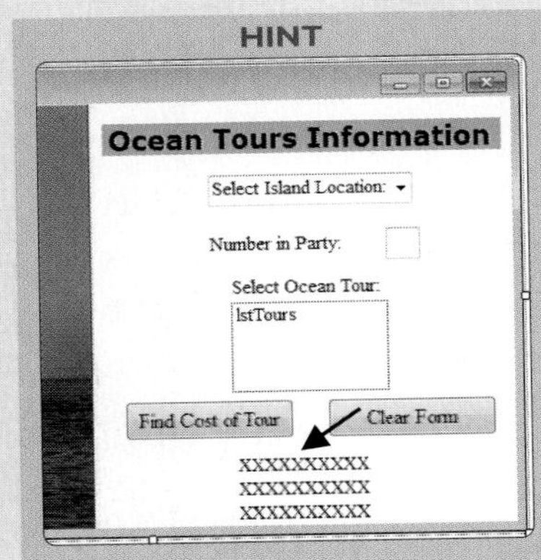

Guided Program Development *continued*

- **Change the Font** Select all the objects on the form except lblTitle and change the font to Times New Roman, size 11pt. Resize any objects as required so that the text is visible. Resize both buttons to (129,31).

- **Set the Visible Properties** Change the Visible property to False for the following objects: lblParty, txtNumberInParty, lblSelect, lstTours, lblMonth, cboMonth, btnFindCost, btnClear, lblTourType, and lblCost. These objects are not displayed until the tour is selected.

- **Set the Accept Button** Click the background of the Windows Form object on its title bar and change the AcceptButton property to the Button object btnFindCost.

- **Set the Cancel Button** Click the background of the Windows Form object on its title bar and change the CancelButton property to the Button object btnClear.

The Form object frmTours is designed (Figure 8-55).

RESULT OF STEP 2

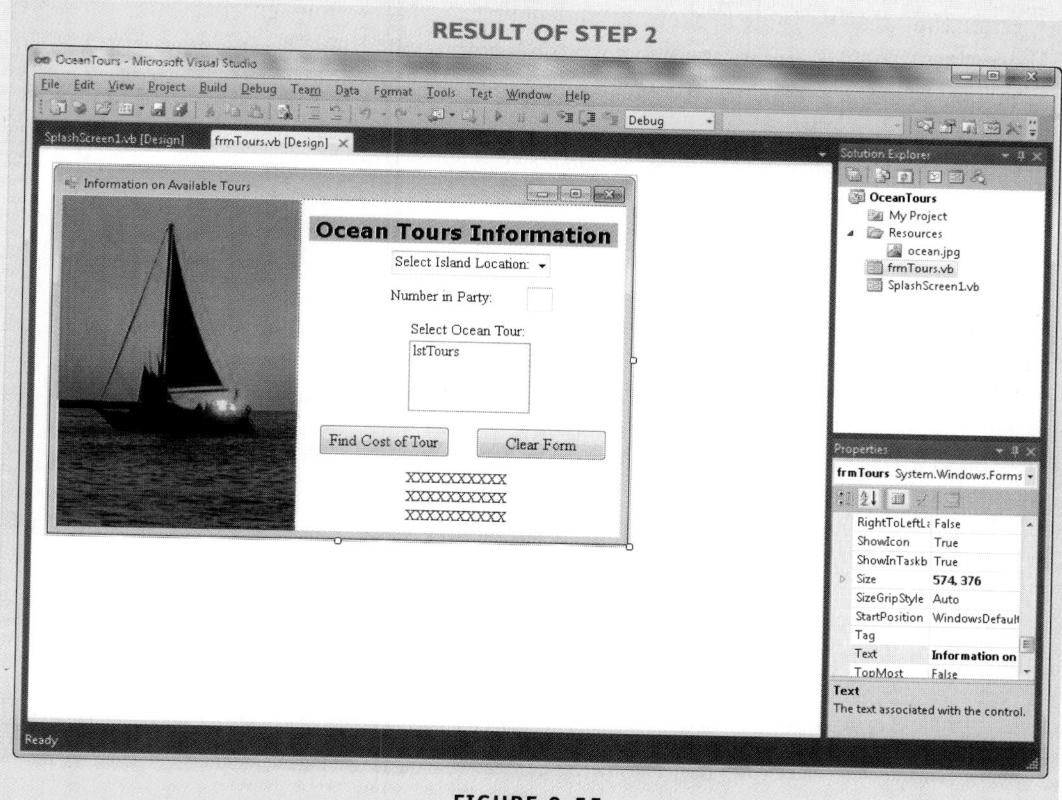

FIGURE 8-55

(continues)

Guided Program Development *continued*

3

- **Code the Comments** Double-click the cboIsland ComboBox object on the frmTours.vb [Design] tab to open the code editing window and create the cboIsland_SelectedIndexChanged Event Handler. Close the Toolbox. Click before the first word in Public Class frmTours, and then press the ENTER key to create a blank line. Insert the first four standard comments. Insert the Option Strict On command following the comments to turn on strict type checking.

HINT

```
' Program Name: Ocean Tours Trip Selection
' Author:       Corinne Hoisington
' Date:         June 22, 2014
' Purpose:      The Ocean Tours Trip Selection application determines the
'               ocean tours available and calculates the cost of the tour.

Option Strict On
```

- **Enter the Class Variables** Following the Public Class header line, enter the class variables required for the program. These class variables are: a) The hours for the length of the tours; b) The types of tours available (deep sea fishing, kayaking, scuba, snorkeling, glass bottom boat, and parasailing).

HINT

```
Public Class frmTours

    ' Class variables
    Private _intTwoHours As Integer = 2
    Private _intThreeHours As Integer = 3
    Private _intFourHours As Integer = 4
    Private _intEightHours As Integer = 8
    Private _strDeepSeaFishing As String = "Deep Sea Fishing"
    Private _strKayaking As String = "Kayaking"
    Private _strScuba As String = "Scuba"
    Private _strSnorkeling As String = "Snorkeling"
    Private _strGlassBottomBoat As String = "Glass Bottom Boat"
    Private _strParasailing As String = "Parasailing"
```

- **Comment the cboIsland_SelectedIndexChanged Event Handler** Enter a comment to describe the purpose of the cboIsland_SelectedIndexChanged Event Handler.

HINT

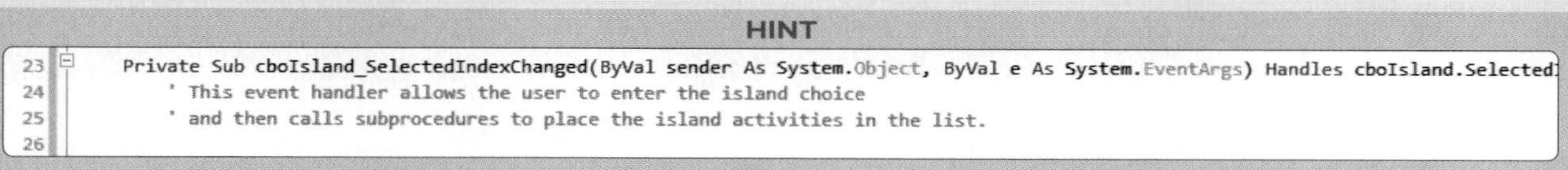

```
Private Sub cboIsland_SelectedIndexChanged(ByVal sender As System.Object, ByVal e As System.EventArgs) Handles cboIsland.Selected
    ' This event handler allows the user to enter the island choice
    ' and then calls subprocedures to place the island activities in the list.

```

Guided Program Development *continued*

- **Code the ValidateNumberInParty Function Procedure** The next step is to code the ValidateNumberInParty Function procedure. Click below the btnFindCost_Click event handler and enter the Function procedure declaration. The Function procedure returns a Boolean value that indicates whether the number the user entered is valid. The value must be an integer value that is greater than 0 and less than 100. A Try-Catch block is used for the conversion to an integer operation to catch any invalid data the user entered. Multiple Catch blocks are used to catch specific exceptions. If an exception occurs, the error message is displayed in a message box, the focus is placed on the txtNumberInParty TextBox object, and the value in the TextBox object is cleared. Write the code for this Function procedure *(ref: Figure 8-48)*.

HINT

```

    Private Function ValidateNumberInParty() As Boolean
        ' This procedure validates the value entered for the number in party

        Dim intPartyNumber As Integer
        Dim blnValidityCheck As Boolean = False
        Dim strNumberInPartyErrorMessage As String = _
            "Please enter the number of people in your party (1-99)"
        Dim strMessageBoxTitle As String = "Error"

        Try
            intPartyNumber = Convert.ToInt32(txtNumberInParty.Text)
            If intPartyNumber > 0 And intPartyNumber < 100 Then
                blnValidityCheck = True
            Else
                MsgBox(strNumberInPartyErrorMessage, , strMessageBoxTitle)
                txtNumberInParty.Focus()
                txtNumberInParty.Clear()
            End If
        Catch Exception As FormatException
            MsgBox(strNumberInPartyErrorMessage, , strMessageBoxTitle)
            txtNumberInParty.Focus()
            txtNumberInParty.Clear()
        Catch Exception As OverflowException
            MsgBox(strNumberInPartyErrorMessage, , strMessageBoxTitle)
            txtNumberInParty.Focus()
            txtNumberInParty.Clear()
        Catch Exception As SystemException
            MsgBox(strNumberInPartyErrorMessage, , strMessageBoxTitle)
            txtNumberInParty.Focus()
            txtNumberInParty.Clear()
        End Try

        Return blnValidityCheck

    End Function
```

(continues)

Guided Program Development *continued*

- **Code the ValidateTourSelection Function Procedure** Click below the ValidateNumberInParty function and enter the ValidateTourSelection procedure declaration. The ValidateTourSelection Function procedure ensures the user selected a tour from the lstTours ListBox object and then returns an integer value for the list selection to the calling procedure. To determine if a tour was selected, the procedure uses a Try-Catch block to convert the selected index value to an integer. If the conversion is successful, a choice was made and the choice is returned. In addition, a Boolean variable in the calling procedure is set to True because the variable was passed ByRef. If the selected index is not converted, the user did not make a choice. An error message box is displayed and the Boolean variable is set to False. One Catch block is used because the only error using the ListBox object is if the user does not select a tour.

HINT

```
Private Function ValidateTourSelection(ByRef blnTour As Boolean, _
    ByRef strTour As String) As Integer
    ' This function ensures the user selected a tour

    Dim intOceanTour As Integer
    Try
        intOceanTour = Convert.ToInt32(lstTours.SelectedIndex)
        strTour = lstTours.SelectedItem.ToString()
        blnTour = True
    Catch Exception As SystemException
        ' Detects if tour not selected
        MsgBox("Select an Ocean Tour", , "Error")
        blnTour = False
    End Try
    Return intOceanTour

End Function
```

Guided Program Development *continued*

• **Code the ArubaFindCost Function Procedures to Find the Cost of an Aruba Island Tour** Click below the ValidateTourSelection Function procedure and enter the ArubaFindCost Function procedure declaration. The purpose of the ArubaFindCost Function procedure is to determine the cost for an Aruba tour. Three variables are passed to the function. Two are passed ByVal: the tour selection and the group size. Tour length is passed ByRef. The ArubaFindCost Function procedure uses the tour selection and group size to determine the cost for the tour based on published rates (*ref: Figure 8-51*). It also changes the values in the tour length field for use in the calling procedure. Write the code for the ArubaFindCost Function procedure.

HINT

```
    Private Function ArubaFindCost(ByVal intTourSelection As Integer, _
     ByVal intGroupSize As Integer, ByRef intTourLength As Integer) As Decimal
        ' This function calculates the cost of the tours to Aruba

        Dim decTourCost As Decimal
        Dim decFinalCost As Decimal
        Dim decArubaDeepSeaCost As Decimal = 199D
        Dim decArubaKayakCost As Decimal = 89D
        Dim decArubaScubaCost As Decimal = 119D
        Dim decArubaSnorkelCost As Decimal = 89D

        Select Case intTourSelection
            Case 0
                decTourCost = decArubaDeepSeaCost
                intTourLength = _intEightHours
            Case 1
                decTourCost = decArubaKayakCost
                intTourLength = _intTwoHours
            Case 2
                decTourCost = decArubaScubaCost
                intTourLength = _intThreeHours
            Case 3
                decTourCost = decArubaSnorkelCost
                intTourLength = _intFourHours
        End Select
        decFinalCost = decTourCost * intGroupSize
        Return decFinalCost

    End Function
```

(continues)

Guided Program Development *continued*

• **Code the JamaicaFindCost Function Procedure to Find the Cost of a Jamaica Island Tour** Click below the ArubaFindCost Function procedure and enter the JamaicaFindCost Function procedure declaration. The purpose of the JamaicaFindCost Function procedure is to determine the cost for a Jamaica tour. It uses the same three passed variables as the ArubaFindCost Function procedure. It also uses similar logic and returns the same values. Write the code for the JamaicaFindCost Function procedure.

HINT

```
    Private Function JamaicaFindCost(ByVal intTourSelection As Integer, _
    ByVal intGroupSize As Integer, ByRef intTourLength As Integer) As Decimal
        ' This function calculates the cost of the tours to Jamaica

        Dim decTourCost As Decimal
        Dim decFinalCost As Decimal
        Dim decJamaicaGlassBottomCost As Decimal = 39D
        Dim decJamaicaParasailCost As Decimal = 119D
        Dim decJamaicaSnorkelCost As Decimal = 59D

        Select Case intTourSelection
            Case 0
                decTourCost = decJamaicaGlassBottomCost
                intTourLength = _intTwoHours
            Case 1
                decTourCost = decJamaicaParasailCost
                intTourLength = _intTwoHours
            Case 2
                decTourCost = decJamaicaSnorkelCost
                intTourLength = _intThreeHours
        End Select
        decFinalCost = decTourCost * intGroupSize
        Return decFinalCost

    End Function
```

Guided Program Development *continued*

- **Code the KeyWestFindCost Function Procedure to Find the Cost of a Key West Island Tour** Click below the JamaicaFindCost Function procedure and enter the KeyWestFindCost Function procedure declaration. The purpose of the KeyWestFindCost Function procedure is to determine the cost for a Key West tour. It uses the same three passed variables as the JamaicaFindCost Function procedure. It also uses similar logic and returns the same values. Write the code for the KeyWestFindCost Function procedure.

HINT

```
Private Function KeyWestFindCost(ByVal intTourSelection As Integer, _
 ByVal intGroupSize As Integer, ByRef intTourLength As Integer) As Decimal
    ' This function calculates the cost of the tours to Key West

    Dim decTourCost As Decimal
    Dim decFinalCost As Decimal
    Dim decKeyWestDeepSeaCost As Decimal = 89D
    Dim decKeyWestGlassBottomCost As Decimal = 29D
    Dim decKeyWestScubaCost As Decimal = 119D
    Dim decKeyWestSnorkelCost As Decimal = 59D

    Select Case intTourSelection
        Case 0
            decTourCost = decKeyWestDeepSeaCost
            intTourLength = _intFourHours
        Case 1
            decTourCost = decKeyWestGlassBottomCost
            intTourLength = _intTwoHours
        Case 2
            decTourCost = decKeyWestScubaCost
            intTourLength = _intThreeHours
        Case 3
            decTourCost = decKeyWestSnorkelCost
            intTourLength = _intThreeHours
    End Select
    decFinalCost = decTourCost * intGroupSize
    Return decFinalCost

End Function
```

(continues)

Guided Program Development *continued*

• **Code the Clear Button Click Event** After the Function procedures that are called from the btnFindCost click event handler have been coded, the next step is to write the code for the Clear Button click event handler. This event handler must reset the Windows Form object and objects on the form so it is displayed the same as when the program starts. This includes resetting the message in the cboIsland ComboBox object, clearing the number in party text box and the tours list box, blanking the labels that display the results, and removing all the objects except the cboIsland ComboBox object from view. Display the Design window and then double-click the btnClear object to open the btnClear click event handler. Write the code for the event handler.

HINT

```
Private Sub btnClear_Click(ByVal sender As System.Object, ByVal e As System.EventArgs) Handles btnClear.Click
    ' This event handler clears the form and resets the form for
    ' reuse when the user clicks the Clear button.

    cboIsland.Text = "Select Island Location"
    txtNumberInParty.Clear()
    lstTours.Items.Clear()
    lblTourType.Text = ""
    lblCost.Text = ""
    lblLength.Text = ""
    lblParty.Visible = False
    txtNumberInParty.Visible = False
    lblSelect.Visible = False
    lstTours.Visible = False
    btnFindCost.Visible = False
    btnClear.Visible = False
    lblTourType.Visible = False
    lblCost.Visible = False
    lblLength.Visible = False

End Sub
```

• **Code the frmTours_Load Event** The last bit of code to write for the Ocean Tours program is the event handler for the frmTours load event. You will recall that when the application begins execution, a splash screen opens first. To display the splash screen longer than by default, you must add a sleep timer. Return to the frmTours.vb [Design] window and double-click the Windows Form object. Assuming you want the splash screen to be displayed for 5 seconds, code the statement to delay program execution for 5000 milliseconds *(ref: Figure 8-16)*.

HINT

```
Private Sub frmTours_Load(ByVal sender As System.Object, ByVal e As System.EventArgs) Handles MyBase.Load
    ' Hold the splash screen for 5 seconds

    Threading.Thread.Sleep(5000)

End Sub
```

Code Listing

The complete code for the sample program is shown in Figure 8-56.

```
' Program Name: Ocean Tours Trip Selection
' Author:       Corinne Hoisington
' Date:         June 22, 2014
' Purpose:      The Ocean Tours Trip Selection application determines the
'               ocean tours available and calculates the cost of the tour.

Option Strict On

Public Class frmTours

    ' Class variables
    Private _intTwoHours As Integer = 2
    Private _intThreeHours As Integer = 3
    Private _intFourHours As Integer = 4
    Private _intEightHours As Integer = 8
    Private _strDeepSeaFishing As String = "Deep Sea Fishing"
    Private _strKayaking As String = "Kayaking"
    Private _strScuba As String = "Scuba"
    Private _strSnorkeling As String = "Snorkeling"
    Private _strGlassBottomBoat As String = "Glass Bottom Boat"
    Private _strParasailing As String = "Parasailing"

    Private Sub cboIsland_SelectedIndexChanged(ByVal sender As System.Object, ByVal e As
System.EventArgs) Handles cboIsland.SelectedIndexChanged, cboIsland.SelectedIndexChanged
        ' This event handler allows the user to enter the island choice
        ' and then calls subprocedures to place the island activities in the list.

        Dim intIslandChoice As Integer

        intIslandChoice = Me.cboIsland.SelectedIndex
        lstTours.Items.Clear()
        Select Case intIslandChoice
            Case 0
                ArubaTours()
            Case 1
                JamaicaTours()
            Case 2
                KeyWestTours()
        End Select
        ' Make items visible in the window
        lblParty.Visible = True
        txtNumberInParty.Visible = True
        lblSelect.Visible = True
        lstTours.Visible = True
        btnFindCost.Visible = True
        btnClear.Visible = True
        lblTourType.Visible = True
        lblCost.Visible = True
        lblLength.Visible = True
        ' Clear the labels
        lblTourType.Text = ""
        lblCost.Text = ""
        lblLength.Text = ""
        ' Set focus on number in party text box
        txtNumberInParty.Focus()

    End Sub
```

FIGURE 8-56 (continues)

```

    Private Sub ArubaTours()
        ' This procedure fills in the possible ocean tours for Aruba
        lstTours.Items.Add(_strDeepSeaFishing)
        lstTours.Items.Add(_strKayaking)
        lstTours.Items.Add(_strScuba)
        lstTours.Items.Add(_strSnorkeling)

    End Sub

    Private Sub JamaicaTours()
        'This procedure fills in the possible ocean tours for Jamaica
        lstTours.Items.Add(_strGlassBottomBoat)
        lstTours.Items.Add(_strParasailing)
        lstTours.Items.Add(_strSnorkeling)

    End Sub

    Private Sub KeyWestTours()
        'This procedure fills in the possible ocean tours for Key West
        lstTours.Items.Add(_strDeepSeaFishing)
        lstTours.Items.Add(_strGlassBottomBoat)
        lstTours.Items.Add(_strScuba)
        lstTours.Items.Add(_strSnorkeling)

    End Sub

    Private Sub btnFindCost_Click(ByVal sender As System.Object, ByVal e As System.EventArgs) Handles btnFindCost.Click
        ' This button event handler determines the cost of the ocean
        ' tour and displays the tour, the cost, and the length

        Dim intGroupSize As Integer
        Dim blnNumberInPartyIsValid As Boolean = False
        Dim blnTourIsSelected As Boolean = False
        Dim intTourChoice As Integer
        Dim strSelectedTour As String = ""
        Dim intIslandChoice As Integer
        Dim intLengthOfTour As Integer = 0
        Dim decTotalCost As Decimal

        ' Call a function to ensure the number of people in the party is valid
        blnNumberInPartyIsValid = ValidateNumberInParty()
        ' Call a function to ensure a tour was selected
        intTourChoice = ValidateTourSelection(blnTourIsSelected, strSelectedTour)
        ' If number of people and the tour selection are valid, calculate the cost
        If (blnNumberInPartyIsValid And blnTourIsSelected) Then
            intGroupSize = Convert.ToInt32(txtNumberInParty.Text)
            intIslandChoice = Me.cboIsland.SelectedIndex
            Select Case intIslandChoice
                Case 0
                    decTotalCost = ArubaFindCost(intTourChoice, _
                                                 intGroupSize, intLengthOfTour)

                Case 1
                    decTotalCost = JamaicaFindCost(intTourChoice, _
                                                   intGroupSize, intLengthOfTour)

                Case 2
                    decTotalCost = KeyWestFindCost(intTourChoice, _
                                                   intGroupSize, intLengthOfTour)

            End Select
            ' Display the cost of the ocean tour
            lblTourType.Text = "Tour: " & strSelectedTour
            lblCost.Text = "Cost: " & decTotalCost.ToString("C")
            lblLength.Text = "Length: " & intLengthOfTour.ToString() & " hours"
        End If

    End Sub

    Private Function ValidateNumberInParty() As Boolean
        ' This procedure validates the value entered for the number in party
```

FIGURE 8-56 (continues)

```
        Dim intPartyNumber As Integer
        Dim blnValidityCheck As Boolean = False
        Dim strNumberInPartyErrorMessage As String = _
            "Please enter the number of people in your party (1-99)"
        Dim strMessageBoxTitle As String = "Error"

        Try
            intPartyNumber = Convert.ToInt32(txtNumberInParty.Text)
            If intPartyNumber > 0 And intPartyNumber < 100 Then
                blnValidityCheck = True
            Else
                MsgBox(strNumberInPartyErrorMessage, , strMessageBoxTitle)
                txtNumberInParty.Focus()
                txtNumberInParty.Clear()
            End If
        Catch Exception As FormatException
            MsgBox(strNumberInPartyErrorMessage, , strMessageBoxTitle)
            txtNumberInParty.Focus()
            txtNumberInParty.Clear()
        Catch Exception As OverflowException
            MsgBox(strNumberInPartyErrorMessage, , strMessageBoxTitle)
            txtNumberInParty.Focus()
            txtNumberInParty.Clear()
        Catch Exception As SystemException
            MsgBox(strNumberInPartyErrorMessage, , strMessageBoxTitle)
            txtNumberInParty.Focus()
            txtNumberInParty.Clear()
        End Try

        Return blnValidityCheck

    End Function

    Private Function ValidateTourSelection(ByRef blnTour As Boolean, _
        ByRef strTour As String) As Integer
        ' This function ensures the user selected a tour

        Dim intOceanTour As Integer
        Try
            intOceanTour = Convert.ToInt32(lstTours.SelectedIndex)
            strTour = lstTours.SelectedItem.ToString()
            blnTour = True
        Catch Exception As SystemException
            ' Detects if tour not selected
            MsgBox("Select an Ocean Tour", , "Error")
            blnTour = False
        End Try
        Return intOceanTour

    End Function

    Private Function ArubaFindCost(ByVal intTourSelection As Integer, _
     ByVal intGroupSize As Integer, ByRef intTourLength As Integer) As Decimal
        ' This function calculates the cost of the tours to Aruba

        Dim decTourCost As Decimal
        Dim decFinalCost As Decimal
        Dim decArubaDeepSeaCost As Decimal = 199D
        Dim decArubaKayakCost As Decimal = 89D
        Dim decArubaScubaCost As Decimal = 119D
        Dim decArubaSnorkelCost As Decimal = 89D

        Select Case intTourSelection
            Case 0
                decTourCost = decArubaDeepSeaCost
                intTourLength = _intEightHours
            Case 1
                decTourCost = decArubaKayakCost
                intTourLength = _intTwoHours
            Case 2
                decTourCost = decArubaScubaCost
                intTourLength = _intThreeHours
```

FIGURE 8-56 (continues)

```
            Case 3
                decTourCost = decArubaSnorkelCost
                intTourLength = _intFourHours
        End Select
        decFinalCost = decTourCost * intGroupSize
        Return decFinalCost

    End Function

    Private Function JamaicaFindCost(ByVal intTourSelection As Integer, _
    ByVal intGroupSize As Integer, ByRef intTourLength As Integer) As Decimal
        ' This function calculates the cost of the tours to Jamaica

        Dim decTourCost As Decimal
        Dim decFinalCost As Decimal
        Dim decJamaicaGlassBottomCost As Decimal = 39D
        Dim decJamaicaParasailCost As Decimal = 119D
        Dim decJamaicaSnorkelCost As Decimal = 59D

        Select Case intTourSelection
            Case 0
                decTourCost = decJamaicaGlassBottomCost
                intTourLength = _intTwoHours
            Case 1
                decTourCost = decJamaicaParasailCost
                intTourLength = _intTwoHours
            Case 2
                decTourCost = decJamaicaSnorkelCost
                intTourLength = _intThreeHours
        End Select
        decFinalCost = decTourCost * intGroupSize
        Return decFinalCost

    End Function

    Private Function KeyWestFindCost(ByVal intTourSelection As Integer, _
    ByVal intGroupSize As Integer, ByRef intTourLength As Integer) As Decimal
        ' This function calculates the cost of the tours to Key West

        Dim decTourCost As Decimal
        Dim decFinalCost As Decimal
        Dim decKeyWestDeepSeaCost As Decimal = 89D
        Dim decKeyWestGlassBottomCost As Decimal = 29D
        Dim decKeyWestScubaCost As Decimal = 119D
        Dim decKeyWestSnorkelCost As Decimal = 59D

        Select Case intTourSelection
            Case 0
                decTourCost = decKeyWestDeepSeaCost
                intTourLength = _intFourHours
            Case 1
                decTourCost = decKeyWestGlassBottomCost
                intTourLength = _intTwoHours
            Case 2
                decTourCost = decKeyWestScubaCost
                intTourLength = _intThreeHours
            Case 3
                decTourCost = decKeyWestSnorkelCost
                intTourLength = _intThreeHours
        End Select
        decFinalCost = decTourCost * intGroupSize
        Return decFinalCost

    End Function

    Private Sub btnClear_Click(ByVal sender As System.Object, ByVal e As System.EventArgs) Handles btnClear.Click
        ' This event handler clears the form and resets the form for
        ' reuse when the user clicks the Clear button.

        cboIsland.Text = "Select Island Location"
        txtNumberInParty.Clear()
        lstTours.Items.Clear()
        lblTourType.Text = ""
        lblCost.Text = ""
        lblLength.Text = ""
        lblParty.Visible = False
        txtNumberInParty.Visible = False
        lblSelect.Visible = False
        lstTours.Visible = False
        btnFindCost.Visible = False
        btnClear.Visible = False
```

FIGURE 8-56 (continues)

```
            lblTourType.Visible = False
            lblCost.Visible = False
            lblLength.Visible = False

        End Sub

        Private Sub frmTours_Load(ByVal sender As System.Object, ByVal e As System.EventArgs) Handles
        MyBase.Load
            ' Hold the splash screen for 5 seconds

            Threading.Thread.Sleep(5000)

        End Sub

    End Class
```

FIGURE 8-56 (continued)

Summary

In this chapter you have learned to create applications using procedures. The items listed in the table in Figure 8-57 include all the new Visual Studio and Visual Basic skills you have learned in this chapter.

Visual Basic Skills

Skill	Figure Number	Web Address for Video
Examine the Ocean Tours chapter project application	Figure 8-2	scsite.com/vb2010/ch8/figure8-2
Add the generic splash screen	Figure 8-5	scsite.com/vb2010/ch8/figure8-5
Pause the splash screen	Figure 8-16	scsite.com/vb2010/ch8/figure8-16
Place a ComboBox object on a form	Figure 8-18	scsite.com/vb2010/ch8/figure8-18
Use Assignment statement to obtain SelectedIndex	Page 576	
Create a SelectedIndexChanged Event	Figure 8-26	scsite.com/vb2010/ch8/figure8-26
Code a Procedure Call and a Sub Procedure	Figure 8-28	
Pass an argument to a called procedure	Figure 8-33	
Pass an argument by value	Figure 8-34	
Passing an argument by reference	Figure 8-38	
Code a Function procedure	Figure 8-40	
Code a Try-Catch Block	Figure 8-44	

FIGURE 8-57

Learn It Online

Start your browser and visit scsite.com/vb2010/ch8. Follow the instructions in the exercises below.

1. **Chapter Reinforcement TF, MC, SA** Click one of the Chapter Reinforcement links for Multiple Choice, True/False, or Short Answer below the Learn It Online heading. Answer each question and submit to your instructor.
2. **Practice Test** Click the Practice Test link below Chapter 8. Answer each question, enter your first and last name at the bottom of the page, and then click the Grade Test button. When the graded practice test is displayed on your screen, submit the graded practice test to your instructor. Continue to take the practice test until you are satisfied with your score.
3. **Crossword Puzzle Challenge** Click the Crossword Puzzle Challenge link below the Learn It Online heading. Read the instructions, and then click the Continue button. Work the crossword puzzle. When you are finished, click the Submit button. When the crossword puzzle is redisplayed, submit it to your instructor.

Knowledge Check

1. Write the line of code that would hold frmSplashScreen for approximately three seconds.
2. What is the name of the property that allows you to place a graphic on the background of the Windows Form object?
3. What is the difference between passing by value and passing by reference?
4. What is the least number of arguments you can pass to a Sub procedure?
5. What is the section of code called that performs a specific task and does not return a value?
6. What is the section of code called that performs a specific task and does return a value?
7. What happens to the variables that were passed by value when you leave a Sub procedure?
8. Name the two types of procedures.
9. How many value(s) can a Function procedure return?
10. Write the Visual Basic statements that will declare a Sub procedure called VotingBooth that receives one variable called intCount. The variable intCount will be changed in the procedure. Write only the first and last lines of the Sub procedure.
11. What is the name of a variable that is passed to a procedure?
12. If you want a copy of a variable passed to a procedure, which way should you pass it?
13. You must have a return statement in a Function procedure. True or false?
14. When multiple arguments are passed to a procedure, the order is not important. True or false?

Knowledge Check *continued*

15. Which type of exception would be detected if you use the conversion command Convert.ToInt32 to convert a non-integer value?
16. Which type of exception would be detected in the code in Figure 8-58?

```
Dim intMultiple As Integer
Dim intProduct As Integer

intMultiple = 2000000000
intProduct = intMultiple ^ 10
```

FIGURE 8-58

17. Which type of exception would be detected if you used the conversion command Convert.ToDecimal to try to convert a letter of the alphabet?
18. If you use multiple Catch blocks in a Try-Catch block of code, how do you determine the order of the Catch blocks?
19. If you include an optional Finally block, it should follow directly after the Try block. True or false?
20. When deciding whether a set of programming steps should be placed in a Sub procedure or a Function procedure, what are three questions you should ask?

Debugging Exercises

1. Fix the code in Figure 8-59:

```
Private Sub btnItemPrice_Click(ByVal sender As System.Object, ByVal e As
System.EventArgs) Handles btnItemPrice.Click
        Dim decPrice As Decimal
        Dim decTax As Decimal

        decPrice = Convert.ToDecimal(Me.txtCost.Text)
        TaxCost(decPrice, decTax)
        lblDisplay.Text("The tax amount is " & decTax.ToString())
End Sub

Private Sub TaxCost(price, tax)
        tax = price * .06
End Sub
```

FIGURE 8-59

(continues)

Debugging Exercises

2. Fix the code in Figure 8-60:

```
Private Sub btnBaseball_Click(ByVal sender As System.Object, ByVal e As
System.EventArgs) Handles btnBaseball.Click
        Dim decHits As Decimal = 200
        Dim decTimesAtBat As Decimal = 498
        Dim decBattingAverage As Decimal

        decBattingAverage=FindRunsBattedIn(decHits, decTimesAtBat)
        lblHits.Text("The batting average is " & _
            decBattingAverage.ToString())
End Sub

Private Function BattingAverage(byVal decHitsCount as Decimal, byVal
decNumberAtBat as Decimal)
        Dim decAverageAtBat as Decimal
        decAverage = decHitsCount / decNumberAtBat
        Return decAverage
End Sub
```

FIGURE 8-60

3. Fix the code in Figure 8-61:

```
Private Sub btnInventory_Click(ByVal sender As System.Object, ByVal e As
System.EventArgs) Handles btnInventory.Click
        Dim intItemNumber As Integer
        Dim decCost As Decimal
        decCost = Convert.ToDecimal(txtPrice.Text)
        DisplayProducts(intItemNumber, decCost)
End Sub

Private Sub DisplayProducts(ByRef decCostValue As Decimal, ByRef intItem As
Integer)
        lblItemDisplay.Text("Item: " & intItem & " Costs: " & _
            decCostValue.ToString())
End Sub
```

FIGURE 8-61

Analysis Exercises

1. What is the output of the code in Figure 8-62?

```
Private Sub btnSevens_Click(ByVal sender As System.Object, ByVal e As
System.EventArgs) Handles btnSevens.Click
    Dim intCount As Integer
    For intCount = 1 To 7
        CalculateSevens(intCount)
    Next
End Sub

Private Sub CalculateSevens(ByVal intCountValue As Integer)
    Dim intResult As Integer
    intResult = intCountValue ^ 3
    lstAnswer.Items.Add(intResult.ToString())
End Sub
```

FIGURE 8-62

2. What is the output of the code in Figure 8-63?

```
Private Sub btnJoke_Click(ByVal sender As System.Object, ByVal e As
System.EventArgs) Handles btnJoke.Click
    DisplayRiddle()
    DisplayAnswer()
End Sub

Private Sub DisplayAnswer()
    lblAnswer.Text = "Because it has a spring in it"
End Sub

Sub DisplayRiddle()
    lblRiddle.Text = "Why should you carry a watch when crossing a
desert?"
End Sub
```

FIGURE 8-63

(continues)

Analysis Exercises

3. What is the output of the code in Figure 8-64?

```
Private Sub btnBedrock_Click(ByVal sender As System.Object, ByVal e As
System.EventArgs) Handles btnBedrock.Click
        Dim strFullName As String = "Fred Flintstone"
        Dim strSecondName As String = "Barney Rubble"

        CountLength(strFullName, strSecondName)
        lblEnd.Text = "My favorite was " & strSecondName
End Sub

Private Sub CountLength(ByVal strFullName As String, ByRef strSecondName As
String)
        lblFirst.Text = "The first name has " & strFullName.Length & "
letters."
        lblSecond.Text = "The second name has " & strSecondName.Length & "
letters."
        strSecondName = "Dino"
End Sub
```

FIGURE 8-64

Analysis Exercises *continued*

4. What is the output of the code in Figure 8-65?

```
Private Sub btnStrangeFacts_Click(ByVal sender As System.Object, ByVal e As
System.EventArgs) Handles btnStrangeFacts.Click
        Dim intHangerLength As Integer = 44
        Dim intMen As Integer = 2000
        Dim intWomen As Integer = 7000
        Dim intValue As Integer

        intValue = Talk(intMen, intWomen)
        lblResponse.Text = "The couple would say " & intValue & " words a
day"
        AverageHanger(intHangerLength)
End Sub

Private Sub AverageHanger(ByVal intHanger As Integer)
        lblPhrase.Text = "The average length of a coat hanger when
straightened is " & intHanger & " inches."
End Sub

Function Talk(ByVal intM As Integer, ByVal intW As Integer) As Integer
        lblPhrase1.Text = "The average man says " & intM & " words a day"
        lblPhrase2.Text = "The average woman says " & intW & " words a
day"
        Return intM + intW
End Function
```

FIGURE 8-65

5. A program contains the procedure declaration shown in Figure 8-66. Write the Function call statement that assigns the returned value to intCubed and passes a variable named intValue.

```
Private Function Cube(ByVal intNum As Integer) As Integer
    Return intNum * intNum * intNum
End Function
```

FIGURE 8-66

6. Write a statement that passes the variable intBase to a procedure and assigns the return value to a variable named intSolution. Write the code that would declare a variable named intPopulation as an Integer. Allow the user to enter the population of their city in a TextBox object named txtCityPopulation. Convert the value to an integer within a Try block. Write a Try-Catch block with an overflow Catch block first, a format exception Catch block second, and a generic exception last. Each Catch block should display a message box explaining the problem with the user's input.
7. Write the code for a Sub procedure named FindHeight that will calculate the total number of inches based on the height of a person when given the feet and inches. For example, if a person is 5'10", they are 70 inches tall. Display the result in a message box.

Case Programming Assignments

Complete one or more of the following case programming assignments. Submit the program and materials you create to your instructor. The level of difficulty is indicated for each case programming assignment.

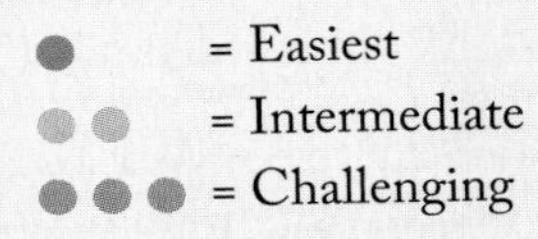

1 ● COMPARE FUEL COST

Design a Windows application and write the code that will execute according to the program requirements in Figure 8-67 and the Use Case definition in Figure 8-68 on the next page. Before writing the code, create an event planning document for each event in the program. The completed Windows Form object and other objects in the user interface are shown in Figure 8-69 and Figure 8-70 on the next page.

REQUIREMENTS DOCUMENT

Date submitted: September 24, 2014

Application title: Compare Fuel Cost

Purpose: This Windows application compares the cost of fuel for a sports utility vehicle with the cost of fuel for a compact car over the life of the vehicles.

Program Procedures: From a Windows application, a consumer can enter the miles per gallon of two vehicles, the cost of gas, the mileage driven each year, and the years that they intend to own the car to calculate total fuel cost for the life of each vehicle. The difference in the cost is also displayed.

Algorithms, Processing, and Conditions:

1. The consumer enters the present fuel price, miles traveled per year, the years of vehicle ownership (years 1–10), and the miles per gallon of a sports utility vehicle and compact car.
2. The same Function procedure will be called twice to calculate the total fuel cost over the life for each car.
3. Display the total cost over the life of the vehicle for each of the two cars and the difference between the two values.

Notes and Restrictions:

1. Validate input by using Try-Catch blocks in separate procedures as needed.

Comments:

1. The picture shown in the application should be selected from a picture available on the Web.
2. The program opens with a splash screen that is displayed for approximately five seconds.

FIGURE 8-67

Case Programming Assignments

Compare Fuel Cost *(continued)*

USE CASE DEFINITION

1. The user views the opening splash screen for approximately five seconds.
2. The user enters the present fuel cost, miles traveled per year, the number of years the vehicle will be owned, and the miles per gallon for their favorite sports utility vehicle and compact car.
3. The user clicks the Compare Life of Vehicle Cost button and the fuel cost per car is displayed.
4. User views the difference in costs between the two vehicles.

FIGURE 8-68

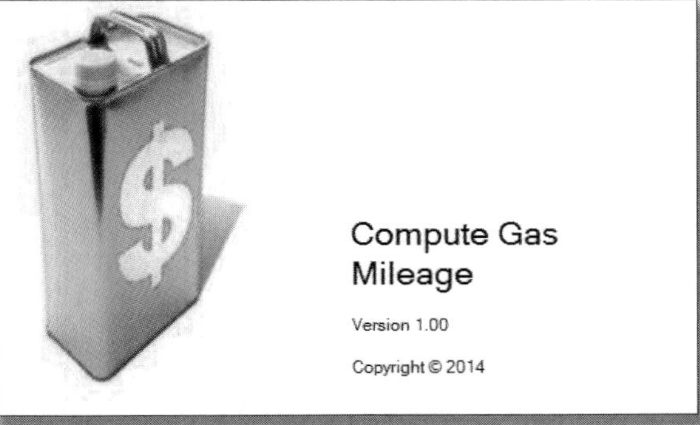

FIGURE 8-69

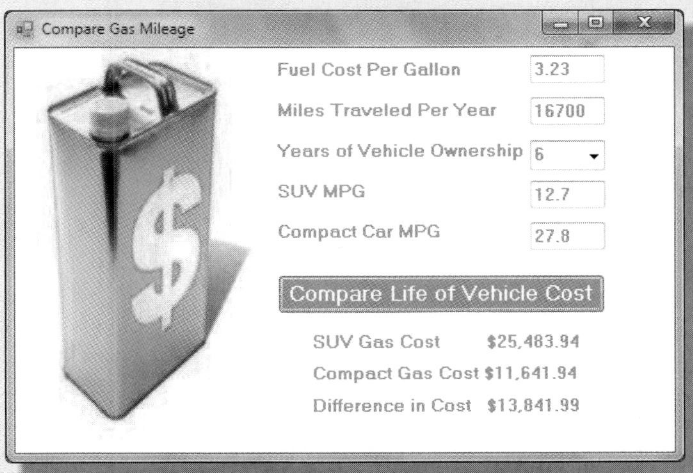

FIGURE 8-70

Case Programming Assignments

2 • ALUMINUM RECYCLING CAMPAIGN

Design a Windows application and write the code that will execute according to the program requirements in Figure 8-71 and the Use Case definition in Figure 8-72 on the next page. Before writing the code, create an event planning document for each event in the program. The completed Windows Form object and other objects in the user interface are shown in Figure 8-73, Figure 8-74, and Figure 8-75 on the next page.

REQUIREMENTS DOCUMENT

Date submitted:	August 11, 2014
Application title:	Aluminum Recycling Campaign
Purpose:	This Windows application calculates the number of cans that must be collected to make the recycling campaign's goal amount and finds the amount earned based on the number of cans collected.
Program Procedures:	From a Windows application, the user can select whether to calculate the number of cans needed to earn a target amount or find the amount earned based on the number of cans collected.
Algorithms, Processing, and Conditions:	1. The user first selects whether they want to compute their collection goal or the amount earned by aluminum collection. 2. After the user selects the recycling option, display the necessary objects based on the selected need. If the user selects the collection goal, request the target amount they hope to earn. If the user chooses to find the amount earned based on their aluminum collection, request the number of cans collected. 3. Based on approximately 24 aluminum cans in a pound and the cost paid for one pound of aluminum cans is currently $0.75, calculate the number of cans to collect to make the goal or calculate the amount of money the collected cans are worth in separate procedures. 4. Display the result for the calculation on the form.
Notes and Restrictions:	1. A Clear Form button should clear the Form. 2. The data the user enters should be validated in Try–Catch blocks in separate procedures as needed.
Comments:	1. The pictures shown should be selected from pictures available on the Web. 2. The application should begin with a splash screen that holds for approximately 4 seconds.

FIGURE 8-71

Case Programming Assignments

Aluminum Recycling Campaign *(continued)*

USE CASE DEFINITION

1. User views opening splash screen for four seconds.
2. User selects whether to calculate the number of cans that need to be collected to make the recycling campaign's goal amount or find the amount earned based on the number of cans collected.
3. User provides the following information: the target amount they hope to earn or the amount earned based on the number of cans collected.
4. User clicks the Find Target Amount of Cans button or Find Amount Earned button and result is displayed.
5. User clicks the Clear Form button to clear the responses.

FIGURE 8-72

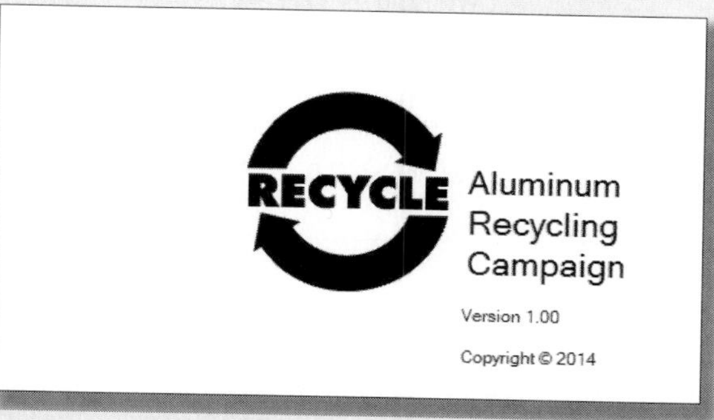

FIGURE 8-73

FIGURE 8-74

FIGURE 8-75

Case Programming Assignments

3 ● BASEBALL TICKET SALES

Design a Windows application and write the code that will execute according to the program requirements and the chart in Figure 8-76, the Program Requirements in Figure 8-77, and the Use Case definition in Figure 8-78 on page 627. Before writing the code, create an event planning document for each event in the program. The completed Windows Form object and other objects in the user interface are shown in Figure 8-79 and Figure 8-80 on page 627.

Type of Ticket	Seat Type	Cost
Season Tickets	Box Seats Lower Deck	$2500 $1500
Single Game Tickets	Box Seats Lower Deck Upper Deck Standing Room Only	$55 $35 $25 $15

FIGURE 8-76

REQUIREMENTS DOCUMENT

Date submitted: June 21, 2014

Application title: Baseball Ticket Sales

Purpose: This Windows application computes the cost of baseball tickets.

Program Procedures: From a Windows application, allow the user to select season or single-game baseball tickets and compute the cost of the tickets.

Algorithms, Processing, and Conditions:

1. The user is requested to select whether to purchase season or single-game tickets from a ComboBox object. The other objects are not visible until the user selects this option.
2. The user is requested to enter the number of tickets needed in a TextBox object.
3. The user is requested to select the type of seats from a ListBox object.
4. One of two Function procedures will be called for season or single-game tickets to compute and pass back the final cost of the tickets.

Notes and Restrictions:

1. A Clear Form button should clear the Form.
2. A Try-Catch block in separate procedures will validate the input.

Comments:

1. The picture should be selected from a picture available on the Web.
2. A splash screen begins this application.

FIGURE 8-77

Case Programming Assignments

USE CASE DEFINITION

1. User views opening splash screen for five seconds.
2. User selects whether to purchase season tickets or single-game tickets.
3. User enters the number of tickets needed and the type of seats based on whether they selected season or single-game tickets.
4. User clicks the Compute Ticket Cost button to display the final cost.
5. User clicks the Clear Form button to clear the responses.

FIGURE 8-78

FIGURE 8-79

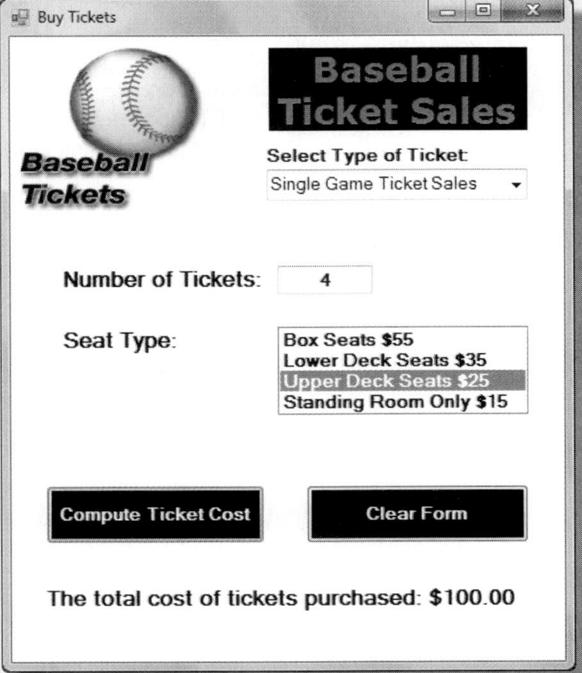

FIGURE 8-80

Case Programming Assignments

4 ●● FRACTIONS CALCULATOR

Design a Windows application and write the code that will execute according to the program requirements in Figure 8-81. Before designing the user interface, create a Use Case definition. Before writing the code, create an event planning document for each event in the program.

REQUIREMENTS DOCUMENT

Date submitted: October 19, 2014

Application title: Fractions Calculator

Purpose: This Windows application allows the user to enter two fractions with the choice of four operations: addition, subtraction, multiplication, or division.

Program Procedures: From a Windows form, the user will enter two fractions (a numerator and denominator for the first fraction and a numerator and denominator for the second fraction).

Algorithms, Processing, and Conditions:

1. The user first views a Windows Application that displays a title, a math graphic, and labels to enter information such as two numerators and two denominators for two fractions.
2. Four radio buttons will display the symbols for a basic calculator (+, − , *, /).
3. When the user enters the required data and selects the mathematical operation, a button displaying an equal sign can be selected to calculate the correct computation.
4. A Sub procedure should be called to handle the input and conversion of the four numbers entered.
5. Using Select Case statements, four Function procedures should be called based on the operation selected. Each Function procedure will calculate the correct operation and return the Decimal value to the calling procedure. The original procedure will print the result.

Notes and Restrictions:

1. The result should be calculated to the hundredths place.
2. The input values should be validated by a Try-Catch block.

Comments:

1. The picture shown should be selected from a picture available on the Web.
2. Do not allow division by zero. Catch this exception with a Try-Catch block.

FIGURE 8-81

Case Programming Assignments

5 MISTY RIVER CAMPGROUND RATES

Design a Windows application and write the code that will execute according to the program requirements in Figure 8-82. Before designing the user interface, create a Use Case definition. Before writing the code, create an event planning document for each event in the program.

REQUIREMENTS DOCUMENT

Date submitted: March 17, 2014

Application title: Misty River Campground Rates

Purpose: This application assists the campground manager to compute the total bill for a camping stay at a campground. The application will calculate the total cost including 7.5% state tourist tax.

Program Procedures: The user can select the type of campground site, number of days, and type of discount program.

Algorithms, Processing, and Conditions:

1. The user first views a Windows form that displays the campground name, a picture of the campground, a ComboBox object requesting the type of site: tent site $20 a night, RV site $35 a night, or cabin rental $55 a night, the number of nights (TextBox object), and if they have one of the following discounts: AAA (10%) or Military (12%).
2. After the information has been entered, a Sub procedure displays the labels: Subtotal Billing Amount for Your Stay, Taxes for Your Stay, and Final Total.
3. Pass the cost of the type of camping site and the number of nights to a Sub procedure to calculate the subtotal of the camp site. Do not display the amount in this procedure.
4. Pass the subtotal and the discount amount to a Function procedure. Determine the subtotal based on the type of discount. Pass the amount back to the calling method.
5. Another Function procedure should compute the 7.5% tax. Pass that value back to the calling method.
6. Pass the subtotal, tax, and final cost to a Sub procedure to display the results.

Notes and Restrictions:

1. The input values should be validated in a separate procedure by a Try-Catch block.

Comments:

1. The picture should be selected from pictures available on the Web.

FIGURE 8-82

Case Programming Assignments

6 ●● CALCULATE YOUR COMMUTE

Design a Windows application and write the code that will execute according to the program requirements in Figure 8-83. Before designing the user interface, create a Use Case definition. Before writing the code, create an event planning document for each event in the program.

REQUIREMENTS DOCUMENT

Date submitted: March 2, 2014

Application title: Calculate Your Commute

Purpose: This Windows application computes the cost of a yearly commute based on car, train, or bus travel.

Program Procedures: From a Windows application, the user selects how they commute to work, and also answers questions based on that commute to compute the cost of traveling to and from work for one year.

Algorithms, Processing, and Conditions:

1. The user first views a Windows application with a title and a ComboBox object requesting the way they commute — car, train, or bus. The other objects on the form are not visible at this time.
2. After the users select the mode of travel, the questions related to that type of travel are displayed immediately.
3. The following customized questions based on the user's choice are requested:
   Car: Daily round trip distance, days worked per month, miles per gallon of auto, cost per gallon of gas, monthly maintenance cost/insurance and monthly parking cost.
   Train: Round trip transit fare, days worked per month.
   Bus: Round trip transit fare, days worked per month.
4. After the values have been validated, calculate the cost of commuting for one year for the selected commuting choice.

Notes and Restrictions:

1. All values the user enters should be validated.

Comments:

1. The picture shown should be selected from a picture available on the Web.
2. A splash screen should open the application.

FIGURE 8-83

Case Programming Assignments

7 ●●● BALANCE A CHECKBOOK

Create a requirements document and a Use Case Definition document, and then design a Windows application based on the case project description in Figure 8-84. Before writing the code, create an event planning document for each event in the program.

Your college wants you to write a Windows Application that students can use to balance their checkbooks. This program will be installed on all computers in the student union. The application should allow the user to enter a starting balance and indicate whether the account has a monthly interest rate. Validate the beginning balance to verify that the number is possible. Allow the user to enter checks, ATM cash withdrawals, and deposits. Also calculate the interest for one month and add the interest amount to the final balance. The user can make multiple debits and deposits and continue until indicating that they are finished making transactions. The interest for the final balance will be added to the last balance after the transactions are completed. Data validation is needed for all input. An opening splash screen will be displayed as well.

FIGURE 8-84

8 ●●● MEDIAN PAY FOR COMPUTER OCCUPATIONS

Create a requirements document and a Use Case Definition document, and then design a mobile application based on the case project description in Figure 8-85. Before writing the code, create an event planning document for each event in the program.

Create a Windows Application that analyzes four job titles in computers from the information listed at the U.S. Department of Labor Statistics Web site found at www.bls.gov. Search for the hourly mean wage and annual mean wage for the national average for the following occupations: Computer Programmers, Computer System Analysts, Computer and Information Systems Managers, and Computer Software Engineers, Applications. Create a Windows form that has a drop-down list of the four occupations. Based on the user's selection, display the current median hourly pay and yearly pay. Also project what the pay will be in five years based on a 3% raise in these present rates per year.

FIGURE 8-85

Case Programming Assignments

9 ●●● POPULATION ANALYSIS

Create a requirements document and a Use Case Definition document, and then design a Windows application based on the case project description in Figure 8-86. Before writing the code, create an event planning document for each event in the program.

The United States Census Bureau would like to you to create a Windows Application that will display the population demographic data for many countries across the world. The Census Bureau has provided the information in the following table.

Country	Last Census (2010) Population	Annual Rate of Population Change Expected	Life Expectancy	Annual Rate of Life Expectancy Change Expected
China	1,323,420,000	0.6%	72.3	0.00023%
France	64,473,140	0.4%	79.6	0.00021%
Mexico	106,535,000	1.6%	75.2	0.00015%
South Africa	47,850,700	−0.3%	43.3	0.00019%
United States	303,232,774	0.9%	77.7	0.00020%

Allow the user to enter a year in the next hundred years and select a country from the list of countries shown in the table. Gather the correct population and other statistics. Calculate the future population and life expectancy for the year entered. Validate all entries. An opening splash screen will be displayed as well.

FIGURE 8-86

ENRICHMENT CHAPTER

Visual Studio Tools for Office

OBJECTIVES

You will have mastered the material in this chapter when you can:

- Use Visual Studio Tools in Microsoft Word
- Create a VSTO Word template
- Add a DateTimePicker object to an application
- Add a table to a Word document
- Add the Actions Pane Control
- Place a ComboBox object in applications
- Calculate payments using the Pmt Function
- Use Math Class methods in mathematical computations

***NOTE: VISUAL STUDIO TOOLS FOR OFFICE INSTALLATION**

Visual Studio Tools for Office (VSTO) is an integrated part of Visual Studio 2010. Both Microsoft Office 2010 and Microsoft Office 2007 are fully supported in Visual Studio 2010.

Introduction

You can use Visual Basic to create applications besides those for the Windows and Web environments. This chapter introduces topics that allow you to develop Office applications using Microsoft Word or Microsoft Excel. In addition to the techniques you have learned thus far to program Windows applications and Web applications, you also can use Visual Studio 2010 to develop code behind Word, Excel, PowerPoint, Visio, Outlook, Project, and InfoPath. The Visual Studio Tools for Office (VSTO) Second Edition is now packaged with Visual Studio 2010, and provides several enhancements including a new visual Ribbon designer for Microsoft Office 2010. The Ribbon designer allows a developer to design an Office Ribbon using the familiar drag-and-drop interface and to interact with the Ribbon using standard .NET code.

Chapter Project

In the sample chapter project, Microsoft Word, the word processing program in the Office suite, is used with Visual Basic 2010 to solve a problem for a car dealership. A local car dealer wants a car sales contract that allows a salesperson to enter the vehicle and buyer information to create a legal contract for the sale of a vehicle. The application will be designed using Microsoft Word to build an information form that is easy to use for the entire vehicle sales team. The Word document should have a Task Pane control on the right side of the screen that the salesperson can use to compute the monthly payment for the vehicle based on the interest rate, the length of the loan, and the amount borrowed.

When the application runs, the contract opens in a Microsoft Word 2010 template as shown in Figure EC-1.

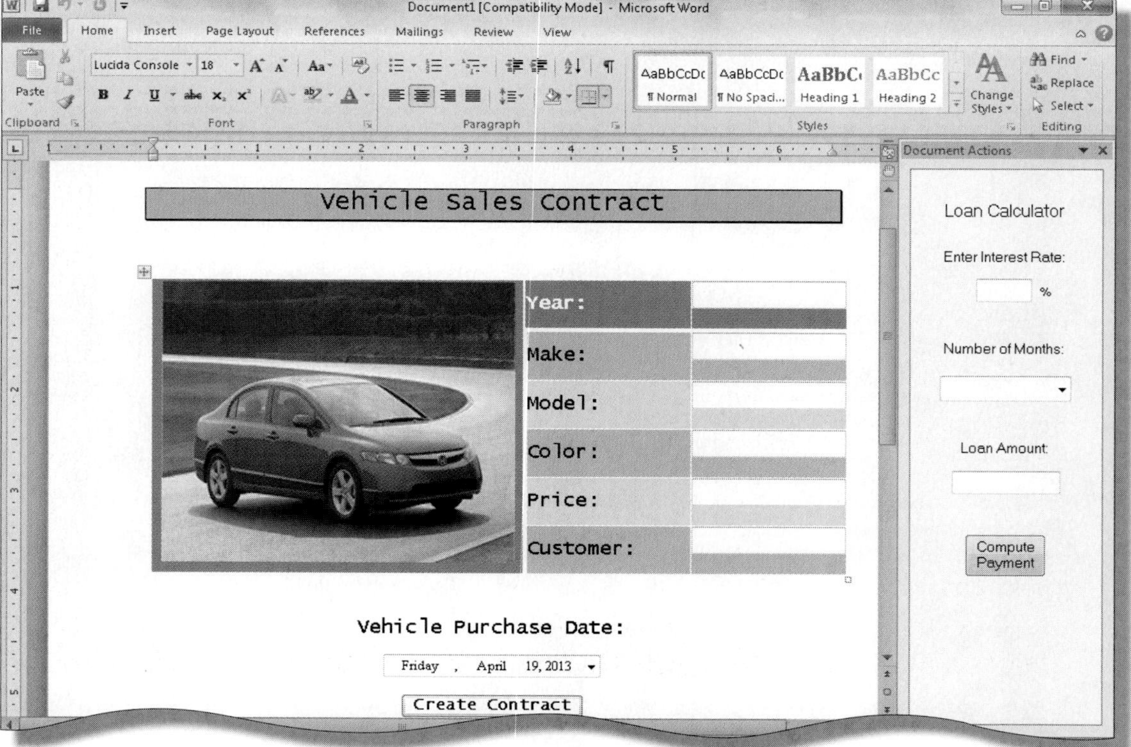

FIGURE EC-1

The salesperson enters the year, make, model, color, and price of the vehicle, and the name of the customer. The salesperson then selects the vehicle purchase date and clicks the Create Contract button. As shown in Figure EC-2, a legal vehicle sales contract is displayed and can be printed and saved. The salesperson also can compute the monthly payments based on the total loan amount, such as $17,000, and the interest rate, such as 9.25%. To do so, the salesperson enters the values requested in the Loan Calculator in the Document Actions task pane on the right side of the window. The salesperson can enter the loan amount directly and select the length of the loan from a box that contains the choices of 12, 24, 36, 48, or 60 months.

ONLINE REINFORCEMENT

To view a video of program execution, visit scsite.com/vb2010/ec and then select Figure EC-1.

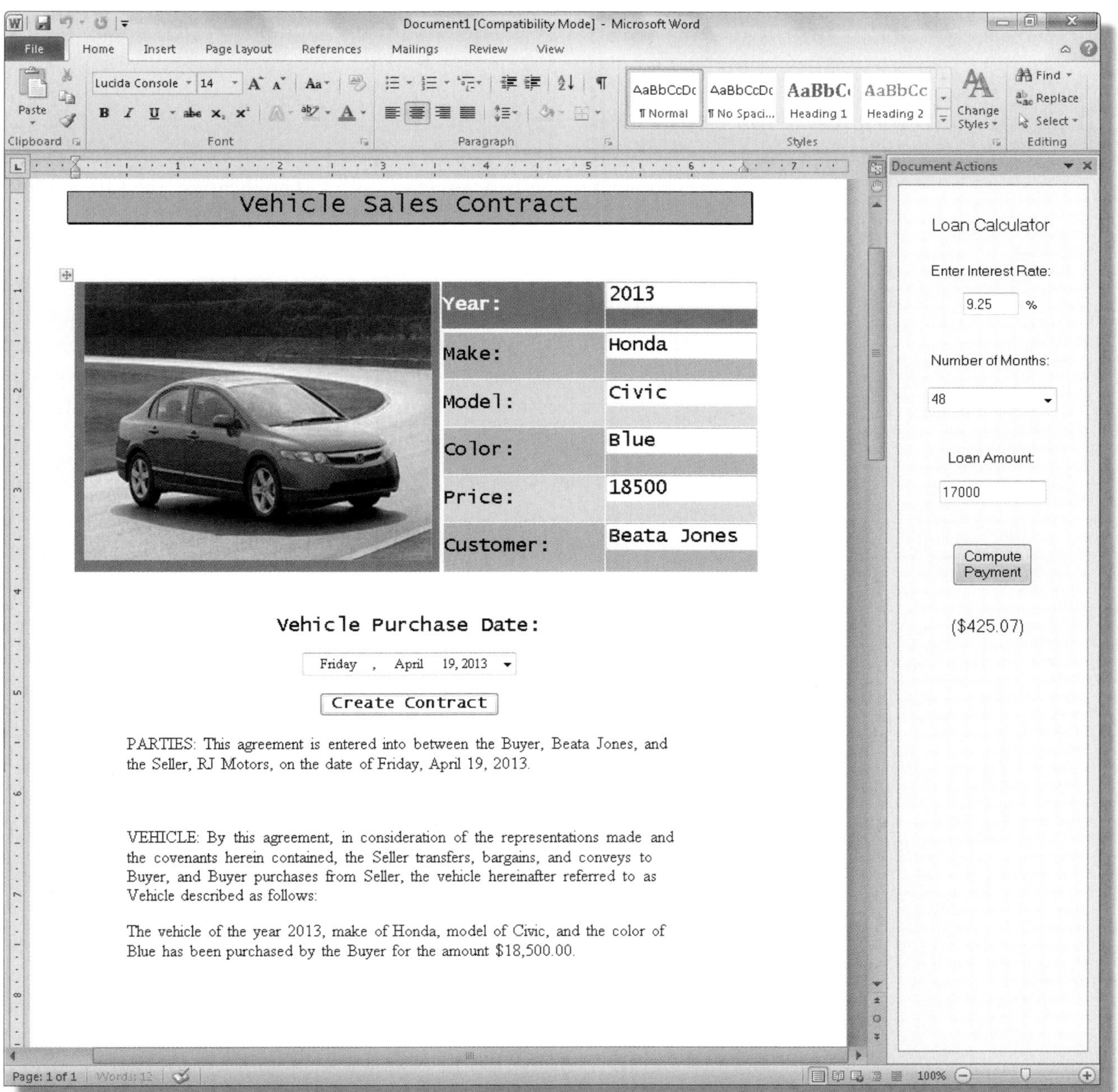

FIGURE EC-2

Programming an Office Document

Microsoft Office 2010 includes software applications that create professional documents used in the business world. Because Microsoft Office has more than a 90% market share, the robust Office environment has been joined with the power of Visual Studio's development facility. **Visual Studio Tools for Office** (VSTO, pronounced "visto") helps you build a Word document or an Excel spreadsheet that contains VB code, allowing you to create automated, customized Office documents that combine the power of Visual Basic with the familiarity of Office. VSTO is a component of Visual Studio 2010 that you can purchase as part of the Visual Studio Team Suite or as an add-on you can download with Visual Studio Professional.

Working with VSTO

Working with Office 2010 documents in VSTO is similar to working with a Visual Basic Windows application. When you start a VSTO application, the Office file (such as a Word 2010 document or Excel 2010 workbook) opens in the Visual Basic IDE, and the document serves as a visual designer. The experience of working with a document in the designer is as close as possible to the experience of working with a Windows form, making it simple to create an interactive document. You can edit and modify a document or workbook using the tools of the Office application. For example, you can use the Undo feature, create Excel formulas, and find and replace text. You also can use the Visual Studio Toolbox to add standard objects such as Label and Button objects to the document or workbook.

Using Templates

When you create your first VSTO application, you indicate whether you intend to create a Word or Excel document or template. A **template** is a special type of Office file that determines the basic structure for a document and can hold text, styles, macros, keyboard shortcuts, custom toolbars, AutoText entries, and other settings. Every Word document is based on a template. When you choose to create a Word document, you select an appropriate template, such as one for a memo or a normal document, which contains styles, formats, and other tools suitable for your purpose.

If you save a document with the file extension .dotx instead of the standard .docx and store the document in the proper place, Word recognizes it as a template. You then can create a new, blank document based on that template, including the styles, text, and other elements you need to create letters, memos, legal documents, Web pages, faxes, or any other kind of document that you use frequently. For example, you might use a home sales template for a real estate company's property listings. The document for each home that a realtor may sell could be based on the template so that all the listings are similar and easy to follow. By making a Word document or template with Visual Basic code behind it, users will feel comfortable with the Word environment while also having the power of the object and class set that Visual Studio provides.

The New Project dialog box in Visual Studio contains many project templates for creating Office 2010 and 2007 solutions such as an Excel Workbook, Word Document, Excel Template, Word Template, Outlook Add-in, PowerPoint Add-in, Visio Add-in, Project Add-in, and SharePoint template.

Creating a VSTO Project

The chapter project, Vehicle Sales Contract, is a VSTO application based on a Word template that allows a car salesperson to create a legal sales contract and compute the cost of monthly payments for a car loan. To create a VSTO application, you can follow these steps:

STEP 1 Start Visual Studio and click the New Project button on the Standard toolbar. In the New Project dialog box, double-click Office and then select 2010 in the Installed Templates pane on the left. In the center section, scroll down and select Word 2010 Template. In the Name text box, type `VehicleSalesContract`.

The New Project dialog box opens (Figure EC-3). The project will be an Office project using the Word template. The name of the project is displayed in the Name text box.

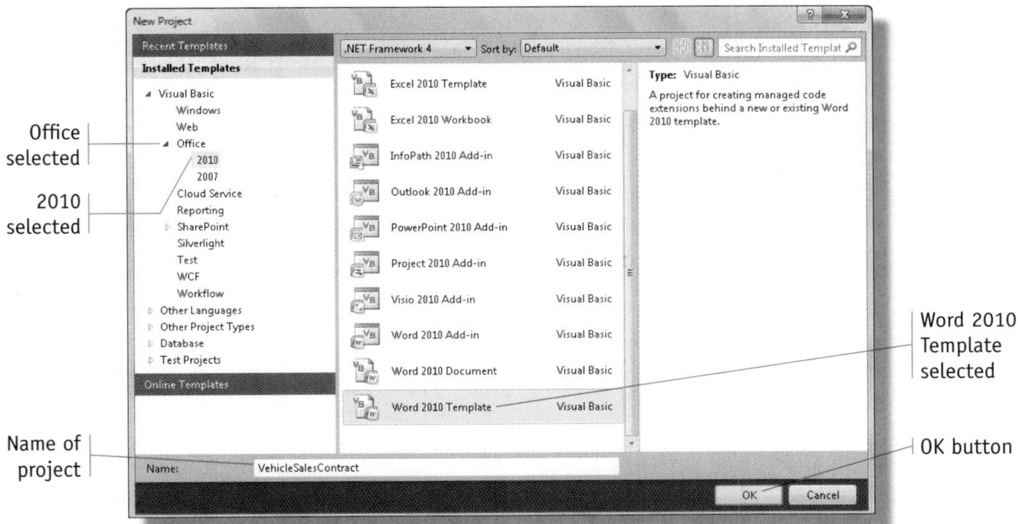

FIGURE EC-3

STEP 2 Click the OK button in the New Project dialog box.

The Visual Studio Tools for Office Project Wizard opens (Figure EC-4).

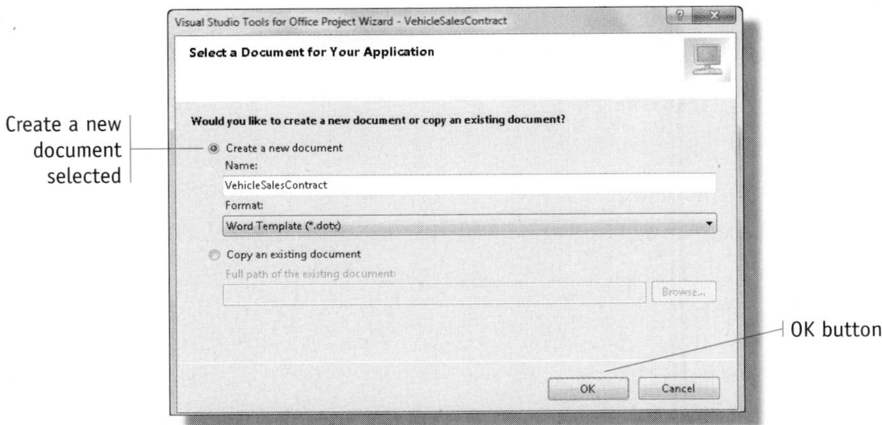

FIGURE EC-4

STEP 3 VSTO can place objects on a new or existing Word document. In this example, if necessary click the Create a new document option button. Click the OK button in the wizard. If necessary, click OK in the warning dialog box.

Visual Studio creates a template named VehicleSalesContract.dotx and opens it, including the standard Word tools, in the Visual Studio window (Figure EC-5). You now can design a Word document and add Visual Basic objects from the Visual Studio Toolbox.

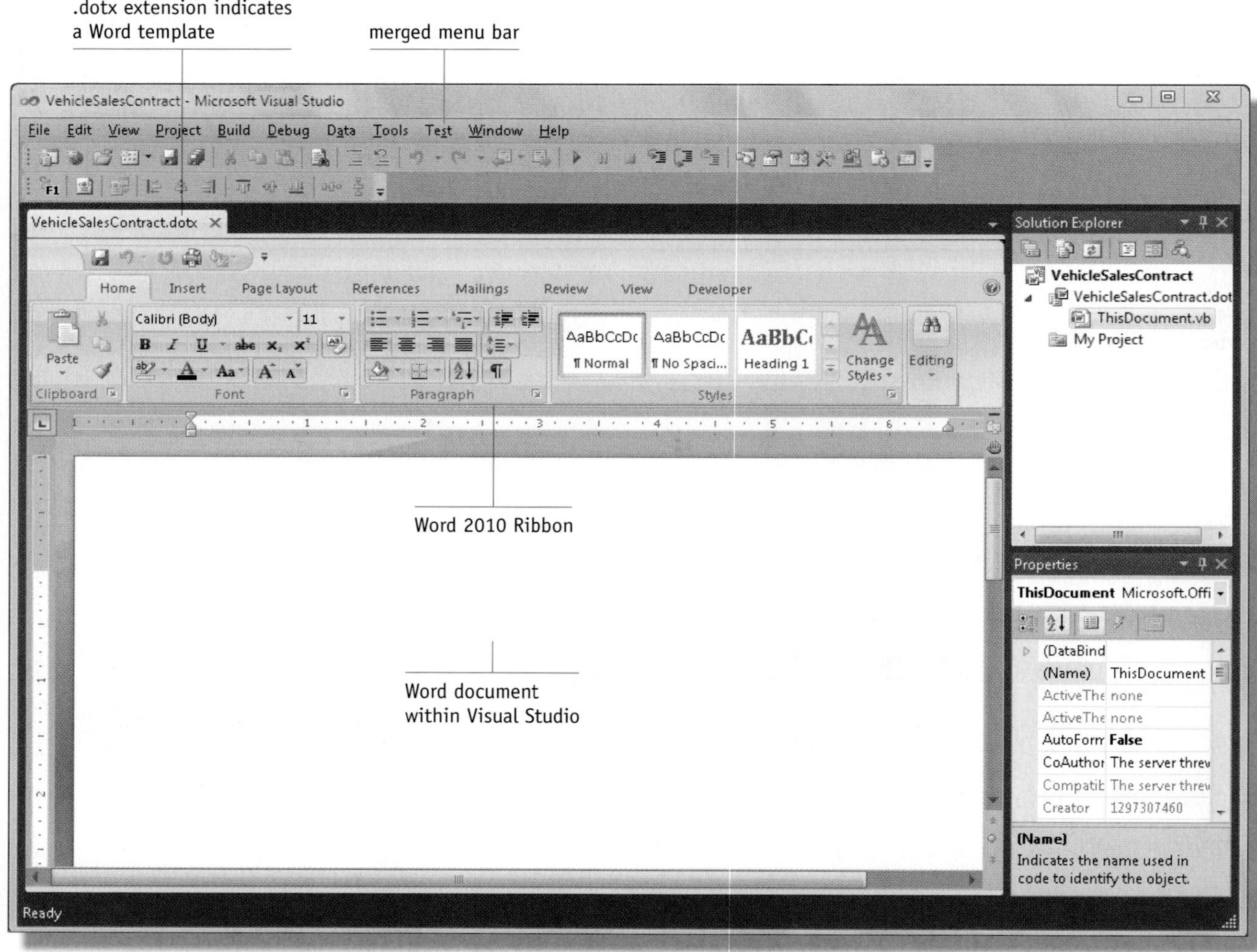

FIGURE EC-5

ONLINE REINFORCEMENT

To view a video of the process in the previous steps, visit scsite.com/vb2010/ec and then select Figure EC-3.

Understanding VSTO Toolbars, Menus, and Ribbons

The Office Ribbon for the selected Office application appears within the Visual Studio window and looks and acts as it does in Microsoft Office (Figure EC-6). Most Microsoft Word 2010 features are also available within Visual Basic 2010.

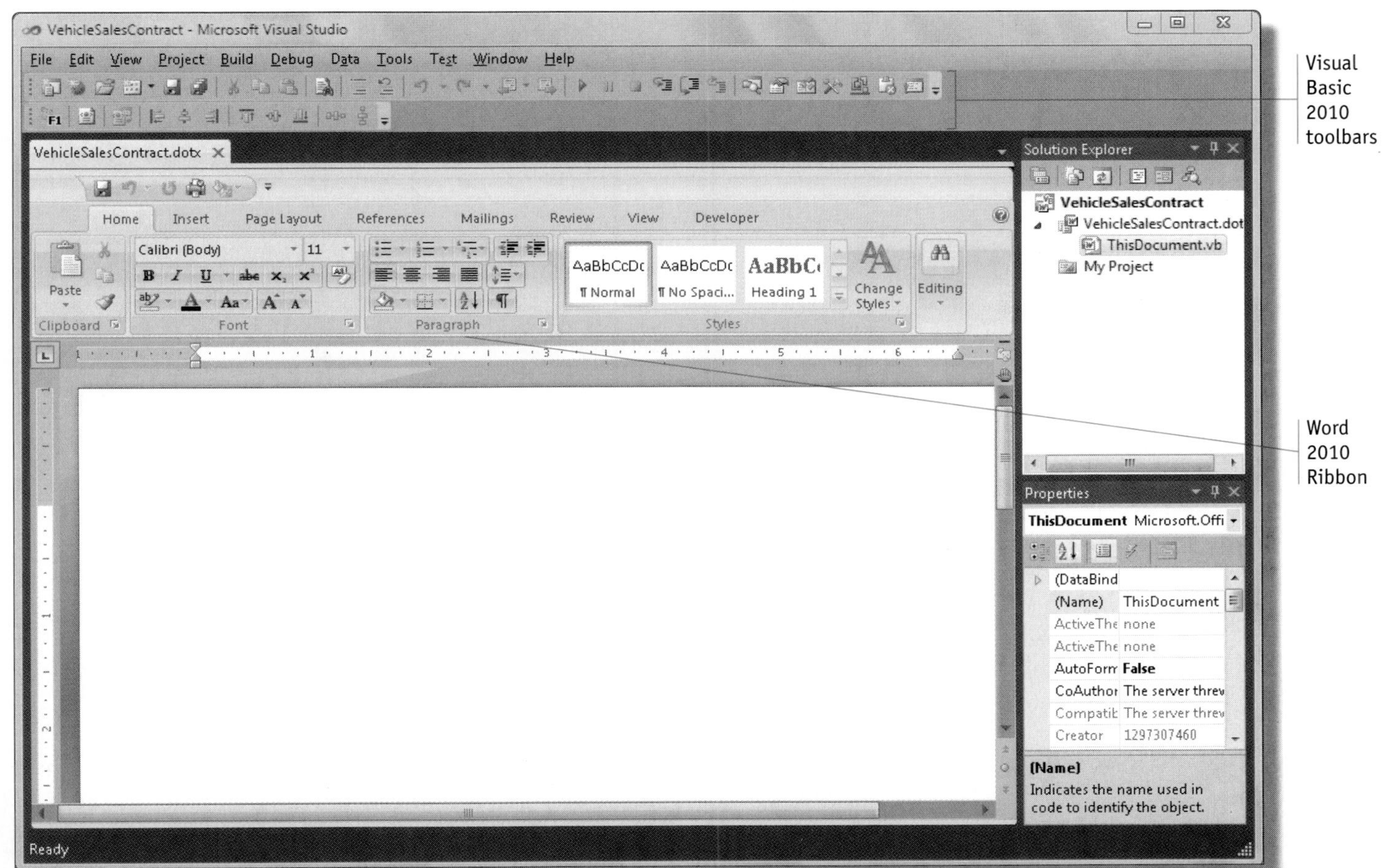

FIGURE EC-6

Using VSTO Design View

When working with Word and Excel templates in VSTO, you work in **Design view**, which enables you to customize the template by adding interactive objects. In addition, you can create Word or Excel documents and drag .NET component objects onto the document, writing Visual Basic code to control the objects.

Using the VSTO Toolbox

The VSTO Toolbox has many of the objects that have become familiar to you in Visual Basic programming. As shown in Figure EC-7, however, the VSTO Toolbox groups objects differently. Most of the objects you will use on a daily basis in VSTO are listed in alphabetic order in the category named Common Controls.

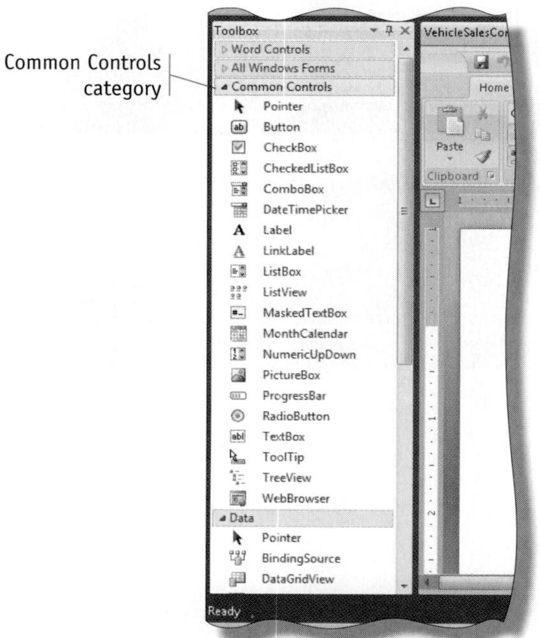

FIGURE EC-7

You can drag objects in the Common Controls category from the Visual Studio Toolbox directly into Word and Excel, as shown in Figure EC-8, and modify the object properties using the Properties window. For example, the TextBox object shown in Figure EC-8 has been dragged from the Toolbox directly to the Word document. You name the TextBox object using the (Name) property.

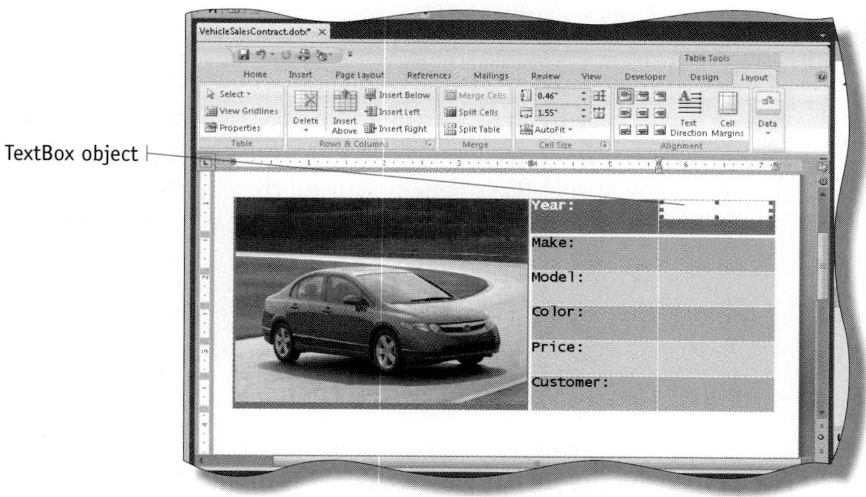

FIGURE EC-8

The GroupBox object is not available in VSTO. If you want two exclusive sets of RadioButton objects in two GroupBoxes, you must write code for the separate sets of RadioButton objects.

Adding a DateTimePicker Object

The **DateTimePicker** object allows the user to select one date from a calendar of dates or times. The DateTimePicker object works in all Visual Studio applications. It appears as a drop-down list with a date or time represented in text (Figure EC-9). When you drag the .NET component onto the Windows Form object, the current date is shown. You can change this date by changing the Value property in the Properties window. The prefix used for a DateTimePicker object is dat.

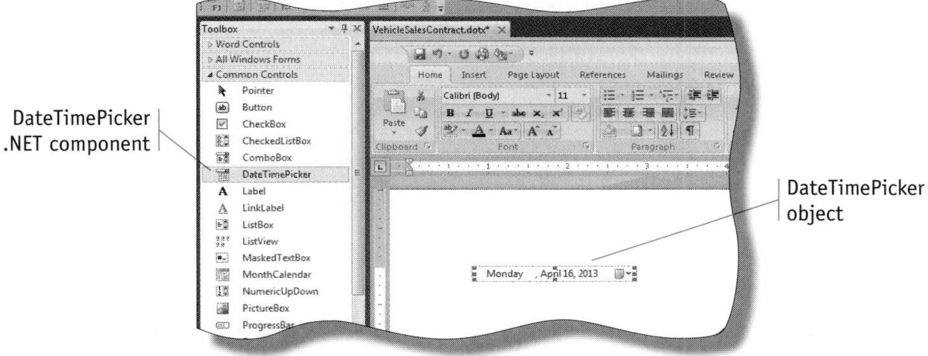

FIGURE EC-9

When you run the application, the user can click the list arrow to the right of the date to view a calendar (Figure EC-10). Using the calendar, the user can select a date and change to a different month. When the user clicks a date in the calendar, the selected date is displayed in the DateTimePicker object. In Figure EC-10, the current date is April 16 but the selected date is April 24.

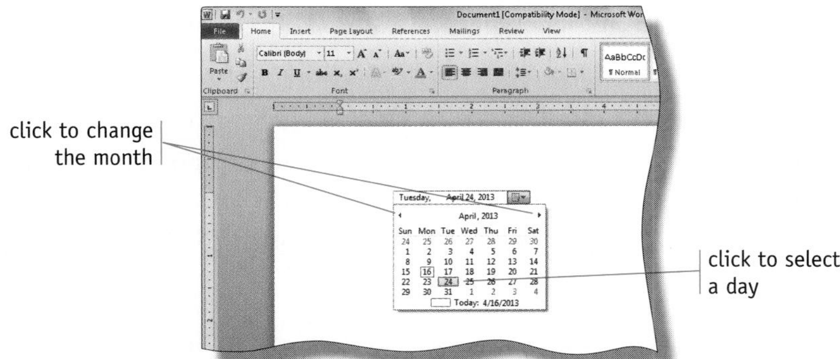

FIGURE EC-10

The selected date in the DateTimePicker can be referenced in code. For example, if the DateTimePicker object shown in Figure EC-10 on the previous page is named datBirthdayMonth, the user's selected birth date can be displayed in a Label object named lblBirthday by using the code shown in Figure EC-11.

```
Private Sub Button1_Click(ByVal sender As System.Object, ByVal e As System.EventArgs) Handles Button1.Click
    lblBirthday.Text = datBirthdayMonth.Text.ToString()
End Sub
```

FIGURE EC-11

If you want to display the day of the week selected in a DateTimePicker in a MsgBox object in a Word document, enter the code shown in Figure EC-12 to display the MsgBox object shown in Figure EC-13.

```
        MsgBox("Your birthday falls on a " & datBirthdayMonth.Value.DayOfWeek.ToString(), , "Birthday")
```

FIGURE EC-12

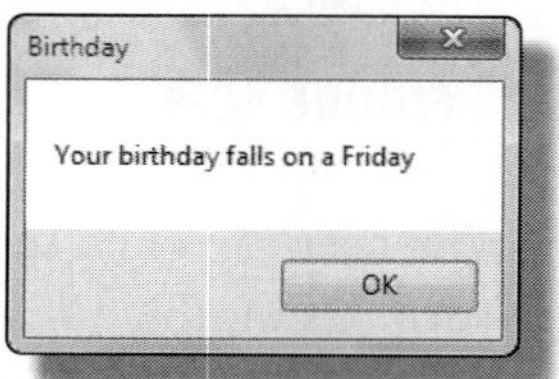

FIGURE EC-13

In Figure EC-13, the DayOfWeek procedure of the Value property returns the day. The ToString changes the returned value to a string for display in the MsgBox.

Adding a Table to a Word Document

Tables, which consist of rows and columns that form cells, can organize information in your document. In a VSTO Word 2010 document, click where you want to insert a table. To add a table to a Word document, you can complete the following steps:

STEP 1 On the Word 2010 Ribbon, click the Insert tab. In the Tables group, click Table.

Word displays a grid so you can select the number of rows and columns you want (Figure EC-14).

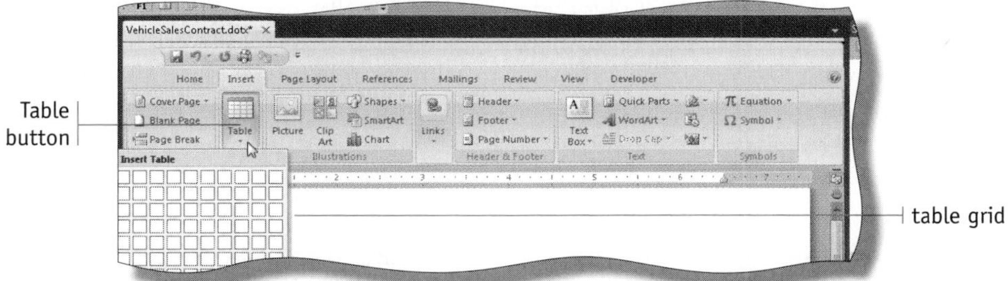

FIGURE EC-14

STEP 2 Drag to select one row and three columns in the grid.

Three cells in the first row of the table grid are selected (Figure EC-15).

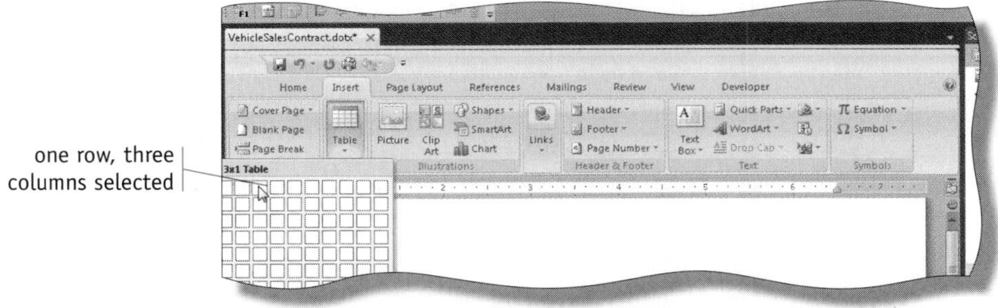

FIGURE EC-15

STEP 3 Release the mouse button to insert the table in the Word template.

A table consisting of one row and three columns appears in the Word template (Figure EC-16).

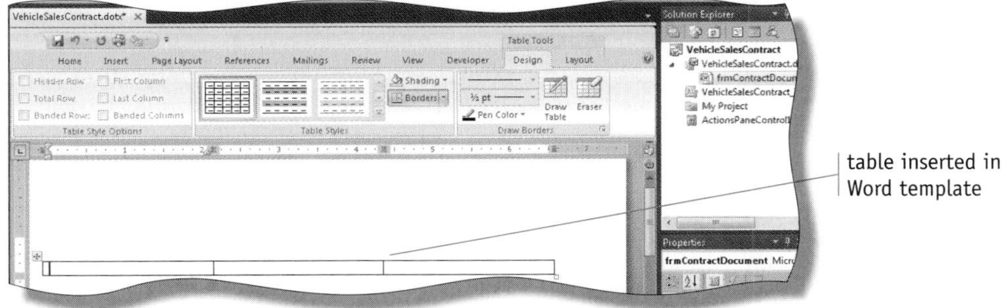

FIGURE EC-16

ONLINE REINFORCEMENT

To view a video of the process in the previous steps, visit scsite.com/vb2010/ec and then select Figure EC-14.

Inserting a Picture and Additional Cells in the Table

To enter text in the table, you can type directly in its cells, advancing from one cell to the next by using the TAB key. You also can place most of the Visual Basic Toolbox objects in a cell, such as a PictureBox or TextBox object. To include an image in the table, you can place a picture in a PictureBox object if you intend to change the graphic image in code, or insert a clip art image or a picture from a file directly into the table cell.

In the following example, the car.jpg image is used. You can download the image from scsite.com/vb2010/ec/images. Save it in a location you will remember. To insert the image, follow these steps:

STEP 1 Click the leftmost cell in the table. Click the Insert tab and then click Picture in the Illustrations group. In the Insert Picture dialog box, locate the car.jpg image file where you saved it. Select the car.jpg image and then click the Insert button to place the image in the table.

Word inserts the car picture in the first cell of the table (Figure EC-17).

FIGURE EC-17

STEP 2 The second and third columns contain one row. To add rows to these columns, first drag across the second and third columns to select them.

The second and third columns are selected in the table (Figure EC-18).

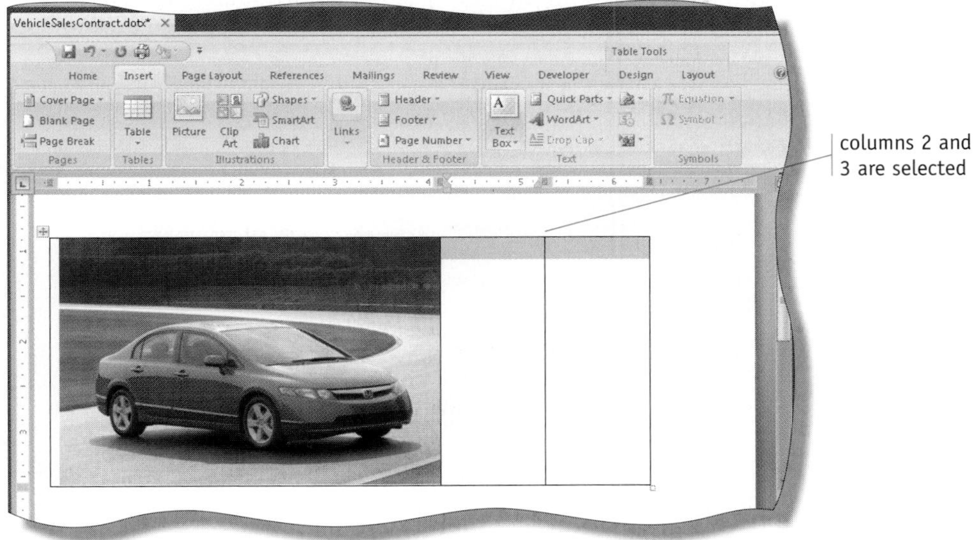

FIGURE EC-18

STEP 3 Click the Table Tools Layout tab. In the Merge group, click Split Cells.

The Split Cells dialog box is displayed (Figure EC-19).

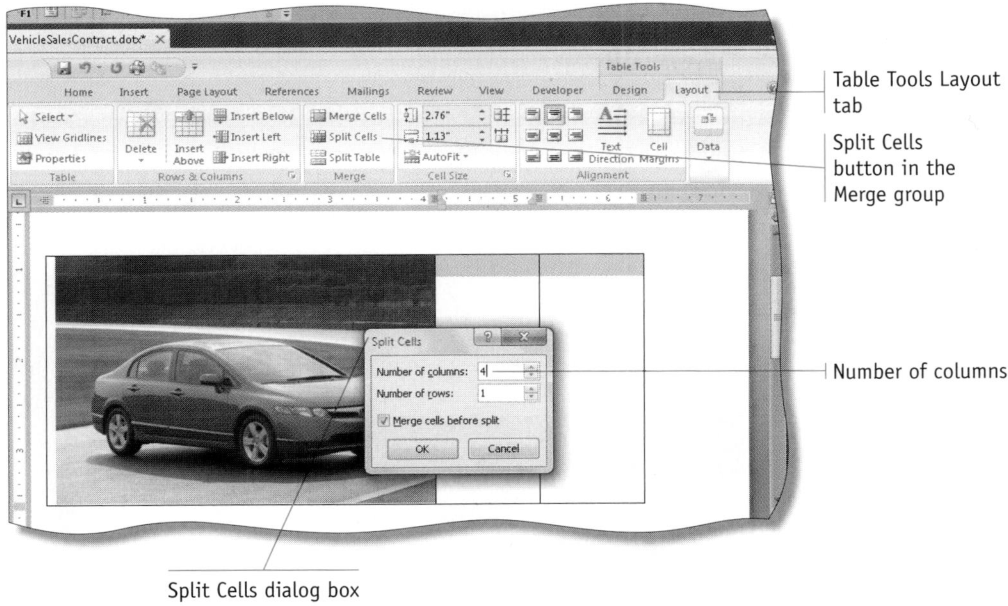

FIGURE EC-19

STEP 4 In the Split Cells dialog box, use the arrows to set the value in the Number of columns list to 2 and the value in the Number of rows list to 6. Click the OK button in the Split Cells dialog box. Click outside the table.

The two right columns now contain six evenly distributed rows (Figure EC-20).

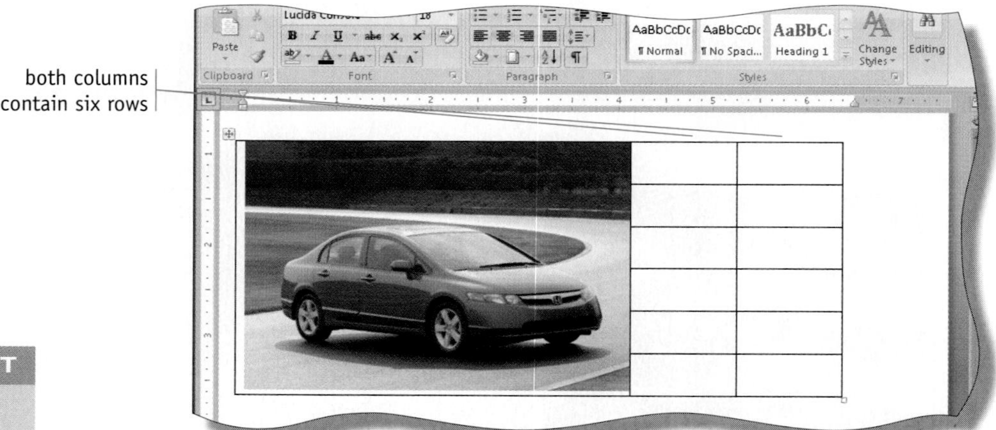

FIGURE EC-20

ONLINE REINFORCEMENT

To view a video of the process in the previous steps, visit scsite.com/vb2010/ec and then select Figure EC-17.

Using Table Styles to Format a Table

You can enter data in the table by typing characters directly into the cells. In the following steps, text has been added to the table.

After creating the table by adding images and text, for example, you may want to add some finishing touches to enhance its appearance. To change the design of a table, Word 2010 has many built-in table styles. To apply styles to a table, you can complete the following steps:

STEP 1 Click anywhere in the table.

The insertion point appears in the table (Figure EC-21).

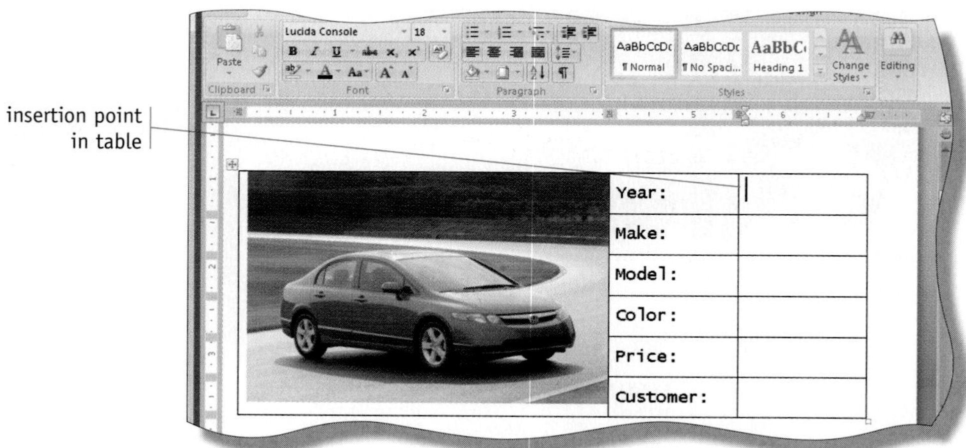

FIGURE EC-21

STEP 2 Click the Table Tools Design tab. In the Table Styles group, click the More button (third arrow). In the Table Styles gallery, scroll down to find the table style named Medium Grid 3 - Accent 1.

On the Table Tools Design tab, the Tables Styles gallery is displayed. The table style Medium Grid 3 - Accent 1 is highlighted (Figure EC-22).

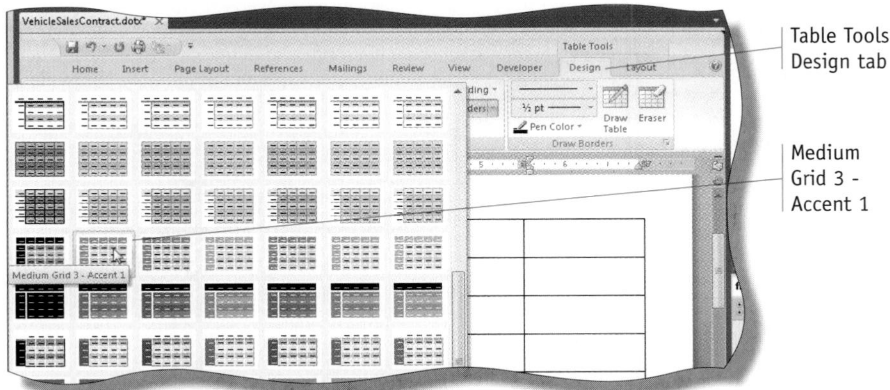

FIGURE EC-22

STEP 3 Select the Medium Grid 3 - Accent 1 table style.

The table format changes to reflect the design of the Medium Grid 3 - Accent 1 style (Figure EC-23).

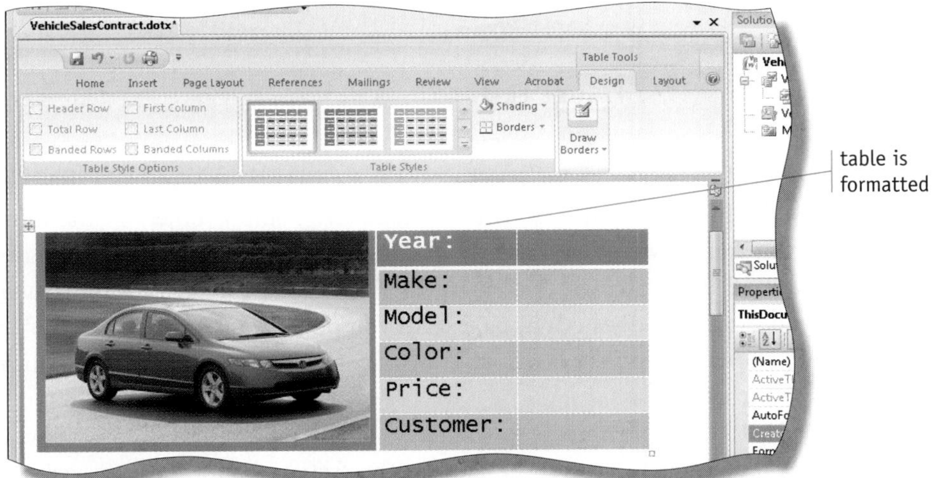

FIGURE EC-23

ONLINE REINFORCEMENT

To view a video of the process in the previous steps, visit scsite.com/vb2010/ec and then select Figure EC-21.

Adding the Actions Pane Control

The **Actions Pane Control** is a customizable task pane that appears in the Office application window. An example of a task pane is the Clip Art task pane, which is shown in Figure EC-24.

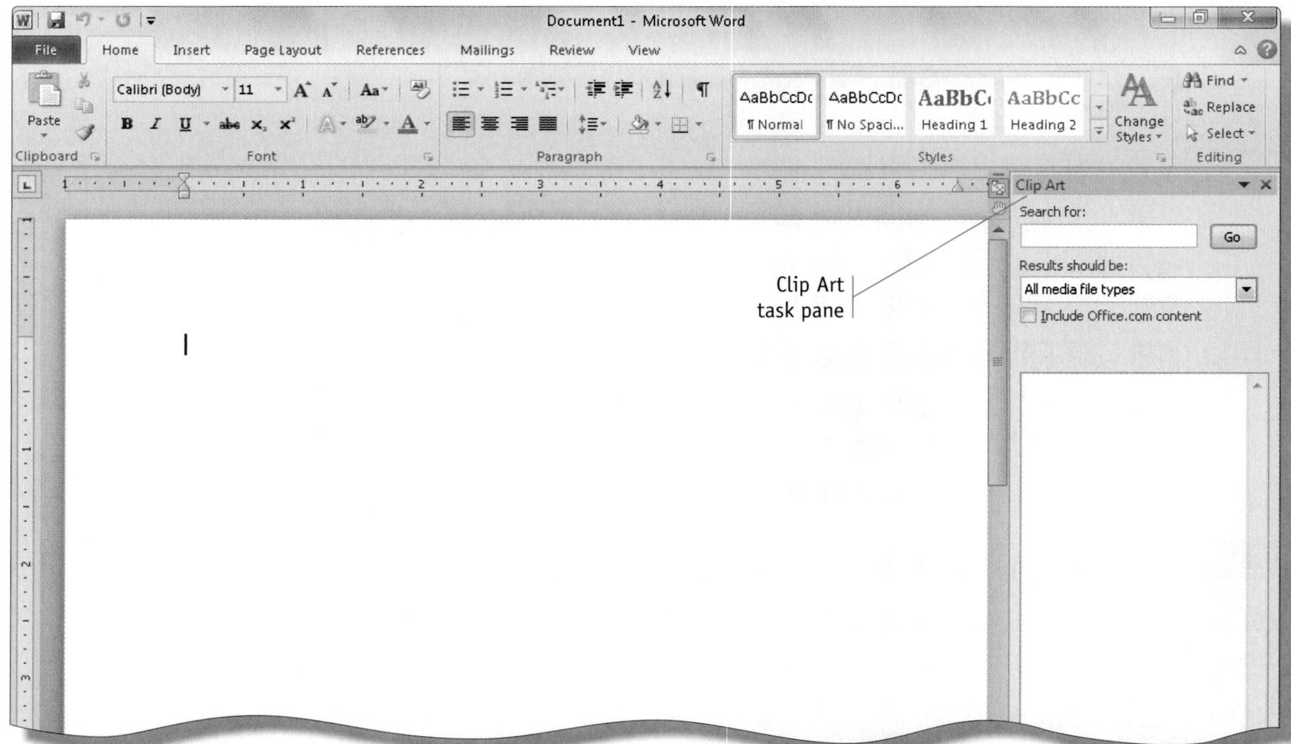

FIGURE EC-24

Using VSTO, you can create a customized Actions Pane Control called the **Document Actions task pane**. You can include any Toolbox object in the Document Actions task pane. To do so, you use the **ActionsPane** object, which acts as a container for Visual Basic objects. Although the ActionsPane object always is available to the executed project, it does not appear until you populate it with Toolbox objects. Once the ActionsPane object is displayed, you can add or remove controls in response to the user's actions.

You can add multiple objects to the ActionsPane object and then write code to respond to events that occur from objects in the ActionsPane. You can create an ActionsPane object in two ways: by coding the ActionsPane object manually, or by dragging a Toolbox control directly onto the ActionsPane object and then coding a one-line request to display the ActionsPane object.

To manually code an ActionsPane object, you can complete the following steps:

STEP 1 Open the code window by clicking the View Code button on the Solution Explorer toolbar. Click inside the ThisDocument_Startup event.

The code window opens and the insertion point appears in the ThisDocument_Startup event (Figure EC-25).

> **HEADS UP**
>
> Two events are included by default when the code window of VSTO is first opened—the ThisDocument_Startup event, which is executed as the Word document is loaded and displayed, and the ThisDocument_Shutdown event, which is executed as the Word document is closed.

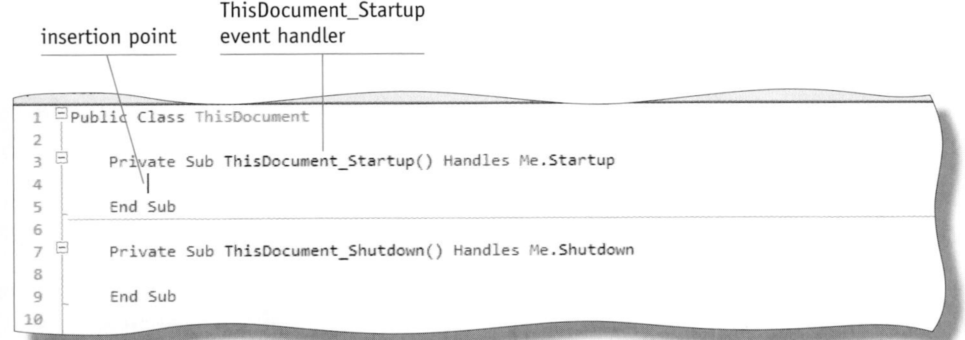
ThisDocument_Startup event handler
insertion point
Public Class ThisDocument
Private Sub ThisDocument_Startup() Handles Me.Startup
End Sub
Private Sub ThisDocument_Shutdown() Handles Me.Shutdown
End Sub

FIGURE EC-25

STEP 2 Type `act` to use IntelliSense to complete the object name ActionsPane. Using IntelliSense, add the statements `.Controls.Add(New DateTimePicker)`. Press the ENTER key and then delete the blank line.

The code (Figure EC-26) adds a DateTimePicker object to the ActionsPane object. By adding a DateTimePicker object to the ActionsPane object, the Document Actions task pane will appear when the application is executed (see Figure EC-27). You must place at least one object inside the Add parentheses to create the ActionsPane object.

```
    Private Sub ThisDocument_Startup() Handles Me.Startup
        ActionsPane.Controls.Add(New DateTimePicker)
    End Sub
```

FIGURE EC-26

STEP 3 Test the application by clicking the Start Debugging button on the Standard toolbar. Click the calendar list arrow in the upper-right corner to open the calendar.

The Word template opens and the Document Actions task pane appears on the right side of the window (Figure EC-27).

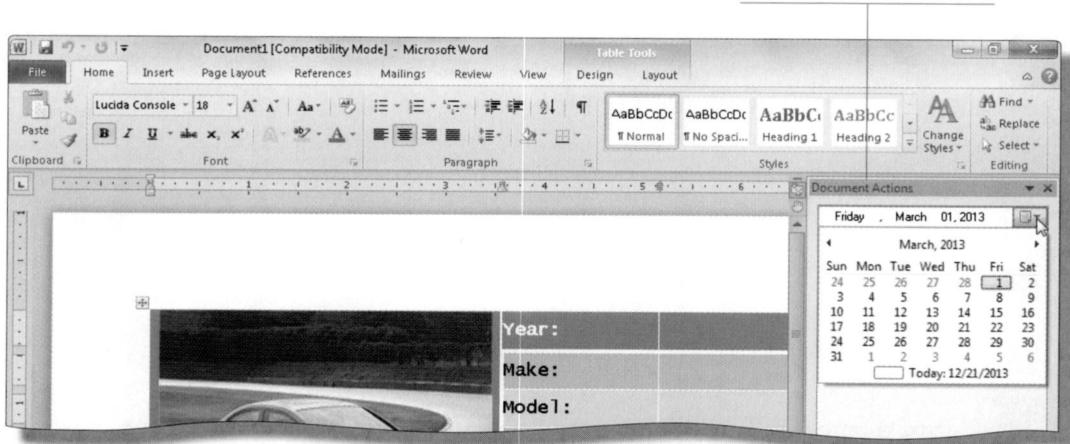

FIGURE EC-27

ONLINE REINFORCEMENT

To view a video of the process in the previous steps, visit scsite.com/vb2010/ec and then select Figure EC-25.

The second way to place an ActionsPane object on the right side of the Word window is to add an Actions Pane Control object in the Visual Studio project window by following these steps:

STEP 1 Click Project on the menu bar and then click Add New Item on the Project menu.

The Add New Item dialog box opens (Figure EC-28).

FIGURE EC-28

STEP 2 Click Actions Pane Control.

In the Add New Item dialog box, the Actions Pane Control icon is selected (Figure EC-29).

FIGURE EC-29

STEP 3 Click the Add button in the Add New Item dialog box.

The Actions Pane Control opens in a new tab (ActionsPaneControl1.vb) in Design view (Figure EC-30).

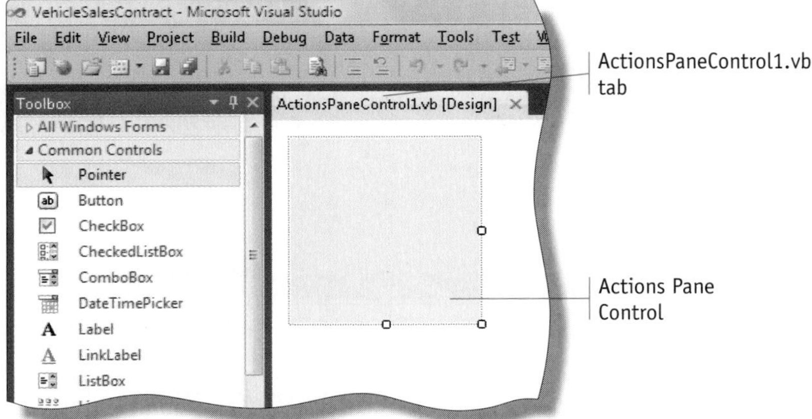

FIGURE EC-30

STEP 4 Drag a Label object from the Toolbox to the Actions Pane Control. Change the (Name) property of the Label object to `lblCalculator`. Change the Text property to `Loan Calculator`, and the Font property to Sans Serif, size 12.

The Label object is placed on the Actions Pane Control (Figure EC-31).

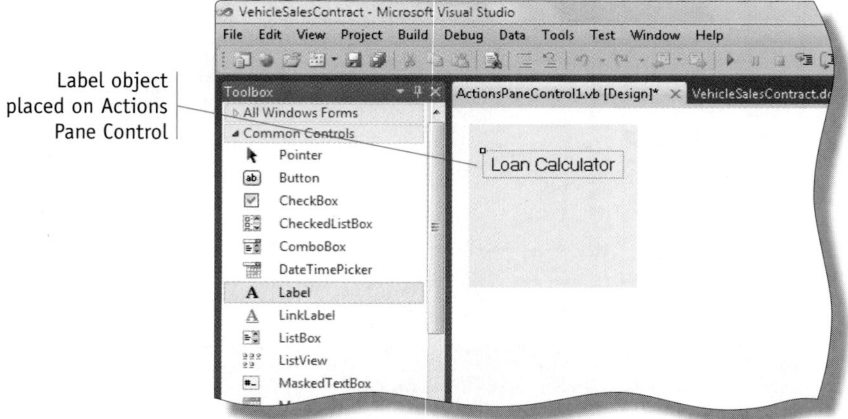

FIGURE EC-31

> **WATCH OUT FOR**
>
> You can resize the Actions Pane Control, but it will still be the standard size on the right side of the Office window when the application is executed.

STEP 5 To display the Actions Pane Control when the application runs, you must code a request to view the Document Actions task pane that is executed when the Word document opens. Click the ThisDocument.vb tab to open the code window for the Word template. Click in the ThisDocument_Startup event, type `act` and use IntelliSense to complete the rest of the line of code shown in Figure EC-32, which opens the Actions Pane Control when the application begins.

The code to open the Actions Pane Control when the document is opened is entered in the ThisDocument_Startup event (Figure EC-32).

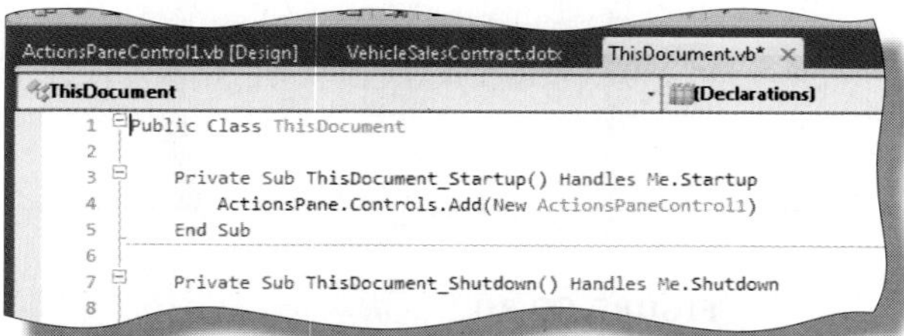

FIGURE EC-32

STEP 6 Click the Start Debugging button on the Standard toolbar to execute the application. Microsoft Word opens with the Document Actions task pane on the right side of the window.

The Word document opens and the Actions Pane Control is displayed on the right side of the window (Figure EC-33).

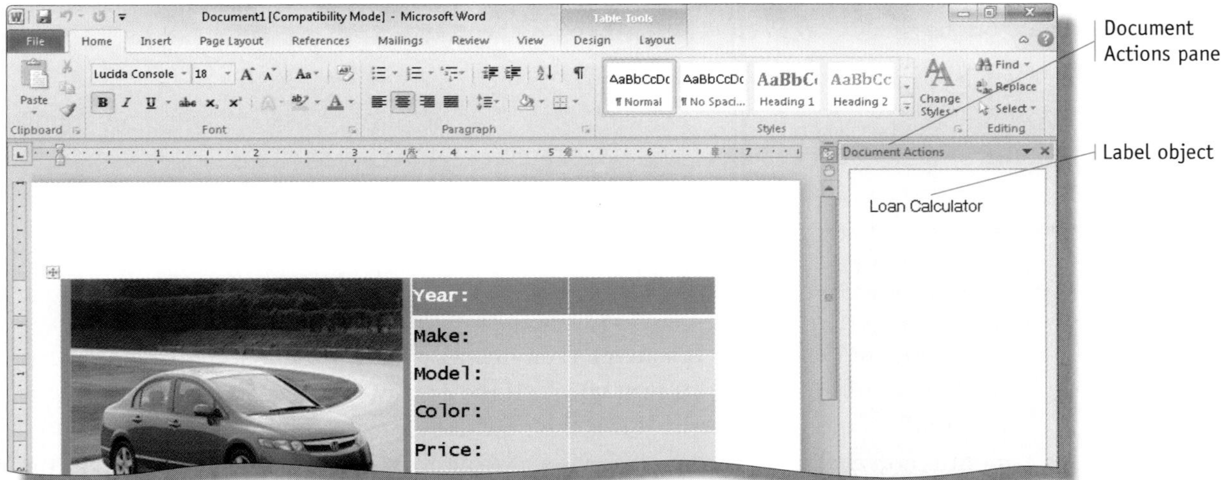

FIGURE EC-33

ONLINE REINFORCEMENT

To view a video of the process in the previous steps, visit scsite.com/vb2010/ec and then select Figure EC-28.

Using a ComboBox Object

You will recall from Chapter 8 that a ComboBox object allows the user to select an item from a list and to enter data as if using a text box. In the Document Actions task pane in the Vehicle Sales Contract chapter project, the user enters the number of months for a loan by either selecting a value from the ComboBox object items list or by entering a value in the text box portion of the ComboBox object. The code must determine that the user has either selected a value from the list or has entered a value in the text box portion.

When the user selects an item from the ComboBox object item list, the **SelectedItem** property for the ComboBox object can be assigned to a variable, as shown by the statement in Figure EC-34.

```
        decLoanMonths = Convert.ToDecimal(cboLoanMonths.SelectedItem)
```

FIGURE EC-34

In Figure EC-34, the SelectedItem property of the cboLoanMonths ComboBox object is converted to a decimal value and is placed in the decLoanMonths.

If the user enters a value in the text box portion of the ComboBox object, the SelectedItem property is assigned a null string and the value the user enters is placed in the Text property of the ComboBox object.

So, to determine if the user selected a value, the program code can check the SelectedItem property. If it is assigned a null string, then either the user entered a value in the text box portion of the ComboBox, or the user did not enter a value. This coding is shown in Figure EC-35.

```
21          If Me.cboMonths.SelectedItem = "" Then
22              If IsNumeric(cboMonths.Text) Then
23                  decLoanMonths = Convert.ToDecimal(cboMonths.Text)
24              Else
25                  MsgBox.Show("Please select the number of months for the loan")
26              End If
27          Else
28              decLoanMonths = Convert.ToDecimal(cboMonths.SelectedItem)
29          End If
```

FIGURE EC-35

In Figure EC-35, the If statement on line 21 checks if the SelectedItem property contains a null string. If so, it next checks if the Text property for the cboMonths ComboBox object is numeric. If it is then the user entered a numeric value for months and that value is converted from a string to a decimal value and placed in the decLoanMonths variable.

If the SelectedItem property contains a null string and the user did not enter a numeric value, then a month has not been entered and the message box is displayed to remind the user to select the number of months for the loan. If the SelectedItem property is not a null string, then the user selected a value from the ComboBox list and that string value is converted to a decimal value and placed in the decLoanMonths variable.

HEADS UP

The ComboBox object also has a SelectedIndex property that returns an integer value corresponding to the selected list item.

Calculating Loan Payments with the Pmt Function

For most people, purchasing a car requires borrowing money from a bank or from the car dealer. In the Vehicle Sales Contract Office application, coding in the Document Actions task pane calculates the monthly payments for a loan on the vehicle when the user clicks the Compute Payment button. To determine the cost of the monthly car payments, a function called **Pmt** performs the mathematical calculation. The Pmt function, which is available in Visual Basic 2010, calculates the payment for a loan based on constant payments and a constant interest rate. To use the Pmt function, you must specify the loan amount, the length of the loan, and the interest rate. The syntax of using the Pmt function in Visual Basic is shown in Figure EC-36 on the next page.

General Format: Pmt function

```
Pmt(Rate, NPer, PV)
```

Rate: The interest rate for the period. For example, if a mortgage payment has an interest rate of 8.5% per year, the rate for the period based on monthly payments would be .085 / 12.

NPer: The total number of payments made over the life of the loan. For example, if a mortgage loan was for 15 years, the number of payments would be 15 * 12 = 180 payments.

PV: The present value of the loan or investment. For example, the present value of a mortgage loan amount could be $150,000. If an investment was made, the present value would be $0.

Optional Formula

```
Pmt(Rate, NPer, PV, FV, Due)
```

FV: Optional — The future value or cash balance you want after the final payment is paid. For example, the future value of a loan is $0 because that is the value after the final payment. However, if you want to save $20,000 over 18 years for your child's education, then $20,000 is the future value. If you do not include this portion, 0 is assumed.

Due: Optional — The due date can be set to either DueDate.EndOfPeriod if the payments are due at the end of the payment period, or DueDate.BegOfPeriod if payments are due at the beginning of the period. If omitted, DueDate.EndOfPeriod is assumed.

FIGURE EC-36

Consider the following two scenarios for using the Pmt function.

First Scenario: You purchase a car and need a loan for $18,500 for four years at an interest rate of 8.9%. The table shown in Figure EC-37 divides the rate by 12 because the yearly rate is divided by the 12 payments, one for each month of the year (that is, one for each payment). The NPer variable is multiplied by 12 because the four-year loan has 48 total payments.

Variable	Operation
Rate	.089 / 12
NPer	4 * 12
PV	18500

FIGURE EC-37

The code written for the first scenario is shown in Figure EC-38:

```
        Dim decRate As Decimal
        Dim decPeriod As Decimal
        Dim decPrincipal As Decimal
        Dim decMonthlyPayments As Decimal

        decRate = 0.089
        decPeriod = 4
        decPrincipal = 18500

        decMonthlyPayments = Convert.ToDecimal(Pmt(decRate / 12, decPeriod * 12, _
            decPrincipal))
```

FIGURE EC-38

The result of the calculation, and the monthly payment amount assigned to decMonthlyPayments, is (459.50), which means you must pay $459.50 per month to pay off a car loan of $18,500 in 4 years with an interest rate of 8.9% per year.

Second Scenario: Your parents want to accumulate $25,000 in 10 years for your brother's college education. They need to know the amount of money they must place in a savings account each month to end up with $25,000 in ten years at an interest rate of 3% per year. The monthly payment is deposited in a savings account at the beginning of each month. The table shown in Figure EC-39 lists FV (Future Value) because that is the money they want to have at the end of ten years.

Variable	Operation
Rate	.03 / 12
NPer	10 * 12
PV	0
FV	25000
Due	DueDate.BegOfPeriod

FIGURE EC-39

The code written for the second scenario is shown in Figure EC-40:

```
        decRate = 0.03
        decPeriod = 10
        decPresentValue = 0D
        decPrincipal = 25000


        decMonthlyPayments = Convert.ToDecimal(Pmt(decRate / 12, _
            decPeriod * 12, decPresentValue, decPrincipal, DueDate.BegOfPeriod))
```

FIGURE EC-40

Guided Program Development *continued*

- **Format the Table** Click anywhere in the table except the car image, and then click the Table Tools Design tab. In the Table Styles group, click the More button (the third arrow). Scroll down and click Medium Grid 3 - Accent 1 *(ref: Figure EC-22)*.

HINT

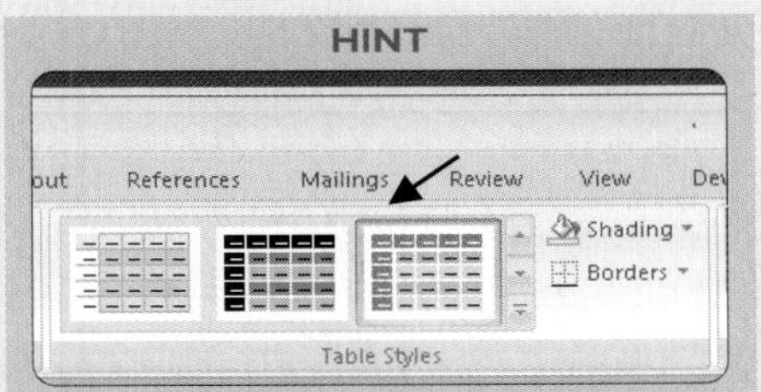

- **Change the Text Alignment in the Table** Click the Table Tools Layout tab. Select the text in the table, and then click the Align Top Left button in the Alignment group.

HINT

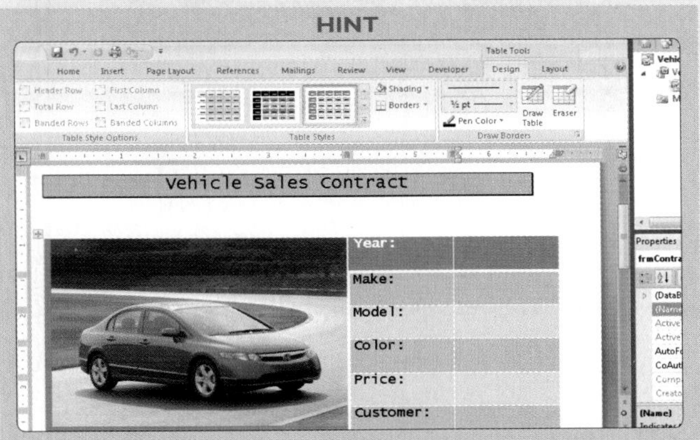

(continues)

Guided Program Development *continued*

The title and table occupy the top of the Word template (Figure EC-47).

RESULT OF STEP 1

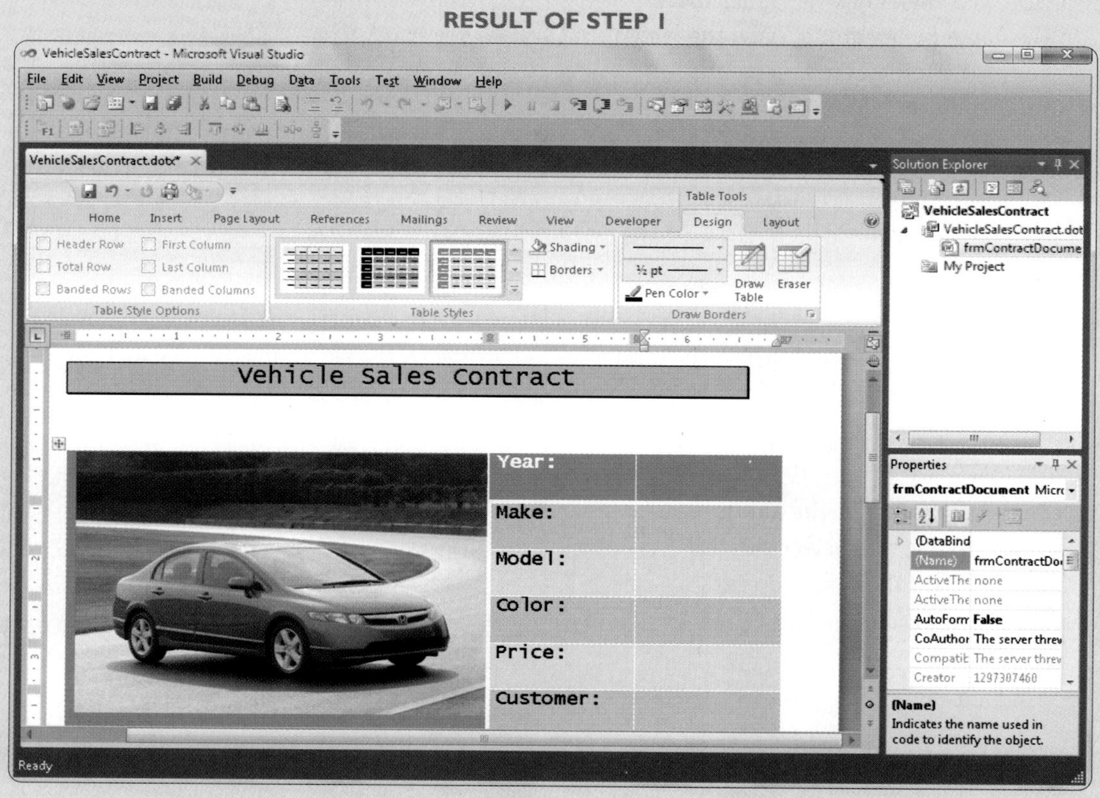

FIGURE EC-47

2

- **Add TextBox Objects to the Table** Open the Toolbox. If necessary, scroll so the rightmost column of the table is visible. Click the top cell in the right column to select it. Drag a TextBox .NET component from the Visual Basic Toolbox into the top cell in the third column of the table. In the Properties window for the TextBox object, name the TextBox object `txtYear`. Change the Font property for the TextBox object to Lucida Console, size 14. Clear the Text property for the txtYear TextBox object. Resize the txtYear TextBox object horizontally to fit in the table cell. Click the Table Tools Layout tab in the Alignment group, click Cell Margins, and then change the default cell margin for the left and right to 0".

HINT

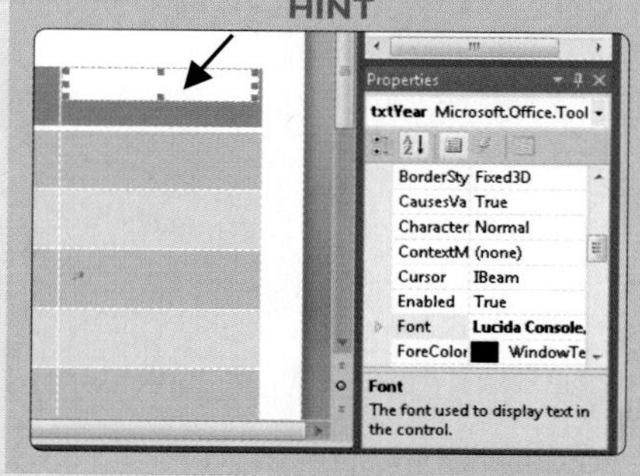

Guided Program Development *continued*

- **Code the Document Actions Task Pane** Click the ActionsPaneControl1.vb [Design] tab and then double-click the Compute Payment button to open the code editing window and create the btnCompute_Click event handler. Code a comment to explain the purpose of the event handler. Enter the code to initialize the variables used on the Loan Calculator on the Actions Pane Control.

HINT

```
Public Class ActionsPaneControl1

    Private Sub btnCompute_Click(ByVal sender As System.Object, ByVal e As System.EventArgs)
    Handles btnCompute.Click
        ' The event handler opens when the user clicks the Compute button
        ' in the Actions Pane. It calculates a monthly payment for a loan
        ' amount based on the length of the loan and the interest rate.

        ' Declare variables
        Dim decRate As Decimal
        Dim decPeriod As Decimal
        Dim decPrincipal As Decimal
        Dim decMonthlyPayments As Decimal
        Dim decMoveDecimal As Decimal = 100D
        Dim decTwelveMonths As Decimal = 12D
        Dim blnPeriodIsValid As Boolean = False
```

- **Validate the Input from the Loan Calculator Is Numeric** Before the monthly payment is calculated, write the code to call the procedure that checks if a valid loan period has been selected or entered and then returns the loan period as a decimal value. Then, write an If statement to check if the txtRate is numeric, the txtLoan is numeric, and the loan period is valid.

HINT

```
        ' Validate that numeric values are entered on the Loan Calculator
        CheckPeriodValidity(blnPeriodIsValid, decPeriod)
        If IsNumeric(txtRate.Text) And IsNumeric(txtLoan.Text) And blnPeriodIsValid Then
```

- **Convert the Rate into a Decimal Amount** Inside the Then clause of the If statement, write the code to convert the value in txtRate to a Decimal data type and then divide the value by the value (100) in the decMoveDecimal variable to convert an amount such as 9.25% to .925.

HINT

```
            decRate = Convert.ToDecimal(txtRate.Text) / decMoveDecimal
```

(continues)

Guided Program Development *continued*

- **Convert the Loan Amount to a Decimal Value** The loan amount in the Text property of the txtLoan TextBox object must be converted from a String data type to a Decimal data type so it can be used in an arithmetic operation. Place the decimal value in the variable named decPrincipal. Write the code to accomplish this processing.

HINT

```
            decPrincipal = Convert.ToDecimal(txtLoan.Text)
```

- **Calculate the Monthly Payment** Write the statement to use the Pmt function to calculate the monthly car payment *(ref: Figure EC-38)*.

HINT

```
            decMonthlyPayments = Convert.ToDecimal(Pmt(decRate / _
                decTwelveMonths, decPeriod, decPrincipal))
```

- **Display the Monthly Payment** Write the statement to display the monthly loan payment in the lblMonthlyPayment Label object.

HINT

```
            lblMonthlyPayment.Text = decMonthlyPayments.ToString("C")
        Else
```

Guided Program Development *continued*

• **Display an Error Message Box if the Input Values Are Not Valid** If the rate, loan amount, or months selection is in error, a message box must be displayed informing the user of the error. In the Else clause of the If statement that checks these values, write the code to display a message box.

HINT

```
        Else
            MsgBox("The Input Entries on the Loan Calculator are Not Valid", , _
                "Error Message")
        End If
```

• **Write the Sub Procedure to Ensure the Loan Period is Valid** To ensure the user either entered a value in the cboMonths ComboBox object or selected a value in the list, the first If statement must test if the SelectedItem property contains a null string. If so, either the user entered a value in the Text property or no selection has been made. If the Text property contains a numeric value, then the entry is valid; the value should be converted to a decimal value and the Boolean variable passed ByRef should be set to true. If the Text property is not numeric, an invalid entry was made and the Boolean variable should be set to False. If the SelectedItem property is not a null string, then a selection was made in the list, so the SelectedItem should be converted to a decimal value and the Boolean variable should be set to true. Write the code to implement this Sub procedure *(ref: Figure EC-35)*.

HINT

```
    Private Sub CheckPeriodValidity(ByRef blnValidity As Boolean, ByRef decMonths As Decimal)
        If cboMonths.SelectedItem = "" Then
            If IsNumeric(cboMonths.Text) Then
                decMonths = Convert.ToDecimal(cboMonths.Text)
                blnValidity = True
            Else
                blnValidity = False
            End If
        Else
            decMonths = Convert.ToDecimal(cboMonths.SelectedItem)
            blnValidity = True
        End If
    End Sub
```

(continues)

Guided Program Development *continued*

The code for the click event of the Compute Payment Button for the Actions Pane Control is completed (Figure EC-50).

RESULT OF STEP 4

```
Public Class ActionsPaneControl1

    Private Sub btnCompute_Click(ByVal sender As System.Object, ByVal e As System.EventArgs) Handles btnCompute.Click
        ' The event handler opens when the user clicks the Compute button
        ' in the Actions Pane. It calculates a monthly payment for a loan
        ' amount based on the length of the loan and the interest rate.

        ' Declare variables
        Dim decRate As Decimal
        Dim decPeriod As Decimal
        Dim decPrincipal As Decimal
        Dim decMonthlyPayments As Decimal
        Dim decMoveDecimal As Decimal = 100D
        Dim decTwelveMonths As Decimal = 12D
        Dim blnPeriodIsValid As Boolean = False

        ' Validate that numeric values are entered on the Loan Calculator
        CheckPeriodValidity(blnPeriodIsValid, decPeriod)
        If IsNumeric(txtRate.Text) And IsNumeric(txtLoan.Text) And blnPeriodIsValid Then
            decRate = Convert.ToDecimal(txtRate.Text) / decMoveDecimal
            decPrincipal = Convert.ToDecimal(txtLoan.Text)
            decMonthlyPayments = Convert.ToDecimal(Pmt(decRate / _
                decTwelveMonths, decPeriod, decPrincipal))
            lblMonthlyPayment.Text = decMonthlyPayments.ToString("C")
        Else
            MsgBox("The Input Entries on the Loan Calculator are Not Valid", , _
                "Error Message")
        End If

    End Sub

    Private Sub CheckPeriodValidity(ByRef blnValidity As Boolean, ByRef decMonths As Decimal)
        If cboMonths.SelectedItem = "" Then
            If IsNumeric(cboMonths.Text) Then
                decMonths = Convert.ToDecimal(cboMonths.Text)
                blnValidity = True
            Else
                blnValidity = False
            End If
        Else
            decMonths = Convert.ToDecimal(cboMonths.SelectedItem)
            blnValidity = True
        End If
    End Sub
End Class
```

FIGURE EC-50

Guided Program Development *continued*

5

- **Code the Vehicle Contract** Open the VehicleSalesContract.dotx Design window and double-click the Create Contract button. In the btnContract_Click Event, write the comments that explain the processing in the event handler. Then, write the code to initialize the variable that will contain the vehicle cost.

HINT

```
Private Sub btnContract_Click(ByVal sender As System.Object, ByVal e As System.EventArgs) Handles btnContract.Click
    ' The btnContract_Click Event displays a legal contract

    ' Declare Variable
    Dim decvehicleCost As Decimal
```

- **Validate All Entries Are Entered** Write the If statement to test the two numeric TextBox objects, txtYear and txtPrice, to confirm their values are numeric; test the TextBox objects txtMake, txtModel, and txtColor to validate that the objects do not contain empty strings; and test the DateTimePicker object to confirm that its value is not an empty string.

HINT

```
        If IsNumeric(txtYear.Text) And txtMake.Text <> "" And _
              txtModel.Text <> "" And txtColor.Text <> "" And _
               IsNumeric(txtPrice.Text) And txtCustomer.Text <> "" And _
               datPurchaseDate.Value.ToString() <> "" Then
```

- **Convert the Price to a Decimal Data Type** Write the statement to convert the price of the car to a Decimal data type. Another way to convert data types is to use the Parse command. You can use Parse in the syntax Decimal.Parse(variable name). If you are converting an Integer, the syntax is Integer.Parse(variable name).

HINT

```
            ' Converts the txtPrice to a Decimal - Parse is supported in VSTO Word
            decvehicleCost = Decimal.Parse(txtPrice.Text)
```

(continues)

Guided Program Development *continued*

- **Display the Legal Contract** Write the code to display the legal contract in the lblParties, lblVehicle, and lblDetails Label objects.

HINT

```
            lblParties.Text = "PARTIES: This agreement is entered into " _
                & "between the Buyer, " & txtCustomer.Text _
                & ", and the Seller, RJ Motors, on the date of " _
                & datPurchaseDate.Text & "."
            lblVehicle.Text = "VEHICLE: By this agreement, in consideration " _
                & "of the representations made and the covenants herein " _
                & "contained, the Seller transfers, bargains, and " _
                & "conveys to Buyer, and Buyer purchases from Seller, " _
                & "the vehicle hereinafter referred to as Vehicle " _
                & "described as follows:"
            lblDetails.Text = "The vehicle of the year " & _
                txtYear.Text & ", make of " & txtMake.Text _
                & ", model of " & txtModel.Text & ", and the color of " _
                & txtColor.Text & " has been purchased by the " _
                & "Buyer for the amount " & decvehicleCost.ToString("C") & "."
```

- **Write the Else Portion of the If Statement** After the Then processing for the If statement is completed, you must write the Else portion of the If statement. An error message box must be displayed if any of the values are incorrect in the document text boxes. Write the code for the Else portion of the If statement.

HINT

```
        Else
            MsgBox("Complete the Table and Select a Date", , "Error Message")
        End If
```

Guided Program Development *continued*

- **Run the Application** When a Word document opens, fill in the information and create the contract.

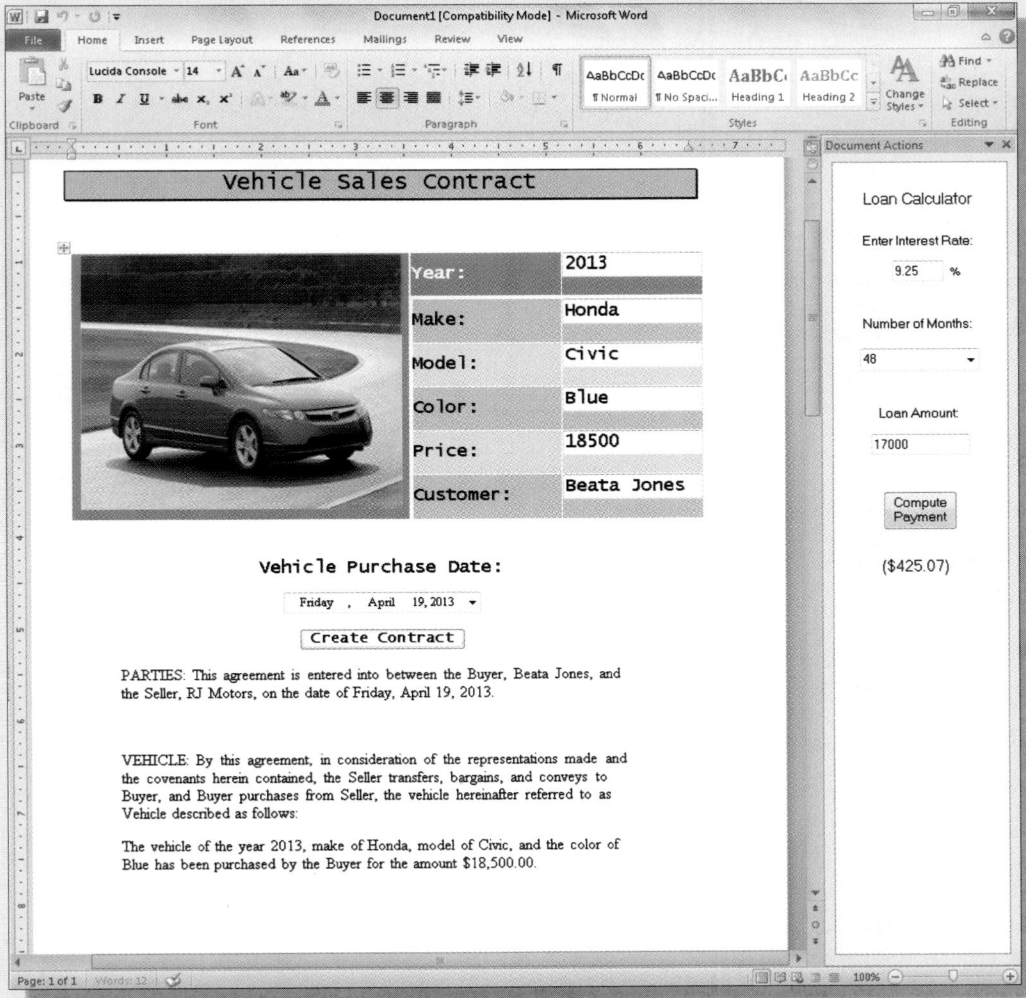

FIGURE EC-51

(continues)

Guided Program Development *continued*

The code for the click event of the Create Contract button for the Actions Pane Control is completed (Figure EC-52).

RESULT OF STEP 4

```
Private Sub btnContract_Click(ByVal sender As System.Object, ByVal e As System.EventArgs) Handles btnContract.Click
    ' The btnContract_Click Event displays a legal contract

    ' Declare Variable
    Dim decvehicleCost As Decimal

    If IsNumeric(txtYear.Text) And txtMake.Text <> "" And _
          txtModel.Text <> "" And txtColor.Text <> "" And _
           IsNumeric(txtPrice.Text) And txtCustomer.Text <> "" And _
           datPurchaseDate.Value.ToString() <> "" Then
        ' Converts the txtPrice to a Decimal - Parse is supported in VSTO Word
        decvehicleCost = Decimal.Parse(txtPrice.Text)
        lblParties.Text = "PARTIES: This agreement is entered into " _
            & "between the Buyer, " & txtCustomer.Text _
            & ", and the Seller, RJ Motors, on the date of " _
            & datPurchaseDate.Text & "."
        lblVehicle.Text = "VEHICLE: By this agreement, in consideration " _
            & "of the representations made and the covenants herein " _
            & "contained, the Seller transfers, bargains, and " _
            & "conveys to Buyer, and Buyer purchases from Seller, " _
            & "the vehicle hereinafter referred to as Vehicle " _
            & "described as follows:"
        lblDetails.Text = "The vehicle of the year " & _
            txtYear.Text & ", make of " & txtMake.Text _
            & ", model of " & txtModel.Text & ", and the color of " _
            & txtColor.Text & " has been purchased by the " _
            & "Buyer for the amount " & decvehicleCost.ToString("C") & "."
    Else
        MsgBox("Complete the Table and Select a Date", , "Error Message")
    End If

End Sub
```

FIGURE EC-52

Summary

In this chapter you have learned to create an Office application using Visual Studio Tools for Office. The items listed in Figure EC-53 include all the new Visual Studio and Visual Basic skills you have learned in this chapter.

Visual Basic Skills

Skill	Figure Number	Web Address for Video
Examine the Vehicle Sales Contract chapter project application	Figure EC-1	scsite.com/vb2010/ec/figureEC-1
Create a Visual Studio Tools for Office application	Figure EC-3	scsite.com/vb2010/ec/figureEC-3
Add a DateTimePicker object to a Form object	Figure EC-9	
Add a table to a Word document	Figure EC-14	scsite.com/vb2010/ec/figureEC-14
Add an image to a Word table	Figure EC-17	scsite.com/vb2010/ec/figureEC-17
Apply Table Styles to format a table	Figure EC-22	scsite.com/vb2010/ec/figureEC-22
Manually code an ActionsPane object	Figure EC-25	scsite.com/vb2010/ec/figureEC-25
Place an ActionsPane object in the Word window to add an Actions Pane Control item	Figure EC-28	scsite.com/vb2010/ec/figureEC-28
Code a ComboBox object on an application	Figure EC-34	
Use the Pmt Function	Figure EC-36	
Use Math Class Functions	Figure EC-41	

FIGURE EC-53

Learn It Online

Start your browser and visit scsite.com/vb2010/ec. Follow the instructions in the exercises below.

1. **Chapter Reinforcement TF, MC, SA** Click one of the Chapter Reinforcement links for Multiple Choice, True/False, or Short Answer below the Learn It Online heading. Answer each question and submit to your instructor.
2. **Practice Test** Click the Practice Test link below the Enrichment Chapter. Answer each question, enter your first and last name at the bottom of the page, and then click the Grade Test button. When the graded practice test is displayed on your screen, submit the graded practice test to your instructor. Continue to take the practice test until you are satisfied with your score.
3. **Crossword Puzzle Challenge** Click the Crossword Puzzle Challenge link below the Learn It Online heading. Read the instructions, and then click the Continue button. Work the crossword puzzle. When you are finished, click the Submit button. When the crossword puzzle is redisplayed, submit it to your instructor.

Knowledge Check

1. Which Office programs can be programmed using VSTO 2010?
2. Office 2010 no longer has menu bars and toolbars. What does Office 2010 primarily use for navigation?
3. What is the name of the VB control that can be placed in the task pane on the right side of an Office window?
4. What is the difference between a Word document and a Word template?
5. What is the file extension for a Word document?
6. What is the file extension for a Word template?
7. Write a line of code that displays the Actions Pane Control on the right side of a window.
8. What procedure should the code for question #7 use?
9. Write a line of code that displays the day of the week determined by a DateTimePicker object named datPayDay in a Label object named lblWeekDay.
10. Write a line of code that displays the date chosen by the user in a DateTimePicker object named datReservation. Print the following sentence in a Label object named lblPlaneReservation. "Your flight will depart on ___________ (date chosen)".
11. Rewrite the command line shown in Figure EC-54 with the ^ symbol.

```
lblDisplay.Text = Math.Pow(4.0, 3.0)
```

FIGURE EC-54

12. Variables should be of the Integer data type to use the Math class methods. True or false?
13. You can place VB controls in a Word table. True or false?
14. Write the statement that assigns the square root of 81.0 to a Label object named lblSquareRoot.

Knowledge Check

15. The formula that computes the area of a circle is Pi * radius^2. Write a VB equation using two Math class methods to compute the area of a circle. Assign this statement to the variable decCircleArea. The radius variable is decCircleRadius.
16. Write a statement that assigns the smaller of two numbers (8.3 and 2.9) to a variable named decLessNumber.
17. Write a line of code that computes the cost of a loan payment made over 15 years for a home mortgage of $175,000 at an interest rate of 6.8%. Assign the payment amount to a variable named decPaymentAmount.
18. Write a line of code that computes the cost of a loan payment for a gaming computer system made over two years for a loan amount of $5000 at 8.9%. Assign the monthly payment amount to a variable named decGameComputer.
19. Write a line of code that computes the amount of money that you need to invest to save $10,000 for a kitchen makeover for your home. You will invest a monthly amount for the next five years at an interest rate of 4% at the beginning of each month. Assign your monthly investment amount to a variable named decKitchenRedo.
20. What is the name of the Math class that computes the absolute value of any number?

Debugging Exercises

1. Rewrite the code shown in Figure EC-55 correctly:

```
Dim firstValue As Integer = 29.25
MsgBox(Math.Round(firstValue)
```

FIGURE EC-55

2. Rewrite the code shown in Figure EC-56 correctly:

```
' The following statement computes a loan
' for 6 years, $16,000 at 12%
loanPayment = Pmt(0.12, 6, 16000)
```

FIGURE EC-56

3. Rewrite the code shown in Figure EC-57 correctly:

```
MsgBox(Math.Max(decFirstValue, decSecondValue, decThirdValue)
```

FIGURE EC-57

Program Analysis

In exercises 1 – 8, evaluate the expression to find the resulting value:

1. Math.Sqrt(16.0)
2. Math.Round(−2.45)
3. Math.Abs(−5.999)

(continues)

Program Analysis *continued*

4. Math.Ceiling(5.01)
5. Math.Floor(−2.2)
6. Math.Max(Math.PI, 3.4)
7. Math.Pow(4.0, 2.0)
8. Math.Min(1.9, Math.E)
9. Determine the output that is displayed in the ListBox object according to the code shown in Figure EC-58:

```
Dim startValue As Decimal
decStartValue = 8.0
lstDisplay.Add(decStartValue)
lstDisplay.Add(Math.Pow(decStartValue, 3.0))
lstDisplay.Add(Math.Ceiling(decStartValue + 0.56))
lstDisplay.Add(Math.Pow(Math.PI, 2.14))
lstDisplay.Add(Math.Max(decStartValue, 7.99))
```

FIGURE EC-58

10. Determine the output that is displayed in the ListBox object according to the code shown in Figure EC-59:

```
Dim decMonthlyPayment As Decimal
decMonthlyPayment = Pmt(0.08 / 12, 7 * 12, 50000)
lstMortgage.Add(decMonthlyPayment.ToString("C"))
```

FIGURE EC-59

11. Write lines of code for each step to determine the monthly payments for a car loan of $21,095 over 60 months at an interest rate 10.9%.

    a. Declare all the variables for the values given: decPrincipal, decMonths, decRate.

    b. Declare a variable named decLoanPayment to hold the monthly payment.

    c. Compute the payment.

    d. Display the payment in a ListBox named lstDisplayPayment.

12. Write code for each step to determine the largest of three numbers.

    a. Declare three variables named decFirstNum, decSecondNum, decThirdNum, and assign the values 5.2, 3.8, and 12.1 to them

    b. Declare a Decimal data type named decTempNum.

    c. Declare a Decimal data type named decLargestNum.

    d. Using a Math procedure, assign the larger of the first and second variable to decTempNum.

    e. Using a Math procedure, assign the larger of decTempNum and decThirdNum to decLargestNum.

    f. Display the largest number as a Label named lblBigNumber.

Case Programming Assignments

Complete one or more of the following case programming assignments. Submit the program and materials you create to your instructor. The level of difficulty is indicated for each case programming assignment.

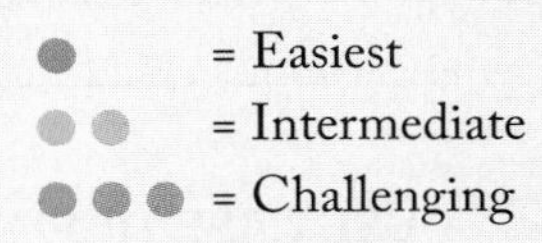

1 ● REAL ESTATE HOME PURCHASE CONTRACT

Design a VSTO application and write the code that will execute according to the program requirements in Figure EC-60 and the Use Case definition in Figure EC-61 on the next page. The output is shown in Figure EC-62 on the next page. Before writing the code, create an event planning document for each event in the program.

REQUIREMENTS DOCUMENT

Date submitted: January 24, 2014

Application title: Home Purchase Contract with a Mortgage Loan Calculator VSTO Application

Purpose: This application uses a Microsoft Word template to allow a real estate agent to create a legal sales contract for property sales and provide a mortgage calculator to calculate monthly payments on the Document Actions task pane.

Program Procedures: In a Word document, the realtor enters the information about the home being purchased and the application creates a home sales contract.

Algorithms, Processing, and Conditions:

1. The realtor first views a Word document that contains a title and a table displaying the home being purchased. The user must enter the home information into the table such as home address, buyer's name, purchase price, city, and state. The date of the closing of the home should also be requested.
2. The right side of the window should display a loan calculator requesting the interest rate, number of months, and the amount of principal being borrowed for the home's mortgage.
3. After entering the required data and selecting the date of closing, the user can click a button to display a legal contract that includes the personalized data of the home purchase.
4. The realtor also can enter data into the loan calculator on the task pane on the right side of the Word window to calculate the monthly payment for the home.

Notes and Restrictions:

1. The home price and the mortgage amount may be different based on the down payment.
2. The mortgage calculator should allow the loan to be paid over 10, 15, 20, or 30 years.

Comments:

1. The picture shown in the table should be selected from a graphic available on the Web.
2. The completed contract could be printed for the customer to view and keep as a legal receipt of purchase.

FIGURE EC-60

(continues)

Case Programming Assignments

***Real Estate Home Purchase Contract** (continued)*

USE CASE DEFINITION

1. User (realtor) enters the home address, buyer's name, purchase price, city, and state. A DateTimePicker object allows the user to select the date of the home closing.
2. User clicks the Create Contract button and the contract with personalized information is printed below the Create Contract button.
3. User enters values into the mortgage loan calculator. (This could also be completed before entering home information.)
4. User clicks the Compute Monthly Payments button on the loan calculator to display the loan amount.

FIGURE EC-61

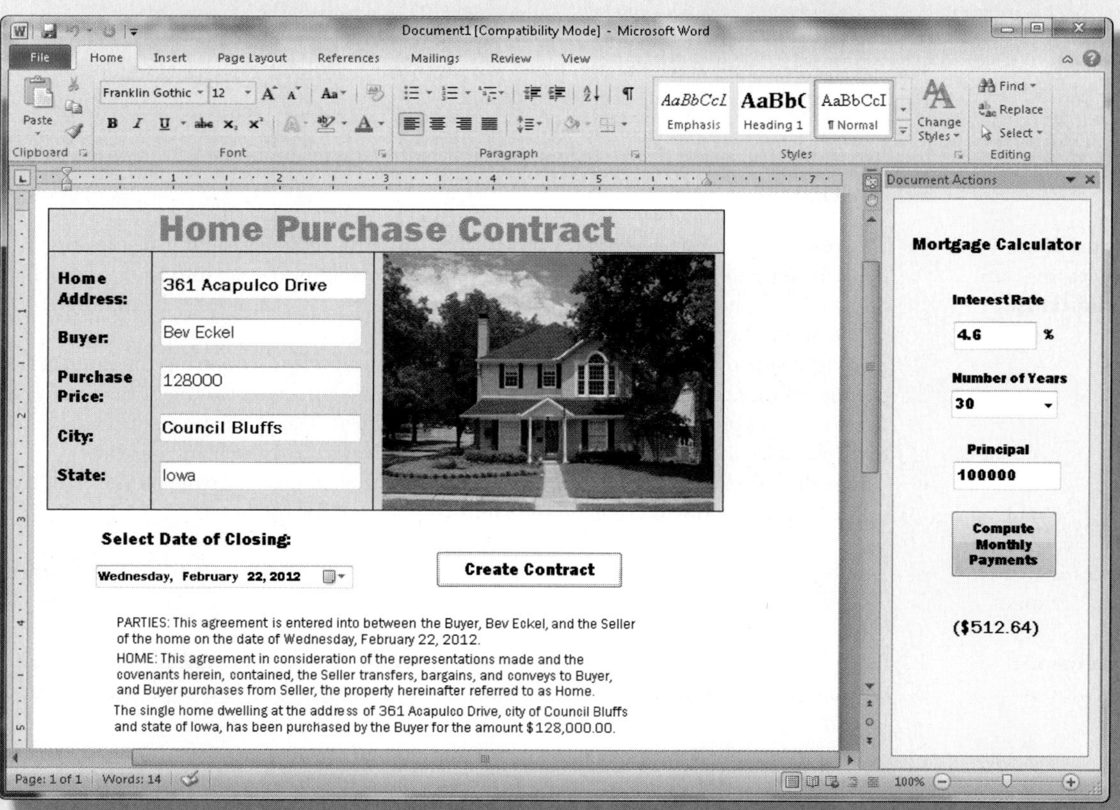

FIGURE EC-62

Case Programming Assignments

2 • BUYING A NEW COMPUTER FOR COLLEGE

Design a VSTO application and write the code that will execute according to the program requirements in Figure EC-63 and the Use Case definition in Figure EC-64 on the next page. The output is shown in Figure EC-65 on the next page. Before writing the code, create an event planning document for each event in the program.

REQUIREMENTS DOCUMENT

Date submitted: April 1, 2014

Application title: Computer Savings Plan VSTO Application

Purpose: This application uses a Microsoft Word template to allow the user to choose one of two computer systems needed for college. The application will calculate the cost, shipping, and tax for the computer system. The Document Actions task pane will calculate how much money the user needs to finance to purchase this system.

Program Procedures: In a Word document, the college student can select one of two computer systems to purchase.

Algorithms, Processing, and Conditions:

1. The user first views a Word template that contains a title and a table displaying two computer systems, their specifications, and cost. The two systems are based on whether you are a computer major (high-end computer) or any other major (average PC).
2. Allow the user to select one of the two systems.
3. The right side of the window should display a loan calculator requesting the interest rate, number of months, and the amount of principal being borrowed for the computer system.
4. When the user selects the computer system, a total amount is displayed. The tax rate is 6.5% and the shipping cost is $55.00.
5. The user enters the interest rate, number of payments (months), and the amount being borrowed into the loan calculator on the Document Actions task pane on the right side of the window to calculate the monthly payment for the computer.

Notes and Restrictions:

1. The user should only be able to select one of the two computer systems.

Comments:

1. The picture shown in the table should be selected from graphics available on the Web.
2. Research the current costs of computers on the Web to determine the price of the two computer systems.

FIGURE EC-63

(continues)

Case Programming Assignments

***Buying a New Computer for College** (continued)*

USE CASE DEFINITION

1. Student selects which of two computer systems will be purchased based on student major.
2. Program displays total cost of the computer.
3. Student enters the interest rate, selects the number of months, and enters the principal into the loan calculator. (This could be completed before selecting the computer information.)
4. Student clicks the Payments button on the loan calculator to display the monthly payment.

FIGURE EC-64

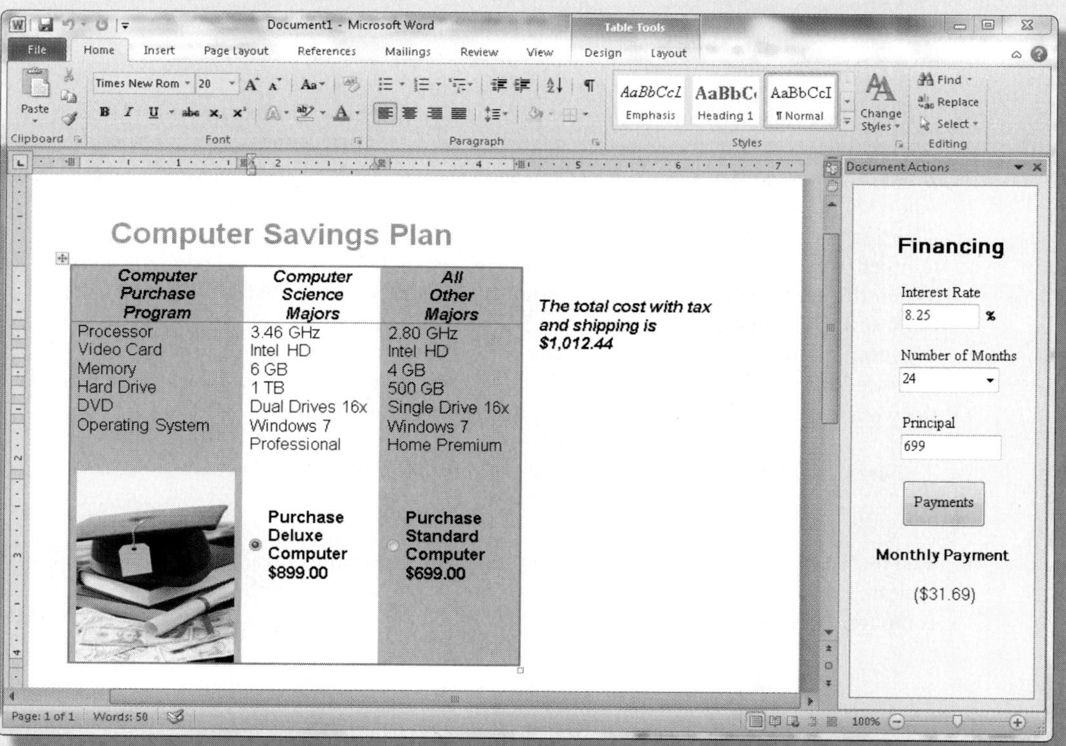

FIGURE EC-65

Case Programming Assignments

3 • SALES COMMISSION FOR FURNITURE STORE

Design a VSTO application and write the code that will execute according to the program requirements in Figure EC-66 and the Use Case definition in Figure EC-67 on the next page. The output is shown in Figure EC-68 on the next page. Before writing the code, create an event planning document for each event in the program.

REQUIREMENTS DOCUMENT

Date submitted: March 4, 2014

Application title: Grand's Furniture Store Commission VSTO Application

Purpose: This application uses a Microsoft Word template to compute the commissions of six employees who work at a furniture store. The application computes the average sales commission, the total sales amount, and the total commission paid rounded to the nearest dollar.

Program Procedures: In a Word template, the store manager can enter the weekly sales amount of the sales people to compute the average sales commission, the total sales amount, and the total commission paid.

Algorithms, Processing, and Conditions:

1. The furniture store manager first views a Word document that contains a title, a table displaying a furniture store logo, and an area for six employee names and their sales amounts. Compute each salesperson's commission based on 7% of the sales amount.
2. The ending day of that week's cycle should also be recorded on the Document Actions task pane.
3. When the user enters the required data, a button can be selected to display the average sales commission, the total sales amount, and the total commission paid. All numbers should be rounded to the closest dollar amount.

Notes and Restrictions: n/a

Comments:

1. The picture shown in the table should be selected from a graphic available on the Web.

FIGURE EC-66

(continues)

Case Programming Assignments

Sales Commission for Furniture Store *(continued)*

USE CASE DEFINITION

1. The furniture store manager enters the names and sales amounts for six sales people. A DateTimePicker object allows the manager to enter the ending date for this week's commissions.
2. The manager clicks the Compute Weekly Commissions Button object to print the information below the Button object.
3. The manager enters the ending date of the week. (This could be completed before entering commission information.)

FIGURE EC-67

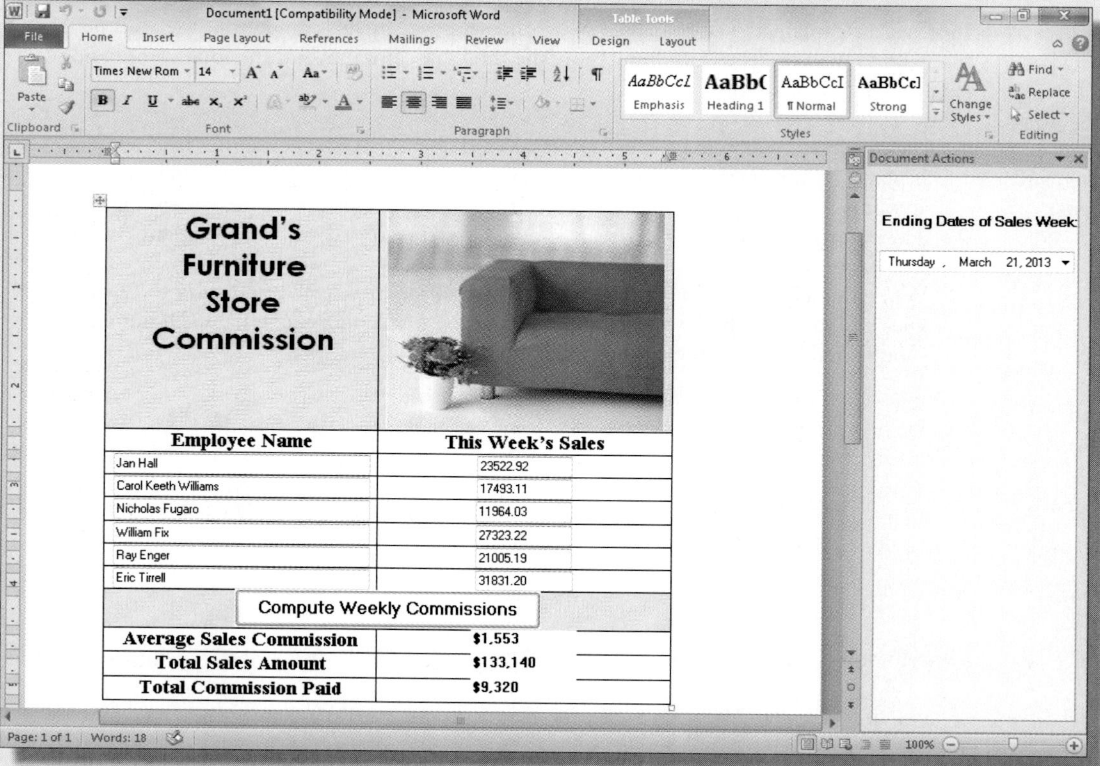

FIGURE EC-68

Case Programming Assignments

4 ●●● OUTFITTERS BIKE RENTAL

Design a VSTO application and write the code that will execute according to the program requirements in Figure EC-69. Before designing the user interface, create a Use Case definition. Before writing the code, create an event planning document for each event in the program.

REQUIREMENTS DOCUMENT

Date submitted: June 2, 2014

Application title: Outfitters Bike Rental VSTO Application

Purpose: This application uses a Microsoft Word document to allow a bike shop owner to create a liability contract for renting a beach cruiser or mountain bike. The application displays the liability contract after the bike renter's information is entered with the price of the day's rental.

Program Procedures: In a Word document, the bike owner enters the bike renter's information and clicks the Create Contract button to display the contract and later print it.

Algorithms, Processing, and Conditions:

1. The user first views a Word template that displays a title and a bike shop picture, and requests the user to enter the renter's name, type of bike (beach cruiser or mountain bike) from a ComboBox object, Helmet (yes or no), Color of Bike, Hours Rented ($5 an hour), Store Location, and Date of Rental (DateTimePicker object) in a table.
2. Display the following contract with the information in the contract as needed:
   I, the Participant (name here), on the date of (date here) freely and voluntarily assume the risks of using the Equipment - (bike type here). Each Participant acknowledges that he/she has executed this Contract and Release. By signing this contract, the renter warrants to Outfitters Bike Rental Company that the bike will be returned in the same condition as rented.
   I agree that I am responsible for any costs associated with unpaid rental/tour fees, damage, and/or theft to the rental/tour Equipment. In such an event I authorize Outfitters Bike Rental Company to charge my credit card in an amount not to exceed $995 per unit. The total cost for today's rental is $XX.XX.

Notes and Restrictions:

1. The pictures shown in the table should be selected from graphics available on the Web.
2. The cost of each hour of rental is $5.

Comments: n/a

FIGURE EC-69

Case Programming Assignments

5 CAR INSURANCE COSTS

Design a VSTO application and write the code that will execute according to the program requirements in Figure EC-71 on the next page. Before designing the user interface, create a Use Case definition. Before writing the code, create an event planning document for each event in the program.

Based on Edmunds.com, the table shown in Figure EC-70 displays the five best insurance rates in the industry.

Make	Model	Style	5 Year Insurance Rate	Vehicle Cost
Chrysler	PT Cruiser	4dr Wagon (2.4L 4cyl 5M)	$4,240	$17,490
GMC	Safari	SLE AWD 3dr Minivan (4.3L 6cyl 4A)	$4,298	$27,440
Dodge	Caravan	SE 4dr Minivan (2.4L 4cyl 4A)	$4,357	$21,130
Saturn	ION	1 4dr Sedan (2.2L 4cyl 5M)	$4,373	$10,430
Pontiac	Sunfire	2dr Coupe (2.2L 4cyl 5M)	$4,389	$14,930

FIGURE EC-70

(continues)

Case Programming Assignments

***Car Insurance Costs** (continued)*

REQUIREMENTS DOCUMENT

Date submitted: May 11, 2014

Application title: Finding the Best Car Insurance Rates VSTO Application

Purpose: This application uses a Microsoft Word template to determine which cars have the best insurance rates. Customers often call the insurance company requesting the best insurance rates on new vehicles. The Document Actions task pane displays a loan calculator to determine the monthly payments for a car payment.

Program Procedures: In a Word template, the insurance agent can find which cars have the lowest insurance rates based on safety tests.

Algorithms, Processing, and Conditions:

1. When a customer calls the insurance agent, a Word template can be opened that displays a ComboBox object containing the make and model of five vehicles with the best insurance rates this year. When a car is selected, a table displays a picture of a car, make, model, style, five-year insurance costs, and purchase price.
2. A Find Lowest button also compares all the insurance costs and displays the result in the table.
3. The Document Actions task pane displays five radio buttons with the names of these five vehicles. Allow the user to select the model and make of the car, the interest rate, and a 2, 3, 4, or 5-year loan. The user enters the number of years instead of selecting the number of years from the list. Display an error message if the user enters more than six years or a negative number. The principal to be financed is also entered. Display the monthly payment.

Notes and Restrictions:

1. The picture shown in the table should be selected from a graphic available on the Web.
2. The information is this year's five best insurance rates from *www.edmunds.com.*

Comments: n/a

FIGURE EC-71

Case Programming Assignments

6 ●● 401K MATCHING CONTRIBUTION INVESTMENT

Design a VSTO application and write the code that will execute according to the program requirements in Figure EC-72. Before designing the user interface, create a Use Case definition. Before writing the code, create an event planning document for each event in the program.

REQUIREMENTS DOCUMENT

Date submitted: January 4, 2014

Application title: 401K Employer Matching Contribution Investment VSTO Application

Purpose: This application uses a Microsoft Word template to allow an employee to see how much their 401K will gain.

Program Procedures: In a Word template, an employee enters their monthly contribution into a company 401K investment program. The result displays the amount that will be in their account at retirement.

Algorithms, Processing, and Conditions:

1. The employee first views a Word template that displays a title, company logo, a table that requests the employee to enter their name and the monthly amount they want to contribute. When an employer offers 401k matching, they are guaranteeing that they will match a certain percentage of the employee's contributions. The local company common match is 50 cents on the dollar, meaning that if an employee invests one dollar in a 401k plan, the employer will match the contribution by contributing 50 cents. The company is currently giving 6% for an investment interest rate. The table in the Word template also requests the number of years until retirement.
2. After entering the requested information, the employee clicks the Compute 401K Value button. The value of the 401K will be displayed with the employer's matching contribution calculated.
3. The Document Actions task pane should display a loan calculator requesting the interest rate, number of months, and the amount of money invested if you were to invest the same amount without having the matching employer contribution.

Notes and Restrictions: n/a

Comments: The logo shown in the table should be selected from pictures available on the Web.

FIGURE EC-72

Case Programming Assignments

7 ●●● AZTEC RENTAL AGENCY

Create a requirements document and a Use Case Definition document, and then design a VSTO application based on the case project shown in Figure EC-73. Before writing the code, create an event planning document for each event in the program:

A home project equipment rental store requests a Word application that allows a sales associate to record customer information, the item(s) rented, and the rental duration (full or half day). The table below shows typical rental items. The document will compute the total rental cost. A picture of the item that is being rented will be displayed. The Document Actions task pane will display a calendar allowing the sales associate to select the beginning date of rental.

Items Rented	Half-Day Cost	Full-Day Cost
Sander	$18.00	$30.00
Wallpaper steamer	$15.00	$24.00
Power washer	$21.00	$36.00
Garden tiller	$27.00	$47.00

FIGURE EC-73

(continues)

Case Programming Assignments

8 ●●● GEOMETRY REVIEW

Create a requirements document and a Use Case Definition document, and then design a VSTO application based on the case project shown in Figure EC-74. Before writing the code, create an event planning document for each event in the program:

> A local teacher wants you to create a practice Word template for students to review calculating the circumference of a circle and the hypotenuse of a right triangle. Allow the student to enter the radius of a circle in the Word template and the two sides of a triangle in the Document Actions task pane. Display the results. Research both formulas needed. Use a Math Class method in each formula.

FIGURE EC-74

9 ●●● ECONOMIC COST OF LIVING

Create a requirements document and a Use Case Definition document, and then design a VSTO application based on the case project shown in Figure EC-75. Before writing the code, create an event planning document for each event in the program:

> A local economist is studying the national problem of the cost of living increase. The current average pay in the United States is $17.77 an hour (U.S. Department of Labor) and has been increasing at 1.9% per year. The cost of living has been increasing at 2.5%. Create a Word template to allow a user to enter a number of years between 5 and 20. Display a ListBox object starting with the present year, average yearly salary (based on 52 weeks a year), and how much you would need to earn per year to keep up with the cost of living increase using the initial average yearly salary as the baseline. Create a Document Actions task pane to allow the user to see the amount they would have in savings if $50 a month were saved over the same period at a four percent interest rate.

FIGURE EC-75

APPENDIX A

Unicode

The 256 characters and symbols that are represented by ASCII and EBCDIC codes are sufficient for English and western European languages (see Figure A-1), but do not provide enough characters for Asian and other languages that use different alphabets. Further compounding the problem is that many of these languages use symbols, called ideograms, to represent multiple words and ideas. One solution to the problem of accommodating universal alphabets is Unicode. Unicode is a 16-bit coding scheme that can represent all the world's current, classic, and historical languages in more than 65,000 characters and symbols. In Unicode, 30,000 codes are reserved for future use, such as ancient languages, and 6,000 codes are reserved for private use. Existing ASCII coded data is fully compatible with Unicode because the first 256 codes are the same. Unicode is implemented in several operating systems, including Windows 7, Windows Vista, Windows XP, Mac OS X, and Linux. To view a complete Unicode chart, see www.unicode.org.

UNICODE KEYBOARD CHARACTERS				
Decimal	**Hexadecimal**	**Octal**	**Binary**	**Character**
32	20	040	00100000	
33	21	041	00100001	!
34	22	042	00100010	"
35	23	043	00100010	#
36	24	044	00100100	$
37	25	045	00100101	%
38	26	046	00100110	&
39	27	047	00100111	'
40	28	050	00101000	(
41	29	051	00101001	)

FIGURE A-1 (continues)

Decimal	Hexadecimal	Octal	Binary	Character
42	2A	052	00101010	*
43	2B	053	00101011	+
44	2C	054	00101100	,
45	2D	055	00101101	-
46	2E	056	00101110	.
47	2F	057	00101111	/
48	30	060	00110000	0
49	31	061	00110001	1
50	32	062	00110010	2
51	33	063	00110011	3
52	34	064	00110100	4
53	35	065	00110101	5
54	36	066	00110110	6
55	37	067	00110111	7
56	38	070	00111000	8
57	39	071	00111001	9
58	3A	072	00111010	:
59	3B	073	00111011	;
60	3C	074	00111100	<
61	3D	075	00111101	=
62	3E	076	00111110	>
63	3F	077	00111111	?
64	40	100	01000000	@
65	41	101	01000001	A
66	42	102	01000010	B
67	43	103	01000011	C
68	44	104	01000100	D
69	45	105	01000101	E
70	46	106	01000110	F

FIGURE A-1 (continued)

Decimal	Hexadecimal	Octal	Binary	Character
71	47	107	01000111	G
72	48	110	01001000	H
73	49	111	01001001	I
74	4A	112	01001010	J
75	4B	113	01001011	K
76	4C	114	01001100	L
77	4D	115	01001101	M
78	4E	116	01001110	N
79	4F	117	01001111	O
80	50	120	01010000	P
81	51	121	01010001	Q
82	52	122	01010010	R
83	53	123	01010011	S
84	54	124	01010100	T
85	55	125	01010101	U
86	56	126	01010110	V
87	57	127	01010111	W
88	58	130	01011000	X
89	59	131	01011001	Y
90	5A	132	01011010	Z
91	5B	133	01011011	[
92	5C	134	01011100	\
93	5D	135	01011101	]
94	5E	136	01011110	^
95	5F	137	01011111	]
96	60	140	01100000	,
97	61	141	01100001	a
98	62	142	01100010	b

FIGURE A-1 (continues)

Decimal	Hexadecimal	Octal	Binary	Character
99	63	143	01100011	c
100	64	144	01100100	d
101	65	145	01100101	e
102	66	146	01100110	f
103	67	147	01100111	g
104	68	150	01101000	h
105	69	151	01101001	i
106	6A	152	01101010	j
107	6B	153	01101011	k
108	6C	154	01101100	l
109	6D	155	01101101	m
110	6E	156	01101110	n
111	6F	157	01101111	o
112	70	160	01110000	p
113	71	161	01110001	q
114	72	162	01110010	r
115	73	163	01110011	s
116	74	164	01110100	t
117	75	165	01110101	u
118	76	166	01110110	v
119	77	167	01110111	w
120	78	170	01111000	x
121	79	171	01111001	y
122	7A	172	01111010	z
123	7B	173	01111011	{
124	7C	174	01111100	|
125	7D	175	01111101	}
126	7E	176	01111110	~

FIGURE A-1 (continued)

APPENDIX B

The My Namespace

Rapid application development (RAD) uses a number of tools to help build graphical user interfaces that would normally take a large development effort. One of the Visual Basic RAD tool innovations introduced in the 2005 version and continued with the 2010 version is the **My** namespace. The My namespace provides a shortcut to several categories of information and functionality and is organized so that you can use IntelliSense to find code elements you use often. Microsoft created the My namespace to make it easier to execute common code patterns that you use when developing .NET applications. By providing a shortcut to the most commonly used .NET Framework Class Library classes and methods, the My namespace helps you retrieve settings and resources that your application requires.

The My namespace feature provides rapid access to the classes and methods through the My classes shown in the table in Figure B-1.

Object	Allows Access to
My.Application	The application information and its services such as name, version, log, and current directory.
My.Computer	The host computer and its resources, and services. My.Computer provides access to a number of very important resources including My.Computer.Network, My.Computer.FileSystem, and My.Computer.Printers.
My.Forms	All the forms in the current project.
My.Request	The current Web request.
My.Resources	The resource elements.
My.Response	The current Web response.
My.Settings	The configuration settings of the user and application level. This object enables great personalization without writing many lines of code.

FIGURE B-1 (continues)

Object	Allows Access to
My.User	The security context of the current authenticated user. The My.User object analyzes the user at runtime, which assists security issues.
My.WebServices	The XML Web services referenced by the current project. Consuming Web services is a necessary ability for modern Web applications.

FIGURE B-1 (continued)

Coding Examples

My is a wrapper that makes accessing the advanced features of .NET easier. For example, you can use the class **My.Application** to determine the version of the current application by using the line of code shown in Figure B-2. Figure B-3 shows the dialog box that displays the version number. You often need to know the latest version of the application to determine whether the application is in final form.

```
MsgBox(My.Application.Info.Version.ToString())
```

FIGURE B-2

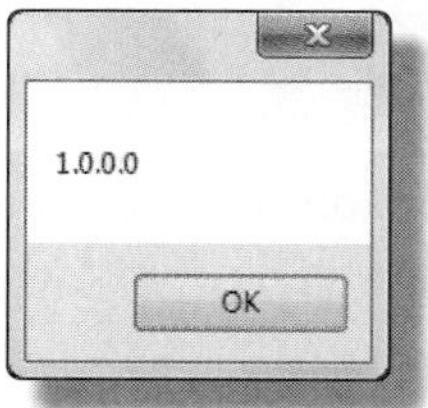

FIGURE B-3

The **My.Application** class can also be used to display the current setting of the culture of a computer. Figure B-4 shows the code you can use to display the culture, which is the language that the computer has been assigned in the language settings. In Figure B-5, the culture is set to English – United States.

```
MsgBox(My.Application.Culture.ToString())
```

FIGURE B-4

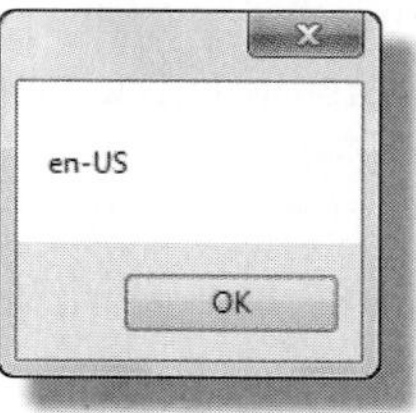

FIGURE B-5

Another class called **My.Computer** can return information about the computer on which the application is deployed, as determined at run time. The My.Computer class provides properties for manipulating computer components such as audio, the clock, the keyboard, and the file system. The My.Computer class can play .wav files and system sounds using the Audio object. You can use the My.Computer.Audio.Play and My.Computer.Audio.PlaySystemSound methods to play .wav sound files and system sounds. The code shown in Figure B-6 plays a .wav file named beachmusic.wav.

```
My.Computer.Audio.Play("C:\beachmusic.wav")
```

FIGURE B-6

A .wav file can also be played in the background when a file named AudioPlayMode.Background is specified, as shown in Figure B-7.

```
My.Computer.Audio.Play("C:\blues.wav", _
                AudioPlayMode.Background)
```

FIGURE B-7

The My.Computer class can access the Clipboard and show what is temporarily stored in the system buffer. For example, if you copied the phrase, "Examples of the My.Computer class", the phrase would be stored in the Clipboard system buffer of the computer. Use the code shown in Figure B-8 to display the contents of the Clipboard in a dialog box as shown in Figure B-9.

```
MsgBox(My.Computer.Clipboard.GetText())
```

FIGURE B-8

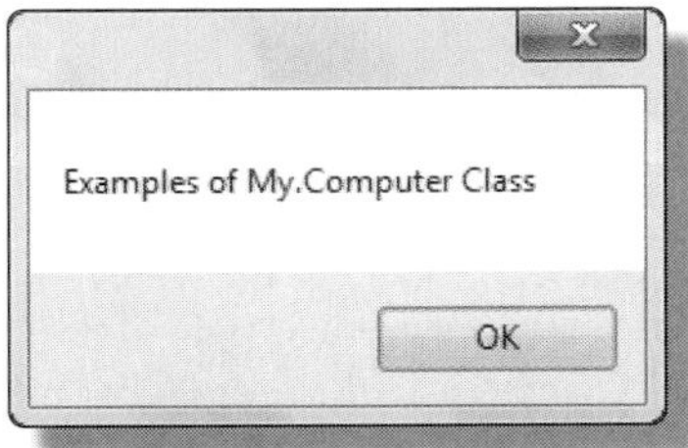

FIGURE B-9

The My.Computer class can access an object that provides properties for displaying the current local date and time according to the system clock by entering the code shown in B-10. Figure B-11 on the next page shows the dialog box that displays the system date and time.

```
MsgBox(My.Computer.Clock.LocalTime.ToString())
```

FIGURE B-10

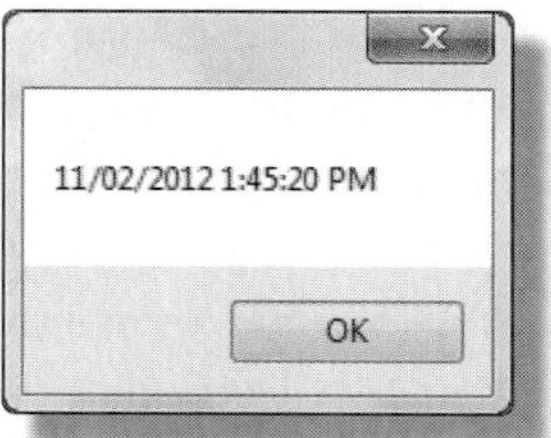

FIGURE B-11

Another My.Computer class determines the current state of the keyboard, such as which keys are pressed, including the CAPS LOCK or NUM LOCK key. The code shown in Figure B-12 provides a true result if the CAPS LOCK key has been pressed. Figure B-13 shows the dialog box that displays the result.

```
MsgBox(My.Computer.Keyboard.CapsLock.ToString())
```

FIGURE B-12

FIGURE B-13

The My.Computer.Mouse class allows you to determine the state and hardware characteristics of the attached mouse, such as the number of buttons or whether the mouse has a wheel. The code shown in Figure B-14 determines if the mouse has a wheel, and Figure B-15 shows the dialog box that displays the result.

```
MsgBox(My.Computer.Mouse.WheelExists.ToString())
```

FIGURE B-14

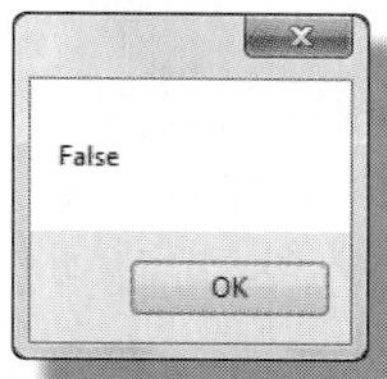

FIGURE B-15

The My.Computer.Network class interacts with the network to which the computer is connected. For example, if the code in Figure B-16 is entered in the code window, the result would be true, as shown in Figure B-17 on the next page, if the computer is connected to an intranet or Internet network.

```
MsgBox(My.Computer.Network.IsAvailable.ToString())
```

FIGURE B-16

FIGURE B-17

You can use the My.Computer.Network class to ping another computer. Ping is a basic network function that allows you to verify a particular IP address exists and can accept requests. Ping is used diagnostically to ensure that a host computer you are trying to reach is operating. The code shown in Figure B-18 determines if the IP address is active, and the dialog box shown in Figure B-19 displays the result.

```
MsgBox(My.Computer.Network.Ping("71.2.41.1"))
```

FIGURE B-18

FIGURE B-19

The My.Computer.Screen object can be used to determine many properties of the screen connected to the computer system. You can determine the properties of each monitor attached to the computer system, including the name, the brightness of the screen, and the working area size. The number of bits per pixel can be determined by the code shown in Figure B-20. In a digitized image, the number of bits used to represent the brightness contained in each pixel is called bits per pixel. Bits per pixel is a term that represents the brightness of the screen resolution. Figure B-21 shows the result of the code.

```
MsgBox(My.Computer.Screen.BitsPerPixel.ToString())
```

FIGURE B-20

FIGURE B-21

The My.Computer.Screen class can also display the current resolution of the user screen, as shown in Figures B-22 and B-23 on the next page.

```
MsgBox(My.Computer.Screen.Bounds.Size.ToString())
```

FIGURE B-22

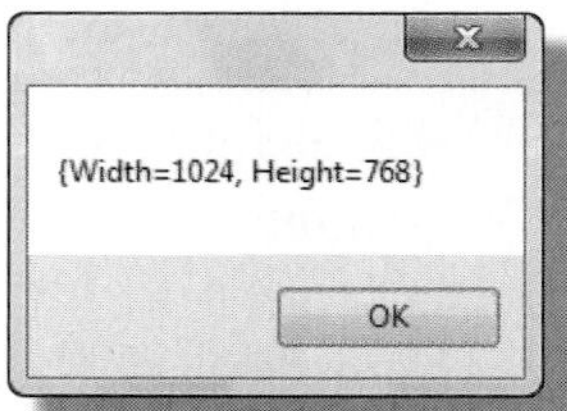

FIGURE B-23

Another class called **My.User** allows you to gather information about the current user. The code example in Figure B-24 shows how to use the **My.User.Name** property to view the user's login name. An application uses Windows authentication by default, so **My.User** returns the Windows information about the user who started the application, as shown in Figure B-25.

```
MsgBox(My.User.Name)
```

FIGURE B-24

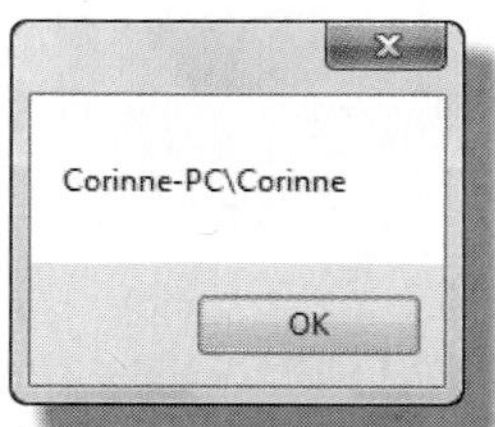

FIGURE B-25

The My namespace also provides a simpler way of opening multiple forms in the same project by using the My.Forms object. If the project includes more than one form, the code shown in Figure B-26 opens a second form named Form2.

```
My.Forms.Form2.Show()
```

FIGURE B-26

APPENDIX C

Naming Conventions

The table in Figure C-1 displays the common data types used in Visual Basic 2010 with the recommended naming convention for the three-character prefix preceding variable names of the data type.

Data Type	Sample Value	Memory	Range of Values	Prefix
Integer	48	4 bytes	−2,147,483,648 to +2,147,483,647	int
Double	5.3452307	8 bytes	−1.79769313486232E308 to +1.79769313486232E308	dbl
Decimal	3.14519	16 bytes	Decimal values that may have up to 29 significant digits	dec
Char	'?' or 'C'	2 bytes	Single character	chr
String	"The Dow is up .03%"	Depends on number of character	Letters, numbers, symbols	str
Boolean	True or False	Typically 2 bytes; depends on implementing platform	True or False	bln

FIGURE C-1

The table in Figure C-2 displays the less common data types used in Visual Basic 2010 with the recommended naming convention for the three-character prefix preceding variable names of the data type.

Data Type	Sample Value	Memory	Range of Values	Prefix
Byte	7	1 byte	0 to 255	byt
Date	April 22, 2010	8 bytes	0:00:00 (midnight) on January 1, 0001 through 11:59:59 PM on December 31, 9999	dtm
Long	345,234,567	8 bytes	−9,223,372,036,854,775,808 to +9,223,372,036,854,775,807	lng
Object	Holds a reference	4 bytes (32-bit) 8 bytes (64-bit)	A memory address	obj
Short	16,567	2 bytes	−32,786 to 32,767	shr
Single	234,654.1246	4 bytes	−3.4028235E+38 to −1.401298E−45 for negative values and 1.401298E−45 to 3.4028235E+38 for positive values	sng

FIGURE C-2

Form Object Naming Conventions

The table in Figure C-3 displays the prefix naming conventions for Form objects. The three-letter prefixes used before variables names are especially helpful when you use IntelliSense.

Object Type	Prefix	Object Type	Prefix
Button	btn	ListBox	lst
Calendar	cld	MenuStrip	mnu
CheckBox	chk	NumericUpDown	nud
ComboBox	cbo	PictureBox	pic
CompareValidator	cmv	RadioButton	rad
DataGrid	dgd	RangeValidator	rgv
DateTimePicker	dtp	RegularExpressionValidator	rev
DropDownList	ddl	RequiredFieldValidator	rfv
Form	frm	TextBox	txt
GroupBox	grp	ValidationSummary	vsm
Label	lbl		

FIGURE C-3

APPENDIX D

Using LINQ with Visual Basic 2010

Introducing Language Integrated Query (LINQ)

LINQ (Language Integrated Query, pronounced "link") is a new feature provided with Visual Basic 2010 and .NET Framework 4.0. LINQ allows you to query data with easily accessible SQL (Structured Query Language) commands within the Visual Basic code window. The addition of LINQ within Visual Studio allows database administrators to use familiar SQL syntax within the Visual Basic programming environment. Many SQL database developers can feel comfortable using their querying skills in the Visual Studio environment. ADO.NET 4.0 supports LINQ queries to manipulate any object associated with database tables using SQL.

The example used in this appendix is the Northwind database, which is provided with the Visual Studio 2010 standard installation. The file is named Northwind.mdf. (Note that this is not the same database as the one included with Microsoft Office Access.) This SQL file is available at for download at scsite.com/vb2010. The Windows application featured in this appendix uses the Northwind SQL database to display the new LINQ to SQL object features. The Northwind database contains a table named Customers, as shown in Figure D-1.

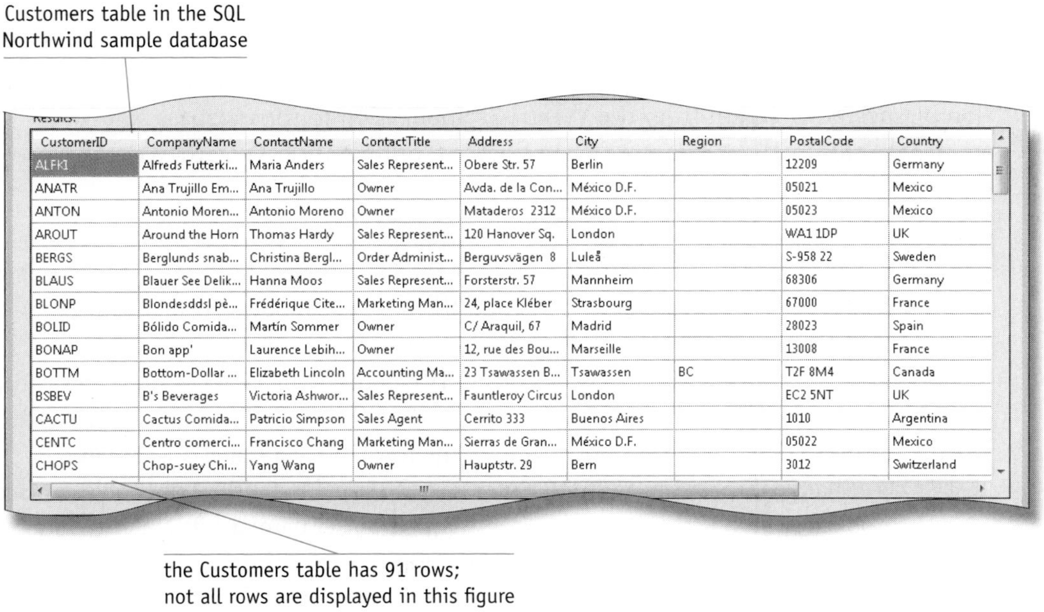

Customers table in the SQL Northwind sample database

CustomerID	CompanyName	ContactName	ContactTitle	Address	City	Region	PostalCode	Country
ALFKI	Alfreds Futterki...	Maria Anders	Sales Represent...	Obere Str. 57	Berlin		12209	Germany
ANATR	Ana Trujillo Em...	Ana Trujillo	Owner	Avda. de la Con...	México D.F.		05021	Mexico
ANTON	Antonio Moren...	Antonio Moreno	Owner	Mataderos 2312	México D.F.		05023	Mexico
AROUT	Around the Horn	Thomas Hardy	Sales Represent...	120 Hanover Sq.	London		WA1 1DP	UK
BERGS	Berglunds snab...	Christina Bergl...	Order Administ...	Berguvsvägen 8	Luleå		S-958 22	Sweden
BLAUS	Blauer See Delik...	Hanna Moos	Sales Represent...	Forsterstr. 57	Mannheim		68306	Germany
BLONP	Blondesddsl pè...	Frédérique Cite...	Marketing Man...	24, place Kléber	Strasbourg		67000	France
BOLID	Bólido Comida...	Martín Sommer	Owner	C/ Araquil, 67	Madrid		28023	Spain
BONAP	Bon app'	Laurence Lebih...	Owner	12, rue des Bou...	Marseille		13008	France
BOTTM	Bottom-Dollar ...	Elizabeth Lincoln	Accounting Ma...	23 Tsawassen B...	Tsawassen	BC	T2F 8M4	Canada
BSBEV	B's Beverages	Victoria Ashwor...	Sales Represent...	Fauntleroy Circus	London		EC2 5NT	UK
CACTU	Cactus Comida...	Patricio Simpson	Sales Agent	Cerrito 333	Buenos Aires		1010	Argentina
CENTC	Centro comerci...	Francisco Chang	Marketing Man...	Sierras de Gran...	México D.F.		05022	Mexico
CHOPS	Chop-suey Chi...	Yang Wang	Owner	Hauptstr. 29	Bern		3012	Switzerland

the Customers table has 91 rows; not all rows are displayed in this figure

FIGURE D-1

Creating a SQL query expression involves three major steps: accessing a connection to the data source, creating a query using LINQ, and executing the query displaying the requested data. You use a query to define which data you want to retrieve from a data source. In addition, you can manipulate the data by sorting, grouping, and filtering it.

When you create a query, you store it in a query variable and initialize it with a query expression. A SQL query expression has three clauses: From, Where, and Select. The "From" clause defines the data source; the "Select" clause defines what is returned; and the "Where" clause (which is optional) lets you refine a search to include only data that meets certain criteria. The general format of a SQL statement is shown in Figure D-2. This example searches the Customers table in the Northwind database for records that contain "Seattle" in the City field.

General Format: SQL Statement

```
From match In db.Customers _
Where match.City = "Seattle" _
Select match
Customers is the name of a table in the Northwind SQL database.
City is the name of a field within the Customers table.
```

FIGURE D-2

This appendix uses the LINQ commands to access data in the Northwind SQL database. Using the Customers table within Northwind, the application will determine which customers are living in the city entered by the user.

Establishing a Connection to a Database

The first step in accessing database information is to establish a connection with the database source, which is named Northwind in this example. You can create a connection by specifying a path from the Windows application to the database source. To connect to the database using the Data Source Configuration Wizard, you can complete the following steps:

STEP 1 With Visual Studio 2010 open, click the New Project button on the Standard toolbar, click Windows under Visual Basic, and then click Windows Forms Application in the Project types pane in the New Project dialog box. Name the project `LinqExample`, and then click the OK button. When the Windows Form object opens, name it `frmCustomer.vb`. Change the Text property to Find Customers by City. Resize the form to a size of 310,342. At the top of the form, place a Label object named `lblCity`. Change the Text property to Enter City Name:. Under the Label object, place a TextBox object named `txtCity`. Place the ListBox object named `lstNames` under the TextBox object. To complete the design of the form, place a Button object named `btnFind` under the ListBox object. Change the Text property to Find Customer(s). Center all objects horizontally on the form. Select all the objects on the form and change the Font property to Arial, size 12. Change any of the other objects on the form to match Figure D-3. Close the Toolbox. Click Data on the menu bar.

The Windows form is created and the Data menu is displayed (Figure D-3).

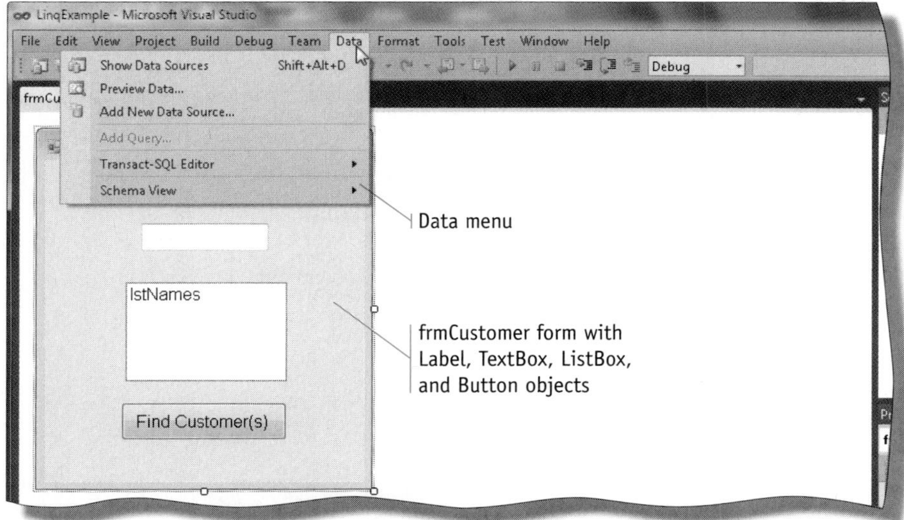

FIGURE D-3

STEP 2 Click Add New Data Source on the Data menu. In the Choose a Data Source Type dialog box, click Database, and then click Next. In the Choose a Database Model dialog box, select DataSet, and then click Next. Click the New Connection button. In the Choose Data Source dialog box, under Data source, select Microsoft SQL Server Database File, and then click the OK button. In the Add Connection dialog box, click the Browse button, and then select the Northwind.mdf database saved on your local machine or USB drive. Click the Open button. The Add Connection dialog box reopens. Click the Continue button in the Add Connection dialog box.

The Choose Your Data Connection dialog box reopens (Figure D-4).

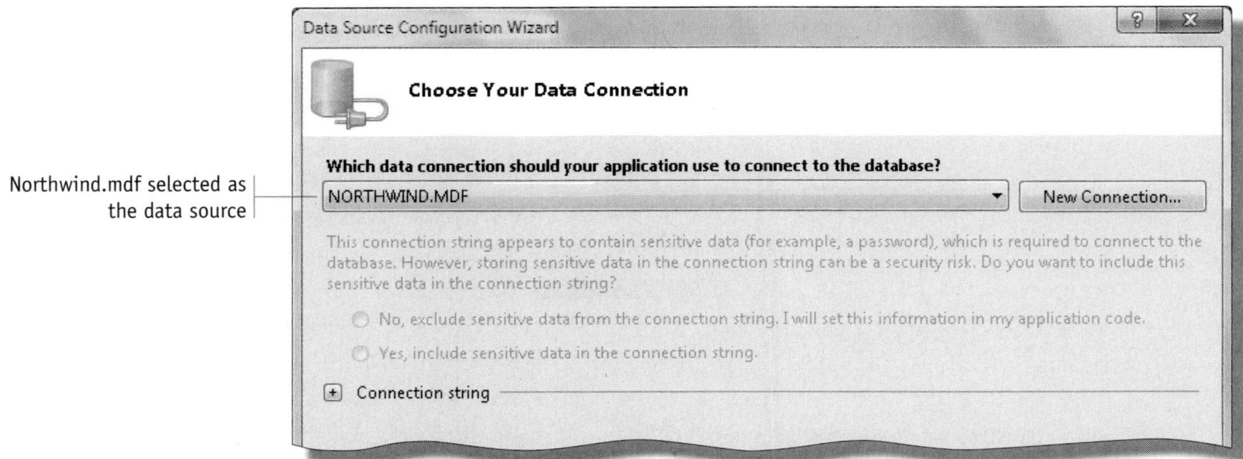

FIGURE D-4

STEP 3 Click the Next button. Click the No button to prevent a copy of the database being created, and then click the Next button. Check the Tables option and click Finish.

The dialog box closes, and a connection to the Northwind database is made. The Solution Explorer displays the DataSet named NORTHWINDDataSet.xsd (Figure D-5).

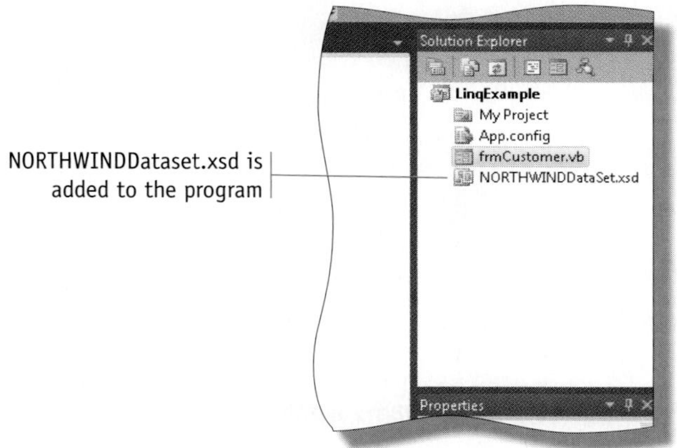

FIGURE D-5

Working with LINQ to SQL

By using LINQ to SQL, you can use the LINQ technology to access SQL databases. Using Visual Basic, you can query, insert, update, and delete information from tables. A LINQ to SQL object needs to be mapped to the database tables. The LINQ to SQL object automatically generates classes for each of the tables, which allows a developer to perform LINQ queries in the code window. To create a LINQ to SQL business object, you can complete the following steps:

STEP 1 In the Solution Explorer window, right-click the LinqExample project. Point to Add and then click New Item. In the center pane of the Add New Item dialog box, select LINQ to SQL Classes. Type `Northwind.dbml` in the Name text box.

The LINQ to SQL Classes item is selected and named Northwind.dbml (Figure D-6).

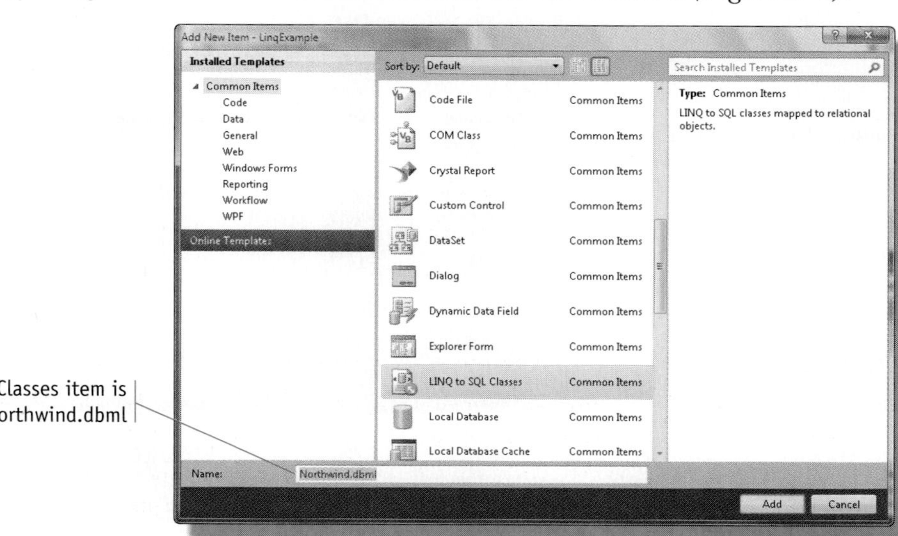

FIGURE D-6

STEP 2 Click the Add button.

The Northwind.dbml LINQ to SQL classes object is added to the project (Figure D-7).

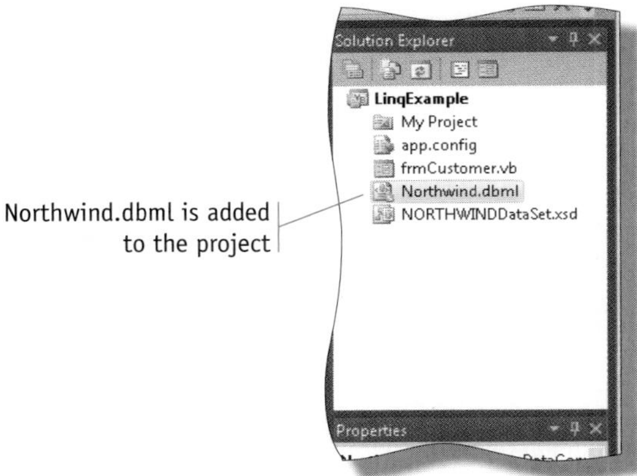

FIGURE D-7

STEP 3 Double-click the Northwind.dbml connection in the Solution Explorer window. The Method Pane is displayed with the tab name Northwind.dbml. Click View on the menu bar, and then click Server Explorer. In the Server Explorer pane on the left side of the window, click the expand icon to expand the Northwind database. Click the expand icon to expand the Tables folder. Drag the Customers table to the Method Pane in the center of the window.

The Customers table is placed on the Method Pane (Figure D-8).

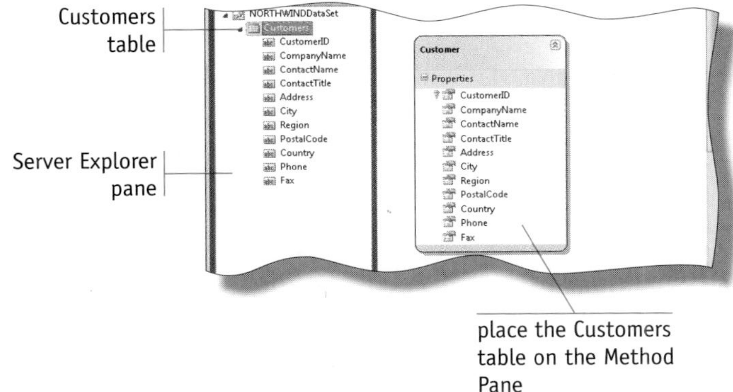

FIGURE D-8

Coding SQL Commands Using LINQ

The purpose of the sample application is to open the Customers table in the Northwind database and to search for the city requested by the user. The name(s) of those customers residing in the matching city will be displayed in the ListBox object called lstNames. Using LINQ, you can use SQL-like commands to query the SQL database. To code using LINQ, you can complete the following steps:

STEP 1 Click the frmCustomer.vb tab. Double-click the btnFind Button object. To create a new method that represents a connection to the database named Northwind, type `Dim db as New nor` in the btnFind click event.

The variable db can access any table within the Northwind database. The NorthwindDataContext object is based on the Northwind.dbml connection. IntelliSense appends the Northwind file name with the ending DataContext to create an object named NorthwindDataContext (Figure D-9).

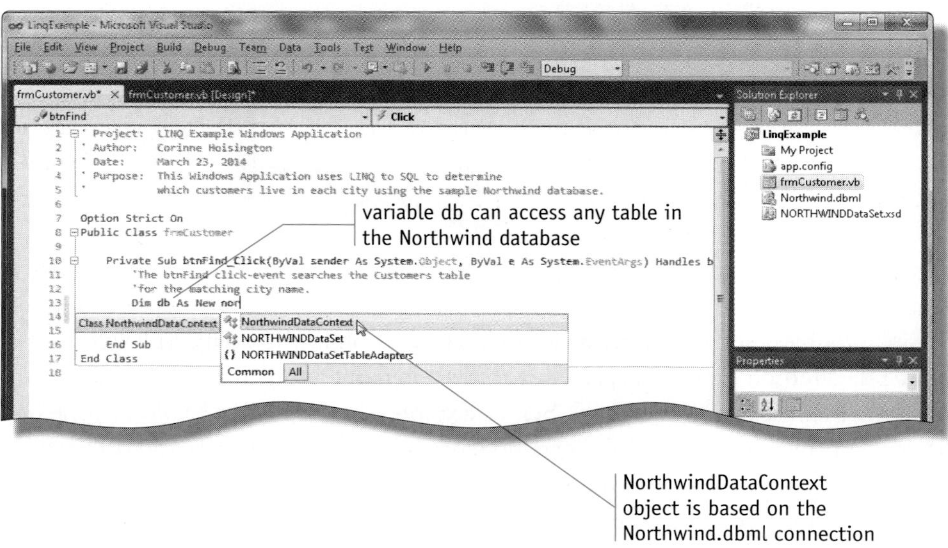
variable db can access any table in the Northwind database
NorthwindDataContext object is based on the Northwind.dbml connection

FIGURE D-9

STEP 2 Select NorthwindDataContext in the IntelliSense window and press ENTER. Type in the code shown in Figure D-10.

The LINQ code is added to the application (Figure D-10).

```
        Dim strCity As String

        strCity = txtCity.Text
        'LINQ code
        Dim matchingCustomers = From match In db.Customers _
                 Where match.City = strCity _
                 Select match
```

FIGURE D-10

After the user has entered the name of the city, the text entered in the TextBox object txtCity is assigned to the variable strCity. Line 18 in Figure D-10 on the previous page initializes a variable named matchingCustomers, which will be assigned to the retrieved records that match the city search string. The From statement determines which database to search. In this case, the variable db connects to the Northwind database, and db.Customers represents the connection to the Customers table within that database. The Where statement is searching for the condition where the city specified in strCity (the city name entered by the user) is equal to the City field in the Customers table. In other words, the Where statement is filtering for records that contain the city name entered by the user. The Select statement assigns the filtered rows that match the entered city name to a variable named `match` for retrieval later in the code.

The last section of code shown in Figure D-11 displays the names of the customers who live in the requested city. The field that is assigned to the customer name in the Customers database is called ContactName. The For Each loop displays each of the filtered rows with the matching city and displays the ContactName field. The SQL statement might match none of the records in the database, one of the records, or many of the records. In the last case, multiple customer names are displayed in the ListBox object named lstNames. The For Each loop repeats until all ContactName fields are displayed within the ListBox object.

```
        'Display matching customers to Listbox object
        For Each customer In matchingCustomers
            lstNames.Items.Add(customer.ContactName)
        Next

    End Sub
End Class
```

FIGURE D-11

Executing the Query

As the application is executed, the user enters a city name in the TextBox object. In the example shown in Figure D-12 on the next page, the user enters the city name of Sao Paulo. The user then clicks the Find Customer(s) button, and the query is executed. The LINQ code connects to the Customers table within the Northwind database and searches for records that have a City field value matching Sao Paulo. The For Each loop then displays each of the customer names found in the matching records in the ListBox object. The application displays the names of four customers who live in Sao Paulo.

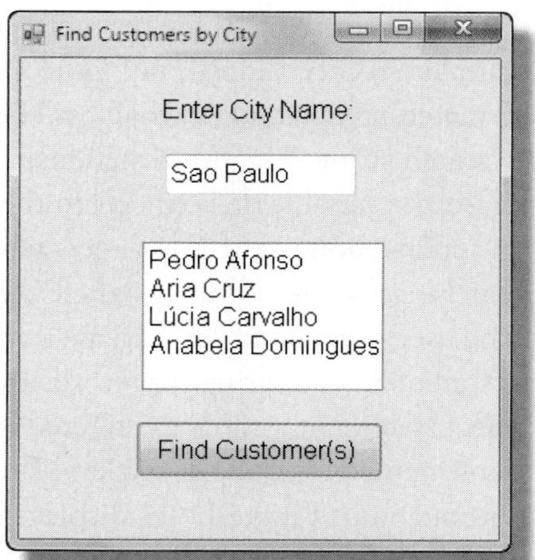

FIGURE D-12

LINQ is a significant addition to the Visual Basic 2010 environment. LINQ provides consistency by defining a set of standard query operators that work across data sources. The deep integration of LINQ into Visual Basic allows developers to be more productive, using the same commands in both the SQL and Visual Basic environments.

APPENDIX E

Using Silverlight with Visual Basic 2010

Introducing Microsoft Silverlight

Silverlight is a browser plug-in that creates multimedia effects within any Web browser, such as Internet Explorer, Mozilla Firefox, Chrome, or Safari. Silverlight Web site multimedia effects include animation, video, and interactivity with images. Silverlight is similar to Adobe Flash, which preceded the Silverlight plug-in, and is considered to be faster and less of a security risk than Flash.

To download the Silverlight plug-in, open the Web page *www.silverlight.net*. This Web page includes samples to view Silverlight in action as well as the link to download the plug-in. The newest version, Silverlight 3.0, is approximately a 4.0 MB download.

You can develop Silverlight applications using Visual Basic 2010. Visual Basic Silverlight is a powerful development platform for creating engaging, interactive user experiences for Web, desktop, and mobile applications, whether users work with the applications online or offline. Silverlight is powered by the .NET framework and is designed to bring a new level of interactivity to your Internet experience.

In this appendix, you will use Visual Basic 2010 to create a Silverlight application that opens in a browser and allows the user to play and stop a video clip. The application includes a video file named space.wmv, which you can download from *scsite.com/vb2010*. When the user opens the application in a browser and clicks the Start button, the space shuttle video begins to play (Figure E-1).

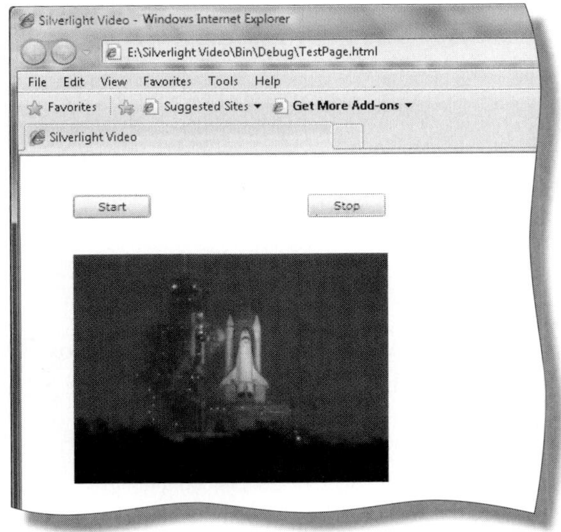

FIGURE E-1

Creating a Silverlight Application

You design a Silverlight application within Visual Studio 2010. When you create a Silverlight application, Visual Studio automatically creates XAML (Extensible Application Markup Language) code, which is assembled by a server to be displayed as a finished application in the browser. To create a Silverlight application, you can complete the following steps:

STEP 1 With Visual Studio 2010 open, click the New Project button on the Standard toolbar. In the left pane of the New Project dialog box, select Silverlight. In the center pane, select Silverlight Application. Name the file Silverlight Video. Click the Browse button and then select the E: drive to save the application on your USB drive.

A Silverlight application is created with the name Silverlight Video (Figure E-2).

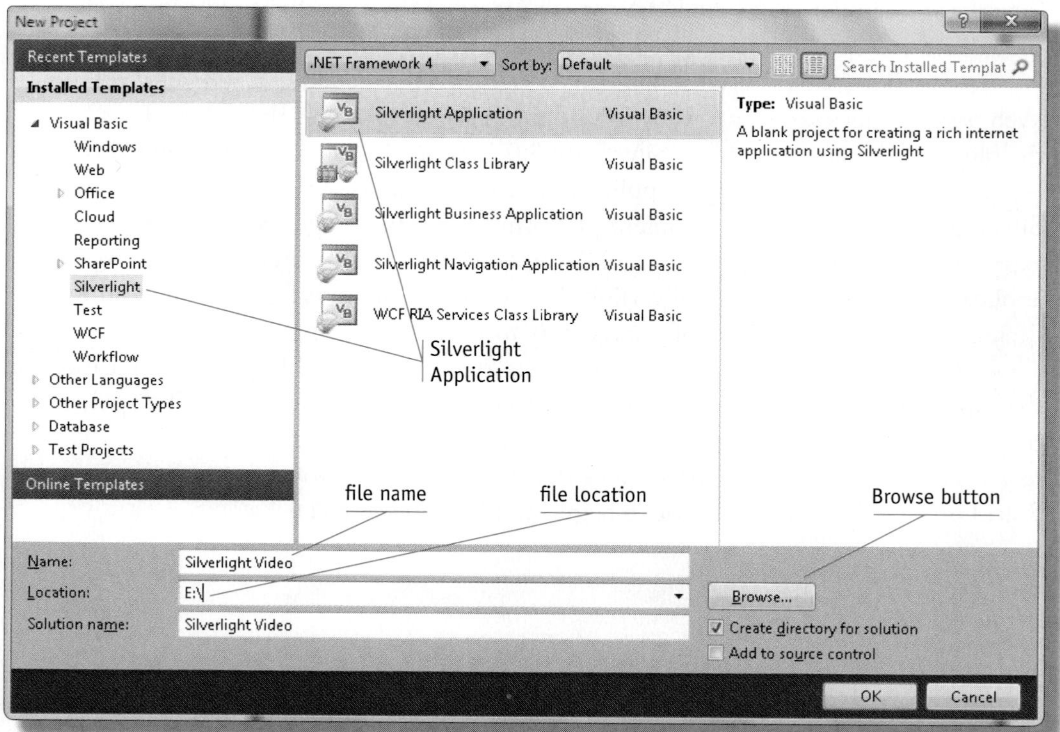

FIGURE E-2

STEP 2 Click the OK button in the New Project dialog box. The New Silverlight Application dialog box opens. Click to uncheck the Host the Silverlight application in a new Web site check box.

The New Silverlight Application dialog box opens. The check box is unchecked (Figure E-3).

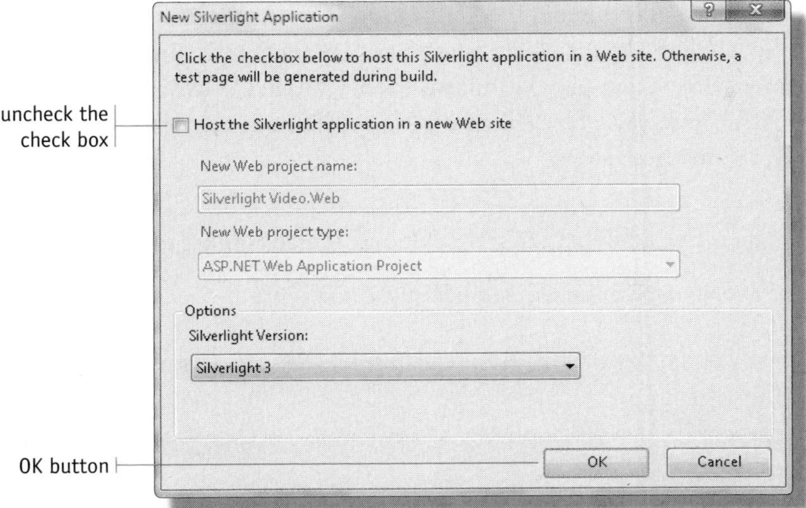

FIGURE E-3

STEP 3 Click the OK button on the New Silverlight Application dialog box.

The Silverlight application opens in Visual Basic (Figure E-4).

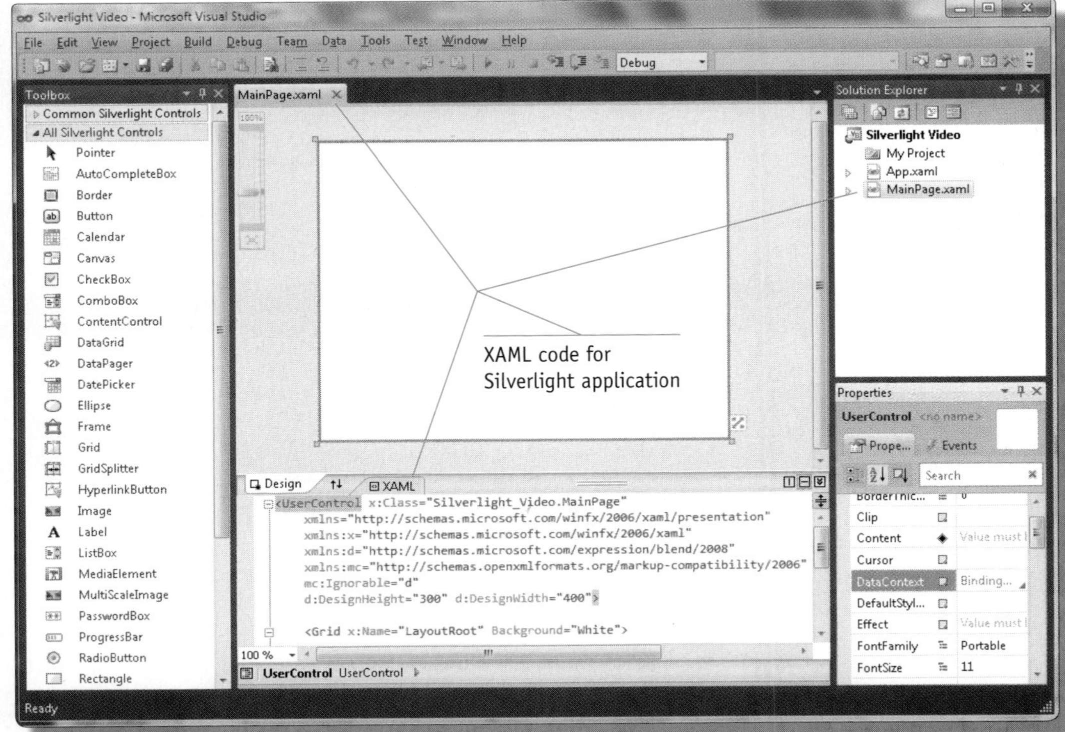

FIGURE E-4

Adding MediaElement Objects

Silverlight supports multimedia files such as audio and video files to play within a browser. The MediaElement object is used to play media files in Silverlight. The MediaElement object can play Windows Media Video (WMV), Windows Media Audio (WMA), and MP3 files. To add a MediaElement object to the Silverlight application, follow these steps:

STEP 1 Open the Toolbox. Drag the MediaElement object to the MainPage form.

The MediaElement appears on the MainPage form (Figure E-5).

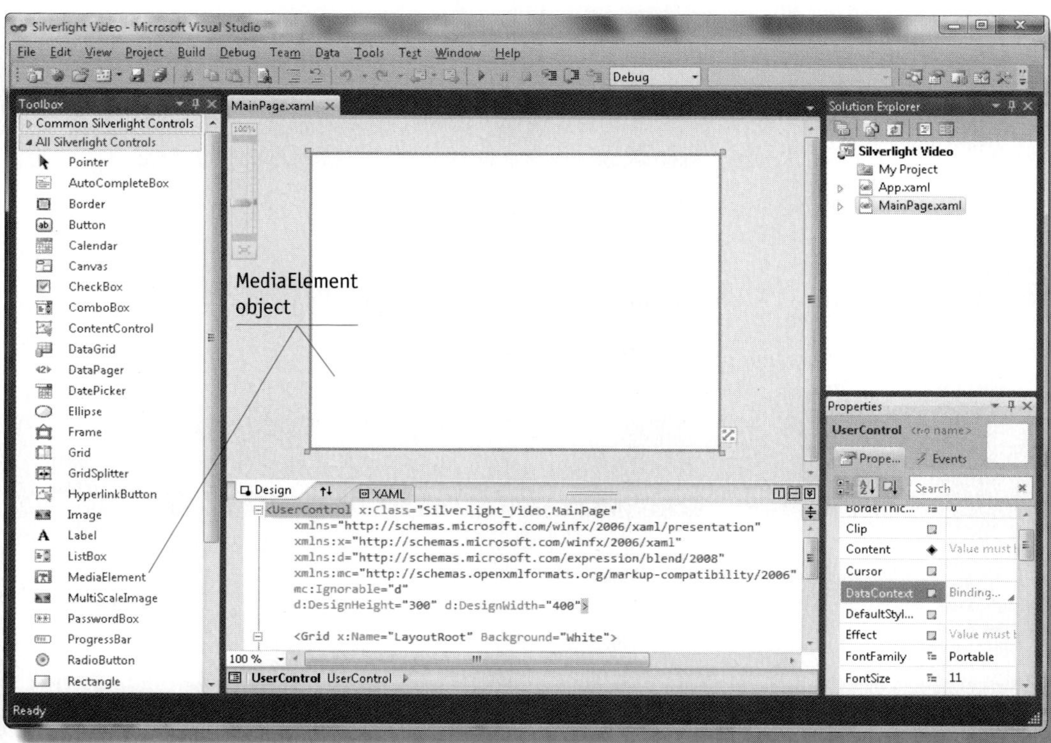

FIGURE E-5

STEP 2 In the Properties window, change the Height property to `200` for the MediaElement object. Change the Width property to `300` for the MediaElement object.

The MediaElement object is resized (Figure E-6).

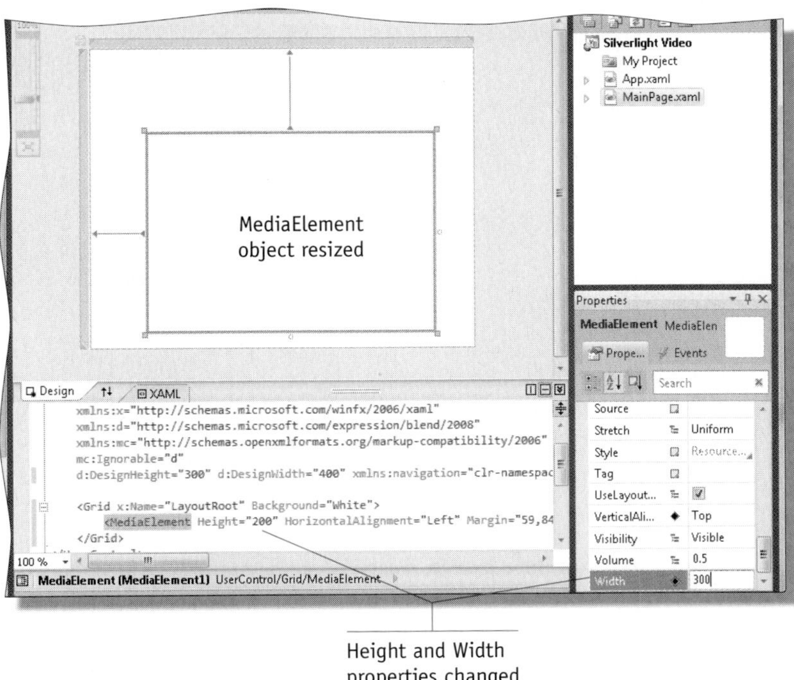

FIGURE E-6

Adding a Video Resource File

The video file that will be played in the Silverlight project must be placed in the Solution Explorer project file to be used within the application. To place the video file in the project, follow these steps:

STEP 1 Download the video file named space.wmv from *scsite.com/vb2010* (Appendix E) to your USB drive. Click the Start button on the Windows taskbar. Click Computer and then double-click the USB (E:) drive. Drag the space.wmv file to the Silverlight Video project name in Solution Explorer.

The Silverlight Video project name is highlighted in Solution Explorer (Figure E-7).

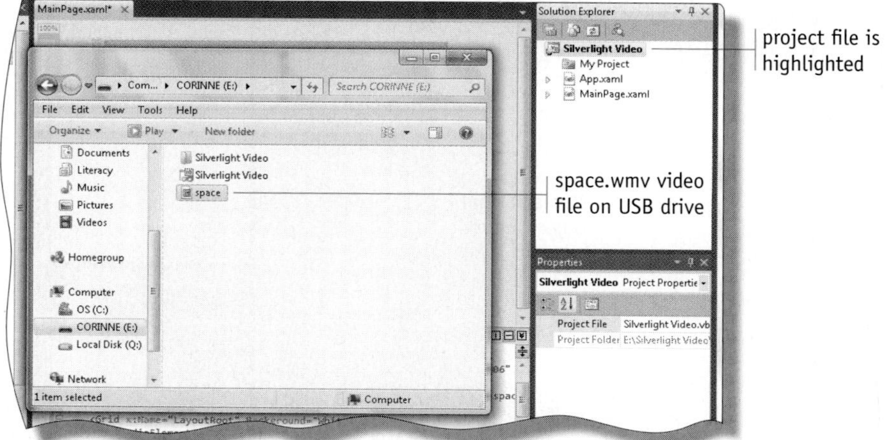

FIGURE E-7

STEP 2 Release the mouse button. The video file is placed within the project.

The Solution Explorer displays the space.wmv file within the project (Figure E-8).

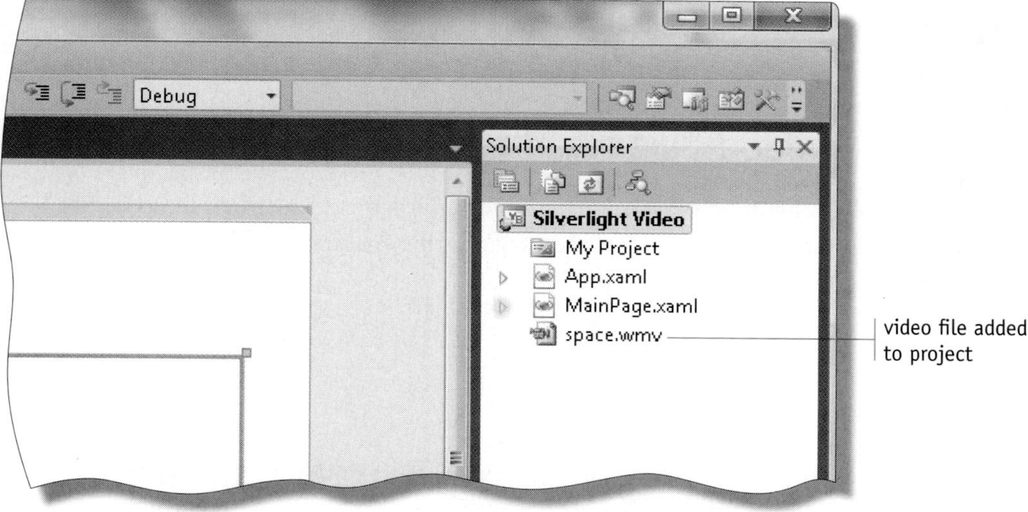

FIGURE E-8

STEP 3 In the Solution Explorer, click the space.wmv video file. In the Properties window, change the Build Action property to Resource.

The Build Action property for the video file is changed to Resource (Figure E-9).

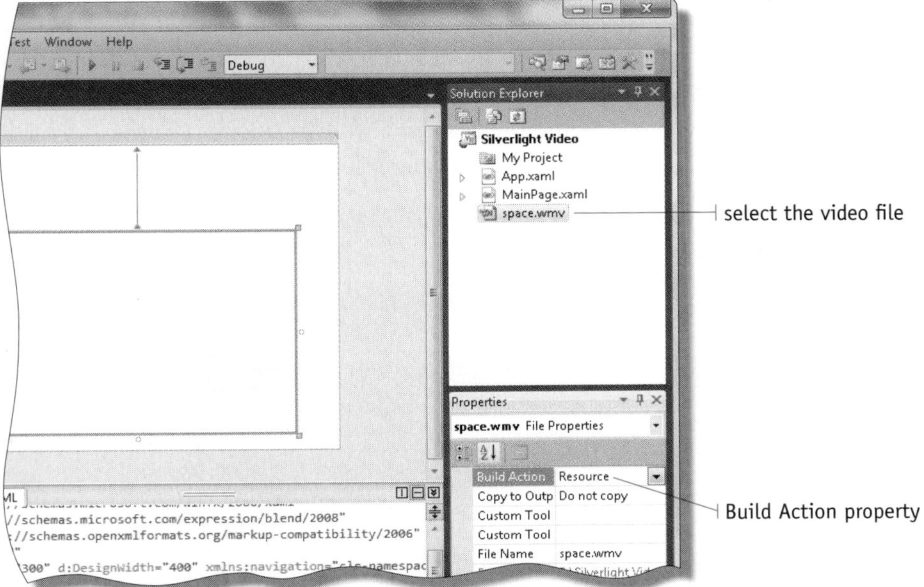

FIGURE E-9

STEP 4 Click the MediaElement object in the center of the MainPage.xaml tab. In the Properties window of the MediaElement object, click to the right of the Source property. Type `space.wmv.` Press Enter.

The Source property of the MediaElement is assigned to the video file (Figure E-10).

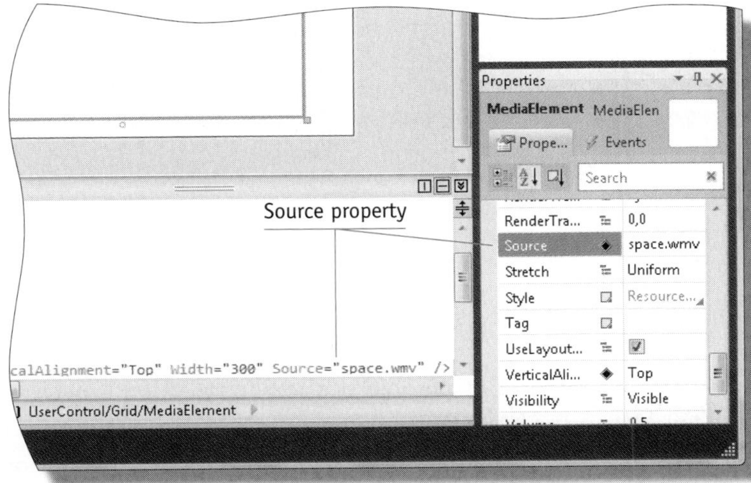

FIGURE E-10

Adding Buttons to the Silverlight Form

The first Button object on the form will play the video file in the browser. The second Button object stops the video from playing. The buttons can be clicked repeatedly. To add Button objects to Silverlight, follow these steps:

STEP 1 Drag two Button objects to the Silverlight form. Name the first button `btnStart` in the Properties window to the right of the word Button. Change the Content property to `Start`. Name the second button `btnStop` in the Properties window to the right of the word Button. Change the Content property to `Stop`.

Two Button objects are placed on the form (Figure E-11).

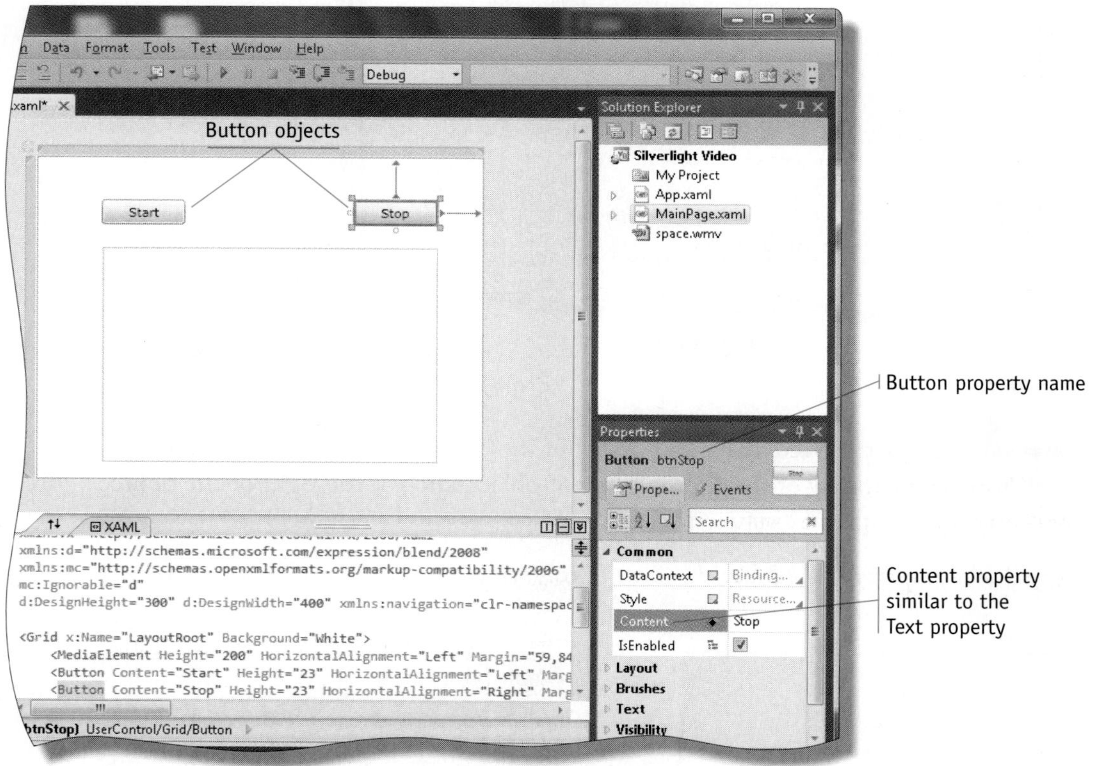

FIGURE E-11

Coding the Video Player

To activate the Start and Stop Button objects, the Start method is necessary to start playing the video. When the Start Button object is clicked, the btnStart click event begins the play method, which plays the video file. When the Stop Button object is clicked, the btnStop click event runs the Stop method to stop the video from playing. To code the Button objects, follow these steps:

STEP 1 Double-click the Start Button object. Type the code shown in Figure E-12.

One line of code is entered for the btnStart event (Figure E-12).

```
' Project:  Silverlight Example Video Player Application
' Author:   Corinne Hoisington
' Date:     March 23, 2013
' Purpose:  This Silverlight Application starts and stops playing a video file.

Option Strict On

Partial Public Class MainPage
    Inherits UserControl

    Public Sub New()
        InitializeComponent()
    End Sub

    Private Sub btnStart_Click(ByVal sender As System.Object, ByVal e As
System.Windows.RoutedEventArgs) Handles btnStart.Click
        MediaElement1.Start()

    End Sub
End Class
```

code the btnStart event

FIGURE E-12

STEP 2 Double-click the Stop Button object on the Silverlight form. Type the code shown in Figure E-13.

One line of code is entered for the btnStop event (Figure E-13).

```
    Private Sub btnStop_Click(ByVal sender As System.Object, ByVal e As
System.Windows.RoutedEventArgs) Handles btnStop.Click
        MediaElement1.Stop()

    End Sub
```

FIGURE E-13

Executing the Silverlight Application

To run the Silverlight application, click the Start Debugging button. A browser will open and load the Silverlight page as shown in Figure E-14.

FIGURE E-14

INDEX

A

E

G

H

N

O

P